To: Stella.

from:- Glynis..''

again.

THE
DECORATOR'S
DIRECTORY

LORRAINE JOHNSON

MICHAEL JOSEPH · LONDON

First published in Great Britain 1981
by Michael Joseph Ltd
44 Bedford Square
London WC1B 3EF

© 1981 Johnson Editions

Editorial Consultant: Phoebe Phillips
Pictorial & Editorial Research: Anne Morgan
Editor: Tessa Clark
Designer: Lorraine Johnson
Filmset by SX Composing Ltd,
Rayleigh, Essex
Printed and bound in
Great Britain

ISBN 0 7181 2008 6

Dedicated to my mother, Ginny, Linda,
and home-lovers everywhere

CONTENTS

It all started when I was doing up a small, terraced house in north London. I wanted two round, Black sinks for the kitchen (Black because I thought I'd never have time to scrub them), and spent what seemed to be an inordinate amount of time finding the importer, and then the distributor.

Frustration built up. Frustration at not being able to find well-designed merchandise easily; frustration with the limited choice offered by most well-known retail outlets; and frustration with what I thought was the suppliers' conservatism.

However, I soon discovered that my frustration was shared by many people. A multitude of wonderful items are made in Britain or imported, but retailers are often understandably reluctant to give precious floor and storage space to products that may have a limited market. As a result, the public doesn't know they exist, and assumes that it has very little choice. *The Decorator's Directory* is an attempt to eliminate at least some of these stumbling blocks. Arranged by supplier, within sections, it describes the merchandise provided by various firms, with illustrations and basic information like prices and measurements. Products range from ceramic tiles to chairs, bathroom suites to carpets, paints to mirrors—everything you need to decorate and furnish a house.

Nearly 1,000 firms are featured, about 50% of the companies we contacted while researching this book; some didn't co-operate, even though no fee was involved. We can only assume that the firms on the following pages, ranging from the smallest cottage industries to large national conglomerates, are rather more willing than the others to help the consumer.

It's obviously impossible to describe every range or product supplied by some of the larger companies. In these cases, we've featured what we consider to be the most interesting and/or useful items. Overall, each section gives a bird's-eye view of the kind of merchandise available from the various suppliers.

If the examples described or illustrated aren't exactly what you want, it's always worth contacting the firm/s concerned and asking for a catalogue and/or your nearest stockist so that you can see their entire range. Information was correct when we went to press, but ranges can be added to, and colours and sizes can change.

We've tried to keep a balance between inexpensive items and products that are definitely at the top end of the market. However, no one is ever rich enough. This becomes even more apparent when you're fitting out a home: desires increase, standards get higher—and prices escalate. Look through this book and decide what you want—then save for it. The difference between a product that's absolutely right and one that you buy in its place isn't just a saving of so many pounds. You'll have to live with your choice, and will be reminded daily of a moment of impatience or weakness. Attaining your goal of perfection will give you pleasure for years to come.

Occasionally, of course, it makes both decorative and economic sense to compromise. For example, a marble-lined bathroom suite with gold-plated taps and accessories is only for the very wealthy. Marble tiles, or marbled wallpaper, and brass fittings create a similar effect—and you'll save literally thousands of pounds.

I hope you'll come back to *The Decorator's Directory* again and again, to solve the dozens of problems that rear their heads when you're pulling together a room—or a house; and that the information in these pages will simplify your task.

AVAILABILITY

We've made every effort to ensure that the merchandise described will be available to readers. But, inevitably, you will sometimes find that a product has been discontinued, usually because it didn't sell well, or because manufacturing costs were so high it was priced out of the market. This happened, maddeningly, to us while we were collecting information for this book. However, it's always worth persevering. The company concerned may just have a few items still in stock, or know of an outlet that has them.

More positively, you may get a recently discontinued product at a large discount—most firms prefer reduced profits to no sale at all; and you could end up with an article that not many other people possess, much like owning a designer's prototype.

Designs within a range can alter slightly from year to year. This applies especially to wallpaper and fabric collections, and is mainly due to changes in fashion, or new decorating trends.

HOW TO USE THIS BOOK

Sections are devoted to areas of usage ('Kitchens') or types of product ('Paint'). Some are sub-divided according to type or function: 'Blinds' includes *Fabric Roller Blinds, Venetian Blinds, Vertical Blinds*, etc; 'Tables' consists of *Dining Suites, Dining Tables* and *Occasional Tables*. Sections, sub-divisions and entries are arranged in alphabetical order.

If you are looking for bathroom accessories, for example, read through *Bathroom Accessories* in 'Bathrooms' to see which firms offer the colour and style you want, at a price you're prepared to pay. When you've made your choice, contact the sales department of the relevant companies—addresses are listed in the 'Suppliers' Index' at the end of the book. They will put you in touch with your nearest stockist, or supply the item direct. It's sometimes possible to get a discount on a product that comes direct from a manufacturing company, but always wait for the firm to offer this reduction. Don't ask for a trade discount unless you are buying in quantity.

Prices: Retail prices, generally for products illustrated, are given where possible, either after the description of a specific item or, if the information applies to all merchandise, on a separate line at the end of the entry. Prices exclude VAT, which has a tendency to fluctuate. Basically, they will enable you to compare costs of items from different manufacturers. Obviously, if two firms have similar products in approximately the same price bracket it's worth contacting both of them for quotations or estimates.

We have sometimes put '*P:* upon application', generally for one of four reasons: the manufacturer, wholesaler or distributor did not want to commit himself or his outlets to a predetermined mark-up (another reason for shopping around); the item is so expensive that it can only be made to order which always involves varying costs; the price depends on the availability of materials—a consideration that applies especially to craftspeople, for example in the 'Special Furniture' section'; or, finally, the merchandise is imported and its price is therefore affected by changes in the rate of exchange.

Prices were correct when we went to press, but inflation means ever-rising costs; it's always wise to allow for this. Similarly, manufacturing costs and the prices paid for raw materials can rise, and this increase is reluctantly passed on to the public.

Measurements: British manufacturers and distributors have not yet gone entirely over to metric measurements, and many still use the imperial system. We give first the type generally quoted by the supplier, followed by its metric or imperial conversion. Inches are rounded to the nearest .5cm, centimetres to the nearest 1/8in; fluid ounces to the nearest 1ml, millilitres to the nearest 1/8 fl oz.

As with prices, measurements are given after the item described or, if they apply to all the merchandise from a particular manufacturer, on a separate line at the end of the entry.

Cross-references: Where relevant we've given these at the end of entries. However, if for any reason you're interested in buying a number of disparate objects from the same firm, check with the 'Suppliers' Index', which lists the sections in which companies' products are described; and the general index at the end of the book. If a reference applies to a sub-division of a section it reads, for example: See also *Dining Tables* ('Tables').

Ranges and Styles: Ranges or collections that incorporate a number of designs, styles, shapes, patterns or pieces of furniture are in capital letters; designs, patterns, etc, are in quotation marks.

Illustrations: These are of products mentioned in the text, and generally come directly after the relevant entry. We've added captions when more than one item is described under a manufacturer; or if the picture is separated from the entry.

SPECIAL THANKS

The author would like to thank the following people for their help in compiling this book:

Phoebe Phillips, who encouraged and backed a crazy idea from day one;

Anne Morgan, who relentlessly, and with unending cheerfulness, pursued the minutiae which drove the rest of us crazy, but without which the book would be useless;

Tessa Clark, who edited and cajoled each and every entry into good shape;

Stanli Opperman, who kindly took time out to photograph the colour illustrations on pages 70, 105, 172 and 279, and the doll's house on the cover;

Alwyn Bailey who shot dozens of samples for the black-and-white pictures;

Catherine Carpenter and Gabrielle Townsend, who sub-edited the book;

Chris Bernstein and John Lawrence, who contributed to it;

Sandra Campapiano, who somehow managed to type it all; and Mr E.J. Allen, Esq.

Finally, if you know of, or find, a supplier that you think should have been included, please write to:

The Decorator's Directory,
Michael Joseph Ltd,
44 Bedford Square,
London WC1.

We will contact the firm concerned in order to make the next edition of *The Decorator's Directory* even better than this one.

INTRODUCTION

Most kitchen appliances are functional rather than decorative, so are outside the scope of this book. The exceptions are the modern and antique kitchen ranges in 'Stoves and Kitchen Ranges'; and the cookers, hobs, refrigerators, etc, all in good colours and/or beautifully designed, described in this section.

Unfortunately, only a very few inspired companies are prepared to go to the enormous trouble involved in producing appliances that are both attractive and technologically advanced.

However, two British companies, Moffat and Tricity, have decor panels to cover built-in freezer and refrigerator door fronts so that they co-ordinate with kitchen units. Finishes are Black, White or stainless steel; and, by arrangement with some kitchen manufacturers, Beige, teak, pine, and lovely brights like Red. In addition Eastham Burco, Miele and Bosch (see 'Kitchens'), have standard appliances that fit their units.

This section also includes a selection of unusual kitchen accessories.

To help you select appliances, a guide to relevant *Which* reports is given below.

WHICH REPORTS

AEG-TELEFUNKEN

Vast range of built-in appliances including 'BP 6.60', the first computer-programmed cooker, and three built-under ovens, some with grills and a rotisserie. Three microwave ovens, and two that combine microwaves and 'Ventitherm' hot air are available, plus four other electric models. Six electric hobs include the 'Vitramic M8.92' in glass ceramic, with a warming plate area and the 'M.61' in Mid-brown enamel. The gas or electric MODULAR HOB system includes a deep-fryer and chromium nickel fluted 'parking' area. Two-tone colour-matched 'KG6.14' gas, 'KM6.24' gas and electric, and 'K6.44' electric hobs come in Mocca (gold), Autumn leaf (mid-brown), and Moss green (olive). Hinged hob covers are available; also matching sinks with wire baskets and chopping boards. Finally there are compatible refrigerators and freezers, plus the 'Santo 3604 KGTC' fridge-freezer.

GAGGENAU ELECTRIC (UK) LTD

A wealth of alternatives, many incorporating new techniques: three electric hot-air wall ovens and a conventional electric model, a microwave unit, a free-standing microwave oven and two electric cookers. Six electric hobs include three in glass ceramic, one of which ('CK052') has a warming area. Two gas hobs and one gas/electric combination are available.

VARIO SYSTEM options include an electric barbecue grill, grill plate and resting surface, and electric fryer that fries fish, meat and desserts without requiring a change of oil. A special hob extractor, mounted between appliances, removes fumes at source. Special hoods include one in matt copper, and versions for concealed, overhead cupboard, and encased, ventilators. Electric or gas standard hobs are available plus a glass ceramic model; all can be enamelled, to match round, square or rectangular sinks, in Mocha (gold), Terre d'Alsace (light brown), Bahama beige, Red, and Majolica (dark brown). Built-in refrigerators, freezers, dishwashers and washing machines are also available.

Gaggenau's barbecue, deep fryer and grill

NEFF (UK) LTD

Wide selection of futuristic – and expensive – appliances for connoisseurs: six electric 'Circotherm' built-in ovens, two built-under 'Circotherm' ovens and an under-counter electric cooker from the LUXURY DESIGNERS range, 'traditional' built-in electric ovens, and four standard electric ovens, three with 'Circotherm' systems. A gas oven comes complete with hob. Hob options in the DOMINO range of stainless steel modular units include a gas hob, electric hotplates, deep-fryer, rectangular plate, warming plate, and 'parking' plate. Matching rectangular, round and round-strainer sinks are available.

The STANDARD range has six stainless steel built-in hobs, a Brown enamelled model and two built-in ceramic hobs, all electric; also a hob for gas. Matching enamelled sinks and gas or electric hobs come in two-tone Burnt sienna, Green haze, and Bitter chocolate, or plain Mocca, Golden sand, Avocado, and Bahama beige. Built-in, built-under, and larger free-standing refrigerators, freezers and fridge-freezers with optional decor panels, two built-in dishwashers, three cooker hoods, and an automatic washing machine complete the range.

Neff's STANDARD electric (top), gas (below) hobs and sinks

PROWODA LTD

Two-tone gas, electric or combination hobs with unique colour-matched control panels. Designed for 3cm (1⅛in) deep worktops, they

Selection from Prowoda's two-tone range

come in Blue pompadour (bright blue), Fern green, Provençal (rusty brown), Terre de Rio (dark brown), Terre de France (golden brown), Red, Val du Loir (light brown) and, unusually, Anthracite (matt black). Matching circular and modular sinks, cooker hoods and oven fasciae come in similar colours. Gas or electric Domino hobs can be mounted singly or in groups, and include a single large rectangular plate. Surrounds are in Terre de France only.

KITCHEN SINKS

BERGLEN ASSOCIATES LTD

Stunning SILKFLEX coloured sinks with matching gas or electric hobs. Three ranges are available, made in West Germany from high-grade seamless sheet steel, vitreous enamelled on both sides. 'Model III' round inset bowls come in Black, White, Sorrento (bright blue), Mocca (dark brown), Avocado, Red, Orange, Golden sand, Stone orange (rust), and Bahama beige. Accessories include a deep basket, drainer basket, soap dispenser and matching tap. A double-bowl inset sink is in the same colours (P: £135).

FRANKE AG

Slick, sleek, Swiss sinks. An extensive selection of stainless steel models includes a small inset bowl. 'Compact', the most unusual style is available with a very deep bowl and a smaller central sink that can be fitted with a matching drainer, draining basket or drainer insert and comes in Cream, Orange red, or Dark brown. A food preparation platter in iroko hardwood is also available. P: sink £135, platter £25.

Franke's 'Compact 125'

The beautifully designed FRANKON-CENTER is a deep sink and draining area with an optional central strainer bowl. Inset, single, or double bowls are available; also a matching electric hob, as well as a chopping board and draining basket. P: sink £140, hob £280.
There's also a very striking range of three inset sinks, two draining boards and two hobs in shaded enamel. Colours are Emerald green, Gold orange, Mahogany brown, and Safari beige. P: sink from £110, drainer £50, hob £280.

GLYNWED BATHROOM & KITCHEN PRODUCTS LTD

LEISURE stainless steel sinks in five styles; also PRISMAFLEX in vitreous enamel. The latter consists of inset bowls in two sizes, and a matching drainer, in a wonderful variety of colours: Harvest gold, Bahama beige, Sepia (dark brown), Autumn (rust), Moss green (light olive), and Sorrento; also White and stainless steel versions. P: bowl £56, drainer £44. Special stainless steel shapes to order.

Glynwed's PRISMAFLEX

B & P WYNN & CO

MAURICE HERBEAU sinks from France. Hammered or smooth brass, copper or matt nickel inset basins come in five styles, with matching taps: double bowl with or without draining board; single bowl with draining board; oval; round; and rectangular. P: £153 smooth copper, £227 hammered.

KITCHEN TAPS

BARKING-GROHE LTD

Five functional sink mixers in chrome-plated solid brass. 'BIFLO', with a high arching spout and quarter-turn levers, is designed for the handicapped, but its fantastically easy-to-grip handles would be useful in any kitchen. P: upon application.

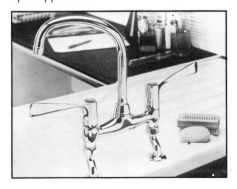

BERGLEN ASSOCIATES LTD

KWC MULTICOLOUR taps in two styles. Surfaces are coated with epoxy lacquer in Stone orange (rust), Avocado, Moss green,

Golden sand, Mocca (dark brown) or Bahama beige (P: £75–£88).
Three chromium-plated taps and a rinse spray attachment are available.

CHLORIDE SHIRES LTD

DA VINCI colour-chromed taps and mixers from a top Italian design team. Acrylic heads are in Harmony brown, Harmony green, Aubergine, Ocean (blue), and Yukon (gold); also chromed versions. P: upon application. *See Bathroom Accessories ('Bathrooms') for illustration.*

SPECTRUM LTD

Cheerful, chunky BALOCCHI taps from Italy. Designed to fit the hand and remain bright and shiny for years, the range includes wall, basin and swan-neck mixers, plus bathroom fittings. Colours – all terrific – are Yellow, Orange, Red, Green, Blue, and Brown; also White and chrome. P: £80.

B & P WYNN & CO

Stunning 'La Picarde' in the style of an old water pump. Designed to match MAURICE HERBEAU sinks, it has a brass or copper cover and swivel head; a single ceramic or wood lever controls the water mix (P: £270).
JULIA single and two-hole mixers, with non-return valves, come in chrome or solid brass, or are finished in matt nickel, old copper, old bronze, polished brass, or gold (P: two-hole mixer £190 chrome–£260 gold).

Wynn's JULIA

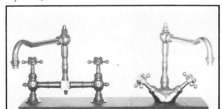

INTRODUCTION

Architectural ornaments, applied after building and/or surface work but before decorating, are a quick and easy way of adding character to a boring box-like room—or an entire house. These non-structural components can also be used cosmetically to hide a multitude of sins.

Rich and varied solutions range from classical or traditional reproductions—typically cornices, architraves, dados, porticos and niches—through authentic but expensive period pieces, to rustic support beams and panelling. Ceiling panels to house lighting, heating and electrical apparatus, or camouflage unsightly cracks or pipes are included; also tiles that can be supported on a grid, or applied directly, to absorb sound and reflect light. (See 'Lighting' for systems specifically designed to illuminate.)

Materials vary from wood (or mock wood) to plaster (or fibrous plaster), foam, fibreglass and new synthetic materials. The real thing—always more expensive—is probably for perfectionists only. (Imitations are hardly noticeable, especially at ceiling height.)

One word of warning: because the choice is so temptingly large, it's only too easy to get carried away, combining redwood screens with Georgian niches topped by illuminated ceilings. As with most decorating schemes, simplicity and compatibility are of paramount importance.

Several firms are willing to help with installation, but anyone with some carpentry skills could do it. Be sure to consult the supplier or manufacturer first—special tools or products may be recommended to make the job easier. A growing number of firms specialize in saving useful and decorative pieces like balustrades, mantelpieces, old tiles, columns, church pews, etc. These are undoubtedly good investments. Four sources at the time of going to press are:

Architectural Heritage of Cheltenham: Possibly the country's grandest selection; stock lists are available.

Architectural Salvage, at the Architectural Press: Index of all types of re-usable building material throughout the UK; it acts as an agency, putting people in search of items in touch with those wishing to dispose of them.

The London Architectural Salvage & Supply Co Ltd: Constant supply of doors, wood block flooring and pitch pine floors, etc; stock lists are available.

Walcot Reclamation: Vast collection of building materials, stoves, fireplaces, and all kinds of wonderful architectural ornaments. Addresses are in 'Useful Addresses'.

This section is divided, according to function or material, into *Plaster and Plaster Effects; Suspended Ceilings;* and *Wood and Wood Effects.*

PRICES AND INFORMATION WERE CORRECT AT THE TIME OF GOING TO PRESS

PLASTER AND PLASTER EFFECTS

ARISTOCAST LTD

Full range of mouldings, including a handsome and unusual pre-fabricated arch (architraves and keystones are optional extras). Other items include three corbels, six panel mouldings, eight pre-cast niches, and four column styles in heights from 6ft 10in (208.5cm) to 7ft 3in (221cm). *P:* upon application.

Aristocast's 'Venetia' niche

CLASSICAL DESIGNS

Another excellent range, from another specialist. Panel mouldings, for walls or ceilings, come in six designs. Attractive, and traditional, they're a worthwhile alternative to expensive wall coverings. The range also includes six centrepieces, three corbels, five columns, seven niches which can be lit from below with concealed strip lighting, 16 cornices, and a prefabricated arch in three sections. *P:* panel mouldings £3 per 150cm (4ft 11in), niches complete with semi-opaque glass base shelf and clear glass intermediate shelf £30–£55, cornices £8.50–£12 per 300cm (10ft), arch up to w 91cm (35⅞in) £175.

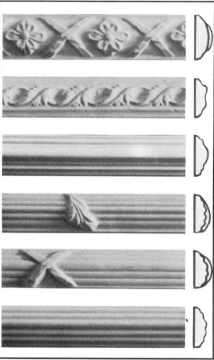

Classical Designs' panel moulding (above), columns (below)

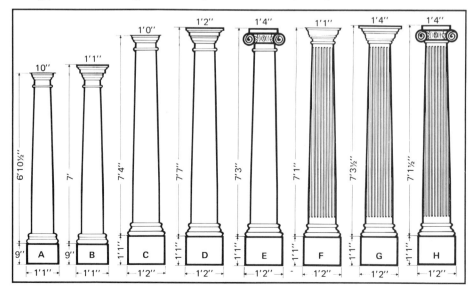

COPLEY CRAFTS

Rigid polyurethane decorations. Exact copies of fibrous plaster originals, they are lighter, cheaper and virtually unbreakable—perfect for home decorators. The range consists of six ceiling roses, two wall brackets, and four decorative cornices in 6ft (183cm) lengths. A very useful little booklet gives fixing instructions. *P:* roses £9–£23, wall brackets £9, cornices £10–£12.

Copley Crafts' ceiling roses: 'Griselda' (top), 'Antonia' (centre), 'Alicia' (bottom)

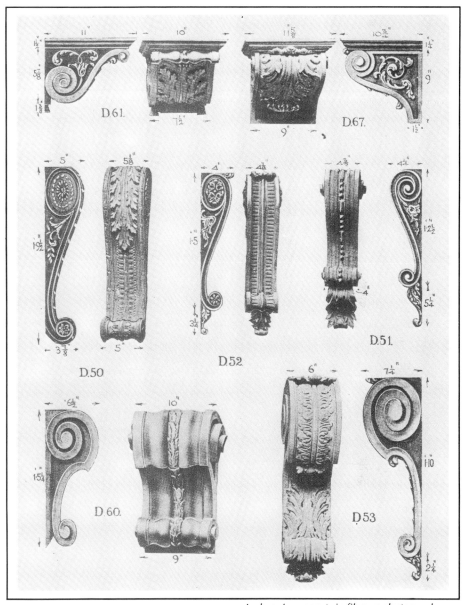

Jackson's supports in fibrous plasterwork

G B GREEN & VERONESE

Small but select range of three elaborate ceiling centrepieces, three niches, four capitals, four panel mouldings (including a very unusual bamboo pole design) and some 50 cornices. *P:* upon application.

Green & Veronese's capitals (below)

GEORGE JACKSON

A wonderfully comprehensive range from the firm who made the castings for Robert Adam's designs in the late 18th century. (These, and other English- and French-style moulds collected over the centuries, are still used today.) The selection includes 32 centrepieces, 15 trusses, 22 capitals, 11 plaques and trophies, 24 niche heads, six strapwork panels, and 71 cornices. Also numerous arches, architraves, columns, dado rails, panels, trusses, etc., covering every aspect of English and French design, from the early 17th to late 19th century. George Jackson also specialize in decoration, gilding, emblazoning, graining and restoration. *P:* upon application.

THOMAS & WILSON LTD

Beautifully conceived collection of fibrous and solid plasterwork, including 15 ceiling roses and 62 moulding/cornicing alternatives. Also numerous enriched and moulded wall panel designs, three column styles, moulded fireplace surrounds, plus dado and skirting mouldings. Everything is made to clients' requirements. (Measurements on Thomas & Wilson's lovely drawings are given in millimetres.) A few of the more unusual designs (including often hard-to-find Gothic archings) are illustrated. *P:* upon application.

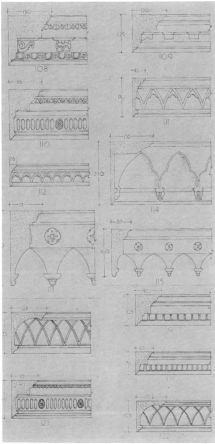

Selection of Thomas & Wilson's cornices in fibrous plasterwork, including several Gothic styles

SUSPENDED CEILINGS

ARMSTRONG CORK CO LTD

Enormous and exciting range of ceiling systems. Made from fire-resistant mineral fibre that reflects light and absorbs sound. Rough-textured TRAVERTONE tiles are painted White. Four designs with surface fissures in varying patterns are available. MINATONE comes in tiles and planks; six face patterns include dotted 'Classic' and grooved 'Caledonia' and 'Hibernia'. MINABOARD, for use with an exposed grid and optional lighting panels, is economical and also comes in six textures. *M:* all 30×30, 60×60cm (11⁷/₈×11⁷/₈, 23⁵/₈×23⁵/₈in), MINABOARD in two additional sizes; MINATONE planks 180×30cm (5ft 10⁷/₈in ×11⁷/₈in). The COLOURLINE SERIES of acoustical tiles is in the 'Celtic' MINATONE texture, in Opal white (palest green), Chrome yellow (gold), and Beige.

The marvellous DESIGNER SERIES is more decorative. Amazing alternatives are mirrored 'Antique Glass', soundproofed by applying polyester film to the standard mineral fibre; boldly textured 'Corkstyle' in natural shades; elegant 'Gold Leaf' with the appearance of hand-crafted parquet, in rich amber tones; and 'Travertone Registry' which incorporates two classically inspired motifs to give an all-over traditional texture. *M:* 30.5×30.5, 61×61cm (12×12, 24×24in).

Modular, open-cell MINAFORM S can form squares or hexagonals, and has excellent acoustic properties. Three patterns are available, to co-ordinate with MINATONE tiles. *M:* 57×30, 117×297cm (22½×11⁷/₈in, 3ft 10¹/₈in ×9ft 8³/₈in).

CERAMAGUARD panels, kiln-fired and finished with acrylic paint, are designed for humid, corrosive conditions unsuitable for conventional ceiling systems, such as over swimming pools. Available plain or with a 'Travertine' surface, they can be washed repeatedly. *M:* 60×60, 61×122cm (23⁵/₈× 23⁵/₈in, 24in × 4ft).

The economical SECOND LOOK ONE range has lay-in panels for use with the TRULOK exposed grid. Score marks simulate a 30×30cm (11⁷/₈×11⁷/₈in) tile. *M:* 60×120cm (23⁵/₈in ×3ft 11¹/₄in).

Most tiles can be mounted on a stable ceiling with adhesives, or fixed to the TRULOK grid system. LUMINAIRE ceilings with integrated lighting panels are also available. *P:* upon application. See also 'Lighting'.

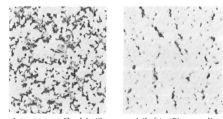

Armstrong Cork's 'Sanserra' (left), 'Fissured' (right) from TRAVERTONE

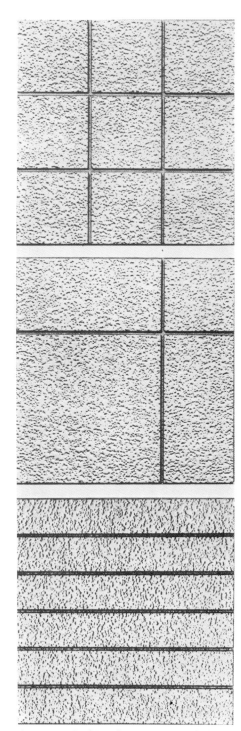

Armstrong Cork's 'Hibernia' (top), 'Caledonia' (centre), 'Celtic' (bottom), all from MINATONE; 'Celtic' also in the COLOURLINE SERIES

PRICES AND INFORMATION WERE CORRECT AT THE TIME OF GOING TO PRESS

Armstrong Cork's 'Travertone Registry' from the DESIGNER SERIES

C+A CEILINGS

Very wide range of illuminated decorative panels, in 14 original and attractive designs suitable for modern or traditional settings. Silver, White, or Gold frames are available; coloured lighting can be incorporated to create special effects. All panels are noise absorbent and insulated. Some can be fitted by the average handyman although C+A provide a free measuring and installation service. *P:* upon application.

DAVID GILLESPIE ASSOCIATES LTD

Unusual ideas for ceilings from a company that's primarily geared to architects, but deliberately steers clear of mass-produced items. ZEROSPAN, made from Zerodec, consists of ceiling coffers and tiles supplied to fit 60×60cm (23⅝×23⅝in) standard grids. Zerodec comes with a standard White textured finish applied to the visible side, but it can be painted or sprayed with most paints and colours, sound-absorbent textured coatings, gilding, and other applied finishes. The hexagonal, triangular and rhombus shapes in HEXADEC (from moulded Zerodec) can be used in an endless variety of patterns to make very unusual ceilings. Mirrored ceilings consisting of inverted, polished aluminium pyramids are also available. Combined with special lighting they can be used to create dazzling effects. *P:* upon application.

Selection of patterns from David Gillespie's ZEROSPAN

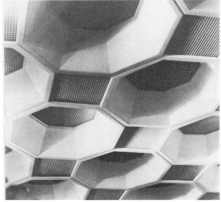

David Gillespie's HEXADEC

LUMITE CEILINGS

Wide range of decorative ceiling panels and frames in very modern geometric designs. LUMITE PVC panels, for rooms where the ceiling cavity requires ventilation, come in seven White textures and four colours: White, Powder blue, Primrose yellow, and Turquoise. Light transmission value is 70% for White panels, slightly less for coloured ones. In addition, there are two opaque wood-grain panels in teak or ash and three acoustic panels with frames in Silver, Gold, White, or Tan. Also fluorescent light fittings. *P:* upon application.

Lumite's PVC 'Daylight' panels with satin silver frames

WOOD AND WOOD EFFECTS

ARISTOCAST LTD

'Tudor cottage' style beams that fit the dimensions of modern houses (maximum length 22ft/671cm). Made from high-density polyurethane foam, and finished in dark oak, they're lightweight, easy to fix, and won't shrink or warp. For maximum effect, moulds are taken from original beams. Joists, corbels, and a very unusual plate rack (in 6ft/183cm lengths only) are also available. *P:* upon application.

CLASSICAL DESIGNS

RICO tiles in varnished or unvarnished wood. Ten designs range from the formally elegant to the asymmetrically modern. Very easily applied to walls (and ceilings) with base laths and mounting tools. Available in pine, larch, rosewood, rustic oak, walnut, teak, ash, oak, anegre, koto, and macore. *M:* 50×50cm (19⅝×19⅝in). *P:* pack of four tiles £14–20.

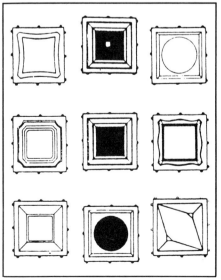

Selection from Classical Designs' RICO

DUROTANIK

Fantastically complete range of carved oak reproductions executed in hard foam, stained in dark oak (other shades upon request). Range includes rough hewn panelling, log and brick or sawn log panels, shingling layer panels, eight beams, and eight brackets. Also joint pieces, adhesives, decorative pegs, etc. *P:* upon application.

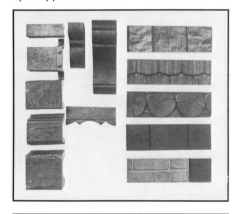

CHARLES HAMMOND LTD

French ROTANE beams from a well-known interior decorating firm. Made from polyurethane, they are absolutely perfect reproductions of wood aged in the Vosges forests. Junction strips, and large and small corbels, are available. *M:* l. 1–6m (3ft 3³/₈in – 18ft 20¹/₄in), sections 6×10–21×23cm (2³/₈×4 – 8¹/₄× 9in). *P:* upon application.

HART OF KNIGHTSBRIDGE

Pine room panelling, to order. An extensive range of pine mantels and surrounds, and a complementary recess or corner cupboard are also available (*P:* upon application). See also 'Fireplaces'.

HOMEWORKS LTD

PANELWORKS panelling, reminiscent of the 18th century. Made from selected fine veneers and solid woods finished with a combination of natural and coloured cellulose, often hand-applied, it can be ordered to fit any shape or size of room. All the necessary mouldings, including cornice, dado and skirting, are supplied. The range also has bookshelves, cupboards, wardrobes, doors (some with glass panels), and radiator casings. Natural versions are available. *P:* w 100 × h 260cm (3ft 3³/₈in × 8ft 6³/₈in) with moulding £525.

MAGNET SOUTHERNS

Numerous panelling products from a huge builder's merchant chain. Timber claddings are available in redwood, whitewood, and cedar, with grooved or plain surfaces, and a choice of ten redwood beads and moulds.

Left to right, from top: Magnet Southerns' whitewood, redwood, dummy grooved redwood, shaped cedar, whitewood weatherboard, shaped cedar timber cladding; below, redwood beads and moulds

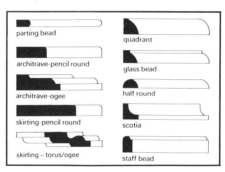

parting bead   quadrant
architrave-pencil round   glass bead
architrave-ogee   half round
skirting-pencil round   scotia
skirting – torus/ogee   staff bead

MAGNALUX panels come in 13 natural wood veneers: teak, rosewood, knotty pine, palado, afrormosia, American black walnut, knotty cedar, oak, cherry, ash, birch, sapele, and elm. Also in six randomly grooved simulated wood finishes: Idaho pine, silver ash, Mai cherry, Pacific elm, American cedar, and Ceylon teak. Panels can be fitted directly on to sound walls with a special adhesive, or attached to a batten system. A flame-retardant finish can be applied, to order only. *M:* 244×122cm (8×4ft). *P:* MAGNALUX natural wood panel £14.50–£20, rosewood panel £25, simulated wood panel £6.

W H NEWSON

Enormous range of architraves, cornices, picture rails, beadings, dados, panel mouldings, astragals, rounds, quadrants, and dowels; also skirtings and mouldings, including some Victorian and Edwardian styles. All potentially useful for applied decoration or restoration purposes. The entire range is illustrated, to show its extent. (You could create your own effect by topping skirting boards with one of the mouldings.) Newson will also make any moulding to order.

MASONITE'S HISTORIC COLLECTION panels authentically reproduce hand-crafted wall panelling. They can be fixed on to smooth walls with a recommended adhesive; or on uneven walls using battens. *M:* 8×4ft (244×122cm). MASONITE also has decorative wall boards in the following textures: Surfstone, Grey or Green Marbletone, White, Red or Tan gold brick, plus Natural or White stone. *P:* upon application.

Left to right, from top: Newson's astragals and panel mouldings; cornices, dados and picture rails; Victorian, Edwardian and period mouldings

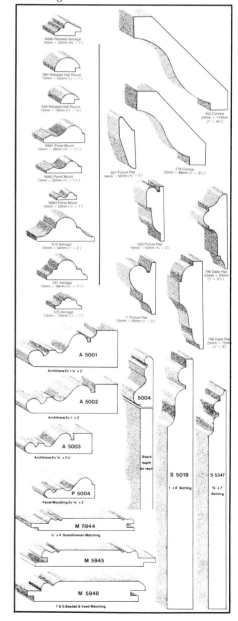

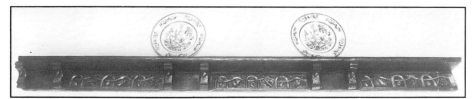

Oakleaf Reproductions' 'Plate Rack' (above) and Tudor door arches (left)

Selection from D & J Simons' ornaments

OAKLEAF REPRODUCTIONS LTD

Absolutely overwhelming selection of nearly 200 pieces, moulded in rigid polyurethane that reproduces every blemish and tool mark on the original. They include everything from beams and corbels (three), friezes, cornices, strip mouldings, adzed planking, columns (six), porticos, 'carved' and linenfold panels (and three rose panels), pilasters, sconces, ceiling roses, pillars and architraves to cartwheels and fake book backs! There are also two Tudor door arches in 6½ft (198cm) or 4ft (122cm) lengths (*P:* £27, £22). All are handfinished to ensure individual character, then stained to a rich oak.

OLD OAK BEAMS come in 6ft (283cm) and 12ft (566cm) lengths; joist corbels and mock bolts are available. 15 wonderfully ornate designs for friezes, cornices and strip mouldings include 'Tudor Rose' and 'Egg and Dart', and unusual 'Plate Rack'. There's a total of 26 different panels including 'Linenfold', in five sizes with matching grooved or floral incised stiles and rails, and plain 'Oak Jacobean', in six sizes with complementary edging strips, friezes, cornices and ceiling moulds. Other panels are carved with motifs that range from a unicorn to more traditional floral patterns. All in a wide variety of sizes. *M:* friezes, cornices, strip mouldings l. 3¾–9½ft (114.5–289.5cm) depending on range/design. *P:* OLD OAK BEAMS l. 12ft×6×6in (366×15×15cm) £50; 'Plate Rack' l. 6ft (183cm) £19.

D & J SIMONS & SONS LTD

Terrific selection of 60 embossed-wood ornaments for walls and furniture, from a small company that pays great attention to detail. Also picture frame mouldings and banister rails. *P:* upon application.

STUART INTERIORS

Accurate facsimiles of Elizabethan and Jacobean woodwork from a specialist firm based in Somerset. The range covers galleries, screens, panelling, mantels (many of them elaborately carved), staircases, and doors. Craftsman-made, in woods like solid English oak, holly, yew, and walnut, they blend perfectly with period surroundings. See also 'Fireplaces'.

SWAN GALLERIES

INSTANT PANELLING range of traditional units in standard widths that fit almost any wall length. They include fireplace surrounds, display cases, columns, bookcases, plain panels, and door units. Frames are made of Siberian pine, panels are blockboard faced with Siberian pine veneer and backed with a toning veneer. The drawings illustrated show some of the options that are available. *P:* upon application.

Swan Galleries' INSTANT PANELLING, including panels, fireplace surrounds, door units and display cases

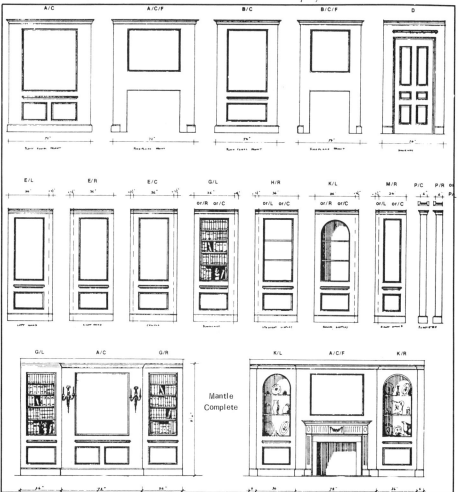

Mantle Complete

INTRODUCTION

The bathroom is often one of the smallest rooms in the house, but there's no reason why it should also be the dullest. On the contrary, it's the place to try out your most exciting and outrageous schemes – no one will stay there long enough to suffer. Foil paper, mirrors, even gloss paint on the walls, will brighten it up. Or go for White walls, sanitaryware and fittings – the cheapest way to create a dramatic effect with towels and accessories providing colour and decorative highlights. You can even repaint an old bathroom suite (see 'Paint'). If you're furnishing from scratch, there's an almost endless choice of styles, ranging from functional High Tech to Victorian Revival.

Bathrooms tend to be short on space, so work with a graph-paper floor plan to find the most suitable lay-out. And, if you're planning basic alterations, remember that toilets are best kept on, or adjacent to, an outside wall, or near the present outlet. Baths and sinks are more moveable, but it makes sense to keep them as close as possible to the present outlet. Baths come in varying widths and lengths – some are only 4×2ft (122×61cm), so even the smallest space can be fitted out in style.

This section covers all the constituents of a bathroom. *Bathroom Accessories and Fittings* range from standard chrome-plated brass taps and mixers to exotic (and expensive) fittings in gold plate, often combined with porcelain or crystal; from plastic accessories through ceramicware to versions made from cultured (reconstituted) marble, and even semi-precious stones. Most manufacturers make their own accessories, but you can mix taps from one firm with a tub from another, providing the plumbing and holes are compatible. Taps, toilet roll holders, towel rails, soap dishes, medicine cabinets, etc can add quite a tidy sum to the basic cost. If you're counting pennies, go for inexpensive co-ordinated plastic accessories in a colour that contrasts or blends with the sanitaryware and bathroom walls.

Sanitaryware includes baths, basins, WCs, bidets, shower trays and vanity units; also wondrous but expensive special ranges, often decorated with borders or painted designs, that can turn a bathroom into a fantasyland. Some more ordinary suites are also available in special depp-dyed colours, so with patience and ingenuity it's possible to get a glamorous effect for a fraction of the cost of the more expensive ranges. White is generally the cheapest colour; hand-painted wares the most expensive. The chart on page 30 gives a breakdown of manufacturers' pastel and deep-dyed shades.

Showers are featured in a separate section, and include both do-it-yourself kits and luxury models. Also a unit which heats water independent of the mains supply.

*The most unusual products from each company are usually illustrated, and prices given accordingly.

BATHROOM ACCESSORIES & FITTINGS

ALBION HARDWARE LTD

Delightfully nostalgic bathroom accessories in brass or chrome, teamed with crystal or porcelain. Each range includes taps, vanity basins, towel rails, paper holders, hooks, toothbrush/tumbler holders and soap dishes. There are three brass or chrome collections: 'Clear Crystal', 'Old Dominion' and 'Georgian Rope'; and three in porcelain: 'Meadow Flower' in Rose, Yellow, and Blue, 'Summer Bouquet', a design of Golden daisies and Green leaves, and 'Village Blue'. Only solid brass is used, chrome-plated or lacquered. *P:* 'Old Dominion' (the most expensive suite), porcelain vanity bowl £160 decorated, £130 plain White, towel rail £20, paper holder £20, hook £8, towel ring £13, toothbrush/tumbler holder and soap dish £15.

ALLIBERT (UK) LTD

Excellent, modern, illuminated mirrors, plus every other imaginable bathroom accessory including a magnetic soap dish and a WC cupboard for storing toiletries. About 30 different bathroom cabinets are also available, each with individual features. Mirror doors have fluorescent or diffused lighting; some cabinets incorporate a razor socket.

GRAND LUXE, the classiest range, incorporates a set of sleekly modern co-ordinated accessories in chrome with clear or 'fine cognac' tinted crystal. Other ranges come in

one of three colour combinations: Beige and Brown, two tones of Green, and Curry (yellow) and Brown. All products are treated with an anti-static process. *P:* SAPONA cabinet with light £45 as illustrated, towel ring and soap holder £3, shelf £6, hinged towel ring £4.

ARMITAGE SHANKS LTD

A wide range of good-looking taps and shower fittings, finished in chrome or gold-plate. STARLITE has a choice of taps or mixers, including the monobloc mixer, with acrylic, onyx marble, or chrome-plated handwheels. SHEERLINE taps are available with clear acrylic, or Brown or Green simulated onyx handwheels. Shower fittings in both ranges can be manually operated, or have thermostatic controls; they can be wall mounted or hand-held. A great range of ceramic accessories is also available: three recessed soap holders, four toilet roll holders, a magnetic soap holder, soap tray, robe hook, towel ring, tumbler and toothbrush unit, toilet brush holder, towel rail bracket, and shelf. *P:* upon application.

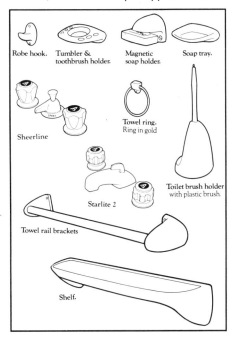

Robe hook. Tumbler & toothbrush holder. Magnetic soap holder. Soap tray. Sheerline. Towel ring. Ring in gold. Starlite 2. Toilet brush holder with plastic brush. Towel rail brackets. Shelf.

BALTERLEY BATHROOMS LTD

Accessories that complement the colours and designs of Balterley's suites including APPLE BLOSSOM and ROMANA GOLD. They come with chromed or lacquered-brass screws; gold-plate is also available. ROMANA GOLD accessories have a hand-applied 22ct-gold edging to contrast with the rich deep tones of the vitreous china. *P:* upon application.

PRICES AND INFORMATION WERE CORRECT AT THE TIME OF GOING TO PRESS

Selection of Balterley's ceramic accessories

BARKING-GROHE LTD

Large, very practical collection of modern, clean-lined taps and thermostatic and regular mixers for baths, basins and showers, plus other plumbing essentials. Unusual designs include the 'Euromix' single-lever basin mixer and the 'Biflo' mixer with swivel nozzle and elbow action (also available as two separate taps).

Most units can be fitted with triangular tap handles, available in crystal, onyx, stainless steel or Brown acrylic. *P:* 'Euromix' and waste £50, 'Biflo' £40.

Barking-Grohe's 'Euromix'

BONSACK BATHS LTD

Enormous range of made-to-order fittings—24 designs include dolphins, reeds, sea shells, festoons and swans. But Bonsack take baths seriously—they also have shelves and trolleys, myriads of mirrors (wall mounted and free standing), wastebaskets, tissue box covers, planters and soft furnishings. They place great emphasis on lighting, and supply matching fixtures. (Both chandeliers can be converted to showers—swans or dolphins spout water!) *P:* upon application.

Bonsack's 'Bow' accessories

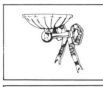

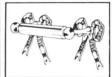

CARRON CO

APOLLO taps and mixers, the best in modern design. Each fitting is available in hand-polished chrome or gold-plate, with hand-wheels in chrome or gold acrylic, chrome, Black styrene, Pink or Brown onyx, and Jade or Burgundy enamel. *P:* upon application.

J & A CARTERS LTD

Sturdy grab bars and safety rails in all shapes and sizes. Each item is ergonomically designed so that elderly or disabled people can use the bath or WC unaided. *P:* from £9.

Carron's APOLLO tap

CHLORIDE SHIRES LTD

Unique coloured chrome taps and mixer sets for bathrooms and kitchens, from a top Italian design team. DA VINCI fittings are capped with tinted acrylic handwheels to tone with the base units. Colours are Harmony brown, Harmony green, Aubergine, Ocean (blue), and Yukon (green). *P:* upon application.

CRAYONNE UK LTD

The best in cheap and cheerful modern bathroom accessories. These nylon shower curtains have weighted hems and come in exciting designs, in wonderful and unusual colours. Also four plain shades: White, Beige, Mid-brown, and Mid-blue. *P:* patterned (2oz nylon) £13, plain (4oz nylon) £11.

Crayonne's shower curtains

CZECH & SPEAKE LTD
'Edwardian' taps, mixers, shower heads and riser pipes in solid brass and gunmetal, with porcelain fittings. (Production methods haven't changed for over a century.) Beautifully hand-finished in polished brass, they can be chrome, nickel, or gold-plated. *P:* '6450' basin mixer with adjustable pop-up waste, from £180 in polished brass, as illustrated.

ENGINEERING CONCESSIONAIRES LTD
Very attractive taps, thermostatic mixers and shower fittings. The innovative 'Enflomix' controls both the flow and temperature of the water from a single lever and comes with a standard or extra-long neck. Also two ranges with simulated onyx handwheels in chrome and gold-plate, and an extensive selection of wastes and traps. Gold-plated waste surrounds (hard-to-find items) are also available. *P:* upon application.

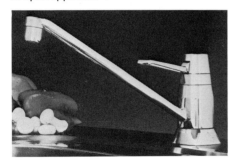

Engineering Concessionaire's 'Enflomix'

GALLERIA MONTE CARLO
Excessively beautiful fixtures and fittings. They include 20 basin sets, 12 complementary tub sets, many with matching showerheads, some of which have crystal handwheels. (How about a dolphin to spout forth your shower?) All in burnished chrome (which looks like pewter) or 24ct gold-plate. Modernists will prefer the 'Sculptured Basin Set' with triangular handles. *P:* upon application.
There's also a hand-painted porcelain range with matching tiles and wallpapers; and basin and tub sets made from semi-precious stones like lapis lazuli, malachite, rose quartz and Black, White, Brown or Green onyx. All are teamed with burnished chrome or gold. All these ranges have matching accessories: towel rails and rings, soap dishes, toilet roll holders, door knobs and drawer pulls, switchplates, hinges, hooks, wastebaskets, etc.
Galleria Monte Carlo also make vanity consoles, benches, towel drapes and shelves in bamboo or Louis XVI reeded gold-plate, brass or burnished chrome. Other delights include the 'Water Nymph' double shelf and towel bar; 17 crystal sconces with gold or silver mounts; crystal ceiling lights; and large matching mirrors. There's also a ribbon, reed and sea shell medicine cabinet, etc. *P:* upon application. See also 'Ceramic Tiles', 'Lighting', 'Wall Coverings'. See page 26 for hand-painted porcelain taps in colour.

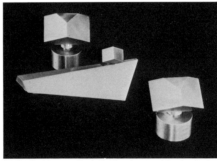

Galleria Monte Carlo's 'Sculptured Basin Set'

PETER D GURNER DESIGNS LTD
Thirteen tap designs in over 50 metal or enamel finishes, complementing this company's absolutely amazing range of fibreglass bathtubs. MEDICI can be finished in gold, bronze, brass, chrome, nickel, copper, antique silver, chocolate, brushed silver, or gunmetal; inlays come in malachite, Chinese lacquer, tortoiseshell, coral, lapis lazuli, mother of pearl, and other precious or semi-precious gemstones. A full range of accessories is also available, including soap dish, towel ring and rail, toilet roll holder, mirrors and knobs. *P:* from £245, to £3,000 for gold and coral taps.

HABITAT DESIGNS LTD
Striking shower curtains in 100% cotton, from the UK's famed purveyors of good taste. LIANA has wavy vertical stripes in Red, Yellow, Blue, and Green on White (*P:* £9.25). CONFUCIUS has overlapping circular patterns in Blue on Off-white (*P:* £11). YACHTING, with a design of Grey boats on squared Blue seas, has matching ceramic tiles and towels (*P:* £11). 100% woven nylon curtains come in four plain shades: Navy blue, Chinese red, Beige, and Brown (*P:* £9.25). See also 'Ceramic Tiles'.

HARRISON-BEACON LTD
Competitively priced accessories in silver anodized aluminium and Black plastic, from a firm that specializes in hardware. Most plastic components can be removed for cleaning, and thoughtful design touches include a toothbrush holder with a place to store toothpaste. There are eight items in the range. *P:* tidy tray £1.70, swing towel rail £4.25.

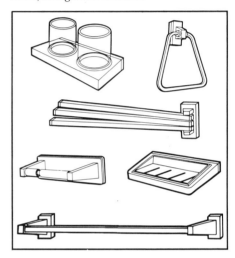

HEATHERLEY FINE CHINA LTD
21 ceramic bathroom accessories, all simply but elegantly designed. Just about everything you could think of, including towel rails, soap dishes, toilet roll holders and storage jars. Colours are Sepia, Avocado, Sun King, Sapphire, Evergreen, Peony, Flamingo, Emerald, Sahara, Cabana, Pampas, Pink, Turquoise, Primrose, Sky blue, and White. There's also a choice of two floral ceramic finishes: 'Summer Song' in pastels and 'Golden Dusk' with a single, sepia, rose motif. *P:* upon application.

IDEAL STANDARD LTD
A wide range of chrome or gold-plated taps, mixers and shower fittings. Some are also available in brass. JETLINE, the most modern range, comes with triangular metal or acrylic handles. The latter are amber-tinted when teamed with gold-plated fittings—unusual and attractive.
PRINCESS ceramic accessories complement the streamlined good looks of Ideal Standard's MICHELANGELO suite, and are available in all the same colours (see chart). *P:* upon application.

Ideal Standard's PRINCESS accessories

JUNEGRADE LTD
Hand-polished, natural mahogany lavatory seats that restore this 'classical' article to its proper status. Each seat comes with all necessary brass fittings, with or without a brass inscription plate. Coloured seats are also available, in a pale natural shade like pine, two shades of Red, Green, Blue, Black, Amethyst, and Orange. *P:* from £30.

MOLNLYCKE LTD
Stylish, practical dispensers for paper towels, soap and toilet tissue, from a Swedish firm. Primarily intended for industrial use, they look attractive—and original—in the home. Available in Green, Blue, Yellow, Brown, and two Reds. *P:* upon application.

PETRATE LTD
Two unusual ranges of stainless steel accessories. KOSMOS, by Geesa, is basically circular, and comes in chrome and gold-plate. Nicely made, if rather expensive, the range consists of a toilet roll holder, shelf, toothbrush holder, towel rail, tumbler holder, soap dish and cloak hook. *P:* toilet roll holder £38, shelf £40, toothbrush holder £19, in chrome. ROYAL CHARISMA, in chrome, has 14 items including a combined toilet roll holder and hook, and a triangular soap dish. *P:* toilet roll holder £5, soap dish £8.

Petrate's KOSMOS shelf (top), toilet roll holder (right), toothbrush holder (left)

S POLLIACK LTD
A staggering array of fittings and accessories, designed to enhance 'Polly's' luxurious bathroom suites and matching tiles. Most three-hole bath, basin and bidet mixer sets are extremely ornate, with swans (several different types), dolphins and even bamboo motifs. Materials like crystal, gold-plate, gemstones, malachite or hand-painted china are incorporated. Matching accessories include bath pulls, soap holders, toilet roll holders,

Polliack's dolphin basin set

tiles, coat hooks, towel rails and towel rings—even WC flush levers.

A quite separate range of fitments, made of attractively turned polished wood, includes a soap holder, toothmug holder, paper holder, towel rail, towel ring, oval mirror and three-branch hanging light for the ceiling. *P:* upon application. See also 'Ceramic Tiles'.

REGENCY BATHROOM ACCESSORIES LTD
Highly decorative taps, mixers and shower fittings finished in gold- or chrome-plate. DIAMOND CUT, a classically elegant design, is probably the most unusual. It's based on a faceted cylinder with panels in Black, Brown, Burgundy, Coral, Green, Blue, gold on gold, or silver on chrome (illustrated with 'Jubilee', Regency's simplest tap). Other ranges, some extremely ornate, feature various motifs from the SWAN to GREEK KEY. REGENCY and GREEK KEY both include towel rails and rings, paper and glass holders, soap dish, wall sconce (also a double version in GREEK KEY), and robe hooks. *P:* upon application.

Regency's DIAMOND CUT mixer with 'Jubilee' taps

SILENT GLISS LTD
Straight or curved shower or bath rails from a firm that specializes in curtainware. All are supplied with wall supports, gliders and stainless steel hooks. Available in anodized natural aluminium or gold finish, the rails are simple—and fast—to fix. *P:* 6100/B (right-angled) for shower tray £8.70, 6100/C/D for baths £25.

SITTING PRETTY LTD
Wooden lavatory seats with a plus. This company specializes in hand-painted monograms, family crests, coats of arms and other special insignia on the lids. The seats come in

solid mahogany, and obeche, an African whitewood that is stained to imitate teak, walnut, rosewood, oak or ebony; or can be coloured Bright red, Dark blue or Green. Sitting Pretty will supply a seat in the finish or colour of your choice, and also wax or French polish. Lacquered or chrome-plated brass fittings; gold-plate is available. For do-it-yourself freaks they offer both types in kit form, including fittings and accessories. *P: mahogany £60, obeche £40, kit £32, motifs from £13 for a monogram to £40 for a coat of arms.*

SPECTRUM LTD

Functional, chunky, I BALOCCHI taps and mixers from Italy. Easy to grip, they come in a range of good, strong colours: Yellow, Orange, Red, Green, Blue, and Brown—plus chrome and White. Units include wall mixer with hand shower, bidet mixer, wash basin mixer, built-in bathtub mixer with hand shower, and wall shower arm with head; also pop-up bidet and bath mixers. *P: upon application.*

Spectrum's I BALOCCHI mixer

ST MARCO'S

Staggering selection of sumptuous imported accessories, in a wide range of prices, designed to transform the drabbest bathroom. All the ranges in St Marco's impressive Sloane Street showroom are very modern, with two exceptions. DORIAN ARTS accessories, in wood or laminated plastic, are either Art Nouveau or fancy French in style—and expensive. They come in White, and walnut; matching bathroom furniture is available in White, with front mouldings, and plain walnut. Some examples from the range are as follows: 7046 mirror (£295), towel handle in two sizes (large £26), towel ring, also two sizes (large £32), bracket for glass or soap (£39), 7039 chandelier in Bohemian crystal (£285), 7050 wall lamp (£140), 7048 footstool (£120), 7031 brush bracket (£65). Nine more lighting, and six mirror, styles are available. The 2000 range is made from metal, looks like turned wood, and

comes in riotous lacquered colours like Red, Pink, Green, Yellow, Plum, and Brown. It includes oval and round mirrors (£55), toilet roll holder (£16), soap and glass holder (£11), coat hook, towel stand, footstool, and three ceiling and three wall light fittings.

St Marco's 2000 soap or glass holder (left), toilet roll holder (right)

Modern PRISMA L, in wood, has all the usual accessories in natural ash, or walnut, plus a toilet seat, wall light and well-lit mirror.
The beautiful, architect-designed CLINIO range includes the single soap dish illustrated (£20), a sponge and soap dish combined, two towel rails, coat hook, toilet tissue and brush holders, footstool, towel rack, and several mirror and medicine cabinet modules complete with lighting.

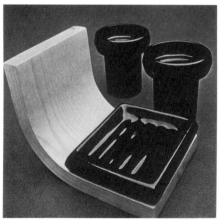

St Marco's CLINIO soap dish

All the usual accessories are available in square-based PRISMA, featuring stainless steel tubing. PASQUINUCCI tinted perspex mirrors with Hollywood-effect rim lighting come in seven styles, in shades of Brown, Champagne, Blue, Green, Gold, and Rose. Space-age ROBERTA in White moulded plastic, with pleasing spherical curves, complements HONEYMOON and MOONLIGHT bathroom furniture and includes everything anyone could possibly want for a vanity top. TANTI NUOVI, in moulded polyurethane, is an even more extensive, but expensive, range of 40 pieces. Last but certainly not least, ACQUA, for High Tech fans, incorporates a steel mesh grid, wood and ceramicware (*P: mirrors from £110, small soap dish £22, shelf and towel rail £40).*

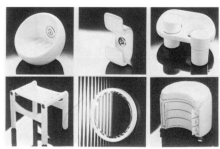

Selection of St Marco's TANTI NUOVI accessories

Lovers of zappy shower curtains will delight in the POSTER range, with brightly coloured, Pop Art style motifs, including comic strips, big cats, Bugattis, droplets, flowers, waves—even *The Sunday Times!* Italian bathroom linen and unusual chrome shaving mirrors are available.

SWEDISH VALVE CO LTD

Wide range of squared-off bathroom fittings. Available in chrome or gold-plate, it includes thermostatic mixers and single lever basin taps. The BRILJANT hand shower head and tube, with bracket fixing or tube clamp, comes in an outstanding selection of colours: White, Black, Blue, Yellow, Curry, Green, Moss green, Olive, Mocha, Bahama beige, Camel, Red, Wine red, and Orange. *P: £10 as illustrated.*

TWYFORDS LTD

Pleasingly designed AZTEC taps and mixers. Made of solid brass, they are finished in chrome or 24ct gold. *P: chrome £55, gold £150.*

Selection of Twyfords' RADIANTE accessories

The RADIANTE range of vitreous china bathroom accessories matches Twyfords' suites. It includes a soap tray, toothbrush holder, towel rail, towel ring, toilet roll holder, toilet brush holder and a long shelf. Available in all Twyfords' colours (see chart). *P:* mirror £39, soap dish £5, shelf £10, towel ring £6.

WINTHER, BROWNE & CO LTD

Swedish pine accessories. Owners of pine-clad bathrooms need no longer be frustrated in their search for competitively priced accessories. This fittings specialist has a soap dish, toothbrush/mug holder, toilet roll holder, and a rack with six coat hooks. (Everything except the rack is supplied polished.) *P:* soap dish £4.60, toothbrush holder £5.10, toilet roll holder £5.30, rack £1.20.

Winther, Browne's toothbrush/mug holder (top), soap dish (centre), toilet roll holder (bottom)

SANITARYWARE

ANDERSON CERAMICS LTD

Beautiful bathroom suites handworked from fireclay. VICTORIANA has an Art Nouveau curlicue in gold against White. (As illustrated the suite retails for about £3,000—wildly expensive—but if you would like it in a solid colour, without the gold finish, it would set you back a mere £1,200.) The mahogany toilet seat and gold-plated taps for the basin and bidet provide the finishing touch.

MERIDIAN ONE, an enterprising and graceful modern range, has a spectacular fibreglass circular bath with club-shaped interior (*P:* bath £710, basin £90, bidet £95, WC £150). The simply styled, but coolly elegant, JESMOND suite is in a special mottled glaze.

Individual items include the extremely attrac-

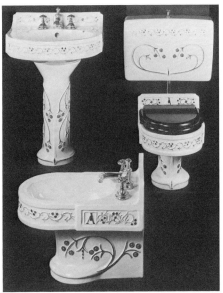

Anderson's VICTORIANA suite

Armitage Shanks' VERSAILLES suite

tive 'alcove' basin— an oval bowl with rectangular surround—an almost hemispherical 'cloakroom' basin for very confined spaces, and 'Harlech 1700', a bath in Beige marble finish. All come with chrome- or gold-plated fittings. MERIDIAN ONE, JESMOND, and the basins are available in Mulberry, Chestnut, Astral blue, Green bronze, White.

ARISTOCAST LTD

Fibreglass baths, basins and shower trays. Although lightweight, they're strong and durable, won't leak or crack and are easily cleaned. The circular 'Libra' bath has a heavily constructed flat base, essential if the bath is also to be used for showering (*P:* £260). The two corner baths, 'Aquarius', and 'Gemini', are available with 'Aristocast integral tiling upstand', which prevents leaks between the bath and the wall(*P:* £180, £190).

An unusual basin shaped like an oyster shell costs about £25, excluding taps. Gold-plated overflow, outlets, grips, chain, etc, are available. See chart for colours.

Aristocast's 'oyster-shell' basin

ARMITAGE SHANKS LTD

An enormous range of simple, good-looking furniture including seven bathtub shapes, 15 basin styles, six shower trays and five WC and bidet options. Also co-ordinating accessories and tap fittings. Very good vanity units in White melamine or mahogany finish—you can choose from louvred or laminate doors, then decide which of their attractive basins will provide the finishing touch. All are available in a large range of colours, including the fashionable deep-dyes (see chart). In contrast to the 'clean lines' approach, VERSAILLES is a 22ct-gold filigree pattern fired on to an Avocado background. It is available on the more expensive baths, basins and bidets, with towel ring, soap tray and toilet roll holder to match. See chart for colours. *P:* upon application.

Armitage Shanks' 'Minerva' vanity unit with 'Seville' fireclay basin

BALTERLEY BATHROOMS LTD
Standard undecorated bathroom sanitary-ware, plus two tempting ranges. APPLE BLOSSOMS juxtaposes a delicate chain of blossoms against a Spring green background. ROMANA GOLD has a 22ct-gold Greek key motif on any of five rich, dark hues or White (see chart). Each item, individually made from deeply glazed vitreous china, receives up to five separate firings in the kiln. Plain and patterned ranges include three baths (one a

corner bath), pedestal, hand and vanity basins, bidet and toilet. All are come in a large range of dramatic shades, including Black (see chart). Every suite has a full range of co-ordinated accessories: wall mirror, tumbler and tooth-brush holder, toilet roll holder, etc. *P:* upon application.

BERGLEN ASSOCIATES LTD
Something completely different—a striking, round seamless steel basin in any Euro-standard colour, is set in a dense Black enamel tub (*M:* diam 27 to 49cm/10⅝ to 19¼in diam, *P:* from £105). This adventuresome firm also imports German-made built-in vanity basins in 18 gorgeous colours including Mushroom, Beige, Lime, Bright orange, Deep red, Coral, two Browns, Bright and Sky blue, Golden sand, Avocado and Forest green, Rose, White, and Black. Six shapes, including the unusual ogee. *P:* £45.

Berglen's round steel basin (above)

Berglen's ogee-shape basin

BONSACK BATHS LTD
Fibreglass baths in every imaginable shape, some very exotic. Godfrey Bonsack has practically turned the bathroom into an art form, albeit a very exclusive and expensive one. The overwhelming visual appeal is backed by sound practical design and, often, innovative engineering—trained craftsmen follow a patented, secret process. Baths are available in one of a thousand matt colours—or the colour of your choice—and 12 'standard' metallic shades: Bright silver, Pale gold, Gold orange, Brilliant red, Purple, Royal blue, Medium blue, Aqua, Lavender, Salmon, Antique brown, and Soft black. Iridescent mother-of-pearl comes in eight shades from predictable Pearly white, through lustrous neutrals, to Red.
Motifs, patterns and borders include fleurs de lis, scrolls, Greek key, rope and lovers' knots, passion fruit, laurel wreaths, daisies, Chinese Ming and Palace Script initials. A bath with under-water massage equipment is available edged with any of these motifs.
Bonsack offer a complete bathroom design service including the preparation of drawings, colour schemes and costs. A huge array of accessories is also available.
P: upon application. See page 25 for Bonsack's 'Egyptian' bathroom in colour.

CARRON CO
Attractively styled bathroom suites in one of three materials: acrylic, cast iron, or pressed steel. Two interesting acrylic baths are 'Granada', a large luxurious affair, and 'Marlborough', with a drop front and contoured backrest. 'Athena', also in acrylic, is a corner bath. 'The Juno', in pressed steel with a vitreous enamel surface, and 'The Atlantis', in acrylic, have roll-front styling. Complementarily styled basins, bidets and WCs coordinate beautifully and boldly in their large

Balterley's ROMANA GOLD suite (left)

selection of colours. 'The Carrina', in acrylic, is an elliptically shaped basin with corner tap position, designed for use in vanity tops. Vanity units come in many different styles, all with moulded doors.

Polystyrene BATH PANELS prevent water collecting between the bath and wall. They come in all Carron's colours, various heights and three styles. A great solution. Of the colours available (see chart) four are exclusive to Carron: Jade, Burgundy, Lagoon, and Aztec gold. Carron also supply stylishly cubic taps. *P:* upon application.

Carron's 'Carrina' acrylic basin

Elliott-Powell's 'Novara' bath and 'Sezanne' vanity top

CHLORIDE SHIRES LTD

Well-designed bathroom suites, for a wide market. Nine baths include the 'Soho' shower bath, a mini-bath and shower in one unit; the 'Chelsea', which has a grab bar for the elderly or disabled; the 'Allegro' with a circular shower area; and the 'Eros', a corner bath. Complementary accessories for all ranges include a vanity bar over the bath for storage. Chloride Shires make five pedestal basins, four for wall mounting and one to fit in a corner; also two shower trays.

The FORMAT 2 range includes a pleasing vanity unit in onyx finish, with a rolled edge, and Chocolate, Olive or White doors. Available in various lengths, it can be fitted with any of three drop-in basins. There's a matching mirrored wall cabinet, and a tall cupboard with shelves, doors and/or drawers.

ROSETTE, the most unusual range, comes in shaded Gold or Lilac, with a choice of two baths, 'Allegro' or 'Eros', two basins, WC and

Chloride Shires' ROSETTE suite

bidet. Distinctive ranges of coloured chrome taps and mixers are also available. *P:* upon application.

ELLIOTT-POWELL LTD

Cultured-marble bathrooms. There are five baths—two ovals in different sizes, two standard shapes, and a bath with a sloping back and seating edge; four shower trays; WC and bidet suites; and ten vanity tops. *P:* 'Novara' sunken bath £700, 'Sezanne' double bowl vanity top £250.

ELON TILES (UK) LTD

A range of ten hand-painted washbasins with co-ordinating flowered taps and accessories, to match this company's gaily patterned glazed terracotta tiles from Mexico. A complementary

towel rack, recessed soap holder, toothbrush and tumbler holder, cloak hook, and toilet roll holder are available. *P:* small round £30, large oval £100; faucet and taps set £135; all accessories £60.

GALLERIA MONTE CARLO

Extensive and exquisitely co-ordinated collection of hand-painted porcelain bowls, with matching taps and accessories. (The same designs are available for oval under-counter bowls.) Classically inspired gold or platinum bandings are optional extras. These uncompromising manufacturers will also supply a complete line of matching accessories: towel bar, wall-mounted soap dish, surface or recessed paper holder, door lever, drawer pull,

Elon's hand-painted basins

switchplate, hook, jar, towel ring, door knob, soap dish, tumbler, wastepaper basket, matching tiles, wallpaper. Galleria Monte Carlo also make a fluted-column china pedestal wash-stand; a wonderfully futuristic stainless steel and marble wash-stand; old-fashioned caned French commodes; and standard or custom-built semi-precious stone vanity tops. A marble basin, bidet and bath, hand-carved into a half-shell shape, is undoubtedly their most expensive range and comes in whatever colour you choose. *P:* upon application. See also 'Ceramic Tiles', 'Wall Coverings'. See page 26 for hand-painted bowls and taps.

Galleria Monte Carlo's stainless steel and marble wash basin

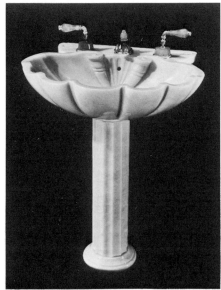

Galleria Monte Carlo's hand-carved marble basin, shaped like a shell

GLYNWED BATHROOM & KITCHEN PRODUCTS

Amazing range of LEISURE vanity basins: two in vitreous enamelled steel, two in acrylic, and 'Tweed', a textured-effect basin and vanity top which comes in White, Green, or Pink/Brown onyx, and Pampas, Sun King, and Avocado marble. It will fit custom-made vanity units (tap holes where required). *P:* 'Leader' £32, 'Tweed' £74 onyx, £83 marble.

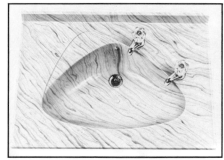

Glynwed's 'Tweed' vanity basin

PETER D GURNER DESIGNS LTD

PLUSH FLUSH range for anyone who wants to sink into a pool of self-indulgence *and* the colour of their choice. There are 12 exotic fibreglass bath shapes, plus WCs, bidets and two shower trays. The very good selection of basins includes two ceramic shapes, four fibreglass models that co-ordinate with baths, and four basins in hand-beaten brass which can be plated in chrome, nickel, brushed nickel, copper, or gold, to order.
2001 spa-water jet bath and shower systems are also available with a push-button automatic system, which fills the bath, that can be operated from the bath or bed. *P:* 'Astoria' sunken bath £450, to 'Kyoto' (virtually a mini-pool) £900.

Gurner's 'Kyoto' bath

IDEAL STANDARD LTD

A very wide selection of sanitaryware including 14 sinks, ten toilets, four bidets, four baths and a shower tray. Two of the best products in the standard ranges are the asymmetrical 'Cleopatra' wash basin, and the 'Nagoya' bath —large enough for two to bath together, not quite a double bath. 'Nagoya' has an elliptical interior with a comfortable backrest at both ends, and is probably best recessed into the floor. Like other Ideal Standard baths, it's made from acrylic sheet.

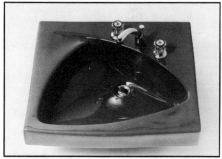

Ideal Standard's 'Cleopatra' basin (above), 'Nagoya' bath (below)

Each item in the striking Italian-style MICHELANGELO range is based on a round-cornered rectangle. All in gleaming ceramic, fired in one of seven non-compromising colours. See illustration on back cover.
P: upon application. See chart.

NORDIC SAUNAS LTD

Intriguing 'bathroom spa'. With the twin advantages of bath and shower, it's a temptingly decadent idea. A powerful built-in circulating pump jets warming streams of aerated water at your body, relaxing muscles and stimulating circulation. Standard colours. Nordic, best known for saunas, solaria and sunbeds, will also make spas to special order. Nordic also market the futuristic BELLINI range from Italy. Made in vitreous china it comes in White, Champagne, Avocado, Blue marine, Bali brown, and Harvest; also two-tone combinations, with White insets in Deep red, Emerald, Cobalt blue, Orange, and Ruby red surrounds. *P:* pedestal basin £110, toilet £210, bidet 480, baths from £300.

Right: Bonsack's exotic 'Egyptian' bathroom, with lotus blossom tiles

Nordic's 'bathroom spa'

PATRICKS OF FARNHAM

Real marble, made-to-measure vanity tops, by a firm that specializes in natural stone. You provide a detailed sketch, and choose one of ten luxurious colours including five variations on White—Black-veined, Rose-veined, Gold-veined, Off-white, and Pure white—plus three Greens. Slabs suitable for wall or floor mounting also available. *P:* 3×2ft (91.5−61cm) slab with polished front edge, overbowl cut out, and three tap/waste lever holes £135.

PETRATE LTD

Wonderfully sculptured range of sanitaryware by Jacob Delafon. Available in soft Antique white only, its futuristic lines are hard to beat. *P:* pedestal wash basin from £240, bidet £120, WC £300.

S POLLIACK LTD

Lavish, luxurious bathrooms that are sometimes even a trifle vulgar in splendidly old-fashioned style. Polliak's most unusual bath, the round 'Chambord Radica', allows two people to sit diagonally opposite each other. The generous overall size of 'Brissac' encloses a tub area with gently sloping sides. In contrast, the lines of the '2000' range are as modern and Italianate as any. CHAUMONT, illustrated with the 'Chinon' bath, is a two-tone Edwardian-inspired suite with moulded borders (*P:* bath £500, WC and cistern £225, bidet £85, basin and pedestal £155). CHATEAU ROUX, with classically fluted pedestals,

Nordic's BELLINI suite

is available hand-decorated or plain (*P:* corner bath £550, WC and cistern £350, bidet £215, basin and pedestal £345). All 'Polly' baths are available in a two-tone rustic finish. Polliack have a large choice of hand-painted, flower-bedecked old-fashioned ranges, and a vast selection of fittings and accessories. See also 'Ceramic Tiles'.

Opposite page: Galleria Monte Carlo's hand-painted taps and basins

Polliack's CHAUMONT (right) with the 'Chinon' bath

RAINBOW PRODUCTS LTD

Five hydrotherapy baths, in a wide range of bathroom colours. Rainbow are specialists in the field and claim increasing popularity for their products. The hydro-system incorporates jets that force a mixture of air and hot water into the bath, giving an all-over massage, dilating the blood vessels, and so helping circulation and improving skin tone.

The SPA BATH range consists of two single baths, a corner bath, a cloverleaf bath and a circular bath. Each is fitted with six adjustable jets, a powerful pump, fingertip controls and a safety circuit breaker. A thermostatically controlled reheating system is also available. The 'Hydro-Massage' system can be fitted to a customer's own fibreglass or acrylic bath. *P:* from £1,100.

Rainbow's HOT TUBS, hand-crafted in timber, can be sunken, half sunken or free standing. Seats are installed at a height that takes full advantage of the hydro-massage jets. Concrete spas, rather like swimming pools, can be made to customer's specifications; available with or without the hydro system. *P:* from £1,700.

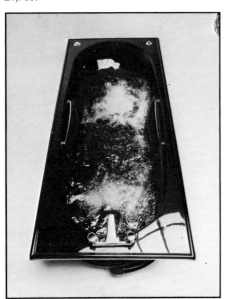

Rainbow's SPA BATH

ROYAL DOULTON SANITARYWARE LTD

A huge selection of clean-lined, modern products made of vitreous china, fireclay or acrylic. 13 basins and WCs, four bidet styles, eight baths and seven shower trays, one for corner fitting, come in a wide choice of colours (see chart) including 15 for the shower trays. The MARBLE LOOK range, made from reconstituted stone bound with resin, produces a convincing luxury finish at a fraction of the price of the real thing.

Baths are available in Beige, Dark onyx or Mink, the tub area set off by an attractively toning-in or contrasting colour underneath. *P:*

Royal Doulton's MARBLE LOOK suite

'Cressida' bath £320, panel extra; double basin £240. The 'Toledo' acrylic shower tray is in Beige marble and Dark onyx.

Vanity units with either single or double, oval or shell-shaped, bowls come in five shades, and two base unit sizes. Panelled cupboard doors have Victorian handles, and the total effect is of effortless, old-fashioned luxury. *P:* double oval basin (illustrated) £230–£265, double base unit £130.

ST MARCO'S

Wonderfully styled Italian sanitaryware that complements St Marco's furniture and accessories. EPOCA and QUADRARCO both have attractively squared-off lines. *P:* QUADRARCO wash basin and column £110, bidet £80, WC £180. There's also a bath that's perfect

St Marco's QUADRARCO suite

for small spaces. Designed for comfort, it comes complete with resting spaces for soap and sponge. *M:* w 2 × 1.4ft (61 × 122cm). *P:* £250.

St Marco's comprehensive catalogue includes a number of products that aren't exhibited in their showroom, for lack of space.

TWYFORDS LTD

Small, practical range from old-established (over a century) manufacturers. Baths are in steel and acrylic. The WC's syphonic flush is quiet and hygienic (Twyfords were pioneers in this field). The RADIANTE basin is outstanding with its unusual circular shape and decorative fluting. The vertically aligned, space-saving BARBICAN basin would make an original choice for a very small bathroom (*P:* £114 with mixer, toilet roll holder). The 'Montrose' corner bath, with a built-in seat, is probably Twyfords' most sumptuous bath (*P:* £545 with side panel, mixer tap and waste).

Twyfords' BARBICAN basin

UAS ENGINEERING LTD

A self-contained, biological toilet system which processes human waste into enriched soil! The 'Humus' is based on principles of natural composting, and requires no water, chemicals or septic tank. Perfect for cottage installation. It will work in any heated bath-

Twyfords' 'Montrose' bath

UAS's 'Humus' toilet system

Vogue's 'Elysian' bath (above),
'Vienna' (below)

corner seat; 'Venetian' has a rounded front and streamlined back rest. *P*: both £390. Vogue also make a drop-in basin and a shower tray, but no bidets, WCs or vanity units.

B & P WYNN & CO

Beautifully hand-painted brass and ceramic-ware, all effortlessly evocative of Continental country life. Basins have matching accessories. FONTAINE LA NORMANDE is predominantly Blue, Gold, or Rose; the matching soap dish, towel holder, tiles, mirror, wall lights and shelf are edged with old gold (*P*: basin and back £172 as illustrated, taps £400).

Wynn's FONTAINE LA NORMANDE basin

room, provided there's a ventilation pipe and an electrical outlet. *P*: £485–795.

VOGUE BATHROOMS

Large range of porcelain-enamelled cast-iron baths that hold their colour, don't scratch easily and feel comfortably safe to use. 'Twingrip' is extra wide and ideal for shower conversion. Luxury 'Elysian' has side tap controls, and chromium or gold-plated fittings with optional matching panels (*P*: £500, including gold-plated taps, etc). For extra safety and accessibility, the 'Atlanta', a small, low-lying bath, is available with hand-grips, grab-rails and a slip-resistant base. Unusual 'Vienna', complete with back rest, is designed for loungers in the bath (*P*: £160). There are also two corner-fitting models in fibreglass and acrylic: 'Bahama' is very angular with a deep

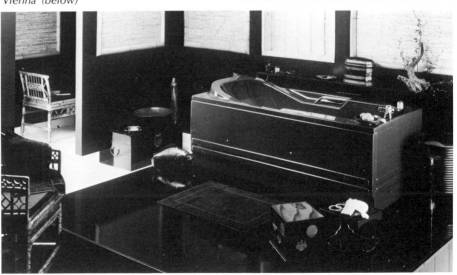

SANITARYWARE MANUFACTURERS	WHITE	PRIMROSE	TURQUOISE	CORAL PINK	SKY BLUE	AVOCADO	SUN KING	PAMPAS	FLAMINGO	BRONZE AUTUMN	MID BROWN	MINK SABLE	HARVEST	DARK BROWN	BRIGHT BLUE	BURGUNDY	PENTHOUSE BLUE	DEEP TURQUOISE	DEEP GOLD	BLACK	OTHER COLOURS
ARISTOCAST LTD	●			●	●	●	●				●				●	●					
ARMITAGE SHANKS LTD	●	●	●	●	●	●	●	●			●		●								'Caspian' (deep turquoise) 'Pompadour' (deep shell pink)
BALTERLEY BATHROOMS LTD	●			●	●	●	●	●	●		●				●		●			●	Emerald, Imperial purple, Spring green (pale lime), Orchid
'Romana gold'	●										●					●	●				Emerald, Imperial purple
CARRON CO	●	●	●	●	●	●	●	●			●			●	●	●	●	●	●	●	Penthouse brown, Jade
CHLORIDE SHIRES LTD	●		●	●	●	●	●	●	●		●				●	●				●	Honeysuckle, Penthouse brown
IDEAL STANDARD LTD	●		●	●	●						●				●	●	●				
'Michelangelo'	●									●	●	●			●	●	●				Moss green
ROYAL DOULTON SANITARYWARE LTD	●	●	●	●	●	●	●	●	●	●	●	●		●	●					●	Honeysuckle, Beige marble, Dark onyx
TWYFORDS LTD	●	●	●	●	●	●		●			●		●								
VOGUE BATHROOMS				●	●	●					●	●		●	●	●	●	●			

Note: Not all manufacturers refer to their colours with the same term so the chart only attempts to describe the shade available.

ROMANE is available with Green, Blue, Rose, or Orange predominant and has optional wall lights, round mirror, and combined soap dish and towel holder. There are many variations on these themes.

The MORTIER range in Cognac or Blue tones also has numerous accessories. Metal fittings are in old gold, old silver, and polished brass. *P:* basin and back £82 as illustrated.

The MONOBLOC range also includes a hand-painted toilet, basin and jug set.

Three tap styles are available with all these ranges, in four finishes: polished lacquered brass, nickel-plated brass, old gold, and old silver. *P:* upon application.

Wynn's MORTIER basin

SHOWERS

GLYNWED BATHROOM & KITCHEN PRODUCTS LTD

LEISURE range of clever, nicely designed showers. 'Fiji' and 'Tahiti' both come with a folding door or two-tone White curtain. 'Hawaii' has a magnetic handset which fixes anywhere on the cubicle wall for height and directional control. 'Bali' is made from polystyrene. The other showers have rigid steel bases, and vitreous enamel or stainless steel walls. All come in nine colours, including White, with manual or thermostatic mixers, and optional instantaneous water-heating systems. *P:* £225–£450, 'Tahiti' £250 with curtain and manual mixer, £275 with folding door.

INSTAFLOW LTD

An instant shower, independent of the mains water supply. 'Instaflow 2000' takes in cold water from the storage tank, pumps out hot water. Six power settings plus a separate controller for fine tuning. *P:* from £310.

MAJESTIC SHOWER CO LTD

An enticing range of shower doors and enclosures from Britain's oldest-established shower enclosure manufacturer. Shaped or square hinged bath screens, with matching fibreglass shower trays are also available. Standard sizes, but Majestic are happy to make special size units. (Trays come in any sanitaryware colour, and special colours may also be made to order.) Tough gold, chrome and brass finishes on the framework complement polished chrome or gold-plate fittings. Safety glass comes in Polished plate, Bronze or Silver tint, Burnished gold or Plain obscure. *P:* corner shower enclosures from £165, trays from £85.

MARFINITY LTD

SILHOUETTE self-assembly kits. You can build your own shower door, or shower or bath side —no special skills or tools are necessary. All kits come to fit widths of 76cm (30in) complete with plastic doors, anodized aluminium frames and fittings. *P:* shower doors from £65, bath sides from £35.

MATKI LTD

Shower (and bath) surrounds that bring a touch of quality and luxury to an area where tough practicality is normally the rule. Folding and sliding doors, on 'equi-sprung' runners, move easily wherever you press them. The top model, 'Aristocrat', has a curved folding door and comes in two sizes. There's a choice of Milky white, Green, Frosted or Smoked 'Polython' doors; top and bottom panels and trays come in Autumn, Avocado, Harvest, Pampas, Sepia, Sky blue, Sun King, and White. Gold or silver frames are available.

The Matki shower base, in slip-resistant fibreglass-reinforced polyester, may be ordered in any standard bathroom colour (*P:* £275 with silver frames, White, Green, or frosted doors).

Matki's 'Aristocrat' shower surround

NORDIC SAUNAS LTD

Shower doors and enclosures made from toughened safety plate glass, framed in silver or gold aluminium. There are three types: pivot, sliding and internally gliding. Also a low-cost fixed screen model with a PVC curtain. Hinged or folding screens are also available to turn a bathtub into a shower (*P: £130*). Glass is normally either 'obscured' or 'smoked', but there are other options on certain models. Fibreglass shower trays come in all standard bathroom colours.

The clean-lined 'President' shower cabinet can be installed almost anywhere. It works off mains cold water pressure, and its 15-litre (26¼pt) hot water storage tank gives five to ten minutes of hot water showering. The cabinet comes complete with manual hot/cold mixer, flexible riser and adjustable hand spray. *M:* h 77½ × w 31½× d 31½in (197×80×80cm). *P:* £500.

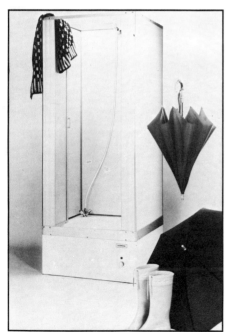

Nordic's 'President' shower cabinet

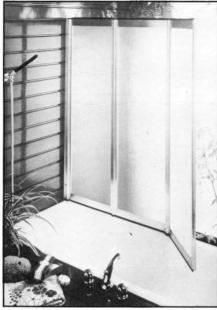

Nordic's folding shower screen

PETRATE LTD

Seven shower enclosures in a variety of sizes with gold or silver anodized framework plus a choice of four acrylic screen patterns. Corner, sliding, folding and swing doors are available. *P:* swing door £230.

Petrate's swing-door shower enclosure

ROYAL DOULTON SANITARYWARE LTD

Three types of shower surround—free standing, built-in, and corner—and two types of bath surround—corner and built-in. All glass is tempered, and is available in a bronze or frosted finish. Frames are high-grade gold or satin aluminium, and there's a special wall adaptor for out-of-line walls. A hinged bath screen for a quick and easy conversion from bath to shower is also available. *P:* bronze glass corner fitting with gold aluminium frame £115.

Royal Doulton's corner shower surround

TWYFORDS LTD

COLORARMOUR screens in laminated patterned glass in an amazing choice of eight colours: Pale gold, Amber, Sepia, Leaf green, Turquoise, Pacific blue, Pink, and Clear. Three models with double-opening doors are available: a corner enclosure; a three-sided model; and an enclosure where the shower provision is 'built-in' with walls on three sides. An alternative is a one- or two-sided enclosure with a curtain rail. *P:* three-sided enclosure £415 in silver finish.

Twyfords' three-sided COLORARMOUR shower enclosure

INTRODUCTION

Modern or traditional, luxurious or simple, the bedroom is the most personal room in your home, a place where you can let your decorative fantasies run wild.

Whatever style you decide on, it's worth spending time, and as much money as you can afford, on the bed – after all, it's where you spend about a third of your life. The base (and mattress) will determine the quality of your sleep, so decide whether you want a simple divan-type, a traditional bed base, pine slats, or an ergonomic wonder.

Headboards set the decorative tone of the room, and can be lacquered or caned, deep-buttoned or leather-wrapped. For real luxury, 'Continental' headboards often incorporate drawers, shelves, and sometimes built-in lights, refrigerators – even a television set.

Beds, the first part of this section, includes brass and four-poster models, sleek pine versions, and space-saving bunk beds.

Bedroom Furniture describes matching suites consisting of a bed or headboard, bedside tables, storage, etc.

*Prices do not include mattresses, unless these are supplied with the bed.

BEDS

ATRIUM

Low-lying MORNA with soft leather upholstery and natural walnut, or Beige or Black lacquer base. Possibly the most Minimal bed on the market, it has a tubular steel frame with two wheels at the head and black rubber feet. Bedside shelves conceal a secret pull-out drawer. *M:* double bed from w 151 × l. 205cm (5ft 9³/₈ × 6ft 8³/₄in), matching headboard w 294 × d 72cm (9ft 7³/₄in × 28³/₈in). *P:* £600, £1,340 with headboard.

The beautiful BOMA range has leather-covered front panels and cushioned head-board, ash or walnut side panels. Handles on bedside cabinet and four-drawer chest are simple leather flaps. MOUNT, finished in polyester lacquer with a leather-centred headboard, also has wonderfully inconspicuous leather handles. Frames and borders are solid wood. Storage solutions include six wardrobes, eight chests of drawers and 23 shelf and/or drawer solutions.

BABY RELAX LTD

Clever FOLDACOT for chic children. With its legs extended it's a bed; when they're telescoped it doubles as a playpen. Plastic feet and castors are supplied, also a mattress. *M:* w 56 × l. 112 × h 39cm (22in × 3ft 8¹/₈in × 15³/₈in). *P:* £61.

DAVID BAGOTT DESIGN LTD

CHELSEA functional four-poster in natural or dark-stained pine, with a slatted pine base. As with all this company's beds, foam, firm-rest or spring mattresses can be supplied. *M:* w 5ft × l. 6ft 8in × h 7¹/₂ft (152.5 × 172.5 × 228.5cm). *P:* £175 as illustrated. A bunk bed and single version are available.

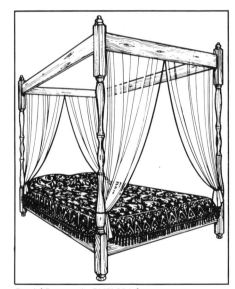

David Baggott's CHELSEA four-poster

Low SPANISH bed in natural or dark-stained pine, with a slatted base and hand-turned corner posts. *M:* w 5ft 3in × l. 7ft (160 × 213.5cm). *P:* £130 as illustrated. Also four-poster and single versions.

PRICES AND INFORMATION WERE CORRECT AT THE TIME OF GOING TO PRESS

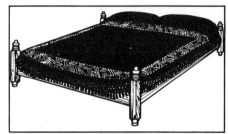

David Baggott's SPANISH bed

The sensible, low-slung SWEDISH bed incorporates two storage drawers. A single bed is available. *M, P:* to order.
See also *Bedroom Furniture.*

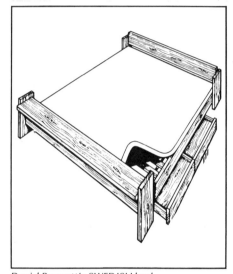

David Baggott's SWEDISH bed

BAKER, KNAPP & TUBBS

Oriental 'Wedding Bed' in walnut pecan with Carpathian elm veneer, faithfully copied from a design of the K'ang period. It must have been quite a wedding. *M:* w 5ft 9¹/₂in × l. 7ft 5¹/₂in × h 6ft 10¹/₂in (176 × 210 × 189cm). *P:* £1,950.

THE BEDCHAMBER

Beautifully hand-painted antique and modern four-posters in pine, mahogany or oak. Beds are available with tester and double valance, or wooden cornice and single valance. Mattress, sprung or foam base, and easily removable curtains can also be supplied. M: double w 5 × l. 6½ × h 7ft (152.5 × 196 × 213.5cm). P: pine from £375, mahogany from £425; curtains made up from £110.

CADO FURNITURE LTD

Chic '442' camp-bed in crosscut beech and canvas. M: w 77 × l. 200cm (30³/₈in × 6ft 6³/₄in). P: £95.

CHARTA FURNITURE LTD

'Cabin Bed', an ingenious bed-study arrangement faced with White and Dark brown melamine, the chipboard ladder in White. M: w 83 × l. 196 × h 156cm (32⁵/₈in × 6ft 5⁷/₈in × 5ft 1³/₈in). P: £330 as illustrated, excluding mattress. Also available as an alcove bed with storage space above, and/or with complementary chests of drawers, wardrobes, dressing table, etc.

PRICES AND INFORMATION WERE CORRECT AT THE TIME OF GOING TO PRESS

Charta's 'Cabin Bed'

MICHAEL J COX

Four-posters in different period styles converted to order from standard beds. Posts and fascia are in pine or mahogany. Draperies can be ruched, ruffled, or styled as a pyramid canopy — Michael Cox's delightful service includes making them in clients' own fabrics. Because each four-poster is made by hand, awkward sizes and spaces can be accommodated. M: post diam 3, 4in (7.5, 10cm), otherwise to order. P: double bed from £300 in pine with net curtains, valance and canopy; £525 in mahogany with client's fabric.

DE LA PLAIN INTERIORS LTD

Striking and unusual 'Bambolettone' from the Italian LE BAMBOLE range by Mario Bellini.

The slanting headboard, an extension of the base, is topped with a separate pillow. The frame is wrapped with foam and padding. A single version is available. Both can be covered in any of de la Plain's wonderful and functional fabrics. M: w 178 × l. 248cm (5ft 10¹/₈in × 8ft 1⁵/₈in). P: £650. See 'Upholstered Furniture' for illustration of LE BAMBOLE.

DEPTICH LTD

'Shaftesbury' brass bed with mother-of-pearl inset in floral motifs, one of a wide selection of Victorian reproductions. M: w 4½–6½ft × l. 6ft 3in (136–198 × 191cm). P: w 4½ft £700 as illustrated. Four-posters, half-testers and headboards are also available. Designs range from plain rod and knob combinations to intricate castings of birds and flowers, some with marble accents. One version combines solid mahogany posts with brass finials and collars. All beds are made from solid brass tubing that has been polished (in two stages), then finished with transparent protective lacquer.

DUCAL LTD

Country-style '9736' in solid pine. It comes with an orthopaedic, interior sprung, or foam mattress. M: w 3ft × l. 6ft 3in (91.5 × 191cm). P: £90. Double bed also available.

WARREN EVANS

Simple, low single and double PINE BEDS. They have slatted bases, no frills, and no

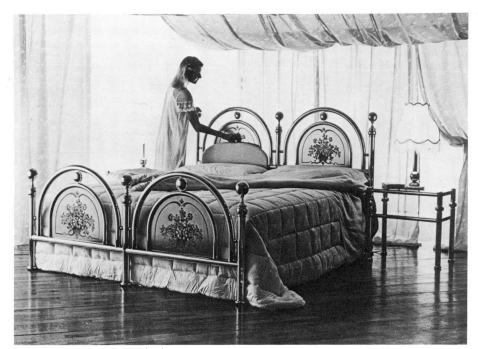

Favorite Interior's PRINCIPE bed

GRAFTON INTERIORS
Empire-inspired 'Daybed 1515' by Hirsch. Upholstered in classical stripes from a selection of high-quality fabrics, it has a hand-lacquered beech frame with gold trim, and feather-filled back cushions. *M:* w 210 × h 97 × d 90cm (82¾ × 38⅛ × 35⅜in). *P:* £875.

DENNIS GROVES
Tubular ZIP bed for devotees of the simple, stylish, industrial look. Made from thin steel tubing, with joints developed by Dennis Groves and produced by Kee Klamp, it comes with a White or Black epoxy resin finish; other colours to order. Top-quality flame-retardant foam mattresses, guaranteed for seven years, can be supplied. Single, double, kingsize and platform versions are available. All beds also come in kit form. *M:* double w 4½ft × l. 6ft 3in (136 × 191cm). *P:* £105.

headboards. *M:* to order. *P:* single from £45, double from £60. Illustration unavailable at the time of going to press.

FAVORITE INTERIOR
Marvellous PRINCIPE kingsize bed in smooth, satin-finish, solid brass. The stove-enamelled headboard, decorated with hand-painted flowers, has an unusual pull-up headrest. *M:* w 5½ft × l. 6ft 3in (168 × 191cm). *P:* £1,400. A matching bedside table is available.

GENERAL WOLFE ANTIQUES
Victorian and Edwardian BRASS BEDSTEADS (left, below) restored by a family firm. The shop is crammed with a vast array of unrestored bed-frames, many with exotic mother-of-pearl, porcelain or mirror inlays, some with full or half canopies; also brass and iron bedsteads. Other period styles are usually in stock, including wooden four-posters, many with original hangings. General Wolfe will also find the bed of your dreams, given a sketch and a budget. Single, double and king-size models are available; also cots. *M:* various. *P:* brass and iron (w 4½ft/136cm) £200 as illustrated, excluding mattress.

GEORGIAN FURNISHING CO
'LS3', a three-panelled headboard with hand-painted Oriental scenes on Red, Brown or Black. Also suitable for use as a screen, it's part of a range of lacquered furniture that includes cabinets, desks, chairs, and chests of drawers. *M:* w 4ft 10in × h 3ft (142 × 91.5cm). *P:* £240.

Bedstead from General Wolfe Antiques (left)

HABITAT DESIGNS LTD
COVENT GARDEN, an updated version of the classical iron bedstead. Made from tough tubular steel, this simple beauty is finished in Chinese red lacquer. The mattress rests on a woven steel mesh base. *M:* w 140 × l. 200cm (4ft 7⅛in × 6ft 6¾in). *P:* £185, with mattress. See overleaf for illustration.

PRICES AND INFORMATION WERE CORRECT AT THE TIME OF GOING TO PRESS

Habitat's COVENT GARDEN bed

HIPPO HALL

'Double Bus' bunk bed for bus-crazy kids, from a firm that specializes in creating environments for children. Made from wood, and painted Bright red, it has chrome rails and a smiling face. *M:* to order. *P:* from £300. 'Castle' and 'House' beds are available; also other furniture to order, to suit clients' whims.

WILLIAM L MACLEAN LTD

Sumptuous hand-crafted, hand-polished headboard. Part of Maclean's beautiful Regency collection, '12-194' comes in natural beech, or tints including Pink, Blue and Green. *M:* w 154 × h 154cm (5ft 1in ×5ft 1in). *P:* upon application. See also *Bedroom Furniture*.

PRICES AND INFORMATION WERE CORRECT AT THE TIME OF GOING TO PRESS

William Maclean's '12-194'

NODUS LTD

Chunky, cottage-style bunk bed in solid pine with brass studs. Part of the DESIGNS IN PINE range, it has a sliding ladder, reversible safety rail — and can be converted to twin beds. Matching pieces include a blanket chest, desk, chests of drawers and wardrobes. *M:* bed w 104 × l. 199 × h 153cm (3ft 4⁷⁄₈in × 6ft 6¼in × 5ft¹⁄₈in). *P:* £135.

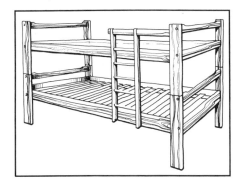

OAKLEAF REPRODUCTIONS LTD

Imposing, 17th-century reproduction four-poster. Made from rigid polyurethane foam, it's an exact copy of an original bed — including carving marks and riven panels. *M:* w 4½ft × l. 6ft 4in × h 6½ft (136 × 193 × 198cm). Other sizes to order. *P:* £610.

OGGI DOMANI

GALAXY bed for space travellers, finished in lacquer, suede or fabric. The arching head-board incorporates a gold-tinted mirror, and bedside tables. The range includes a dressing table, and wardrobe with mirrored doors. *M:* w 9ft 9in × l. 6½ft (297.5 × 198cm). *P:* ivory lacquer £850.

ROOKSMOOR MILLS

Very versatile bunk bed in beech. It can be separated to form twins, or zipped together to make a double bed. Soft, firm or extra-firm mattresses are supplied. *M:* w 2½, 3ft × l. 6ft 3in × h 4ft 9in (76, 91.5 × 191 × 144.5cm). *P:* £255.

Rooksmoor's bunk bed

Magnificent PINE BED, with hand-turned posts. By Ernest Inder, it's supplied in four easily assembled sections, with a firm or extra-firm mattress. Complementary pieces are a wardrobe, mirror, bedside table, dressing table and stool. *M:* bed w 5ft 5in × l. 7ft 1in (165 × 216cm). *P:* from £400. Also cane beds.

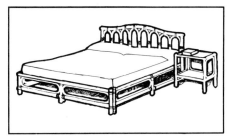

Rooksmoor's PINE BED

JAMES SECCOMBE LTD

'JS2000' in Propathene, a strong light plastic. The dust-free, non-allergenic and self-ventilating mattress is made from hospital-quality foam perforated to vary in density and 'give' around the hips and shoulders. The headboard and frame fit firmly on to the base. The removable velour-upholstered headboard panel comes in Brown, Camel, Blue, Old Rose, and Dane gold; the frame is White or Honey. Glass-topped side tables. *M:* as illustrated w 214.4 × l. 196.4cm (7ft × 6ft 5½in). *P:* £400. Also available without headboard, side-tables. Options include four under-bed storage drawers, and mirrored trim around the base. 'JS3000', and 'JS4000' with side tables, have totally upholstered headboards and surrounds in velour, Dralon or leather.

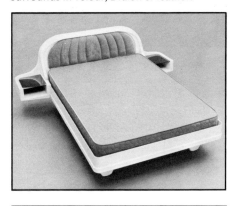

SLEEPEEZEE LTD

'Concept Two' bunk bed that separates into two singles, in polished hardwood, natural

pine or White. Mattresses have firm 'Tensicoil' springing. *M:* w 91.5 × l. 191 × h 148.5cm (3ft × 6ft 3in × 4ft 10½in). *P:* from £370 including mattresses.

'Twosome' space-saver in polished hardwood, glowing honey pine or White. The lower bed is pulled out and raised to the same level as the top one. *M:* w 97 × l. 205cm (3ft 2⅛in × 6ft 8¾in). *P:* both from £325 including mattress.

Sleepeezee's 'Twosome'

SLUMBERLAND LTD

'Dream Master' bunk bed with childproof, lockable catches. Easily converted to two singles, it has unusually good mattresses, made from specially developed 'Posture Springing' between layers of Slumberland's 'Slumbafoam' and covered with a hardwearing Jacquard fabric. Optional drawers have castors and dustproof lids. *M:* w 84 × l. 198 × h 145cm (33in × 6½ft × 4ft 9⅛in). *P:* £400 plus drawers (£40 each).

SPACE-SAVING BED CENTRE

'Divanette Twin de Luxe Bunk Bed' that can be conventionally stacked, or separated into twins. In addition, one bed can be folded down (complete with sheets and blankets) and tucked underneath the other. Metal bars underneath the steel mesh base can be adjusted for firmness or springiness. Two 5in (12.5cm) thick fabric-covered foam mattresses

are supplied. *M:* w 2ft 9in × l. 6ft 5in × h 3ft 1in (84 × 195.5 × 94cm). *P:* from £190.

Space-Saving Bed Centre's 'Divanette Twin de Luxe Bunk Bed'

Solid 'Pine Twin' beds with firm, slatted wood bases and foam mattresses. One bed can be folded down to slide under the other on castors. *M:* w 2½ft × l. 6ft 3in (76 × 191cm). *P:* pair £210.

Space-Saving Bed Centre's 'Pine Twin'

STAPLES & CO LTD

Splendid '524' four-poster with gleaming, delicately reeded solid brass uprights and

turned ornaments. Illustrated with Nottingham lace curtains and bedspread, it also comes in White, Black or Brown enamelled steel, with brass top rails and ornament. Good range of widths. *M:* w 4½ft × l. 6ft 3in × h 6ft 9in (137 × 191 × 206cm). *P:* £400 as illustrated overleaf, lace £200 extra.

'Ashdown' is solid English ash with veneered ash panels. It comes complete with canopy, slatted base, one of Staples' justifiably famous spring interior mattresses, and Dorma curtains in two designs: 'Sherwood' (illustrated) in Green and Biscuit, and 'Peking', another floral, in shades of Brown. Both can be co-ordinated with bedlinen, quilt covers, roller blinds, and curtains. Single and double beds only. *M:* w 5ft × l. 6ft 3in × h 6½ft (152.5 × 191 × 198cm). *P:* £700.

Staples' 'Ashdown'

Solid mahogany 'Gainsborough' with Nottingham lace curtains and bedspread. It has a hand-finished headboard, turned footposts. Double and kingsize only. *M:* w 4½ft × l. 6ft 3in × h 7ft (137 × 191 × 213.5cm). *P:* £400, lace £200 extra.

Staples' 'Gainsborough'

STOKECROFT ARTS

Functional but pleasing BUNK BED. Hand-made to order in solid pine, with integral head and foot ladders, the frame is jointed, dowelled and glued — no screws, nails, etc. The bed comes with or without mattresses; matching storage boxes are available. *M:* as illustrated w 3ft × l. 6ft 4in × h 5ft 4in (91.5 × 193 × 162.5cm). *P:* £160, mattresses £42 each.

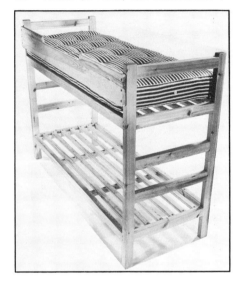

STORAGE-BOX BED, a simple solution to the ever-present problem of where to keep things. Like the bunk bed it's hand-made in solid pine, with independent suspension, and comes with or without a mattress. *M:* w 2½, 3, 4, 4½, 5ft × l. 6ft 7in (76, 91.5, 122, 136, 152.5 × 202.5cm). *P:* £155–£190, mattress £45–£110.

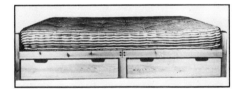

Stuart Interiors' four-poster

STUART INTERIORS

Made-to-order four-poster (left, below) from specialists in Elizabethan and Jacobean furniture. The epitome of 17th-century grandeur, it's designed to take a modern-sized mattress. All beds come in solid oak, with holly, yew or walnut contrasts. Normally they are made by craftsmen in the Stuart workshops and re-assembled *in situ*. *M:* to order. *P:* £2,000 as illustrated.

TRANNON MAKERS

Unique support system in Red or Black stained ash, by David Colwell. 'Doubled Slats' provide uniform resilience across the full width of the bed; the slatted platform, made from three reversible and interchangeable sections (to compensate for uneven wear), ensures a flat but yielding surface with no depression in the centre. Flat components are easily assembled with removable dowels. Double and kingsize versions only. *M:* w 4½, 5, 5½ × l. 6½ft (137, 152.5, 168 × 198cm). *P:* from £325.

VERARDO

Rounded, sculptural 'Giada' finished in Beige or Black lacquer, from a selection of gorgeous (and expensive) beds. *M:* w 177 × l. 211cm (5ft 10in × 6ft 11in). *P:* upon application. Others, in the same finishes, are simply rounded 'Fulvia' with brass strips, 'Yoko' with a brass-edged pagoda-shaped headboard, and 'Manola' with a rectangular headboard edged with two brass strips. See also 'Storage'.

PRICES AND INFORMATION WERE CORRECT AT THE TIME OF GOING TO PRESS

WOOD BROS FURNITURE LTD

Sweet OLD CHARM cradle in solid oak. The child's name is carved inside a heart motif, by one of the firm's master craftsmen. The cradle is a limited edition, although technically part of an extensive range of bedroom, dining-room and sitting-room furniture. *M:* w 3ft × l. 17¾ ×h 29in (91.5 × 45.5 × 73.5cm). *P:* £270.

'Great Bed of Ware', a scaled-down version of the original in the Victoria & Albert Museum. Probably the crowning glory of the 120-piece OLD CHARM range, it's made from hand-polished and shaded hand-carved oak in light oak,Tudor brown or antiqued finish. *M:* w 6ft 11in × l. 6ft 7in × h 7½ft (211 × 200.5 × 228.5cm). *P:* £1,930, antiqued £2,050. There's a wide choice of complementary storage furniture.

FURNITURE

AUSTINSUITE FURNITURE

Perfectly plain, potentially continuous, BAHAMA wardrobe system. Finished in Ivory, with inlaid brass trim, it locks together instead of being fixed to the wall. Three matching bedside chests, mirrored door fronts, five dressing tables, and padded headboard units are also available. *M:* five-door wardrobe as illustrated w 247.6 × h 225 × d 59.6cm (8ft 1½in × 7ft 4⅝in × 23½in). *P:* £420.

Austinsuite's BAHAMA

DAVID BAGOTT DESIGN LTD

Comprehensive range of modern pine furniture, including four-posters, bunk beds, and storage units: wardrobes, chests of drawers, chests, etc. *M:* double wardrobe w 3½ft × h 6ft 1in × d 22in (107 × 185.5 × 56cm), chest of drawers w 3½ft × h 24¾ ×d 22in (107 × 62.5 × 56cm). *P:* £130, £45.

BAKER, KNAPP & TUBBS

Fine Queen Anne-style bed and chest of drawers from a firm that specializes in high-quality reproductions. The bed, '590', has reeded columns ending in carved-leaf posts; the chest has fretwork detail on the top frieze, chamfered corners, and ogee bracket feet. *M:* bed w 5ft 5in × l. 6½ft × h 6ft 8in (165 × 198 × 201cm), chest w 3ft 2in × h 5ft 7in × d 18in (96.5 × 170 × 46cm). *P:* bed £600, chest £900.

BAMBOO DESIGNS

F RANGE cane furniture that combines today's styles with yesteryear's sturdiness. Designed by David Sage, and made in the Far East, pieces are lacquered or painted to order. A single headboard is available; also complementary fabrics and wallpapers. *M:* headboard w 150 × h 71cm (4ft 11in × 28in), dressing table w 112 × h 74 × d 53cm (3ft 8⅛in × 29⅛ × 20⅞in). *P:* £140, £230.

Baker, Knapp & Tubbs' Queen Anne-style bed and chest of drawers

Bamboo Designs' F RANGE

DALVERA

Marvellous COLLEZIONE THAI bed and bedside table with cane grid frames. It also comes in a walnut or pearl lacquer finish. A single bed is available, and complementary JAMILA two- or three-door wardrobes and a chest of drawers. *M:* bed w 180 × l. 200cm (5ft 10½in × 6ft 6¾in). *P:* £260.

Simple but pleasing range. MALAYSIA, in natural, walnut, or Black lacquered finish, includes a bedside table with drawer, single-door wardrobe with a mirror and four drawers, writing or dressing table with two drawers, chair with natural caned seat (available with or without arms), and a single or double bed with a cane surround and metal spring frame. *M:* single bed w 3ft 2in × l. 6ft 3in (96.5 × 191cm), single-door wardrobe w 3ft 5in × h 6½ft × d 23in (104 × 198 × 58.5cm). *P:* £150 plus foam mattress £35, £250.

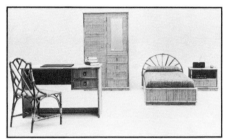

Dalvera's MALAYSIA

DUCAL LTD
Country-style BELLAMY pine furniture that blends well with genuine antiques. This very comprehensive range also includes two-drawer dressing tables with optional mirrors, a wardrobe with four fitted shelves, four-drawer chest of drawers, stool, three-drawer bedside cabinet, and a single bed. *M:* double bed w 137 × l. 190cm (4½ft × 6ft 2¾in), six-drawer chest of drawers w 86 × h 119 × d 44cm (33⅞ × 3ft 10⅞in × 17⅜in), hanging wardrobe w 95 × h 183 × d 58cm (3ft 1⅜in × 6ft × 22⅞in). *P:* £115, £190, £260.

J T ELLIS & CO LTD
Sensible GRADUATE range designed for dormitories but also perfect for homes. Chipboard carcases are veneered in teak or beech; fronts and tops can be faced with White, Cinnamon, Coffee, Cream, Tropical blue, French green or Brazil brown Formica.

Ducal's BELLAMY

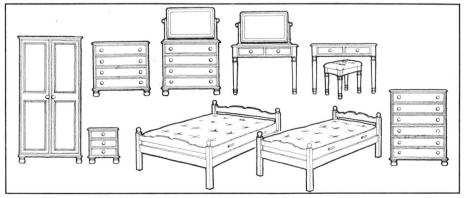

Drawer joints are dovetailed, cupboard doors can be hung right or left. The range consists of six drawer units, five wardrobes, five desks, three bookcases, three mirrors, a bedside table, under-bed storage drawer, single bed, and vanity unit with towel rail. *M:* wardrobe as illustrated w 90 × h 230 × d 60cm (35⅜in × 7ft 1⅝in × 23⅝in). *P:* upon application.

Ellis' GRADUATE

FAVORITE INTERIOR
BAROQUE suite with overtones of Fontainebleau — just right for a little château in the suburbs. Made from solid wood, it's hand-carved with scrolls galore, hand-

painted, and gilded. Drawers are lined with oak. *M:* bed w 175 × l. 190 × h 148cm (5ft 8⅞in × 6ft 2¾in × 4ft 8¼in), wardrobe w 320 × h 230 × d 60cm (10½ft × 7ft 1⅝in × 23⅝in). *P:* £10,000 for all pieces illustrated.

FSI FURNITURE
CANE RANGE in solid wood decorated with woven cane. It comes in natural pine, light or dark mahogany or natural or Black-stained beech, coated in clear satin lacquer or natural beeswax. The range consists of a single or double headboard, made-to-measure chest of drawers, three bedside tables, and the very unusual option of wardrobe doors in a full range of standard sizes. *M:* headboards w 30in–6½ft × h 16½in (76–198 × 42cm), chest of drawers w 28 × h 23½ × d 16in (71 × 40.5 × 59.5cm), wardrobe doors w 12–24in × h 18in–6½ft (30.5–61 ×46–198cm) in 6in (15cm) increments. *P:* headboards £28–£58, chest of drawers £100, wardrobe doors £18–£49.

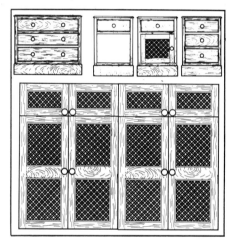

GAUTIER LTD
Futuristic TITAN range for children. A budding space traveller's dream come true, it also includes three shelves, a chest of drawers and a secretaire storage unit. Pieces are in laminate-faced board with Cobalt blue bands. *M:* beds w 119 × l. 225cm (3ft 11in × 7½ft), wardrobe w 110 × h 184 × d 41cm (3ft 7in × 6ft × 23in). *P:* £260, £130. Also a 'racing car' bed.

Well-made WINCHESTER suite from France. Marvellously evocative of the early 19th century, this reproduction furniture comes in finely finished cherry veneer with period brass pulls. It also includes a double bed, bedside table, three-door wardrobe, mirror and writing desk. *M:* bed w 3ft 3in × l 6ft 10in (99 × 208.5cm), wardobe w 3ft 11in ×h 6ft × d 26in (119.5 × 183 × 66cm). *P:* upon application.

Gautier's WINCHESTER

GIORGETTI
'6124' headboard and storage units, part of an unusually well-made rattan suite. Units come in lacquered or polished solid wood, with caned panels. A bedside table, mirror and two chests of drawers are also available. *M:* headboard w 180.5 × h 123cm (5ft 11½in × 4ft ½in), chest of drawers w 106 × h 78 × d 49cm (3ft 5¾in × 30¾ × 19¼in). *P:* £350, £550.

GRAFTON INTERIORS
Impressive but simple POSTUMIA bed by Ca 'Onorai, with integral side tables and matching mirrored wardrobe. Its metal base is topped with rosewood; the wardrobe is in Black anodized aluminium. Also available in White, Black or Charcoal laminate with matching or Bright green trim. *M:* bed to order, wardrobe w 165 × h 120 × d 45cm (3ft 11¼in × 5ft 5in × 17¾in). *P:* £400, £850.

Grafton's POSTUMIA

Simple but lush ZINDO range in lacquered leather. Vaguely Oriental but ultimately sleek, all pieces, including the matching lamps, come in eight colours with solid brass accents. *M:* bed w 208 × l. 228cm (6ft 9⅞in × 7ft 5⅞in), bedside table w 60 × h 45 × d 40cm (23⅝ × 17¾ × 15¾in). *P:* £1,290, £370.

Grafton's ZINDO

HUBBINET FURNITURE LTD
ELYSEE wardrobe, part of a large French-styled range. Finished in lustrous White, pieces have panels in White, Pastel pink, French grey, or White or Grey with Gold highlights. Drawers have serpentine or straight fronts; wardrobes

and chests are equipped with castors. The range also includes a one-door wardrobe, headboards, chests of drawers, dressing table, and cheval mirror. Wardrobes (all with mahogany stained interiors) are fitted with locks. *M:* w 8ft 6¾in × h 7½ft × d 22in (261 × 228.5 × 56cm). *P:* £650.

INTERLÜBKE LTD
Gorgeous modular MEDIUM PLUS range finished in natural or Black-stained ash, Brazilian mahogany, or Red, Cream or Grey-white lacquer, with matching wood, lacquer, polished granite or travertine tops, and bronzed or chrome handles. Beautifully crafted, it includes beds, headboards with concealed reading lights, and wardrobes with gliding doors. Units have strip pulls. *M:* beds w 90–200 × l. 190–210cm (35⅜in–6ft 6¾in × 6ft 2¾in–6ft 10¾in). *P:* upon application.

Other systems from these pioneers in modular furnishing include ENVIRONMENT 121 for small, multi-purpose rooms. In Grey-white lacquer only, it includes fold-away beds, chests with tops that reveal mirrors and fronts that open out to form secretaires, and reading lights built into headboards or wall panels. STORAGE WALL units are available in Grey-white laminate only, with doors in a host of finishes including mirror, fabric and grass paper as well as lacquer and woods. They can be fitted with shelves, drawers, hanging rails, tie racks, etc.

KESTERPORT LTD
'Flor de Luna' bed, one of the three styles in the BAMBOO range of 24-ct gold-plated, solid brass furniture. Matching night tables, low and high bookcases, chairs and a coatstand are available. Double bed only. *M:* w 174 × l. 195cm (5ft 8½in × 6ft 4¾in). *P:* £588. See overleaf for illustration.

PRICES AND INFORMATION WERE CORRECT AT THE TIME OF GOING TO PRESS

Kesterport's 'Flor de Luna'

William Lawrence's CANTERBURY

KINGSHALL FURNITURE LTD

Good-looking MILITARY range, based on the classical campaign chest, from a firm that specializes in well-made reproduction furniture. Made from the finest solid mahogany, with mahogany veneers and solid brass fittings, it consists of a simple headboard with brass-edged corners, in three sizes, a bedside chest, two- and three-door wardrobes, an eight-drawer tallboy, a four-drawer chest of drawers, and a kneehole dressing table with triple mirror. Other chests, and a four-poster, to order. *M:* tallboy w 3ft 8in × h 4ft 7in × d 21in (111.5 × 139.5 × 53.5cm), dressing table w 3½ft × h 31 × d 20in (106.5 × 78.5 × 51cm). *P:* £575, £425.

LABLANC LTD

Exclusive POMPADOUR suite with hand-carved, hand-decorated wood frames. One of six French-style ranges, it comes in six lacquered shades; other colours, and special upholstery fabrics, to order. *M:* headboard w 168.5 × h 142cm (8ft 9¾in × 4ft 8in), dressing table w 159 × h 172 × d 54cm (5ft 2⅝in × 5ft 7⅝in × 21¼in). *P:* £650, £1,500.

PRICES AND INFORMATION WERE CORRECT AT THE TIME OF GOING TO PRESS

LaBlanc's POMPADOUR

WILLIAM LAWRENCE & CO LTD

Competitively priced CANTERBURY with mahogany veneers, antique-finish brass handles, and mouldings in South African redwood. Mirrors have bevelled edges. The range also includes three other wardrobes, a pedestal dressing table, chests of drawers and a bedside cabinet. The headboard can be upholstered. *M:* headboard w 3, 3½, 4½, 5ft (91.5, 106.5, 136, 152.5cm), dressing table as illustrated w 5ft × h 28½ × d 17½in (152.5 × 72.5 × 44.5cm). *P:* from £35; £215.

WILLIAM L MACLEAN LTD

BAMBOO SUITE from a firm that specializes in Georgian and Regency reproductions. Pieces are made from solid beech which is hand-polished, or stained in one of Maclean's pastel shades; natural wooden stains can also be supplied. The furniture illustrated is only part of a huge selection in beautifully made simulated bamboo — including three more headboard styles. *M:* four-poster as illustrated w 150 × l. 215 × h 220cm (4ft 11in × 7ft × 7ft 2¾in), chest w 100 × h 74 × d 50cm (3ft 3⅜in × 29⅛in × 19⅝in). *P:* upon application.

William Maclean's BAMBOO SUITE

MANHATTAN

Striking TAMARIND range. 'Antique' cork panels are highlighted by round mahogany knobs with shanks covered in Black leather; edgings are mahogany veneer. An enormous selection of units includes wardrobes, chests of drawers and cupboards, two dressing tables, five low bedside units, headboards, and mirrors. *M:* double wardrobe w 100 × h 225 × d 62cm (3ft 3⅜in × 7ft 4⅝in × 24⅜in), double three-drawer chest of drawers w 100 × h 70.5 × d 47.5cm (3ft 3⅜in × 27¾ × 18¾in) *P:* £300, £200.
SAVANNAH has Snow, Chamois or Dusk melamine surfaces with cherry wood trim, and complementary integral worktops in cherry wood veneer. Simpler TUXEDO is in the same shades, with plain, semi-circular handles in solid cherry wood.
Pieces for all three ranges are supplied flat with instruction leaflets, except chests of drawers and cupboards; or Manhattan will arrange installation. A free planning and design service is available.
See page 43 for TAMARIND in colour.

MFI FURNITURE CENTRES LTD

Simply designed, carefully machined self-assembly GEMINI. Made from unfinished chipboard, these cheap and potentially cheerful units can be painted, stained or varnished. A dressing table, bookcase, bedside cabinet, ottoman, three- and five-drawer chests and double and single wardrobes are available. *M:* wardrobe w 36¼in × h 4ft 11in × d 18¼in (92 × 150 × 46.5cm). *P:* £27.95.

OGGI DOMANI

Circular revolving BORA bed — practically a way of life. Finished in suede, leather or fabric it has a high mirrored canopy fitted with drawers, refrigerator and a light and sound system that includes a colour television set, digital clock and cassette player. The dressing table has a matching upholstered chair. *M:* w 10ft 4in × l. 9ft (315 × 274.5cm). *P:* suede £3,950.

SHASTON FURNITURE LTD

SHASTON units finished in crisp White or teak-effect melamine, teak carcase with White doors, White carcase with teak doors, or

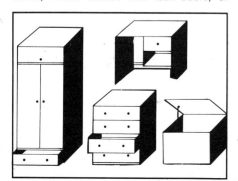

White with gold-beaded moulding. 35 units include 12 bookcases, six chests of drawers, five wardrobes and a desk; all are supplied fully assembled. *M:* '201' double wardrobe with drawer w 76 × h 184 × d 50cm (30in ×6ft ½in × 19⅝in), '11' four-drawer chest w 76 × h 95 × d 40cm (30in × 3ft 1⅜in × 15¾in), '20' box ottoman w 76 × h 46 × d 46cm (30 × 18 × 18in), '22' desk w 91 × h 74 × d 40 (35⅞ × 29⅛ × 15¾in). *P:* from £110, £68, £32, £39.

SOLENT FURNITURE LTD

Sensible ALPHABET for bedrooms, finished in Oyster or Parchment laminate with solid natural oak trim and handles. It also includes a bed base with two drawers, vertical shelving, five other wardrobes and an illuminated mirror. *M:* wardrobe w 80 × h 200.4 × d 57.8cm (31½in × 79in × 22⅞in). *P:* £135

STAG CABINET CO LTD

Competitively priced MINSTREL with rich cherry mahogany veneers and brass ring pulls. A wide range of wardrobes, chests of drawers, dressing tables, bedside cabinets, etc, is available. *M:* wide chest of drawers w 32in × h 3ft 8½in × d 18in (81.5 × 107 × 46cm). *P:* £120.

Stag's MINSTREL (above), TEMPO (below)

Practical TEMPO self-assembly modular storage furniture, finished in White or Mid-brown melamine accented with solid beech handles. It also includes a top box, small cupboard, bookcase, headboard, chest of drawers, etc. *M:* wardrobe w 30¼in × h 5ft 7in × d 21¼in (76.5 × 170 × 54cm). *P:* £70.

UNIFLEX FURNITURE LTD

Comprehensive ULTIMA 82 fitted furniture in White with teak or mahogany tops. The range includes a wide selection of wardrobes, dressing tables, chests of drawers, mirrors, and headboards covered in Oyster velvet or to order; also pieces for young adults — study units, for example. *M:* dressing table w 100 × h 132 × d 45cm (3ft 3⅜in × 4ft 4in × 17¾in). *P:* £140 as illustrated.

VERARDO

'SCHEHERAZADE', an outrageous specimen from a range of bedrooms in real or imitation suede. Not for the timid or impecunious, it's available in Bright red, Soft blue, Lilac, Grey, Tan, Rusty gold, Mid-blue, Brown, Persimmon, Rust or Olive real suede; and Beige, Tan, Mushroom, Light brown, Rust, Dark brown, Persimmon, Slate grey, Wine, Light blue or Navy imitation suede. It comes complete with a built-in radio/digital clock, Philips stereo cassette and telephone; a refrigerator, ashtrays, mirrors and revolving mattress are optional extras. Some units can be finished in rosewood-effect, or Beige or Black lacquer. *M:* diam 230cm (7ft 6⅝in). *P:* upon application.

Right: Manhattan's TAMARIND

INTRODUCTION

Forget nets. Forget curtains. Forget unlovely views. Consider blinds. They're not clanky, metal dust traps any more. Blinds have blossomed into arguably the cheapest, most functional, yet handsomest window treatments going. They can be slats or panels, silk-screened or air-brushed, wooden or pper, patterned or plain, ruched or cane, sheer or opaque, vertical or horizontal, aluminium or plastic, pleated, made to order, or made at home. They also work as room dividers, fire-proofers, draught excluders or light controllers.

Basically, most blinds function in one of two ways: with a spring-tensioned roller mechanism, or linked by cords that are operated with pulleys.

If you're handy, you can make your own roller blind with a do-it-yourself kit — most fabrics can be used, prepared with special spray-on-stiffeners. Or a company will do this custom job for you. Alternatively, a number of artists specialize in hand-painting blinds — imagine Italianate gardens at your window — and only you will know about the brick wall 5ft away.

Corded versions include vertical blinds, also called vertical drapes, and pull-up Austrian and Roman blinds for swags-of-fabric fans. The standard Venetian variety includes wooden and cane versions for rustic rooms, and anodized stainless steel, or plastic, for a purely functional effect.

Whatever you choose, blinds are the best beginning to a beautiful window. And, if you get bored, or richer — or if your style changes —you can add curtains later. Because blinds are becoming so popular, prices are keenly competitive, especially for plain colours.

This section is divided into plain and patterned *Fabric Roller Blinds, Paper and Wood Blinds, Specialist Products* for double-glazed windows, insulation, etc, plastic, aluminium and wooden *Venetian Blinds*, and smooth and textured, plain and printed *Vertical Louvres*.

*Prices are based on the following measurements: vertical louvre blinds 3 × 7ft (91.5 × 213.5cm), all others 3 × 4ft; or the nearest size available.

See also 'Useful Addresses'.

FABRIC ROLLER BLINDS

BLIND ALLEY LTD

Unique roller blinds from a specialist company. They'll adapt tile or wallpaper designs, create one-off hand-painted or air-brushed blinds, print sales messages, make up in your own fabric. Their large range of silk-screened designs can be made to measure in the colour of your choice. Plain blinds are available in more than 100 colours. Blind Alley are open on Sundays, will even visit you if you're in the London area. *P:* plain colours £20.

Left: Luxaflex's FINEBLINDS

Left to right, top to bottom: Blind Alley's 'Bamboo Trellis', 'Shell Scallop', 'Sunrise', 'Traditional Flowers', 'Double Palm with Grass', 'Odeon'.

CLEAN BLINDS LTD

CENTURYAN plain and printed roller blinds. Designs include several bright optical prints and modern florals, plus seven border designs. The bottom edge can be straight or shaped. Plain fringes come in Brown, White, Green, or Gold; bobble fringes in Brown, Blue, White, or Pink. White or Gold edging braid is available, and there is the unusual option of Cream macramé lace (on straight bottom blinds only). See chart for plain colours. *P:* plain £20, patterned £25.

DEANS BLINDS LTD

Competitively priced, custom-made blinds with a spring roller mechanism. Available in a few tiny florals in browns and creams, a modern Navy-and-White design, and 18 plain colours (see chart). *P:* £15.

FILTRASOL LTD

19 plain colours (see chart) plus some pleasant small floral designs: 'Laura Brown', a small Brown and White overall print; 'Berrie', an etching-like line drawing of fruit clusters and leaves in sepia; 'Grassland', an unobtrusive White-on-White pattern; and 'Clouds', a delightful scattering of cumulus. Some patterned blinds have matching curtain fabrics, available on request. Four decorative fringes and trims (all White), two scalloped edges. *P:* £14.

GAYLINE LTD

Outstanding selection of plain colours—23 clear, strong shades (see chart). Patterns include the usual bright florals, and some pleasant border prints. 'Poppy', 'Fleur', 'Countryside', and 'Cornucopia' are especially attractive. No special trims or finishes, but prices are competitive. Gayline offer a money-back guarantee if you don't like your blind after a week's home trial. Also some uncoated matching fabrics. *M:* w 70in (175cm), minimum order 5yd (450cm). *P:* plain £17.

SUSANNE GARRY LTD

Sheer fabric blinds, a speciality of this Walton Street interior designer. Mainly floral motifs, sometimes subtly shaded, but usually White-on-White. Matching opaque fabrics are available for upholstery and curtains. All products are made to measure and therefore fairly expensive. *P:* upon application. See also 'Partitions'.

W A HUDSON LTD

ROLLS FABRIFIX kit with all the necessary fittings except fabric. In addition, twist, trellis or bobble fringe trimmings are available in White; also a tassel or Turk's head pull. Fabric sprayed with ROLLS FABRIFIX stiffening solution becomes wrinkle-free when mounted on rollers and sufficiently fray-resistant to dispense with hemming the sides. The spray will treat 2 to 2.5 sq m (c 21½ to c 27 sq ft) of fabric, depending on weight and absorbency. *M:* roller w 60, 90, 120, 180, 245cm (23⅝, 35⅜, 47¼, 70⅞, 96½in); trim 90, 120, 150, 180cm (35⅜, 47¼, 59, 70⅞in). *P:* roller £2.75–£11.50, stiffener £2.25, trims £1.10–£1.75.

LUXAFLEX LTD

A good variety of patterns and plain colours. Finishes include scalloped and fringed trims with matching pelmets. For a completely integrated effect, the Vymura Interior Designer Collection offers matching blinds (in Vymura fabrics), curtains and wallpapers that tone with

Luxaflex's 'Jessop'

painted walls. Pretty 'Jessop', illustrated with matching wallpaper in reversed colours, comes in in three colourways. Unpatterned blinds are available in three textures: SHANTUNG in Cream, Beige, and Lemon; LINENWEAVE in Champagne, Beige, Brown, and Dark green; TERYLENE in Camel, Coffee, and Chocolate. In addition, there are 100% cotton blinds in 35 shades (see chart). *P:* £18. Marvellous PICTURE GALLERY printed blinds are also available. *P:* upon application.

Left to right, top to bottom: Luxaflex's 'Patchwork', 'Cornfield', 'China Moon' from Picture Gallery; 'Country Style'

MAYFAIR BLINDS
Spongeable SOMBRERO BLINDS. Several attractive designs include 'Victoria', a lacy pattern on Peach, Pale blue, or Rose; 'Lille', Gold and Rust flowers on Brown; 'Clivendon', a William Morris-style motif in Yellow/Gold/Rust on Chocolate; 'Meadow', a hedgerow border design on Brown or Blue; and 'Beech Leaves', an overall design very subtly printed in Rust, Olive, or Beige on a pinoleum ground. Also four plain colours: Brown, Beige, Ochre, and Yellow. *M:* w 91.5cm, 122cm, 183cm (36, 48, 72in); standard drop 183cm (72in). *P:* £15.

Mayfair's 'Beech Leaves' (left) and 'Lille' (right) from SOMBRERO

Miracles' airbrushed 'Flamingo and Sunset'

MIRACLES LTD
Exotic, one-off blinds. The team of artists united under Miracles' banner will airbrush any of their, or your, designs on to pinoleum slats, or fabric (the latter is slightly more expensive). Palm trees, birds of paradise, landscapes and seascapes are favourites. *P:* depends on complexity of design.

PEEL & CAMPDEN LTD
Competitively priced PANAROLA roller blinds in cotton or cotton/polyester, with woodspring roller and bottom lath. They come in eight plain colours, and 12 floral designs in-cluding 'Pompom' (green and yellow chrysanthemums), 'Daisy' (greens and golds), and 'Autumn Leaves' (spice shades against white). Delivery is within seven days of order, with fitting instructions. *P:* £15.

JAMES ROBERTSHAW & SONS LTD
Mainly cane and wooden blinds. This firm will also make laminated blinds from your own material, fixed to a spring roller with all fittings. Shaped edges and fringes are available. Fabric must be 2in (5cm) wider and 12in (30.5cm) longer than the finished length. Keep it rolled, not folded, so that it doesn't crease before laminating. *P:* £12 with client's fabric.

SOUTH WALES BLIND CO LTD
Two attractive ranges. Roller blinds are co-ordinated to Dorma bedlinen and curtains designed by Mary Quant. They come in lovely border prints and unusual plain colours: Coffee brown, Flanders blue, Mulberry, and Conifer (avocado). Others come in nine clear colours and patterns, and include four shaped finishes, lace trims, patterned braids, bobbles, fringes and tassels. This manufacturer will provide a remarkable 'Hotline' service: ready-made blinds (which can be trimmed to your requirements) are delivered within one or two *days* from receipt of order. *P:* £15. See also 'Soft Furnishings'.

SUNSTOR LTD
Over 90 designs, many of which can be ordered in different colourways. They include bold stripes, bright abstracts, tasteful florals, scenic effects, and elegant border prints and plain colours. Special designs for kitchens and childrens' rooms—'Bongo' is a colourful

Sunstor's 'Fruitex' (top left), 'Window Box' (top right), 'Moulin' (bottom)

jungle print in light-excluding fabric. 'Moulin' is an Art Nouveau style pattern in Orange and Brown on White, from the CUSTOM MADE range; 'Window Box' comes in White and shades of Brown on Beige; 'Fruitex' in Beige on Cream, White on Off-white, or White on Grey, can be used as a blackout blind. All blinds are custom-made with a wide choice of trims, laces and scallops. *P:* plain £17.

SUNVENE LTD
13 plain shades (see chart) plus a fairly large range of florals. The plain polycottons can be shaped and trimmed with a White fringe or bobbles. Patterns include some sweet, small-scale motifs and three border designs, of which 'Waves Champagne' is the most striking. Waterproof, mothproof vinyl blinds are available with optional scalloped edges but no trims. *P:* upon application.

SUNWAY
Made-to-measure blinds from one of Britain's best-known manufacturers. Both the COLOURWAVE range and MATCHMATES (which co-ordinates with the attractive Sanderson TRIAD collection) have a very wide choice of designs. The ROLLDOWN CURTAIN range is attractively lacy; THAI is elegantly oriental. Good choice of shaped finishes, trims, pull cords, etc. *P:* upon application.

VIXEN-SMITH LTD
Outstandingly adventurous modern designs, gorgeously hand-printed from the LIVING DAYLIGHTS, AURORA, and VIXO CARE collections. LIVING DAYLIGHTS patterns can be printed on most standard plain colours, and shaped (seven options) and/or decorated at the bottom. There are 19 bold and beautiful designs like 'Stars' on Navy, 'Cheetahs' on Cream, and 'Palm Trees' in Brown on Champagne. Vixen-Smith also offers a similarly wonderful collection of 24 patterns including bold borders, and some photographic reproductions. 'Everglades', 'Clovelly', 'Sunflower', 'Poppy', 'The Wave', 'Fuji', 'Clouds', 'Landscape' and 'Flower Pots' are examples. Similar designs are available on vertical louvres. *P:* £28.

Vixen-Smith's 'Cheetahs'

FABRIC ROLLER BLINDS IN PLAIN COLOURS	WHITE	YELLOW	LT GREEN	BT GREEN	AVOCADO	LT BLUE	MID BLUE	LT GREY	CREAM	CHAMPAGNE	SAND	COFFEE	DK BROWN	ORANGE	GOLD	RED	PURPLE	DK GREY	NAVY	AQUAMARINE	ROSE	PINK	DK GREEN	RUSSET	BLACK
CLEAN BLINDS LTD 'Centuryan'		•	•		•	•					•	•	•	•	•	•	•				•	•		•	
DEANS BLINDS LTD	•	2	•		•	•	•	•	•	•	•	•	•	•	•	•	•	•							
FILTRASOL LTD	•	2			2	•	•			•	•	•	•	•	2	•				•	•	•	•	•	
GAYLINE LTD	o	•	3	•	•	•	•			•	•	•	•	•	•	2	•			•	•	•	•	•	•
LUXAFLEX LTD		2	2		2	•	2	•	•	2	2	2	•	2	2	2		•	2	•	•	•	2		
MAYFAIR BLINDS			•							•			•	•											
PEEL & CAMPDEN LTD 'Panarola'	•	•			•		•				•	•	•						•						
SOUTH WALES BLIND CO LTD				•	•		•				•	•	•	•	•						•				
SUNSTOR LTD	•	•	•		•	•	2	•	•	•	•	•	•	•						•	•		•		
SUNVENE LTD	•	•	•		•		•	•			•	•			2					•	•	•			

Vixen-Smith's 'Stars'

PAPER AND WOOD BLINDS

CIEL
Not cheap, but very unusual. These pinoleum pull-up Roman pleated blinds, from a firm of interior decorators, are made to measure from wood slats. *P:* £25.

EATON BAG CO
Natural-coloured split bamboo cane roller blinds. They look attractive, fit in with almost any style of decor—and are very reasonably priced for made-to-measure blinds. Ideal if you want privacy, need to let some light in and hate net curtains. Whole bamboo and rattan blinds are also available. The drop length is limitless. *M:* up to 8ft (225cm). *P:* £11.

HABITAT DESIGNS LTD
Roll-up French slatted wood blinds. They come in Natural, Brown, Green, or Blue and with brackets, cleat and full fixing instructions. *M:* (2 first) 32×40in (81×102cm), 36×80in (91×204cm), 40×80in (81×204cm), 44×80in (112×204cm), 48×80in (122×204cm). *P:* £15.

MARVIC TEXTILES LTD
Unique range of natural wood slats woven together using natural and man-made yarns, in clear colours. The material can be hung in a variety of ways: Roman fold, duofold, cord and pulley, or as draperies. They're supplied with a plain or elaborate valance, and made to order in virtually any colour, to any size. *P:* £56.

Marvic's 'Quincy' Roman blind

JAMES ROBERTSHAW & SONS LTD
Natural pinoleum (split cane) in three styles: a roll-up blind with taped edges raised by pulleys; a reefed or Roman blind, with untaped edges, that pulls up in layers; and a roller blind, with taped edges, which can be mounted on spring rollers for an extra charge. *P:* £11. They're also available printed with brightly coloured floral patterns like 'Blue Belle', 'Climbing Orange', and 'Red Poppy'— perfect for giving a conservatory-feel to any room (*P:* £15). A handsome Roman (pull-up) blind in wood is another distinctive product. The natural colours create a warm, striped effect and its thickness makes it a good insulator.

Robertshaw's 'Blue Belle'

T F SAMPSON LTD

PLEATEX paper blinds with crisp accordion pleats, made to measure from specially processed, cellulose-based paper. Practical yet fantastically inexpensive, with trouble-free pulleys and a brake mechanism, they are perfect for glass-roofed extensions and conservatories because of the paper's high insulating properties. Colours are translucent Ivory or Pure white, plus Flame red, Indigo blue, and Spinach green. Printed versions are available to order. *P:* £15.

SILENT GLISS LTD

Elegant CASCADE CURTAINS, usually available only from expensive interior decorators. So far as we know, this manufacturer is the only large company to make this type of blind —not exactly a roller blind, it's operated by a pulley and cord system. They come either custom-made or in kit form to make up at home. The fabric is pulled up into loose pleats by means of cords threaded through a series of rings on the back. Full instructions are provided should you want to have a go, and the manufacturers say anyone who can make ordinary curtains will have no trouble with these blinds. *M:* finished width 110–139cm (43³/₈–54³/₄in); all drops up to 300cm (118in). *P:* upon application.

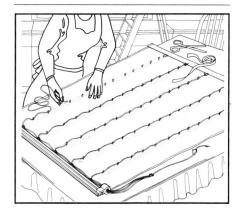

SPECIALIST PRODUCTS

FABER BLINDS LTD

Two ranges, METALET 25 and MINIMATIC, for installation between double glazing, allowing excellent light/heat control (*M:* slats 2.5 or 3.5 cm/1 or 1³/₈in). For a complete blackout, there's 1800 X-RAY, which can be operated manually or electrically. They're also perfect for skylights or slanted windows. *P:* upon application.

PEEL & CAMPDEN LTD

Audio-visual and blackout Venetian *and* roller blinds. Details and prices upon request.

PERMA BLINDS LTD

The RIDALUX blackout roller blind can be combined with a Venetian blind to give light control or a complete blackout. RIDANETT, a simpler version, is for use where 100% light exclusion is unnecessary, and is ideal if a roller blind is required between double glazing. Both come in various fabrics. Audio-visual (70–80% blackout) blinds are also available, in Matt black or Dark green. *P:* upon application.
Perma also makes a noise-reducing blind approved by the British Standards Institute and manufactured to BS 3415.

RMC PANEL PRODUCTS LTD

THERMOBLIND insulated shutters, in a variety of decorative finishes, including plastic, wood, fabric, and laminates. Very effective in preventing heat loss, they are a legitimate alternative to double glazing. Simple to install, they also provide a measure of security against intruders. *M:* to order. *P:* £35.

VENETIAN BLIND SERVICES (STAFFS)

Aluminium framed BLACKOUT BLIND featuring blind box, channels and bottom rail in black anodized aluminium. Cord operated, it can be fitted within or outside window recesses. *M:* maximum size 300×300cm (118×118in). *P:* upon application.

VENETIAN BLINDS

CLEAN BLINDS LTD

Blinds in a wide selection of unusual shades (see chart), made from a special aluminium alloy with maximum resistance to corrosion (*M:* slats 2in/5cm, *P:* £19). This firm will also clean and/or renovate clients' blinds.

ERICSON BLINDS LTD

Slimline blinds in 17 plain colours, plus gold and silver. They're also available in six wood-effect finishes: walnut, sandalwood, teak, birch, rosewood, whiteoak. Seven days' free approval. Fast delivery—blinds are despatched with 48 hours. *M:* slats 1³/₈in (3.5cm). *P:* £12.

PRICES AND INFORMATION WERE CORRECT AT THE TIME OF GOING TO PRESS

VENETIAN BLINDS	WHITE	MAGNOLIA	IVORY	FAWN	OYSTER	EGGSHELL	YELLOW	BEIGE	GOLDEN BROWN	PINK	RED	ORANGE	BURNT ORANGE	CHESTNUT	DK BROWN	LT BLUE	MID-BLUE	NAVY	MINT	AQUA	LT GREEN	BRIGHT GREEN	AVOCADO	LIME GREEN	DK GREEN	LT GREY	GREY	BLACK	VIOLET	SILVER	GOLD
CLEAN BLINDS LTD	●		●	●			●	●		●	●	●				●			●	●	●	●		●		●		●	2	●	●
ERICSON BLINDS LTD	●	●	●	●		●	●									●	●			●	●					●	●			●	●
FABER BLINDS LTD	●	●	●	●			●									●	●	●		●	●					●		●			●
FILTRASOL LTD 'Quality' (2in/50mm)	●	●	●	●	●	●	●	●	●	●	●	●			●		●	●								●	●				
'Quality' (1³⁄₈/35mm)	●	●	●	●				●	●						●		●									●					
'Economy'	●	●	●					●	●						●				●	●	●	●									
GAYLINE LTD 'Economy 50'	●		●	●			●	●		●		●		●	●	●	●		●	●	●	●				●	●				
'Classic'	●		●	●			2	●	●	●	●					●	●			●	●						●				
'Princess'	●	●	●	●			2	2	●	2	2	●	2		2	2	2	●		2	2	2	2	●	2	2	●				
LUXAFLEX LTD 'Fineblinds'	●	●	●	●			●	●	●	●	●			●		2	●	●		2	●	●	●	●	●	●	●	●			●
PEEL & CAMPDEN LTD 'Panorama'	●	●	●	●			●	●		●	●			●		2	●			2	●	●	●	●	●	●	●	●		●	●
PERMA BLINDS LTD	●			●		2	●			2	●	●				●	●		●	●	●	●		2	●	●	●				
T F SAMPSON LTD	●	●	●		●		●	●			●	●				●	●	●			●					●	●	●		●	●
SOUTH WALES BLIND CO	●	●	●			●	2	●	2	●	●	●				●	●		●	●	2	●		●		●	●	●		●	●
'Carefree' & 'Consort' (2in/50mm)	●	●	●				2	●		●	●	●			●	●	●		●	●	2	●		●		●	●	●			
'Carefree' & 'Consort' (1³⁄₈in/35mm)	●		●	●			●	●	●	●	●					●	●				●					●	●				
SUNVENE LTD	●	●	●			●	●		●	●	●				●	●	●			●					●		●			●	●

FABER BLINDS LTD

25 clean colours plus Black, and White (see chart). The FABER EDITION combines two, three or four colours in the same blind to give a highly colourful, or restrained and subtle, effect. *M:* slats 1³⁄₈, 2in (3.5, 5cm). *P:* £23.

FILTRASOL LTD

QUALITY and ECONOMY made-to-measure blinds in two widths of slat. The wider slat is available in 19 colours; the narrower in ten. Both come with matching head and bottom rails. *M:* slats 1³⁄₈, 2in (3.5, 5cm). *P:* £18.

GAYLINE LTD

Two types of Venetian blind: ECONOMY 50 has lighter, more modern styling; CLASSIC is traditional with a square box heading. Both ranges are available in plain shades (see chart) or in more than one colour for striped and border effects. Competitive prices. Seven-day free approval period. *M:* slats 1³⁄₈, 2in (3.5, 5cm). *P:* ECONOMY £17; CLASSIC £22.

LUXAFLEX LTD

One of the largest colour ranges in Venetian blinds: 45 colours including some fabric and wood-effects, and a number of good, strong, deep shades (a refreshing change from the usual pastels). Another outstanding feature of FINEBLINDS is a plastic slat control rod instead of the annoying cord. The DECORMATCH range has a choice of two combinations of stripes, available in nine colourways. *M:* slats 1, 1³⁄₈, 2in (2.5, 3.5, 5cm). *P:* £20–£26. See page 44 for colour illustration of FINE BLINDS.

PEEL & CAMPDEN LTD

PANORAMA stove-enamelled blinds in 24 colours with automatic cord lock-on mechanism. They're guaranteed for five years and delivered with fitting instructions, brackets and screws. Up to three colours can be combined in a blind; there's a 10% surcharge for four or more. Head and bottom rails in White only. Delivery within two weeks. *M:* slats 1³⁄₈, 2in (3.5, 5cm). *P:* £16, 10% extra for 1³⁄₈in slats. SIESTA tailor-made plastic blinds are much less expensive than conventional Venetian blinds, and are lightweight, rustproof and easier to hang. They're available in Yellow, Blue, Green (pastels), and White with matching head and bottom rails. *M:* slats 1½in (3.5cm); maximum 8×6ft (244×122cm). *P:* £14.

PERMA BLINDS LTD

An unusually extensive range of blinds for different situations, including external use and partial blackout. NOVOLUX is for installation between double glazing. CONTINENT is the most popular domestic blind. All ranges are available in 27 colours. *M:* slats 1, 1¾, 2in (2.5, 4.1, 5cm). *P:* £20.

T F SAMPSON LTD

Good range from a firm that's justifiably famous for its fantastically inexpensive pleated paper blinds. Unusually, slats are suspended on Terylene threads instead of tape. Treated against rust, most sizes come in 18 non-fade colours. 2.5cm (1in) slats are in White and Silver only; 3.5cm (1³⁄₈in) and 5cm (2in) versions are available in Matt and Gloss black. *M:* slats 2.5, 3.5, 5cm (1, 1³⁄₈, 2in). *P:* £12.

SOUTH WALES BLIND CO LTD

A particularly wide choice of Glamorline blinds. CAREFREE is the least expensive, CONSORT a slightly heavier-duty type. PRINCESS is a more luxurious blind with colour-matched head and bottom rails and—an unusual refinement—colour-matched cords and laces. The VOGUE range of multi-colour blinds is available in nine styles, each with different colour combinations. *M:* slats 3.5, 5cm (1³⁄₈, 2in). *P:* VOGUE £20.

SUNVENE LTD

Stove-enamelled blinds in 22 shades, with automatic cord lock. Up to six colours can be combined in a blind at no extra charge. There's a five-year guarantee, and credit facilities are available. Venetian blind laundry service too. The manufacturers say their blinds can be fitted using only a screwdriver. *M:* slats 1³⁄₈, 2in (3.5, 5cm). *P:* upon application.

TIDMARSH & SONS LTD

Beautiful TIMBERSHADE blinds made from best quality Western red cedar, specially selected for its grain, stability and lightness. They come in natural, redwood, dark grain or white grain finish, with high-strength Terylene tapes and cords in complementary shades. The blinds are operated with a single cord, rod and handle, but an electric motor is available. Wood-slat blinds have a deeper stack than standard Venetians when raised—about 3in (7.5cm) per 12in (30.5cm) of blind drop. Delivery free. *M:* slats 1¹¹⁄₁₆in (4.3cm). *P:* £47.

VERTICAL LOUVRE BLINDS

BAUMANN FABRICS LTD
Three ranges, made from a special flame-retardant yarn that shrivels up and extinguishes itself in case of fire. The staggering SIERRA collection comes in a rainbow choice of 40 colours; louvre edges are finished, but not artificially stiffened or vinylized, so the fabric's character remains unchanged (*M:* louvres 12cm/4¾in).
Knitted NEVADA consists of translucent strips (*M:* louvres 5in/12.5cm); FRETRIC can combine strips from both other ranges. Cleaning instructions are supplied. *M:* w 36 ×h 84in (91.5×213cm). *P:* £75–£85.

CLEAN BLINDS LTD
CENTURYAN vertical blinds, especially suitable for large windows, where light control is critical. They come in Rose pink, Jaffa, Mink, White, Maize, Avocado, Citrus, Light green, Kingfisher (olive). *M:* louvres 3½, 5in (9, 12.7cm). *P:* 5in £22–£28, 3½in 15% extra.

FABER BLINDS LTD
Stoutly made and hard-wearing blinds backed by two failsafe features—a draw-control which avoids snarl-ups and a built-in braking device. Louvres are made from dust-resistant fabric in seven textures and several shades: Cream, Beige, Stone, Bright green, Orange, Yellow, and Azure blue. *M:* louvres 12.7cm (5in). *P:* £25–£30, depending on texture.

FILTRASOL LTD
Five ranges span a good choice of fabrics: PASTEL, close-woven and plain; SHANTUNG, a silk-effect; SUNSHADE, a more textured weave; FASHION, a heavier hessian-type weave; and SAFEDRAPE, a finer-textured weave. They come in seven or ten colours, depending on the range (see chart). All blinds are weighted, chainlinked and specially treated to resist dust, and come with an aluminium self-lubricating handrail. *M:* louvres 3½, 5in (9, 12.7cm). *P:* £33.

GAYLINE LTD
Relatively inexpensive blinds, in a choice of three fabrics and 18 colours. SHANTUNG is a textured fabric in six shades while FLAME-GUARD and RADIANCE, also in six colours each, are closer woven and flame resistant. Seven-day free approval period. *M:* louvres 3½, 5in (9, 12.7cm). *P:* £32.

GLAMORLINE LTD
26 colours, and three fabrics: SUNTEX, a shantung weave; SUNWEAVE, a flame-resistant finely woven bouclé texture; and FLAMEX, a close-woven plain textured fabric, also flame-resistant. *M:* louvres 3½, 5in (8.9, 12.7cm). *P:* £35.

LUXAFLEX LTD
An unusually large selection of fabrics in pleasant, unobtrusive, earthy colours: SUN-GLASS, a close-woven plain fabric finish in White and Beige (*M:* louvres 5in/12.7cm); SHANTUNG, shantung weave in White, Natural, Orange, Pale beige-yellow, and Brown (*M:* louvres 5in/12.7cm); SPICE, a coarser woven fabric in White and Natural (*M:* louvres 4in/10cm); TERYLENE, close-woven, narrow, ribbed effect in Ice white, Chestnut brown, Moss green, Honey gold, and Tropical sand; and ALUMINIUM, plain metallic in Natural grey, Bronze, Mushroom, and White (*M:* louvres 4in/10cm). BOUCLE, a more open-weave plain fabric, and SUPERTWIST, a more obviously textured open-weave finish, come in ten colours (see chart) (*M:* BOUCLE 5in/ 12.7cm).

PERMA BLINDS LTD
Very good fabrics and colours, plus a useful speciality: all Consul Vertical blinds can be fitted inside double-glazing, and controlled from inside when it's closed. Available in six fabrics: PERMAGLASS, a closely woven bouclé effect; SHANTUNG, textured silk weave; POLYESTER, a slightly smoother weave; and SPICE, a heavier-weight woven fabric. All these come in two widths. PERMAWEAVE, more highly textured, has four attractive tweedy designs in Off-white shades. PERMATELA is patterned. All blinds can be supplied in lengths of up to 500cm (16ft 5in). *M:* louvres 8.9, 12.7cm (3½, 5in) except PERMAWEAVE, PERMATELA 12.7cm (5in) only. *P:* PERMAGLASS, SHANTUNG 12.7cm (5in) louvres £29.

SALTREE VERTICAL BLINDS LTD
Vinyl or shantung-weave louvres in White, Lemon, Light blue, Pink, and Lime green. SPICE, a heavier-grade fabric, is available in White and Buckwheat. Maximum width is 16ft 6in (503cm). *M:* louvres 3½, 5in (9, 12.7cm). *P:* upon application.

SILENT GLISS LTD
One of the most expensive ranges, but worth every penny. LAMELLA blinds come in an outstandingly wide selection of colours, including the bright primaries (see chart) which no other manufacturer seems to think the English

Silent Gliss' 'Poggio Fiorito'

public will like. (Silent Gliss is a Continental company, and probably the world's largest manufacturer of curtain track.) Excellent and unusual patterns include 'Poggio Fiorito'; 'Linee', a narrow Blue-and-White stripe; 'Maggia', a subtle all-over texture; 'Grano', a row of waving corn; and 'Fili d'Erba', tall green grasses. In the right setting these high-quality blinds are elegant and effective. All blinds come in 100% cotton or polyester fabric, and can be tracked to fit into any available corner. *M:* to order. *P:* upon application.

SUNVENE LTD

VISTA blinds in fabric, PVC or aluminium. SHANTUNG weave comes in White, Beige, Primrose yellow, and Green; GLASSFIBRE in White, Champagne, Brown, Tango, Yellow, and Green; SPICE (hessian texture) in White, Tweed (beige), and Oatmeal. *M:* louvres 4, 5in (10, 12.7cm). *P:* upon application.

VERTIKA INTERNATIONAL LTD

Spongeable, fireproof louvres that can be hung by an amateur. The GLASSFIBRE range comes in five textures and a wide variety of colours (see chart), and White net. Colours include White, Cream, Beige, Sand, Sage, Grey, Orange, and Brown. *M:* louvres 8.9, 12.7cm (3½, 5in). *P:* 5in £28–£32, 3½in 15% extra.

VIXEN-SMITH LTD

And now for something completely different —AURORA printed louvre blinds. 12 designs, most in more than one colourway, are available on any of 40 plain fabrics.

VERTICAL LOUVRE BLINDS	WHITE	CREAM	OATMEAL	SAND	YELLOW	COFFEE	GOLD	DK BROWN	RUST	ORANGE	RED	PINK	WINE	NAVY	MID-BLUE	LT BLUE	AQUA	LT GREEN	BT GREEN	DK GREEN	AVOCADO	LT GREY	DK GREY	BLACK
BAUMANN FABRICS LTD 'Sierra'	●	2	2	2	3	2	2	2	2	3	●	2	2	2	●	●	●	2	2	2	2	●	●	●
FABER BLINDS LTD 'Vertical'	●	●	●	●		●	●	●		●						●		●	●			●		
'Supervertical'	●	●	●	●		●	●	●		●						●		●	●			●		
FILTRASOL LTD 'Pastel'	●	●		●						●												●		
'Shantung'	●			●	●	●	●	●	●												●			
'Sunshade'	●	●		●	●	●	●									●					●			
'Fashion'	●		●		●		●		●								●				●			
'Safedrape'	●			●	●		●		●	●	●					●	●				●			
GAYLINE LTD	2	2	2	2		●	2	●	●							●	●	●				●		
GLAMORLINE LTD	3	●	●	2	2	2	2	2	●					●		2	2			●	●	●		
LUXAFLEX LTD 'Boucle'	●	●	●	●	●	●	●	●	●	●													●	
'Supertwist'	●		●	●		●	●	●	●												2	●		
PERMA BLINDS LTD 'Permaglass'		●	●				●	●									●							
'Shantung'	●		●		●											●						●	●	
'Polyester'	●		●		●	●			●							●								
'Spice'	●	●	●		●		●	●																
SILENT GLISS LTD Cotton	●	●	●	●	●	●	●	●	●	●	●					●		●	●					●
Polyester	●	●	●	●	●	●			●	●	●			●	●	●		●	●	●	●	●	●	

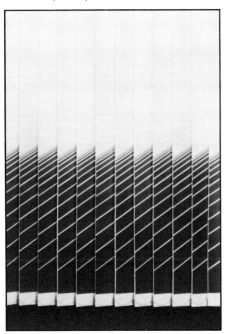

Geometrics, palm trees, waves, Greek keys, ripples, swirls, stripes, butterflies, porpoises and more make their way across the base of the blind—if you want to make your window a focal point, this is the answer. (40 undecorated colours are also available).
M: louvres 3¾, 5in (9.5, 12.7cm). *P:* £34–£52, plus £12–£20 with decorative border.

S C WILLIAMS LTD

Contract-quality blinds in a wide range of colours and materials, including a flame-resistant fabric. *M:* to order. *P:* upon application.

PRICES AND INFORMATION WERE CORRECT AT THE TIME OF GOING TO PRESS

Vixen-Smith's 'Tall Diagonals' (left), 'The Wave' (right)

INTRODUCTION

An inspired choice of carpeting can do more to create a harmonious interior than almost any other aspect of furnishing. The same colour and texture throughout a small house will give a feeling of spaciousness and unity. Different tones or even textures will define spaces and set apart rooms or areas.

Wool, traditionally the supreme carpet yarn – and the most expensive – is still unchallenged in many areas. It can be dyed to the widest range of colours (over 1,500), holds them better than other fibres, and won't easily catch fire. It cleans well and is certainly the hardest-wearing yarn. Wool carpets are usually mothproofed. 100% wool, or a mix of 20% nylon (for strength) and 80% wool are favoured by quality manufacturers – afford it if you can.

Hardwearing acrylics (Acrilan, Courtelle, Dralon, Orlon) are most like wool, but soil more easily and are also fairly expensive.

Flame-resistant modacrylics (Teklan) are comparatively new, and used primarily for contract carpeting. Domestic use will no doubt increase.

Nylon (Bri-Nylon, Enkalon, Celon, Dupont, Antron, Timbrelle) is tough and fire-resistant. It can be used on its own, or to add strength to blends.

Polyesters (Dacron, Terylene, Trevira) come in good, pleasant colours, but are only moderately hardwearing.

Polypropylene (Ulstron, Merkalon, Olefin, Propathene) is mainly used for hardwearing, low-priced carpets like plush piles. Stain-resistant, and relatively static-free, it has a slight sheen.

There are basically two types of pile: long or short cut pile; and loop pile used in Wilton, tufted or Brussels weave carpets. Both are capable of endless variation, especially when they are combined in sculptured or textured carpets.

Loop pile, made from a continuous series of loops, comes in a range of textures from thick and nubbly to closely curled.

Velvet pile, also called velour, is very closely cut and used mainly for plain or mottled effects.

Long shag pile, with all strands cut to the same length (½–4in/1.3–10cm) is perfect for modern settings. Twist or hand-twist pile, with a definite twist or kink built into the yarn, has a pebbly look. Most common in plain carpets, it's sometimes combined with other piles to create various textures.

Sculptured pile uses different heights to make 'carved' patterns in Wilton or tufted carpets. Cut and loop piles can be combined with sculpturing.

Manufacturing methods vary, as does the complexity of the designs they create. However, the quality of a carpet ultimately depends on the fibre used.

Axminster carpets are normally highly patterned. Up to 35 colours can be combined, giving an almost endless variety of designs.

Wilton patterns are simpler, as the looms take a maximum of only five colours. But Wiltons are also the most durable, strongest, and often the most expensive carpets on the market because of the high amount of pile woven into the backing.

Tufted carpets, a relatively modern invention, can be plain or patterned. Individual lengths of yarn are inserted into a pre-woven backing, creating a looped or cut-pile texture. The backing is coated twice to hold the tufts. The first tufted carpets were made from cheap synthetics. Happily they now come in better fibres, as well as wool.

Fibre bonded carpeting, sometimes called 'needleloom' or 'needlepunch', is used mainly for tiles. Dense, felt-like layers of fibres are pushed into a backing impregnated with a bonding agent to hold them together.

Cord carpets can be woven or tufted, with a low-loop uncut pile. Bonded cords have a mass of fibres fixed to a hessian back and, usually, a rigid upper surface. Cords are generally very hardwearing – and about half the price of Wiltons. Look for natural and synthetic fibre mixes.

Fake grass isn't strictly carpeting, but we've included two companies who make gorgeous artificial grass that never needs mowing, is impervious to weeds, isn't slippery when wet, and comes in different colours. Imagine vacuuming the lawn, or hosing down the playroom.

The carpet industry is gradually changing to metric widths of 1, 2, 3 and 4 metres, but the change will be slow. Shops sometimes give prices for square yards *and* square metres. There is about one-fifth more carpeting in a square metre than in a square yard.

Some carpets are still made on looms with traditional broadloom widths. The most common are 9ft (274.5cm), 12ft (366cm), 15ft 457.5cm) and 18ft (549cm). Body carpets, the trade's name for the 'narrow' strips used as runners on stairs and in halls, is 27in (68.5cm) and 3ft (91.5cm) wide. Try to avoid using it in rooms; the joins are never really invisible (unless it's tufted).

A new, simple grading scheme for all woven and tufted-pile carpets makes it easy to select suitable carpets for different areas – there's no need to use the same expensive carpeting throughout the house. Many manufacturers make the same colours in different weights: light domestic (bedrooms only), medium domestic (light traffic areas), general domestic (sitting rooms), heavy domestic (hallways and landings), and luxury domestic. Contract quality is specifically for public places, but also useful at home in hallways and other high-traffic areas. Unfortunately, it's not always available in relatively small quantities.

This section is divided into the following types of carpeting: *Berber; Coir, Coconut, Maize, Rush and Sisal; Cord; Flecked; Indoor/Outdoor; Made-to-Order; Patterned; Sculptured Pile; Shag; Tiles; Wilton* (chart).

*Prices exclude fitting and underlay.

BERBER CARPETING

ABINGDON CARPETS LTD

ROYAL KINGDOM tough twist-pile carpets in 80% wool and 20% polyamide. They're available in three characteristically flecked practical colours—Bokhara (dark brown), Fawn, and Hemp. *M:* w 12ft (366cm). *P:* sq yd £11.

W & R R ADAM LTD

Two gorgeous Berber ranges in 100% new wool: BERBERY TWIST for heavy domestic use; BERBERY DELUXE for luxury contract use. Both qualities come in undyed colours that range from off-whites to browns: 76 Champagne, 77 Oyster, 78 Granite, 79 Honey, 80 Koala, 81 Lovat. *M:* w 12ft (366cm). *P:* sq yd £15–£18.

AFIA CARPETS

Very competitively priced Berbers, in pure wool. There are four natural shades, from Beige to Mid-brown, plus a bright Grass green. Carpets are available backed with heavy density rubber, or unbacked if you prefer underfelt. Delivery throughout the United Kingdom. *M:* w 13ft (396.5cm). *P:* sq yd £7.25.

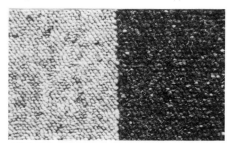

Afia's Beige Berber (left), Mid-brown (right)

AXMINSTER CARPETS LTD

DARTMOOR, a super-heavy Axminster Berber made from 100% pure new wool. It comes in Stone, discreetly patterned with two toning shades, Medium fawn and Pale green. *M:* w 27in, 3, 12ft (68.5, 91.5, 366cm). *P:* sq yd £14.

FORBO TAPIJT BV

Incredible range of Berbers, distributed by a Netherlands-based firm. Some synthetic fibres (Acrilan) are available; the others are pure wool. LARISSA is a looped-pile, 100% Acrilan, foam-backed Beige carpet with a slightly tweedy look (*P:* sq yd £8).

PADIRAC, also a looped pile, is made from 85% Acrilan and 15% animal hair; it has an all-over salt and pepper effect, in Ivory and Rust and Beige, and is foam-backed (*P:* sq yd £8). There is a wide selection of all-wool carpets. MANILLA, a low level loop, comes in a range of Chocolate browns, with a foam back (*P:* sq yd £10).

ARMADA is backed with polyester, has much

larger loops and combines Ivory, Rusts, and warm Browns in its highly textured surface (*P:* sq yd £12). PADERNA has the same surface texture as ARMADA, but blends Ivory, Beige, and Tan, and is slightly more expensive (*P:* sq yd £13).

ARADAN's more irregular looped surface has a distinctive olive tinge (*P:* sq yd £13).

ASTRABAD, a Wilton woven loop carpet also with an irregular pile, combines larger areas of Beige and Tan (*P:* sq yd £16.50).

MAXIM is the ultimate shag carpet, bursting with Brown-flecked Ivory yarns three-quarters of an inch deep. It looks like a most beautifully groomed sheep (*P:* sq yd £21).

Finally, there's ESMERALDA—it just has to be the thickest, loopiest and knobbliest carpet on the market (*P:* sq yd £31).

M: all carpets w 13ft 1½in (400cm).

GASKELL BROADLOOM CARPETS LTD

Three superb ranges. Distinctive CRAGSMAN is a heavy quality looped-pile carpeting spun from 100% pure new wool by a method unique in the United Kingdom. It comes in the usual browns (two) and light beiges (three), and also Lovat (olive), and Smalt and Zaffre (two cobalt blues). *M:* w 12ft (366cm). *P:* sq yd £10.

JERBA has larger loops, and is not technically a Berber—it's woven from a blend of 80% acrylic fibre and 20% natural wool. It's available in five natural colours from Creamy white to Mid-brown, including a gorgeous Silvery grey. *M:* w 13ft 1½in (400cm). *P:* sq yd £7.

RUSTICANA, the top range, is 100% new wool. Similar to CRAGSMAN, it has chunkier loops and comes in a large range of natural shades from Creamy white to Dark chocolate, and Silver. Uniquely, some beiges and mid-browns have been accented with strands of contrasting shades like Shell (salmon), Cinnamon, Sepia, and Tweed (orange). *M:* w 3, 12, 15ft (91.5, 366, 454.5cm). *P:* sq yd £12.

Gaskells ask you to not mix pieces from different batches as there will be slight colour variations and also mention that because of the random blending to produce the *au naturel* effect, some slight line effects may be present.

All of these carpets are mothproof and flame resistant.

Gaskell's RUSTICANA (left), JERBA (centre), CRAGSMAN (right)

Top to bottom: Forbo's LARISSA, PADIRAC, PADERNA, MAXIM, ESMERALDA

HUGH MACKAY & CO LTD

Amazing all-wool Wilton Berbers. Designs are primarily bold geometrics, each combining no more than four colours from a total of 20 natural, undyed shades. (Who would have thought there are 20 differently coloured sheep?) *M:* w 27in (68.5cm). *P:* sq yd £24.

THOMSON SHEPHERD (CARPETS) LTD

Simple but stunning collection of Berbers, all in 100% wool co-ordinated with complementary Sanderson fabrics and wall coverings. MORESQUE I has three subtle geometric designs: 'Lattice', 'Chevron', and 'Diamond', each in three natural colours—White, Flaxen beige, and Sandalwood. The illustration shows 'Chevron' teamed with a quilted-effect cotton matelassé fabric which is also available in three toning Berber shades. *P:* sq yd £28.

In MORESQUE III, different thicknesses of Berber yarns are used in cut and looped piles,

Thomson Shepherd's 'Chevron' from MORESQUE 1

PRICES AND INFORMATION WERE CORRECT AT THE TIME OF GOING TO PRESS

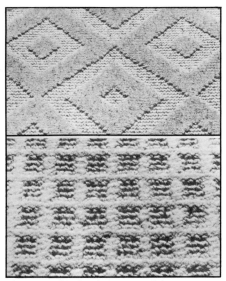

Thomson Shepherd's 'Diamond' from MORESQUE 1 (top), 'Checkpoint' from MORESQUE 111 (bottom)

in four two-tone designs. 'Strata' is Stone white, Beige, and Sandalwood; 'Trellis', 'Mosaic', and 'Checkpoint' come in White and Sandalwood. *P:* sq yd £30.
M: both ranges w 12ft (366cm).

TINTAWN LTD

Five ranges from the people who probably pioneered the Berber look of ultra-natural colour and texture in carpeting.
THATCHER, woven on simple flat looms from new wool, with 20% nylon for durability, is available in a good range of shades, from dark to light: Kestrel brown, Brown ale, Norfolk reed, Wheatmeal, Rickstraw, Barley beige, and Silvermoth (pale grey). *P:* sq yd £16.
WOOLWARP, an all-wool pile in Brussels weave, with a coarsely looped surface, comes in Moorland (a blend of brown and grey), Homespun (oatmeal grey), and White ram (a lovely bleached ivory). *P:* sq yd £20.
The most luxurious and expensive Berber is SHEPHERDWEAVE, designed, say the manufacturers, for palaces and embassies

Tintawn's SHEPHERDWEAVE

(presumably not for shepherds). A heavy Brussels weave carpet in 100% virgin wool, it's available in Barbary brown, Jacobs fleece (grey-brown), Mountain grey, Woolpack (caramel), Border burling (beige flecked with brown), Shetland tan (beige), and Swaledale white. *P:* sq yd £24.
M: all ranges w 3, 9, 12ft (91.5, 274.5, 366cm).

COIR, COCONUT, MAIZE, RUSH, AND SISAL CARPETING

JAYMART RUBBER & PLASTICS LTD

Terrific selection of competitively priced natural grass carpeting. BRUSH-OFF, in 100% coir with PVC backing, comes in natural Fawn, Red, Dark green, Moss green, Whisky, Gold, Anthracite, Light brown, and Dark brown, in four qualities. Latex-backed PANAMA ROYALE is in natural. *M:* both w 100, 200cm (3ft 3⅜in, 6ft 6¾in). *P:* sq m £8–£15, £4.50. AJENGO plain coconut matting is also in natural only (*M:* w 46–213.5cm/18in–7ft, *P:* sq m £1.60.

Jaymart's PANAMA ROYALE

ROOKSMOOR MILLS

Classically woven rush and maize mats made to measure to the nearest square foot and joined, almost invisibly, with 'unbreakable' twine. They come in 12in (30.5cm) squares, each made of smaller squares in alternate natural shades to produce the distinctive appearance of natural matting. RUSH MATTING, made from natural seaside grasses, is the best of the three qualities normally available. These inexpensive, natural floor coverings can be easily cleaned with soap and water, and are not adversely affected by damp. Damaged squares can be replaced (the manufacturers also supply a needle and twine with every order, for running repairs). *M:* mats 9×6, 12ft (274.5×183, 366cm). *P:* £15, £30.

E RUSSUM & SONS LTD

Tough, coconut fibre carpets and tiles, backed with a sheet of vinyl chloride—perfect for high traffic areas. Cut edges won't fray (unlike mattings with a woven backing), and the plastic base is impermeable to water, loose dirt and dust. Colours are Natural (tan), Red gold

(orangey-gold), Anthracite (dark slate grey), and Green (dark olive); not all sizes are available in all shades. *M:* mats 1200×100, 200cm (39ft 4½in×13ft 3⅜in, 6ft 6¾in); tiles 50× 50cm (19⅝×19⅝in). *P:* mats sq m £11–£15; tiles £2.75–£3.20 per tile.

PETER SMITH ASSOCIATES LTD

PSA CUTFAST plastic-backed coir pile matting, cut and supplied without finishing in natural and a choice of eight colours: Russet (burnt orange), Gold, Charcoal, Green (slightly olive), Natural (tan), Red, Whiskey (sandy orange), and Dark brown. *M:* 1100×100, 200cm (34ft 1⅛in×3ft 3⅜in, 6ft 6¾in). *P:* sq m £10.50–£13.50.

BRUCE STARKE & CO LTD

Hardwearing 100% coir carpeting. It's anti-static, flameproof, easy to lay, and won't fray. The TROPICAL range is tough, latex backed, and comes in natural colours and four textures. HAMELIN matting and tiles are available in Natural, Red, Olive green, Cognac, Brown russet; and a wonderful wavy-line pattern in Black on Red, Light blue on Blue, and Dark brown on Natural. Tiles also come in Anthracite. *M:* w 100, 200cm (3ft 3⅜in, 6ft 6¾in); tiles 50×50cm (19⅝×19⅝in). *P:* upon application.

Left to right, top to bottom: Bruce Starke's '3', '1', '7', '5' from TROPICAL

TASIBEL (LONDON) LTD

Inexpensive TASITWEED sisal carpeting with foam backing. (Sisal is a little softer, and possibly less tough, than coir.) The TASITWEED 2300 and 2800 ranges are gorgeous bold weaves—2300 in Brown, Rust, Beige, Off-white, and Chocolate; 2800 with more variegated mixes like Green and Beige, Brown laced with Sepia, Chocolate with Brown, and Sand with Rust. *M:* w 200cm (6ft 6¾in). *P:* sq m £7–£7.50. TASITWEED 1100, 1200 and 1300, less gutsy in texture, are available in similar colours. The 1100 is woven in four combinations: Olive/Pale green/Beige, Rust/White/Deep chocolate, Brown/Sepia/White, and Rust/Sepia/White. *M:* w 200cm (6ft 6¾in). *P:* sq m £4.80. The 1300 comes in similar combinations, the 1200 in plain Natural, Sand, and

Left to right, top to bottom: Tasibel's TASITWEED 1200, 1100; BROADWAY; TASITWEED 2300, 1300, 2800

Chocolate (*M:* both w 380, 400cm/12ft 6in, 13ft 1½in, *P:* sq m £4.80).

BROADWAY is more expensive but incorporates chevron designs. In Off-white, Rust-streaked Brown, and Brown-streaked Cream. *M:* w 400cm (13ft 1½in). *P:* sq m £7.25. TASITWEED comes in rolls (minimum order three rolls unless you want to pay the variable sisal tariff).

Tough, rustic COCO PANAMA ROYALE matting is in a natural colour only. It's very inexpensive, and the latex backing means cut edges won't fray. *M:* w 200, 400cm (6ft 6¾in, 13ft 1½in). *P:* sq m £4.25.

ANJENGO THREE SHAFT COCO MATTING is slightly inferior in quality, but unbelievably cheap. Fawn only. *M:* w 18, 27in, 3, 4½, 6ft (46, 68.5, 91.5, 137, 183cm). *P:* sq yd £1.60.

CORD CARPETING

DLW (BRITAIN) LTD

Two ranges of cord carpeting, made from synthetic fibres, with high-density foam backing. Colours are autumnal, and the carpets have a slight sheen when laid. RO 828, in 100% polypropylene, is for general domestic use and comes in nine colours. There are seven variations on brown: 828–60 (Mid-brown), 828–66 (slightly more Orange), 828–70 (Copper brown), 828–10 (Rust), 828–46 and 828–45 (two beiges), and 828–42 (Champagne). Also two greens—828–22 (Pale sage) and 828–30 (Mid-olive). *M:* w 200cm (6ft 6¾in). *P:* upon application.

HANNOVER, a loop-pile, cord-type carpeting in 100% anti-static polyamide, is suitable for heavy domestic use. It's available in three greens and seven browns: 1151–30 (Bright olive), 1151–33 (Gold-flecked olive), 1151–35 (Soft sea green), 1151–40 (Pale champagne), 1151–45 (Grège), 1151–46 and 1151–64 (Soft tans flecked with Light beige), 1151–66 (Sienna flecked with Copper), 1151–67 (Tan flecked with Orange), and 1151–76 (Tan with Orange and Gold). *M:* w 400cm (13ft 1½ins). *P:* upon application.

GILT EDGE CARPETS LTD

ENDURA made from 50% nylon and 50% polyester. Recommended for areas subject to wear and heavy soiling, it's available in two qualities, each in 14 colours. 'Super Endura' comes in a range of browns: Sandstone, Walnut, Cinnamon, Terracotta, Chestnut, Caramel, Koala, Desert gold, and Champagne; also three greens—Everglade, Larch, and Sage—Denim, and Graphite (*P:* sq yd £6.50).
Less expensive 'Endura' carpets are available in Antelope, Caramel, Sandalwood, Walnut, Chestnut, Desert gold, Amber gold, Sandstone, Cherry red, Baltic blue, deeper Pacific blue, Everglade, Indigo (purple), and Pampas green (*P:* sq yd £5.25).
M: both ranges w 3, 6, 12ft (91.5, 183, 366cm).

GREENWOOD & COOPE LTD

CORMAR foam-backed cord carpeting, in two qualities, both for general domestic use. Made from man-made fibres, it's good value for money. 'Klondyke', slightly variegated, is in Meraklon BCF, a polypropylene fibre. It has a slight sheen, but is much less expensive than the animal fibres traditionally used for cord carpets. Colours include Peat, Ocelot (paler brown and beige), Bamboo (tawny beige), Russet (orange and gold), Pewter, Bracken (tan and pale grey), Ivy (apple green and brown), Clematis (sky and navy blue), and Cinnabar (wine red and rose). *P:* sq yd £5. 'Homecord', slightly more expensive, is made from 100% polypropylene and is available in 12 lovely colours including Ivory, a unique white laced with silvery-grey. Other shades are Squirrel (dark brown), Rust, Camel (warm tan), Sand (greeny-gold), Barley (beige and light brown), Pebble (beige), Conifer, Olive, Cherry, Grey (mid), and Blue (dark green and royal blue). *P:* sq yd £6.50.
M: w 3, 9, 12ft (91, 274, 366cm).

HOMFRAY CARPETS LTD

EUROPA anti-static nylon cord carpeting for high traffic areas. Its 'Voracel' sponge cushion backing won't crumble, doesn't smell of rubber and is guaranteed to last as long as the carpet. It comes in Copper, Brown, Maize, Red, Blue (deep ultramarine), Iris green (olive), Fawn, and Bracken. *M:* w 12ft, 13ft 1½in (366, 400cm). *P:* sq yd £3.50.

ROOKSMOOR MILLS

Very competitively priced COUNTY foam-backed cord carpeting, made from 100% polypropylene and supplied cut to length. It's available in 11 lovely shades: Off-white, Silvery grey, Golden yellow, Aquamarine, Turquoise, Sea green, Olive green, Dark olive, Dark brown, Pewter, and Burnt orange. *M:* w 18, 27in, 3, 4½, 6, 7½, 9, 10½, 12ft (46, 68.5, 91.5, 137, 183, 228.5, 274.5, 320, 366cm). *P:* sq yd £7.20.

SOMMER ALLIBERT (UK) LTD

Budget-priced, needlepunch STAR SCALA cord carpet made from 100% polypropylene with foam backing. Suitable for domestic or light contract use, it comes in a very good selection of 14 colours: Light gold, Light orange, Dark gold, Dark orange, Maroon, Light beige, Dark beige, Light grey, Grey, Petrol blue, Sky blue, Heather (tan), Brown, and Dark green. *M:* w 200, 400cm (6ft 6¾in, 13ft 1½in). *P:* upon application.

A F STODDARD & CO LTD

Beautifully tasteful RANNOCH or SUPER RANNOCH carpeting in 40% wool/hair, 50% viscose and 10% nylon, suitable for general domestic use. 'Natural' colours predominate in the Wilton cords: Manilla (soft beige), Oatmeal (darker beige), Bullrush (dark brown), Pewter (light grey), Graphite (charcoal grey), Avocado (olive green), Sage (soft green), Brick (red-orange) and Rose grey (burnt red). Soft 'Stripes', all subtly lovely are produced in a unique tweed, cut-pile cord carpet, by combining two of these shades: Avocado tweed (Avocado and Sage), Brick tweed (Brick and Rose grey), Pewter tweed (Pewter and Manilla), and Graphite tweed (Graphite and Bullrush). *M:* w 27in, 12ft (68.5, 366cm). *P:* sq yd £5.50, £7.50.

Stoddard's 'Stripes' from SUPER RANNOCH

TRETFORD CARPETS LTD

INTERLAND cord carpeting in 80% animal hair, 15% nylon and 5% viscose, mothproofed to European standards. Intended for heavy domestic use, it comes in 37 of the most beautiful colours available. Neutrals: Biscuit, Oatmeal, Maize (soft gold), Double cream, Wild rice, Mushroom, Milk chocolate, Bronze, Burnt oak, Coffee bean, Dapple grey, Larch, and Silver birch. Warm colours: Curry powder, Jonquille, Sunflower, Pomegranate,

Russet, Lobster, Orange squash, Burnt orange, Cedar, Apricot, and Peach. Cool colours: Bracket (olive), Broom, Lettuce leaf, Clover green, Lichen, Evergreen, Peacock, Sky blue, Lagoon blue, Cornflower, Lilac, Blackberry, Deep purple. Samples from your local dealer, or write to Tretford. *M:* w 100, 200cm (36ft 3³⁄₈in, 6ft 6³⁄₄in). *P:* sq m £8.50.

Tretford's INTERLAND

FLECKED CARPETING

ABINGDON CARPETS LTD
KNIGHTSBRIDGE two-tone twist carpeting with rubber backing, made from 40% Courtelle acrylic, 40% Evlan viscose and 20% nylon. It comes in 13 shades: Oatmeal, Beige, Sandstone, Silver birch, Topaz, Mink brown, Greengage, Forest green, Olive, Burma green, Blue, Rose, and Lacquer red. *M:* w 18, 27in, 3, 4½ft (46, 68.5, 91.5, 137cm). *P:* sq yd £8.25.

ASSOCIATED WEAVERS LTD
ARMADA high-density foam-backed carpeting for heavy traffic areas. Made from 50% polyamide and 50% polypropylene, it comes in nine highly textured tones: Berber, Lama, Stone, Honey, Whisky, Coffee, and Teak (all striated neutrals which show very little dirt or wear), Orange, and Moss. *M:* w 400cm (13ft 1½in). *P:* upon application.

OLLERTON HALL DECORATING SERVICE
SPECKLY HEN carpeting in foam-backed 100% polypropylene. Very good value, it's guaranteed for seven years, and can be supplied in any width or length in 6in (15cm) multiples. There are six colourways, all flecked with dark versions of the overall shade: Tan/Beige, Tan/Gold, Brown/Gold, Olive/Sage, Brown/Beige, Brown/Orange. *M:* maximum 75ft (22.8m) × w 13ft 1in (399cm). *P:* sq yd £4.60.

PRICES AND INFORMATION WERE CORRECT AT THE TIME OF GOING TO PRESS

A F STODDARD & CO LTD
TELSAX and TELSAX SUPER MARL carpeting for very heavy domestic use, in 70% Acrilan and 30% nylon. Unusually soft, but ultimately practical, it comes in nine comparatively vibrant shades, all with a darker fleck in the same colour group: Brown, Fawn, Olive, Green, Blue, Gold, Orange, Turquoise, and Red. *M:* w 12ft (366cm). *P:* sq yd £8.50.

THOMSON SHEPHERD (CARPETS) LTD
DEBUTANTE tonal Wilton, its overall texture designed to conceal wear and tear. Made from 80% wool and 20% nylon, it's suitable for heavy domestic use, and comes in Antelope/Fawn, Sand/Beige, Gold/Russet, Red/Dark red, Blue/Green, Moss green/Olive, Aubergine/Dark blue, Fuschia/Red, Rust/Red, Autumn tan/Bronze, Stone/Beige, and Milk/Brown. *M:* w 3, 9, 12ft (91.5, 274.5, 366cm). *P:* sq yd £10.

INDOOR/OUTDOOR CARPETING

THE GREENSWARD CO
LAZYLAWN artificial grass for everything from grassy wall-coverings to cricket wickets and football pitches. The light range, suitable for walls, is available backed or without backing, in Olive and Emerald green (*M:* w 3ft/91.5cm, *P:* sq yd £2.25–£3.50).
Medium-weight LAZYLAWN, for domestic use, comes in a variety of textures and colours (*M:* w 4ft 11in/150cm, *P:* sq yd £3.50–£5.50).
The heavy-weight range includes a curly, mossy 'grass' (*M:* w 6ft 6³⁄₄in/200cm, *P:* sq yd £6–£9).
TAPLAY grass tiles are also available—combined with paving stones, they make for a care-free patio (*M:* 19⁵⁄₈×19⁵⁄₈in/50×50cm, *P:* sq yd £3.50). Other delights include an imitation putting or chipping green. The manufacturers will provide the adhesive and carpet tapes necessary for a professional job.
Greensward also make a fake thatch in Beige, Butterscotch, Chestnut, Lagoon blue, Salt and pepper, Red (*M:* w 4ft 11in/150cm, *P:* sq yd £6).

JAYMART RUBBER & PLASTICS LTD
GRASSHOPPER all-weather artificial grass in 100% polypropylene, from a firm that specializes in economy flooring. It won't mildew or rot, and is guaranteed not to fade for five years. Available in three qualities, in rolls or cut. *M:* w 110–122, 200–206cm (3ft 7³⁄₈in–4ft, 6ft 6³⁄₄in–6ft 9¹⁄₈in). *P:* sq m £7–£11.

PEEL & CAMPDEN LTD
FORBO GARDEN artificial grass made from polypropylene. Small 'feet' make it unnecessary to cement it into place, and guard against slipping. Slightly more expensive than other 'grass', it's ideal for cement or similar hard

surfaces. Available in Grass green and Earth brown, FORBO GARDEN is guaranteed against fading. *M:* w 6ft 6³⁄₄in (200cm). *P:* sq yd £8.

PETER SMITH ASSOCIATES LTD
ASTROTURF, the original artificial lawn. Designed for indoor or outdoor use, it was originally developed in the USA for sports stadiums. Available in rolls or cut lengths, it comes in three colours: Green, Rusty brown and Gold. *M:* w 3ft (91.5cm). *P:* sq yd £16. VERDANT, a less plastic 'lawn', has a shorter pile (*M:* w 4ft 11in/150cm, *P:* sq yd £9).

MADE-TO-ORDER CARPETING

BOSANQUET IVES LTD
Absolutely lovely designs from a firm that specializes in custom-made carpets. Available only through interior decorators, they can be made in any width, pattern or colour combination. *P:* upon application. See page 69 for a selection of designs in colour.

C P CARPETS (KIDDERMINSTER)
Patterns or plain shades from one of the few manufacturers able to produce special colourings and designs in traditional Wilton carpeting. Velvet, twist, loop or traditional textures are available, to any length. C P Carpets will also arrange fitting. *M:* w 27in, 3ft (68.5, 91.5cm). *P:* upon application.

HUGH MACKAY & CO LTD
A total of 250 colours (that's 35 million design permutations), from a company that makes consistently arresting carpets. There are nine qualities of Wilton, each of which can combine up to five colours. Delivery is about eight weeks. A reproduction service is also available: an Adam period all-wool rug based on a design at the Victoria and Albert Museum was made recently for a client. Carpets can be supplied in Brussels weave or velvet pile, for the same price as the normal Wilton, and they are willing to tackle any design you want for a carpet or run. *M:* to order. *P:* upon application.

MERCIA WEAVERS LTD
Eight grades of Wilton in 80% wool and 20% nylon, from the carpet division of Parker Knoll, the famous furniture manufacturers. There's a choice of 108 standard colours, and no minimum yardage requirement. Designs are never discontinued. Grades range from very heavy general contract quality to carpeting for heavy domestic/contract use. *M:* w 27in, 3ft 3³⁄₈in (68.5, 100cm). *P:* upon application.

TURBERVILLE SMITH
Patterned Wilton carpets combining up to five colours in various grades, from London's

oldest carpet retailers (established 1825). Primarily contract carpeting suppliers, catering especially to architects, Turberville Smith have agreed to be included in this book. They will weave any design you like (their sample book illustrates 96 patterns), in small quantities if necessary. A complete after-care service is available. *M:* w 27in, 3ft (68.5, 91.5cm). *P:* upon application.

WILTON ROYAL CARPET FACTORY LTD
Five grades of Wilton carpeting in any colour you want. There's no minimum yardage but the looming charge, which decreases as the quantity increases, isn't totally absorbed until about 40 linear yards (36.4 metres). *M:* w 27in, 3ft (68.5, 91.5cm). *P:* sq yd £16–£24.

PATTERNED CARPETING

AFIA CARPETS
Stunning carpets from all over the world, displayed in a beautifully laid-out store at 81 Baker Street in London. Afia also periodically commission new designs. Examples are the collections by Linda Barron, better known as a fashion designer, and Robert Wallace, an American who gained recognition for his hand-made tapestries, rugs and carpets. LINDA BARRON designs, some of the most unusual on the market, range from the neat precision of 'Mosaic' and 'Crossed Line' to the undisciplined appeal of 'Clouds', 'Shapes', and 'Curved Lines'. All are made from 80% wool/20% polyamide. Each of the six designs comes in three pastel, medium and strong colour groups—a total of 18 shades. The pastels use Mushroom, Cream, Dusky blue, and Pink, the medium range relies on Grey-green, Rust, Cream, Blue, and Amber, while Dark blue, Rust, and Grey predominate in the strong group. Her designs are also available in the colourway of your choice. *P:* yd £32.

Left to right, top to bottom: 'Shapes', 'Crossed Lines', 'Curved Lines', 'Mosaic', 'Tweed', 'Clouds', all by LINDA BARRON for Afia

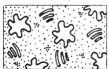 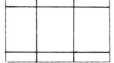

 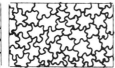

The ROBERT WALLACE collection is based on 18th-century needlework motifs. There are five designs: 'Wild Fruit', 'Stria', 'Treillage', 'Cotillion', and 'Rose du Bois'—each available in 12 colours, in either Brussels weave or velvet pile finish. *P:* yd £29.

'Treillage' by ROBERT WALLACE for Afia

Afia also market 'Private Designs', by three world-famous designers: Manuel Canovas, Halston, and Jack Lenor Larsen. Canovas, one of France's top fabric designers, has turned his talents to creating beautiful—if fairly expensive—carpets, all in 100% pure wool. Designs include 'Pamprilles' (abstracted leaves and flowers in Pale green and Lilac on White), 'Cassandre' (rose medallions on a trellis in Beige and Ecru tones), 'Adrien' (three-dimensional 'op' pattern in Black, Grey, and White), 'Fraises' (plump, Red strawberries on Cream, naturally), and 'Arcadie' (Pale pink and Green birds, elegantly exotic, fly over a Cream ground). Also four geometrics—'Flavie' (Grass green and Ink blue), 'Kali' (Beige rectangles), 'Antinoe' (Peach), and 'Trajan' (Mushroom and Ivory). Delivery takes three weeks, but it's worth the wait. *P:* yd £38.
HALSTON, who dresses the beautiful people, has designed a uniquely coloured and textured collection. His 'Suede Look' carpets, in dense Antron nylon, are available in 26 shades. *P:* sq yd £29.
Finally, there's the LARSEN collection of three-dimensional Jacquard Wiltons with small innovative shapes in pastel tones on Cream backgrounds. Co-ordinating borders are also available. 'Quadrangle 1001' and 'Metropolis' are both geometrically inspired. 'Happiness' has soft swirling shapes. *P:* yd £35.
Afia's EVERGREEN range, in pure wool, comes in ten beautiful designs. All in pastels like Peach, Ecru and Pistachio, although you can select your own colours. Motifs include tulips, butterflies, scattered waterlilies and beribboned or bedecked trellises. *P:* yd £28.
M: w 27in (68.5cm); HALSTON 'Suede Look' w 12ft (366cm). See page 69 for a selection of Afia designs in colour.

ASSOCIATED WEAVERS LTD
Velvety textured carpeting with geometric designs, at prices that won't break your budget. There are three ranges in 100% polyamide with foam backing, all suitable for high-traffic areas. NAPOLI, based on a smaller square within a square, comes in lovely subdued duotones of Browns, Greens, and Reds. SNOWFLAKE and MONA, both strict florals, are available in similar colourways. *M:* w 400cm (13ft 1½in). *P:* upon application.

AXMINSTER CARPETS LTD
A huge range of traditionally patterned carpets from specialists in Axminsters, at Axminster in Devon. All are 100% mothproofed wool, and manufactured to the highest quality. 'Shell-burst', a sort of Punk-style spatter, has overtones of the 1950s, while 'Panel Persian' is a classic design in Fawn, Red, or Green colourways. 'Egyptian' is an unusual pattern in spice tones. 'Turkey Red' has a Bright red ground accented by other primaries; 'Adam Panel' combines Fawn medallions and Gold scrollwork on a Dark red ground; 'Kashan' is Nutmegs and Cinnamons on White. 'Exeter' has small medallions in Lichen green, Tans, and Rust on a ground of Soft green and White; it also comes in a predominantly Brown colourway. These are only a few of the designs available from these experts. *M:* w 27in, 3, 9, 12ft (68.8, 91.5, 274.5, 366cm). *P:* sq yd £12–£20.

Left to right, top to bottom: Axminster's 'Turkey Red', 'Adam Panel', 'Kashan', 'Exeter'

PRICES AND INFORMATION WERE CORRECT AT THE TIME OF GOING TO PRESS

BLACKWOOD MORTON & SONS LTD

A very large and varied selection of Axminsters. There are three ranges in 80% wool and 20% nylon. Persian-inspired motifs predominate in SORRENTO, in Browns, Beiges and Golds; 'Seichur Panel', in Cream, is an unusual and beautiful design. The scrolls and leaves of MATRIX are more typical Axminster patterns. HEBRIDEAN is a very abstract collection: the inspiration for designs is reflected in their names: 'Rock Pools', 'Sand Dunes', and 'Moorland'. All come in tasteful Tans, Creams, and Olives. Less expensive carpeting is made from 40% wool, 40% viscose (Evlan) and 20% nylon.

HYVAL is more abstract than AXMOR, but both have the scrolls and swirly leaves associated with Axminster weaves. KINTYRE and WOVAX, the cheapest ranges, are in man-made fibres. Both are more brightly coloured than the other BMK ranges. However, KINTYRE includes several 'calmer' patterns like 'Dutch Floral Scroll', 'Persian Screen' and 'Persian Vase'. *M:* w 91.5cm (3ft). *P:* upon application.

BROCKWAY CARPETS LTD

High-quality TERRA FIRMA in 80% wool and 20% nylon. 'Hyperion' is a subtly coloured scroll pattern; '1/1543', an unusual dark Oriental motif on a soft ground of Beige and White. There are also several modern geometric designs with Browns predominating. *M:* w 3, 12ft (91.5, 366cm). *P:* sq yd £19.50.

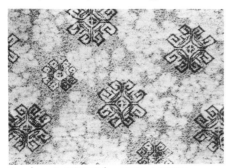

Brockway's '1/1543' from TERRA FIRMA

THE CARPET MANUFACTURING CO LTD

Unusually varied and wonderful designs, from one of the UK's major manufacturers. SALOPIAN includes several designs manufactured 70 years ago, and recently discovered in CMC files. In 80% wool and 20% nylon, it's suitable for heavy contract use. The patterns include several real beauties. 'Emperor', a hexagonal Persian, is in soft Blues and Greens on a Rust ground; 'Sultan' combines shades of Red, Green, Blue, and White; 'Pasha' is a strong Forest green and Royal navy on a Bright red ground; 'Emir' has a mixture of Navy and Light tans on an Orange russet ground. 'Vizir' is the most delicate design, with Soft greens, Sky blues, and Rusts on a Creamy background.

'Rustic' and 'Wild Briar' are both Art Nouveau-influenced stylized florals in spice tones. Victorian motifs include 'Cheltenham' in Ecru and Beige on a Rust ground; 'Victoria', Dark green and Russet on Ecru; and 'Balmoral', Dark green on Oriental red. *M:* w 27in (68.5cm). *P:* sq yd £20.

Left to right, top to bottom: Carpet Manufacturing Co's 'Emir' from SALOPIAN, 'Coffee Cream', 'Heather Tweed' from DEBRETT, 'Octagine' from KARA-VAN

Designs in the equally lovely DEBRETT Wilton range are slightly less complex, woven from a maximum of four shades in 80% wool/20% nylon. In total contrast to SALOPIAN, all patterns are geometrically based. They include 'Coffee Cream', Tan and Cream on Rich brown; and 'Heather Tweed', Soft gold or Green on Cream. *M:* w 27in, 3, 12, 15ft (68.5, 91.5, 366, 457.5cm). P: sq yd £29. KARA-VAN, another range of geometrics, is made from 100% acrylic. Designs include 'Octagine' in Oyster white, Beiges, and Browns, or Soft yellow. *M:* w 12ft (366cm). *P:* sq yd £14.

CARPETS OF WORTH LTD

CORINTH and ACROPOLIS ranges, each consisting of classic Axminster designs, in 100% Acrilan. Illustrated are two CORINTH designs: 'Dresden', a Jacobean-inspired floral design, delicately coloured in Soft blues, accented with Beige and Grey shades; and 'Antoinette', a Louis XIV panel chintz with Gold and Russet bouquets and festoons on a Brown ground. The AFGHAN range, in 80% wool and 20% nylon, has much lower-key colourations. 'Kasak', a Shivran design on a Dark blue

ground, is particularly appealing. *M:* w 3, 12, 15ft (91.5, 366, 457.5cm). *P:* upon application.

Carpets of Worth's 'Dresden' (left), 'Antoinette' (right) from CORINTH

GASKELL BROADLOOM CARPETS LTD

HIBERNIA contract quality carpeting in 80% wool and 20% nylon. Natural shades only—strict small-scale plaids and checks are executed in various combinations of Whites, Beiges, Browns, and Blacks. Don't think of these colours as strictly conference-room shades; they work anywhere. *M:* w 3, 12, 15ft (91.5, 366, 457.5cm). *P:* sq yd £12.50.

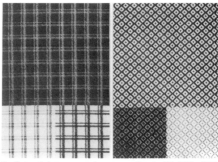

Left to right, top to bottom: Gaskell's '56', '12', '64', '49', '85', '84' from HIBERNIA

GILT EDGE CARPETS LTD

A huge selection of patterned Axminsters in a wide variety of prices. They include 'Kashmiran' in Tan, Gold, Salmon, and Browns on a light ground; and 'Tabriz', a Persian pattern with traditional Golds, Tans, and Cream on a Dark royal blue or stunning Russet ground. There are dozens of traditional Axminster designs in HALLMARK, GUILDHALL, and SHIREHALL, made from 80% acrylic and 20% nylon. Illustrated is 'Masquerade', with roses and trelliswork in Off-whites through Brown on a ground of Warm reds. *M:* w 3, 12ft (91.5, 366cm). *P:* sq yd £10–£15.

Right (top): Gilt Edge's 'Masquerade' (left), 'Kashmiran' (right)

HOMEWORKS LTD
JACK LENOR LARSEN range of fantastically patterned, fantastically beautiful, and very expensive, carpeting. Mainly in 100% pure new wool, they are perfect for heavy domestic use. Nine designs, including swirls, checks and jacquard patterns, complement plain carpets in the collection. Textures range from Wilton velvet to low loop. 'Quadrangle', with 10×10cm (4×4in) looped patchwork squares set in a cut-pile ground is the most unusual. *M:* w 69–104cm (27¹/₈in–3ft 5in) depending on design. *P:* sq m £42–£75.

'Quadrangle' by JACK LENOR LARSEN for Homeworks

MARY FOX LINTON LTD
COOMBE carpeting in wonderfully simple geometric designs, made from 100% wool. The patterns, in Brussels weave or the smoother Wilton texture, combine two or three colours. Illustrated are 'Kew', 'St. James', 'Hyde', 'Holland' and 'Regent' (inspired by London's famous parks). 13 co-ordinating fabrics and eight matching wallpaper and tile

designs are available. All carpets are woven to clients' specifications, and Mary Fox Linton will also create special designs and/or matching border motifs. *M:* w 27in (68.5cm). *P:* m Brussels weave £20, Wilton £18. Small surcharge on orders under 40m (43¾yd).

HUGH MACKAY & CO LTD
Axminsters from a traditional company famous for its custom-made contract carpets. WOLSINGHAM and CONNOISSEUR (which combines thick felted yarn with a velvety pile to give unusual textural interest) are both based on typical motifs: swirling leaves and intricate florals. Made from 80% wool and 20% nylon, they come in Blue, Green, Rust, and Brown tones. *M:* w 3, 12ft (91.5, 366cm). *P:* sq yd £15, £20.

Hugh Mackay's CONNOISSEUR

In addition, there's the CATHEDRAL range designed for heavy domestic use, which consists of 14 designs. Illustrated are: 'Kenwood', a classic Adam panel in Rich reds; 'Lismore', a delicate Art Nouveau pattern in shades of

Above: Hugh Mackay's 'Kenwood' (left), 'Lismore' (right) from CATHEDRAL

Left, top to bottom: Mary Fox Linton's 'Kew', 'St James', 'Hyde', 'Holland', 'Regent' from COOMBE

Terracotta with a hint of Red; and 'Sultan', an Indian-style motif in Red, Blue, Green, and Gold. These are only a few from this collection (which should not be confined to the lobbies of four-star hotels). *M:* w 27in (68.5cm). *P:* upon application.

Hugh Mackay's 'Sultan' from CATHEDRAL

COUNTERPOINT is a positively awe-inspiring range of perfectly co-ordinated, wonderfully coloured Axminsters, in 24 patterns. You can choose the design according to the scale and purpose required in each room and the colour flow will harmonize throughout—a possibility formerly available only to the very wealthy few. Made from 80% wool and 20% nylon, suitable for heavy domestic use, it comes with Blue, Gold, Brown, Green, or Burgundy predominating. *M:* w 27in, 12ft (68.5, 366cm). *P:* sq yd £19. See page 69 for two designs from this range in colour.

SUPER PLUSMIN includes several tartans, or Hugh Mackay will weave your own in up to five colours. Big cat skins and python textures are also available in this small range. *M:* w 27in, 12ft (68.5, 366cm). *P:* upon application.

MERCIA WEAVERS LTD

Three simple beauties, in 80% wool and 20% nylon. Intended for designers and interior decorators, they can be woven in over 108 standard colours, and are available in five contract qualities. 'Sequin' is patterned with two-colour dots, 'Catspaw' marked with nine-point, single-colour prints, 'Honeycomb' has a hexagonal all-over grid in two colours. *M:* w 68.5, 100cm (27in, 3ft 3³/8in). *P:* sq m £20–£30. See page 69 for 'Catspaw', 'Honeycomb' in colour.

Mercia Weavers' 'Sequin'

NAVAN CARPETS LTD

ARDEE Wilton carpets, originally developed for the American commercial market. Made of 80% wool and 20% nylon, they're not cheap—

Hugh Mackay's COUNTERPOINT

but they're certainly some of the most beautiful patterned carpets on the market. Triangular motifs include 'Pyramids', with Olive and Beige on Creamy yellow ground or Brown and Burgundy on Raspberry. Square designs are also available, such as 'Square Mesh' in Light coffee and Apricot overlaid with a Rust grid, and 'Dot-n-Dash', with Lime or Red dots connected by a White grid on Dark green or Burnt red. *M:* w 12ft (366cm). *P:* sq yd £15. See page 69 for 'Dot 'n' Dash' in colour.

Navan's 'Pyramids' (left), 'Square Mesh' (right) from ARDEE

THOMSON SHEPHERD (CARPETS) LTD

Hardwearing CITATION Axminster carpeting, in unusually subtle shades, to match Sandersons' William Morris wallpapers. Made from 80% wool and 20% nylon, it's suitable for heavy domestic or general contract use. 12 patterns range from the classic, Morris-influenced 'Golden Fly', 'Chrysanthemum', and 'Granville' to 'Poppy', a more stylized floral design. 'Patchwork' is especially striking with flower motifs in the form of a honeycomb. *M:* w 3, 12ft (91.5, 366cm). *P:* sq yd £17.

Thomson Shepherd's 'Golden Lily'

Thomson Shepherd's 'Chrysanthemum' (top), 'Granville' (bottom)

The amazing DELTIC range of authentic Scottish tartan designs is for the plaid mad. This Axminster carpeting, made from 80% wool (some from Scotland's famous black-faced sheep) and 20% nylon, is suitable for heavy contract use. The range includes 'Royal Stewart', 'Ancient Buchanan', 'Hunting Ross', 'Dundee', 'MacPherson', 'Clan MacDonald', 'Wallace', 'MacKenzie'. *M:* w 27in (68.5cm). *P:* yd £14.

TEMPLETON CARPETS
Non-swirly patterned carpets designed by Mary Quant, in 100% Dralon, suitable for general domestic use. This very unusual and stylish range includes 'Freckles', a tiny geometric in Greens or Browns, 'Moorland', a plaid in heathery Browns, 'Marrakesh', a mixture of Olive and Spice shades, 'Ludo' in Dark brown with Red dots on Beige, 'Jigsaw' in pastels and 'Hampton Court' in Fudge, Cream and Chocolate. *M:* w 3, 12ft (91.5, 366cm). *P:* sq yd £12.

Templeton's 'Hampton Court' by Mary Quant

TINTAWN LTD
LOOMTUNE carpeting in a small herringbone pattern. Made from 20% nylon/20% fine animal hair/60% wool, it's backed with dense latex and suitable for any domestic use. Available in seven lovely mixes of Beige with Cream, Gold, Dusty pink, Cornflower blue, Leaf green, Brown, or Olive. *M:* w 3, 9, 12ft (91.5, 274.5, 366cm). *P:* sq yd £14.

Tintawn's LOOMTUNE

TOMKINSONS CARPETS LTD
Good selection of Axminster carpeting. Two ranges, ROYAL WINDSOR and ROYAL DEVON, epitomize Axminster designs, with complex patterns woven in the softest of shades. All in hardwearing 80% wool and 20% nylon, except ROYAL WINDSOR which is 100% Acrilan, and suitable for heavy domestic use. *M:* w 3, 12, 15ft (91.5, 366, 457.5cm). *P:* upon application.

ULSTER CARPET MILLS LTD
Axminster carpeting in 80% wool and 20% nylon. GLENDUN and GLENMOY both consist of eight traditional designs with repeats every 3ft (91.5cm). Patterns in the IN-STOCK COLLECTION are bolder and simpler, without background shading, like '2085' in Beige, Orange, Burnt red on Chocolate. *M:* w 27in, 12ft (68.5, 366cm). *P:* sq yd £16–£18.

YOUGHAL CARPETS LTD
Gorgeous CARRAIG collection of softly patterned, heather-coloured carpets, and co-ordinating plains. Made from 80% wool and 20% nylon, they are suitable for heavy domestic use. Six designs include 'Glengarry Check' incorporating colours from the selection of plain shades: Violet slate, Violet grey, Antelope fawn, Spring beige, Coffee beige,

Pink beige, Thistle rose, Quartz rose, Oriental green, Chinese jade, Pigeon grey, and Willow grey (*M:* w 12ft/366cm, *P:* sq yd £12). See page 69 for 'Glengarry Check' in colour.

SCULPTURED PILE CARPETING

ASSOCIATED WEAVERS LTD
'New Mood' collection of luxurious, but fairly inexpensive, sculptured and slightly shaggy carpets. They're made from 100% polyamide (nylon) fibre, treated with 'Scotchgard' to counteract static electricity and stay clean longer. Suitable for general domestic use.
The LOTUS range is available in Twilight mist (beige), Bisque (goldy-beige), Dry champagne (mid-brown), Coral rose (rosy beige), Pewter, Chiffon green (light olive), Spring green (grass green), Crystal blue (blue-grey), Creole tan (red-brown), and Java brown (dark brown). Each colour incorporates several similar shades, creating a textural effect that can add years to the carpet's 'wear'. ORIENT, also subtly textured, is made from the same fibre. It comes in 14 shades from Sahara beige to Bracken (dark brown). Other colourways include Tobacco, Chestnut, Salmon (burnt orange), Cyclamen pink, Wild mink, California gold, Sage green (olive green), Mint green (grass green), Bayleaf green (pale green), Polar blue (blue-grey), Everest grey, and Seal skin (champagne).
M: both ranges w 12ft (366cm). *P:* upon application.

BLACKWOOD MORTON & SONS LTD
Carpets in 52% acrylic, 28% modacrylic and 20% nylon. There are two sculptured motifs: 'Aviemore', a flower-and-swirl pattern; and 'Gold Thistle', a more geometric square enclosing a motif. Both are available in Spring white (ivory), Buckskin (beige), Caramel, Mink (mid-brown), Peat brown, Tan (burnt orange), Moss green, Chestnut (rust red), and Red currant (bright red). 'Gold Thistle' also comes in Saffron, Jade (soft green), Satinwood gold (orange-gold), Dusky rose, and Forest green (dark green). *M:* w 3, 9, 12, 15ft (91.5, 274.5, 366, 457.5cm). *P:* upon application.

MARY FOX LINTON LTD
Cut- and loop-pile 100% wool carpeting, virtually invisibly seamed–the height of sculp-

Mary Fox Linton's 'Trellis'

tured success. It isn't cheap, but you can have any colour or two colours you wish, edged with solid pile or a woven design. Motifs include 'Trellis', 'Wood Mews', and 'Versailles'. *M:* w 27in (68.5cm). *P:* yd £20 (small surcharge on orders under 40m (43¾yd)).

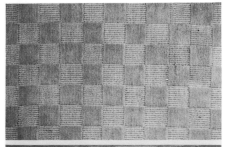

Mary Fox Linton's 'Wood Mews' (top), 'Versailles' (bottom)

TAMESA FABRICS LTD
Calm, cool designs in a mixture of Brussels and Wilton twist weaves. Made from 80% wool and 20% nylon, all carpets, including 'Perugia' in Off-white, reflect this company's bias towards neutrals, and its skill in achieving understated good looks. *M:* w 27in (68.5cm). *P:* m £19. See also 'Wall Coverings'.

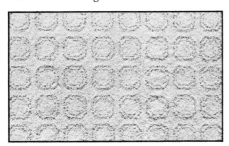

Tamesa's 'Perugia'

WILTON ROYAL CARPET FACTORY LTD
Real beauties from a traditional company that's climbed on the Berber bandwagon. Made from 50% wool and 50% acrylic, they come, unusually, in eight shades from dark Blackthorn (chocolate), through Mahogany, Walnut (mid-brown), Teak (grey-brown), Oak (green-beige), Ash (blue-beige), and Beech (beige), to attractive, and popular, light Sycamore (champagne). *M:* w 91, 183, 274.5, 366, 453cm (3, 6, 9, 13ft). *P:* sq m £21.

SHAG CARPETING

ASSOCIATED WEAVERS LTD
SARI NEW MOOD deep-pile carpeting, slightly mottled to give a rich appearance (and show dirt less). Made from high lustre nylon, it's treated with 'Scotchgard' and backed by a seven-year guarantee. Suitable for heavy domestic use, it comes in nine handsome colours: Twilight mist, Coral rose, Creole tan, Dry champagne, Java brown, Spring green, Chiffon green, Crystal blue, and Pewter. *M:* w 12ft (366cm). *P:* upon application.

BLACKWOOD MORTON & SONS LTD
TUNDRA shag carpeting inspired by Scandinavian Ryor rugs (originally used as wraps and cushion covers rather than floor coverings). Made from a three-ply yarn of 80% wool and 20% nylon, it looks as though it's been hand-knotted. Available in a huge range of neutrals plus Bright red, Pastel blue, and White; also two flecked colourways—Tan and Cream, and Beige and White—for a really rugged look. You can order the exact length you need. *M:* w 3, 9, 12, 15ft (91.5, 274.5, 366, 457.5cm). *P:* upon application.

FORBO TAPIJT BV
100% anti-static polyamide shag ANTILLA in a very nice range of colours: Silvery grey, Light beige, Pink, Blue, Camel, Mauve, Olive, Dark beige, Dark brown, and Light green. *P:* sq yd £17.50.
Also an unusually long looped shag-type carpet, BELLEVUE, made from 100% Trevira (anti-static polyester). It comes in similar shades: Natural, Green, Grey-green, Camel, Pink, Pearl grey, Chestnut, Blue, Grey-beige, and Havana. *P:* sq yd £16.
M: both ranges w 13ft 1½in (400cm).

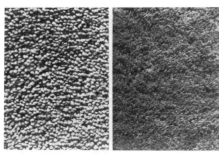

Forbo's BELLEVUE (left), ANTILLA (right)

GREENWOOD & COOPE LTD
Three shag carpetings in man-made fibres. The very usable CARESS low-shag range is made from Dacron and comes in Platinum cream (off-white), Mink (beige), Honey (light gold), Koala, Antelope, Coffee cream, Sable brown, Flame (red-orange), Old rose, Forget-me-not, Celadon (pale green), and Silver birch. *P:* sq yd £8.50.

ZENITH, a luxury domestic carpet in Timbrelle is guaranteed for seven years. It's available in Parchment, Buttermilk (palest yellow), Oyster (beige), Sandalwood, Chocolate, Fern (pale green) and Corinth (rose pink). *P:* sq yd £16. Finally, the luxurious SHANTUNG range is made from Sylkharesse, which has a pleasing patina and a very soft finish, unlike most man-made fibres. It comes in seven soft hues: Rice, Sampan beige, Papyrus (pinky beige), Tea (rose beige), Sultana (rusty beige), Bengal rose, and Jade green (palest green). *P:* sq yd £16.
M: all ranges w 3, 9, 12ft (91.5, 274.5, 366cm).

Greenwood & Coope's SHANTUNG

HATEMA (UK) LTD
Carpeting made from 100% cotton—an exciting development, introduced here by a subsidiary of one of the Netherlands' largest textile manufacturers. There are three competitively priced ranges, all inherently moth-

Hatema's cotton carpeting

proof, treated with 'Scotchgard', and available in a stunning range of colours for general domestic use. TOPEKA is a thick twist-loop carpeting, PLANTAGE has finer loops, and DAKOTA is a soft velour with a foam back (*P:* sq m £12).
Six different textural structures are also available in Ecru (off-white) (*P:* sq m £11–£18).
MONAST ultra-chunky shag carpeting, in pure virgin wool with jute backing, is suitable for high traffic areas. Not cheap, but it's a really unusual and luxurious floor covering. It comes in Off-white, Grey-beige, Beige, Light sand, Sage green, Dusty rose, and Steel grey. *P:* sq m £35. Hats off to these innovators.
M: all ranges w 400cm (13ft 1½in).

TINTAWN LTD
SOUBRETTE, lovely, luxury shag carpeting from a firm traditionally associated with Berbers. Available in a wide range of shades, with names as exotic as the colours themselves. From the palest: Snow (creamy-white), Gold, Honey, Cashmere (mushroom), Cedar (tan), Doeskin (mid-brown), Coral bisque, Tokay (rose red), Garnet, Spiece (dark brown), Blue hussar (deep ultramarine), Pompadour (bright blue), Bluemoon (light blue), Greensleeve (dark green), Linden (forest green), Moselle (light olive), and Stardust (grège). *M:* w 3, 9, 12ft (91.5, 274.5, 366cm). *P:* sq yd £18.

TILES (CARPETING)

DLW (BRITAIN) LTD
Two needlepunch ranges, with the familiar 'curly' surface texture, both for heavy contract use. POLO, the more expensive, is made from 100% polypropylene and comes in Blue, Gold, Orange-red, Olive, Grass green and three Browns. STRONG has a larger selection of colours including Grey-brown. *M:* rolls w 200cm (6ft 6¾in), tiles 40×40, 50×50cm (15¾× 15¾, 19⅝×19⅝in). *P:* upon application.

DUNLOP SEMTEX LTD
FLOORMAKER carpet tiles in two qualities: Springtex and Superpile. Both are made from 100% polypropylene, with a specially designed backing that keeps the tile flat. Springtex comes in 11 lovely colours: Cairngorm brown, Beaver brown, Dusky brown, Brendon brown, Morland tweed, and Caramel. Other shades are Exmoor (gold), Green (olive), Denim blue, Beacon blue (royal blue), and Cleveland rust. Superpile is available in nine similar colours. *M:* 12×12in (30.5×30.5cm). *P:* pack of nine £7.

GASKELL BROADLOOM CARPETS LTD
Carpet tiles in three qualities. Inexpensive HIGH LEVEL loose-lay tiles are made from 100% polypropylene, and are without backing, or foam-backed. Suitable for general domestic use. Surface texture is soft, and slightly curly. They come in 12 colours: Oatmeal, Caramel, Burnt almond, Bitter chocolate, Golden brown, Russet, New Cypress green, Saffron, Pacific blue, Pomegranate (orange), Grenadine red, and Blueberry. Available in packs of nine, or as individual tiles. Also by the metre. *M:* 33.3×33.3, 50× 50cm (13⅛×13⅛, 19⅝×19⅝in). *P:* sq m £6.
HUSKITILE, made from 50% nylon, 40% polypropylene and 10% viscose, is coarser, tougher—and more expensive. For heavy contract use, the range comes in 12 autumnal tones. *M:* 50×50cm (19⅝×19⅝in). *P:* sq m £7.
HOPSCOTCH 'easy-lay' carpet tiles are in 100% Fibrite. They come in 12 similar colours. Tiles in packs of nine cover one square yard. *M:* 30.5×30.5cm (12×12in). *P:* sq m £4.

GERLAND LTD
Inexpensive HARMONIE needlepunch carpeting, from a manufacturer better known for vinyl floorings. Made of 50% polypropylene and 50% nylon, with 100% polypropylene backing, and treated to resist dirt and stains, it's suitable for contract use. Available in Chamois, Sand, Copper (gold), Brick, Green, Blue (slate), Grey, and Chestnut. *M:* 200× 200cm (6ft 6¾in × 6ft 6¾in). *P:* sq m £4.50.
NORSEMAN 75 and 75 PLUS are low-cost fibre-bonded carpeting and carpet tiles in 100% polypropylene, suitable for high-traffic areas. They come in Light steel, Charcoal, Sisal, Beech brown, Coffee brown, Bronze yellow, Spanish orange, Cedar green, Florentine blue, Scarlet, Orient red, and—unusually—Royal purple. *M:* w 137, 274.5cm (4½, 9ft), tiles 45× 45cm (17¾×17¾in). *P:* upon application.

HEUGA UK LTD
Probably the largest selection of carpet tiles on the market. The top range, 415 ELITE, is made from 100% wool. It comes in three warm and neutral shades: Ermine (beige), Arctic fox (darker beige), and Mink (tan). 430 HORIZON, a twist-pile carpet tile in 70% acrylic and 30%

nylon, is in ten autumny colours, from Moonglow (sea green), to Aurora (brick red). The LUX S and HEARTH ranges are more like traditional 'hairy' carpet tiles. Both are in a tough combination of animal hair, nylon and viscose; LUX S is slightly softer, HEARTH is a little cheaper. LUX S is available in Heuga's favoured autumn shades, plus Lime green and Sea green. HEARTH colours are darker versions of the same tones.
The following tiles are much stronger, suitable for heavy contract use, and slightly more expensive. The luxurious 550 SUPERLOOM range is made from 80% wool and 20% nylon. It comes in Navy blue, Bright blue, three Olive greens, two Russets, Dark brown, Gold, and Beige. 425 HERITAGE, another twist-pile carpet tile, has a more textured effect. In 70% acrylic and 30% nylon, it's available in ten muted earth'y tones. 550 HARVEST, a loop-pile carpet tile, made from an extremely resilient acrylic/nylon yarn, has a rougher stippled texture. Colours are based on neutrals with tasteful Browns, Greys, and Tans predominating. The 580 OLYMPIC range has the same knobbly texture, but with a slight sheen, and is less expensive. It's made of 100% Antron 111, which has permanent static control, is highly fire resistant and conceals moderate quantities of dirt. It comes in two Greens, Rust, Mercury blue, Grey, two Golds, and three Browns. 575 GRANDE is another slightly textured range. Soft, tufted, cut-pile tiles in 100% nylon look like velvet, and also have a slight sheen. Earth tones predominate. 535 ACADEMY is a plain twist-pile at a fraction of the price of the 580 OLYMPIC. It's made in 100% Timbrelle and available in good colours which include three Greens (one with blue tones), and a whole range of Browns. 610 STRATA has virtually no pile, but is a hardwearing needlefelt range in Grey, Red, three Greens, and three Browns.
The two toughest ranges are FLOR S in 55% nylon, 27.5% animal hair and 17.5% viscose, and FELT S, which is more hairy and made from 95% animal hair. FLOR S has more shades than any other range, and the colours are brighter, from Maple (orange-red), to Cedar (a blue-black). The FELT S spectrum is much darker, with Navy, Forest green, Sea green, and seven other dark neutrals.
M: all ranges 50×50cm (19⅝×19⅝in). *P:* upon application.

TUFTED CARPET TILES LTD
One of the widest selections of carpet tiles in the country, all backed with woven polypropylene. There are three classically 'hairy' ranges, suitable for general domestic or contract use. MOSS, the least expensive, is made from 45% animal hair, 35% nylon, 10% viscose and 10% other fibres, backed and ready to lay. Fairly soft, though characteristically 'hairy', it comes in nine colours: Pearl (light tan), Moonstone (mid-tan), Tiger's eye (milk-chocolate brown), Amethyst (olive green), Emerald, Opal (blue-green), Topaz (light copper), Ruby, and

Graphite (charcoal flecked with white). *P:* sq yd £6.75.

Next is TRIDENT, in 40% animal hair, 40% nylon, 10% viscose, and 10% other fibre, specifically for contract use. It's available in Blue slate (black mixed with sea blue), Garnet (wine red), Sunset (copper), Quartz (gold), Jade (olivey green), and four browns—Coral (light tan), Marble, Mosaic, and Earth (dark brown). *P:* sq yd £7.50.

TRON, an ultra-tough carpet tile in the same fibres, is ³⁄₈in (1cm) thick. It comes in six practical earth tones: Chartreuse (olive green), Rum (dark brown), Champagne (mid-brown), Whiskey (golden brown), Cognac (copper brown), and Malt (similar to Rum but flecked with white hair). *P:* sq yd £8.50.

The following ranges have a smoother look: TUCA LOOP, made from 69% Acrilan, 30% Modacrylic and 1% static control thread, is a very tightly woven looped tile, with latex backing. Suitable for high-traffic areas. Very 'natural', without the usual synthetic fibre sheen, it's good value for money. Available in Sand stone (tan), Sun glow (russet red), Brown ochre (terracotta), Silk green (grass green), Leaf green (olive green), Dove grey (grège), and Burnt sienna (dark brown). *P:* sq yd £8.50.

TUF, in 80% acrylic and 20% nylon, is very soft and slightly 'curly' in texture. Suitable for heavy domestic use, it comes in Mocca (mid-brown), Sylvan green (mid-olive), Mexican gold (bright gold), Flame (burnt orange), and Autumn beige (warm yellowy-beige); also two duotones: Mid-brown (yellow and brown fibres), and Thrush brown (white and brown). *P:* sq yd £10.50.

TUF's less-textured cousin, SUPER TUF, is made from the same fibres but feels much tougher. For heavy contract purposes, it's available in Redwood (reddish-brown), Burnt oak (dark brown), Sun king (light copper), Agate (russet red), Strand olive (gold), Lombardy green (dark olive green), and Fawn (light tan). *P:* sq yd £11.

Tuca's DECOR range in 69% Acrilan, 30% Modacrylic and 1% static control thread, ³⁄₈in (1cm) thick, is suitable for contract use and represents real luxury in man-made fibre tiles. Each tile combines two tasteful shades: Rosewood (dark brown) and Taffy (mid-brown), Rosewood and Sun copper (burnt red), Cypress (olive) and Peru natural (light brown), Charcoal and Peru natural. This tile, when laid, looks like wool. *P:* sq yd £13.

The high-quality SPECTRUM range, in 80% wool and 20% nylon, combines two colours in each tile: Sage (olive) and Mint, Lignum (dark brown) and Mushroom, Chocolate (mid-brown) and Rust, Sage and Mushroom. *P:* sq yd £14.25.

Tuca's EXECUTIVE range of tough, superb-quality carpet tiles in the 'Berber' (undyed wool) colour range is also made from 80% wool and 20% nylon. Very densely woven, for heavy contract use, it comes in nice neutrals. *P:* sq yd £15.50.
M: 19⁵⁄₈×19⁵⁄₈in (50×50cm).

WILTON MANUFACTURERS	YELLOW	GOLD	OLIVE	PALE GREEN	BRIGHT GREEN	DARK GREEN	TURQUOISE	DARK BLUE	BRIGHT BLUE	PALE BLUE	PURPLE	PINK	RED	RUST	PALE ORANGE	IVORY WHITE	BEIGE	TAN	BROWN	DARK BROWN	BLACK	GREY
ABINGDON CARPETS LTD 'Royal Kingdom'; 80%wool/20% polyamide. *P:* sq yd £10		●	●		●					●		●		●			●		●	●		
W & R R ADAM LTD 'Forest Hills'; 10% Courtelle/20% nylon. *P:* sq m £12		●	●	●								●							●			
'De Luxe Wilton'; 100% wool. *P:* sq m £24																●	●	●	●	●		●
ASSOCIATED WEAVERS LTD 'Florence'; 50% polyamide/50% polyester. *P:* upon application		●	●	●		●			●	●	●					●	●	●	●	●		
BRINTONS CARPETS 'Bell Twist'; 80% wool/20% nylon. *P:* sq m £14	●	●	●	●	●					●	●						●					
DLW (BRITAIN) LTD 'RN 1205'; 70% polyamide/30% polyacrylic. *P:* upon application			●	●									●				●	●	●			
FORBO TAPIJT BV 'President'; 100% worsted wool, foamback. *P:* sq m £25		●	3	3						●	●								●			
'Ambiance'; 100% polyamide, foamback. *P:* sq m £15		●	3		●						●					●	2	●	●	●		
'Mimosa'; 100% polyamide, foamback. *P:* sq m £13	●					●		●	●	●		●				●	2	●	●	●	●	●
'Antilla'; 100% Sylkharesse. *P:* sq m £21			●	●					●	●	●						●	●	●			
'Bellevue'; 100% Trevira. *P:* sq m £19			●						●		●					●	2	●	●			
GEORGIAN CARPETS LTD 'Gina', 'Farmer George', 'Georgian Manor'; 100% wool. *P:* sq yd £15, £18, £25	●	●	●	●			●		●		●	●	●	●		●	●	●				
GILT EDGE CARPETS LTD 'Wessex', 'Wessex Junior'; 80% wool/20% nylon. *P:* sq yd £21, £16	●	●	●	●			●	●						●			●					
'Wessex Twist'; 80% wool/20% nylon. *P:* sq yd £16		●	●	●			●										●					
'Loktwist'; 80% Acrilan/20% nylon. *P:* sq yd £13.50		●			●						●	●	●				●					
OLLERTON HALL DECORATING SERVICE 'Super Solid', 100% polypropylene. *P:* sq yd £5	●	●			●					●		●				●	●					
'Dense Super Twist'; 100% polypropylene. *P:* sq yd £7		●	●	●						●						●	●					
ROOKSMOOR MILLS 'Magic Carpet'; 100% wool. *P:* sq yd £6	●	●	●			●		●			●	●				●	●		●			
A F STODDARD & CO LTD 'Supersax Twist'; 80% wool/20% nylon. *P:* sq yd £14.50	●	●	●		●					●				●			●					
'Telsex'; 50% wool/50% nylon. *P:* sq yd £8.50		●	●		●		●										●					
'Iona'; 80% wool/20% nylon. *P:* sq yd £12	●	●	●				●		●	●		●	●				●					
TEMPLETON CARPETS 'Admiration Twist'; 80% wool/20% nylon. *P:* sq yd £19		●	●							●			●	●		●	●		●			●
'Cosmopolitan'; 80% wool/20% nylon. *P:* sq yd £16.25			●					●	●			●					●		●			
THOMSON SHEPHERD (CARPETS) LTD 'Hostess', 'Super-hostess'; 80% wool/20% nylon. *P:* sq yd £13.50, £16	●	●	●	●	●	●			●	●	●					●	●					
TINTAWN LTD 'Shearing'; 100% wool. *P:* sq yd £20																●	●	●	●			
WILTON ROYAL CARPET FACTORY LTD 'Charte'; 80% wool/20% nylon. *P:* sq yd £14	●	●	●			●		●	●			●	●			●	●		●			●

INTRODUCTION

Think tiles. They can replace carpets, with or without underfloor heating; line walls and even ceilings; cover tables and working surfaces; and be used for hearths, decorative cornices, patios.

Introduced to Europe from Moorish Spain and North Africa, glazed ceramic tiles were traditionally relegated to the floors and walls of chilly bathrooms and institutional halls. Modern tiles are still made from the same material – the most practical, long-lasting and easily cleaned available – but their appearance has changed drastically.

True, there are still the traditional designs: hand-painted Blue and White tiles for kitchens, transfer-printed Victorian flowers for fireplaces; and Spanish and French Provençal shaped floor tiles in warm, classic terracotta. But there are also deep fashion colours, mosaics in multi-faceted patterns, tiles that combine to make delightful pictures of orange trees in tubs, abstracts, geometrics in sharp Black and White, and soft, smudgy tones in rectangular blocks.

The basic practical consideration is whether a surface requires heavy- or light-duty tiles. Always check the suitability of a range with the manufacturer or supplier, to save endless trouble later. Similarly, outdoor tiles are particularly hardwearing, and normally frostproof; those for swimming pools and fountains must stand up to water – and every kind of weather. Heavy-duty and outdoor tiles, some with non-slip surfaces, generally come in quiet colours and patterns. Usually laid in large areas, they're designed to be unobtrusive and conceal dirt.

A vital word: tiles must be accurately and carefully laid – a job the supplier will usually do, although it may double the cost. Hand-made versions backed, often unevenly, with clay can be particularly difficult to handle. Most mass-produced tiles are quick and easy to lay; a good handyman can do a perfectly adequate job.

Tiling is permanent. So, if a bathroom is tiled to match bedroom wallpaper, or a vanity top complements a fabric, buy extra paper or fabric to replace or repair the originals.

*Floor tiles are generally 15–20mm ($5/8$–$3/4$in) thick; wall tiles 6–11m ($1/4$–$3/8$in).

SALLY ANDERSON (CERAMICS) LTD

Two basic wall tile ranges. Ten striped and curved GEOMETRIC patterns, and ten related ONE-STEP-ON designs based on feathers and foliage, in 26 colours. Matching plain slip-resistant floor tiles are available. Sally Anderson will also design and make special orders. *M:* $4^1/4 \times 4^1/4$, 6×6in (10.5x10.5, 15.2×15.2cm), or to order. *P:* GEOMETRIC sq yd £9–£10.50; ONE-STEP-ON sq yd £11–£12.50; floor tiles sq yd £10.50–£12.50.

PRICES AND INFORMATION WERE CORRECT AT THE TIME OF GOING TO PRESS

Sally Anderson's 'Willow Tree' from ONE-STEP-ON

LAURA ASHLEY LTD

Sweet but sensible range of wall or floor tiles, made in Italy to co-ordinate perfectly with Laura Ashley's fabrics, wallpapers and soft furnishings. Five floral prints, one neat geometric, and 13 plain colours: White, Cream, Sand, Mustard (bright yellow), Apple, Moss, Sapphire (light blue), China blue (bright blue), Smoke (blue-grey), Rose, Burgundy, Terracotta, and Saddle (light brown). Suitable for high-traffic areas, tiles can be bought singly or by the square metre. *M:* 20×20cm ($7^7/8 \times 7^7/8$in). *P:* sq m £15. See also 'Fabrics', 'Soft Furnishings', 'Wall Coverings'. See page 70 for 'C150', 'T232' in colour.

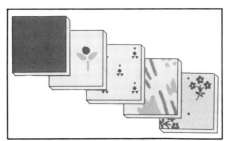

Left to right: Laura Ashley's plain, 'P767', 'S49', 'L631', 'R150' tiles

---

BARBEE CERAMICS LTD

Marvellous porcelain mosaic wall and floor tiles by Sinter of Italy, imported and distributed by Barbee. Square STANDARD (*M:* 1.9×1.9cm/$3/4 \times 3/4$in) and round SATELLITE (*M:* diam 1.8cm/$3/4$in) come in 18 gorgeous colours with gloss, eggshell and matt finishes. Round SOLARIS (*M:* diam 4cm/$1^5/8$in) and square RC4 (*M:* 4×4cm/$1^5/8 \times 1^5/8$in) are available in 12 shades with matt or semi-matt finishes.

Other ranges include glazed EMBRI-FAVORIT, with a distinctive irregular surface; it comes in a good range of earth tones plus two Blues (*M:* 10×20cm/4×$7^7/8$in). SAN SALVO, a classic Provençal shape with a nice mottled surface is

in Mid-brown, White, Light brown, Cream, and Brick red (*M:* 20×15cm/$7^7/8 \times 5^7/8$in). The EPOCA range includes ornate 'Kay 6' in a combination of Cream, Brown, and Golden yellow (*M:* 25×25cm/10×10in). *P:* upon application.

Barbee's 'Kay 6' from EPOCA

A BELL & CO LTD

Genuine Dutch hand-painted tiles for walls, or fireplace surrounds. Six traditional Blue and White designs: 'Windmill', 'Children at play', 'Small landscapes', 'Ships', 'Shepherds', and 'Spider corner' with a small flower in each corner (*M:* 13×13cm/$5^1/8 \times 5^1/8$in, *P:* tile £2.50–£2.90).

Less expensive hand-painted reproductions are available — a plain tile and a selection of Dutch landscapes in Blue or Maroon on an Off-white ground with 'spider' corners (*M:* 10×10, 15×15cm/4×4, $5^7/8 \times 5^7/8$in, *P:* landscape tile £1.60, £1.80).

See page 70 for 'Windmill' in colour.

BOYDEN & CO LTD

Exclusive French, Italian, and British ranges. French mosaics by BRIARE, for walls and floors, are mounted on paper or wire mesh. They come in marvellous colours, and a variety of shapes: 'Pastilles', 'Variation', and 'Galets' are round; 'Gemmes' is hexagonal; 'Triton' is four-sided, and 'Diffusion 24' is a small square. 'Sialex', a square, is matt finished, with or without a relief design (a small square within a diamond). Seven co-ordinating borders include Greek key and chequerboard effects. *M:* sheets 30×30cm ($11^7/8 \times 11^7/8$in). *P:* 'Gemmes', 'Diffusion 24' sq m £20, others upon application.

Unusual 'Tapestry' wall tiles, and co-ordinating 'Caractère' and 'Byzance', look like small petit point pictures. Four designs are available: baskets of Blue or Orange flowers, a bunch of rosy apples, a circle of Pink posies, and baskets of Blue and Pink flowers. *M:* 7.5×7.5cm (3×3in). *P:* tile £1.08.

Boyden's 'Diffusion 24' (small squares), 'Sialex' from BRIARE

CACTUS AND PALME consists of four plant designs in Green, and one plain Matt white tile. 'E30' is a cactus flowering in a pot; 'E31' shows cactus clumps, 'E33' is a flower pot, and 'E35', a palm. M: 30×20cm (11⁷/₈×7⁷/₈in). P: sq m plain £36, patterned tile £5.

The beautiful and comprehensive Italian range of MARAZZI wall and floor tiles includes good unpatterned tiles: 'Metropoli' in 18 solid colours, except Black (M: 30×30cm/11⁷/₈×11⁷/₈in); 'Garden' rectangular tiles in Tan or Brown (M: 30×60cm/11⁷/₈×23⁵/₈in); octagonal 'Contee', for floors only, in Cream, Sand, and Rust (M: 30×30cm/11⁷/₈×11⁷/₈in). Squares are 'Bosco' in eight colours (M: 15×15cm/5⁷/₈×5⁷/₈in), and 'Elba' in 11 (M: 20×20cm/7⁷/₈×7⁷/₈in). Co-odinating floral and patterned tiles are available. P: sq m £10–£18.

More exotic floor tiles are 'Brasil' in seven warm tones with a slightly mottled effect (M: 30×40cm/11⁷/₈×15³/₄in); lightly glazed Florentine-shape 'Provencale' in Cream, Sand, and Brick (M: 20×30cm/7⁷/₈×11⁷/₈in); and oblong '2000' in 13 mottled colours (M: 10×20cm/4×7⁷/₈in). '3000', in White, Cream, Olive, Rust, and Coffee, has matching tiles, perfect for stair treads, with parallel lines along one edge (M:20×30cm/7⁷/₈×11⁷/₈in). P: sq m £14–£20.

Unusual CLASSICA wall tiles are 'Vendemmia 1 & 2' with bunches of Golden grapes, and Olive vine leaves; 'Intreccio', an undulating White on White pattern; 'Mignon 1 & 2', in White on Brown, with long-stemmed tiny flowers; and 'Capriccio 1 & 2', crisp Blue stripes on White. M: 20×30cm (7⁷/₈×11⁷/₈in). P: sq m £15, to order only.

ASTRALE floor and wall tiles are sharply geometrical with overlapping triangles, bold circles and thin stripes, in Brown on Gold or Light blue on Navy. 'Perseo 1 & 2', 'Cigno 1 & 2' and 'Michelangelo 2 & 3' are illustrated. Country-style 'Bahamas' wall tiles have hand-painted flowers including daisies and anemones on a crackled Cream ground. Smaller 'Emilia' also has hand-painted flowers, on the same ground, in more than nine designs. 'Girasole Verde' from CERAMIAL is a sunflower in a circle. M: all 20×20cm (7⁷/₈×7⁷/₈in). P: sq m £8–£12. See page 70 for 'Variation', 'Diffusion 24', 'Tapestry', 'R16 Pommes', 'Girasole Verde', 'Cactus', 'Cactus Pot', 'Palme', 'Palme Pot' in colour.

Above, left to right, from top: 'Perseo 1 & 2', 'Cigno 1 & 2', 'Michelangelo 2 & 3', all from Boyden's ASTRALE

Below: Boyden's 'Mignon 1 & 2' (left), 'Capriccio 1 & 2' (right) from CLASSICA

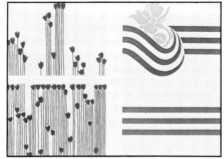

MAURICE BROWN LTD
Hand-printed tiles to complement five designs in their lovely REGENT PARK COLLECTION of fabrics and wallpapers. 'Sandmarks' has an all-over network; 'Daisy Sans' is a pert single flower; simple 'Mini Orchid' and 'Maxi Orchid' are stylized; and 'Bamboo Shoot' has a leaf-wrapped trellis. All in one or two colours, to order, on White: Navy, Rose, Apricot, Baby blue, Red, Brown, and Yellow. M: 6×6in (15.2×15.2cm). P: sq yd one colour £18.50, two colours £23.

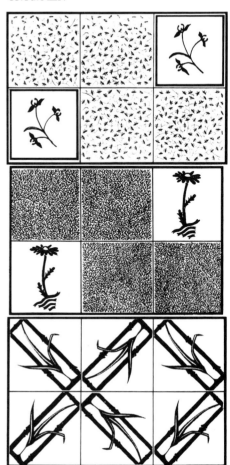

Maurice Brown's 'Mini Orchid' and 'Maxi Orchid' (top), 'Sandmarks' and 'Daisy Sans' (centre), 'Bamboo Shoot' (bottom)

CAPITAL CERAMICS
CAPRICORN DE STEENBOK floor tiles from the Netherlands. Made from hard-wearing, frost-proof stone, for indoors or out, they come in Old Brown, Beige-brown, Anthracite, Ivory white, Orient blue, Red-brown, Sahara beige; also speckled versions in Orient blue, Berber beige, Blue, Beige-brown, Red-brown, Bronze green and Ivory white. M: 8¹/₂×8¹/₂, 12¹/₈; 12¹/₈×12¹/₈in (21.6×21.6, 30.8; 30.8×30.8cm). P: tile from £1.80.
Matching wall tiles (M: 4¹/₈×4¹/₈in/10.4×10.4cm) and integrated strip and skirting tiles are available.

CASTELNAU MOSAICS & TILES
Quarry floor and wall tiles, including ends of ranges at special prices, from a shop that specializes in their supply and installation. P: sq m floor from £6.75, wall from £3.75.
Anna Wyner can be commissioned through

Castelnau. She usually works in Byzantine *smalti*, a Venetian mosaic material, which she combines with vitreous glass, marble, stained glass and ceramics. *P:* £2,500 for *c* 16 sq ft, including designing, supplying and pre-casting, but fees depend on the work involved.

Castelnau mosaic mural by Anna Wyner

CERAMIC CONSULTANTS LTD

RYE floor and wall tiles from a small factory that specializes in colour matching. 40 standard patterns are available in more than 50 glazes and 70 colours.

BORDER TILES, hand-printed in more than 90 brilliant colours for walls and 20 subtle shades for floors, are designed to frame plain or decorated tiles. Their patterns include florals, geometrics, and Victorian and Far Eastern motifs. 'Willow Pattern' is edged with bamboo, with a butterfly in each corner.

There's also a hand-painted 18th-century style FLOWER series, botanically incorrect but utterly charming. All have a double-line circle enclosing different flowers in Indigo, Cobalt, Blue, Green, Olive green, Denmark green, Damson, Lavender, Pink, Tan, Yellow, or Dark grey on White. Special colours to order. Ceramic Consultants will also match fabrics and supply murals to order.

M: 6×6in (15.2×15.2cm). *P:* sq yd from £16. See page 70 for 'Border Trail', 'RYE flower', 'Blazer', 'Willow Pattern', 'Solid Green glaze', 'Forget-me-Not', 'Borderline' in colour.

CERAMIQUE INTERNATIONALE

Subtly shaded wall tiles. MONSOON in Bright blue, Beige, Brown, Gold, and Rust. Co-ordinating grass and flower patterns are available. *M:* 15×15cm (5⁷/8×5⁷/8in). *P:* sq m plain £14.30, patterned £14.80.

GERMINAL rectangular tiles have matching tiles decorated with different grasses. Four pale colours are available: Ivory, Pink, Grey, and Sand. *M:* 20×7cm (7⁷/8×2³/4in). *P:* sq m plain £23.30, patterned £25.70.

CIEL (CHRISTOPHER LAWRENCE TEXTILES & LIGHTING LTD)

Small but interesting selection of tiles from a well-known interior design shop. All are available in more than 40 colours on an Off-white ground; many co-ordinate with Ciel fabrics. 'Rice' is spattered; 'Dotty' has small random blobs, in one colour; 'Nella' has fern stalks; and 'Zig Zag' has four alternating colours. *M:* 6×6in (15.2×15.2cm). *P:* sq yd from £17.

Ciel's 'Dotty' (left), 'Zig Zag' (right)

DOMUS LTD

Marvellously modern Italian tiles including four in the 'high-duty' flooring category for kitchens, bathrooms, etc. '3302' is a chequer-board in Tan or Dark green with Brown, plus Grey or Beige with White. (*P:* sq m £18). 'EG' has diagonal lines with floral motifs and comes in Mid-green, Saxe blue, or Dark brown on a White ground (*P:* sq m £15). '172' is Beige with a grid border in Terracotta, Royal blue, or Bright green (*P:* sq m £15). '2844'/'2845' and '2836' are subtly shaded plaids in Beige, Green, or Blue (*P:* sq m £16.50). *M:* all 20×20cm (7⁷/8×7⁷/8in).

Domus also have many lighter 'low-duty' tiles for walls or light-traffic areas. 'Harlequin' is White, with small pastel triangles in each corner, to give just a subtle hint of colour (*P:* sq m £35). 'DRD' tiles are the traditional Florentine shape with a central spray of flowers and Lime green leaves, on a Cream background. Tiles are edged in the same colour as the flowers: Rust, Lilac pink, and French blue; also Peach pink flowers with Lime green edging. Co-ordinating tiles in Cream, with colour edging only, are available. *P:* floral sq m £25, co-ordinating tile £1. *M:* both ranges 20×20cm (7⁷/8×7⁷/8in).

The striking SE range of Black and White geometric patterns includes Black or Blue horizontal lines etched on White with four, eight, 16 and 32 lines (*M:* 20×20cm/7⁷/8×7⁷/8in, *P:* sq m £30).

The B range has thicker Black lines on White; some are reversed (White on Black), while 1B is plain Black (*M:* 13×26cm/5¹/8×10¹/4in, *P:* sq m £28).

'1510' tiles, White with Black triangles in each corner, combine to create a classical design. '2865', a White octagonal pattern on Black, is a chequerboard effect. *P:* both sq m £28. '3302', another chequered motif, is in Tan and Brown (*P:* sq m £18). *M:* all 20×20cm (7⁷/8×7⁷/8in).

Natural terracotta clay tiles include squares and oblongs. 12-sided '333' is available to order. *M:* 10×20, 20×20–50×50cm (4×7⁷/8, 7⁷/8×7⁷/8–19⁵/8×19⁵/8in). *P:* sq m £28.50. Brightly coloured glazed versions are Orange 'V96' and Yellow 'V98' (*M:* 10×20, 20×20cm/ 4×7⁷/8, 7⁷/8×7⁷/8in, *P:* sq m £36.50).

'Valentino' tiles have single Blue, Pink, or Green flowers scattered on White. 'Mandarin' forms a beautiful orange tree mural complete with leaves and fruit — your own orangery. *M:* 20×20cm (7⁷/8×7⁷/8in). *P:* sq m White £18.90, patterned £25.50.

See page 70 for '2836', 'EG', and '3302' illustrated in colour.

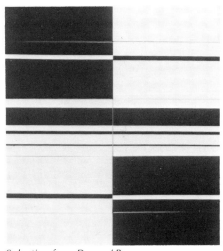

Selection from Domus' B range

ELIZABETH EATON LTD

Imported tiles reminiscent of Continental country life. Handsome floor tiles from France are hand-made and woodfired. Shapes include a rectangle and diamond, squares in two sizes, and six classic Provençal variations. *M:* small square 10×10cm (4×4in), diamond 15×27cm (5⁷/8×10⁵/8in). *P:* sq m £16–£23.

IRICERAM clay floor tiles from Spain are available plain or with a central burn mark, and have pleasingly random depths of colour. Ten shapes. *M:* hexagon diam 11, 20cm (4³/8, 7⁷/8in). *P:* sq m burnt £17, plain £15.

Very expensive French wall tiles, hand-made with slightly rounded edges, come in 28 rich, slightly mottled, glazed shades. *M:* 10×10cm (4×4in). *P:* sq m £40–£46.

Selection from Elizabeth Eaton's French floor tiles

ELON TILES (UK) LTD

Beautifully rustic, contemporary tiles from Mexico. They're all hand-made, so surfaces undulate and colourations vary. Three unglazed ranges are available for floors.

CARILLO glazed wall tiles come in 17 wonderfully vibrant shades: Pure white, Mexican white (off-white), Mustard, Yellow, Intense yellow, Parrot green (lime), Green (emerald), Blue, Dark blue, Plum, Mauve, Pink, Red, Terracotta, Orange, Chocolate, and Black. Special sizes and shapes to order. *P:* sq yd £22.

The range also includes 45 exquisitely charming decorative tiles. Simple, cheerful motifs like florals, geometrics, fruit, vegetables, and numerals are hand-painted in bright 'peasant' colours including Orange, Bright blue, Yellow or Green, on Off-white. Suitable for worktops, the tiles have matching edging and corner pieces. Special colours and sizes can be supplied, to order. *P:* sq yd £33. *M:* 4×4in (10×10cm). See also 'Flooring'. See page 70 for five decorative tiles in colour.

GALLERIA MONTE CARLO

SHERLE WAGNER collection of hand-crafted, hand-painted—and correspondingly expensive — wall and floor tiles. Designed to co-ordinate with the Galleria's outstanding bathroom suites, they come in six patterns, many with different tiles within each design to create various effects. 'Summer Garden' has leaves, flowers and butterflies in a combination of Green, Blue, Rust or Gold on White; 'Ming Blossoms' is sprays of tiny White flowers on Yellow, Mid-blue, Rose pink, or Brown; and six different 'Waterlilies' all have Pink flowers and Mid-green leaves on a Royal blue background. For an excessively opulent effect, PLATINUM and GOLD TILES, coated with the genuine metals, come plain or in two sculptured designs: a raised circular motif etched with fan-shaped lines or concentric circles. *M:* all 8×8in (20.5×20.5cm). *P:* upon application.

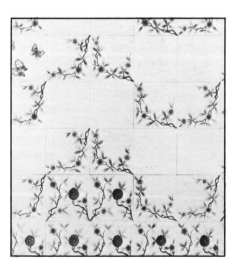

Galleria Monte Carlo's 'Summer Garden' (left below), 'Water Lily (top), 'Ming Blossoms' (above)

FREDA GOITEIN

Mosaics to order from an artist who specializes in portraits and industrial scenes. Freda Goitein will design, or translate, any motif into a mural or wall covering. *M:* murals from 20×30in (51×76cm); wall coverings to order. *P:* from sq ft £60; portraits from £300.

GRAFTON INTERIORS

Ornate and exotic FAB GLASS tiles designed to form large wall panels. Far Eastern florals in White, Red or Black are printed on a contrasting ground in one of the same colours, then decorated in Gold. *M:* 20×20cm (7⅞×7⅞in). *P:* tile from £6. See page 71 for illustration.

ELEANOR GREEVES

Hand-screenprinted ceramic wall tiles, suitable for worktops and fireplace surrounds, made by Eleanor Greeves, an ex-architect. Patterns, 20 in all, are beautifully based on

Selection of carpets (right):
Hugh Mackay's 'Design 771' from COUNTERPOINT (1)
'Curved Lines' (2) and 'Mosaic' (3,6) by LINDA BARRON for Afia
Afia's 'Tweed' (4)
'Mosaic' and 'Tweed' conbined (5)
Afia's Berber (7)
Mercia Weavers' 'Catspaw' (8)
'Fraises' by MANUEL CANOVAS for Afia (9)
Bosanquet Ives' 'Keltic Fret' (10), 'Denizen' (11), sample border (12), 'Floral Diamond Lattice (13), 'Warton' (14), 'Spot' (15), 'Sloane' (17), 'Chad' (19), 'Bamboo' (20)
Selection from Afia's EVERGREEN (16, 18), Afia's 'Curved Lines' (21)
Mercia Weavers' 'Honeycomb' (22)
Bosanquet Ives' sample border (23)
Selection from Afia's EVERGREEN (24, 25)
'Edinburgh' (26)
Hugh Mackay's 'Design 773' (27), 'Design 786' (28) from COUNTERPOINT
Navan's 'Dot-n-Dash' from ARDEE (29)
Youghal's 'Glengarry Check' from CARRAIG (30)

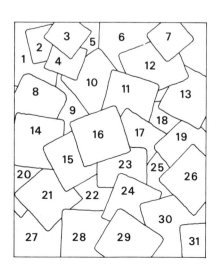

Selection of tiles (left):
Habitat's 'Mikado' (1)
Boyden's 'Diffusion 24' (2)
Elon's 'Indian' (3), 'Daisy May' (4), 'Cross' (5)
Langley's 'Intense Green' (6)
World's End's 'Border One' (7)
Domus' '2836' (8)
Ashley's 'C150' (9)
Elon's 'Damask' (10), 'Seville' (11)
Boyden's 'R16 Pommes' from BRIARE (12)
World's End's 'Open Field' (13)
Sheppard's 'Cat and Geranium' (14)
Boyden's 'Tapestry' tiles (15, 16, 17)
Ceramic Consultants' 'Border Trail' (18)
Boyden's 'Girasole Verde' (19)
Ceramic Consultants' 'RYE flower (20)
World's End's 'Dot' (21), 'Open Field Border'
and 'Linear Flower Border' (22)
Sheppard's 'Landscape' (23)
World's End's 'Palm' (24)
Sartor's 'Mayfly' (25)
Ceramic Consultants' 'Blazer' (26)
Ashley's 'T232' (27)
Boyden's 'Cactus' (28)
Bell's 'Windmill' (29)
Ceramic Consultants' 'Willow Pattern' (30)
Domus' 'EG' (31)
Sartor's 'Iris' (32)
Habitat's 'Yachting' (33)
Boyden's 'Cactus Pot' (34)
Ceramic Consultants' solid green glaze (35)
Polliack's 'Bouquet' (36)
World's End's 'Diagonal Weave' (37)
John Lewis' 'Trigon' (38)
Ceramic Consultants' 'Borderline' (39)
Boyden's 'Palme' (40)
World's End's 'Victoriana' (41), 'Daffodils' (42)
Ceramic Consultants' 'Forget-me-Not' and
'Borderline' (43)
Mary Fox Linton's 'Cognac' (44)
Domus' '3302' (45)
Polliack's 'Fiore Verde' (46)
World's End's 'Greek Key' (47)
Boyden's 'Variation' (48), 'Palme Pot' (49)

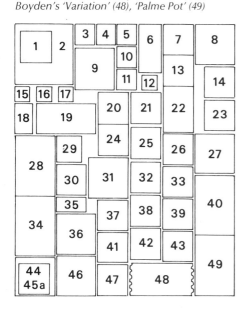

flora. They include 'Cranesbill', 'Clematis', 'Marigold', and 'Daisy'. Colours are Mid-blue, Lead blue, Buff, Grecian brown, Turquoise, Sage, Olive, Lemon, Rust, and Amber, on White. Some designs incorporate two colours. A ceramic colour card is available, and samples can be supplied for the cost of a single tile, plus postage. M: 4¼×4¼, 6×6in (10.5×10.5, 15.2×15.2cm). P: sq yd smaller tiles one colour £33, two colour £40; sq yd larger tiles one colour £24, two colour £31.

Left to right, from top: Eleanor Greeves' 'Cranesbill', 'Clematis', 'Marigold', 'Daisy'

Grafton's FAB Glass

HABITAT DESIGNS LTD
Patterned and plain wall tiles from Britain's well-known purveyors of good taste. Patterns, all on White, are 'Dandelion' and 'Nettle' in Green and Yellow; 'Redcurrant' in Red; 'Mikado' with Blue arrows forming squares; and 'Yachting', designed to co-ordinate with shower curtains and towels, in Grey and Light blue with a thick Blue border. Plain tiles come in Pure white, Bright red, Cobalt blue, and Plain cream. M: 15×15cm (5⅞×5⅞in). P: pack (⅔ sq yd) plain £5.50; 'Redcurrant', 'Mikado' £11.25; 'Nettles', Dandelion', 'Yachting' £14. See page 70 for 'Mikado' and 'Yachting' in colour.

H & R JOHNSON TILES LTD
Comprehensive selection of ceramic tiles, at amazingly low prices, from Britain's largest manufacturer. Plain 'MG' wall tiles, in 20 colours can be used alone or to complement other designs.
'Fireflash' unglazed rectangular floor tiles, with matching skirting, come in Fireflash red, Harvest flash, Coffee flash, Sierra flash, and Pepper. PASTORAL wall tiles in Pearl or Fawn with a sketchy Brown edging also come with a central daisy duo in White, Pampas (pale) green, Gold, Moss (olive), Pompadour (pink), or Sepia.
LAKELAND wall tiles have floral edgings on a slightly mottled Off-white ground. Two designs are available: 'Coniston', with a leaf at each corner and in its centre panel, in Gold, Rust, or Brown; and 'Derwent' edged with a Green or Blue garland. Both can be combined with plain 'Windermere' or with 'MG' tiles in Lotus blue (light blue), Light Stone, French beige (caramel), Golden tan (rust), Sepia (dark brown), Pampas, Avocado, or Bitter Green (light avocado).

Johnson's 'Coniston' from LAKELAND

The CRISTAL 200 range for interior walls and light-duty flooring includes 'Crackle Parchment' with Brown crazing on a Cream ground; and slightly textured 'Nimbus Blue' (light aqua), 'Nimbus Harvest' (gold), 'Nimbus Brown' (caramel) and 'Nimbus Champagne' (gold on off-white). 'Scroll' and 'Bryony' are florals on 'Crackle Parchment'. Classical 'Obidas', 'Belem' and 'Miranda' are predominantly earthy tones of Cream, Gold, or Pale olive. 'Clemente', in plain speckled Brown, also comes with three co-ordinating patterned designs in Fawn or Green.
WORKTOP TRIMS, designed for 21in (53cm) deep kitchen units, are ideal for wood-edged tile worktops, and bathroom or kitchen surfaces. Supplied as straight trim, internal mitres or corner pieces, they come in 'Nimbus Champagne', 'Nimbus Magnolia' (textured off-white), 'Burnt Gold' (spattered gold), and 'Bramble Burnt Gold' with a leaf design on a spattered Gold ground.

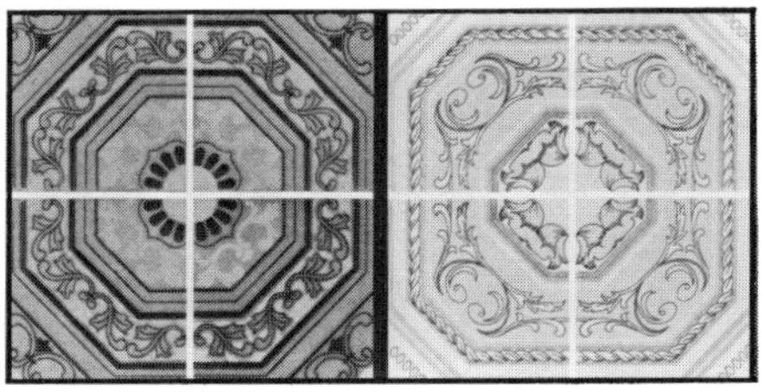

Johnson's 'Obidas' (left), 'Belem' (right) from CRISTAL 200

The NEW MOOD series features three geometric tiles: striped 'Parallel' and 'Linear'; and 'Swirl', a giant curlicue in Pampas or Brown on White.
M: all 6×6in (15.2×15.2cm) except 'MG' $4\frac{1}{4}$×$4\frac{1}{4}$in (10.8×10.8cm), 'Fireflash' 8×4in (20.5×10cm). *P:* sq yd £9–£11.

Johnson's 'Parallel' (left), 'Swirl' (right) from NEW MOOD

LANGLEY LONDON LTD

Vast selection of tiles, including some excellent French and German imports. Ten ranges made in France by Villeroy & Boch are stocked; five feature decorated wall tiles, with complementary plain tiles also suitable for floors. The DIAMANT range, in vitrified glazed mosaic, consists of octagons and square inserts that combine to form a classic 'octagon and dot' pattern. Octagons are Matt white, or decorated with one of three designs to complement the different coloured squares: three fruits (grapes, loganberries, pineapples) for Russet; three wild flowers for Green; three kitchen items (preserves, grinder, jars) for Blue. Plain octagons and squares come on sheets of perforated paper ready for grouting; decorated tiles are supplied in packs of 12, four of each design. *M:* octagons 7.3×7.3cm, ($2\frac{7}{8}$×$2\frac{7}{8}$in), squares 2.5×2.5cm (1×1in), sheets 30×45cm ($11\frac{7}{8}$×$17\frac{3}{4}$in). *P:* sheet £4, sq m £25, decorated tile 80p.

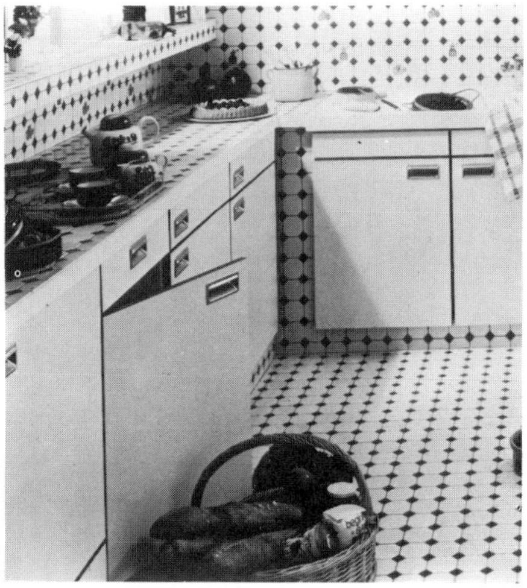

Langley's DIAMANT

CANTON has one plain tile and four with landscapes inspired by Chinese drawings, designed to form a frieze (*M:* 30×20cm/$11\frac{7}{8}$×$7\frac{7}{8}$in, *P:* sq m plain £30, patterned tile £6).
ENGLISH GARDEN includes plain White 'S10', and delicate 'S14' in White with a Grey-white tree (*M:* 30×20cm/$11\frac{7}{8}$×$7\frac{7}{8}$in, *P:* sq m plain £30, patterned tile £3).
The three tiles in the ETUDE range are 'Meadow Grass' and 'Bell Flower' in Olive, Orange or Fuschia on a Cream ground, and a plain version in Cream (*M:* 30×20cm/$11\frac{7}{8}$×$7\frac{7}{8}$in, *P:* sq m plain £22, patterned £32).

Langley's ETUDE

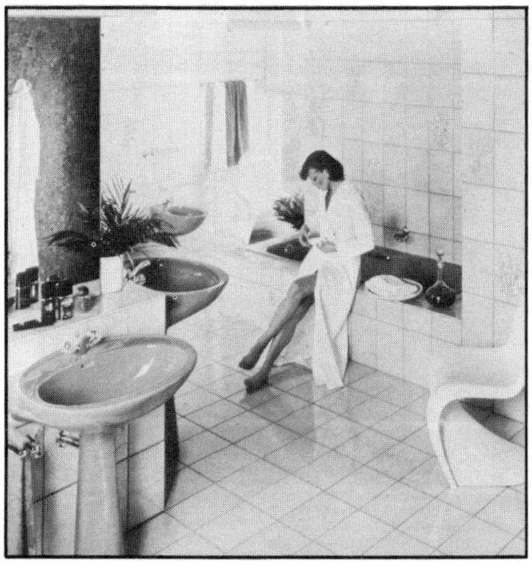

PALISY heavy-duty floor tiles, with naturalistic striations, are frost resistant for use indoors or out. The largest is available in White, Cream, Beige, Sand, and Coffee, the smaller sizes also in Grey, and Green. *M:* 5, 10×20; 20×30cm (2, 4×$7\frac{7}{8}$; $7\frac{7}{8}$×$11\frac{7}{8}$in). *P:* sq m £17.50–£21.
FLORENCE tiles, in vitrified ceramic mosaic, are also for interior or exterior use. Wall and floor versions are available. Colours, which vary attractively in depth, are Desert gold, Orange, Sea shell, and Green for bathrooms only; Golden brown, Brown-beige, Variegated bronze, and Sand beige can be used anywhere in the house. Tiles are mounted on paper mesh sheets. *M:* 52×31.5cm ($20\frac{1}{2}$×$12\frac{1}{2}$in). *P:* sq m £25.50, except Golden brown £21, Orange £27.50.

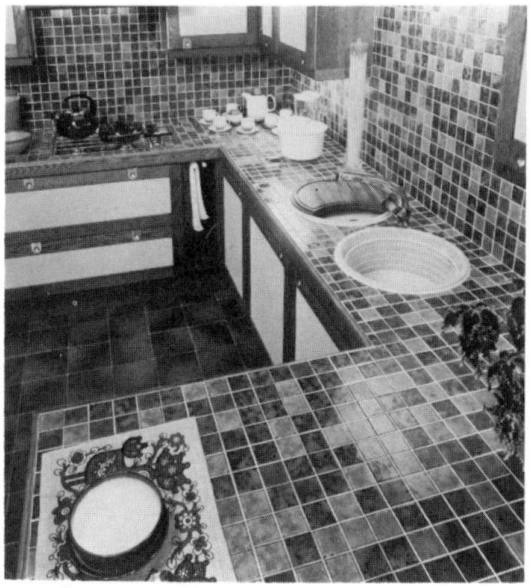

Langley's FLORENCE

ROCKY glazed floor, skirting and staircase tiles are available as squares or elongated hexagons, and come in four mottled colours: Ice gold for medium-stress areas; and Volcanic white, Aztec brown, and Tempered bronze, all with a more durable glaze, for heavy duty. *M:* square 19.7×19.7cm ($7\frac{3}{4}$×$7\frac{3}{4}$in), hexagonal oblong 29.5×9.6cm, ($11\frac{5}{8}$×$3\frac{3}{4}$in). *P:* sq m £11.
CORONA hexagonal floor tiles, made from slightly textured vitrified terracotta, are for indoor or outdoor use (*M:* 30×26cm/$11\frac{7}{8}$×$10\frac{1}{4}$in, *P:* sq m £26).
Glazed PROJECT RANGE floor and wall tiles are resistant to chemicals and come in semi-matt White, Walnut, and Sorrel; and high gloss Oyster, Mink, French blue, Coral, Bracken, Almond, and Sandalwood (*M:* 19.8×6.5cm/$7\frac{7}{8}$×$2\frac{5}{8}$in, *P:* sq m £9).
Villeroy & Boch also make unglazed floor and wall tiles. 'Algier Brown' and 'Algier Beige' are a Florentine shape, 'Biscarosse', 'Biscaye' are simple ogees. In earth tones only, supplied on perforated paper sheet. *M:* 6×6, 7.5×9.8cm ($2\frac{3}{8}$×$2\frac{3}{8}$, 3×$3\frac{5}{6}$in). *P:* sq m £18.50.
Langley also stock equally marvellous ranges from Buchtal. GLAZED CERAMIC WALL FACINGS are frostproof, colour fast and

maintenance free. Real stunners, the tiles come in 50 colours, including five intensive glazes: Yellow, Orange, Red, Green, and Blue. (Crazing can occur with these glazes, but doesn't affect performance.) *M:* 24×11.5, 24×5.2cm (9³/8×4¹/2, 9³/8×2in), intensive glazes in large size only. *P:* sq m £14.50–29, intensive glazes sq m £33. Buchtal also do Terracotta-toned tiles, specifically for stairs.

Hardwearing RUSTIC floor and wall tiles come in a good selection of shaded colours: Brown-aubergine, Colorado (russet), Grandezza (coffee), Bianco (cream), Attica (bronze), Patrician red (deepest burgundy), Piccolo (sand and rust), Tobacco (bronze and brown), Ocean (turquoise and brown), Cognac (tan and beige), Tropica (olive and brown), and Orient (gold and brown) (*M:* 19.4×9.4, 19.4, 24×5.2, 11.5, 24cm/7⁵/8×3³/4, 7⁵/8, 9³/8×2, 4¹/2, 9³/8in; also hexagonal tile to complement square 24×11.5cm/9³/8×4¹/2in, *P:* sq m £17–18).

UNGLAZED FINE GRAIN wall and floor tiles are frostproof, fireproof, resistant to acids and alkalis, immune to bacteria — and much else! They come in three variegated colours: Off-white, Light brown, and Old brown. *M:* 24×5.2, 11.5cm (9³/8×2, 4¹/2in). *P:* sq m £13.50–14.70. Also matching step tiles, cove skirtings, external and internal angles.

The unique and striking KERAION range comes only in large sizes. There's a choice of 19 rich shades for wall tiles, all with a marbly luminescent face created during firing. For floors or walls, there are 12 colours, mainly earth tones except for Koln (deep green) and Jakarta (deep blue). *M:* 30, 60×60cm (11⁷/8, 23⁵/8×23⁵/8in). *P:* sq m 60×60cm from £47.

Six types of SINZIG non-slip ceramic floor tiles, for High Tech fans, are available in Grey and White. Surfaces are smooth, textured, or studded, some with a speckled finish. *M:* 15×15cm (5⁷/8×5⁷/8in). *P:* sq m £16.50–24.50. Langley stock other tiles, primarily for industrial use, many of which are also suitable for specific areas like swimming pools. A design service is available to anyone interested in decorative murals or special finishes. See page 70 for 'Intense Green' from GLAZED CERAMIC WALL FACINGS in colour.

Langley's SINZIG waffle-studded tiles

PRICES AND INFORMATION WERE CORRECT AT THE TIME OF GOING TO PRESS

JOHN LEWIS LTD

Four charming wall tiles, from a well-known department store. 'Trigon' has thin White lines accented with tiny Green dots, on Beige; 'Lattice' is overlapping diagonals in Light blue or Green with darker accents, on White; 'Bamboo' is a Light green trellis with darker leaves, on White; and 'Wisteria' is Bright yellow flowers clinging to a Bright blue trellis. *M:* 6×6in (15.2×15.2cm). *P:* sq yd £18. See page 70 for 'Trigon' in colour.

Left to right, from top: John Lewis' 'Lattice', 'Bamboo', 'Wisteria', 'Trigon'

MARY FOX LINTON

Wall tiles that complement three of the 14 abstract designs in Mary Fox Linton's collection of fabrics and wallpapers. 'Cognac', 'Richemont' and 'Biron' come in one, two, or three colours from a choice of 25 shades. *M:* 4¹/2×4¹/2, 6×6in (11.5×11.5, 15.2×15.2cm). *P:* sq yd from £18. See page 70 for 'Cognac' in colour.

MARLBOROUGH CERAMIC TILES

Four ranges of wall tiles. Long-stemmed flowers and leaves proliferate on CHAMPFLEUR and PASTORALE, both available with undecorated plains. CHAMPFLEUR in palest Willow green, Coral, Oyster or Azure, PASTORALE in Willow green or Oatmeal.

Marlborough's CHAMPFLEUR

More modern BUBBLES and PARALLELS are available in Brown, Honey, Oatmeal, Oyster, Azure, Coral, Willow green, Jade, and Turquoise. Some tiles come only in boxes of 72; an extra 10% is charged if a box has to be split. *M:* 6×6in (15.2×15.2cm). *P:* sq yd £10–£14. Matching plain floor tiles are available in Coral, Willow green, and Oyster. (*M:* as above, *P:* sq yd £18).

Marlborough's BUBBLES (top), PARALLELS (bottom)

MAW & CO

Individual wall tiles made with the TUBELINE process, based on a 17th-century technique. (Small seams of clay are squeezed onto the surface, like icing, to form outlines and the tiles are then hand-painted with coloured glazes.) Murals can be commissioned. *M, P:* upon application.

MAJOLICA tiles include birds, scenes from Charles Dickens' novels, Victorian street scenes, knights (inspired by brass rubbings), and four tiles depicting the seasons; 'Isadora', Art Nouveau in style, is predominantly Blue or Brown. (*M:* 9×9in/23×23cm, *P:* tile £15).

Maw's 'Isadora' from MAJOLICA

MIRACLES LTD

Modern Op Art floor and wall tiles consisting of small squares in Greens, Blues, Reds, and Yellows create a chequered effect. Rainbows and palm trees are also available. *M:* 20×20cm (7⁷/₈×7⁷/₈in). *P:* sq m £30.

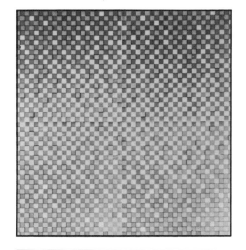

PILKINGTON TILES LTD

Wide selection from one of Britain's major manufacturers. Wall tiles, made by Pilkington's 'Universal' system, have spacer lugs on all four edges, with two adjacent edges fully glazed so that all tiles can also be used for edges or corners. Plain tiles come in an amazing 33 colours, including six different whites. *M:* 4¼×4¼, 6×6in (10.5×10.5, 15.2×15.2cm). *P:* sq yd £7–£8.

Patterned wall tiles include AZTEC, WOODLAND, HARMONY, NEAPOLITAN, ALPINE, and RIMINI, all with an abstract flower motif. AZTEC is in Gold, Ebony or Jade; WOODLAND in Autumn (tan) and Spring (gold); HARMONY in Blue, Tan, Pink, Olive, and Chocolate; NEAPOLITAN in Autumn, Avocado, and Chocolate; ALPINE in Spruce, Oyster, and Sorrento; RIMINI in Chocolate, Sorrento, Olive, and Gold; with matching bordered tiles. *M:* 6×6in, (15.2×15.2cm). *P:* sq yd patterned £9–£15. QUEENSBERRY has four

Pilkington's WOODLAND

designs: 'Chintz' in Olive, Sorrento (blue), or Chocolate; 'Bouquet' with Dark brown bouquets on a Honey or Ivory ground; delicate 'Lace' in Plum on White; and 'Salome', an Art Nouveau motif in Chocolate or Blue on White (*M:* 6×6in/15.2×15.2cm, *P:* sq yd £15). Inexpensive FIORI has a central motif in Chocolate, Olive or Tan on Cream; matching plain Cream tiles are available (*M:* 4¼×4¼in/10.8×10.8cm, *P:* sq yd £7.65). BRETON, designed for counter tops as well as walls, comes in six shades: Flame (red), Sand (gold), Sea (turquoise), Earth (brown), Sky (cobalt), and Cloud (off-white). Co-ordinating patterned tiles have animal or leaf motifs. *M:* 4×4in (10×10cm). *P:* sq yd plain £15.80, patterned £16.20, animal tile 60p.

From top: Pilkington's 'Lace', 'Bouquet', 'Salome', 'Chintz' from QUEENSBERRY

DORSET unglazed floor tiles, for indoors and out are available in Black, Red (terracotta), and Chocolate, plus spattered neutrals: Dorset rockface (tan), Dorset stone (beige), and Dorset granite (rust). Fully vitrified tiles come

Pilkington's 'Dorset Four Square' (top), 'Dorset Four Square Plain' (bottom)

in three speckled colours on Off-white: Blue flint, Grey flint, and Isotope grey. Textured non-slip styles are: 'Pinhead' in Grey, 'Studface' and 'Surefoot' in Dorset stone (beige), 'Dorset Four Square' and 'Dorset Four Square Plain' in Beige or Grey. *M:* 6×6in (15.2×15.2cm). *P:* sq yd £6–£8.50.

Antique style CLASSIC floor tiles are resistant to impact, heat, crazing, fading, water and solvents. 'Corinth' and 'Florence' can be used alone, or combined to form four-tile designs. 'Pergamino', with a central flower motif in Beige, Olive, or Amber, has a matching plain tile bordered in Brown. *M:* 8×8in (20.5×20.5cm). *P:* sq yd 'Florence' £16.20, 'Pergamino' £16.40.

Softly mottled PENTHOUSE CO-ORDINATES come in Pink, Fawn, Gold, White, and Olive (*M:* 6×6in/15.2×15.2cm, *P:* sq yd £10).

DANIEL PLATT & SONS LTD

Hardwearing floor tiles particularly appropriate for commercial use, with an anti-slip ribbed, short-faced or studded finish. Square, rectangular and hexagonal versions come in Red, Black, Buff, Chocolate, and various blends. Coved skirtings, angles, channels and fittings, step treads and fittings are also available. *M:* 10×10, 15×15; 7.5, 20×10cm (4×4, 5⁷/₈×5⁷/₈; 3, 7⁷/₈×4in), hexagons 15×15cm (5⁷/₈×5⁷/₈in) only. *P:* upon application.

S POLLIACK LTD

Hand-painted and transfer-decorated floor and wall tiles to match this company's luxurious bathroom suites. Flowers predominate in the hand-painted collection, in Red, Blue, Green, or Brown, with Green leaves. Plain White 'Cane' has a beige border; gold inlay tiles match the 'Belle Epoque' suite. Transfer tiles have a fine White trellis ground overprinted with daisies, dog roses, a single floral motif, or multi-coloured flowers. Plain White trellis tiles are available. *M:* 8×8in (20.5×20.5cm). *P:* hand-painted 'Cane', or gold inlay tile £7.50, transfer tile £2, plain sq yd £22.50. See also 'Bathrooms'. See page 70 for 'Bouquet' and 'Fiore Verde' from the hand-painted collection in colour.

RAGNO ITALIAN CERAMIC TILES LTD

Stunning collection of Italian tiles — a total of 34 ranges, including eight outstanding wall tiles. MAIOLICHE D'ARTE consists of five designs, all on White, plus a plain White version. 'Faenza AO1/AO' are Grey-blue, Dark blue and Mustard yellow on White. 'Deruta' is Blue on White. 'Vietri' has small Orange flowers and Green leaves on a Brown grid. 'Urbino' has Pink flowers, and 'Gubbio' is Yellow flower heads with small Green leaves. *M:* 15×15cm (5⁷/₈×5⁷/₈in).

The TROPICI range includes fish, flying geese,

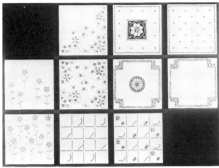

Left to right, from top: Ragno's 'Gubbio', 'Faenza', 'Urbino', 'Deruta', 'Vietri' from MAIOLICHE D'ARTE

and flowers. 'Onda' is a stylized wave in Aqua and Black on White; 'Coriandoli' combines stripes and dots in Blues and Gold on White. *M:* 20×20cm (7⁷/₈×7⁷/₈in).

PRIMAVERA has floral motifs on Bright yellow, Cobalt blue, Brown, Peach, Beige or Grey grounds (*M:* 20×20cm/7⁷/₈×7⁷/₈in). TREVIRA has classical designs in Gold on mottled Beige (*M:* 15×15cm/5⁷/₈×5⁷/₈in); NUOVE MARIE and SMERALDO are more ornate, each with three richly patterned designs in earth tones (*M:* both 20×20cm/7⁷/₈×7⁷/₈in).

HOLIDAY terracottas are made in mottled Beige, Sand, or Rust and in 15 patterns — a selection of borders, geometrics and florals (*M:* 20×20, 25×25cm/7⁷/₈×7⁷/₈, 9⁷/₈×9⁷/₈in).

REGIONI, for Op Art fans, has receding parallel lines on bright grounds: Orange, Olive, Blue, Gold, and Brown. Matching plains are available. *M:* 20×20cm (7⁷/₈×7⁷/₈in). NILO and PERGAMENA, with mock-crazed earthy grounds look hand-painted. Both plain or flowers.

Unpatterned ranges include two with rippled surfaces. MODUR is in Olive, Gold, Brown, Blue, and Red (*M:* 20×10cm/7⁷/₈×4in); MORATOM, in Off-white, Cream, and Tan, comes in a mottled or striated version (*M:* 20×30cm/7⁷/₈×11⁷/₈in).

The most unusual tiles, ALPI, look like wood for an effect of luxurious parquet flooring. Five designs are available in natural wood tones, all beautifully and naturalistically executed. *M:* 20×20cm (7⁷/₈×7⁷/₈in). *P:* sq m from £10.

Left to right, from top: Ragno's 'Cervinia', 'Sestriere', 'Bormio', 'Livigno', 'Parquet' from ALPI

SARTOR

Wall tiles that co-ordinate with Sartor fabrics and wall coverings. 'Iris' flowers, 'Mayfly' with small Dark green insects and 'Bamboo' with Green leaves, are all on White. *M:* 6×6in (15.2×15.2cm). *P:* sq yd £29. See page 70 for 'Iris' and 'Mayfly' in colour.

CHRISTINA SHEPPARD

Hand-painted, made-to-order tiles. Techniques include *graffito*, with a wide range of glazes, as well as traditional brush strokes. Christina Sheppard prefers to design for specific purposes — tabletops, fireplaces, kitchen and bathroom walls, etc. Colouring varies, so no two tiles are ever exactly the same. *M:* 4×4, 6×6in (10×10, 15.2×15.2cm). *P:* £1.50–£2. See page 70 for two tiles in colour.

SLOANE SQUARE TILES

Hand-painted wall tiles available singly, or as panels, in any colour, design and/or material chosen by the customer. The illustration shows a 35-tile panel in soft shades of Pink, Blue, and tones of Grey-green on creamy White (*M:* 2½×3ft/76×91.5cm, *P:* £150).

H & E SMITH LTD

HEXAGONAL glazed floor tiles for light-traffic areas, in Ironstone (black), Stardust (white), Chestnut (terracotta), Harvest (sand), and Lincoln (emerald green). There are also dazzling metallic oblong, square and hexagonal tiles with embossed designs. 'Shield' has a raised circle, and matching ribbed tiles. Colours are Bronze, Tinsel (dark red), Ironstone (black), and White. *M:* 6×6in (15.2×15.2cm). *P:* upon application.

Smith's 'Shield' (centre), with matching ribbed tiles

GEORGE WOOLLISCROFT & SON LTD

Architectural floor and cladding tiles. Unglazed MODMET 200, for interior or exterior floors, comes in good, earthy colours: Rustic blend (red and brown), Beech blend (copper and brown), Ironstone (terracotta), and Sand blend (beige and brown). Compatible 'S021' skirting tiles, with external angles, are available. *M:* 20×20cm (7⁷/₈×7⁷/₈in). *P:* sq m £13.

WORLD'S END TILES

Terrific collection of modern geometric, and period floral, wall tiles. Each design can be screened in any of 28 colours, on any colour ground! 'Dot' has a White ground covered with dots; an overlay on one side of a bordered version has festoons, etc., in darker shades of the main colour. Popular Victorian 'Palm' shows bamboo, palm leaves and a sunburst, 'Daffodils' are bright and cheerful, 'Half Tone' is plain, with just tiny dots within a fine border line. In 'Fleur de Lys' the classic emblems alternate with three dots. 'Victoriana' has Gothic overtones. 'Linear Flower', in two colours on a plain ground, has a border enclosing wild flowers and berries. 'Diagonal Weave' is a trellis effect.

Most tiles have co-ordinating border versions. 'Open Field' can be used with 'Border One', and with square 'Open Field Border'.

In addition, any patterns can be printed in gold such as 'Greek Key' — very effective but expensive. To reduce the overall cost, one row of gold-patterned tiles can be combined with matching plains.

M: all 6×6in (15.2×15.2cm), border tiles 6×3in (15.2×7.5cm). *P:* sq yd one colour £16.50, two colours £18. See page 70 for 'Dot', 'Palm', 'Daffodils', 'Victoriana', 'Open Field', 'Border One', 'Open Field Border', 'Linear Flower Border', 'Diagonal Weave', 'Greek Key' in colour.

INTRODUCTION

There's probably nothing so soothing as the soft tick of a clock, evoking more leisured days gone by. More practically, clocks are both functional and very much part of the overall decorative scheme in any room. They come in a wide variety of shapes, sizes and types: ultra-modern digital display clocks, pleasing big-faced school clocks, 'antique' long-case models, carriage and dome clocks — and more. Movements vary from traditional eight-day spring mechanisms to the less troublesome quartz working.

For genuine antiques, see 'Useful Addresses' for our list of dealers and restorers. But be warned — sound models usually command high prices. Although reproduction clocks are by no means cheap, they're usually less expensive and combine traditional techniques with modern accuracy and reliability.

*Measurements given in this section refer to clock heights, unless otherwise stated.

BILLIB FURNITURE (UK) LTD

Two ranges of reproduction long-case clocks. Exclusive INTERCLOCK has high-quality Black Forest and Flemish workings. 12 distinctive styles, in a variety of wood finishes, include

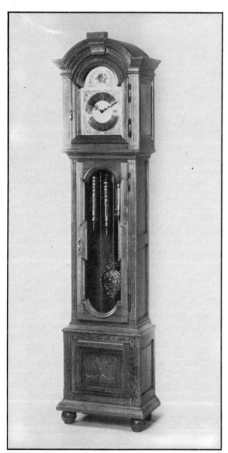

Billib's 'Canterbury'

'Kent' in oak, and maple, and 'Canterbury' in oak, and cherry (*M:* 'Kent' h 7ft 1½in/217.5cm, 'Canterbury' h 7ft 2½in/220cm, *P:* 'Kent' £1,400, 'Canterbury' £1,300, additional chimes extra). The less expensive Danish WESTMINSTER range also offers 12 styles, finished in mahogany, light or dark walnut, oak, teak, or rosewood depending on the model. Cabinets in both ranges have glass-panelled doors (some with leaded panes) to reveal the interior brass weights. Two wall hanging clocks are also available: 'Waltham' in mahogany, and 'Andover' with a gong strike, in mahogany, and oak (*M:* h 3ft 9in/114.5cm, *P:* £360).

GURDON BURNETT

Marvellous timepieces by a craftsman who likes to make clocks for specific environments. Gurdon Burnett will work in any scale, within a strict budget or in the most exclusive materials available. Sleek, pure designs include the perfect travel clock shown in colour on page 79. It houses a silver structure overlaid with yew, a silver face with red-gold hands, and a quartz movement. Silver hinges allow complete, compact folding. *M:* h 6½in (16.5cm). *P:* £350 as illustrated in colour, other clocks from £100.

CLIVE BURR

Lovely clocks, often in silver and wood, by a silversmith turned clockmaker. The fine example illustrated in colour on page 79 has a dark kingwood and light sycamore frame, and silver front with dark oxidized silver squares (*M:* h 5in/12.5cm, *P:* £300 as illustrated in colour, other clocks from £50).

CHRISTON CLOCKS LTD

Unique and stylish collection of reasonably priced quartz-battery wall and table clocks in chromium-plated steel, polished brass, and satin aluminium. Traditional styles include a ship's clock, and small or large station clocks in pine, and mahogany. Among the more modern items are a 'Hoop' clock with satin aluminium base and glass dome, the 'La Posh' table clock, essentially a stainless steel strip, and a variety of boldly styled wall clocks. *M:* diam 18×13cm (7¹/8×5¹/8in), diam 15×22cm (5⁷/8×8⁵/8in). *P:* £40, £30.

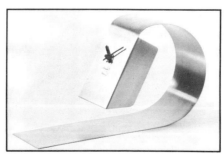

Christon's 'La Posh'

Christon's 'Hoop'

CLASSIC GARDEN FURNITURE LTD

Enchanting selection of wall clocks from a company that specializes in cast iron. All are nicely made, and not prohibitively expensive. The 'C81' Dutch wall clock with ornamental top piece is finished in walnut and brass (*M:* h 2ft 1in/63.5cm, *P:* £65). The 'C104 Sallander' wall clock in burr walnut and brass has a marvellous sunburst pendulum, and the phases of the moon on top of the arched dial (*M:* h 21in/52.5cm, *P:* £110). 'C105', a cased wall clock with a charming hand-painted face and dial also shows the moon's phases (*M:* h 3ft/91.5cm, *P:* £180). All clocks are eight-day duration, with strikes on the hour and half hour.

Classic Garden Furniture's 'C81', 'C104 Sallander', 'C105'

CRAYONNE UK LTD

Quartz-battery wall clock with easy-to-read numerals and a second-hand. It comes in two sizes, the smaller in Brown, and White, the larger also in Deep green. *M:* diam 6½in (16.5cm), 9in (23cm). *P:* £16, £19.

Crayonne's wall clock

DORON CLOCKS

Wall, mantel, and long-case clocks. 'Vienna' is a regulator style long-case clock with a spiral gong which strikes the hours and half hours. It comes in two sizes in a mahogany finish, the smaller also in Black. *M:* h 2ft 9in (84cm), 3ft 9in (114.5cm). *P:* £189, £300. Grandfather and grandmother clocks with mahogany veneer cases, eight-day weight-driven movements, and brass-finish weights, chain, and pendulum bob are particularly attractive. The 'Thanet' grandmother clock and 'Gothic' grandfather have three chime options. *M:* 'Thanet' h 6ft (183cm), 'Gothic' h 6ft 4in (193cm). *P:* £415–£475, £675–£795.

ENGLISH CLOCK SYSTEMS

Standard range of 12 conventional wall clocks intended primarily for commercial use. The 'School Clock' is attractive and functional with a circular, grained aluminium dial and Black bar-type hands (*M:* diam 6, 8in/15, 20.5cm, *P:* £25, £30). An unusual double-sided, ceiling suspension clock can be fitted with any dial in the range. *M:* diam 12in/30.5cm, *P:* £80).
Digital display wall clocks, also designed for commercial or industrial use, would look very stylish in a modern house, but are by no means inexpensive. All come in White, and Brown, with White digits on a Black ground. Green, Yellow, Red, and Blue cases can be supplied at extra cost. *M:* diam 31–33cm (12–13in). *P:* £90–£240, special case £5.

PRICES AND INFORMATION WERE CORRECT AT THE TIME OF GOING TO PRESS

English Clock System's 'School Clock'

GOODFELLOWS CLOCKS

Reproduction wall and long-case clocks from a family firm which employs traditional techniques passed down through many generations. Seven styles are available, in beautifully veneered mahogany with a choice of wooden or glass-panel doors and brass dials designed by Goodfellows.
The detail illustrated below is from one of the most attractive long-case clocks, with a solid brass dial. Its curled mahogany base with line ebony inlay has been French-polished by hand and it has an Urgos movement. *M:* h 6½ft ×w 20in (198×51cm). *P:* £500, wall from £250, long-case £400–£1,500.

Goodfellows' '4PGM56U' long-case clock

M & I J HARRISON LTD

Wall clock, and long-case model, from a firm best known for its custom-designed kitchens. Both have eight-day German movements with a bell strike, and come in light or dark stained pine cases with brass detailing. *M:* long-case h 6ft 1in (185.5cm), wall h 2ft 6in (76cm). *P:* long-case £390, wall £130.

SHANDON CLOCKS LTD

Nicely designed battery-operated clocks in well-made metal cases. Wall clocks include square '3958' with a chromed case (*M:* h 12in/30.5cm, *P:* £100); computer-numbered digital '3940' in brushed stainless steel; and '3960' with a Black face, White numerals, and chromed case (*M:* both diam 7½in/19cm, *P:*

£20). Carriage-style '3952' has a brass or chrome case (*M:* h 6in/15cm, *P:* brass £70, chrome £60); '3953', a more modern table timepiece on a stainless steel strip, looks like half a large wristwatch (*M:* h 9in/23cm, *P:* £40).

SMALLCOMBE (IMPEX) LTD

Possibly the most complete selection of British-made long-case and bracket clocks on the market. The less expensive ENGLISH ELEGANCE range consists of nine models. 'Warwick', 'Hereford', 'York', and 'Sandringham' come with Westminster chime(*M:* h 127, 162, 188, 203cm/4 ft 2 in, 5ft 4in, 6ft 2in, 6ft 9in, *P:* £288, £392, £505 or £555 (mahogany/yew or walnut), £473). HUTT AND HOLLAND has five exclusive styles in solid timber, all hand-carved and hand-made to order (*P:* £685–£1,700).

Left to right: Smallcombe's 'Warwick', 'Hereford', 'York', 'Sandringham'

SMITHS INDUSTRIES CLOCK CO

Probably the widest range of modern British clocks on the market, from a company that's a household name. It includes carriage, mantel, anniversary, kitchen, wall, alarm, and commercial clocks. Most have the new quartz movement, and all are guaranteed for one or two years. A very attractive school clock has Roman numerals in pine and mahogany (*M:* h 30cm/11⁷/₈in, *P:* £460). Illustrated are: 'Dumbarton', a quartz-movement wall clock with a sapele case and Roman numerals (diam 30cm/11⁷/₈in, *P:* £43.50); 'Trinity Pendulum', battery-operated with a mahogany wall case and hinged bezel (*M:* h 47cm/18½in, *P:* £60); and 'Lantern', an unusual crown-topped carriage clock with a grained and polished brass case (*M:* h 24.5cm/9¾in, *P:* £65). Other well-designed models are the brass-cased 'Marine' wall clock (*M:* diam 10cm/4in, *P:* £25);

and 'Derby', a round kitchen clock with large, bold numerals and moulded case, available in White, Brown, Avocado, and Orange (*M:* diam 20.5cm/8in, *P:* £23).

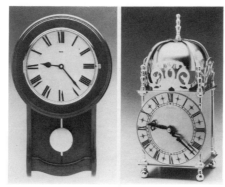

Smiths' 'Trinity Pendulum' (left), 'Lantern' (right)

Smiths' 'Dumbarton' (left), 'Marine' (right)

Smiths' 'Derby'

WOOD BROS FURNITURE LTD

Solid oak grandfather clock with a leaded front, linenfold panel cabinet, and brass dial. Part of the enormous OLD CHARM furniture range, it comes in three finishes: light oak, Tudor brown, and antique oak. *M:* h 6ft 7in (200.5cm). *P:* £760 (antique oak £790).

PRICES AND INFORMATION WERE CORRECT AT THE TIME OF GOING TO PRESS

Opposite page: Wood and silver clock by Clive Burr (top), folding model by Gurdon Burnett (bottom)

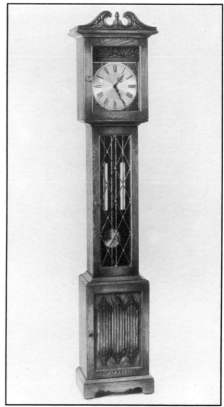

Wood Bros' OLD CHARM grandfather clock

CHRISTOPHER WRAY'S LIGHTING EMPORIUM LTD

Functional 'Brass Wall Clock' from this purveyor of pretty reproduction lighting. Very competitively priced, it has bold numerals and a classical face which can be sign-written to order. *M:* diam 17in (43.5cm). *P:* £30.

INTRODUCTION

Take a seat – and take your choice from a selection in plastic, fibreglass, cane, bamboo, ash, leather, brass, pine, mahogany, wickerwork, enamelled metal, tubular steel, canvas or fabric.

Always make sure a chair is the right size for the room, and surrounding furniture. Dining chairs, for example, should have a seat height that's comfortable in relation to the height of the table; and the arms of a carver chair should slide easily under the table top. (The latter is especially important if space is limited.)

This section includes everything from strict, straight-backed dining chairs to leather-slung models and partially upholstered pieces; also chairs that have been ergonomically designed for specific purposes, fold-away versions, and comfy rockers. Styles range from beautifully accurate reproductions, to totally 20th-century classics. Prices vary as much as the chairs themselves – from £8 to £350. See also 'Special Furniture', 'Upholstered Furniture'.

ANTOCKS LAIRN LTD

Tough, but sculpturally interesting, seating unit. 'Abacus 700' by David Mellor is designed for public or domestic use, indoors or out. The strong, steel wire mesh seat rests on crossed tubular supports which are available chromed, or nylon-coated for use outdoors. The foam-filled seat pad is covered with fabric or PVC. *M:* w 24 × h 27 × d 24in (61 × 68.5 × 61cm). *P:* £60–£70 depending on covering. Also available without arms.

ARAM DESIGNS LTD

'MI 16', a curvaceous beauty on a polished, chromium-plated tubular steel frame. The seat, back and armrests are woven cane. *M:* w 22 × h 33 × d 33in (56 × 84 × 84cm). *P:* £200. Also available without arms.

Left: De la Plain's 'Diagolo' chairs
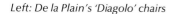

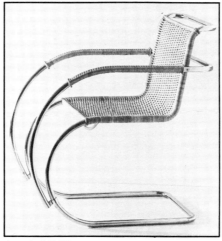

Aram's 'MI 16'

A sleek beauty by a famous triumvirate, one of many Modern Movement pieces from Aram, 'Basculant' by Le Corbusier, Pierre Jeanneret and Charlotte Perriand has a seat and adjustable back in calfskin, leather or canvas, hide armrests stretched on a chromium-plated tubular steel frame. *M:* w 23¾ × h 26 × d 26in (60 × 66 × 66cm). *P:* £290. See 'Upholstered Furniture' for illustration.
BISCIA polished chrome stacking chairs can be upholstered in fabric or leather. *M:* w 25½ × h 29¹/₈in (65 × 74cm). *P:* fabric from £45, leather £99.

Aram's BISCIA

'Cesca' a 20th-century classic, by Marcel Breuer, has a polished tubular steel frame, cane seat and back framed in ebonized bentwood. Much copied, so beware of cheaper and less sturdy imitations. *M:* w 18¼ × h 31½ × d 22¼in (46.5 × 80 × 56.5cm). *P:* from £200. It also comes without arms and can be supplied fully upholstered, or with fabric or leather inset panels.
'Coray 1939', a lightweight, stacking armchair for inside and outside by Hans Coray, was designed — you guessed it — in 1939. It has a rustproof aluminium frame finished in anodized silver, with matching perforated

Aram's 'Cesca' (left), 'Coray 1939' (right)

shell, and White cast rubber feet. *M:* w 20½ × h 29½ × d 20½in (52 × 72 × 52cm). *P:* £100
The 'Londra' chair has a collapsible polished chrome frame slung with natural canvas. The front bar is solid beech. *M:* w 31½ × h 28³/₈ × d 27¹/₈in (80 × 72 × 69cm). *P:* £71.

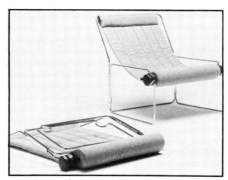

Aram's 'Londra'

'Stam' by Mart Stam is a tubular classic with a polished chromium-plated tubular steel frame. Seat and back are Tan or Black coach hide. *M:* w 19½ × h 33¾ × d 25½in (49.5 × 85.5 × 65cm). *P:* £350. Also available without arms.

Aram's 'Stam'

Designed in 1925, and still going strong, 'Wassily' by Marcel Breuer has a polished chromium-plated tubular steel frame; seat, back and arm straps are in Tan, Dark brown, or Black coach hide, or White canvas. *M:* w 31 × h 28 × d 28in (78.5 × 71 × 71cm). *P:* coach hide £410. (A similar, less expensive, version is available: £160 in canvas, £210 in leather.)

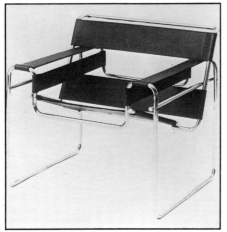

Aram's 'Wassily'

ASH & CO

'Balestrini' by Anthony Hooper, a sophisticated folding chair for contract and domestic use. The beautifully constructed wooden frame is in natural ash and chromed metalwork. Leather or canvas upholstery is available. *M:* w 63 × h 72 × d 60cm (24⁷/₈ × 28³/₈ × 23⁵/₈in). *P:* £250 leather.

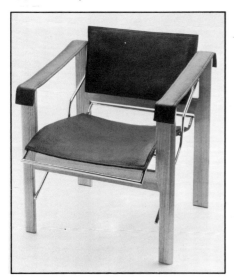

ASHLEY FURNITURE WORKSHOPS

Folding 'Campaign Chair' with a polished mahogany frame that adjusts to six sitting positions. One of many exceptionally well-

made reproductions from this company, it dates from the 19th century. Leather upholstery comes in an outstanding selection of colours: 120 in matt leather, 12 in glazed, and 15 in hand-antiqued leather. *M:* w 23½ × h 40 × d 32in (59.5 × 101.5 × 81.5cm). *P:* £225.

Ashley's 'Campaign Chair'

Magnificent facsimile of the first steel rocker, exhibited by R.W. Winfield of Birmingham at the Great Exhibition of 1851. The flat steel frame is finished in brushed metal, upholstered in the same fine leathers as the 'Campaign Chair'. Supplied in kit form, the rocker is easily assembled. *M:* w 24 × h 42 × d 35in (61 × 107 × 89cm). *P:* £200.

Ashley's steel rocker

ASTON WOODWARE

Low-back settle, made-to-order in good quality oak or elm. It can be supplied pegged through, or with flush ends; with a solid or tongue-and-grooved back. Finishes range

from natural to a dark stain; or the wood can be polished, to order. *M:* to order. *P:* ft £18; ends £22.50 each.

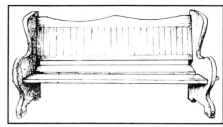

Aston's low-back settle

Two stool styles from a range of five. All are made with beech tops and elm legs. *M:* w 10 × h 18–27 × d 6in (25 × 46–68.5 × 15cm). *P:* £9.45–£10.50.

Aston's stools (above), Windsor (below)

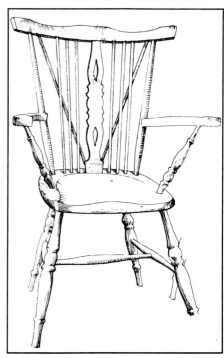

Hand-made Windsor (left, below) with a pierced splat centre. It's part of a range of country chairs, mainly in oak or elm, with spindle backs, from a firm that makes cottage-style pub furniture. *M:* w 21 × h 35 × d 18in (53 × 89 × 46cm). *P:* £100.

ATRIUM

Bauhaus-inspired TECTA cantilevered arm-chair and chaise-longue. Both have a chromed tubular steel frame strung with White or Black polypropylene 'wickerwork'. *M:* armchair w 63 × h 70 × d 78cm (24⁷/₈ × 27¹/₂ × 30³/₄in), chaise-longue w 60 × l. 60 × h 66cm (23⁵/₈ × 63 × 26in). *P:* both £360. Matching chairs in the range include dining chairs with or without arms, a bar stool, and a high-back chair. Fabric or leather cushion upholstery is an optional extra. See 'Upholstered Furniture' for illustration.

H J BERRY & SONS LTD

Reproduction spindleback Lancashire chair with a rush or loose cushion seat, from a firm of traditional chairmakers. It comes in medium or dark stains, or a 'heavily distressed' finish at extra cost. *M:* w 22¹/₂ × h 42¹/₂ × d 18in (57 × 108 × 46cm). *P:* £100. A traditional rocking chair, and a child-sized version 30in (76cm) high, are also available.

'29', a charming reproduction of a rush-seated saddle stool. *M:* w 30¹/₂ × h 11 × d 13¹/₂in (77.5 × 28 × 34.5cm). *P:* £70. A 15in (38cm) high footstool, also with a rush seat, is available.

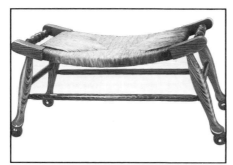

Berry's saddle stool

BLC TRADITIONAL COUNTRY FURNITURE LTD

Pleasing smoker's bow chair. Made from matured pine or seasoned beech, it has nicely turned legs and splats. *M:* w 18 × h 31 × d 19in (46 × 79 × 49cm). *P:* £45. Other styles include a spindleback and a fiddleback.

CADO FURNITURE (UK) LTD

'142', an updated director's chair in light beechwood with a canvas seat and back. *M:* w 68 × h 88 × d 54cm (26³/₄ × 34⁵/₈ × 21¹/₄in). *P:* £90. A low-slung deck-chair with adjustable headrest and optional footstool is also available.

Space-age '265' is an easy chair with adjustable neck-rest, and footstool, by Sten Ostergaard. Made from nylon reinforced with fibreglass, its silky gloss finish is anti-static and won't delaminate. This futuristic beauty comes in White, Brown, or Beige, with nylon stretch

fabric covers. Upholstered armrests are optional. *M:* w 35 × h 37³/₈ × d 35in (89 × 95 × 89cm). *P:* £350.

Cado's '142' (above), '265' (below)

CIANCIMINO DESIGN LTD

'Orlando' with a tapered, satin steel frame, and brass fittings. Suede upholstery only, in any colour selected by the customer. *M:* w 21 × h 34 × d 21in (53.5 × 86.5 × 53.5cm). *P:* £135. See overleaf for illustration.

CLASSIC GARDEN FURNITURE LTD

Unusual 'C97' stool with a swivel tractor seat. In cast iron, it can be made to order in any height. *M:* w 17 × h variable × d 13in (43 × 33cm). *P:* painted from £38.
'C100', 'C101', 'C102', are classic bentwood chairs selected from two dozen modern and traditional styles. Rocking chairs, bar stools, tables, coat racks and a baby's high chair are also available. *M:* diam 16–16¹/₂ × h 30–39in (40.5–42 × 76–99cm). *P:* £25–£40. See overleaf for illustration.

Ciancimino's 'Orlando'

Left to right, from top: Classic Garden Furniture's 'C97', 'C100', 'C101', 'C102'

THE CONRAN SHOP LTD

Low-backed KARTELL bar stools in metal and plastic. The seat is Black, legs are Red. *M:* w 33 × h 88 × d 33cm (13 × 34⅝ × 13in). *P: £85.*
Stylish 'La Tripolina' folding chair, from Citterio, with an ash frame, and natural, Orange, Yellow or Red canvas seat. *M:* w 25 × h 125 × d 80cm (9⅞ × 49¼ × 31½in). *P: £75.*

DE LA PLAIN INTERIORS LTD

'Diagolo' design-your-own chairs (almost). Frames are in walnut, Black leather, or chrome, seats in lacquer, ten shades of leather in several qualities, or the customer's own fabric. *M:* w 53 × h 80 × d 54cm (20⅞ × 31½ × 21¼in). *P: £70–£140, £100 in customer's own fabric. See page 80 for colour illustration.

DESIGNERS GUILD

Delightfully evocative cane chairs, two with upholstered backs, made to the Guild's specifications in the Far East, and finished in

clear lacquer. Unlike many cheaper versions, all have firm seat supports. Feather-filled cushions have zip-fastened covers, with piped edges, in Designers Guild fabrics. *M: various. P: £86–£205.* For a truly unique piece, coloured lacquers and stains can be applied at extra cost. See also *Occasional Tables* ('Tables'), 'Plants and Planters', 'Shelving'.

MARTIN J DODGE

'C16' solid mahogany Adam-style spiderback carver and side chair with marquetry centre panels. *M:* as illustrated w 24 × h 40 × d 29in (61 × 102 × 73.5cm). *P:* carver £230, side chair £200.

'C23' and 'C24', two very fine reproduction Regency chairs, with cane seats. 'C23' on the left is painted and carved; 'C24' is lacquered and gilded. *M:* 'C23' w 22 × h 33 × d 20in (56 × 84 × 51cm), 'C24' w 22 × h 34¾ × d 20¾in (56 × 88.5 × 52.5cm). *P: £320.*

Martin J Dodge specialize in reproduction tables and chairs, beautifully made from the best quality wood. Other styles include a Sheraton cross-splat, and Regency and Chippendale chairs, plus Hepplewhite balloon and lyre backs and a simple Georgian style. All are available with or without arms.

ENVIRONMENT DESIGN

'Break' by Mario Bellini. This high-backed chair has a steel frame, feather and polyurethane foam padding. Covering is fabric with leather piping, or leather. *M:* w 56 × h 85 × d 51cm (22 × 33½ × 20in). *P:* fabric from £265. Also available without arms.

Environment's 'Break'

Simple but elegant '412 Cab' by Mario Bellini, inspired by the original hansom cab (c 1834). The steel frame is covered in tough, saddle-stitched hide in Natural (tan), Black, Blue, Green, and two Reds. *M:* w 47 × h 80 × d 47cm (18½ × 31½ × 18½in). *P:* £180.

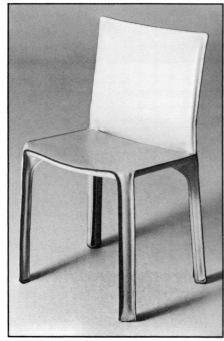

Environment's '412 Cab'

'Hill House No. 1' by Charles Rennie Mackintosh. The ultimate ladderback, this striking chair was designed by the famous

Scottish architect/designer in about 1900. One of eight reproductions by Cassina in Italy, it has an ashwood frame and ebony finish. *M:* w 40.5 × h 140.5 × d 39cm (16 × 55¼ × 15³/₈in). *P:* £300.

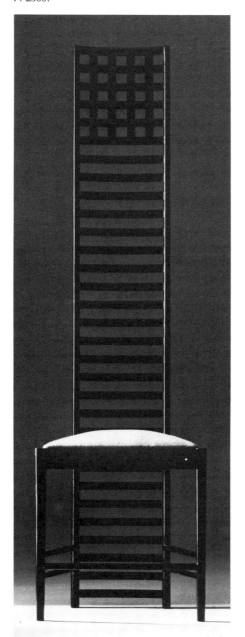

Environment's 'Hill House No. 1'

ERCOL FURNITURE LTD
'473', a double bow rocker in pine. One of four streamlined traditional designs it is also available in a darker stain. The seat cushion is optional. *M:* w 60 × h 103 × d 76cm (25⁵/₈ × 40½ × 30in). *P:* from £140.

Ercol's '473' rocker

ESTIA DESIGNS LTD
Wonderful 'E32CH' folding chair to match an equally wonderful table, from one of the country's most exciting design firms. Ideal for anyone who can never get quite comfortable, it has over 50 height and seat-angle permutations, from dining to low-down sitting. The natural canvas seat is stretched on a tubular steel frame finished in Red, Brown, Green or Yellow epoxy. *M:* w 21 × h variable × d 21in (53.5 × 53.5cm). *P:* £16, four £60. See *Dining Tables* ('Tables') for illustration.

FORMA LTD
'Anna', a rustic folding chair with a natural beech frame and caned seat. *M:* w 45 × h 85 × d 41cm (17¾ × 33½ × 16¹/₈in). *P:* £25. Also available with a woven rush seat or Black-stained frame.

Forma's 'Anna' (left); 'Gamma' (right) described overleaf

'Gamma' (illustrated overleaf) has a tubular chrome frame, and woven cane seat and back with natural or Black-stained surrounds. *M:* w 46 × h 80 × d 42.5cm (18 × 31½ × 16³/₈in). *P:* £30. Also available without arms.

Chic, futuristically rounded 'Joint', designed by Guzzini is inexpensively moulded in Brown or White plastic. It can be plain or upholstered. *M:* w 44 × h 80 × 44cm (17³/₈ × 30¾ × 17³/₈in). *P:* £40 plain, £65 upholstered.

Forma's 'Joint'

Unusual 'Plusia' has a rectangular caned seat and back surrounded in chrome and set in a natural or Black-stained wood frame. *M:* w 49 × h 76 × d 32.5cm (19¼ × 30 × 12¾in). *P:* £35.

Forma's 'Plusia'

The director-style 'Regista' armchair has a natural beech frame, Beige canvas seat and back. *M:* w 47.5 × h 84 × d 39.5cm (18³/₈ × 33 × 15³/₈in). *P:* £27. Also available without arms.

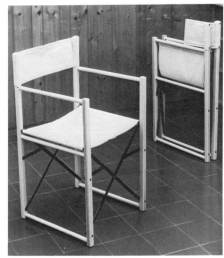

Forma's 'Regista'

GEORGIAN FURNISHING CO

Handsome Chippendale reproduction in solid Indonesian walnut. 'C7A' has the characteristic square leg and hand-carved back. *M:* w 25 × h 39 × d 21in (63.5 × 99 × 53.5cm). *P:* £255. Several other beautifully made reproductions are also available.

'C11L', a very unusual armchair. Hand-carved in solid Indonesian walnut, with bird's head detail, it can be upholstered in hide or damask. *M:* w 30 × h 40 × d 26in (76 × 101.5 × 66cm). *P:* hide £580.

Georgian's 'C11L'

Lovely lacquer LQACS chair with cabriole legs, and hand-painted motifs on a Red, Brown or Black ground. Upholstery is damask. *M:* w 21 × h 38 × d 21in (53.5 × 96.5 × 53.5cm). *P:* £185. An armchair version is available. See 'Storage' for illustration.

Giorgetti's '6143' (top), '6142' (bottom)

GIORGETTI

'6142', '6143' (left, below) chairs from Italy. Possibly the most attractive and faithful Art Nouveau reproductions on the market, with carved backs and characteristic flowing lines, they can be upholstered in fabric or leather. Wood is highly polished and hand-worked. '6141', the most deeply upholstered, has cushions everywhere and a comfortable high back; '6142' is almost Chinese in appearance; and low-backed '6143' is a chic dining chair. *M:* '6141' w 100 × h 95 × d 86cm (39³/8 × 37³/8 × 33⁷/8in), '6142' w 79 × h 100 × d 73cm (31¹/8 × 39³/8 × 28³/4in), '6143' w 70 × h 83 × d 69cm (27¹/2 × 32⁵/8 × 27¹/8in). *P:* from £775, £450, £550.

HAG (UK) LTD

'2009' hobby chair — the black-and-white illustration really doesn't do justice to this simple beauty. The seat and base are in natural or dark pine, or can be stained Red, Yellow or Green. Back and seat are press-moulded in 1.2cm (½in) wood. *M:* w 41 × h 52.5 × d 41cm (16¹/8 × 20³/4 × 16¹/8in). *P:* £45.

CHARLES HAMMOND LTD

'Jacob Fauteuil', upholstered in 'Java Jungle', a Lee Jofa fabric. *M:* w 58 × h 98 × d 57cm (22⁷/8 × 38½ × 22½in). *P:* £115, excluding fabric.

Charles Hammond's 'Jacob Fauteuil' (left), 'Louis X111' (right)

'Louis XIII' carver with mahogany-stained fine beech frame, upholstered in Charles Hammond's own 'Clayton Mill' fabric. *M:* w 57 × h 112 × d 68cm (22½ × 44¹/8 × 26³/4in). *P:*

from £60. Also available without arms, it comes in a variety of finishes including White.

'Sunbury Park' carver. A Chippendale-style classic, it's upholstered in Charles Hammond's exclusive patchwork fabric. *M:* w 61 × h 97 × d 62 (24 × 38¹/8 × 24³/8in). *P:* £150. Also available without arms, and with brass feet.

Charles Hammond's 'Sunbury Park'

JOYCE HARDY

Pleasing wheelbacks, made to order from recycled pine on Joyce Hardy's pine-stripping premises. *M:* w 15, 17 × h 33 × d 18in (38, 43.5 × 84 × 46cm). *P:* £30, carver £45. See also 'Storage', *Dining Tables* ('Tables').

HILLE INTERNATIONAL LTD

'Polo', designed by Robin Day for outdoor as well as indoor use — holes allow rainwater to drain away. The one-piece shell, in easily maintained moulded polypropylene, comes in strong colours that won't fade: Flame red,

Yellow, Emerald green, Black, and White. *M:* w 54 × h 70 × d 52cm (21¼ × 27½ × 20½in). *P:* upon application.

Hille's 'Polo'

HOMEWORKS LTD

WOODWORKS dining chairs. Six styles include 'L 15' and oval-backed '7413', both reminiscent of classic French furniture; and more rustic pieces like rush-seated 'C500', and '7411' with a square caned back, rush seat. Some chairs have upholstered sides and backs. Hand-carved solid oak or cherry frames look as though they've faded with age. *M:* 'L 15' w 26 × h 39 × d 26in (66 × 99 × 66cm), '7413' w 24 × h 39 × d 24in (61 × 99 × 61cm), 'C500' w 19 × h 34 × d 18in (48.5 × 86.5 × 46cm), '7411' w 24 × h 36 × d 24in (61 × 91.5 × 61cm). *P:* upon application.

Left to right, from top: Homeworks' 'L15', '7413', 'C500', '7411' from WOODWORKS

INTERSPACE

Ergonomically designed VERTEBRA chairs by Castelli that allow office workers to sit comfortably at their desks. (On average, most people move six times per hour.) The first range to take these movements into account, VERTEBRA is the result of spending £1.4 million, and tooling up for three years. Frames have sprung joints covered with flexible neoprene tubing; seats and backs are shock-resistant polypropylene, upholstered with polyurethane foam and covered in fabric. Numerous styles are available. *M:* w 57.5 × h 89.5–101 × d 65.5 × base diam 66cm (22¾ × 35¼–39¾ × 25¾ × 26in). *P:* from £360 as illustrated.

Interspace's VERTREBRA chairs

JARDINE LEISURE FURNITURE LTD
Aluminium 'R2' carver for garden rooms. In White only, it's from a selection of reproductions made from cast-iron originals. *M:* w 16 × h 33 × d 15in (40.5 × 84 × 38cm). *P:* £32. Also available without arms.

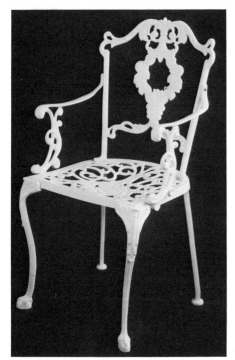

JAYCEE FURNITURE LTD
Solid oak corner seating. In Old English, Middleton or Antique oak finishes, it's part of the immense TUDOR range of sitting- and dining-room furniture. Backs feature authentically hand-carved panels. *M:* large bench w 127 × h 84 × d 56cm (50 × 33 × 22in), corner unit w 66 × h 84 × d 66cm (26 × 33 × 22in). *P:* £240, £138.

'Queen Anne' oak chairs upholstered in Fawn Dralon or tapestry print, frame finishes as for corner seating. *M:* both w 53.9 × h 109.3 × d 44.7cm (21⅛ × 43⅛ × 17⅝in). *P:* side chair from £116, carver from £130. Eight other styles include ladderbacks, wheelbacks and a smoker's bow chair.

JUST DESKS
Victorian swivel chair from the LONDON COLLECTION of reproduction study or library furniture. One of four classic styles, all upholstered in deep-buttoned leather in a choice of colours, it has reeded legs, brass studs. *M:* w 24 × h 34 × d 23in (61 × 86.5 × 58.5cm). *P:* £195. See also 'Desks'.

KINGSHALL FURNITURE LTD
Gorgeous, reproduction Georgian wavy-line ladderbacks, part of the KNIGHTSBRIDGE collection. Made from solid mahogany, they are beautifully hand-finished and upholstered. *M:* armchair w 25 × h 37 × d 18in (63.5 × 94 × 46cm), side chair w 22 × h 36 × d 18in (56 × 91.5 × 46cm). *P:* from £260, £215. See also *Dining Tables* ('Tables').

Just Desks' swivel chair

Kingshall's wavy-line ladderback

VINCENT LLOYD LTD
'Standhelp', an ergonomically designed perch that takes the strain out of long periods of standing. Obviously perfect for assembly lines, it would be equally at home in the kitchen. *M:* w 37 × h 100 × d 29cm (14½ × 39⅜ × 11⅜in). *P:* £75.

Vincent Lloyd's 'Standhelp' (left), 'Steifensand' (right)

The 'Steifensand' typist's chair (left, below) has an exclusive, variable backrest and seat angle adjustments, twin-wheel braking castors, and height adjustment. *M:* w 46 × h 88 × d 45 × base diam 56cm (18 × 34⅝ × 17¾ × 22in). *P:* £96. Complementary 'Executive' and stacking chairs are also available.

WILLIAM L MACLEAN LTD

'47/197', a Louis XV-style chair with graceful legs and splats in hand-carved, hand-polished in natural beech. This specialist firm will finish and upholster any of their reproductions to order. *M:* w 51 × h 93 × d 51cm (20 × 36⅝ × 20in). *P:* upon application.

William L Maclean's '47/197'

A sophisticated little Louis XVI side chair, '47/292', made from painted solid beech, hand-polished to an authentic finish, complements Maclean's lovely collection of French and Regency reproduction furniture. *M:* w 46 × h 87 × d 49cm (18 × 34½ × 19¼in). *P:* upon application. Natural or pastel-tinted wood is also available, and all furniture can be finished or painted to order, or simply hand-waxed. Chinese-style '47–314' has a complicated fretwork back and simulated bamboo legs. An unusual addition to this company's Chippendale-inspired range, it is also available with arms, and can be lacquered to order. *M:* w 54 × h 105 × d 49cm (21¼ × 41⅜ × 19¼in). *P:* upon application. A solid beech Louis XVI-style armchair,

William L Maclean's '47/292' (above), '47/314' (below)

'48/221' has padded arms and seat, a caned back and antiqued frame. *M:* w 58 × h 97 × d 65cm (22⅞ × 38⅛ × 25½in). *P:* upon application.

William L Maclean's '48/221'

Handsome, Oriental '48/514' is part of a gorgeous collection. It comes in Black lacquered beech, with a caned seat and spattered paintwork back. *M:* w 55 × h 104 × d 47cm (21⅝ × 41 × 18½in). *P:* upon application.

William L Maclean's '48/514'

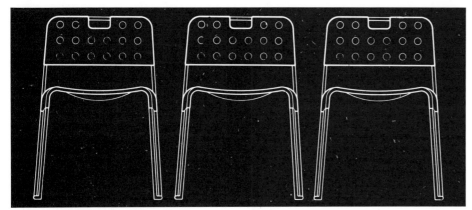
OMK's 'Stack S1'

OMK DESIGN LTD
'Stack S1', a High Tech stacking classic. The tubular frame is in polished chrome or epoxy; the pressed steel seat and back come in Green, Yellow, Red, Black, or White. *M:* w 21 × h 29 × d 20in (53.5 × 73.5 × 51cm). *P:* £32.

PEL LTD
Distinctive PLEXUS seating by Glickman and Hollington, one of four contract-quality ranges intended to re-establish this company — famous in the 1930s — in the forefront of contemporary design. Oval-section steel frames support unique sculptured upholstery moulded in one piece for maximum comfort. Pure wool covers come in seven colours. *M:* armchair w 64 × h 75 × d 70cm (25¹/₈ × 29¹/₂ × 27¹/₂in). *P:* £90.
'PPI-FR', a pyromaniac's nightmare. This

polypropylene shell chair, from a firm that specializes in contract furniture, is virtually fireproof. Terracotta only. *M:* as illustrated w 49.5 × h 82 ×d 51cm (19³/₈ × 32¹/₄ × 20in). *P:* £9.

PEL's 'PP1-FR'

T SAVEKER LTD
'V1254', a tip-up wooden seat with spring lifting action. *M:* diam 32cm (12⁵/₈in), d 5cm (2in) when tipped up. *P:* £8.

HENRY SERVENTI LTD
Stylish 'Togo' with a sprung chrome frame. The vinyl seat comes in a wide range of colours. *M:* w 51 × h 76 × d 56cm (20 × 30 × 22in). *P:* from £75.

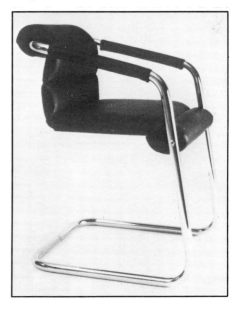

STUART INTERIORS
Classic Windsor chair with cabriole legs. Made from yew, it's just one example of fine workmanship from a Somerset-based firm that specializes in beautifully crafted 16th-

and early 17th-century reproduction furniture and woodwork. *M:* w 25 × h 40 × d 23in (63.5 × 101.5 × 58.5cm). *P:* £300.

FREDERICK TIBBENHAM LTD

Sturdy sensible 'C25' hall seat, the perfect solution to storage and seating problems. Like all furniture from these specialists in fine oak reproductions, it's finished in Stuart brown or Jacobean. *M:* w 36 × h 42 × d 20in (91.5 × 107 × 51cm). *P:* £275.

Tibbenham's 'C25'

Ornately carved and beautifully made 'C73' Stuart side chair and its companion 'C73A' armchair, in solid oak. Leather seats are finished with brass nail heads. *M:* 'C73' w 23 × h 46 × d 20in (58.5 × 117 × 51cm). *P:* £300. Five other similarly styled chairs are available.

Tibbenham's 'C73' (left), 'C73A' (right)

Traditional, ladderback 'C83' side chair and 'C83A' armchair, with authentic rush seats. *M:* 'C83' w 18½ × h 37 × d 15½in (47 × 94 × 39.5cm), 'C83A' w 21½ × 42 × d 16in (54.5 × 106.5 × 40.5cm). *P:* £100, £120. A more expensive, leather-seated version has plain horizontal slats.

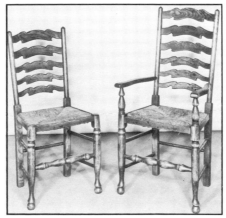

Tibbenham's 'C83' (left), 'C83A' (right)

WILLIAM TILLMAN LTD

Gorgeous, Regency-style 'Model RC'. In mahogany, with gracefully curved legs and back, it's typical of this company's high-quality reproductions. *M:* w 18½ × h 33½ × d 18½in (47 × 85 × 47cm). *P:* £180. A Hepplewhite-style dining chair, with a pierced back and upholstered seat, comes with or without arms.

TOGGLE MOULDINGS LTD

'TW3' swivel chair and 'TW5' stool with a PVC seat, in White, Red, Yellow, Light stone or Dark brown moulded glass-reinforced plastic. Special colours to order. *M:* 'TW3' w 47 × h 73 × d 47cm (18½ × 28¾ ×18½in), 'TW5' diam 40

× h 45cm (15¾ × 17¾in). *P:* £52, £30. Other pieces in this extensive range include a chair without the swivel base, stacking and dining chairs, tables and a high stool.

Toggle's 'TW3' (left), 'TW5' (right)

TRANNON MAKERS

'C1' recliner that folds flat or adjusts to one of three seating positions. From a selection of simple, hand-made furniture designed by David Colwell, it has a steam-bent, hand-turned ash frame finished with natural lacquer, or stained Red or Black; seat and back are made from naturally resilient rattan battens. *M:* w 24 × h 38 ×d 35in (61 × 96.5 × 89cm). *P:* £120. Also available with tweed upholstery for an extra £25.

Lightweight 'C2' folding chair, by David Colwell, with an English cowhide seat, and steam-bent, hand-turned ash frame and back in the same finishes as 'C1'; feet have Black rubber skids. Locked open with the turn of a threaded wooden knob, it folds to a depth of 9in (23cm) — and still stands upright — for storage. *M:* w 23 × h 29 × d 19in (58.5 × 73.5 × 48.5cm). *P:* £90.

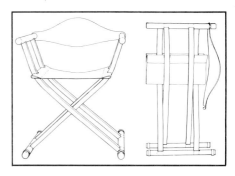

R TYZACK LTD

Mahogany '1013A' carver and '1012' side chair, two fine examples of the chairmaker's art, copied from Thomas Chippendale's original designs. Also available with straight legs, they can be upholstered in fabric or hide. *M:* '1013A' w 26 × h 39 × d 26in (66 × 99 × 66cm), '1012' w 22 × h 38 × d 23in (56 × 96.5 × 58.5cm). *P:* £450, £320. Other mahogany period chairs from these specialists in 18th- and 19th-century reproductions include a Hepplewhite-style lyre-back with pierced slats.

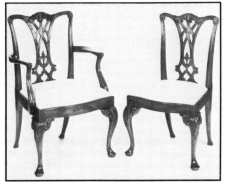

Tyzack's '1013A' (left), '1012' (right)

Regency-style '1015A' and '1014', an armchair and side chair, have sabre legs and side frames. Available in three mahogany finishes, each has an inlaid boxwood stripe on the back. *M:* '1015A' w 21 × h 34 × d 23in (53.5 × 86.5 × 58.5cm), '1014' w 18 × h 33 × d 21in (46 × 84 × 53.5cm). *P:* £160, £130. Other variations on the Regency theme are '5020' with hand-carved rope stays, '5024' with a showood back, and '5026' with seat and back fully upholstered. All with or without arms.

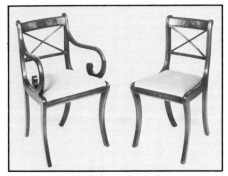

Tyzack's '1015A' (left), '1014' (right)

Sweet, small-buttoned '1032' in mahogany has turned back and front stretchers. *M:* w 19 × h 32 × d 20in (48.5 × 81.5 × 51cm). *P:* £270. A deep-buttoned version is available with arms and also as a two-seater sofa. These, and most pieces from this well-known firm, are covered in antiqued hide, or to order.

A deep-buttoned reproduction Victorian rocking chair, '1059' is beautifully made in solid mahogany, covered in hand-antiqued

Tyzack's '1032' (left), '1059' (right)

hide or the customer's choice of fabric. *M:* w 23 × h 38 × d 35in (58.5 × 96.5 × 89cm). *P:* hide £450. Also a matching footstool.

'1061', a simple, graceful reproduction of an early 19th-century Trafalgar chair, has 'sabre' front legs. Upholstered in leather or fabric, it comes with or without arms. *M:* w 21 × h 34 × d 22in (53.5 × 86.5 × 56cm). *P:* antiqued hide £260 as illustrated.

Tyzack's '1061' (left), 'Gainsborough' (right)

The classic 'Gainsborough' reproduction chair also comes with plain hide upholstery. *M:* w 26 × h 39 × d 25in (66 × 99 × 64cm). *P:* deep-buttoned £450. It can have a swivel base, and fully upholstered side arms. The 'Dorset' chair, a Victorian favourite, also comes with or without a swivel base.

WESTNOFA (LONDON) LTD

'Cox' by Ingmar Relling, possibly the ultimate 'director's chair'. Very comfortable, with a laminated beech frame, it's upholstered in leather, or natural canvas. *M:* w 78 × h 76 × d 61cm (30¾ × 30 × 24in). *P:* leather £180.

'Inka', a gorgeous recliner by Peter Opsvik, with leather or fabric armrests and upholstery. The solid beech frame is natural, or stained rosewood, teak or Black. *M:* w 67 × h 93 × d 78–105cm (26³⁄₈ × 36⁵⁄₈ × 30¾–41³⁄₈in). *P:* leather £310.

Westnofa's 'Inka'

'Junior', a simple beauty with leather or fabric upholstery and sling arms, natural or stained beech frame. This conference chair by Ingmar Relling would make a luxurious dining chair. *M:* w 62 × h 68 × d 66cm (24³⁄₈ × 26¾ × 26in). *P:* leather £200.

Westnofa's 'Junior'

'Tiara Two' by Ingmar Relling, with leather sling arms and upholstery in three qualities; also a matching footstool. *M:* w 69 × h 100 × d 85cm (27¹⁄₈ × 39³⁄₈ × 33½in). *P:* from £250. A low-backed version is available; and complementary coffee-tables.

Westnofa's 'Tiara Two'

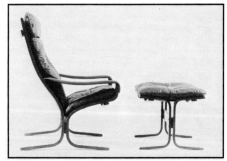

INTRODUCTION
Every household needs a desk for dealing with bills and correspondence.

Look for smooth-running drawers, a comfortable height, and sufficient storage space for supplies. The working surface should be a practical size, and covered in an appropriate material—easy-to-clean laminates are best for heavy use, while gold-tooled leather tops are for luxury only.

The desks in this section range from period reproductions, often updated with built-in filing drawers, to models that are part of ranges designed for office use.

If matching chairs or storage systems are described elsewhere in the book, we refer you to the relevant section.

BAKER, KNAPP & TUBBS
Very unusual partners' desk, '3640', from a firm that specializes in fine reproductions. Copied from a late Georgian original, it has a hand-coloured leather top hand-tooled in 24-ct gold. The two doors are fitted for files; drawer fronts are hinged doors. *M:* w 76 × h 30 × d 46in (193 × 76 × 116.5cm). *P:* £6,270.

Marvellously elegant hand-decorated reproduction of a William & Mary secretaire. Made from maple and finished in Red, Black and Gold lacquer, it's authentic down to its painted feet and oriental pulls. *M:* w 39 × h 89½ × d 19½in (99 × 227.5 × 49.5cm). *P:* £6,060.

BRITISH THORNTON LTD
Clever DOUBLE TOP desk/drawing table. A section of the flat work surface rotates to reveal the drawing board. *M:* w 120 × h 70 × d 60cm (47¼ × 27½ ×23⅝in). *P:* £155. Larger versions are available; also matching screens and tables.

CARSON OFFICE FURNITURE LTD
LINK 900 desk, part of a simply designed range of unit office furniture which could also be used in the home. All kinds of permutations include side panels in Brown laminate, front panels in Sandstone and tops veneered in anigré, a pale West African hardwood. Drawer fronts come in wood veneer, or Lime green, Sky blue, Orange, Red, Yellow, White or Sandstone laminate. Matching units include table tops, drawer units in a multitude of sizes, corner units, and bookcases and cupboard units with hinges or tambour shutter doors. *M:* desk w 170 × h 72 ×d 70cm (66⅞ × 28⅜× 27½in), low storage unit w 97.5 × h 72 × d 51cm (38 × 28 × 20in), both as illustrated. *P:* £260, £155.

G C FURNISHINGS LTD
Gorgeously simple 'ST 180' desk from the stunning INTERFUNCTION range. Intended for office use, it would be perfect in a modern home. Finishes are Grey-white or textured 'graphite' laminate; a rounded rim made from aluminium sections joins the top and sides. *M:* w 180 × h 75 × d 78cm (70⅞ × 29½ × 30¾in). *P:* Grey-white £150. Also other sizes and drawer arrangements. See also 'Storage'.

GEORGIAN FURNISHING CO
'A38' desk in solid wood. Quartered bamboo veneer adds interest to its simple lines. Drawer pulls and feet caps are solid brass. *M:* w 50 × h 30 × d 26in (127 × 76 × 66cm). *P:* £700.

Georgian's 'A38' (above); 'BC1' (below), see overleaf for description

Tiny beauty veneered in Indonesian walnut. 'BC1' has hand-carved cabriole legs, solid brass fittings. *M:* w 26 × h 37 × d 19in (66 × 94 × 48.5cm). *P:* £600.

CHARLES HAMMOND LTD
Five-drawer KINGSTON HALL desk or dressing table, part of Charles Hammond's large range of Chinese Chippendale inspired furniture. *M:* w 122 × h 74 × d 52cm (48 × 29¹/₈ × 20½in). *P:* £340. Other pieces include a three-drawer dressing or console table, a kidney-shaped dressing table, bedside tables, chest of drawers, and Chippendale-style coffee and lamp tables. All pieces can be stained, painted or decorated to order.

M & I J HARRISON LTD
Sturdy KNEEHOLE desk with nine separate drawers, nicely made in pine. The company specializes in pine furniture and kitchens. *M:* w 50 × h 32 × d 22in (127 × 81.5 × 56cm). *P:* £275.

JAYCEE FURNITURE LTD
Hand-carved and waxed secretaire from the huge TUDOR range of sitting- and dining-room furniture. In solid oak, it comes in Old English, Middleton and Antique oak finishes. *M:* w 99 × h 102 × d 47cm (39 × 40¹/₈ × 18½in). *P:* £560.

Kingshall's 'MD/1' desk, 'CH/1' chair

Jaycee's TUDOR secretaire

JUST DESKS
Writing desk from the LONDON COLLECTION of study furniture veneered in burr walnut, Honduras mahogany or bird's eye maple, with solid brass drawer pulls. The gilt-edged leather top comes in a choice of colours. *M:* w 48 × h 30 × d 24in (122 × 76 × 61cm), or to order. *P:* £225.

Just Desks' writing desk (above), pedestal desk (below)

A pedestal desk from the LONDON COLLECTION is veneered in burr walnut or lighter bird's eye maple. The top is covered in gilt-edged hide in a selection of colours. Drawers, all with locks, include one fitted for suspension files. Handles are solid brass. *M:* w 60 × h 30 × d 36in (152.5 × 76 × 91.5cm). *P:* £550. Smaller sizes are available; also a matching filing cabinet.
Contradicting its name, this specialist firm also supplies other period-style pieces for the well-equipped library or study. See also 'Chairs'.

KINGSHALL FURNITURE LTD
'MD/1' desk and 'CH/1' chair (opposite), in highest quality mahogany accented with solid brass fittings. Part of the MILITARY range, these hand-finished pieces are available with Green or Brown hide. *M:* desk w 48 × h 30 × d 28in (122 × 76 × 71cm), chair w 23 × h 37½ × d 20½in (58.5 × 95.5 × 52cm). *P:* £625, £205.

WILLIAM L MACLEAN LTD
'19/76' Louis XV writing desk from an extensive and beautiful range of French reproduction furniture. In solid beech, with hand-carved detail and reeded legs, it can be tinted to order. *M:* w 114 × h 75 × d 58cm (44⅞ × 29½ × 22⅞in). *P:* upon application.

Norman's 'M84' (below)

N NORMAN LTD
'M84' desk in mahogany (left, below); also available in yew. The gold-tooled leather top comes in Green, Gold, Black, Red, Pink, or Parchment. *M:* w 48 × h 30 × d 24in (122 × 76 × 61cm). *P:* £450. A more traditional pedestal desk is available.

PIRA LTD
Inexpensive 'Bacla Studio' writing desk in White, Red or Brown moulded plastic with a chromium-plated tubular steel frame. *M:* w 118 × h 73 × d 66cm (46½ × 28¾ × 26in). *P:* £89. '

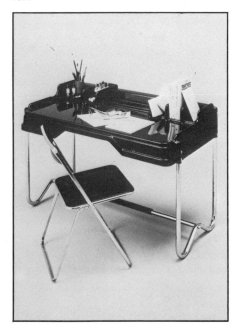

WILLIAM TILLMAN LTD
'Model LI', a fine Chippendale-style six-drawer partners' writing table in mahogany. The gilt-tooled leather top comes in Faded green, Dusky rose, and Tangerine. *M:* w 72 × h 30 × d 44in (183 × 76 × 111.5cm). *P:* £1,760. A simpler Hepplewhite style, also leather-topped, has slim, tapered legs.
'Model N' Hepplewhite-style partners' desk —

the ultimate in fine reproductions. In solid mahogany, it has a gilt-tooled leather top in the same shades as 'Model LI'. *M:* w 63 × h 30 × d 41in (160 × 76 × 104cm). *P:* £2,300.

Tillman's 'Model N'

R TYZACK LTD
Generous '2010' pedestal desk in mahogany with a gold-tooled leather top. *M:* w 66 × h 30 × d 39in (167.5 × 76 ×99cm). *P:* £1,100. Also three smaller versions.

WOOD BROS FURNITURE LTD
Fine OLD CHARM pedestal desk, from a huge range of Tudor reproductions in solid oak. Richly hand-carved with a silver-embossed leather top, it comes in light oak, Tudor brown or a special antique finish. An integral filing cabinet drawer can be fitted on the left or right. *M:* w 54 × h 31 × d 30in (137 × 78.5 × 76cm). *P:* £450, antique finish £510. Matching pieces include tables, a bookcase, individual wall units — and a grandfather clock.

INTRODUCTION

The choice of textile designs has widened immeasurably over the past ten years. Gone are the days when you were limited to classic floral patterns or sensible plain shades. Today the spectrum ranges from letters of the alphabet to zebras, small dots to landscapes, neat posies to bold florals, shiny glazed cotton chintzes to matt, nubbly wools, and from revivals of prints based on early Chinese patterns to Art Deco flamboyants.

Colour and design may be the most obvious considerations when selecting a furnishing fabric, but scale, texture and fibre content are equally important, and should influence your final decision.

Too large a pattern will dwarf a small room, so the size of the design repeat is critical; check this with the manufacturer. Similarly, combining more than one pattern – or the same pattern in more than one size – can lead to disaster unless they're carefully designed to co-ordinate with each other, and other furnishings. In addition, the textures need to work together.Ideally shop with paint and carpet swatches of the room in question, plus pieces of any other fabric or wallpaper in use.

Man-made fibres are generally less expensive than natural yarns, but develop dust-attracting properties. For easy maintenance, choose a fabric that combines both types of fibre. Cotton is normally the least expensive natural material, followed by linen and wool. Silk-based velvet and brocade cost the most. Printed fabrics are more expensive than plains, for obvious reasons, while special designer ranges, produced in relatively small quantities, are usually the dearest.

Most designs come in one of six widths – 36, 40, 45, 48, 54, 60in (90, 100, 115, 122, 136, 150cm) – printed or woven to ½–1in (1.2–2.5cm) of the selvage on each side.

Chair and sofa covers should be made from a durable fabric, in the best quality you can afford. Ideally, it should be dark or patterned, especially if the furniture will get lots of wear. Buy enough to make easy-to-clean, protective arm pads – important if you decide on an extravagantly pale shade.

Curtains can be made of virtually any fabric, from lightweight cheesecloth to the heaviest velvets. If money is tight, opt for an interesting (and inexpensive) sheer – preferably not nylon net – or blinds, and invest in curtains at a later date. Whatever material you select, buy extra for matching piping on cushions, and to repair small damages.

*For reasons of space, only overall manufactured widths are given; for design widths, check with the firm concerned.

See *Co-ordinates* ('Wall Coverings') for matching fabrics and wall coverings; see also 'Wall Coverings' for fabrics that can be applied to walls.

ANNA'S CHOICE

Lovely lace curtain panels, and pretty prints in pure cotton, from the mail order division of Margo International Fabrics. Nine lace patterns, all in beautiful Ecru (off-white), include 'Butterfly' with song birds and butterflies (*M:* h 200, 300 × w 120cm/78¾, 118, 47¼in, *P:* £11, £16). Most are supplied as panels, but 'Rosebud' and 'Cherubs' are sold by the metre (*M:* w 45in/115cm, *P:* m £3, £6).

Prints include 'Printemps', 'Fleur' and 'Petit-fleur' glazed chintzes in muted Gold/Green/Lilac or Dusty lilac/Rose/Sea green (*M:* w 45in/115cm, *P:* m £6).

Anna's 'Butterfly' (top), 'Printemps' (bottom)

GP & J BAKER LTD

Beautiful, traditional prints, many originated nearly a century ago by founders George Percival and James Baker. Linens, unions, twills, cottons and chintzes are printed with designs from diverse, often 18th-century, sources like original American documents, a Chinese vase in the Victoria & Albert Museum, an Indian fabric, a French child's bodice, and a Chinese silk robe in the Baker collection. Happily, prices are competitive. *P:* £6–£15. Some have matching wallpapers. 'Han' and 'Hankow', adaptations of an early 18th-century Chinese design, are illustrated with a plain co-ordinated linen weave. All come in Beige, Mid-

brown, Dark brown, Pale green, Blue green, and Light gold. *P:* m 'Hankow' £13.15, 'Han' £11.50.

Exciting matching plain glazed chintzes are available in 44 shades plus nine quilted versions—a bonus usually confined to expensive decorators. They include 'Nonesuch Palace' and 'Zerand', both slightly glazed, very distinctive, and absolutely beautiful. *P:* m from £8.50 for plain unquilted fabrics.

Other plains include Dupions in 99 colours, 14 with matching quilting and wall coverings (*P:* m from £6).

M: w 140cm (55in). See page 105 for 'Nonesuch Palace', 'Zerand' in colour.

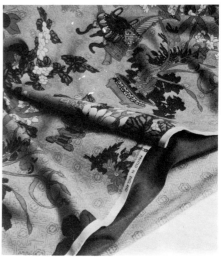

Baker's 'Hankow' (top) and 'Han' (bottom) with matching plain fabric (centre)

Wm H BENNETT & SONS LTD

Real silk fabrics—amazing value and quality at fantastically competitive prices. Six natural undyed textures are available: 'Pongee 4017', 'Shantung 4020', 'Tussah 1603' (*P:* m £1.75); 'Noil 5053' (*P:* m £2); 'Ya Kiang' in bleached Off-white, or Natural beige, twill effect (*P:* m £2.50, £2.95); and 'Satin 2050' (*P:* m £2.30). Also fine shirt stripes in various combinations (*P:* m £5.50).

Prints include '1905', sweet nosegays on Black, Pale pink or White (*P:* m £3.30), and more modern 'Habotai' on Apricot, Beige, Sky blue, Pale green or Pale grey (*P:* £3.10). 'Macclesfield' silk stripes, for really heavy-duty upholstery, comes in cool colourways (*P:* m £4.90).

Plain spun silk, silk chiffon and other variations are available, but stock varies so send for samples, or outline your requirements. Minimum order for each shade and quality is 3m; prices quoted are for cut lengths of 3m to 15m (considerable reductions for 22m to 45m). *M:* w 90cm (36in).

PRICES AND INFORMATION WERE CORRECT AT THE TIME OF GOING TO PRESS

Selection of silks from Bennett

BLOSSOM LTD

Softly springlike blossoms, hand-painted on heavy, glazed pure cotton. Three designs, all on White with Green leaves, are available: 'African Violet' in Yellow, Pink or Violet; 'Kathy's Carnation' in Apricot, Pink, Sky blue or Yellow; and 'Tea Rose' with Apricot, Sky blue or Yellow bunches. All are available with smaller scale co-ordinating fabrics. *M:* w 48in (122cm). *P:* m £11–£13. See page 105 for 'Tea Rose' in colour.

Left to right: Blossom's 'Kathy's Carnation', 'Tea Rose', small 'African Violet', small 'Tea Rose', 'African Violet'

BOUSSAC DISTRIBUTION (UK) LTD

Traditional, classical designs updated with modern colourways, from a leading French manufacturer, mainly in pure cotton. Very bold florals predominate, with some tiny country-style designs and a few up-to-the-minute patterns. A wonderful, large abstract-ed flame print comes in original colour combinations. Marvellously glazed and marbled 'Garde' is in Green/Cobalt blue/Purple, Dusty rose/Brown/Turquoise, Cobalt/Black/Red, Grey/Rose/Green, Forest green/Brown/Purple, and Navy/Purple/Grey (*P:* m £8).

Plain printed moirés abound, in Teal blue, Grey-white, Green, Soft brown, Burgundy, Rust, Navy, Light blue, Light grey, Beige, Peach, and Soft gold (*P:* m £5.50). Ever-classical 'Florentin' striped designs come in Sky blue/Grey, Gold/Brown, Rose/Burgundy, Grey/Peach, and Yellow/Orange gold, accented with thinner White stripes (*P:* m £6).

Contemporary motifs include 'Galapiat', a most beautiful and unusual nursery design; Sky blue drawings are on Off-white, between panels in a multitude of pleasing colours (*P:* m £5). 'Artifice' and 'Paillettes', also wonderfully modern, have scattered small shapes on Cream, Peach, Pale blue, Pale lilac or Pale green (*P:* m £5).

Boussac's showrooms are definitely worth a visit in your search for the perfect fabric. *M:* w 130–140cm (51¼–55in).

Left to right from top: Boussac's 'Florentin', 'Galapiat', 'Paillettes', 'Garde', 'Artifice'

CIEL (CHRISTOPHER LAWRENCE TEXTILES AND LIGHTING LTD)

Exclusive custom-printed cottons, many designs by John Stefanidis. Most are simple geometric and abstract prints in one or two

Selection of Ciel's fabrics

colours. CIEL has a wonderfully expressed obsession with large and small zig-zags, as well as hedgehogs, hippos and elephants. *M:* w 122cm (48in). *P:* m £8–13. Some matching tiles, and hand-painted tables, lamp bases and lampshades. See also 'Ceramic Tiles', 'Lighting', 'Tables'. See page 105 for 'Baskets', 'Foretide Bamboo', 'Small Grid' in colour.

COMBE MANOR FABRICS

Lovely high-quality fabrics, screen printed by hand. Drawn mostly from original 18th- and early 19th-century documents, motifs range from neat geometrics to medium-scale florals, several with bordered designs. Clean, fresh colours include Coral, Grass green, Light blue, Olive, and Rust, generally on White or Ecru (unbleached) cotton, but any colourway will be supplied on request. Designs can be printed on White or Ecru voile (avoiding the nasty net syndrome), or special fabrics to order. A glaze can be applied to any pattern. Coombe Manor will coat fabrics in plastic for practical tablecloths, blinds, etc, or back them with paper for wall coverings—and are pleased to help with design problems. *M:* w 120cm (47¼in). *P:* m £8–£12.

Selection of Combe Manor's prints

THE CONRAN SHOP LTD

Bright and beautiful, reasonably priced fabrics. Designs are mostly up to the minute, all on pure cotton. 'Crisalde' is in Grey/Sky/Charcoal or Peach/Aqua/Yellow, with co-ordinating 'Marmo' and 'Pluma' in the same colourways (*P:* all m £6.25). 'Everyday Little Dots' is Grey/Salmon, Bright red/Green/Blue, and Soft pink/Blue/Green (*P:* m £6.75). 'Lida' has very subtle colourations in Black/Beige/Mushroom, Olive/Aqua/Sea green, and Rose/

Sea green/Peach (*P:* m £7.25). Other designs include 'Birthday' with Pink, Blue or Yellow flowers and Bright green stems on White (*P:* m £6.75); 'Bristles' with brush strokes in Soft green or Bright pink on White (*P:* m £6.75); 'Fireworks' and 'Criss Cross' with a Pale green or Bright pink ground (*P:* m £6.75); and very traditional 'Fleur de Lys' in Dusty pink/Brown or Rose/Sea green/Sky, on Cream (*P:* £7.25). The Conran Shop will make fabrics into blinds, curtains, etc, to order.

Upholstery-weight plains include ribbed 'Bamboo' in Baby blue, Light peach or Nutmeg (*P:* m £7.50); 'Maltu-a-Maddu', a thicker rib in Off-white (*P:* m £8.75); and 'Alicante' and 'Alicante Angles', chic, Cream-on-Cream geometrics (*P:* m £8.20).
M: w 55in (140cm).
See page 105 for 'Everyday Little Dots', 'Lida', 'Fleur de Lys' in colour.

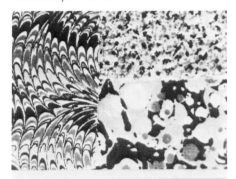

Left to right, from top: Conran's 'Pluma', 'Crisalde', 'Marmo', 'Alicante', 'Alicante Angles'

ELIZABETH EATON LTD
TISSUS D'HELLEMMES embroidered edgings to match chic checks, stripes, etc in pure cotton. What must be the sweetest border on the market is illustrated. *M:* border d 18cm (7¹⁄₈in), fabric w 150cm (60in). *P:* m border £5.50, fabric £10.50.

February Fabrics' 'Adam'

FEBRUARY FABRICS LTD
Fantastically flamboyant designs in upholstery-weight pure cotton, or linen union. 'Adam' is a floral extravaganza in Beige on Mid-brown, Soft green on Beige or Mushroom on Peach. 'Daisy' has White, Yellow-centred flowers with Green stems, on Beige, Chocolate or Grass green.

Other patterns include 'Paisley' in Grey-blue, and wonderfully complex 'Islam' with Blue or Brown predominating. 'Blackberry', a lovely country-style fabric, is in Tan/Rose/Beige, Salmon/Green/Purple, and Khaki/Salmon/Dark green, all on a trellis ground. 'Primrose' has bouquets in Salmon/Brown or Sea green/Pale gold on a basket-weave ground. Bold Art Nouveau 'Waterlily' is Rust/Salmon/Brown or Beige/Brown/Pink.
M: w 54in (136cm). *P:* m £6–£6.90. See page 105 for 'Blackberry' in colour.

FOURSQUARE DESIGNS
Essentially contemporary upholstery fabrics. Some are designed for contract purposes, so are perfect for the heaviest domestic use; most are competitively priced, unlike many mainly imported collections. 'Kuadrat' a very unusual but practical sheer in acrylic with silk slub texture is in Off-white, Beige, and Dark brown (*M:* w 120cm/47¼in, *P:* m £7). Flame-proof 'Beta' and 'Gamma', in 20% wool, 10% linen and 70% modacrylic, are stripes and plains (*M:* w 130cm/51¼in, *P:* m £11).

'Brighton', 'Holiday', 'Tivoli' and 'Moves' are seaside-inspired designs from Ole Kortzau, the famous Danish textile designer. All are in uncompromisingly bright colours, on 47% cotton and 53% viscose. 'Moves', a simple but beautiful stunner, comes in plain shades with White stripes, or White with coloured stripes, in Brown, Red, Bronze, Yellow, Beige, Lilac, Green, Black, Turquoise or Grey. *M:* all w 120cm (47¼in). *P:* m £7.

'Lise' and 'Lotte', in slightly sheened pure cotton satin, have similarly simple irregular stripes at 1in (2.5cm) intervals (which could co-ordinate with 'Moves'), plus a matching

Foursquare's designs by Ole Kortzau

check. Colours are Grass green, Gold, Orange, Beige, Brown, Grey, Blue, Navy, Red or Turquoise, on White. A jungly stripe, also on cotton satin, comes in White, Black or Yellow on White, or Beige, Orange or Dusky pink on darker same-coloured grounds. *M:* all w 120cm (47¼in). *P:* m £6.

Tough plains include pure woold 'Mikla' in gorgeous heathery tones with matching soft stripes and checks (*M:* w 150cm/60in, *P:* m £20). 'Bondal', a good, natural-looking cloth in 55% wool, 31% viscose and 14% polyester, comes in ten similar tones with co-ordinating stripes (*M:* w 130cm/51¼in, *P:* m £15). 'Inka' woollen velvet with cotton backing, one of the hardest wearing cloths on the market, is in 21 wonderful shades (*M:* w 130cm/51¼in, *P:* m £28).

Pure cotton PARALLEL LINES is for geometric fans: 'Roxy', 'Rockies' and 'Origami' are small-scale designs in Red, Yellow, Loden (green), Light blue or Grass green on White (*P:* m £7). 'Pistage', in pure woven cotton, comes in plain, softer seaside shades with striped borders (*P:* m £5). *M:* all w 120cm (47¼in).

Selection from Foursquare's PARALLEL LINES

A luscious range of neutrals (variations on Beige) features one raw silk and four self-textured cottons (*M:* 90cm/36in, *P:* m £7 silk, £5 cotton). At the other end of the scale, ANNE COLLIN's 1950s prints are hand-printed on White cotton in shades of Yellow, Pink, Blue, and Purple, with Black accents (*M:* w 130cm/51¼in, *P:* m £12).

'Tindale Fell' curtain fabric, made in England, is a delightful landscape pattern for anyone who fancies a glimpse of rolling hills at their windows. In pure cotton satin it comes in Brown, Teal blue, Grey, and Olive, with matching polyester sheers (*M:* w 150cm (60in). *P:* m £9.

See also *Co-ordinates* ('Wall Coverings').

Foursquare's 'Tindale Fell' (left)

SUSANNE GARRY LTD

Unique sheer fabrics, most with matching opaques. Part of the German INTERIUR range, the majority are woven from man-made fibres; 'Silberling', for example, is 62% polyester and 32% viscose (*M:* w 150cm/60in, *P:* m £22). Designs are mainly distinctively Oriental, with wheat sheaves, bull rushes, ferns and bonsai predominating. See also *Co-ordinates* ('Wall Coverings').

Susanne Garry's 'Siberling' from INTERIUR

GASKELL BROADLOOM CARPETS LTD

HARVEST range, to complement this company's extensive collection of natural wool carpets. The same heavy yarns, all moth-proofed and at least 89% wool, are crochet-knitted to form chunky fabrics. Perfect for curtains, they can also be stretched as room dividers. Four designs are available, each in six colourways from darkest Brown to creamy Beige. *M:* w 48in (122cm). *P:* from m £10.

GRAHAM & GREENE LTD

Three co-ordinating prints, each on a different scale, designed by Francis Ronaldson. 'Jungle', 'Paw' and 'Star' come in heavy and regular weight pure cotton, both suitable for upholstery. These lovelies are in Airforce blue, dark Forest green, Burnt red, Peach or Cream, overprinted on Cream or Peach. *M:* w 50in (127cm). *P:* m £5.75, £5.95.

Matching ready-made scatter cushions are available with or without piping; also knitted versions in the same three designs. See page 105 for 'Jungle', 'Paw', 'Star' in colour.

Left to right: Graham & Greene's 'Jungle', 'Paw', 'Star'

CHARLES HAMMOND LTD

Lovely country house chintzes and linen unions; also a wide selection of fabrics from all over the world, including silks, silk velvets, and hand-woven designs from France.

The following are pure cotton. 'Guelder Rose' is in Dark green/Green, Light green, Coral/Green, Coral, Blue, and Lime/Green, all on Brown, with two co-ordinating fabrics, a border and a plain trellis (*M:* w 120cm/47¼in). 'Ribbon and Trail Trellis' combines flowers and ribbons in Pink/Turquoise on Mushroom, Orange/Green on Cream, Turquoise/Apricot on Mustard, Turquoise/Apricot or Green/Coral on Stone, Apple green/Pink, Yellow/Turquoise, Pink/Olive, Orange/Yellow or Pink/Plum on White. 'Rosamund' is Blue/Green on Cream, Pink/Green on Dark brown, Coral/Green on Beige, and Pink/Green or Blue/Yellow on White (*M:* both w 137cm/54¼in). 'Liu', a glazed chintz comes in Blue/Green or Coral/Green on Pale green, and Coral/Tan on Beige; Blue/Pink on Beige is also available in linen union (*M:* w 130cm/51¼in). 'Zig-zag' is Pink/Blue on Cream, and Pink/Green on Pale turquoise (*M:* w 136cm/54in). *P:*

Left to right, from top: Charles Hammond's 'Guelder Rose', 'Guelder Trellis', 'Ribbon and Trail Trellis', 'Rosamund', 'Liu', 'Zig-zag'

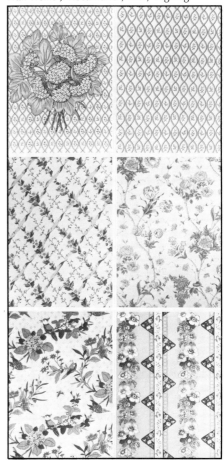

all m £8.50, except 'Guelder Rose' and co-ordinates £8.80.

Charles Hammond is the exclusive UK agent for very special—and very expensive—LEE JOFA hand-blocked chintzes and linens. Patterns are predominantly traditional, brought up to date with contemporary colours. The range includes Indian crewel embroideries, and some co-ordinating wallpapers.

Fabrics, many hung at full curtain length, are displayed in the firm's showroom together with a pleasing array of antiques, reproduction and upholstered furniture, lamps and light fittings, prints and cushions.

A good selection of machine and hand-made co-ordinating cords, tassels, etc, is available. The company also undertakes upholstery, and makes curtains in its own workshops.

NICHOLAS HASLAM LTD

Bright, airy cottons, designed by this talented interior decorator; patterns incorporate flowers and stripes. 'Hyacinthe' is in realistic Green, with light Lilac flowers on the palest Green, Lavender on Pale lavender, or Pea green with Pink flowers on White. M: w 56in (142cm). P: m £12.

H A S TEXTILES LTD

Gorgeously plush pure cotton printed velvets, suitable only for the grandest settings, in a myriad colours and designs. Also 'antique' velvets in 40 shades, ribbed in ten. M: w 122cm (48in). P: m £25–£35. Very high-quality printed brocades and damasks, chintzes and cotton satins, also in rich traditional patterns, are another speciality. '5149' has Rose or Turquoise predominating on Cream; '5256' is Paisley-style motifs in Grey, Coral or Turquoise and Mushroom on Light beige. M: both w 130cm (51¼in). P: from m £6, '5149', '5256', £8.50.

Panel designs, on pure cotton, are probably the most unusual. Wide fabrics, divided into squares, give a stylish but inexpensive patchwork quilt effect. Three very different designs are available: 'Manoir 50122' with sweet flower tops, hearts and stripes in Gold/Coral/Blue-grey/Soft green or Gold/Dusty rose/Dusty violet/Charcoal, both on White; more sophisticated 'Manoir 50533' in Wine, Blue, Loden (green), Brown or Charcoal, on Creams; and 'Samanda' in Salmon, Olive, White or Light Grey on Black. M: w 130cm (51¼in). P: m £5.50, £6.

Left to right, from top: H A S Textiles' 'Samanda', 'Manoir 50533, 50555, 50122'

HEAL & SON LTD

Fabrics for the 1980s from this well-known home furnishing store on Tottenham Court Road. Subtly coloured abstract and geometric shapes predominate, all on flame-retardant pure cotton. Heal's designs include 'Tako' by Dina Shagman-Goldstein in Brown/Mushroom, Blue/Pink or Green/Putty, on White; 'Fantasia' by Haydon Williams in Turquoise/Grey, Gold/Green or Orange/Brown, on White; P A Fawcett's 'Hawkweed' in Loden (green)/Olive, Yellow/Tan, Red/Loden or Tan/Brown, on Beige; cotton satin 'Mystique' with streaks of Sky blue, Salmon, Mushroom or Old gold; and 'Checkers' in Black/White, Cinnamon/Beige, Grey/Steel, Mushroom/Beige or Olive/Loden. M: w 122cm (48in). P: m £5, except 'Mystique' £9.25.

Heals also provide a curtain-making and upholstery service.

Left to right, from top: Heal's 'Tako', 'Fantasia', 'Mystique', 'Checkers'

HOMEWORKS LTD

Marvellous, essentially modern fabrics. French PLACIDE JOLIET, in wool and man-made fibre, has brightly coloured plains plus 33 co-ordinating designs, including large and small-scale checks and herringbones. 'Vezac', made from 55% polyester and 45% wool, is a deck chair stripe in wonderful colours: Bright green, Soft turquoise, Beige, Celadon green, Blue, Rose, Dusty pink, Dusty apricot, Gold, Bright yellow, and Red. Also co-ordinating checks and stripes. M: w 140cm (55in). P: m £9.

The American JACK LENOR LARSEN range consists of more than 95 designs in gorgeous textures and colours (M: various, P: m £13–£46).

WICKERWORK fabrics from California include bold, but nicely coloured pure cotton prints, with the emphasis on marvellously stylized geometrics; co-ordinating plains are available (M: w 130cm/51¼in, P: m £12–£18).

Selection from Homeworks' 'Crystal Palace' by JACK LENOR LARSEN

MARGO INTERNATIONAL FABRICS LTD

Mainly modern designs in hardwearing fibres, lovely colourways. Although supplied only to the trade through curtain makers, retailers, contract furnishers, etc, these fabrics are certainly worth chasing.

Plain 'Beaulieu', in 88% viscose and 12% flax, with a slightly nubbly surface, comes in Wine red, Soft cocoa, Rose, Sea blue, Soft turquoise, Pale olive, Rust orange, Copper yellow, Soft gold, Light tan, Mid-brown, and Beige-white (M: w 130cm/51¼in, P: m £10). 'Shiant', a complex geometrical design on pure cotton, is predominantly Rose/Pink, Gold/Primrose, Salmon/Shell, Sea green/Mint, Teal/Pale blue, Navy/Pale blue or Chocolate/Dusty rose (M: w 136cm/54in, P: m

£7). 'Canna' and 'Rhum' are small and large-scale versions of the same pattern, on a ribbed, linen-type mixture of 55% flax and 45% cotton. 'Canna' comes in Copper/Rust, Teal/Sky blue, Loden (green)/Light olive or Chocolate/Cocoa, all on Beige. *M:* both w 130cm (51¼in). *P:* both m £7.

Margo's 'Canna' (left), 'Rhum' (right)

'Genoa', a gorgeous Art Deco revival design, is in soft velour velvet-finish pure cotton, in Grey/Salmon and Navy/Olive on Brown, Tan/Salmon/Sand, and Rust/Copper/Forest (*M:* w 140cm/55in, *P:* m £20). 'Canute-Meikle' in 55% flax and 45% cotton, with Burnt red on ribbed Beige, is for anyone who favours the primitive or ethnic look (*M:* w 130cm/51¼in, *P:* m £7).
Barbed wire is the surprising—but effective—inspiration for co-ordinating 'Rhode Island' and 'Bantam', in pure cotton. Both come in Beige, Light blue, Light green, Dusty rose, and Salmon pink. *M:* w 136cm (54in). *P:* m £7. See page 105 for 'Shiant', 'Bantam' in colour.

Margo's 'Genoa' (top), 'Canute-Meikle' (bottom)

MARVIC TEXTILES LTD
Plain and printed moirés from the UK's largest specialist in these fabrics; also other exquisite Continental textiles. Manufacturers include Dubly, Europe's largest producer of velvet; Montessuy, whose excellent collection includes velours and velvets, plus piqués and suede fabrics; and Haas who make plain upholstery and curtain materials in a wide variety of textures.
Moirés are 'Moiré Bouquet' in 58% cotton and 42% rayon, printed with trails of flowers (*M:* w 128–130cm/50¼–51¼in, *P:* m £13); and 'Moiré Chanel' in 46 colours (*M:* w 128cm/50¼in, *P:* m £8.50). Both can be paper-backed. The more unusual French MISA range of exquisite striped designs, in hemp and rayon, is suitable for the finest upholstery (*M:* w 130cm/51¼in, *P:* m £12).
COLEGRAM COLLECTION pure acrylic piqués have chic geometrics in Off-white only (*M:* w 145cm/57in, *P:* m £35). In the Deschemaker PIC ET PIC range, five piqué designs in up to five colours incorporate both florals and geometrics; 'Cypris' is illustrated (*M:* w 130cm/51¼in, *P:* m £31). HORIZON chintzes, also from Deschemaker, come in six colourful Oriental patterns: 'Psyché', 'Chensu', 'Macao', 'Katmandou', and 'Percel Sérénité' which can be quilted (*M:* w 120–140cm/47¼–55in, *P:* m £17–£28). FRIVOLE, eight tapestry designs, is from the same manufacturer.
Dupion mixes include SHANTUNG BALI in

Marvic's 'Cypris' from the COLEGRAM COLLECTION

52% Dupion, 41% acetate, and 7% linen; available in a grand total of 101 colours, it can be paper-backed for walls, foambacked for upholstery or quilts (*M:* w 125cm/49¼in, *P:* m £11, paper-backed £13). The soft, linen-like TOILE collection, in 35% cotton and 65% Dupion, is in 83 shades (*M:* w 145cm/57in, *P:* m £12).

PRICES AND INFORMATION WERE CORRECT AT THE TIME OF GOING TO PRESS

Wondrous velvets include DUBLY STRIPE printed and embossed stripes in cotton and man-made fibres (*M:* w 130cm/51¼in, *P:* m £28); MONTESSUY waterproofed and crease-resistant viscose velours in 80 shades (*M:* w 130cm/51¼in, *P:* m £36); pure linen velvets in 50 colourways (*M:* w 140cm/55in, *P:* m £40); and 'antique' velvets, also in linen, in 30 colours (*M:* w 140cm/55in, *P:* m £27). More sensibly priced ranges are 100% Dralon OMEGA and CHOPIN, each in 12 shades (*M:* w 130cm/51¼in, *P:* m £8.50). Also BEDALE curtain and MARQUIS upholstery pure cotton velours, in 20 shades (*M:* w 125cm/49¼in, *P:* m £10.50, £13.50).
French and German printed velvets are real stunners. The former, in cotton and man-made fibres, have discreet dots in Olive, Forest, Rust, Beige, Ivory or Burgundy, on a dark ground (*M:* w 136cm/54in, *P:* m £15). RASCHEL features herringbone patterns, cross-hatches, zig-zags and prints, in terrific colours (*M:* w 140cm/155in, *P:* m £23).
German TOLMAC velvets, in 100% Dralon, come in 67 colours, plus embossed designs. A guide on how to match patterns to historical periods is available. Clients' own patterns can be embossed for an extra £2.50 a metre (minimum 50m). *M:* w 140cm (55in). *P:* m £25.
Marvic Textiles also stock plain chintzes in easy-care 50% cotton and 50% Dacron, in 38 colours (*M:* w 125cm/49¼in, *P:* m £4). Wonderful natural textiles include French 'Hoggar', a most beautiful, pure wool, woven chequerboard design (*M:* w 140cm/55⅛in, *P:* m £34); and a 100% silk upholstery fabric in 23 colours (*M:* w 127cm/50in, *P:* m £31). A mixture of 68% silk and 32% Dacron also comes in 23 shades (*M:* w 120cm/47¼in, *P:* m £13).
A selection of beautiful bargains in Whites and Beiges is intended for interior decorators and designers who want special shades dyed to order, but the fabrics are perfectly usable in their natural state. Pure cotton Indian repps come in nine White or Beige variations, and nine textures (*M:* w 122cm/48in, *P:* m £5–£7.50).
GAZELLE suede fabric is real textural luxury made from 36% cotton, 11% viscose and 53% acrylic, in 20 lovely shades.
Most fabrics, except the sheerest silks, can be paper-backed for an extra £2.20 a metre.

MOORHOUSE & REYNOLDS
Slightly outrageous, very stylish, colourfast cottons from a printing workshop with on-the-spot design and retailing services; screen printing is in public. Patterns include some pop, some punk, some wavy stripes—the workshop explores ideas and techniques that would be impossible in a more commercial environment.
Among the designs, all on White, are 'Home Sweet Home' in Turquoise green, Brown or Black (*P:* m £5.25); 'Spot The Ball' in Bright yellow, Black or Red (*P:* m £5.75); 'A Rose Is a Rose' in Magenta, Brown, Green or Turquoise

green (*P:* m £3.75): and 'Ancient and Modern' in Coppertone, Chocolate, Bright yellow or Turquoise green (*P:* m £7.25).
M: w 48in (122cm). *P:* m up to £9.

Above, Moorhouse & Reynolds' 'Home Sweet Home'; below, 'Spot The Ball' (left), 'Ancient and Modern' (right)

NICE IRMA'S FLOATING CARPET LTD
No floating carpets, but all sorts of pleasing, and inexpensive, pre-shrunk, colourfast fabrics. Hand-loomed Indian cottons sold as bed-covers but perfect for curtains, are printed with hand-carved wooden blocks. Designs include a Red butterfly on Yellow, a Khaki and Black medieval print, Green and Turquoise lotus blossoms, a Rose and Black floral pattern, and Blue-green/Wine flowers on Pale blue, or Brown/Red on Cream. Great value, they come in three sizes. *M:* w 72, 90× 108; 114×122in (183, 228.5×274.5; 289.5× 310cm). *P:* £6–£8.
'Raj' cottons, much more tribal and highly textured, are predominantly Cream/Beige/ Cream or Brown/Cream (*M:* w 36in/90cm, *P:* m £3). For incredible value 'Sanganere', also cotton, is a Provençal-style print of bright, small flowers on darkish grounds of Forest green, Wine red, Royal purple or Midnight blue (*M:* w 36in/90cm, *P:* m £2).
Nice Irma also has deepest Burgundy or Midnight blue rayon velvets scattered with exotic flowers (*M:* w 39in/99cm, *P:* m £4).

PRICES AND INFORMATION WERE CORRECT AT THE TIME OF GOING TO PRESS

Selection of Pallu & Lake's fabrics

THE OLLERTON HALL DECORATING SERVICE
Woven French tapestries for cushion covers, chair backs, etc. Five subtly coloured hunting scenes are available. *M:* 18×18in (46×46cm). *P:* £11, slight discount for quantity.

PALLU & LAKE FURNISHINGS LTD
Damasks, brocades, chintzes and all kinds of hand-prints from a specialist firm founded by Pierre Maisonneuve in 1927. The company is the exclusive agent for Casals (French),

Zumsteg (Swiss) and Brunschwig & Fils (American) fabrics, and numerous UK manu-facturers. Renowned for their prints, Pallu & Lake also have a very expensive and exclusive range of hand-woven silks and velvets. The company is an associate member of the Historic Housing Association.
At a more commercial level, the American CHARLESTON COLLECTION is based on designs from South Carolina. Stunning patterns, derived from Chinese and uniquely American motifs, are printed on glazed cotton. Available in original colours as well as contemporary combinations the range includes marvellous chintzes, flame patterns, light and heavy textures—and 60 plain chintzes. In the illustration the tablecloth is 'King Street Stripe' in Corals/Sea green/Sky blue on Off-white; the walls and curtains are 'Sunbriar', a Jacobean floral in the same colourways; and the dining chairs are uphol-stered in Louis XVI 'Argyll', a soft cotton weave, in Coral. Other tonalities are Celadon (light green), Beige, Pearl (pale blue-grey), Black, Indigo (rich navy), and Lacquer red. *M:* all w 54in (136cm). *P:* m £11.95. See page 105 for 'King Street Stripe' in colour.

PARKER KNOLL TEXTILES LTD
Overwhelming selection of unpatterned co-ordinates: cotton velour velvets in 81 colours, 40 textures and weights; 150 Dupions; and linen-like polyester in 40 shades.
Parker Knoll also stock some very unusual printed fabrics. Pure cotton CASADIMA, for upholstery, has 12 co-ordinating designs

based on Javanese wax prints, in beautiful colourways: Blue grey/Rust, Burgundy/Olive/Muted blue, Wine/Navy/Brown, Forest green/Sage/Brown, Wine/Aubergine, Wine/Dark grey/Light grey, all on Soft gold; Chocolate/Blue on Mushroom, Red/Green on Bronze, and Deep red/Soft gold and Wine/Teal blue/Aqua/Beige on Black. Three designs can be used as panels. *M:* w 120cm (47¼in), 'panel' designs w 90cm (36in). *P:* m £8.

Selection from Parker Knoll's CASADIMA collection

Beautiful glazed chintzes, in pure glazed cotton, include overtly Oriental 'Primrose Dragon', 'Primrose Symbol' and background 'Primula'. Colours are Black on Light grey, Rust on Dark beige, Violet on Blue-grey, and Orange-red on Pink. *M:* w 130cm (51¼in). *P:* m £7.50. 'Laburnum', sweeter but dramatic, has Rose, Sage or Cream flowers delicately scattered, or striped, on Black. Other combinations are Sage/Soft pink/Pale blues, Red/Pale green/Lilac/Baby blue, and Blue-grey/Ochre/Olive/Rust, all on Cream, Red/Pink/Lilac/Baby blue on Soft or Pale green, Soft blues on Pink, and Ochre/Olive/Rust on Blue-grey. This exquisite range is available machine-quilted. *M:* w 130cm (51¼cm). *P:* m £13. See page 105 for 'Primrose Dragon' in colour.

QUENBY PRINTS

Competitively priced pure cottons, suitable for the most down-to-earth bedsitter or the grandest country house, designed by Edith de Lisle and hand-printed in Lancashire. Seven of 14 stunning designs are: 'Petit Plumes', 'Mixed Stripe', 'Textured Stripe', 'Malenita', 'Single Plumes' and 'Solid Stripes'. Colours are pre-dominantly Shell pink, Lemon yellow, Bright peach, Blue, Stone beige, Ruby red or Grass green. 'Perricholi' is overprinted with Gold or Silver. *M:* w 47–48in (119.5–122cm). *P:* m £7–£8, 'Perricholi' £20. See page 105 for 'Perricholi' in colour.

Quenby's 'Malenita', Malenita Border' by Edith de Lisle

M R RECTOR LTD

Wide selection including coloured woven acrylics, ribbed and crushed velours, plain dyed satins, knitted Dralon, Dralon and pure cotton velvets (in 25 shades), and some flame-retardant fabrics. Unusual 'Countess Ribbed Velour', in 70% triacetate and 30% nylon, is in Light mink, Peacock blue, Aztec gold, Copper, Sage green, Mahogany or Claret red (*M:* w 120, 190cm/47¼, 74¾in, *P:* m £5, £7). DUCHESS CRUSHED VELOUR, in the same colours, has a similar sheen. *M:* w 120cm/47¼in, *P:* £6).
Most flame-retardant fabrics are tweedy modern stripes in popular Browns, Oranges or Olives, but they include a plain, only slightly textured, range in 21 colours including bright primaries. Made from Teklon and mod-acrylic, the fabrics' flame-retardant quality is unaffected by cleaning or washing. *M:* w 120cm (47¼in). *P:* m £6.50.

RUSSELL & CHAPPLE LTD

Tough cotton duck upholstery fabric. Various weights come in Orange, Yellow, Red, Royal, Navy, Brown, Black, and Khaki; waterproofed in Blue, and Green. *M:* w 34in (86cm). *P:* m from £1.30.
Really inexpensive curtaining includes thick White cotton yarns woven with Beige jute (*M:* w 36, 48, 54in/90, 122, 136cm, *P:* m £1.30–£1.90); and unbleached calico sheeting (*M:* w 36, 72in/90, 183cm, *P:* m 47p, £1.07). Hessian is available in three qualities, 21 colours (*M:* w 69cm/27in, *P:* m from 32p). Best of all, Fawn curtain lining is really inexpensive (*M:* w 48in/122cm, *P:* m 92p).
Russell & Chapple also stocks stage cloths, boat covers, and primed and unprimed canvas, in its olde-worlde premises.

IAN SANDERSON TEXTILES LTD

Patterned and plain fabrics, plus small-scale co-ordinates. Plains include 'Moresque' heavyweight moirés in 26 shades (*M:* w 130cm/51¼in, *P:* m £8); and tough linen-weave 'Thor', 85% viscose and 15% linen, in 27 shades (*M:* w 130cm/51¼in, *P:* m £10). Co-ordinating 'Jasper', in 30% rayon, 13% linen and 54% cotton, has four floral borders (*M:* w 120cm/47¼in, *P:* m £5).
Probably the most unusual and useful range, pure cotton PREMIER, woven in England, is stunningly simple. Four patterns and a matching plain are available in each colourway. Colours are Lime green/White, Peach/White, Beige/White, Beige/Pale blue, Red/Royal blue, Royal blue/Lime green, Royal blue/White, Orange/Beige, and Pale blue/White. *M:* w 136cm (54in). *P:* yd £12.

Selection from Ian Sanderson's PREMIER range

MICHAEL SZELL LTD

Distinctive fabrics with dramatic, mainly large-scale motifs for grand settings: paisley designs, grasses, pineapples, elephants, etc. Although Michael Szell mainly supplies leading interior decorators, he is happy to design for and/or sell to private customers. All fabrics are printed to order, but large samples are displayed in his showroom.
Patterns can be applied to cotton, voile, velvet, moiré or raw silk, in colours specified by the client. 'Maytime', 'Ananas', 'Windsor' and 'Perseus' are just four examples.
M: to order. *P:* m from £10 cotton to £25 silk.

From top: Michael Szell's 'Maytime', 'Ananas', 'Windsor', 'Perseus'

TARIAN DESIGN LTD

Highly individual fabrics with the emphasis on bold, modern design, first launched in 1977. Geometric and abstract plant motifs predominate. Ten prints on shrink-resistant, pure cotton include 'Assam' in Grey, Green or Pink, and 'Checkmate' by Jennifer Howard in Greens, Lilac sand, Dusty pinks or Apricots (*M*: w 122cm/48in, *P*: m £7.50). All can be treated with a flame-retardant finish.

Some cottons, and many other fabrics, have matching sheers—a very unusual feature. Generally in natural and man-made fibres, they come with an overall raw silk effect, White-on-White patterns, or subtle woven designs.

Luxurious printed velours, in pure cotton, come in four designs, primarily in neutral colours (*M*: w 122cm/48in, *P*: m £25).

Tarian's 'Assam' (left), 'Checkmate' (right)

TISSUNIQUE LTD

Exquisite, but expensive, French and Swiss textiles. The PIERRE FREY range includes marvellous, sensible and practical fabrics in pure cotton: classical ticking stripes in 25 colours on traditional White; gingham checks and coordinating plains in seven shades: and plaids and checks (*M*: w 130–140cm/51¼–55in, *P*: m £14–£18). Tough but subtle 'Amélie', in 64% cotton and 36% viscose with little woven spots, is in 24 soft tones including White and four Beiges (*M*: w 130cm/51¼in, *P*: m £14). Pure cotton 'Gordes' is for people who like the look of needlework; perfect for covering chair seats where the real thing would be prohibitively expensive, it comes in six plain shades (*M*: w 128cm/50¼in, *P*: m £26).

Great PIERRE PATIFET tapestry weaves are perfect for heavy-duty upholstery. Closely woven, but not inexpensive, designs include several big stripes, in 100% viscose; also 'Rhapsodie' with minuscule checks in nine colour combinations, 'Seductur' with woven diagonals, 'Furioso' with chevrons, and 'Chicome' with Op Art checks, all in 51% viscose and 49% cotton; plus ten White-on-White or Beige-on-Beige patterns (*P*: all m £20). Quilted-effect pure cottons in 12 delightful designs feature boats, birds, florals, dots, stripes and cherries, have raised patterns on White (*P*: m £36).

LES GRANDS IMPRESSIONISTES large-scale traditional chintzes come in 24 designs, some glazed, some unglazed, all lovely (*P*: m £25–£30). *M*: all w 140cm (55in).

PRELLE & CIE's elegant, and fantastically expensive, chintzes, brocades, and tapestry designs are undoubtedly Tissunique's most exclusive fabrics. One of them, 'Patron', has a classical central motif on a needlepoint ground—the perfect answer to the problem of renewing dining-chair seats. In 50% acrylic, 38% viscose and 12% linen, it comes in Gold on Red, Dark blue, Beige, Gold or Green (*M*: w 64cm/25in, *P*: m £40). Expensive, but a metre would refurbish two seats.

MANUEL CANOVAS fabrics are equally inspiring. They include wonderful tapestry weaves with geometric and abstract floral designs, plus nubbly, thick, soft combinations of wool and cotton, and wool and acrylic, in rich shades like Wine red, Deep navy, Forest

green, Dark brown, and Beige/Ivory (*M*: w 130cm/51¼in, *P*: m £50–60).

'Ceres', a good upholstery fabric in 56% cotton and 44% viscose, with textured criss-crossing diagonals, comes in an amazing array of 68 colours (*P*: m £12). 'Toile Indian', a silky slub in 100% viscose, is available in 120 shades (*P*: m £15). *M*: both w 130in (51¼in).

WATTS & CO LTD

Unique collection of nine Victorian designs, beautifully woven in pure silk, or wool and cotton. Inspired by architect Augustus Pugin, their colours conform as closely as possible to the original colourways. Fabrics can be specially woven, and have been used in restoration schemes throughout the country. *M*: w 48in (122cm). *P*: upon application. See also 'Wall Coverings'.

Selection of fabrics (right):
Pallu & Lake's 'King Street Stripe' (1)
Graham & Greene's 'Jungle' (2), 'Paw' (3), 'Star' (4)
Quenby's 'Perricholi' (5)
Fabric Shop's 'Springtime' (6)
Conran's 'Fleur de Lys' (7), 'Lida' (8)
Fabric Shop's 'Chelsea Green' (9)
Parker Knoll's 'Primrose Dragon' (10)
Baker's 'Nonesuch Palace' (11)
Fabric Shop's 'Diamond Trellis' (12)
Ciel's 'Foretide Bamboo' (13), 'Baskets' (14)
Tamesa's 'Albany' (15), 'Bamboo' (16)
Blossom's 'Tea Rose' (17)
February Fabrics' 'Blackberry' (18)
Baker's 'Zerand' (19)
Margo International's 'Bantam' (20)
Ciel's 'Small Grid' (21)
Conran's 'Everyday Little Dots' (22)
Margo International's 'Shiant' (23)

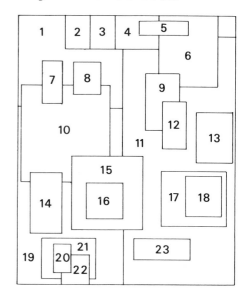

INTRODUCTION

Every home should have one. It doesn't matter whether a fireplace is traditional or modern, original or reproduction.

An open fire can be economical in the country where wood is free, or cheap; but it will never be the world's most efficient heating method – too much heat goes up the chimney. However, many fireplaces can be adapted to take a back boiler which will heat domestic water, and warm radiators throughout the house.

Two words of warning. First, installing a new fireplace is a job for a reliable expert. Shoddy workmanship or inappropiate materials can result in chimneys or floors catching fire. Second, always get the chimney swept and, ideally, relined before using re-opened fireplace – caked soot is a major hazard.

Fireplace Accessories includes grates, sometimes called fire baskets (usually if they burn wood) or dog grates; fire irons or companion sets (tongs, poker and shovel); fire dogs or andirons to support burning wood on the hearth; and wood baskets.

Mantels and Surrounds deals with complete fireplaces, and/or their constituent parts: the decorative mantel; the protective surround in a fireproof material like cast iron, marble, stone or tiles (sometimes with an interlining in one of these materials); and the hearth or base. See also 'Stoves and Kitchen Ranges'.

FIREPLACE ACCESSORIES

ACQUISITIONS (FIREPLACES) LTD

Antique and reproduction grates and accessories. Stock varies, but the cast-iron 'Adam-style Shell Grate' is always available. Designed to complement the 'Peace and Plenty' surround, it can be fitted with a coal-effect gas fire. *P:* £295. Other items include antique fire baskets, and the 'Mildmay' reproduction dog grate (*P:* £210). Original brass or cast-iron fenders, coal buckets, fire irons, trivets, fire guards, and companion sets are always available. See *Mantels and Surrounds* for 'Peace and Plenty' illustration.

ARCHITECTURAL HERITAGE OF CHELTENHAM

Antique grates. A good range of accessories including fire dogs, fire baskets and fire backs, fenders and brassware is usually also available from these architectural salvage specialists. *P:* upon application.

A BELL & CO LTD

Very good range of accessories including brass fire dogs, and brass and wrought-iron companion sets and fire irons. Fire guards are 'SG4' in plain wire mesh, 'SG5' with triangular sides, and 'SG3' in plain wire mesh on two small legs,

Left: Selection from Machinka (see 'Wall Coverings')

decorated with two horizontal brass strips (*P:* £25, £10, £27). There are also two brass coal scuttles: 'A12' shaped like a helmet, and 'A13' a plain scoop (*P:* £30, £27).

Fire baskets come in 'French', 'Adam', 'Regency', and 'Georgian' styles, in armour bright with brass details. *P:* upon application. Two period dog grates are available: '3526' has a one-piece cast-iron canopy, buffed to a semi-armour bright finish to match the front of the grate; '3527' comes with a sheet-metal canopy covered in brass, armour bright sides and brass feet. *P:* upon application. Plain bar grates suitable for logs, and canopy dog grates, are available in cast iron, sheet metal, and brass.

Wrought-iron companion sets include 'BC21' and 'BC31/4' with brass handles (*P:* £33, £28). 'A10' fire irons have urn-shaped handles, 'A11' are fancier, both in brass (*P:* £33, £30).

Fire dogs include unusual 'Tudor' in armour antiqued bright finish, and 'Cherub' in fine cast iron with a sprayed finish (*P:* upon application). 'Urn-top' and 'Splay leg' are in brass (*P:* £30, £28).

CARVED PINE MANTELPIECES LTD

More than 25 grates. Suitable for open fires, they can be converted for electricity or gas, with mock coal or logs, at extra cost. *P:* £70–£450. Other accessories include a wide range of antique fenders, fire irons, fire dogs and fire screens. More mundane items such as reed asbestos or iron linings, marble surrounds and hearths, and brass edgings are available in various sizes. Also fine mesh fire curtains (*P:* £50 up to w 24in/61cm including tensioned runner; then £1 per 1 in/2.5cm).

Selection of Bell's accessories

CLASSIC GARDEN FURNITURE LTD

'Adam' is the more unusual of the two fire backs available. Inspired by the designs of Robert Adam it has three panels decorated with Greek urns and leaf scrolls. 'C76' is a more ordinary reeded design. *M:* both w 30× h 36in (76×91.5cm) plus side panels w 16, 18in (41.5, 46cm). *P:* 'Adam' £135; 'C76' £100. Other smaller fire backs are mainly 17th-century designs decorated with Tudor roses, lions and unicorns, crowns, crests, and shields. Sizes vary. *P:* £30–£75.

Classic Garden Furniture's 'French' grate, 'Adam' fire back

Distinctive fire dogs include 'Wellington', 'Regency', 'Brass Regency', 'Brass Colonial', 'Tudor', 'Warwick', and 'Adam Sunflower' (*P:* £40–£50).

Fire baskets are available in a Georgian style in polished steel and brass with a solid back; also in 'Spanish', 'Fleur-de-lis', 'Cromwell', and 'Castle' which incorporates an ornamental fire basket. The 'Adam' dog grate comes with a firebrick back and is finished in polished iron or brass (P: iron £125, brass £150). The 'French' grate in black, or polished iron, is illustrated with 'Adam Sunflower' fire dogs and an ornamental panel with a leaf pattern above the back (P: black £115, polished £135). Fire irons are in black wrought iron, brass, polished brass, and with rosewood handles (P: £30).

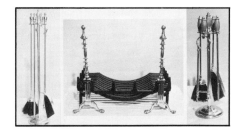

Classic Garden Furniture's 'Adam' grate with 'Adam Sunflower' fire irons (top), 'Wellington' fire dogs (above); below, left to right, 'Urn' fire irons, brass 'Colonial' fire dogs, brass and rosewood fire irons

DAVEY & JORDAN

FIRECRAFT hand-made, wrought-iron accessories. They include 13 fire baskets, some of which incorporate fire dogs. Designs are generally plain, but the corners of some models are topped with decorative balls, points, clubs, and open spirals. 'FB6' and 'FB10' have solid fire backs, while 'Fireset' incorporates an ash tray under the front feet (P: £60, £75, £30). Made-to-order canopies come

in copper, and matt black steel. Brass fire screens come in three styles, or to order. Two companion sets have unusual open spiral decoration on the handles. A black set, and a burnished one, both on stands, are also available. *P: £95, £30, £95.*

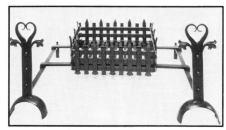

Davey & Jordan's 'FB5' duck-egg basket (top), 'FB7' grate (bottom)

INTEROVEN LTD

Grates and other accessories from a cast- and wrought-iron specialist. Grates come in 'French', 'Castle', 'Adam', 'Apollo', 'Regency', and 'Chestnut' styles (P: £36–£98). Six fire baskets include 'Buckingham' and 'Hertford' in hand-finished wrought iron (P: £46–£53, £29–£35). Fire dog styles are 'Wellington', 'Regency', and 'Ball' (P: pair £35–£40). Dog grates include 'Stourbridge' in polished or matt black cast iron (P: £45–£68).

Left to right, top to bottom: Interoven's 'Chestnut', 'Regency', 'Adam', 'Apollo'

PETIT ROQUE LTD

Possibly the widest selection of grates on the market: 12 for burning logs, 30 for coal or logs. Designs range from classical to modern, and come in metals including wrought iron and bright polished steel with brass trim. 'Gothic', 'Adam', and 'Georgian' fire dogs are available in matt black, and polished bright iron, 'Ball' and 'Lion' andirons in brass. There are three fire backs in cast iron, and five companion sets in polished brass, and black wrought iron. P: upon application. The 'SM576' fire screen with central arched panel is the most elegant in the range (P: £70).
The 'Log-a-Hoop' holds cut logs and two fire irons while 'Log Rest 559' is probably the most unusual accessory—a semi-circular curve of polished brass. A brass-strapped wooden tub is also available for storing small logs at the fireside. P: £30.
Canopies come in polished brass or copper, with a slightly beaten, plain or rustic finish, and in stainless steel. Alternatively, they're available in Black or White enamel. Easily installed smoke hoods, in plain brass, copper, and stainless steel come in four shapes.
Finally, the CONVECT-O-HEATER woodburner is probably Petit Roque's most unusual product. A small fan blows room air into the burner through hollow tubes below, above, and behind the fire, then expels the heated air back into the room, overcoming fireplace 'draw' and boosting warmth. The CONVECT-O-HEATER can be installed in any normal fireplace opening. P: £75.

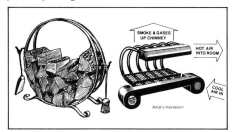

Petit Roque's 'Log-a-Hoop' (left), CONVECT-O-HEATER (right)

PURITAN FORGE LTD

Large range of accessories, including the exclusive 'Instamount' fire curtain. Drawn across the fireplace opening, it gives protection against sparks and falling logs—with no loss of heat. Made of 20-gauge black mesh, with manual pulls, it opens and closes on a glide rod held in position by spring tension. A decorative top bar in satin black or polished brass disguises the rod which is custom-made to fit square or arched fireplaces. (A kerb bar to match the top bar is available.) Up to 24in (61cm) the curtain draws from one side only; over this width two curtains are provided and draw from the centre. P: upon application.
Fire baskets come in nine designs including 'Georgian' and 'Chestnut', both suitable for period mantels. 'Castle' and 'Fleur de Lys' in-

corporate fire backs. *P:* £25–£60.
Three fire dogs are also available: 'Tudor' in polished cast iron, 'Warwick' in polished iron and brass, and 'FDC3' in brass (*P:* pair £45).

Puritan Forge's 'Instamount' fire curtain

RENZLAND & CO

Well-made, custom-built wrought-iron accessories, including six fire baskets, six companion sets and log and coal trays. The 'CS/31/4' companion set is available with stainless steel or teak handles (*P:* £20). Renzland specialize in metalwork for domestic and commercial use, but will also undertake shot blasting at their works or on site, cleaning brickwork, timber, metal, etc, painting, repairs, and welding. Stove enamelling at their factory.

Renzland's 'CS/31/4' companion set, and fire basket

SALEMINK LTD

Exquisite hand-made brass and copper fireside accessories. All pieces are beautifully made, carefully finished and generously proportioned. No fire dogs or andirons, but there's a total of 35 log or coal-holders, including nine copper coal buckets with Blue-and-White china handles, plus numerous other styles in copper and brass, with or without legs. If you're after the pleasing gleam of either metal, be sure to take a look at their wares. *P:* brass trough with china handles £6–£12, lion's head pot with legs £22–£45.

JAMES SMELLIE LTD

Canopies in hand-hammered copper or brass, plain or hand-hammered stainless steel, and steel finished black. Only the highest quality heavy-gauge metal is used. There are four basic shapes: 'Westbury', 'Stratton', 'Cromwell', and 'Monmouth', all designed to fit above a dog grate in an open fireplace and lined in front with asbestos and sheet steel. All are made to order. *P:* from £65. Three made-to-order cooker hoods are available.
14 fire baskets include, unusually, a number of reproductions from genuine old patterns. Most are sold with built-in fire dogs. '3979' has a tip-up grate for clearing ash (*P:* £101). Two decorative reproduction 17th-century fire backs are also stocked (*P:* £47, £64).

Smellie's '3979' fire basket

MANTELS AND SURROUNDS

ACQUISITIONS (FIREPLACES) LTD

Tempting original and reproduction fire-places. Originals range from Early Victorian to Art Nouveau, and are highly decorative, especially the Art Nouveau cast-iron examples with hand-painted tiled inserts. Edwardian pine surrounds with complementary cast-iron inserts, often tiled, are also available, plus exclusive reproduction mantels, understandably less expensive, made with moulds taken from original castings. 'Peace and Plenty', illustrated, features the Greek goddess of the harvest on each side (*P:* £595). 'Serpentine' (*P:* £585), 'Adam-style shell grate (*P:* £255), and 'Regency' style (*P:* £575) mantels and sur-rounds are also available. Reproductions can be in burnished cast metal or painted.

Acquisition's 'Peace and Plenty' fireplace and 'Adam'-style grate

AINSTY FACTORING CO LTD

Good selection of fireplaces from a firm that's specialized in slabbing since 1936. The model illustrated combines stone and slate. *P:* £130.

ARCHITECTURAL HERITAGE OF CHELTENHAM

Fireplaces from a conservation-minded firm that specializes in architectural salvage. Their ever-changing stock sometimes includes models with ornate wood carvings; also English and French marble mantels. *P:* carved wood, £700–£2,000, marble £300–£1,500.

Architectural Heritage's carved wood surround

ARISTOCAST LTD

Fibreglass mantels, with real Continental marble surrounds in Beige, Green, or Black. All designs are taken from original period mantels while two, the 'Kensington' and 'Knightsbridge', can be made to measure. Available in one piece for all types of fires, or with gas or electric entry points. *P:* mantel £99, marble surround and hearth £230 ('Bayswater', illustrated, is the most inexpensive).

Aristocast's 'Bayswater' fireplace

A BELL & CO LTD

Extensive range of mantels and surrounds combining polished marble, slate and other stones. Also marble, whitewood, and natural pine reproductions. Simple hole-in-the-wall fireplaces (also made to measure) are faced in stainless steel, copper, or bronze. Polished marbles for hearths and facings can be sup-plied in White, Rose, Grey, Grey-Green, Dark green, Dark beige, Dark red, and Black. All made to measure. *P:* upon application.

PRICES AND INFORMATION WERE CORRECT AT THE TIME OF GOING TO PRESS

There are also two attractive suspended, metal fireplaces. The PICO-BELL FIRE, an angular sheet-metal appliance, is attached to the wall by only two fixing bolts (*P:* from £285). The PORT-A-BELL FIRE is designed as an outside barbecue, but works well as a free-standing fireplace, on a superimposed hearth. Bells also have a wide selection of accessories and a very comprehensive range of cleaning and sealing compounds. See also 'Useful Products'.

Bell's PORT-A-BELL FIRE

T F BUCKLE (LONDON) LTD

Pine reproduction mantels, and a much more extensive collection of antique wood, stone, and marble mantels (often in Louis XV style). Stock varies but fire backs, grates, fenders, spark guards and fire irons are normally avail-able. *P:* wood from £100, marble from £400.

ROSEMARY CAMDEN

'Marble' fireplaces, painted by an ex-portrait painter who trained and exhibited extensively

Marble fireplace by Rosemary Camden

in her former capacity. Rosemary Camden can marbleize any substance—wood, stone, metal, even marble itself. A great way to get a 'marble' fireplace without ripping out the old one. *And* it's considerably cheaper than the real thing. *P:* upon application.

CANLIN DEVELOPMENTS

Two very unusual products. 'Cameo', a real problem-solver, is a gracefully arched cast-iron surround incorporating a grate and shell-shaped firebasket; it can be recessed into a wall or fitted under a mantel (*P:* £380).
'Cog' is completely different—an outstandingly contemporary built-in fireplace with polished alloy facets and sculptural appeal (*P:* from £460).

Canlin's 'Cameo' grate (above), and 'Cog' (below)

CARVED PINE MANTELPIECES LTD

More than 40 mantels in Russian pine, suitably coloured and waxed. There's a varied selection of beautiful designs depicting urns, flowers, festoons, etc. Also some elaborately carved models including 'Pyrton', a most ornate piece (*P:* £700). All designs can be made to measure. Marble slips, surrounds and hearths come in a good choice of colourations. A wide range of antique marble mantelpieces is normally available; also accessories.

Carved Pine's 'Pyrton' mantel

CHESTER METAL CO LTD

Copper, stainless steel, brass, and/or aluminium fireplaces from a specialist firm that prides itself on its made-to-order service. Illustrated are a wall sculpture fireplace in mirror-bright stainless steel (*P:* £500); and stunning brass canopy, surround and fender, beautifully crafted and fitted into a period mantel (*P:* £300). Noble efforts! All fireplaces are installed by Chester Metal.

Chester Metal's brass fireplace

Chester Metal's wall sculpture fireplace

DELABOLE SLATE CO LTD

Custom-built fireplaces in lovely, natural slate. The stone is supplied from Delabole's own quarry and cut to order. *P:* upon application.

EMSWORTH FIREPLACES

Large selection of period pine mantels (supplied primed White) with polished marble surrounds. Modern 'patchwork' or slabbed fireplaces, wood-burning stoves, and a few hole-in-the-wall designs are also available, plus ceramic tile mantels reminiscent of the late 1940s, all made to order. Brass, copper, and stainless steel canopies come in four styles. Free delivery to many counties. Numerous wrought-iron and cast-iron accessories are also available. *P:* upon application.

PRICES AND INFORMATION WERE CORRECT AT THE TIME OF GOING TO PRESS

FEATURE FIRES LTD

Specially commissioned fireplaces that suit clients' specifications, decor and requirements, from a firm that specializes in their design, supply and fitting. In timber and/or sheet metal, all fireplaces come fully fitted or in do-it-yourself kit form. Quotations are accompanied by a sketch. *P:* upon application.

GALLEON-CLAYGATE LTD

Huge range of reproduction and modern surrounds in polished or riven marble, sandfaced or smooth briquettes, ceramic tiles, slate, quartzite, etc. Mantels come in hardwood, and fibreglass. There are over 100 surrounds, or they can be made to order. Fire baskets and built-in fire screens are also available. *P:* upon application.

HART OF KNIGHTSBRIDGE

Carved pine mantels, some very imposing and ornate with a great deal of carved detail. All come in natural, waxed, or White finish. 'Kenwood', 'Louis', 'Canterbury', 'Clovelly', 'Bradwell', and 'Melton' are some of the best designs from these specialists. Made-to-measure fireplaces can be supplied, and Hart will install matching panelling. Eight grates suitable for electric fireplaces are available. *P:* £150–£700 including marble surround and hearth. See also 'Architectural Ornaments'.

Right: Jackson's 'Louis XVI-1780' (top), 18th-century 'Adam' (centre), 19th-century 'Regency' (bottom) fireplaces

GEORGE JACKSON

Exact reproductions of antique fireplaces: four 17th-century, four early 18th-century, seven 18th-century Adam designs, three 19th-century, one Louis XV, and three Louis XVI. The timber surrounds are enriched with applied composition ornamentation hand-pressed, in many cases, from the original, reverse-carved, wood box moulds designed and carved for Robert Adam. *P:* upon application.

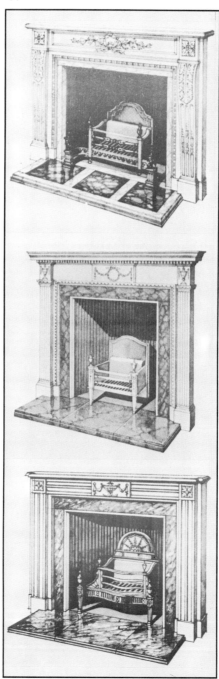

KEDDY HOME IMPROVEMENTS LTD

Scandinavian warm-air open fireplaces. Fresh outside air is brought in through a separate channel, heated, and expelled into the room to boost the warmth provided by the open fire. One of the fireplaces is combined with a central heating unit.

SUPERFIRE, probably the most efficient open fireplace available, burns any solid fuel including peat and turf. Made of leca (expanded clay) it comes in six different sizes and shapes, and is the most common warm-air fireplace in Europe, where it's been on the market for more than 20 years. SUPERFIRE is supplied complete in kit form and is easy to assemble and install. It can be used as it is or with any surround and/or mantel of your choice. *P:* £350–£700.

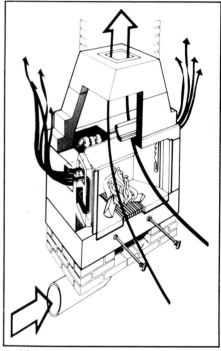

Keddy's SUPERFIRE

The WINDFIRE wood-burning open fireplace is easily installed provided there's a chimney. Made in high-grade steel, it has double walls for heating air efficiently. It comes in kit form, but is not for novice do-it-yourself enthusiasts. Optional smokestacks, straight up or through the back, are available. *P:* £400–£450, matt black chimney cover £50–£80.

The IMPULS HEATING SYSTEM, a fireplace system combined with a central heating unit, can be installed anywhere a chimney can be fitted. It will burn most solid fuels and can be used as it is, or with a mantel and/or surround. There are two types. The hot air model has a separate distribution outlet for another four rooms, and is an ideal complement to an electric heating system. The hot water model supplies full central heating, and can be combined with other systems so that when the fireplace is burning the other heating unit automatically shuts off. *P:* £700–£850.

Keddy also supply the ISO-KAERN chimney system. It consists of outer chimney castings made of leca mixed with cement and cast like concrete, and inner flue liners. Made of pumice, the liners are resistant to any conditions a domestic heating appliance can produce. An insulated, stabilizing filling is poured between the castings and liners during installation. A good selection of diameters is available. *P:* upon application.

Keddy's WINDFIRE

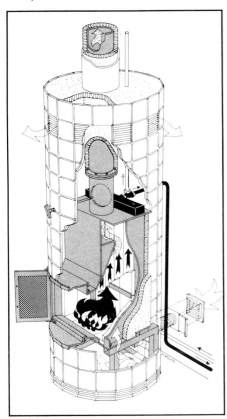

Keddy's IMPULS HEATING SYSTEM

MARBLE HILL GALLERY

25 hand-carved, traditional, reproduction pine mantels. Available waxed, or unwaxed for painting, they come in a good stock of popular sizes but can be made to order provided the proportions aren't altered. Marble slips and hearths can be supplied. Antique Louis XV and Louis XVI marble mantelpieces as well as a good range of antique fenders, fire irons and fire screens are available; brass grates suitable for fires can be fitted with electric bars, glowing coals, or gas logs. *P:* reproduction mantels £100–£300, slips, hearths from £50.

MINSTER FIREPLACES

Handsome, reproduction Tudor, Edwardian and Georgian fireplaces in reconstructed or natural stone (the latter primarily from Minster's own quarries in Somerset). Also traditional stone and/or brick fireplaces. Portland, Ham, Doulting, and Light or Dark Purbeck stones are available, all tooled or rubbed. 'Dillington', with a moulded spandrel, is illustrated. *P:* £395–£530. Fireplaces can be custom-built—upon receipt of a rough sketch Minster will submit a finished design and quotation. Fire baskets, fire backs and throat units can be supplied.

Minster's 'Dillington' fireplace

PARKER FIREPLACES

Do-it-yourself reproduction fireplaces in kit form with some very unusual features. BUCKINGHAM has a solid English walnut mantel polished, in the traditional way, with beeswax and turpentine. It's fitted with a marble hearth, reeded surround, brass frame and hearth plate. *P:* upon application. LANDLEY is similar, but with a carved, waxed

pine mantel (*P:* £400). BURGHLEY must be the most unusual, with a *solid* rosewood surround and mantel, and natural York stone hearth, sides and back (*P:* upon application). Several ivory-coloured mantels with gilt ornamentation, and both Portuguese and Italian marble hearths, are also available. Mantels, surrounds and hearths can be supplied separately.

Parker also make 'Therm-O-Flame' gas log fires, and an extensive range of cast-iron accessories.

PATRICKS OF FARNHAM

Very large range of mantels, most of them copies or adaptations of 18th- or 19th-century originals. They range from simple Regency designs suitable for smaller rooms, to more ornate 18th-century mantelpieces in the style of William Kent. Seven hand-carved pine mantels come uncoloured, unwaxed, White, or with a mahogany finish. Dimensions are flexible so the mantels can be altered to fit existing openings.

Modern random-stone fireplaces, and several traditional designs in natural stone including Cotswold, Ancaster, York, Portland, and from the Forest of Dean, are available. ETON is in fine rubbed Ancaster stone with reeded iron surround (*P:* £650). All frames come in brass, copper, or stainless steel.

Hearths and shelves can be supplied in polished Belgian fossil, a very durable slab, and Patrick also stock more than 30 marbles, and three slates. Accessories include a varying selection of fire baskets, fire frets, fire dogs and decorative firebacks.

Patrick's ETON

PETIT ROQUE LTD

Eight period mantels in hand-carved pine. Also three styles in polished marble. Style A, specifically designed for open fires, complies with building regulations. Styles B and C are purely for decoration—cracking and smoking may result if they're used with a fire, and heat loss can be excessive. Available in sheet form, the marble comes in light creamy Beige with faint Orange/Brown markings, Green with Dark green and Black markings, and Burgundy wine with White, Green/Grey and Dark maroon. *P:* upon application.

M A POPE (FIREPLACES) LTD
Extensive selection of fireplaces, in materials that include York, Cheshire, Portland, Sicilian, and Ancaster stone. These can be custom-built (design and estimate are free of charge). Also a small range in marble, and three makes of reproduction fibreglass mantels. Pine mantels come in varying sizes, and a choice of 20-plus standard models. Hearths and slips in reconstructed marble, or polyester resin 'marble', custom-made French brick fireplaces, gas log fires, and brass fire frames are also available. *P:* upon application.

JAMES SMELLIE LTD
Made-to-order HOLE-IN-THE-WALL fireplaces with copper, stainless steel, or bronze surrounds and optional canopies. All are designed to accommodate Smellie's 'Firex' grate which burns all solid fuels, and can be used with virtually any fireplace, *and* fitted with one of two boilers. *P:* £100–£130 as illustrated, with 'Firex' grate.
Traditional stone, and brick fireplaces, made to order, are available.

Smellie's HOLE-IN-THE-WALL

SOLAR FIREPLACES LTD
Custom-built fireplaces in a patchwork of different stones, slates and marbles. Cottagey styles topped by metal canopies and oak beams are favoured. *P:* upon application.

Stuart Interior's mantel and surround

STARLING MANTELS LTD
Very competitively priced period fibreglass mantels. Suitable for all types of fire, they're light, strong, and easily cleaned with soap and water. Nine styles range from 'S100', the simplest design, with reeded panels, to 'S600', the most ornate, with festoon decoration on the top plaque. Only four screws are required to fix the mantels. Reconstructed marble interiors and hearths are also available, in six neutral shades from the palest beige, Perlato Royal, to the darkest green, Verdi Polcevera. *P:* mantels £120–£130, surround and hearth £125.

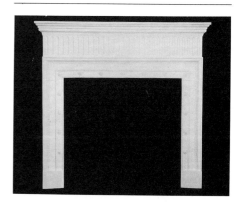

Starling's 'S100' (right)

STUART INTERIORS

Ornately carved oak mantels and surrounds with yew or holly inlays or carved and/or simply chamfered stonework pieces, from a firm of conscientious reproduction specialists. *P:* upon application.

SWAN GALLERIES

Nine made-to-measure hand-carved pine mantels decorated with festoons, shells, flowers, urns, and other classical motifs with pine panelling and mirrors to match. Also reproduction grates, suitable for coal or log fires; they can be fitted with electric bars and glowing 'coal'. Marble slips and hearths in a good range of colours are also available. *P:* mantel £160, grate £250, hearth and slip from £180, mirrors from £250. See also 'Architectural Ornaments'.

Swan Galleries' 'Culross' mantel

THEALE FIREPLACES LTD

Custom-built fireplaces in Cotswold and Yorkshire stone, Cumberland green slate, plain slate, and brick. Also plain or fancy reproduction carved pine mantels supplied unfinished, polished or whitened, complete with marble interior slabbed for installation. *P:* upon application.

VERINE PRODUCTS & CO

Faithful reproductions of 18th-century mantels. Made in fibreglass they won't crack, warp or distort with heat or humidity. 12 designs are available, all suitable for solid fuel, gas or electric fires, and can be supplied with 'marble' inserts made from polyester resin, in five convincing shades: Pakistani Onyx (apple green with brown, red and white veins), Verde Tinos (dark and light green veined in white), Bruno Scuro Napoleon (dark brown with white

and wine veins), Pompeiano (white veined in cream and brown), and Nero Portoro (black with red and white veins). Brick is also available, in a warm terracotta colour, for use with all the mantelpieces. The 'Fluted Adam' mantel allows clients to choose from a selection of decorative elements such as eagles, urns, goats' heads, etc. 'Zodiac', the most unusual design, is embellished with the 12 astrological signs, based on ancient drawings. 'Louis', serpentine-fronted, and decorated with shell mouldings, is based on a Louis XV original; in two sizes. 'Westminster' is carved from designs in William Paine's book on decorative details, published in 1774. Surrounds come in White, except for 'The Empire' which is also available in a light wood finish. *P:* mantels £140–£180, surround and hearth £175–£350.

Verine's 'Zodiac' (above), 'Louis' (below)

WALCOT RECLAMATION

All kinds of second-hand building materials and architectural items. These dealers also stock used RAYBURNS, British and Continental wood and coal stoves, Georgian,

Regency, and Victorian cast-iron fireplaces, ornamental tiles, and surrounds. A selection from their ever-changing stock is illustrated. *P:* free-standing stoves £30 (unrestored), £200 (restored); Victorian mantels with tile surrounds £100–£150 (restored).

MR WANDLES' WORKSHOP

Original late 19th-century fireplaces which once graced the rooms of London's suburban villas and artisan terraces. Made from cast iron, sometimes with beautiful original tile surrounds, they've been restored to their former deserving splendour by Mr Wandle & Co. Finishes are shotblast, brilliant polish, black lead, and matt or eggshell black; or fireplaces can be painted to order. A good range of fenders, coal buckets, fire irons, fire backs, and other accessories is always available. Mr Wandle will also arrange a complete fitting service. *P:* £125–£300.

INTRODUCTION

As any successful interior decorator knows, the secret is attention to detail. Whether a scheme is modern or period, city-chic or country charming, it's imperative to get the fittings right. A conscientious painting job can be spoilt by the wrong door fittings. (The perfect time to consider their colour and shape is when you're repainting.) A fine piece of Georgian furniture is wrecked when stainless steel drawer pulls are used. If expensive curtains are sloppily hung, the care lavished on choosing the right fabric is totally wasted. Finally, always be sure screws match fittings – chrome fitments with brass screws, or vice versa, spell disaster.

This section is divided according to function — into *Cabinet*, *Curtain* and *Door* fittings. The first two sometimes overlap: keyhole covers (escutcheons) match door knobs which match coat hooks which match drawer pulls. Curtain fittings include easy-to-install telescopic rods and more complicated pelmet arrangements. *Specific measurements aren't given for cabinet and door fittings — most come in standard sizes.

*The range of an extendible rod or pole is indicated with a hyphen: 12–20in/30.5–51cm. For standard curtain fittings, 'to' is used to indicate a selection of widths: 24in to 4ft (61 to 122cm).

CABINET FITTINGS

GALLERIA MONTE CARLO

49 sumptuous pulls. They complement equally gorgeous door levers and knobs, push plates, bar pulls, light switch plates, coat hooks, escutcheons, etc. All are available in 24ct gold-plate, brushed chrome, and antique pewter finishes. *P:* upon application.

GRANT SLIDES LTD

Wide selection of drawer slides. The '222 Duo-Rail' fits into normally wasted space under the drawer, and requires no side mounting space. Also door slides. *P:* upon application.

HARRISON-BEACON LTD

Six pulls and handles, part of an extensive range of hardware clearly illustrated in Harrison-Beacon's well-designed catalogue: flush pull in chrome-plated brass (*P:* two £1.25); satin anodized extruded aluminium handle (*P:* two £1.13); satin anodized aluminium cylinder lock door pull (*P:* 80p); '812' black or chrome-plated tubular steel bow handle (*P:* upon application); and '2445' anodized aluminium sliding door pull (*P:* two 57p). The '712' card frame in brass (*P:* 43p) is available with a matching pull (*P:* 82p). Also door fittings, mirror fixtures, brass hinges, and three castors: 'Rotaglide' with plate or socket fixings for use on carpets; 'Slimline' for light furniture; and 'Supercastors' for heavier pieces. All in chrome, the latter two also in grey. *P:* four £5.80, £4.60, in chrome.

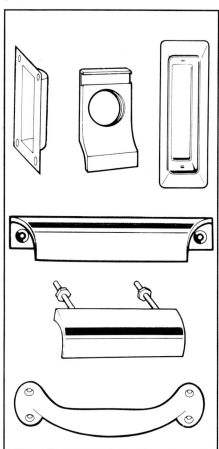

Left to right, from top: Harrison-Beacon's flush, cylinder lock, and sliding door pulls; aluminium handles; tubular steel bow handle

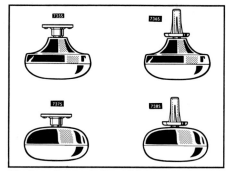

Harrison-Beacon's 'Rotaglide' castors showing shapes and types of fitting

HEATHERLEY LTD

See *Door Fittings* for plain and flowered drawer pulls.

B LILLY & SONS LTD

Good basic pulls, rod mounts, coat hooks, etc. The MODERN range of knobs, handles, and finger pulls comes in traditional, and more streamlined, functional, designs in brass, bronze, chrome, and silver anodized finishes. *P:* 45p–£2.

A great range of reproduction ANTIQUE cabinet handles comes in a variety of highly decorative, and some plainer, styles, all illustrated, all wonderful. Polished brass, and relief finishes. *P:* 55p–£2.

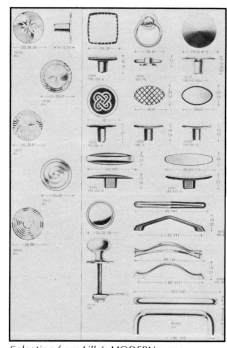

Selection from Lilly's MODERN range

PRICES AND INFORMATION WERE CORRECT AT THE TIME OF GOING TO PRESS

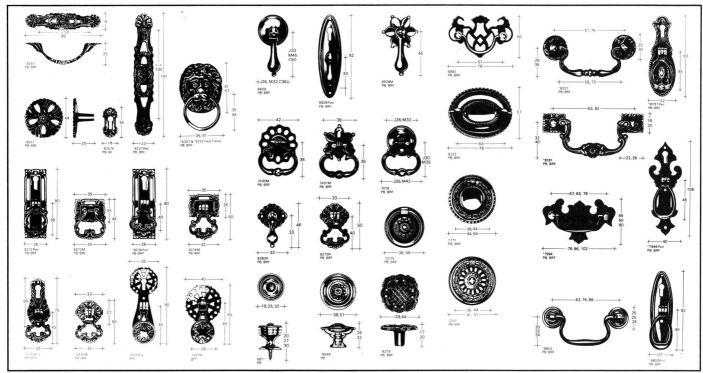

Lilly's ANTIQUE range

PANAVISTA LTD

The most comprehensive collection of cabinet fittings on the market: over 100 items. Panavista are sole agents for Amerock cabinet hardware. MODERN knobs and pulls come in anodized, antique English, and copper finishes (*P:* 66p–79p). PROVINCIAL, an elaborately leafy design, comes in gold on ivory, or finished in bright brass (*P:* 59p–£1.12). COLONNADE is a starker, Georgian, brass range. COLONIAL Gothic-style fittings in black, and hammered-effect bright brass, are ideal for heavier wardrobes or chests (*P:* hinges (pair) 79p–£2.02).

Panavista's COLONIAL range

Panavista's PROVINCIAL range

PERKINS & POWELL LTD

Beautiful, polished brass COBDEN range, from a firm that's well known for high-quality marine fittings. It includes a cupboard knob, in three sizes, a locking catch and a coat hook. Three flush drawer pulls, five hinges, three latches, five door hooks, and other equally useful but more obscure fittings, from the marine range, come in polished brass, chromium plate, satin chromium plate or B.M.A. finish. *P:* upon application. See also *Door Fittings* for COBDEN range.

PRICES AND INFORMATION WERE CORRECT AT THE TIME OF GOING TO PRESS

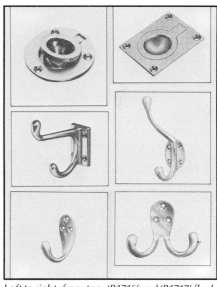

Left to right, from top: 'B1716' and 'B1717' flush rings, 'B1116', 'B3055', 'B3159', 'B2349' hooks from Perkin & Powell's marine range

VALLI & COLOMBO LTD

Drawer pulls and knobs, part of a stunning selection of Italian imports. A selection from six of Valli & Colombo's 12 awe-inspiring designs is illustrated: 'A18', 'A121', 'A120' and 'A15' come in cast bronze, 'A28' and 'A22' in 'Nikrall' alloy. *P:* drawer handles 60p–£1.60. See overleaf for illustration.

Left to right, from top: selections from Valli & Colombo's A18, A28, A120, A121, A15, A22

WINTHER, BROWNE & CO LTD

Drawer fittings, including an exclusive and unusual collection of unpolished wooden pulls and handles in afrormosia and iroko. Plain turned knobs, in various sizes, come in oak, pine, and beech. Winther, Browne also make door fittings, and WINBRON embossed hardwood ornaments for wardrobes, fireplaces, furniture, etc. *P:* 10p–70p.

WOODFIT LTD

Extensive selection of modern and traditional knobs and handles, in aluminium, die-cast metal, solid brass, and wood. Also a good range of period brassware handles with decorative escutcheons; and door fittings. More functional products include aluminium handles for kitchen drawers and cabinets, mechanical drawer runners, and guides to prevent heavy drawers tipping forward when opened. *P:* upon application.

PRICES AND INFORMATION WERE CORRECT AT THE TIME OF GOING TO PRESS

CURTAIN FITTINGS

ANTIFERENCE LTD

Wide range of curtain-hanging solutions, including two inexpensive plastic tracks that will bend around corners and bays. MONORAIL comes in plain white, or with gold trim, in standard lengths that can be cut to size. It's sold in packs complete with all fitments. *M:* w 4 to 9ft (122 to 274.5cm). *P:* pack £1.75–£3.50
DECORAIL is available in four styles, two with fleur-de-lis finials, and is sold in exact lengths for straight runs or bends up to 9ft (274.5cm). Internal cording can be fitted and a lighter track, for net curtains, can be added with extension brackets. *P:* ft 42p–48p with fittings.

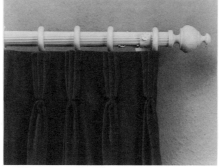

Antiference's DECORAIL (top), 'Sherwood' from KIRSCH in wood-textured steel

DECORPOLE traditional hardwood curtain poles come complete with rings and brackets in warm walnut, natural, and white. Extra brackets, rings and finials are available. *M:* w 4 to 10ft (122–305cm), diam 1³/₈in (3.5cm). *P:* £14.50–£23.50. KIRSCH metal curtain poles, in ready-assembled kits with internal cording, can be adjusted telescopically for an exact fit. Five styles include the following finishes: alumigold, antique gold, brass and antique brass; also white and wood-textured steel in natural walnut. Two matching tie-backs are available, in brass. *M:* 4ft 2in–7½ft, 7½–12½ft (127–228.5, 228.5–381cm). *P:* £27, £38. *M:* w 30in to 22½ft (76 to 686cm), diam 1, 1³/₈in (2.5, 3.5cm). Internally corded but concealed curtain rails are also available. CONTEMPORARY RAIL, totally hidden behind the pleated curtain heading, comes in two

strengths: 'Regular' and 'Double Duty', both in straight, telescopically adjustable lengths. Alternatively, they can be made to measure and/or formed to fit bays. *M:* w 12 to 16ft (366 to 488cm). *P:* 16ft £3.50–£8.10.
SWANGLIDE, and SUPERFINE, are supplied corded in set lengths for straight runs (*M:* w 28in to 18ft 8in/71 to 569.5cm, *P:* up to 48in £4.50, £7.25).
TENSION RODS, slim, oval telescopic action rods, are a neat way to hang nets (*M:* w 16in to 6ft/40.5–183cm, *P:* w 16–24in/40.5–61cm £2).

ARQUATI

Striking, high-quality wooden curtain poles and pelmets, designed and made in Italy. Three types of pole are available, all supplied complete with fittings: JUNIOR for small windows and lightweight curtains (*M:* w 4 to 7ft/122 to 213.5cm, *P:* £11–£18); SENIOR for larger windows and heavier curtains (*M:* w 6 to 12ft/183 to 366cm, *P:* £18–£27); and a corded version of SENIOR in the same sizes. All come in white, natural, and dark walnut. Components (wooden ring and eye, pole ends, support bracket and pole) can be bought singly or separately. Spare brackets and heavy duty support plug(s) are also available.
TRIPLO curtain track is fully corded and made to measure. There are three models: for tall headings, conventional headings, and vertical louvre blinds. Exceptionally, they come in seven finishes: white, dark walnut, and light walnut, all with aluminium; and plain white, dark walnut, walnut, and natural wood. The track can be jointed at right angles if requested. *P:* upon application.
Four pelmet ranges are available in exquisitely shaped wood, made to measure in the UK and supplied with built-in pre-corded tracks. A total of 15 classic designs come in any of five finishes: ivory/gold, antique pine, light walnut, medium walnut, and antique walnut. Pelmets are made with a 5½in (14cm) turn at each end, or completely straight. *P:* upon application.

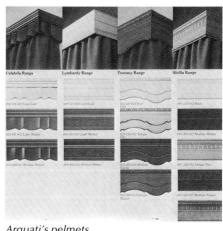

Arquati's pelmets

FABER BLINDS LTD

A good choice of fittings from a company well known for its blinds. FABER 66 anodized aluminium track is available straight, or can be shaped to any curve provided the inside radius is a minimum of 7.7cm (3in). There are numerous varieties of cord pulls so that several curtains can be mounted on the same rail. *P:* upon application. FOLK POLE DE LUXE, made from Scandinavian pine in natural, and dark oak finish, is ribbed along its length and comes with matching wooden rings. Fixing is concealed by an adjustable wooden bracket. *M:* w 130 to 390cm (4ft 3¼in to 12ft 9½in), diam 3cm (1¹/₈in). *P:* £13–£27 complete.

CORNICHE, designed for contract use, combines a wooden pelmet and aluminium track. Supplied in kit form, with all fittings, it comes in seven styles. They range from '42114', a traditional raised floral and leaf design in a soft gilt finish, to '3294', a simple grooved profile with prominent ridges in 'gold leaf' (natural and dark oak versions—'3298' and '3292'—are also available). For modern settings, '1618' is a plain white pelmet which can be painted to match any setting. '1620' is the same design, in ivory with linen-look facing edged with fine 'gold' line. For more ornate schemes, '1603', in white, has a raised centre frieze of a leafy garland picked out in gold. *M:* w 3 to 13ft (91.5 to 396.5cm). *P:* upon application.

CORNICHE pelmets are available by the foot, for covering a door or window trim.

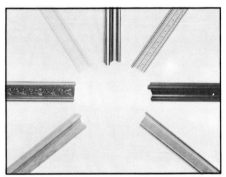

Clockwise from left: '3298', '42114', '1618', '3294' '1603', '3292', '1620' from Faber's CORNICHE

D & H FACTORS LTD

Internally corded TRACK DE LUXE from France, specially designed for heavy curtains. Long popular with professionals, it's equally suitable for the do-it-yourself market. Supplied in packs, with all fittings, it comes in gold, silver, and white, in standard lengths that can be cut to size. *M:* w 4 to 12ft (122 to 366cm). *P:* £13.50–£25. The BARONESS curtain tie-back set includes decorative metal cord holders.

GRABER

Five curtain poles in brass, antique brass, antique gold, antique white, wood grain, and chrome, on a heavy-duty steel or tarnish-free aluminium base. Corded or uncorded, they are available in a range of diameters, in standard lengths. Some are supplied complete with ball-bearing pulley sets for heavy curtains, all come with fittings, and instructions. *M:* w 24in to 20ft (61 to 610cm). *P:* upon application.

HARRISON-BEACON LTD

Extensive and unusual range of curtain tracking systems. TUDOR wooden poles, in dark walnut or natural finish, are available uncorded or ready-corded in standard lengths (*M:* w 5, 6, 8, 10ft/152.5, 183, 244, 305cm, diam 1¼in/3cm, *P:* uncorded £18–£30, corded £24–£36). CORNICE poles in aluminium with gold-effect anodized finish have real brass rings (*M:* w 4 to 12ft/122 to 366cm, diam 1, 1½in/2.5, 4cm, *P:* £11–£35). RINGSLIDE is similar, but plainer; made from steel, with polished brass-effect finish, it comes ready-corded in four sizes (*M:* w 30in to 20ft/76 to 610cm, diam 1in/2.5cm, *P:* £9–£27). MARQUIS, in the same sizes and material, is also ready-corded but is finished with an engraved finial in bright or antique brass, or Brittany oak (*P:* £17–£48).

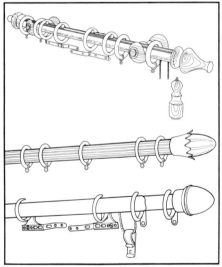

Harrison-Beacon's TUDOR (top), CORNICE (centre), RINGSLIDE (bottom)

There are also three less obvious tracking systems. SUPERDRAPE, made from extruded aluminium with nylon fittings, comes in a silver or gold-effect finish. It's particularly suitable for corners or bays, as it can be bent to fit so that there's no additional strain on brackets. SUPERWHITE and SUPERCREST are both in rigid PVC, the latter with a gold-toned Greek key pattern running its length. *M:* w 4ft to 16ft 5in (122 to 500.5cm), diam 1¹/₈in (3cm). *P:* £1.60–£6.50 including fittings.

Right (top): Harrison-Beacon's SUPERCREST (left), SUPERDRAPE (top right), SUPERWHITE (bottom right)

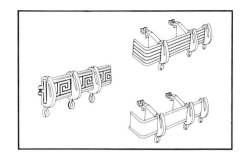

W A HUDSON LTD

Great curtain poles from a firm that's been making them for 75 years. REGENCY is in reeded aluminium with gilt finish or glossy white plastic over a strong metal tube. Brackets, rings and pineapple finials are in matching white or golden brass. *M:* w 120 to 360cm (3ft 11¼in to 11ft 9¾in), diam 1.9, 3.2cm (¾, 1¼in). *P:* £9.75–£22.

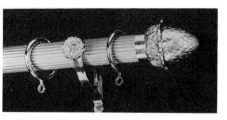

Hudson's REGENCY curtain pole

SUPERGLIDE, a reeded rail, is available in gold, silver, and white acrylic finish, on aluminium. Strong, but easily curved around bay windows, it's simple to fit and available corded or uncorded. *P:* 125–500cm (4ft 1¼in to 16ft 4⁷/₈in) uncorded £4–£14 silver, £5–£18 white.

MINIGLIDE, a satin silver anodized aluminium or white acrylic rail, pre-drilled for fixing, is supplied corded or with cord control set. Seven sections are available, for top or face fixing. Supplied complete with fittings it comes in standard lengths. *P:* 125–500cm (4ft 1¼in to 16ft 4⁷/₈in) corded £10–£15.

MAJORGLIDE, a very heavy-duty rail for contract use, is supplied to size in aluminium alloy with satin silver finish. *P:* from m £2.

NYLASTIC, made from PVC with a steel core, is an easily curved, all-purpose inexpensive rail for use behind pelmets. Various cord control sets are available. *P:* rail with metal bracket m from £2. Finally, STAYWHITE is a lightweight metal rail suitable for light fabrics. Made from anodized aluminium, in satin silver finish, it can be corded and bent by hand. *P:* m £1.95 complete.

M: SUPERGLIDE, MINIGLIDE, NYLASTIC, STAYWHITE w 125 to 300cm (4ft 1¼in to 9ft 10¹/₈in) in 25cm (9⁷/₈in) lengths, up to 500cm (16ft 4⁷/₈in) in 50cm (19⁵/₈in) lengths.

Wood and brass poles are made to clients' specifications. Wooden versions are available with wood or brass rings and brass brackets, and are finished in white enamel, stained and

varnished mahogany, and medium oak (*M: diam* 2.5, 3.2, 4, 4.5cm/1, 1¼, 1½, 1⅞in). Brass poles are plain or reeded, with solid brass finials in ball, pineapple, spear point, and fleur-de-lis shapes (*M: diam* 2.5, 3.2, 4, 5cm/1, 1¼, 1½, 2in, reeded diam 4, 5cm/1½, 2in only). Reeded aluminium poles come in a white acrylic or gilt anodized finish, with brass ball or pineapple finials (*M: diam* 5cm/2in). *P:* upon application.
Additional fittings are available for all rails, and can be supplied separately.

HUNTER-DOUGLAS LTD

LUXAFLEX decorative poles and tracks. Wooden poles come in walnut and natural finishes (*M:* w 4, 6, 8ft/122, 183, 244cm, diam 1in/2.5cm, w 6, 8, 10, 12ft/183, 244, 305, 366cm, diam 1⅜in /3.5cm, *P:* upon application).
Metal poles are in two styles: 'Wellington' in antique or bright brass, or plain 'Salem' in bright brass only (*M:* w 30in to 22ft 8in/76 to 691.5cm, diam ⅜, 1, 1⅜in/1, 2.5, 3.5cm, *P:* upon application). There are four plastic tracks: corded SUPREME, fluted WHITE PACEMAKER, GOLDEN PACEMAKER for pinch or pencil pleats, and CHAMPION for straight runs or bays (*M:* w 3 to 10ft/91.5 to 305cm in 1in/2.5cm increments; larger sizes to order, *P:* upon application).

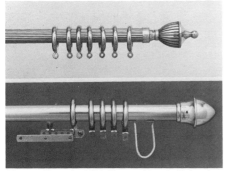

Hunter-Douglas' 'Wellington' (top), 'Salem' (bottom) from LUXAFLEX

STANLEY CURTAIN COMPANIONS LTD

Probably the widest selection of corded and non-corded curtain rods on the market—a total of 21 designs. Also eight styles of curtain hook and 14 pleating tape options.
A good range of ready-corded, extendible tracks is available. GINA, a functional, non-decorative model for walls or ceilings, comes complete with cord tension pulley (*M:* w 30in–3ft 11in/76–119.5cm to 12ft 10in–24ft 9in/391.5–755cm, *P:* £6.50–£23). Plain styles in heavy gauge metal include SPLENDID, SHADOW, and SYMPHONY. All come in the same shape, but a variety of finishes: SPLENDID in gleaming brass, SHADOW in polished gunmetal (shiny dark brown), and SYMPHONY in satiny gold. *M:* w 30in–3ft 11in (76–119.5cm) to 10½ft–

11ft 9in (320–358.5cm). *P:* £15–£48. Reeded metal rods include ANTIQUE in dark antique brass finish, ARISTOCRAT in polished brass (both illustrated with an acorn-shape reeded finial), and HAWTHORNE in gleaming brass, illustrated with a plain finial (*M:* w 30in to 13ft/76 to 396.5cm, diam 1⅜in/3.5cm, *P:* £15–£47).
Classic, budget-priced CAFÉ RODS are finished in brass. Round or moulded rings are available. Suitable only for lightweight curtains, they're also extendible and are supplied in packs with accessories (excluding rings). *M:* w 30in–3ft 11in (76–119.5cm) to 5ft 7in–9ft 10in (170–300cm), diam ½ to 1in (1.2 to 2.5cm). *P:* £3–£12.

From top: Stanley's SHADOW, SYMPHONY, ARISTOCRAT, HAWTHORNE, SPLENDID (gleaming brass), ANTIQUE, SYMPHONY

A total of 11 solid wooden rods is available. Corded versions are CLASSICA and VENEZIA both with shaped ends, in walnut and white; also CLAUDIA in walnut and LOUISA in white, both with spheroid finials. *M:* w 5ft 11in to 11ft 2in (180.5 to 340.5cm), diam 1⅜in (3.5cm). Non-corded rods are thick CASTELLANA and thin SOPHIE, both in walnut finish. *M:* CASTELLANA w 5ft 3in to 11ft 2in (160 to 340.5cm) diam 1½in (4.5cm); SOPHIE w 4ft 5in to 6ft 7in (134.5 to 200.5cm), diam ⅞in (2.2cm). *P:* CASTELLANA £31–£60; SOPHIE £8–£13.50. SARA is cordless, CLASSICA corded. Both are reeded and come in walnut finish. *M:* w 5ft 1in to 11ft 2in (155 to 340.5cm), diam 1⅜in (3.5cm). *P:* £17–£31, £25–£43. Round-end rods include CLARA in natural, CARLOTTA in walnut, and BIANCA in white, all cordless (*M:* w 5ft 3in to 11ft 2in/160 to 340.5cm, diam 1⅜in/3.5cm, *P:* £17–£31). All above with rings and fittings included. EMILY, a slimmer, budget-priced rod, comes unfinished, ready to paint or stain (*M:* w 3ft 11in to 7ft 11in/119.5 to 241.5cm, diam 15/16, 1⅛in/2.4, 3cm, *P:* £7–£18). Extra rings 80p for 4.

Towel rails to match EMILY and SOPHIE are available (*M:* w 19⅝in/50cm, *P:* £3.50, £4.30). Also extra rings, brackets, finials and tie-backs for all ranges.

Stanley's CLASSICA, SARA, VENEZIA, SARA, VENEZIA (bottom row), round-ended CASTELLANA, CARLOTTA (top)

SWISH PRODUCTS LTD

Large range of curtain track systems. SOLO-GLYDE, and SOLOGLYDE REGAL with crown-shaped finials, are for inexpensive gathered headings (*P:* m 85p). DELUXE is designed for deep headings, DELUXE IMPERIAL for pencil or twin pleats (*P:* m £1.50–£2). NYLONGLYDE incorporates a pelmet track, and lightweight FURNIGLYDE is for net curtains (*P:* m 90p, 75p). NOVAPOLES has the looks and style of a wooden pole, but the easy installation and cost advantages of a plastic track. Three versions are available, two in matt brass (one reeded), and the third in a wood grain with 'acorn' finial. *M:* w 175 to 300cm (5ft 8⅞in to 9ft 10⅛in), diam 3, 3.5cm (1⅛, 1⅜in). *P:* from £7. Individual fittings also available.

Swish's DELUXE (top), NOVAPOLE (centre), DELUXE IMPERIAL (bottom)

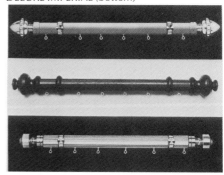

WINTHER, BROWNE & CO LTD

Wooden curtain rods in two styles, from a firm that makes all kinds of wooden ornaments. In hardwood or Swedish pine, they're supplied complete with brackets, rings and finials. *M:* w 3, 6ft (91.5, 183cm), diam 1in (2.5cm). *P:* £7.75, £10.60.

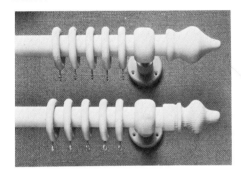

DOOR FITTINGS

ALBION HARDWARE LTD

Three distinctive ranges of internal door fittings. Each consists of door levers or pull handles, cabinet knobs, finger plates and escutcheons. The hand-made LIMOGES porcelain range comes in plain White, and White edged with a Gold line or decorated with a Blue floral or Gold fleur-de-lis motif, all on hand-polished solid brass mountings; also White edged in Slver, on polished chromium-plated mountings. CORONET, a superb collection of individually made fittings in Crystal clear or Smoky haze acrylic, is available faceted or smooth, as illustrated. The transparent handles are cut from solid acrylic blocks, and hand-finished. Mountings are polished or satin brass, or chrome. The more elaborate marble-like CRYSTALCUT range comes in green onyx, or alabaster. Solid brass mountings are trimmed with a decorative rope design. *P:* upon application.

Albion's CORONET range

Albion's CRYSTALCUT range

GALLERIA MONTE CARLO

Sherle Wagner collection of elaborate period door fittings, from a Continental firm that specializes in exclusive bathrooms and fixtures. Galleria Monte Carlo also has branches in Paris and Monte Carlo. The extensive selection includes 24 door levers, 32 door knobs, four push plates, six back plates, six bar pulls, three latches, three escutcheons, seven light switch plates—and 50 drawer pulls. Starkly simple, futuristic DIMENSION is the outstanding exception to a host of highly decorative, rather baroque fittings. *P:* upon application.

Galleria Monte Carlo's back plates (left), push plates (right)

HARRISON-BEACON LTD

Comprehensive selection of hardware, including two ranges of well-made brass door furniture polished to retain a warm glow. VICTORIAN has clean, simple lines; GEORGIAN, the traditional rope edging. *P:* VICTORIAN octagon knob £8.25, finger plate £4.15; GEORGIAN mortice knob set £11, finger plate £8.65.

PRICES AND INFORMATION WERE CORRECT AT THE TIME OF GOING TO PRESS

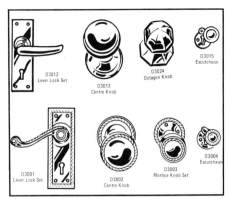

Harrison-Beacon's VICTORIAN (top), GEORGIAN (bottom) ranges

HEATHERLEY FINE CHINA LTD

Porcelain drawer and cupboard knobs, finger plates and escutcheons. There's a good choice of six floral designs on White, and Ivory: 'Festoon' in Pink/Sage, 'Floral Chintz' in Pink/Green/Blue/Yellow, 'Chintz Rose' in Rose/Gold, 'Apple Blossom' in Peachy-red/Olive, 'Blue Bouquet' in bright blues, and 'Dogwood' in Yellow/Gold/Olive. Gold line on White or Black is also available, plus plain White. *P:* escutcheon £1, mortice set £9 (undecorated slightly cheaper).

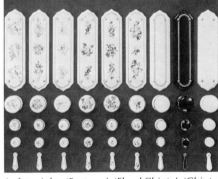

Left to right: 'Festoon', 'Floral Chintz', 'Chintz Rose', 'Apple Blossom', 'Blue Bouquet', 'Dogwood', Gold line on White, Gold line on Black, plain White fittings from Heatherley

HOPE WORKS LTD

Craftsman-made wrought-iron fittings, from a firm that's been making them for over 100 years. Faithful reproductions of 19th-century styles, all fittings come in matt black, and armour bright finishes, obtained by using powder coating (more durable than paint and slightly more expensive than matt black). Authentically forged square-headed screws are supplied where appropriate. Illustrated are four lever handles: 'A2747-1', 'A3298-1', 'A3141-1', and 'A2918-3', compatible with pull handles, bolts, and drawer knobs. *P:* pair £11. See overleaf for illustration.

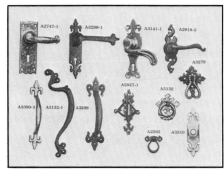

Selection of Hope Works' lever handles and pulls

B LILLY & SONS LTD

Functional fittings including bolts and chains, escutcheons, finger plates, card frames, hinges and latches. Most come in brass, bronze, chromium-plated, and silver anodized finishes. The award-winning SADLER 'M' SERIES range of mortices, knobs, key covers and spindles is the only door furniture approved and licensed by the British Standards Institute. Mainly exterior fittings, it also includes strikingly simple levers and locks for interior doors. Knobs in soft silver anodized steel are illustrated. *P:* £4.25–9.50.

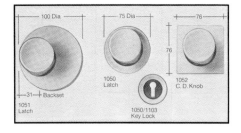

NEWMAN-TONKS HARDWARE LTD

Beautifully chunky, clean-lined STEDEN polished brass door fittings. The superb mortice knob and lever handles are complemented by an indicator bolt and elegantly

Newman-Tonks' 'Status' range

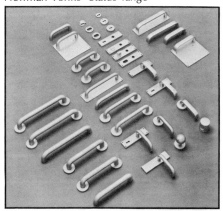

Newman-Tonks' STEDEN range

simple pull handles. 'Status' (also from STEDEN) is a much wider selection of more functional architectural hardware in satin-finished stainless steel, and aluminium. The modern 'Cambrian' suite in anodized aluminium, and gracefully distinctive 'Regency' in brass with rope-design trim, are both outstanding. *P:* upon application.

PERKINS & POWELL LTD

Striking, and very comprehensive, COBDEN range in polished brass. It includes pulls, latches, centre knobs, handles and door knockers; also niceties like a bell push and coat hook. *P:* upon application.
Other fittings include knobs, letter plates, door pulls and sash stops, fasteners and hooks, in polished, chromium plate, satin chromium plate or B.M.A. finishes.

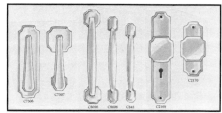

Left to right: Perkins & Powell's door knockers, handles and knobs from COBDEN

ROTHLEY BRASS

Period door fittings, hand-finished, in solid brass and lacquer. Elegant GEORGIAN has a traditional rope-effect border; VICTORIAN is plain and functional. LOUIS, ADAM and QUEEN ANNE feature exceptionally elaborate designs. *P:* upon application.

Rothley's LOUIS (left), QUEEN ANNE (right) door fittings

VALLI & COLOMBO LTD

Three spectacular, unusual and comprehensive ranges of fittings that harmonize with all styles of decor and share the outstanding features expected of Italian design. GAUDIA, MEDICEA, and NOVIA come in chunky solid brass; door and drawer fittings co-ordinate to perfect a room or scheme. All three ranges also include lever handles, keys, escutcheons, window pulls, coat hooks, switch covers and door plates. Glorious and numerous hinges, handles and pulls are available. *P:* pair lever handles NOVIA £11.

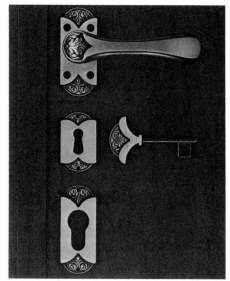

Selection from Valli & Colombo's NOVIA range

WOODFIT LTD

Stockists with a vast mail-order catalogue offering a huge selection of useful products, including an elegantly plain range of highly polished, hand-finished solid brass door fittings. Fittings for sliding doors include light and heavy-duty selections. Folding door components, and locks, hinges and handles for glass doors are also available.

Right: Amtico's 'Mountsorrel'

INTRODUCTION

Decorating begins at ground level. Whatever your lifestyle—or budget—it's imperative to get the floor right.

Before laying any kind of flooring, make sure the subfloor is sound. Remove protruding nails from timber, fasten loose boards, and level the surface if necessary. Concrete, brick or tile floors must also be smooth, and free from damp.

This section is divided according to material. *Cork Floor Tiles* range from unsealed products (the cheapest) which must be coated before use, through waxed tiles that need occasional recoating, to hard-wearing, trouble-free versions finished with polyurethane or vinyl (the most expensive). All vary in thickness. *Rubber Flooring* is sound absorbent, and relatively inexpensive.

Stone Flooring can be slate, reconsituted marble, marble, or lava-derived materials. Although it can feel cold, it's undeniably handsome—and requres virtually no maintenance. Sizes and thicknesses vary enormously.

Vinyl Sheet Flooring ranges from flexible, unbacked sheeting to more costly, harder wearing cushioned versions. *Vinyl Tile Flooring*, normally uncushioned, is coloured right through and generally inexpensive. Relatively easy to lay, both forms need regular repolishing.

Hardwearing *Wood Flooring* consists of parquet tiles, and more expensive timber planking. Both types can add to the value of your home.

CORK FLOOR TILES

ALLIANCE FLOORING CO LTD

Competitively priced, unsealed cork tiles, in a light shade only (*M:* 12×12in/30.5×30.5cm, *P:* sq yd £2.75–£3.50 depending on thickness.)

MUNDET CORK & PLASTICS LTD

JOINTITE cork tiles in a particularly large range of sizes. They're unfinished, ready for waxing, sealing and waxing, or coating with a synthetic resin seal, and can be supplied tongued and grooved if they're over $5/16$in (8mm) thick. Also cork strips, in varying widths, for borders or creating 'deck' effects. Both come in an unusually wide selection of thicknesses, in light, medium or heavy density according to intended use. Several natural shades range from Light tan to Dark brown. Covered skirtings and special stair heads are also available. Mundet will install, and finish, if required. *M:* tiles 12×12in (30.5×30.5cm), also 9×9in (23× 23cm), 36×12in (91.5×30.5cm) and other sizes. *P:* upon application.

Left: Wicanders' 'Strip Oak'

NORTHERN CORK SUPPLIES LTD

Cork tiles in mottled Red, Blue, Green, Brown, Yellow, and Natural, with a tough gloss finish. Northern will mail a sample pack of 20 different tiles for a £2 deposit (plus postage) which will be refunded, or deducted from any order over £5, when the pack is returned—a really helpful, and unique, service.

They also supply some leading branded flooring materials, at the lowest possible prices. *M:* 18×9in (46×23cm). *P:* sq yd £3.30.

VIGERS STEVENS & ADAMS LTD

Extra-thick ROBINSON HEAVY DUTY CORK TILES for the heaviest domestic or commercial use. They come in three finishes. Synthetic resin is probably the hardest wearing, and requires the least maintenance. Wax-impregnated tiles have to be re-waxed and polished from time to time. 'Sanded' tiles are ready for finishing with a polyurethane sealer. All are available in light, medium and dark colours, also variegated narrow and broad strip patterns in varying shades, giving an unusually extensive range of design possibilities. CARVELLE tiles, finished with a very hardwearing flexible synthetic resin, are tough and easy to maintain. They come in light, medium and dark shades, with up to three sub-shades in the light and medium colours.

M: 30.5×30.5cm (12×12in), other sizes available to order in ROBINSON range. *P:* upon application.

WICANDERS (GREAT BRITAIN) LTD

CORK-O-PLAST, possibly the most popular cork floor tile on the market although it's more expensive than waxed or unsealed products. Each tile consists of four layers: a PVC underside (to keep out moisture), a layer of cork, a decorative layer of cork veneer, and finally an easy-to-clean, resilient clear PVC layer. Uniquely, there are 11 different patterns: 'Natural', a medium shade; 'Natural Expand' with darker exposed flecks; 'Smoke', a dark brown; 'Smoke Expand' dark/light brown; 'Character', a light cork 'parquet' effect of small irregular rectangles; 'Classic', a light, larger patchwork effect; 'Colorite Green' and 'Colorite Red' light, expanded cork designs with the relevant colour showing through the natural gaps; 'Accent', a light, more heavily textured natural effect; 'Checker' light, irregular small squares in alternate directions; and 'Harmony', similar to 'Natural Expand' but with larger dark patches. *M:* 30×30cm (11$7/8$× 11$7/8$in), except 'Accent' 90×15cm (35$3/8$× 5$7/8$in) only, 'Natural' and 'Natural Expand' also 90×15cm (35$3/8$×5$7/8$in). *P:* sq m £11–£15. CORKTEX natural cork tiles are less expensive, and less exciting. The CORKTILE range of sanded, ready-to-seal tiles comes in two thicknesses. *M:* both ranges 30×30cm (11$7/8$× 11$7/8$in). *P:* sq m CORKTEX £5.50; CORKTILE £3.50. All Wicanders tiles are supplied in packs of nine.

Wicanders' 'Harmony' from CORK-O-PLAST

RUBBER FLOORING

GERLAND LTD

GERFLEX 3S rubber tiles, for contract use, made from highly resistant, odourless, anti-slip rubbers. METRO TILES come in three surface effects: 'Round Stud' in Black; 'Square Stud' in Marine blue, Chocolate brown or Burnt orange; and 'Pastilles', a combination of raised circles and lozenges in Black, Dark green, and Brick red. *M:* 75×75cm (29½×29½in). *P:* sq m £16–£20.

Gerland's 'Pastille' (top left), 'Round Stud' (right), 'Square Stud' (bottom left), all from METRO TILES

JAYMART RUBBER & PLASTICS LTD

Possibly the world's largest selection of rubber anti-slip flooring and mats. Products include studded and textured floor tiles in a choice of colours: Dark brown, Black, Grey, Green, and Olive. *M:* 50×50, 100×100cm (19⁵/₈×19⁵/₈in, 3ft 3³/₈× 3ft 3³/₈in). *P:* from £10 sq m.

Also sheet flooring in a variety of designs—studded, chequered, ribbed, and even marbled. It's available in a reasonable selection of colours: Black, Brown, and Grey, plus Green, Red and Blue in some ranges. Smaller mats will be cut to size. *M:* 10, 20m × 120, 140cm (32ft 9³/₄in, 65ft 7¹/₂in × 3ft 11¹/₄in, 4ft 7¹/₈in). *P:* from £6 sq m (Black £4). 'Safe-T-Step', a combined rubber stair nosing and round-studded stair tread and smooth riser, is useful for making steep wooden stairs safe (*M:* w 100cm/3ft 3³/₈in, *P:* m £7.50).

Jaymart's chequered (top), broad-ribbed (bottom) flooring

STONE FLOORING

CATHEDRAL WORKS ORGANISATION

CAMAIEU floor tiles come in an amazing array of sizes and can be combined to form more than 100 designs, successfully incorporating the contrasting colours of 'Comblanchien' and 'Larrys' stone (*M:* square 30×30cm/11⁷/₈× 11⁷/₈in, rectangle 30×15cm/11⁷/₈×5⁷/₈in, diamond 17.5×20cm/6⁷/₈×7⁷/₈in, strips 30× 7.5cm/11⁷/₈×3in, *P:* sq m square £15, rectangle £13, diamond, strip £16). A beautiful, highly polished finish costs sq m 88p.

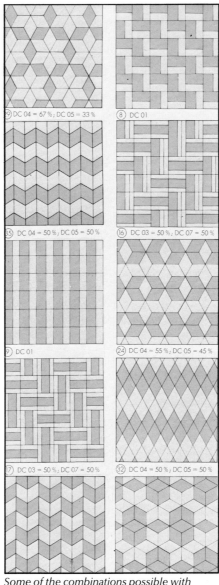

Some of the combinations possible with Cathedral Works' CAMAIEU tiles

DELABOLE SLATE CO LTD

Slabs and tiles from a quarry that has been producing high-quality slate for over 400 years. They make handsome, hardwearing floor coverings suitable for indoor and outdoor use. Colours range from Grey to Grey-green or Grey-blue.

Slabs come in 'standard' sizes, or special shapes can be cut to order. Finishes vary from the natural split face to a sawn or relatively fine ground finish. *M:* w 18in × 1¼in thick (46× 3cm), random lengths up to 5ft (152.5cm). 'Quarries' or tiles are smaller rectangular pieces with natural split faces and sawn edges (*M:* 6×6in/15×15cm to 12×12in/30.5×30.5cm or 6 to 12in/15 to 30.5cm wide in random

lengths 1 to 1½×width, ¼ to ³/₈in/6mm to 1cm thick—or thicker). DELASLATE split-faced Blue slate paving is supplied in pre-packed units of 21 stones (a square yard) that form a standard interlocking random rectangular pattern or an interlocking rectangular coursed pattern (standard width, random length). *M:* ³/₈in (1cm) thick. Crazy paving is also available, but is probably most suitable for outdoor use. *P:* all products upon application.

ELON TILES (UK) LTD

Three ranges of floor tiles. Very handsome LAVA STONE TILES, in traditional earth tones, are also suitable for walls. PRECAST PAVERS, used on Mexican sidewalks, are decorated or plain. Suitable for high-traffic areas, they blend well with other decorated tiles in the Elon collection. Striking MARBLE TILES are brilliantly grained, with Pink or Grey tones. *M:* 4×4, 8×8in (10×10, 20.5×20.5cm), MARBLE TILES also 4, 6×12in (10, 15×30.5cm). *P:* upon application.

Elon also have a fine and colourful range of Mexican glazed terracotta tiles.

See also 'Ceramic Tiles'. See page 70 for decorated Elon tiles in colour.

MARBLE PANELS LTD

Fine panels in granite and real marble. A special backing makes them stable for use as flooring. Granite comes only in natural shades; marble is predominantly Green, Pink, Brown, or Beige. *M:* to order. *P:* sq m marble £96–£165, granite £130–£185.

PETIT ROQUE LTD

Finely polished slate or marble and sandstone tiles. Slate comes in Green (*P:* tile £9.15, £19.70) and Black (*P:* tile £4.10, £7.80). *M:* both 18×12, 18in (46×30.5, 46cm). Marble and sandstone tiles are in Perlato (beige), Patricia Verde (green), Goldstone, and Rosso Levanto (rose red) (*M:* 20×15in/51×38cm, *P:* tile £13.60–£16.30 depending on shade).

VINYL SHEET FLOORING

ARMSTRONG CORK CO LTD

Marvellous vinyl floorings, wide enough to be installed without seams in all but the largest rooms. ARMSTRONG DIY 400 CUSHIONED VINYL is especially suitable for laying yourself. It's flexible, easy to cut and requires no tape or adhesive to hold it down at the edges. Five patterns: 'Medallion', a bold tiled effect with a medallion motif in Terracotta, Tan, Natural, Beige, and Blue; 'Orlando' Spanish or Provençal tiles in warm natural colours—Terracotta, Beige, White, and Bronze; 'Fiesta', a small square tile pattern in Green, Blue, Brown, Mink, and Gold; 'Avalon', an overall marble effect in White, Beige, Green, and

Pink; and 'Terrace' 'bricks' in Cream, Beige, Burnt red, and Soft green. *P:* sq m £4.

PREMIER CASTILIAN is very hardwearing with an extra-thick cushioned inner layer and a strong backing that make it suitable for laying over a variety of sub-floors. Subtle shading and deep embossing create a warm, natural look. There are eight patterns: 'Casino', a classic Provençal shape, incorporates a surface pattern, in White, Beige, Soft gold, Terracotta and Soft green; 'Parquet' comes in two wood tones, pine and oak; 'Portofino' and 'Palamos' are both in naturalistic earth shades, the former Provençal shaped, the latter square; 'Woodspice', a more complex parquet design, is in two brown shades; 'Chantilly' is an ornate tile pattern in Cream or Beige; 'Domingo', an unusual Moorish design, comes in Cream, three tans, an Olive green and an unusual Sea blue; and 'Texture' is an overall marble effect in Beige, Brown and Off-white. *P:* sq m £6.50.

ARMSTRONG ACCOTONE is similar, and also very hardwearing, but more moderately priced. It comes in seven designs: 'Patio', an attractive textured brick effect in Black, Off-white, Mid-brown, Tan, Golden brown, and Dark brown; 'Woodstock', a traditional wood block design in light and medium tones;

Armstrong's 'Casa Bella' from OLYMPIA

'Ceramica', a geometric tile pattern in predominantly Green or Tan shades; 'Moravian Inset', a pleasant combination of small square plain and patterned tiles, with Blue, Beige, Tan, and Mid-brown as the dominant colours; 'Tenerife', a large, ornate floral tile design in four shades of Brown/Tan/Beige; 'Merida', a richly coloured smaller tile effect in Tan, Beige, Gold, and Deep brown; and, finally, 'Marbella', an all-over marble pattern in Off-White, Warm beige, and Tan. *P:* sq m £4.25.

Armstrong's 'San Marino' from SUNDIAL

OLYMPIA is available in four designs, all in earth tones. Three are inspired by tiles, one is a parquet pattern. *P:* sq m £7.50.

SUNDIAL comes in soft earth shades, in three patterns: the usual Provençal shaped tiles; smaller versions including 'San Marino', and 'Arabesque' square tiles. *P:* sq m £7.

M: all ranges w 200, 400cm (6ft 6¾in, 13ft 1½in).

DLW (BRITAIN) LTD

TRILUXE high-quality cushioned vinyl flooring made in Germany, wide enough to be laid wall-to-wall without seams in most rooms. There are four patterns: three are inspired by Provençal motifs, the fourth is an unobtrusive all-over terrazzo effect. All come in three or

DLW's '8741' terrazzo pattern from TRILUXE

PRICES AND INFORMATION WERE CORRECT AT THE TIME OF GOING TO PRESS

four warm, natural, earthy shades ranging from greens through beiges to terracottas. *M:* w 400cm (13ft 1½in).

MARMORETTE is a very hardwearing marbleized lino, suitable for high-traffic areas. 17 colours include several shades of neutral Greys and Beiges, a bright Red, two Blues, Black and a good Tan. *M:* w 200cm (6ft 6¾in). Marbleized PVC is also available, in rolls or tiles. It comes in cool Beige, Sand, Coffee, Cream, Grey and Grey-green. *M:* marbleized PVC, rolls w 60cm (5ft 3in), tiles 30×30, 50×50cm (11⅞×11⅞, 19⅝×19⅝in). *P:* all products upon application.

DUNLOP SEMTEX LTD

Very reasonably priced, good quality VYNOLAY sheet vinyl, in 20 colours and designs. Patterns are mainly attractive 'tiles', but simulated wood block effects and small geometrics are also available. Suitable for do-it-yourself. *M:* w 6ft (183cm). *P:* sq yd £4.

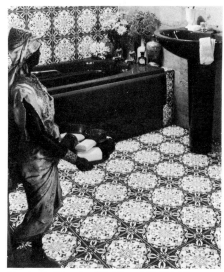

Dunlop's 'Caspian Tile' from VYNOLAY

GERLAND LTD

Enormous selection of very high-quality flooring. Reasonably priced GERFLOR 4000 cushioned vinyl is suitable for a wall-to-wall, seamless fit. Designs, based on French Provençal tiles, come in pleasant, subtly shaded, natural colours. 'Cezanne' is available in Brick, Beige, and Ochre; 'Sierra', alternating large and small tiles, is in Beige, Chamois, Sienna, and Copper; 'Antibes' and 'Solar' are more complicated tile patterns in lovely natural tones including russets and golds; 'Fontainebleau' is a contrasting wood block effect in two light wood tones; 'Elysee', a more elaborate parquet design, is also in two shades—Chestnut and Cedar. *M:* w 400cm (13ft 1½in). *P:* sq m £7.

Tough, top-quality GERFLOR CUSHIONFLEX has 12 patterns, three based on classical tile motifs: 'Alhambra' in Sienna, and Flame; 'Casbah' in Copper; and 'Picardie' in Blue, Beige, Brown, and Ochre. The range also includes 'Parquet' in Oak; 'Cadiz' terracotta tiles in Sandstone, and Ivory; 'Cork' in medium and light shades; 'Disco', a bold abstract design in Brown and White; 'Forum' 'marble slabs' with small inset diagonals in Black on White, and Brown on Off-white; 'Bologna', a random rectangular stone slab effect in Beige, and Gold; and 'Etna', an overall marbleized effect in Beige. *M:* w 200cm (6ft 6¾in). *P:* sq m £7.

Gerland's 'Cezanne' from GERFLOR 4000

GERFLOR DIPLOMA is as wide as 4000, but less expensive. It has a reasonable selection of patterns, mainly 'natural' stone, tile, wood, and mosaic effects. 'Oporto' is simulated cork slabs in two browns; 'Ascot' parquet effect comes in Oak or Elm; 'Florence' is the familiar Provençal tile in Sienna, Brick, and Ivory; 'Ravenna' is a plain earthenware tile in Beige, Orange, Honey, and Rust; 'Strada' stone mosaic effect is in Sable (sand), Emerald, Granite, and Bronze; 'Provence', another traditional French 'earthenware' tile design, is in Copper, Orange, Sandstone and Cognac. *M:* w 400cm (13ft 1½in). *P:* sq m £5.50.
'Easy-lay' GERFLOR VISA fibreglass-reinforced

Gerland's 'Oporto' from GERFLOR DIPLOMA

Gerland's 'Alhambra' from GERFLOR CUSHIONFLEX

vinyl flooring can be loose-laid without adhesive, and is very moderately priced. Patterns are: 'Medina' small Moorish tiles in Ochre, Marine (blue), Flame (brown), and Copper; 'Palmyra', another interlocking tile design, in Sandstone, Ochre, and Copper; 'Chatelet' wood block effect in Oak; 'Malta', a plain tile pattern in Brown, Regency (pale green), Copper, and Sandstone; 'Minos', a modern abstract design in Jade (green on beige), Savannah (tan on beige), and Cognac (dark brown on tan); and 'Veneto' square tiles with small insets in Chamois, Bronze, Copper, and Ochre. *M:* w 200cm (6ft 6¾in). *P:* sq m £5. Inexpensive GERFLOR STANDARD cushioned

Gerland's 'Medina' from GERFLOR VISA

vinyl consists mainly of simulated tile designs with a pleasantly natural look. Among the best of the ten patterns are: 'Sorrento' large Provençal tiles in Copper, Ochre, Ivory, and Brick; 'Tudor' hexagonal tiles in Copper, and Orange; 'Algarve' highly decorated motifs with Olive, Brown, or Burnt orange predominating; 'Provence', another mellow earthenware design, in Copper, Sandstone, and Cognac; 'Italian Marble' Beige travertine; 'Cartel', a smaller version of 'Sorrento', in Beige, Gold, Green, Terracotta, and Sable; and 'Parquet' in Pine, and Teak. *M:* w 200cm (6ft 6¾in). *P:* sq m £5.40.
GERFLOR BRAVO high-quality foam-cushioned flooring, wide enough for a seamless fit, comes in four designs only: 'Alicante', an abstract floral in Beige, and Cream; 'Labrador', a lovely textured hexagonal in the same

shades; 'Agora' large 'stone' squares in beige and tan tones; and 'Granada' Mediterranean floral tiles in Olive, Russet, and Blue-green colourways. *M:* w 400cm (13ft 1½in). *P:* sq m £9.

CLASSIC marbled vinyl is much more typical, and comes in an amazing total of 16 shades from whitest White to blackest Black, with plenty of primaries like Red and Cobalt blue in between, streaked with Grey/White. Also available in tiles. *M:* w 200cm (6ft 6¾in), tiles 30×30cm (11⅞×11⅞in). *P:* sq m £5.

MARS, the most unusual range, is a felt-backed vinyl flooring with a slightly stippled surface. It comes in Beige, Grey, Gold, Sea green, Aqua, Orange, and Brick red. *M:* w 200cm (6ft 6¾in). *P:* sq m £3.50.

NAIRN COATED PRODUCTS LTD

Three cushioned vinyl ranges in extra-wide as well as normal widths.

ARENA DE LUXE, the top collection, comes in eight naturalistically coloured patterns including wood plank 'Madeira' in light, medium and dark tones; 'Minoa' square, stone-textured tiles in Beige, Gold, Tan or Rust; and 'Capri', a stone effect with a diamond shape cut into a square, in Light beige, Slate grey, Light sand or Tan. *P:* sq m £6.

CUSHIONFLOR DELUXE, a comprehensive middle-priced range, has a multitude of patterns—23 designs include traditional tile and terrazzo effects, plus marble and stone. (*P:* sq m £5.50.)

Budget CLASSIC SEAMFREE has 12 designs in 30 colourways, including woodblock, un-glazed and patterned tiles, rush matting, terrazzo and minibrick effects (*P:* sq m £4.50). *M:* w 2, 4m (2yd 6¾in, 4yd 13½in).

Nairn's 'Capri' from ARENA DE LUXE

SOMMER ALLIBERT (UK) LTD

A very wide range of floor coverings.

BALASOFT, the top range, in extra-thick, textured, double vinyl backed with heavy-duty compressed foam is warm and soft to the tread, and extremely hardwearing. Patterns are: 'Aztec', a shaded brick effect in Cream, Slate, and Rust; 'Scandinavian Wood' simulated parquet; 'Marbella' small Provençal tiles and 'Octavian' octagonal and square tiles, both in Beige, Rust, Olive, and Gold; 'Florentine' unusual mosaic-inspired tiles in Cream, and Mushroom; and two florals—very subtle 'Geisha' in Brown/Rust, and Yellow/Beige, and 'Jacobean', a more colourful, complex pattern with Honey, Blue, or Olive predominating. *P:* m £4.50.

TRICONFORT tough flexible flooring, originally designed for contract use, is now available to the public in wonderfully simple, subtle patterns and colours: 'Travertine Tile' in Grey; 'Aztec' earthenware tiles in Honey; 'Herringbone' marble tiles in Beige; 'Cork Tile' in Light and Mid-brown; 'Oak Plank'; 'Dark Brick' and 'Light Brick'; 'Dark Woodblock Oak'; 'Hexagon' and 'Honeycombe' hexagon tiles, both in beige/brown shades. Textured pales are also available: 'Tweed' in Green, and Beige; 'Flake' in White-specked Beige; 'Jaspe' sandstone in three beiges; and 'Travertine' in Sand, and Raw silk (white). 'Basketweave', by far the most unusual design, consists of small checks in Cream, Beige, Dark brown, Green, and Chestnut. *P:* m £3.60–£3.80.

Less expensive BALASTAR also comes in a good selection of designs. Highly patterned 'Victorian Tile' is in Rust, Green, and Blue; 'Cloud' is an overall Creamy-beige fleck; 'Corinth', a small, interlocking curved tile pattern, comes, unusually, in Pale pink only; 'Quarry' is in natural Sand; 'Dutch Tile', a small Provençal shape, comes in Grey, Green, Gold, and Beige; 'Portuguese Cork', 'Woodblock' and 'Devon Tile' are all available in realistic shades. 'Rustic Stone', a stone effect sporadically decorated with leaves, comes in Mushroom, and Tobacco. *P:* m £2.70.

Sommer say BALANOR, a flexible, luxury floor covering, is especially easy to lay. It comes in an enormous selection of patterns, most with naturalistic tile effects. Squares are: 'Quarry' in Nut brown, and Midnight blue; 'Greek Tile' in Gold, and Sandy brown; and 'Cottage Brick' in Flame, and Moss. Floral-bedecked squares include 'Moroccan Tile' in Brown, and Tangerine; 'Avignon' in Stone; 'Regency Tile' in Blackberry, or Cornflower, on a White ground; and 'Malvern', a more modern motif in Green, and Brown. Popular hexagonal designs are 'Provence' in Honey, and Old brick; 'Dutch Tile' in Tan; and two smaller-scale patterns—'Tomette' in Mushroom, Autumn gold, Russet, and Spruce green, and 'Wood Plank' in Natural only. The most unusual pattern is 'Concorde' with small interlocking shapes in Salmon, Stone, or Pacific blue (turquoise). *P:* £3.15.

Finally, the FLOORMATE do-it-yourself range

has seven patterns: 'Marble' is in Beige; 'Woodblock' and 'Cork Tile', in natural colourations; 'Malaga' in Olive, Orange, and Brown, and 'Jeddah' in Tan are both Mediterranean tile shapes. More ornate designs are 'Athenian' in Cream, Green, and Beige; and 'Floral' in Aubergine, Gold, and Blue. *P:* m £2.70.

M: all ranges w 200cm (6ft 6¾in). See also 'Wall Coverings'.

VINYL TILE FLOORING

AMTICO (NATIONAL PLASTICS) LTD

AMTICO vinyl tiles, definitely the most expensive on the market. They come closer than any others to achieving the beauty of 'natural' flooring materials—special 'grouting' and beautiful hand-finishing mean that no two tiles are exactly the same. Extremely hardwearing, they're often used in shops, banks, restaurants, etc. AMTICO tiles come in a great range of classical, modern and realistic designs, and several colourways: 'Esplanade' large Spanish-inspired brown-etched ceramic tiles with a herringbone border in White, Cream, and Brown; 'Mountsorrel' perfectly plain, very convincing square tiles, in White, Brick red, and Orange-red; 'Chateau', 'New Chateau' and 'Antique Chateau' Provençal tiles with alternating plain and textured areas, in Cream, White, Brick red, Burnt orange, Russet, and, unusually, Black; 'Bucks County', a similarly textured smart herringbone brick design in White, Black, Tan, and Slate blue; 'Oxford Brick' like 'Bucks County', but for domestic use only, in Cream, Brick red, and Red-orange; and 'Tudor Brick', consisting of three alternating squares of bricks in White, Brick red, and Orange. There are also two simulated wood block designs: 'French Parquet' lovely etched wood tiles in White, and Brown; and 'Trianon' interlocking motifs in Brown. 'Renaissance' plain marbleized stone-effect tiles come in White, Black, Cream, Pale gold, and Green/Yellow; it's also available in a larger size into which the normal, smaller tiles can be set diagonally for contrast. 'Pantheon' is a cool classical pattern in White, Off-white, and Salmon beige; 'Phoenicia', a simple geometric of large squares edged in small ones, is in White, Cream, and Pale gold; elegant 'Lorenzo' resembles incised travertine marble in White, Off-white, and Light salmon; 'Amsterdam' comes in the same shades. 'Lorenzo Travertine' is marbleized, in Cream, and Off-white. 'Harmony', a more typical design, has marbly streaks on a plain background of White, Black, Pale grey, Beige, Dark green, Cream, Yellow, Yellow-green, and wonderfully bright Blue.

For purists, there are also absolutely plain tiles in Black, or White—perfect for the ever-popular chequered floor used in foyers, hallways, etc, or for the drama of solid black or white floors.

Amtico's travertine-effect 'Lorenzo'

Amtico's 'Amsterdam'

Amtico will provide special shapes and strips, provided they can be cut from a 91cm (3ft) square; and will match colours and produce special designs if the order is big enough.
The company sells a liquid floor cleaner and wax dressing for their floors. (We've tried them both and they're the best.)
M: 30.5×30.5cm (12×12in), 'Renaissance' also 91.5×91.5cm (3×3ft). *P:* sq m £21–£25. see page 123 for 'Mountsorrel' in colour.

ARMSTRONG CORK CO LTD
PLACE 'N' PRESS vinyl tiles. They're available smooth, or embossed for hard wear and easy maintenance. Patterns are: 'San Roque' Spanish tile design in natural Terracotta, Tan, White, and Cream; 'Palatial' terrazzo marble chip effect in Natural cork, Alba beige, Corsica olive, Lemon, and cool White; 'Bradford Brick' in Red, and White; 'Travertine Marble' in Cream, and Beige; 'Woodblock' in Light oak, and Teak; 'Bisque' octagon tiles in Bronze, Cream/Beige, and White; and 'Tivoli' in White, Green, Gold, and Tan/Brown. Tiles come in packs of 11, covering a square metre. *M:* 30×30cm (11⁷/₈×11⁷/₈in). *P:* pack £6.

Clockwise from top centre: Armstrong's 'San Roque', 'Palatial', 'Bradford Brick', 'Travertine Marble', 'Woodblock', 'Bisque', and 'Tivoli' (centre), all from PLACE 'N' PRESS

DLW (BRITAIN) LTD
High-quality marble-effect tiles, for heavy domestic or commercial use. They come in nine subtle shades: two greys, one beige-yellow, five beige-browns, and one soft sea green. *M:* 30×30, 50×50cm (11⁷/₈×11⁷/₈, 19⁵/₈×19⁵/₈in). *P:* upon application.

DUNLOP SEMTEX LTD
Inexpensive, easy-to-lay DUNLOP SELFLAY tiles. Available in packs of 16, they come in 12 marble-effect colours: Mediterranean blue, Charcoal, Capri blue, Silver birch, Honey, Tangerine, Mexican maize, Yellow, Tan, Chocolate, Sage green (pale beige-green), and Lime green. *M:* 9×9in (23×23cm). *P:* £2–£2.50. DUNLOP CRAFTSMAN SUPER are heavier, more expensive, and are supplied in nine-tile packs. Nine marble-effect colours include: Tobacco, Cinnamon, White gold, Sicilian grey, Kingfisher, Mustard, and Silver birch. *M:* 30×30cm (11⁷/₈×11⁷/₈in). *P:* pack £2.50–£3. ARISTOCRAT self-adhesive tiles are particularly easy and convenient to lay. Four of the five patterns are large, decorative floral tiles. 'Woburn' comes in Terracotta, and Chocolate brown, in packs of nine. *M:* 30.5×30.5cm (12×12in). *P:* pack £5.25.

PRICES AND INFORMATION WERE CORRECT AT THE TIME OF GOING TO PRESS

Dunlop's 'Woburn' from ARISTOCRAT

GERLAND LTD
Six good ranges. Hardwearing ARDOISE tiles, suitable for contract use, simulate slate convincingly with raised non-slip graining. 'Slates' are cut in varying directions from large plaques to obtain 32 different reliefs, giving a very geometric look to the finished floor. *M:* 40×20cm (15³/₄×7⁷/₈in). *P:* sq m £19.
CLASSIC heavy-duty tiles come in 16 plain colours, all with a slight marbled streak: White, Grapefruit, Cognac, Redcurrant, Ash grey, Bracken (warmer grey), Lime green, Liffey green, Pearl grey, Mid-grey, Riviera (blue), Marine blue, Cotswold beige, Chamois, Peat, and Black. *M:* 30×30cm (11⁷/₈×11⁷/₈in). *P:* sq m £5.
ARCHITECTON is similar but the marble effect is more subtle. The tiles are primarily designed for contract use, but the strong plain colours should also appeal to domestic users. 12 shades: White, Imperial blue, Light grey, Redcurrant, Cotswold beige, Old gold, Ash grey, Sage green, Dark grey, Black, Chocolate, and Tango (orange). *M:* 30×30cm (11⁷/₈×11⁷/₈in). *P:* sq m £4.25.
Flexible DECORTILE, and DECORSTIK (self-adhesive) tiles are much thinner, and intended for do-it-yourselfers. Available in packs covering 5sq m (c 54sq ft) they're easy to lay and cut. Both come in nine colours: Ivory, Dove grey, Black, Old gold, Chateau green, Imperial blue, Palmyra stone (pink-beige), Tango (orange), and Havana (deep brown). *M:* 25×25cm (9⁷/₈×9⁷/₈in). *P:* DECORTILE sq m £3.05; DECORSTIK sq m £4.25.

WOOD FLOORING

ALLIANCE FLOORING CO LTD

Do-it-yourself parquet flooring at reasonable prices. Felt-backed, pre-sanded and beautifully sealed hardwood mosaic panels are available in a variety of woods: kempas, afzelia, red meranti (redwood), walnut, agba, iroko, mahogany (sapele), Burma teak (standard, and Haddon Hall pattern), and oak (*M:* 4½×4½in/ 11.5×11.5cm, *P:* sq yd £4–£7). Kiln-dried, tongued and grooved hardwood strip overlay is also available in Tasmanian oak, Canadian oak, mahogany (sapele), Canadian maple, and iroko (*M:* w 2in/5cm, *P:* sq yd £6.50–£9.50).

ILFORD PARQUET CO LTD

Competitively priced pre-sanded wood mosaic panels, suitable for do-it-yourself. They come in a basketweave pattern of 16 sections, each containing five strips of wood: Burma teak, iroko, afzelia, or red meranti (redwood). Ilford Parquet also supply adhesives, panel pins, sealers, skirting edgings, cork inserts and threshold strips, all reasonably priced. *M:* panels 18×18in (46×46cm). *P:* panels sq yd £5–£6.50.

PAR-K-PLY LTD

Laminated strip flooring, each strip bonded with phenolic adhesive and sealed with a non-slip satiny resin. A unique interlocking system of rounded 'ears' makes them very easy to lay, and suitable for do-it-yourself. Although the sub-floor must be flat, the flooring can go over almost any base material. It comes in oak and African utile (a reddish wood), the latter in shorter as well as standard lengths—perfect for herringbone and basketweave patterns. Panel pins and adhesive are also available. *M:* 35¼×2¾in (89.5×7cm), African utile also 13¾×2¾in (35×7cm). *P:* sq yd £7–£8.50.

SURREYBOARD CO LTD

Felt-backed, hardwood parquet flooring tiles for do-it-yourself. Their outstanding feature is a special double-sided adhesive tape which enables the floor to be laid without the usual messy bitumen adhesive (but the latter is available). The tiles are ready-sanded, but not sealed, and come in juniper, mahogany, iroko (African teak), oak, Burma teak, and agba (African oak). Surreyboard will also provide matching mouldings, polish, wax remover, and sanding blocks. *M:* 18×18in (46×46cm). *P:* sq yd £7–£10.

Surreyboard's parquet tile (detail)

Solid tongue-and-grooved oak blocks for laying in classic 'herringbone' or 'brick bond' patterns are available. *M:* 2⅝×10⅜in (6.5× 26.5cm). *P:* sq yd £15.

VIGERS STEVENS & ADAMS LTD

Good choice of flooring. PARKIFLEX easy-to-lay flexible parquet flooring panels are designed for do-it-yourself installation. In iroko (African teak), sapele and mahogany combined, each block contains 16 alternately laid smaller sections of parallel fillets. Panels should be sealed with the manufacturer's compatible floor sealer. *M:* 46×46cm (18× 18in). LAMELLA OVERLAY prefinished laminated strip flooring is made from two layers of softwood, and one of hardwood, with tongued and grooved sides and ends. It comes in oak, ash, brown acacia, and beech. Panels are laid on an underlay of cork and bitumen for good insulation. This very hardwearing and resilient floor normally needs to be laid by a specialist. *M:* 300×13.7cm (9ft 10⅛×5⅜in). Skirting and doorway strips are also supplied. For high-quality flooring, kiln-dried hardwoods are available as unsealed strips interlocked by tongued and grooved edges, in random lengths. *M:* 100–250cm (3ft 3⅜in–8ft 2⅜in). Traditional parquet strips, in tongued or grooved blocks, can be laid in a variety of patterns. *M:* 23×7.5cm (9×3in). Both are available, with skirtings and thresholds, in a number of woods including gerjun, iroko, merban, maple, and oak.

VISTAWOOD hardwood mosaic flooring comes in panels made up of opposite grained sections containing four or five fillets. Suitable for very heavy traffic areas like schools and sports halls, it's virtually indestructible in a domestic setting. *M:* 46.3×46.3cm (18⅛× 18⅛in). FELTWOOD hardwood mosaic flooring is similar, with a felt backing. *M:* 46× 46cm (18×18in). Both should be installed by a specialist. *P:* all products upon application.

Vigers Stevens' PARKIFLEX flooring

WICANDERS (GREAT BRITAIN) LTD

WOODLINE pre-finished oak hardwood flooring. It's impregnated with oil and wax and subjected to infra-red heat for a long-lasting, attractive sheen which shows up the beauty of the natural grain. There are three styles. 'Cumberland' square parquet blocks are made of fillets laid in one direction, and come in Chestnut brown. *M:* 12×12in (30.5×30.5cm). *P:* sq yd £12. Cottage-style 'Village Plank' strips, in random widths and a good choice of lengths, look as if they're pegged down, but can be glued or nailed in place. They're available in two tonalities: Mellow brown and Old English mellow brown. *M:* 12in–5ft×random width 3, 5, 7in (30.5–152.5×7.5, 12.5, 17.5cm). *P:* sq yd £17. 'Strip Oak', a bold grained planked floor, comes in Natural and Gunstock shades. *M:* 9in–8ft×2¼in (23–244×5.5cm). *P:* sq yd £13–£16.

The PERMAGRAIN range, made with a special process by which oak is sealed with liquid acrylic polymer that has been forced into the porous structure, is exceptionally hardwearing. Designed for contract (or commercial) use, it is perhaps over-specified for domestic purposes, but would certainly provide a handsome floor with several lifetimes of wear. It comes in four shades of grained oak. Fillets in each section are laid parallel to create one-directional, or tesselated, effects. *M:* 12×12in (30.5×30.5cm). *P:* sq yd £18. Adhesives, trowels and wax conditioner are available for all products.

See page 124 for 'Strip Oak' in colour.

Wicanders' 'Cumberland' from WOODLINE

INTRODUCTION

Kitchens today are light years removed from their Victorian counterparts. The traditional larder or pantry has been overtaken by refrigerators and freezers. Floors are often cork, tiled or vinyl instead of stone or wood. The cooking range that could take up an entire wall has been fragmented into split ovens and hobs, eye-level grills and a host of gadgets. Nevertheless, it's still possible to opt for either a traditional or modern approach, depending primarily on the material used for cabinet fronts.

Basically, there are five surfaces: solid wood, usually protected with a coat of clear sealer; wood veneer – thin sheets glued on to a cheaper base board – similarly protected and sometimes combined with solid wood frames; mock wood in plastic laminate; and coloured laminates (the trade term for plastic laminates), in a matt finish or with the ultimate shine of lacquer look-alike gloss laminate. Solid wood kitchens are generally the most expensive, matt laminate the cheapest.

Although there is no such thing as a cheap kitchen, there are ways to cut the costs. If you're starting from scratch it's worth remembering that today's kitchen unit is essentially a simple box mounted on a plinth and fitted with shelves, wire storage baskets, racks, etc. Make your own housing, and fit the cabinets with the accessories you need. If you already have the units, and simply want to change the doors, invest in new drawer and door fronts in solid pine or oak, or go in search of discarded doors and/or panels from an architectural salvage supplier.

If none of these options appeal, be prepared to part with a fair amount of cash. This can be substantially reduced if you invest in a self-assembly kitchen – dealing direct with the manufacturer ensures good value for money and, although it may not be the cheapest kitchen on the market, it will almost certainly cost less than its 'fitted' counterpart. Whether you go for self-assembly, or prefer to have your kitchen installed by an expert, first do an accurate floor plan, complete with measurements of all furniture and appliances that will be part of the new room. Alternatively, the manufacturer will arrange for a kitchen planner (his agent) to do the groundwork and installation.

Accessories include a wide choice of coloured hobs, decor panels for refrigerators and freezers (to match cabinet fronts), etc. See 'Appliances'. Even sinks and taps have come a long way. Gone are the days when the former were heavy, White troughs. Today sinks come in virtually any shape, can be inset into worktops, and are in every imaginable colour – bright Blue, blazing Yellow, beaten copper. Draining boards, as part of the sink, or draining baskets which drop in, are also available. Taps are coloured, Edwardian or industrial.

PRICES AND INFORMATION WERE CORRECT AT THE TIME OF GOING TO PRESS

Lighting is another important design element. Most manufacturers make matching panels to conceal strip lights mounted on top cupboards, but other lighting is also necessary. See also 'Lighting'.

Once all these details have been finalised, discuss your requirements with a supplier. Usually, after taking accurate measurements, he will provide a plan and written quotation. It pays to shop around – or even ask more than one installer to quote on the same kitchen.

The following section includes over 40 manufacturers. Text about each firm describes the company's general approach, and focuses on outstanding ranges or details. (Most companies make matt laminate kitchens, but some offer pleasing handles or unusual colours). The charts that follow the text give details of the finishes, handles and worktops in each range, with a sketch illustrating a typical top drawer/bottom cupboard combination. Worktops are laminates unless otherwise stated, and come in one of three ways: square edged, post formed or round-edged, or edged with solid wood to match base cabinets. (A few companies that make only a limited number of ranges have not been charted; appropriate details are given in the text). Study these charts once you have decided on the style, and look through the company's brochure. The section ends with descriptions of some outstanding *Kitchen Accessories*.

Measurements differ slightly from company to company; once you have decided on the kitchen you want, it's really up to you or the planner to work out how you can fit the units into the given space.

Opposite, left to right, from top: Stained glass by David Pearl, Amber Hiscott (both Wind's Eye Studios), Robina Jack, Mark Angus

*Prices are based on a combination of the following items. (If a specific width was not available, the nearest, larger, width was used). 45cm (17¾in) base unit with drawer; 90cm (35⅜in) sink base with two doors; half carousel with two baskets; 90cm (35⅜in) hob base with two doors; oven housing unit (oven h 87.6cm/34½in); single 45cm (17¾in) wall unit; double 90cm (35⅝in) wall unit; single 60cm (23⅝in) wall unit.

*In the 'Finishes' column of the charts, edgings are specified only if a choice of special stains or effects is available. Many manufacturers do standard wood edgings and trims.

ALLMILMÖ LTD

Beautiful kitchens from a consistently stylish manufacturer. 40 front designs are available with over 500 cabinet types in all—probably the largest selection on the market. At least two kitchens are unique: CONTURA EDELWEISS, with an undulating ribbed surface and soft matt finish, and FUENEN CARREE, which has an intricate square-orientated design in laminate inside a light oak surround. Allmilmö make wood kitchens in an equally impressive variety of designs. Visual appeal is well matched by conscientious attention to detail, like a special clip-on plinth with a built-in flexible floor seal to prevent liquids running under cabinets. See page 161 for CONTURA EDELWEISS in colour.

Allmilmö's FUENEN CARREE

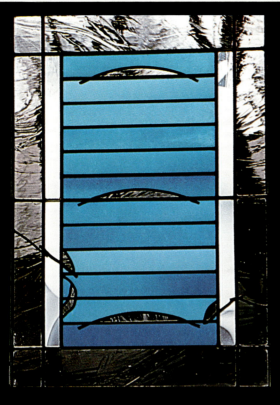

ALNO (UK) LTD

Attractive range of fitted kitchens with individual design details like special handles, and many imaginative storage ideas. Unusual, space-conscious furniture for the dining area consists of an L-shaped upholstered wooden bench (back rests match the kitchen tables), a wooden table and two free-standing chairs. An excellent idea for a spare corner—and the perfect complement to an Alno kitchen.

ARCLINEA UK LTD

Four modern, functional ranges from an Italian manufacturer. H85, the most unusual, has plain laminate fronts, in White, Sand, or Wood; cylindrical red plastic pulls are the only accent. SILVA M30 is for rustic fans.

Unusual storage options include small spice drawers, and a pull-out chopping trolley. Other, more standard fittings are equally sensible and beautiful. Like most Italian companies, Arclinea produce a brochure full of ideas for layouts and colour schemes.

ASKO FINNTERNATIONAL LTD

Marvellously up-to-the-minute Scandinavian pine kitchen. LAPPONIA is panelled (vertically on doors and drawer fronts, horizontally on walls) with solid pine or pine laminate worktops. Handles are bold wooden knobs. Other matching storage options are available, as well as a dining table and chairs. This sauna-like range is for anyone who likes their pine modern and practical.

ROBERT BOSCH LTD

Good-looking kitchens with excellent storage solutions like corner and spice units, plus matching cornices and rounded end units. Bosch's sensible policy is to concentrate on only 15 ranges—slightly fewer than some of their German competitors—while still offering a comparatively wide selection of designs. Fronts come in a good range of finishes including Wenge, a darkish wood. The company's brochure shows how their units can be used effectively for storage or room division in living or dining areas, to blend with the kitchen.

BULTHAUP UK

Extraordinarily large selection of tasteful designs, from a top-of-the-market German manufacturer. 17 ranges are available in a wide variety of finishes. CONTUR, the most unusual, has softly rounded edges surrounding the interior grid, and comes in 20 finishes: four natural wood shades, three hand-dragged colours (Polar white, Soft azure, and Black-brown), nine polyurethane-covered fronts (Polar white, Soft azure, Graphite, Light grey, Maple yellow, Salmon red, Pearl white, Iris green and Terra brown), and four with White laminate centre panels edged in White,

Alno's ALNOPART (above); Asko Finnternational's LAPPONIA (below)

Azure, Graphite, or natural wood. Unusual treatments for solid wood include White with Blue moulded edges (BURGUNDY and BRITTANY) and hand-dragged White with Gold (PROVENCE).

Some cabinet fronts can be ordered undrilled, i.e. without handles, to be personalized with the customer's choice of pulls, knobs, etc. Similarly, some can be supplied sanded only, ready for staining, painting, polishing, etc. Special stains cost an extra 7%. See page 152 for CONTUR in colour.

CROSBY KITCHENS LTD

Three high-quality, self-assembly kitchens (a combination that's none too common). The solid wooden range is made from imported alder, a Canadian timber, stained and finished by hand. For a relatively small manufacturer Crosby make a good range of accessories including wire storage baskets, drawer liners, cornices and spice racks.

Left: Siematic's 5005S in White

THOMAS EASTHAM & SON LTD

Fully integrated fitted kitchens from Eastham Burco, who also make high-quality cookers, refrigerators, washing machines and dishwashers. The kitchens will readily accommodate Eastham's, and other manufacturers', appliances. Worktops come in a variety of finishes, with round or square edges. Imaginative ancillary furniture includes peninsular wall units and breakfast bar extensions. A planning kit comes with the brochures; if you send a sketch, and £5, their kitchen planning department will produce a detailed layout.

J T ELLIS & CO LTD

Useful selection of moderately priced kitchens, some specifically intended for builders, developers and local authorities. CHEVIOT DE LUXE, the top range, has a real wood carcase with dark oak outside, mahogany inside. A full range of accessories is

Eastham's COTTAGE

available including stainless steel or coloured sinks, and an inset ceramic chopping board; also some good storage ideas such as divided and lined cutlery drawers.

Left: J T Ellis' CHEVIOT (top), CHEVIOT DE LUXE (bottom)

ENGLISH ROSE KITCHENS LTD

Beautifully made kitchens from an extremely conscientious British firm. Craftsmanship is the keynote, with the emphasis on the very highest quality hardwood frames, the thickest laminates, and doors and drawers that open

English Rose's FRAMEY (below)

and close silently. An impressive number of manufacturing processes and inspections ensures a constant standard. Modern space-saving devices like apothecary drawers are available, plus worktop cutting boards, stainless steel or coloured sinks, and some round-edged laminate worktops. For a really personal touch, clients can specify any one-off oddity they fancy—English Rose will try to oblige.

FORMAT KITCHENS
Attractive collection of kitchens with the emphasis on manufacturing precision and technical excellence. There are 12 ranges, all beautifully made. Wood fronts are resistant to damp and water, drawer interiors are rounded with no joints or corners where dust or dirt can accumulate, stainless steel hinges are noise-less and adjustable. 17 worktop materials are available including four in earthy ceramic tiles, and 16 sink styles. FLANDERN, one of the top ranges, can be supplied with a very unusual leaded glass door front. Many additional features can be supplied—including a radio/cassette recorder.

GEBA KITCHENS LTD
Good quality, solid kitchens. There are 24 ranges (like most German manufacturers, Geba cover a lot of ground), many of them in wood. The most striking of these wooden wonders are POMPADOUR and DU BARRY, both with magnificent hand-carved wood panels, and EXQUISIT, with Black-stained slats accented by cubic aluminium pulls. Worktops are rounded or square-edged laminates, or tiles. Oak edging is available. Additional units, and accessories like plate racks and spice shelves, cover every conceivable storage requirement.

GREENCRAFT
Craftsman-made kitchens in pine, solid oak and mahogany. Originally known for pine kitchen furniture, Greencraft deal direct with customers and price their products accordingly. WELLINGTON, in wood, is based on the classic campaign chest with brass corner edging and recessed ring pulls. Oriental-style KNIGHTSBRIDGE has a pencil-thin cane laminate surface. Worktops are available in eight basic patterns, or can be made to order. They come with rounded edges, or with mahogany or oak edging strips to match kitchen units. Options include a choice of 12 sink styles, some with drainer inserts and chopping board, additional handles and knobs so non-built-in furniture can match cabinets, and a good assortment of wire basket storage items.

PRICES AND INFORMATION WERE CORRECT AT THE TIME OF GOING TO PRESS

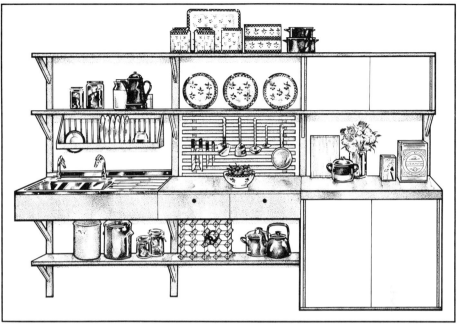

Habitat's STUDIO (above)

Greencraft's WELLINGTON (below)

GROVEWOOD PRODUCTS LTD
Well-designed, good quality kitchens to suit most tastes and budgets. They range from modern ranges like SL to traditional styles like TOWN AND COUNTRY, and can be fitted (by arrangement) or self-assembled. Many

Grovewood's SL

imaginative storage ideas make the most of every inch of space. Worktops have round or square edges, with solid wood edgings in some ranges.

HABITAT DESIGNS LTD
Simple, economical STUDIO system of cabinets. Units are attached to uprights which are fixed to the wall. Uprights, brackets, drawer fronts and edgings are in fine-grained British Columbian pine; worktops, shelves and cupboard doors are White melamine. Ten units, including upper and lower cupboards, a utensil rack, worktops, sink unit and plate rack, are supplied in packs. *M:* 'Pack One' (two uprights, three shelves) h 198 ×w 107 ×d 30cm (77⅝×42½×11⅞in); 'Pack Four' (worktop with two drawers) h 110 × w 55 × d 18cm (43⅜×21⅝×7⅛in). *P:* £53, £48.

M & I J HARRISON LTD
Made-to-order pine kitchens, based on a single, attractive panel design. Competitively priced, they come in natural, medium or dark finish, with brass handles. An impressive array of wire-framed storage solutions is available. See also 'Tables'.

HOMEWORKS LTD
Five beautifully and conscientiously designed Boffi kitchen ranges, perfect down to the last detail. Unusual handles, for example, include cool cylinders of solid elm for DOGU, and bronzed metal hemispheres for D76. Finishes include glossy lacquers, natural woods and traditional matt laminates. LA CUCINA, designed for contract use, is so nicely

M & I J Harrison's pine kitchen

executed in Dove grey laminate and light pine, with ridged plastic pulls, that it would look good in any home.

A huge selection of storage solutions and accessories includes unusual ideas like a small step-ladder mounted on lower door backs, and built-in wooden chopping boards. Boffi rate highly for simple, stunning products.

Homeworks' LA CUCINA from Boffi

HYGENA LTD
Simple, modern self-assembly kitchens in laminate, plus one in wood. Screw holes are pre-drilled, and all door backs match door fronts. Surprisingly, RICHMOND QA in oak is less expensive than the laminates, which come

in extremely attractive colours. Worktops are available in 12 standard lengths, or to order, and are round or square-edged, with timber edging, or prepared for ceramic tiles. Hygena claim to be the only manufacturer to offer a three-year guarantee with self-assembly kitchens.

JUST DOORS
Kitchen unit doors in solid kiln-dried pine finished with up to seven coats of clear melamine lacquer. They come in three standard sizes to fit most wall cupboards, and base units that can take a 19.5cm (7⅝in) plinth, 7.5cm (3in) thick worktop and have a 0.5cm (³/₁₆in) gap between door and worktop. Concealed hinges make the doors suitable for units made from melamine-faced chipboard. Fitting instructions are supplied. *M:* h 62.5cm (24⅝in) × w 39.5, 49.5, 59.5cm (15¾, 19¾, 23¾in). *P:* standard doors from £18; made-to-order up to h 80cm (31½in) × w 60cm (23⅝in) from £22.

LADYLOVE KITCHEN UNITS
Six modern kitchens with laminate or simulated wood fronts. Ladylove concentrate on a comparatively limited range of designs, but this includes the V.I.P., probably the only ventilated kitchen units on the market. Also the SLIDEAWAY with sliding doors—although these are unfashionable, demand has remained constant. The G.B. EXECUTIVE range is self-assembly, others come fully assembled.

LEICHT FURNITURE LTD
Seemingly infinite number of kitchen designs: 31 high-quality ranges, with 86 different fronts. TRADITION is available in Green-stained

wood, an interesting and perhaps slightly daring finish. As with many German-made kitchens, laminates come only in White, Sand, Yellow, and Green. Imaginative storage solutions include options like spice drawers, open wine cubicles, small shelf divisions, and a tall pull-out cupboard with access from front and back.

Leicht's TRADITION 2

MANHATTAN
Tasteful, modern kitchens. All ranges are matt laminated, except for No. 7, a pleasing, panelled wooden design. Some useful storage units are available; unusual accessories include a ceramic chopping board. Worktops have rounded or square edges.

PRICES AND INFORMATION WERE CORRECT AT THE TIME OF GOING TO PRESS

Manhattan's No 3

MAYFAIR KITCHENS

Good selection from a quality British manufacturer. VINTAGE 80 has a very unusual feature: the laminate panels can be reversed, virtually giving two kitchens for the price of one. Mayfair are well known for having introduced a number of original storage features, some of which have been copied: the carousel corner unit, a tall roll-out unit, pull-out tables with telescopic supports, etc. Options include four stainless steel sinks, six round sinks in vitreous enamel, leaded or smoked-glass door fronts, a scratch- and heat-proof glass worktop saver, and decor panels.

MFI FURNITURE CENTRES LTD

Self-assembly kitchens from a firm whose trademark is no-nonsense value for money. GEMINI, in unfinished chipboard, is a real money-saver. Two units are available, for £10 (wall) and £15 (base). *M:* wall h 47 × w 100 × d 31.1cm (18^1/$_2$×39^3/$_8$×12^1/$_4$in), base h 83 × w 100 × d 48.5cm (32^5/$_8$×39^3/$_8$×19^1/$_8$in). Some ranges are virtually indistinguishable from those of much more expensive manufacturers. The range of accessories includes a cutlery tray, laundry basket, wine rack and door storage racks. All worktops have rounded front edges and a curved splashback.

MIELE CO LTD

Handsome fitted kitchens, superbly integrated with Miele's technologically advanced cookers, washing machines, dishwashers, etc. Unusual designs include PROGRAMME 25 with cane laminate edged in solid oak, and very unusual semi-circular oak pulls; and PROGRAMME 24 with vertically panelled fronts in Black-stained oak and smart cubic aluminium pulls. Brochures and advertisements show men preparing food—good news for feminists. See also 'Appliances'.

Mayfair's MAGNUM (above); Miele's PROGRAMME 25 (below)

MOORES FURNITURE DIVISION

Cleanly designed self-assembly kitchens, easy to assemble—and easy on the pocket—including a specially designed range for the disabled. MOROCCO is especially attractive, with a warm, leather-texture finish offset against a subtly matching wood trim; while CLASSIC comes in a nice array of gloss laminate shades. Storage provisions are simple but effective. Standard worktops have square edges, but rounded (or post-formed) versions are available with some finishes.

MFI's 'Burma teak effect' kitchen

POGGENPOHL UK LTD

Beautiful, and totally functional, kitchens from the archetypal German kitchen manufacturer. Special features include storage provision for French loaves, and a built-in radio with nine-position intercom. The style is mainly modern but a few more traditional ranges are available, including FP, RP, MC and MA. CF, FP and ML can be supplied in a rustic, Green-stained wood. Worktops are wood-edged, rounded or squared, with or without splashbacks, or tiled on site. They come in six laminates, four tile colours, Wenge (parquet wood), Corian (beige mock marble), Glasal (grey-flecked stainless steel), and rippled stainless steel. There's also a huge choice of round or rectangular sinks: 25 styles in stainless steel, and five in Yellow, Olive, or Dark brown enamel. Other options include a wooden breakfast bar and corner bench or dining suite, two extractor hoods and numerous appliance housings.

Poggenpohl's 'MA 89' in rustic oak

PRIOR UNIT DESIGN

Custom-built pine kitchens, but customers can specify any other wood. Fronts are made from kiln-dried timber, interiors finished in White laminate. Doors, hung on brass hinges, are fitted with brass knobs. Prior will provide laminate or other worktops, or design units to incorporate existing tops. Any necessary equipment can be supplied, including up-to-date kitchen aids like micro-wave ovens and deep fryers; also, hand-made copper hoods. Quotations, based on accurate drawings of floor plans, are free.

SHASHTON FURNITURE LTD

Two factory-built kitchens. Door fronts are slatted pine or more formal moulded afrormosia laminated on to melamine-faced board. A huge selection of units and appliance housings, including some wall cupboards with glass-fronted doors, is available. P: pine £660, afrormosia £820. A small range of accessories includes a slide-out towel rail, wire basket carousel, bottle rack, waste bin, and cutlery tray. Melamine worktops can be supplied, with rounded or wood edges.

SIEMATIC UK LTD

Very special fitted kitchens from a company that specializes in imaginative styling. They include 8008 RA—probably the first ever rattan kitchen, with diagonal slate in a broad oak frame and striking convex drawer fronts; and the very unusual 4004 GR with Red handles and

trims. Other stylistic pluses include beautiful dining area solutions for the 1001 AL and 3003 R ranges: two oblong tables and one round one, in solid wood, and matching chairs with removable rush seats (M: to order, P: upon application). Chairs have round legs, and backs that curve slightly upwards; or legs with rounded edges, and straight backs. Available with or without arms, they come in Delft blue and Sepia. There's also the perfect corner seating unit with solid oak arms and legs and rush seats, finished to match most kitchen units. Worktops have square or round edges, come in lightly textured laminates, solid wood, slate and polished granite. Storage options and accessories include wall and

Siematic's 8008 RA

display units with small spice drawers, moulded cornices, and hook boards. The well-produced Siematic brochure is both sensible and inspiring. See page 134 for 5005 S in colour.

SOLARBO FITMENTS LTD

Self-assembly kitchens made from top-quality pine. Good value, they come in two styles: the 300 with narrow panels, and the slightly more expensive 500 with wider ones. Ranges can be mixed to fill awkward spaces. The solid pine is polymer sealed, and all hinges are invisible. Pine, brass and White porcelain knobs are sold separately, also solid chased, and 'Colonnade', brass pulls. (P: pine knob 40p–solid chased brass pull £3.70, with a wide range of prices in between.) Inset or surface-mounted sinks, in chrome nickel steel only, are available in nine styles. WEARITE laminate worktops are supplied moulded or flat and come in seven colours: Alpine white, Golden leaves, Venetian marble, Linen grey, Coffee, textured Olive green, and textured Bitter chocolate. The good range of storage options and accessories includes a vacuum cleaner rack, solid pine spice shelves, and a solid marble chopping board (M: 46×38cm/18×15in, P: £15). Solarbo will build to clients' exact requirements.

SOLENT FURNITURE LTD

Self-assembly kitchens, three in solid wood, plus ANTELOPE in laminate with striking inverted triangle handles in solid oak. Unusually, the wood kitchens include a rosewood veneer range, with the precious South American hardwood also on the inside of the doors. Standard worktops have rolled edges, but square edges are available. There are four stainless steel sinks, plus circular inset bowls in Mocha brown to complement all ranges. Accessories include a teak chopping board and wire baskets, and a good range of storage units.

Solent's ANTELOPE

STATELY HOME KITCHENS LTD

Elegant, reasonably priced, wooden kitchens, panelled in attractively grained solid American red oak. Designs are exclusive to Stately Home. Some units are available with leaded glass doors, and various appliance and top-mounted cabinet and lighting housings can be supplied. Laminated worktops have solid oak edgings.

STONEHAM & SON (DEPTFORD) LTD

British-built SILHOUETTE kitchens. All nine ranges are solid and conventionally elegant. Cabinet fronts in the 200 and 400 ranges are edged with exotic African hardwoods like utile or afrormosia, and the 600 range has striking wrought-iron handles and fittings. The 1000 range, in oak-edged laminate, comes with light or medium oak-effect worktops. Imaginative accessories include coloured chrome taps, 16 stainless steel sinks, and single enamelled bowls in Emerald green, Gold-orange, Mahogany brown, and Safari beige. Storage options include a dresser unit with spice drawers for all ranges.

TIELSA (UK) LTD

Fifteen kitchens from a German manufacturer. Striking designs include ALPINA in Green-stained oak with a fine Red line to highlight the panelling. Other stains for oak kitchens include Black, and Antique white (a very delicate, almost light grey, shade). Worktops are laminate, with a rounded front, or edged with solid oak or aluminium. Stainless steel and enamel sinks are made by Franke. Cooker canopies come in two styles, and numerous appliance housings can be supplied. Nice finishing touches include an oak-edged tile working surface, pegged wall boards, turned plate racks, and rows of tiny spice drawers. See page 151 for AROSA in colour.

Tielsa's ALPINA

SEE CHARTS AT THE END OF THIS SECTION FOR FURTHER DETAILS OF EACH RANGE

Stoneham's SILHOUETTE 600

TIFFANY KITCHENS

Good selection of kitchens, including several varieties in panelled wood (this German manufacturer's strong point). MODUS is outstanding, with chequerboard inset panels surrounded by solid wood. Worktops are round, square or wood-edged. Pleasing accessories include spice drawers and plate racks for most ranges. All kitchens are guaranteed for five years.

WHITELEAF FURNITURE

Three kitchens. Two are available in wood processed in Whiteleaf's Buckinghamshire mill using the latest vacuum kilning method, and all units are partly built by hand. The OAK kitchen is particularly attractive, with clean lines and optional smoked-glass door fronts. A

Whiteleaf's OAK

matching table, chair and sideboard are available. HAMPDEN, in Formica only, is self-assembly. Formica worktops in a wide range of finishes, are square-edged; wood edges are available. There's a good range of storage units, plus a free kitchen planning service. See also 'Tables'.

WINCHMORE FURNITURE LTD

Attractive, wood-panelled self-assembly kitchens. ASHLEY, in oak, has Formica door panels in 'woven grass' or Ruby red. Laminate worktops are unusually tasteful (no swirly designs), with rounded edges. Edgings are available in wood to match any kitchen, and can be inlaid with a choice of three plain or patterned tile designs, or supplied ready for clients' own worktops. Winchmore will replace a worktop section with a 60cm (23⅝in) wide chopping board in 'sugar rock'

Winchmore's ASHLEY

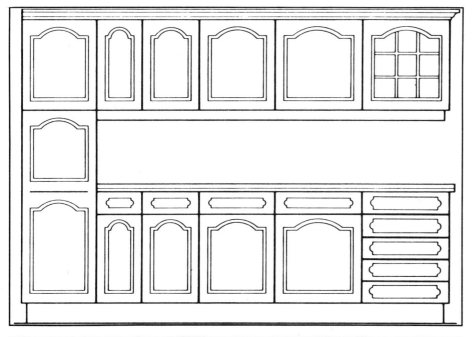

Woodfit's oak kitchen (left)

maple, with a rounded edge. The most unusual feature of all kitchens is the complete absence of handles or pulls—gold-finish hinges (Black on COLONIAL) are the only visible fittings. Units can be left as they are, or clients can choose their own handles. Accessories include two extractor hoods, a plate display rack, two covings and/or lighting valances in solid wood to match unit doors. See also 'Fittings'.

WOODFIT LTD

Doors for kitchen units and wall cupboards, made from top-quality kiln-dried American solid oak. Drawer fronts and full-height doors are also available. Great for anyone who wants to build new units from scratch, or simply improve existing ones, the range includes a glass-fronted door, usually found only in the most expensive kitchens; solid oak mouldings for cornices, and concealing lights; edging for worktops; and a matching turned oak knob. *P:* drawer front £6.50, glass-fronted door £38–£43, worktop moulding m £2.50, knob 80p.

WOODSTOCK

Made-to-measure kitchen island units and worktops in Canadian maple. Virtually unknown in the UK, this splendid hardwood develops a fine patina with age and use. Unlike a lacquer or polyurethane finish, it can be renewed—by rubbing the relevant area with wire wool and re-oiling it—making Canadian maple perfect for a heavily used working surface. (Oil costs only £1.25p for 8oz/280ml—try renewing any other working surface for that!) *M:* worktops, tables up to l. 305cm (10ft). Matching tables and chairs, and chopping boards, are also available.

WORKSHOP WONDERLAND

Handsome, all-wood, PANACHE modern kitchens made to clients' specifications. Workshop Wonderland is a group of British furniture designers who work in close co-operation with customers. Beautifully matching veneers for doors and drawer fronts come in natural or black ash, natural, dark or medium oak, and natural, red or brown mahogany. Accessories like carousels and wire baskets are readily available, but clients can order any addition they wish—including furniture for a dining area. PANACHE isn't cheap—but custom-made products never are. See overleaf for illustration.

PRICES AND INFORMATION WERE CORRECT AT THE TIME OF GOING TO PRESS

Woodstock's Canadian maple kitchen (left)

Workshop Wonderland's PANACHE

Wrighton's COTSWOLD

F WRIGHTON & SONS LTD

Beautifully designed kitchens from a company that could reasonably claim to be the UK's foremost kitchen manufacturer. (Wrighton are regular Design Council Award winners.) Decpol polyester, a particularly notable innovation, is made by an exclusive process that produces a brilliant, mirror-like finish. Other features are a sensible and sensitive collection of worktop finishes, including three inlaid tile tops—and the opportunity to choose your own. There are 11 stainless steel sinks, and a popular round inset version in Orange enamel. Taps come in six styles, with an optional spray attachment, all in chrome. A wide range of storage facilities is available, plus two ventilation systems for the optional cooker hood.

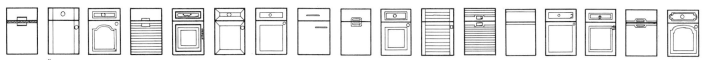

ALLMILMÖ: *Bamboo Ceragrip, Edelweiss, Micado Ceragrip and Oslo; Bornholm; Camargue; Contura Bamboo and Contura Edelweiss; Florenz and Venecia; Fuenen and Fuenen Carree; Goteborg; Gravel; Gravel, Olive, Savanne and Softline Japan; Moselle; Nevada; Nordland; Oak Reproduction; Oxford; Piemont; Sand and Tabac; Toscana*

ALLMILMÖ	PANELS	FINISHES	HANDLES	WORKTOPS
BAMBOO CERAGRIP	Laminate (oak edgings	Textured: Matt Beige	Recessed Pulls	Square, Round-edged Laminates: White, Beige, Brown; Morocco decor: Off-White, Mid-brown, Olive, Dark olive; Slate: Brown, Grey; Woodblock: Light, Dark
BORNHOLM	Oak Veneer	Light Stain	Solid Oak Knobs	AS ABOVE
CAMARGUE (L)	Solid Oak	Light, Medium, Old Brown Stains	Solid Oak Knobs	AS ABOVE
CONTURA BAMBOO, CONTURA EDELWEISS	Laminate (oak edgings)	Beige	Solid Oak Pulls	AS ABOVE
EDELWEISS	Laminate	White	Chrome Pulls	AS ABOVE
FLORENZ (L)	Solid Oak	Antique Brown Stain	Metal Pulls	AS ABOVE
FUENEN, FUENEN CARREE	Laminate (oak edgings)	Beige Linen-textured, Beige and Black Chequer—front	Solid Oak Knobs	AS ABOVE
GÖTEBORG	Oak Veneer	Medium Stain	Solid Oak Knobs	AS ABOVE
GRAVEL	Laminate (oak edgings)	Linen-textured: Beige	Solid Oak Recessed Pulls; Solid Oak Pulls	AS ABOVE
MICADO CERAGRIP	Laminate (oak edgings)	Textured: Matt beige	Recessed Oak Pulls	AS ABOVE

MOSELLE	(L)	Solid Oak	Medium Brown Stain	Solid Oak Knobs	AS ABOVE
NEVADA		Solid Oak Slats	Wenge (dark brown) Stain	Square Metal Knobs	AS ABOVE
NORDLAND		Oak Louvres	Wenge (dark brown) Stain	Recessed Wood Pulls	AS ABOVE
OAK REPRODUCTION		Laminate	Textured: Light, Medium Stains	Recessed Plastic Pulls; Metal Strips	AS ABOVE
OLIVE		Laminate	Linen-textured: Olive green	Recessed Plastic Pulls; Metal Strips	AS ABOVE
OSLO	(L)	Oak Veneer	Light Stain	Recessed Plastic Pulls	AS ABOVE
OXFORD		Mahogany Veneer	Red Mahogany	Brass Knobs	AS ABOVE
PIEMONT		Solid Oak	Medium Old Brown Stain	Burnished Metal Ring Pulls	AS ABOVE
SAND		Laminate (oak edgings)	Textured: Beige/Light, Dark Stains	Recessed Wood Pulls	AS ABOVE
SAVANNE		Laminate	Wicker-Textured: Beige	Recessed Plastic Pulls	AS ABOVE
SOFTLINE JAPAN		Laminate (oak edgings)	Silk-Textured: Beige	Recessed Wood Pulls	AS ABOVE
TABAC		Laminate (oak edgings)	Textured: Olive/Dark Stain	Recessed Wood Pulls	AS ABOVE
TOSCANA	(L)	Solid Oak	Medium Stain	Wood Knobs	AS ABOVE
VENECIA	(L)	Solid Wood	Hand-painted Lacquer: Gold, Brown	Burnished Metal Pulls	AS ABOVE All prices upon application

(L) Indicates Leaded Glass Door Option   (T) Indicates Tinted Glass Door Option

ALNO: *Alno 80 Hom; Alno 80 Hob; Alnoplus Mel and Alno 80 Mel; Alnorond; Alnoplus Hom; Alnotop; Alno 80 Meg; Alno 80 Meg; Alno 80; Alnoform; Alnopart; Alnoclass; Alnostil*

ALNO		PANELS	FINISHES	HANDLES	WORKTOPS
ALNO 80 HOM (£940–£1010)	(T)	Laminate	Sand, Yellow, Green	Recessed Simulated Wood Pulls	Laminates: White, Sand, Olive, Light green, Brown; White Slate effect; White Granite effect; Olive Marble effect; Simulated Light, Brown, Reddish-brown Oak; Simulated Light, Brown, Reddish-brown Parquet
ALNO 80 HOM (£940–£1010)	(T)	Simulated Wood	Light, Brown	Recessed Simulated Wood Pulls	AS ABOVE
ALNO 80 HOB (£1010)	(T)	Laminate (wood uprights)	Bast beige, Bast yellow, Bast green	Wood Pulls	AS ABOVE
ALNO 80 HOB (£1010)	(T)	Simulated Wood	Light Oak, Brown Oak	Wood Pulls	AS ABOVE
ALNOPLUS MEL (£1270)	(T)	Laminate	Carre white, Carre sand	Anodized Metal Strips	AS ABOVE
ALNOROND (£1270)		Laminate	Parchment beige, Parchment green	Wood Pulls	AS ABOVE
ALNOPLUS HOM (£1380)	(T)	Laminate (wood uprights)	Linen-look: White, Green, Yellow	Recessed Simulated Wood Pulls	AS ABOVE
ALNOTOP (£1680)	(T)	Wood Veneer	Light Oak, Brown Oak Stains	Turned Wood Knobs	AS ABOVE
			Bamboo beige	Porcelain Knobs	AS ABOVE
ALNO 80 MEL (£1700–£1800)	(T)	Laminate	White, Green	Anodized Metal Strips	AS ABOVE
ALNO 80 MEG (£1700–£1800)	(T)	Oak Veneers (Oak Frames)	Light, Brown Stains	Antiqued Brass Rings	AS ABOVE
ALNO 80 MEG (£1700–£1800)	(T)	Oak, Pine (Wood Frames)	Light Oak, Brown Oak, Natural Pine	Antiqued Brass Rings	AS ABOVE
ALNO 80 (£1800)	(T)	Oak Veneer (Oak Frames)	Light, Reddish-brown Stains	Wood Knobs (metal stud inset)	AS ABOVE
ALNOFORM (£1930)	(T)	Oak	Light, Brown, Dark Stains	Turned Wooden Knobs	AS ABOVE
ALNOPART (£1930)	(T)	Oak Veneer	Light Brown, Reddish-brown Stains	Wood (metal stud inset)	AS ABOVE
ALNOCLASS (£2220)	(L)	Oak	Light Brown, Reddish-brown Stains	Antiqued Brass Pulls and Rings	AS ABOVE
ALNOSTIL (£2220)	(L)	Oak Veneer	Classic German Oak	Antiqued Brass Knobs	AS ABOVE

(L) Indicates Leaded Glass Door Option   (T) Indicates Tinted Glass Door Option

ARCLINEA		PANELS	FINISHES	HANDLES	WORKTOPS
GAMMA 30 (£1160–£1260)	(S)	Wood Veneer, Laminate	Veneers: Teak, Ash, Pitch, Pine; Laminates: White, Cricket green, Nile grey	Metal Strips	Laminates: White, Dark brown
GAMMAPIU (£1270)	(S)	Walnut, Oak	Natural	Metal Strips	AS ABOVE
SILVIA M30 (£2140)	(S)	Walnut	Natural	Walnut Knobs	AS ABOVE
H85 (£1040–£1140)	(S)	Wood, Laminate	Wood: Cherry; Laminates: White, Savana	Red Plastic Knobs	AS ABOVE
(S) Indicates Smoked Glass Door Option					

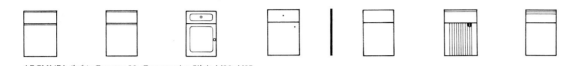

ARCLINEA (left): Gamma 30; Gammapiu; Silvia M30; H85
BOFFI (right): AL 15 and La Cucina; D76 Natural; Dogu Natural; Toys; Xila Natural, Xila Polyester and Xila Walnut

BOFFI	PANELS	FINISHES	HANDLES	WORKTOPS
AL 15	Laminate	White	Self-handles	Laminate: White; Stainless Steel; Solid Wood
D 76 NATURAL	Oak Slats	Natural; Dark Stain	Bronzed Metal Pulls	AS ABOVE
DOGU NATURAL	Solid Elm Slats	Natural	Solid Elm Cylindrical Pulls	AS ABOVE
LA CUCINA	Laminate, Pine	Laminate: Dove grey; Natural Pine	Dove Grey, Pine-look Plastic Pulls	AS ABOVE
TOYS	Wood Veneer	Walnut, Ash	Metallic Knobs	AS ABOVE
XILA NATURAL	Ash	Patinated Veneer	Self-Handles; Recessed Pulls	AS ABOVE
XILA POLYESTER	Polyester-treated Wood	Lacquer: White, Deep blue, Forest green, Black, Red	Self-Handles; Recessed Pulls	AS ABOVE
XILA WALNUT	Moabi Walnut	Patinated Veneer	Self-Handles; Recessed Pulls	AS ABOVE All prices upon application

BOSCH: Exquisit AS3; Exquisit GB 703; Exquisit GR3; Exquisit GT3; System HK3; Exquisit KL3; Exquisit KL 803; System LK3; System PA3; Exquisit PT 1003; Exquisit RF3; Exquisit RS3; System SB603; Exquisit SL3; Exquisit SL903

BOSCH		PANELS	FINISHES	HANDLES	WORKTOPS
EXQUISIT AS3 (£2000)	(L)	Oak	Antique Stain	Brass-plated Rings	Laminates: Montana white, Alabama brown, Manila green, Romantica blue/White, White, Tundra green, Romantica yellow/Beige, Oregon brown; Oak Strip effect; Oak End-grain effect; Oak Planking effect; Light Oak effect; Slate effect; Granite effect
EXQUISIT GB 703 (£1150)		Laminate (wood-effect trim)	Bahama beige, Jura white/Wenge (dark brown), Bahama beige, Linen beige, Linen green, Pampas green/Oak	Recessed Wood-effect Pulls	AS ABOVE
EXQUISIT GR3 (£1610)		Oak Veneer	Light, Medium, Dark Stains	Recessed Solid Oak Pulls; Burnished Metal Rings	AS ABOVE
EXQUISIT GT3 (£1610)		Laminate (solid oak trim)	Bernina white, Maringa beige, Maringa yellow, Maringa green	Solid Oak Strips	AS ABOVE
SYSTEM HK3 (£1450)		Oak Veneer	Light, Medium Stains	Wood Knobs	AS ABOVE
EXQUISIT KL3 (£1610)		Wenge, Pine	Natural	Aluminium, Wenge Strips	AS ABOVE
EXQUISIT KL803 (£1251)		Laminate (wood-effect trim)	Bahama beige, Jura white/Wenge; Bahama beige, Linen beige, Linen green, Pampas green/Oak	Wood-effect Strips	AS ABOVE
SYSTEM LK3 (£1310)		Laminate (solid oak trim)	Reedgrass green Hessian beige	Oak-effect Loops; Solid Oak Knobs	AS ABOVE
SYSTEM PA3 (£1350)		Beechwood	Brown	Beechwood Knobs; Metal Knobs	AS ABOVE

	PANELS	FINISHES	HANDLES	WORKTOPS
EXQUISIT PT1003 (£1310)	Laminate (oak-effect trim)	Andel green, Tobaco beige, Wallis white, Jasmine yellow	Oak-effect Pulls	AS ABOVE
EXQUISIT RF3 (£1820)	Oak	Medium, Light Stains	Medium Oak Knobs; Brass-plated Rings	AS ABOVE
EXQUISIT RS3 (L) (£2000)	Oak	Medium, Maron (Mid-brown) Stains	Oak Knobs; Brass-plated Rings	AS ABOVE
SYSTEM SB603 (£900)	Laminate	White, Beige, Yellow, Green	Medium, Light Oak-effect Knobs, Loops, Inset in Medium or Light Oak Effect	AS ABOVE
EXQUISIT SL3 (£1610)	Wenge	Natural	Metal Strips with Ring Pulls	AS ABOVE
EXQUISIT SL903 (S) (£1310)	Laminate	Jamaica brown, Aswan yellow, Rhodes green, Sapporo White	Metal Strips with Ring Pulls	AS ABOVE

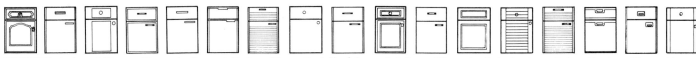

BULTHAUP: *Andorra, Brittany and Burgundy; Compact; Contour; Diagon; Fjord; Fjord; Formoak; Inline and Linare; Laminate, Laminate–Oak and Laminate–Wenge; Meran; Natural Cork/Wenge; Normandy and Provence; Oak Jalousette; Oak Lamelle; Oak Profile; Soft Profile; Spessart*

BULTHAUP	PANELS	FINISHES	HANDLES	WORKTOPS
ANDORRA (L) (£2010)	Solid Oak	Smoked natural, Structured, Patina antique Stains	Old Tin, Brass Knobs	Wood-edged Laminates: White, Linen decor green, Linen decor brown, Wenge (dark brown) mosaic, Decor travertine (beige), Decor granite (grey), Endgrain decor natural, Wenge domino, Oak domino; Round-edged Laminates: Dark brown, Quartz sand, Oak decor
BRITTANY (L) (£2010)	Solid Oak	Provence brown (mid-brown), Patina antique, Lasur green, Hand-dragged white	Undrilled; Old Brass Knobs; Ring Pulls; White China Knobs	AS ABOVE
BURGUNDY (L) (£1990)	Oak	As 'Brittany'	As 'Brittany'	AS ABOVE
COMPACT (£960)	Laminate	White	Undrilled; Chrome, Brown, Oak Pulls; Ceramic, Wood Knobs	AS ABOVE
CONTUR (£1430–£1600)	Wood (wood edgings) Laminate	Laminates: Azur, Polar beige, Graphite, Light grey, Maple yellow, Salmon red, Pearl white; Wood: Natural, Provence brown, Mahogany brown, Wenge	Undrilled; Black, White China Knobs	AS ABOVE
DIAGON (£1950)	Lacquered	Lacquers: Polar beige, Light grey, Pearl white, Azur, Graphite, Iris green (light green), Maple yellow, Terra brown, Salmon red	Undrilled; Black Laminate Pulls	AS ABOVE
FJORD (£1430–£1600)	Polyurethane	As 'Contour'	Integrated pulls	AS ABOVE
	Oak Veneer	Sanded only; Natural; Mahogany, Provence, Rustic brown and Special Stains		
FORMOAK (£2300)	Wood Veneer Louvres (solid oak edgings)	Natural, Provence brown, Mahogany brown, Wenge Stains; Lacquers as 'Linare'	Integrated pulls	AS ABOVE
INLINE (£1050)	Laminate	As 'Contour'	Undrilled; Chrome, Black Grip-handles; Metal Knobs	AS ABOVE
LAMINATE (£1700)	Laminate	Matt: Light sand	Undrilled; Sand Laminate Pulls	AS ABOVE
LAMINATE-OAK LAMINATE-WENGE (£1800)	Laminate (wood edgings)	Matt: White, Brazil brown, Sierra (gold), Maroon	Undrilled; Wenge (dark brown), Solid Oak Pulls	AS ABOVE
LINARE (£1100)	Textured Laminate, Polyester Laminate	Horizontally Textured Laminates: Polar beige, Pearl white, Light grey, Azur, Graphite, Iris green, Terra brown, Maple yellow, Salmon red; Linen-textured Laminates: Natural; Polyester Laminates: Quartz grey	Undrilled, Oak Chrome, Black grip handles	AS ABOVE

PRICES AND INFORMATION WERE CORRECT AT THE TIME OF GOING TO PRESS

KITCHENS

	PANELS	FINISHES	HANDLES	WORKTOPS
MERAN (£1430–£1540)	Wood Veneer, Laminate	Veneers: Sanded only; Natural; Smoked natural; Provence brown Stains; Laminates: as 'Contour'	Undrilled; Wood Knobs	AS ABOVE
NATURAL CORK/ WENGE (£2200)	Natural Cork (Wenge edgings)	Natural	Solid Wenge (dark brown) Pulls	AS ABOVE
NORMANDY (L) (£1820–£1900)	Oak	As 'Brittany'	Brass Knobs; Ring Pulls; White China Knobs	AS ABOVE
OAK JALOUSETTE (£1820–£1900)	Solid Oak	Sanded only; Natural; Mahogany brown, Provence brown, Rustic oak, Wenge, Special Stains	Undrilled; Wood Knobs	AS ABOVE
OAK LAMELLE (£2300)	Solid Oak Slats	Untreated; Natural; Rustic; Provence (brown), Mahogany brown, Wenge Stains	Undrilled; Solid Oak Pulls	AS ABOVE
OAK PROFILE (£1250)	Laminate (oak edgings)	Limone, Sahara: Textured: Jap beige, Jap green, Cotton (sand)	Solid Oak Pulls, Natural, Peat, Wenge stains	AS ABOVE
PROVENCE (L) (£2090)	Wood Veneer	Sanded only; Provence brown, Patina antique, Special Stains; Hand-dragged White w/Blue or Gold moulding	Brass Rings	AS ABOVE
SOFT PROFILE (£1250)	Laminate (oak edgings)	Hemp-textured: Natural, Reed (green-beige) edgings	As 'Oak Profile'	AS ABOVE
SPESSART (£1470–£1790)	Horizontal Wood Veneers (solid oak edgings)	Sanded only; Rustic natural, Smoked natural, Provence brown, Special Stains	Undrilled; Wood Knobs; Pulls to match finish	AS ABOVE
VENEER (£2200)	Oak Veneer	Untreated; Natural; Stone; Chestnut, Peat, Pistachio (bright green), Wenge Stains	Undrilled; Chrome, Oak Pulls; Ceramic Knobs	AS ABOVE
WOOD GRAIN LAMINATE (£960)	Laminate	Rustic Oak	Wood Knobs	AS ABOVE

CROSBY	PANELS	FINISHES	HANDLES	WORKTOPS
CANADIAN (L) (£1040)	Alder (Canadian timber)	Natural	Wood Knobs	Laminates: Sun beech, Spring bouquet, Arctic meridian, Tropical meridian (soft checks), Classic onyx, Vellum
CELESTE (£790)	Laminate (mahogany edgings)	Conifer, Country cotton (beige), Champagne, Corn (yellow)	Sculptured Mahogany Grips	AS ABOVE
UNIVERSAL (£680)	Laminate	Olive green, Mushroom, White, Parchment, Light Oak; Textured: Hessian	Integrated Metal Grips (against mahogany cappings)	AS ABOVE

(L) Indicates Leaded Glass Door Option

CROSBY (left): Canadian; Celeste; Universal
EASTHAM BURCO (right): Cottage; E-Line Oak; E-Line Teak; E-Line Laminate and Polyester; Hallmark; Select Oak and Teak; Select Laminate

EASTHAM BURCO	PANELS	FINISHES	HANDLES	WORKTOPS
COTTAGE (L) (£880)	Reversible Laminate (solid oak frames)	Cork/Beige Leather, Barley/ Green Leather	'Antique' Brass Ring Pulls	Wood-edged Laminates: Greenline tile, Leatherette
E-LINE (£850–£1050)	Oak	Natural	Oak Knobs	Square-edged Laminates: Damask, Classic onyx, Smoky marble, Bitter chocolate; Round-edged Laminates: also Autumn tile, Green block marble
	Teak	Natural	Teak Knobs	AS ABOVE
	Laminate	Textured: Yellow pampas, Oatmeal parchment, Peppermint, Oyster, Russet, Sage	Brown Metal Pulls	AS ABOVE
	Polyester	White, Biscuit, Bitter chocolate	Brown Metal Pulls	AS ABOVE
HALLMARK (£1050)	Reversible Laminate (solid oak frames)	Quartered Oak/Natural	Solid Oak Knobs	Wood-edged Laminates: Buckingham Tile (Terracotta), Classic onyx, Green block marble
	AS ABOVE	Hopsack/Sanderson Triad 'Polka' Floral Pattern		AS ABOVE
	AS ABOVE	Antique Cork/Caneweave		AS ABOVE

SELECT (£670–£850)	Oak	Natural	Aluminium Strips; Wood Pulls	Square-edged Laminates: Classic onyx, Orange damask, Teak, Bitter chocolate, Grey criss-cross, Avocado, Sunflower; Round-edged Laminates: Autumn tile, Green block marble, Sienna brown, Textured white
	Teak	Natural	AS ABOVE	AS ABOVE
	Laminate	Arctic white, Peppermint oyster, Burnt almond, Topaz, Yellow pampas, Oatmeal, Parchment, Teak	AS ABOVE	AS ABOVE

(L) Indicates Leaded Glass Door Option

ELLIS	PANELS	FINISHES	HANDLES	WORKTOPS
CHEVIOT (£980–£1440)	Oak Veneer, Laminate (oak edgings)	Veneers: Dark Oak, Light Oak; Laminates: Woven Grass, White, Chocolate	Antique Brass	Laminates: Teal, Pine, Autumn onyx, Pamela brown, Blue corinth, Oyster textured, Cork, Diced oak, Lemon damask, Saffron tile, Travertine stone, Jacobean teak, Planked teak, White, Olive, Gold, Chocolate, Mushroom, French green, Tropical blue, Cinnamon, Leather, Woven grass
GRAMPIAN (£890)	Teak Veneer	Teak	Brass Knobs	AS ABOVE
METROPOLITAN (£470–£500)	Melamine-faced Chipboard	Gold, Pine, Olive, White	Aluminium, Plastic Strips	AS ABOVE
PENTLAND (£580–£740)	Laminate	Tropical blue, Leather, Cinnamon, French green, Chocolate. Optional Round-edged Doors, Worktops	Aluminium, Plastic Strips	AS ABOVE

ELLIS (left): Cheviot; Grampian; Metropolitan; Pentland
ENGLISH ROSE (right): Cheltenham; Framey; Harrogate; Infinite Fluted Oak; Infinite Laminate; W Range; W Range; W Range

ENGLISH ROSE	PANELS	FINISHES	HANDLES	WORKTOPS
CHELTENHAM (£1800)	Oak	Dark, Light, Saffron Stains	Cast Metal Pulls	Laminates, Gloss: Snow-white, Spanish marble (rose), Turkish mosaic (off-white), Venetian marble (grey-white), Avocado marble, Bronze tableau, Natural hessian; Matt: Classic onyx, Sienna onyx, Sienna topaz, Orange damask, Checkerboard oak, Saffron tile, Antique cork
FRAMEY (£1200)	Laminate (oak edgings)	Gloss: White, Walnut, Harvest, Wedgwood blue, Doeskin, Ivory, Dusty olive; Matt: Paprika, Spice, Caramel; Textured: Barley, Oatmeal, Gourmet oak	Oak Pulls	AS ABOVE
HARROGATE (£1550) (L)	Oak	Dark, Light, Saffron Stains	Metal Pulls, Knobs	AS ABOVE
INFINITE (£1480–£1740)	Fluted Oak	AS ABOVE	Wood Pulls; Metal Knobs	AS ABOVE
	Laminate (birch frames)	Gloss: White, Walnut, Harvest, Wedgwood blue, Doeskin, Ivory, Dusty olive; Matt: Snow white; Paprika, Spice; Textured: Barley, Oatmeal, Oak, Brown; 'Infinite' Leatherette: Beige, Olive, Bronze	AS ABOVE	AS ABOVE
W RANGE (£1100)	Laminate	As 'Framey' or 'Infinite'	Solid Oak Pull; Silver or Gold Anodized Strip; Silver or Bronze Knobs	AS ABOVE

(L) Indicates Leaded Glass Door Option

FORMAT: Bretagne; Decora; Duo-Forma; Euro-Forma; Flandern; Oranien; Pro-Forma; Rondella; Royal; Structura (see overleaf for chart)

FORMAT		PANELS	FINISHES	HANDLES	WORKTOPS
BRETAGNE (£1750)	(L)	Oak	Rustic, Antique Stains	Metal Pulls, Knobs	Laminates, Plain: Cream, Brown; Textures: Brown, Green, Beige, Black or Beige marble; Oak or Teak wood mosaic, Gold or Olive swirls; Tiles: predominantly Olive, Gold, Beige
DECORA (£1100)		Laminate	Wood-textured: Natural, Rustic	Metal Pulls	AS ABOVE
DUO-FORMA (£1200)		Laminate (wood trim)	Linen-textured: Beige, Yellow	Oak Pulls	AS ABOVE
EURO-FORMA (£1300–£1640)		Oak Veneer, Laminate	Veneers: Chestnut, Light, Red; Laminates: Beige, Yellow, Green	Recessed Ceramic Grips	AS ABOVE
FLANDERN (£1870)	(L)	Oak	Rustic (mid-oak) Stain	Metal Knobs	AS ABOVE
ORANIEN (£1230)		Oak	Light, Rustic Stains	Wood Pulls	AS ABOVE
PRO-FORMA (£1640)		Oak Louvres	Red, Light, Chestnut, Rustic Stains	Oak Knobs	AS ABOVE
RONDELLA (£1100)		Laminate	Creamy yellow, Beige	Recessed Plastic Grips	AS ABOVE
RONDELLA 200 (£900)		Laminate	White, Off-white, Apple green, Mocha	Metal Strips	AS ABOVE
ROYAL (£1920)	(L)	Oak	Natural	Cast Metal Pulls	AS ABOVE
STRUCTURA (£1100)		Laminate (wood edgings)	Shantung-silk Textured: Creamy yellow, Stone	Wood Grips	AS ABOVE
(L) Indicates Leaded Glass Door Option					

GEBA: *Chinon; Contura, Montana, Prestige and Rondo; Dekora and Futura; Du Barry; Exquisit; Favorit Griff; Favorit Knopf and Gabella Bast: Lamelle and Ranch; Moderna; Perfecta; Louis Philippe; Pompadour; Regence II; Richelieu; Royal; Rustica; Scandia; Variant; Verona; Village*

GEBA	PANELS	FINISHES	HANDLES	WORKTOPS
CHINON ANTIQUE (£1510)	Solid Oak	Malaga Stain	Metal Pulls	Laminates, Textured: Beige, Sand, Mustard, Opal, Green, Brown Granite, Black marble, Brown/Black
CHINON WEISS (£1840)		Dragged White Paintwork	White Plastic Knobs	
CONTURA (£960)	Laminate (wood edgings)	Textured: Sand/Light Oak Stain	Recessed Wood Pulls	AS ABOVE
DEKORA (£960)	Laminate	Off-white, Light green	Recessed Wood Pulls	AS ABOVE
DU BARRY (£1840)	Solid Cherry	Natural	Metal Knobs	AS ABOVE
EXQUISIT (£1100)	Oak Veneer	Brown, Black Stains	Aluminium, Brown Plastic Pulls	AS ABOVE
FAVORIT E-GRIFF (£1100)	Oak Veneer	Natural Malaga Stain	Recessed Wood Pulls	AS ABOVE
FAVORIT-KNOPF (£1100)	Oak Veneer	Natural Malaga Stain	Oak Knobs	AS ABOVE
FUTURA (£960)	Laminate	Off-white, Light green	Recessed Metal Pulls	AS ABOVE
GEBELLA BAST (£1400)	Laminate (wood edgings)	Beige hessian Laminate/Dark brown Stain	Brown Plastic Knobs	AS ABOVE
LAMELLE (£1300)	Solid Oak	Natural	Oak Knobs	AS ABOVE
MODERNA (£960)	Laminate	Off-white	Beige Plastic Pulls	AS ABOVE
MONTANA (£960)	Laminate	Sepia brown, Forest green	Metal Pulls	AS ABOVE
PERFECTA (£960)	Laminate	Textured: Cream, Olive Green	Oak Pulls	AS ABOVE
LOUIS PHILIPPE (£1630)	Wood Veneer	Red Cherry	Plastic Knobs	AS ABOVE

	PANELS	FINISHES	HANDLES	WORKTOPS
POMPADOUR (£1670)	Hand-carved Oak	Natural Antique Stain	Metal Pulls or Knobs	AS ABOVE
PRESTIGE (£960)	Laminate	Cream	Recessed Malaga Oak Pulls	AS ABOVE
RANCH (£1260)	Solid Oak	Malaga Stain	Wood Knobs	AS ABOVE
REGENCE II (£1300–£1440)	Solid Oak	Malaga Stain	Metal Pulls; Oak Knobs	AS ABOVE
RICHELIEU (£1790)	Solid Oak	Golden brown	Metal Pulls	AS ABOVE
RONDO (£1100)	Oak Veneer	Natural	Recessed Ceramic Pulls	AS ABOVE
ROYAL (£1100)	Laminate (wood edgings)	Cream/Malaga Oak Stain	Recessed Wood Pulls	AS ABOVE
RUSTICA (£1500)	Solid Oak	Natural Malaga Stain	Metal Knobs or Pulls	AS ABOVE
SCANDIA (£1500)	Solid Oak	Natural	Wood Knobs	AS ABOVE
VARIANT (£830)	Laminate	Off-White, Light green, Dark brown	Metal Strips	AS ABOVE
VERONA (£960)	Laminate (wood edgings)	Cream/Malaga Oak Stain	Recessed Wood Pulls	AS ABOVE
VILLAGE (£1300–£1440)	Solid Oak	Natural Malaga Stain	Wood, Metal Knobs	AS ABOVE

GREENCRAFT: *Blenheim and Lancaster; Chelsea, Knightsbridge, Mayfair and Westminster; Montrose; Pembroke and Stirling; Wellington*

GREENCRAFT	PANELS	FINISHES	HANDLES	WORKTOPS
BLENHEIM (£1350)	(L) Oak	Dark Stain	Antique Bronze Pulls	Laminates: Dark brown, Red, Light green, Yellow, Dark green, Beige, White, Swirl, Marble
CHELSEA (£800)	Laminate	Sycamore	Plastic Strips	AS ABOVE
KNIGHTSBRIDGE (£800)	Laminate	Pencil Cane	Plastic Strips	AS ABOVE
LANCASTER (£1350)	(L) Oak	Light Stain	Antique Bronze Pulls	AS ABOVE
MAYFAIR (£700)	Formica	White, Amber, Olive, Blue, Cinnamon, Russet, Coffee cream	Plastic Strips	AS ABOVE
MONTROSE (£860)	Pine	Natural	Solid Brass Knobs	AS ABOVE
PEMBROKE (£1270)	(L) Oak	Dark Stain	Antique Bronze Pulls	AS ABOVE
STIRLING (£1270)	(L) Oak	Light Stain	Antique Bronze Pulls	AS ABOVE
WELLINGTON (£1571)	Mahogany	Natural	Recessed Brass Pulls	AS ABOVE
WESTMINSTER (£800)	Laminate	Sycamore	Plastic Strips	AS ABOVE
(L) Indicates Leaded Glass Door Option				

GROVEWOOD: *Daintymaid; Impact 2; Original 1; Original 2; SL; Traditional Pine and Town and Country*

GROVEWOOD	PANELS	FINISHES	HANDLES	WORKTOPS
DAINTYMAID (£840)	Laminate	Mushroom, Blue birch, Grovewood white, Catkin, Bronze koa, Maize, Planked hickory, Honeysuckle	Aluminium Strips	Laminates: Green pampas, Grey damask, Block teak, Block beech, Creme marble, Classic onyx, White antiqua, Parchment, Buffalo, Yellow cascade, Pearl oyster, Mandalay teak
IMPACT 2 (£600)	Laminate	Oak, White	Aluminium Strips	Laminates: Classic onyx, Vellum, Yellow, Mandalay teak, Oak

Right: Tielsa's AROSA in oak with Antique white stain

ORIGINAL 1 (£720)	Melamine	Honey beech, Honey maple	Solid Pine Strips	AS ABOVE
ORIGINAL 2 (£720)	Melamine (pine edgings)	Buttermilk, White/Pine	Solid Pine Strips	AS ABOVE
SL (£1320)	Laminate (wood edgings), Wood Veneer	Laminates: Parchment, Buffalo, Gold leather, Caramel, Shagreen (white haze); Veneers: Teak, Oak	Wood Strips'	As 'Daintymaid'
TRADITIONAL PINE (£950)	Pine	Polyurethane-sealed: Natural, Honey	Recessed Pine Strips	Laminates: Yellow cascade, Oak, Mandalay teak, Classic onyx, Vellum
TOWN & COUNTRY (£950)	Hardwood		Brass Knobs	

HYGENA	PANELS	FINISHES	HANDLES	WORKTOPS
CONTOUR (£910–£990) (S)	Polyester Gloss Laminate	Textured: Tan hide, Greengage, Apricot yellow rift, Cream vellum, Dark chocolate; Polyester Gloss: Honey beige, White, Coalport blue, Cinnamon, Caramel	Recessed Oak, Ivory Finish, Mahogany Pulls	Laminates: Hessian (off-white), Atlanta marble (grey-white), Teak block, Stripped oak, Rustic planked oak, Onyx, White honeycombe, Laurel leather, Vellum, Natural oak marquetry (inlaid), Dark oak marquetry (inlaid), Bracken leather
HARMONY (£1050–£1240)	Laminate (elm edgings)	White, Mushroom, Mink, Oyster, Sandalwood, Hazel; Textured: Vellum, Woven grass, Natural, Medium elm	Solid Elm Pulls	Round, Wood-edged Laminates: Onyx, Almond, Brown ochre, Sepia marble, Saffron tile, Natural or Rustic planked oak, Dark English tile
QA (£580)	Laminate	Country Mint, Seasoned teak, Polar white, Tuscan leather (beige)	Recessed Plastic Pulls	Laminates: Atlanta marble (grey-white), Hessian (off-white), Stripped oak, Lemon damask, Teak block, Onyx, Rustic planked oak
QA RICHMOND (£870)	Veneer Laminate (American oak trim)	American Oak: Natural, Medium Stain; Laminate: Straw	American Oak Pulls	AS ABOVE

(S) Indicates Smoked Glass Door Option

HYGENA (left): Contour; Harmony; QA; QA Richmond **LADYLOVE** (right): GB; GB Executive; Slidaway; Superb; System 'A' deLuxe; V.I.P.

LADYLOVE	PANELS	FINISHES	HANDLES	WORKTOPS
GB (£490)	Laminate	White, Olive green, Planked Teak	Metal Strips	Square-edged Laminates: Planked teak, Buckingham tile, Milano marble, Cremo marble, Pine, Grey crisscross, White, Natural teak, Grey broadcloth; Round-edged Laminates: Block teak, Block beech, Orange damask, Onyx marble
GB EXECUTIVE (£640)	Laminate	Vellum-textured: Sand, Sage	Metal, Wood Strips	AS ABOVE
SLIDAWAY (£430)	Laminate	White, Danish Teak, Olive green, Sun orange	Metal Pulls	AS ABOVE
SUPERB (£600)	Laminate	Golden; Textured: Sand, Sage	Wood Strips	AS ABOVE
SYSTEM 'A' DELUXE (£450)	Laminate	White, Teak, Olive green, Orange, Pine	Metal Strips	AS ABOVE
V.I.P. (£570)	Laminate	Planked Teak, Golden, White, Olive green, Sun orange	Aluminium Strips	AS ABOVE

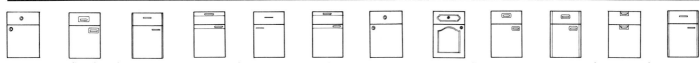

LEICHT Gamundia: Chic; Chic G; De Luxe; De Luxe H and De Luxe GR; Gamundia; Kontura; Nova; Rustica 2 **LEICHT Lux:** Bosca G; Bosca K; Interform H; Interform S; Interlux; Interlux H; Kent; Matura Lux; Matura 2; Matura K; Multiform; Multiform G; Ronda; Royal; Scandia; Tradition; York

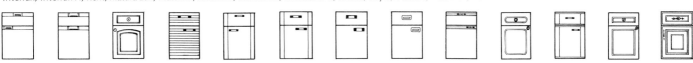

Left: Bulthaup's CONTUR in Natural

LEICHT GAMUNDIA		PANELS	FINISHES	HANDLES	WORKTOPS
CHIC (£870)		Simulated Wood	Pine, Larch	Recessed Wood Handles; Wood Pulls	Laminates: White, Light-grey, Oak parquet block wood, Cork, Light yellow, Light green, Teak grain, Olive, Quartz, Coral, Tabac, Brown-green. Available with wood edges to match units
CHIC G (£870)		Laminate	Hessian Textured: Ivory	AS ABOVE	AS ABOVE
DE LUXE (£840)		Laminate (oak edgings)	Beige, White, Reed green	Oak Pulls	AS ABOVE
DE LUXE H & DE LUXE GR (£1000)		Laminate, Simulated Wood	Laminates: Maize, White, Ivory, Reed green, Hessian; Simulated Wood: Light	Oak Strips	AS ABOVE
GAMUNDIA (£790)		Laminate	White	Metal Pulls	AS ABOVE
KONTURA (£1320)		Solid Oak	Natural	Natural, Mid-brown Wood Strips	AS ABOVE
NOVA (£880)		Simulated Oak	Light Oak	Solid Oak Knobs	AS ABOVE
RUSTICA 2 (£1800)	(L)	Solid Oak	Natural; Hand-stained Maron (mid-brown)	Solid Oak Knobs	AS ABOVE

LEICHT LUX		PANELS	FINISHES	HANDLES	WORKTOPS
BOSCA G (£1440)		Oak Veneer (solid oak edgings)	Natural; Maron Stain	Recessed Solid Wood Pulls	AS ABOVE
BOSCA K (£1230)	(S)	Laminate (oak edgings)	Beige, Sand/Maron Stain; Beige, Simulated Wood/ Natural	Recessed Solid Oak Pulls	AS ABOVE
INTERFORM H (£1330–£1410)	(S)	Laminate	Sahara beige, White, Platane gold	Recessed Solid Oak Pulls	AS ABOVE
INTERFORM S (£1330–£1410)	(S)	Laminate	White, Beige	Oak Pulls	AS ABOVE
INTERLUX (£1150)		Laminate (oak edgings)	Sand, Bambus, Maygreen	Metal Strips	AS ABOVE
INTERLUX H (£1150)		Laminate (oak edgings)	White, Beige, Sand, Maron, Maygreen, Hessian beige	Solid Oak Strips	AS ABOVE
KENT (£1930)	(L)	Solid Oak	Hand-stained Maron	Antiqued Metal Pulls	AS ABOVE
MATURA LUX (£1470–£1710)		Slatted Oak	Natural; Maron, Dark Brown, Stains	Solid Oak Pulls	AS ABOVE
MATURA 2 (£1470–£1710)		Wood	Natural; Black, Maron Stains	Solid Oak Pulls	AS ABOVE
MATURA K (£1470–£1710)	(S)	Laminate (wood edgings)	Hessian beige/Natural; Mid-brown Stains	Solid Oak Pulls	AS ABOVE
MULTIFORM (£1030)		Laminate (oak edgings)	Linen Textured: Savanna green, White, Hessian beige, Bamboo gold, Flaxen/Light, Dark Oak Stains	Recessed Oak Pulls	AS ABOVE
MULTIFORM G (£1030)		Laminate (oak edgings)	AS ABOVE	Wood Pulls	AS ABOVE
RONDA (£1290)		Laminate (oak edgings)	Rustic, Green, Yellow, Sahara	Oak Pulls	AS ABOVE
ROYAL (£1820)	(L)	Mahogany Veneer (solid mahogany edgings)	Natural; Red mahogany, Maron Stains	Mahogany Knobs	AS ABOVE
SCANDIA (£1820)		Oak-edged Fibre	Natural; Mid-brown	Oak Pulls	AS ABOVE
TRADITION (£1710)		Veneer (solid wood edgings)	Natural; Mid-brown, Moss-green Stains	Wood Pulls	AS ABOVE
YORK (£2050)	(L)	Solid Wood	Hand-stained Antique, Chestnut	Antiqued Metal Pulls	AS ABOVE
(L) Indicates Leaded Glass Door Option			(S) Indicates Smoked Glass Door Option		

MANHATTAN: *1 and 2; 3; 4; 5; 6; 7 (see overleaf for chart)*

PRICES AND INFORMATION WERE CORRECT AT THE TIME OF GOING TO PRESS

MANHATTAN	PANELS	FINISHES	HANDLES	WORKTOPS
1 (£550)	Laminate	White	Brown Plastic Strips	Laminates, Round-edged: Textured: White, Moss green (pattern); Plain: Chamois, Beaver brown; Square-edged: White Milano marble, Saffron/Brown floral, Panama beige grass (check); Textured: White, Moss green (pattern); Plain: Chamois, Beaver brown
2 (£610)	Laminate	Natural Teak, Beech, Knotty Pine, Honey, Smoke, Avocado	Brown Plastic Strips	AS ABOVE
3 (£770)	Laminate	Delphinium blue, Chamois, Inca gold, Mink, Marsh oak, Cottage oak, Paprika, Beaver brown, Ermine white, Catkin green	Satin Aluminium Strips	AS ABOVE
4 (£770)	Laminate	AS ABOVE	Aluminium Strips; Aluminium Pulls	AS ABOVE
5 (£830)	Laminate (ash edgings)	Chamois, Paprika, Beaver brown, Ermine white, Catkin green	Solid Ash Pulls	AS ABOVE
6 (£830)	Laminate (teak edgings)	Chamois, Inca gold, Beaver brown, Ermine white, Catkin green	Solid Teak Pulls	AS ABOVE
7 (£1000)	Wood Veneer (solid mouldings)	Medium Oak Stain	Solid Oak Knobs	AS ABOVE

MAYFAIR	PANELS	FINISHES	HANDLES	WORKTOPS
CHAMPAGNE (£740)	Laminate	Olive, Bitter chocolate, Honeydew, Coffee, Sunbeech, Rust	Bronze, Silver Metal Strips	Square-edged Laminates: Olive, Bitter chocolate, Coffee, Sunbeech, Rust, Olive cascade, Classic onyx, Rustic brown, Lemon damask, Greyleaves, Travertine, Kosmo brown, White linen, Cream ripple. Kosmo brown, White linen, Cream ripple also available with round edges
MAGNUM (£760)	Polyester	Lime green, Bottle green, Fawn, Ice, Chocolate, Russet, Black, White	Bronze, Silver Metal Strips	AS ABOVE
ORIGINAL VINTAGE (S) (L) (£1000)	Teak Veneer	Natural	Teak Knobs; Metal Pulls	AS ABOVE
VINTAGE 80 (S) (L) (£1130)	Reversible Laminate (oak edgings), Wood Veneer, Cane	Laminates: Moroccan green/Moroccan red, Hessian Weave/Cream Ripple; Veneers: Natural, Jacobean Oak, Teak; Traditional Cane; Edgings: Natural; Jacobean Brown stain	Natural, Dark Wood Knobs; Metal Pulls	AS ABOVE

(L) Indicates Leaded Glass Door Option	(S) Indicates Smoked Glass Door Option

MAYFAIR (left): Champagne and Magnum; Original Vintage; Vintage   **MIELE** (right): Programme 21; 24; 25; 26; 29; 30; 31; 34

MIELE	PANELS	FINISHES	HANDLES	WORKTOPS
PROGRAMME 21 (£1250)	Laminate	Pearl white, Madras brown	Aluminium Strips	Laminate: White embossed
PROGRAMME 24 (£1960)	Oak	Black	Metal	AS ABOVE
PROGRAMME 25 (£1810)	Laminate, Oak	Laminate: Cane Weave; Oak: Natural	Oak Rings	Laminate: Tobacco brown
PROGRAMME 26 (£1900)	Ash	Stained Natural	Wood Knobs	Laminate: Sand
PROGRAMME 29 (£1320)	Laminate (oak edgings)	Sylt beige	Oak Strips	Laminate: Rustic oak (oak edgings)
PROGRAMME 30 (£1020)	Laminate	Sahara beige	Recessed Aluminium Pulls	Laminate: Tobacco brown
PROGRAMME 31 (£1020)	Laminate (wood edgings)	Green/Oak, Shell yellow/Wenge (dark brown) Stain	AS ABOVE	Laminate: White
PROGRAMME 34 (£1660)	Wenge Veneer	Natural Wenge (dark brown)	Aluminium Pulls	Laminate: White embossed

PRICES AND INFORMATION WERE CORRECT AT THE TIME OF GOING TO PRESS

MFI	PANELS	FINISHES	HANDLES	WORKTOPS
BURMA (£330)	Laminate	Burma Teak	Metal Strips	Laminates: Onyx, Chocolate, Teak
CONTINENTAL (£310)	Laminate	White, Mint	Metal Strips	AS ABOVE
COTTAGE (£360)	Oak Veneer	Natural	Wood Knobs	AS ABOVE
GEMINI WALL UNIT £10 BASE UNIT £10	Chipboard	Unfinished	Round Chipboard	AS ABOVE
TUDOR (£510)	Solid Oak	Natural	Wood Knobs	AS ABOVE

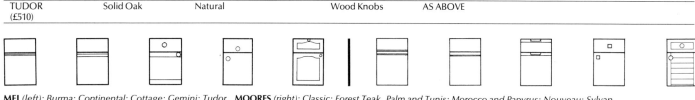

MFI *(left): Burma; Continental; Cottage; Gemini; Tudor* **MOORES** *(right): Classic; Forest Teak, Palm and Tunis; Morocco and Papyrus; Nouveau; Sylvan*

MOORES	PANELS	FINISHES	HANDLES	WORKTOPS
CLASSIC (£600)	Laminate	Gloss: White, Coral red, Mint green, Midnight blue (turquoise), Chocolate brown	Aluminium Strips	Laminates, Plain: Polar white; Textured: Dark chocolate, Moss green, Classic onyx, Vellum, Nordic pine, Regal teak, Grey linette, White antiqua, Sunbeech. Textured worktops are available with rounded edges
FOREST TEAK (£580—£680)	Laminate	Woodgrain, White	Aluminium Strips	AS ABOVE
MOROCCO (£390)	Laminate (wood edgings)	White; Leather-textured: Beige	Recessed Wood Strips	Laminates, Plain: Polar white; Textured: Dark chocolate, Moss green, Classic onyx, Vellum. Textured worktops are available with rounded edges
NOUVEAU (£390)	Laminate	Textured: Magnolia, Mint green, Harvest gold, Jet (black)	Metal Pulls	AS CLASSIC
PALM (£350)	Laminate	Gloss: Olive green, White	Aluminium Strips	AS MOROCCO
PAPYRUS (£390)	Laminate (wood edgings	White; Leather-textured: Beige edgingss	Recessed Wood Strips	AS MOROCCO
SYLVAN (£910)	Solid Wood	Pine, Iroko	Solid Brass Knobs	AS CLASSIC
TUNIS (£350)	Laminate	Gloss: Mushroom, White	Aluminium Strips	AS MOROCCO

POGGENPOHL: *CF; CG; CH; CR and HR; FM; FP; FR; MA; MC; ML; MS; NR; RP*

POGGENPOHL	PANELS	FINISHES	HANDLES	WORKTOPS
CF (£1370)	Reeded Laminate (oak edgings)	Quartz beige/Light, Dark, Moss green	Recessed Wood, Metal Pulls	Laminates: White-beige, Leaf-green, Tobacco brown, Blossom white, Quartz paprika, Dark planked oak, Grey-white, Beige with marble effect, Solid teak, Wenge parquet, Oak parquet; Tiles: White, Beige, Yellow-brown, Red honeycombe
CG (£1120)	Laminate	Pearl white, Apple green, Honey yellow, Quartz beige	Metal Strips	AS ABOVE
CH (£1370)	Laminate	Curry, Gold, Honey yellow, Quartz beige, Blossom white, Palm green, Tobacco brown	Recessed Aluminium Pulls	AS ABOVE
CR (£1690–£1820)	Laminate (oak edgings)	Beige/Light, Dark Brown Oak Stains	Solid Oak Pulls	AS ABOVE
FM (£1690)	Oak Veneer	Light Oak Stain	Oak Knobs	AS ABOVE
FP (£1820)	Wood	Mahogany, Leaf green Stains	Wood, Bronze-coated Brass Knobs	AS ABOVE
FR (£1690)	Oak Veneer (solid oak frames)	Medium brown, Light Oak Stains	Wood Knobs	AS ABOVE
HR (£1690–£1820)	Wood Weave Laminate (solid oak edgings)	Light, Dark Oak Stains	Solid Oak Pulls	AS ABOVE
MA (£2240)	Solid Oak	Antique (medium brown) Stain	Brass with Pewter Finish Rings	AS ABOVE

MC (£2130)	(L) Solid Oak	Light, Dark Brown Stains	Brass, Brass with Pewter Finish, Wood Knobs	AS ABOVE
ML (£1700)	Solid Oak	Moss green, Fumed, Light Oak Stains	Wood Knobs	AS ABOVE
MS (£1820)	Solid Wood (metal edgings)	Mahogany, Light Oak, Black Oak, Burnt Chestnut Stains	Silver-coloured Metal Pulls	AS ABOVE
NR (£1690–£1820)	Net-structured Laminate (oak edgings)	Light, Dark Brown/Light, Dark Brown Oak Stains	Bronze-edged Oak Knobs	AS ABOVE
RP (£2240)	Cherrywood Veneer	Natural	Brass Knobs	AS ABOVE

(L) Indicates Leaded Door Front Option

SIEMATIC: *4004; 6006; 7007; 1001 AK and 1001 FE; 1001 AL and 1001 NE; 2002L; 3003R; 4004 K; 4004 GR and 4004 GRL; 5005 SC; 5005 SE, 5005 SEL and 7007 SE; 8008 ME, and 8008 RA (without the textured front)*

SIEMATIC	PANELS	FINISHES	HANDLES	WORKTOPS
4004 (£950)	Laminate	Matt, Ribbed: Reproduction Pine, Sahara brown, Teak, Alaska white, Atlas sand, Tonga beige, Maize yellow, Mango green	Aluminium Strips	Laminates: Mosaic oak effect; Domino pattern in solid Wenge, Solid oak finish; Parquet effect in oak finish; Slate-top effect; Black/White or Brown/White polished granite; Textured: White, Brown, Red, Olive, Beige
6006 (£1280)	Laminate	Gloss: Sunshine yellow, Light grey, Grape green	Aluminium Strips	AS ABOVE
7007 (£1630)	Oak Veneer slats	Light Oak, Medium Brown Stains	Hand-turned Wood Knobs	AS ABOVE
1001 AK (£2600)	(L) Wood	Lacquer: Frisian blue	Porcelain Knobs	AS ABOVE
1001 AL (£2600)	(L) Wood	Lacquer: Hand-dragged Off-white with Delft-blue, Sepia brown frieze	Porcelain Knobs	AS ABOVE
1001 FE (£2510)	(L) Solid Vosges Wood	Hand-rubbed Flemish brown Stain	Hand-turned Wood Knobs	AS ABOVE
1001 NE (£2280)	(L) Solid French Oak	Medium Brown Stain	Hand-turned Oak Knobs	AS ABOVE
2002L (£1820)	Oak Veneer (solid oak uprights)	Light Oak/ Medium Brown Stain	Solid Oak Pulls	AS ABOVE
3003R (£1980)	Oak Veneer	Light oak, Medium Brown Stains	Hand-turned Wood Knobs	AS ABOVE
4004 K (£1140)	Laminate (oak edgings)	Matt, ribbed: Sand white, Paloma white, Java beige, Savannah brown, Jade green, Natural oak, Natural reproduction pine	Recessed Oak Pulls	AS ABOVE
4004 GR (£920)	Laminate, Veneer	Laminates, Matt, Ribbed: Alabaster white, Gobi sand, Bahama beige, Topaz yellow, Light oak; Veneer: Chestnut oak Stain	Natural, Red, Brown Tubular Aluminium Pulls; Natural, Medium Brown Oak Pulls	AS ABOVE
4004 GRL (£1000)	Laminate (oak edgings)	Matt: Bahama beige, Gobi sand/Silver-coloured Metal, Light oak, Dark Brown Stains	AS ABOVE	AS ABOVE
5005 SC (£1460)	Laminate	Matt, Ribbed: Snow white, Saffron yellow, Citrus green, California sand, Bali beige	Chrome-coloured Pulls	AS ABOVE
5005 SE (£1460)	Laminate (oak edgings)	Matt, Ribbed: Jasmine white, Sunda wood, Saffron wood, Citrus wood, Nevada wood	Recessed Oak Pulls	AS ABOVE
5005 SEL (£1620)	Laminate (oak edgings)	Matt, Ribbed: Lily white, Florida sand, Honey gold, Reed green, Samoa Beige	Oak-coloured Laminate Pulls	AS ABOVE
7007 SE (£1700)	Oak Veneer	Light Oak Stain	Recessed Laminate Pulls	AS ABOVE
8008 ME (£2250)	Solid Oak	Natural	Solid Oak Knobs	AS ABOVE
8008 RA (£2550)	Rattan (oak frames)	Dark Brown Stain, White	Solid Wood Knobs	AS ABOVE

(L) Indicates Leaded Glass Door Option

SOLENT	PANELS	FINISHES	HANDLES	WORKTOPS
ANTELOPE (£630)	Laminate (oak edgings)	Stone (beige)	Oak Pulls	Laminates, Textured: Gerona olive, Castille stone, Delft blue (light blue), Onyx marble, Planked teak, 'Stella' Gold/Brown Textured geometric print. Onyx marble, Planked teak and 'Stella' are available with square edges
OAK (£870)	Oak Veneer	Natural	Antiqued Metal Ring Pulls	AS ABOVE
PINE (£680)	Pine	Melamine Coating	Solid Wood Knobs	AS ABOVE
ROSEWOOD (£770)	Rosewood Veneer	AS ABOVE	AS ABOVE	AS ABOVE

SOLENT *(left): Antelope; Oak; Pine; Rosewood* **STONEHAM** *(right): 101; 200; 201 and 300; 400; 401; 600; 800; 1000*

STONEHAM	PANELS	FINISHES	HANDLES	WORKTOPS
SILHOUETTE 101 (£1450)	Solid Oak	Rustic Light, Rustic Stains	Antique Brass Finish Pulls	Laminates: Lemon damask, White marble, Black slate, White slate, Planked teak, White hessian, Golden green, Rawhide, Honeycomb, Golden brown, Palomino
SILHOUETTE 200 (£1250)	Wood Veneers (solid afrormosia, utile edgings)	English ash, American red cherry	Circular, Rectangular Recessed Metal Handles	AS ABOVE
SILHOUETTE 201 (£1280)	Oak Veneer (solid oak edgings)	Rustic Light, Rustic Stains	Turned Oak Knobs	AS ABOVE
SILHOUETTE 300 (£1280)	Laminate (oak edgings)	Pencil Cane, Woven Grass/Light, Rustic oak Stains; Textured: Sable, Olive pampas/Light, Rustic oak Stains	Turned Oak Knobs	AS ABOVE
SILHOUETTE 400 (£940)	Laminate (afrormosia edgings)	Natural hessian, White eldorado leather, Natural linen, Antique eldorado leather	Rectangular, Recessed Metal Handles	AS ABOVE
SILHOUETTE 401 (£930)	Laminate (oak edgings)	As 'Silhouette 300'	Oak Pulls	AS ABOVE
SILHOUETTE 600 (£1010)	Laminate	Classic white crystal, Planked Oak	Wrought-iron Hinges, Pulls	AS ABOVE
SILHOUETTE 800 (£890)	Laminate	Forest oak, Polar crystal, Cream crystal, Havana (beige) crystal, Coffee crystal, Gold crystal, Laurel (green) crystal, Mandarin (red-orange) crystal	Aluminium Strips	AS ABOVE
SILHOUETTE 1000 (£940)	Laminate (wood edgings)	As 'Silhouette 800'	Light, Medium Solid Oak Strips	AS ABOVE

TIELSA: *Aera; Alpina; Ariane; Arosa; Bavaria; Carat; Castell, Eden and Merano; Fiesta; Futura; Gamma; Nova; Taiga; Tosca*

TIELSA		PANELS	FINISHES	HANDLES	WORKTOPS
AERA (£1520)		Oak Veneer	Mellowed Natural Tint; Mahogany, Wenge (dark brown) Stains	Solid Oak Knobs	Laminates, Textured: White sand, Coral red, Curry, Rush green, Tobacco brown, Dark brown marble with Curry grain, Green; Simulated/Imitation Finishes: Natural or Dark antique oak block; Stone white or green slate; Natural oak plank; Medium oak parquet
ALPINA (£2300)	(L)	Oak (contrasting piping)	Natural/Black piping; Leaf green Stain/Red piping	Oak Knobs	AS ABOVE
ARIANE (£1360)		Laminate (oak edgings)	Linen-textured: White diamond, Sapphire amber, Topaz, Aquamarine, Coral/Natural; Romanisch, Wenge, Mahogany Stains	Oak Pulls: Natural; Romanisch, Wenge (dark brown), Mahogany Stains	AS ABOVE
AROSA (£2020)	(L)	Oak	Natural; Antique White, Antique turquoise, Flemish Stains	Pewter Rings; Oak Knobs	AS ABOVE

	PANELS	FINISHES	HANDLES	WORKTOPS
BAVARIA (£1520)	Oak Veneer	Mellowed Natural Tint; Natural; Antique, Wenge Stains	Solid Oak Knobs	AS ABOVE
CARAT (£950–£1140)	Laminate (oak edgings)	White pearl, Sand, Sahara, Simulated oak, Simulated antique oak, Simulated green oak	Strips: Aluminium; Natural; Romanisch Oak Stain	AS ABOVE
CASTELL (L) (£2020)	Oak	Mid-brown Stain	Antique Brass Knobs	AS ABOVE
EDEN (FRAMED) 1 (£1920)	Oak Veneer (oak edgings)	Natural	Solid Oak Knobs with Metal Centres	AS ABOVE
EDEN (STILED) 2 (£1920)	Oak Veneer (oak edgings)	AS ABOVE	AS ABOVE	AS ABOVE
FIESTA (£1450)	Laminate (oak edgings)	White, Beige Linen, Rush green, Yellow	Solid Oak Pulls	AS ABOVE
FUTURA (£1190)	Laminate	Sand, Beige Linen, Rush green, Deep yellow	Aluminium, Wood Strips	AS ABOVE
GAMMA (£1690)	Oak Veneer (oak edgings)	Natural; Natural Tint; Antique, Black Stains (with aluminium handles)	Recessed Solid Oak Pulls	AS ABOVE
MERANO (£2300)	Oak	Mid-brown Stain	Antique Brass Knobs	AS ABOVE
NOVA (£1190)	Laminate	White, Curry (deep yellow), Brown	Recessed Chrome, Simulated Oak Pulls	AS ABOVE
TAIGA (£1200)	Laminate (wood edgings)	Maize Grass Cloth, Jade Grass Cloth, Brown Grass Cloth/Natural; Wenge Stain	Simulated Wood, Plastic Pulls	AS ABOVE
TOSCA (£1920)	Oak	Vertical Strips: Natural: Antique Stain	Self-handles	AS ABOVE

TIFFANY	PANELS	FINISHES	HANDLES	WORKTOPS
7000 (£1220)	Laminate (oak edgings)	Light, Dark Oak, Cream, Sand beige, Dark Beige/Natural	Solid Oak Knobs	Round, Square, Wood-edged Laminates, Textured: Beige, Green, Rust; Plain oak effect, Parquet effect, Black marble effect. Or tiles supplied by customer
9000 (£1500)	Oak Veneer	Light, Rustic, Green Stains	Solid Oak Strip Handles	AS ABOVE
CLASSIC (£1880)	Solid Oak	Rustic, Chestnut Stains	Metal-centred Wood Knobs	AS ABOVE
MODUS (S) (£1640)	Oak Veneer	Light, Rustic Stains, Chequerboard Centre Panel	Solid Oak Pulls	AS ABOVE
OPTIMA (£1100)	Laminate (oak edgings)	Sand, Lime/Natural, Rustic Stains	Recessed Oak Pulls	AS ABOVE
PLANTINA (S) (£1350)	Laminate (oak edgings)	Leather effect: Beige/Chestnut Stains	Recessed, Chestnut-stained Oak Pulls	AS ABOVE
RESIDENZ (£2150)	Solid Oak	Chestnut Stain	Bronzed Pulls	AS ABOVE
ROMANTICA (L) (£1810)	Solid Oak	Light, Rustic Stains	Solid Oak, Antiqued Metal Knobs	AS ABOVE
RONDO (£1500)	Oak Veneer	Light, Rustic Stains	Solid Oak Pulls	AS ABOVE
VARIO (£1350)	Laminate (wood edgings)	Sand, Cream/Mid-brown, Dark Brown Stains	Recessed Oak-colour Plastic Pulls	AS ABOVE

TIFFANY *(left): 7000; 9000; Classic; Modus; Optima; Plantina and Rondo; Residenz; Romantica; Vario* **WHITELEAF** *(right): Hampden; The Oak Kitchen; 4000*

WHITELEAF BURCO	PANELS	FINISHES	HANDLES	WORKTOPS
HAMPDEN (£570)	Formica	Orange, Green, Planked Oak, Vellum, Planked Teak, Planked Pine	Metal strips	Formica: Lemon damask, Onyx marble, Vellum, Planked oak, Planked pine
THE OAK KITCHEN (£1350)	Solid Oak	Natural	Recessed Pulls	Formica: Oakwood veneer laminate, Onyx marble, Vellum, Saffron tile, Autumn stone, Sepia onyx marble, Antique Eldorado leather, White slate, Charcoal slate; Oak with solid oak edging; or tiling provision
WHITELEAF 4000 (£810–£1070)	Solid Beech, Formica	Beech: Natural; Dark Stain; Planked Teak, Planked Pine, Planked Oak, Formica: Vellum, Fresh olive, Honeydew (gold), Spice brown, White	Wood Knobs; Metal Strips	Formica: Sepia onyx marble, Classic onyx marble, White slate, Charcoal slate, Saffron tile, Lemon damask, Antique Eldorado leather, Autumn stone, Buff seaspray, Vellum, Planked teak, Planked pine, Planked oak

WINCHMORE		PANELS	FINISHES	HANDLES	WORKTOPS
BARTON (£1870)	(L)	Solid Oak	Natural	None	Venetian, Beige Valencia, Braganza, or Adriatic marble; Brown or Latigo leather, Almond Atlantis, Golden Linagrain, White slate, Butcher's Grain
COLONIAL (£1580)		Pine	Natural; Melamine: Honey, Dark Oak/Black hinges, Spruce green/Brass hinges	None	AS ABOVE
CULFORD (£1380)		Hardwood	Natural; Melamine: Honey, Cherry, Nut brown	None	AS ABOVE
DALHAM (£1680)		Maple	Natural	None	AS ABOVE
RISBY (£1680)		Oak	Natural	None	AS ABOVE
SPANISH (£1450)	(L)	Hardwood	Natural; Melamine: Honey, Cherry, Nut brown	None	AS ABOVE
SUDBURY (£1380)	(L)	Hardwood	Natural; Honey, Cherry, Nut brown	None	AS ABOVE

WINCHMORE *(left): Barton; Colonial; Culford and Sudbury; Dalham; Risby; Spanish*
WRIGHTON *(right): California; Cornwall; Gimson; Pugin; Cotswold; Herald and Pageant; Nash; Voysey; Waltham*

WRIGHTON		PANELS	FINISHES	HANDLES	WORKTOPS
CALIFORNIA (£790)		Decpol Polyester, Melamine, Laminate	Polyesters: Paris blue, White, Bitter chocolate, Stone, Pompeian red, Fawn, Buttercup yellow, Bottle green; Textured Melamine: Stone, Terre Vert (olive); Laminates: White, Pine, Teak, Rosewood	Aluminium Strips	Laminates: White, Celestine marble, Sackcloth; Simulated woods: Pine, Teak, Rosewood; Veneer Laminates: Natural oak, Elm
CORNWALL (£950–1070)		Decpol Polyester, Veneer Laminate	Polyesters: As 'Californian'; Veneer Laminates: Natural Elm, Oak	Aluminium Strips	Laminates: White, Stone, Frost marble, Victorian marble, Oporto cork, Padua tile, Olive green, Teak; Veneer Laminates: Natural elm, Oak
GIMSON (£1690–1880)	(S)	Solid Oak (oak edgings)	Natural; Russet Stain	Wood, Victorian Brass Knobs; Bronzed Drops	Laminates: White, Stone beige, Frost marble, Victorian marble, Oporto cork, Diced oak, Padua tile, Olive green, Himalayan teak; Laminated Veneers (with solid wood edges): Natural oak, Russet oak, Natural elm, Mahogany or Frost marble; Tiles (with wood edges): White, Chamois, Breton flame
PUGIN (£2010)	(S)	Solid Oak (oak edgings)	Natural; Russet Stain	Wood, Victorian Brass Knobs; Bronzed Drops; Recessed Brass Ring Pulls	AS ABOVE
COTSWOLD POLYESTER (£1690–1880)	(S)	Oak Veneer, Decpol Polyester (oak edgings)	Veneers: Natural; Russet Stain; Polyesters: White, Stone, Pompeian red, Bottle green, Jet black	AS ABOVE	AS ABOVE
HERALD (£1110)		Decpol Polyester (teak strips)	White, Pompeian red, Stone, Fawn, Aubergine, Buttercup yellow, Bitter chocolate, Jet black, Bottle green, Paris blue	Teak Strips	AS ABOVE
NASH (£1470)		Veneer Laminate (oak edgings)	Natural oak, Russet Stain	As 'Gimson'	AS ABOVE
PAGEANT (Polyester) (£1060–1180)		Decpol Polyester	As 'Herald'	Aluminium Strips	AS ABOVE
PAGEANT (Veneer) (£1060–1180)		Veneer Laminate	Natural Elm, Oak	AS ABOVE	AS ABOVE
VOYSEY (Polyester) (£1310–1660)		Decpol Polyester (teak, mahogany edgings)	White, Stone, Pompeiian red, Jet black, Bottle green/Teak; White; Jet black; Mahogany	Victorian Brass, Teak, Mahogany Knobs; Bronzed Drops	AS ABOVE
VOYSEY (Wood) (£1310–1660)		Teak Veneer (solid teak edgings), Mahogany Veneer (solid mahogany edgings)	Natural	AS ABOVE	AS ABOVE
WALTHAM (£1210–1460)		Decpol Polyester, Wood Veneer, Veneer Laminate	As 'Herald'	Aluminium Strips	AS ABOVE

Right: Allmilmö's CONTURA EDELWEISS

INTRODUCTION

Fabrics, wallpaper, carpeting and furniture are all important, but lighting finally brings a room alive and should be your first consideration when decorating.

Start by making a sketch of the room, showing windows and doors, fireplace, etc. Add the main pieces of furniture, working surfaces like kitchen units or desks, and decorative items (display shelves or cabinets, pictures or plants). Then mark existing electrical points. List special activities like model-making or sewing, and specific objects that deserve highlighting. This plan will help you decide how much light you need, and where the fittings should go, depending on the quality of natural light, and your colour scheme. Sketch additional electrical points that may be necessary. Finally, consult a qualified electrician who will advise you, and also install new points (not a do-it-yourself job).

Obviously, special rooms have special needs. Kitchens need two levels of lighting: overall ceiling illumination, and specific lights for work surfaces which are often under overhead cupboards. Spotlights can be used for sink and/or stove illumination. Wall mounted, or fixed on track systems, they're useful in any working room.

The dining-room is another special case. An attractive rise-and-fall pendant over the table gives a low, soft atmospheric light; well-placed wall lights are important, especially over a serving table or sideboard. Bedrooms need overall lighting (with dimmer control as a luxury) and bedside lights, at eye level or higher, for reading in bed. Plastic or glass units that won't be affected by steam are best for bathrooms: enclosed fittings flush with the ceiling would be a good choice. Pull-cord switches are absolutely essential for safety, unless wall switches are outside. A low-voltage razor point is the exception.

Sitting- and living-room lighting depends on your lifestyle—and the impression you want to create. Downlights, round or square metal canisters recessed or semi-recessed into the ceiling, or ceiling mounted, cast pools of light. Uplights, their reverse, are equally dramatic. Standard and free-standing lamps, and table lights, are more conventional but no less effective. (Do remember, trailing wires can be very dangerous—another reason for planning light points with an electrician.)

Other lighting choices include surface fittings mounted directly on to walls or ceilings, and recessed fittings let into the space above the ceiling.

* Measurements always include shades, unless otherwise stated; and refer to the maximum dimension (the base of a shade, for example).
* Depth is the projection from the wall.
* Maximum wattage is given.
* Some firms list lighting of the same kind in series numbers based on size, etc.

Left: Selection from Maurice Brown's KOSTKA ceramic table lamps

ADEPTUS DESIGNS LTD

Functional, well-designed lighting from a great design-oriented retail firm. The 'D3R' cone-shaped hanging lamp and holder, with Black rubber trim and rise/fall mechanism, comes in White and Brown (*M:* diam 38cm/15in, *P:* £14; 100 watts). The 'CL' shade, also cone-shaped, is in Red, Green, Yellow, Brown, and White (*M:* diam 30cm/11⁷/₈in, *P:* £5; 75 watts).

Adeptus also have a marvellous range consisting of a clamp spot and a switched wall, table or floor standard light in White, Brown, and Black. Individual units can be fitted to the following: 'TK3' track system in White (*M:* w 100cm/3ft 3³/₈in, *P:* £20); 'SC' or 'MC' clamp (*P:* £6.50, £7); 'S6' or 'M6' floor standard base (*M:* both h 126cm/4ft 1¹/₈in, *P:* £18.50, £19); 'S4' or 'M4' table standard base (*M:* h 12¹/₂in/31.5cm, diam 4in/10cm, *P:* £8.50, £9.50); and the 'AAC' anglepoise in White, Green, Brown, Black, or Red (*M:* 3ft 3in/99cm, *P:* £13; 60 watts).

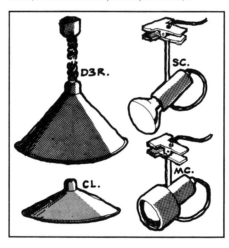

ANGLEPOISE LIGHTING LTD

Versatile, well-designed fittings from a famous name generally associated with the much-copied classic found in studios, offices and workshops. Most would look good in a modern home. The Anglepoise '3-33' table lamp with a spring-loaded angle adjuster is simple, yet stunning, with a Black, White, Signal red, Cadmium yellow, or Bright green shade on a Black ribbed base (*M:* maximum h 27in/69.5cm, *P:* £20). The ever-beloved aluminium '90', with clamp, comes in Black, White, Red, Dark green, Light green, Beige, Dark brown. An illuminated magnifier, telephone, microphone or rivet gun holders, and classic table or pedestal base lamps are also available, plus stabilizing accessories like screw-down bases and wall brackets. *M:* maximum h 30in (76cm). *P:* £21. 60 watts.

Right, left to right, from top: Aram's 'Foglio', 'AOY', 'Tau', 'Relemme'

Anglepoise's '3-33'

ARAM DESIGNS LTD

Specialized range of highly unusual and dynamic light fittings. The 'Arco' standard lamp, a gorgeous classic, has a marble base and a stainless steel arc that ends in a spun aluminium shade (*M:* h 250cm/8ft 2³/₈in, arc diam 200cm/6ft 6³/₄in from lamp support to edge of shade, *P:* £300). 'AOY', a very unusual all-glass uplighter is a clear glass cylinder with a white opal interior and amber or black glass (*M:* h 60cm/23⁵/₈in, diam 30cm/11⁷/₈in, *P:* £300). 'Foglio' by Tobia Scarpa is the epitome of curvy simplicity in white enamelled, polished chrome, or brassed steel (*M:* w 37cm/14¹/₂in, d 9.5cm/3³/₄in, *P:* from £40). 'Tau', a marvellously slick polished aluminium light, comes with or without a rise/fall mechanism, in White only (*M:* diam 36cm/14¹/₈in, *P:* with rise/fall mechanism £90). 'Relemme', a wonderfully simple lamp, is available with a White, Brown, or Red globe accented by a black rubber ring at the base, and matching ceiling rose and weight. A rise/fall mechanism is optional. *M:* diam 38.5cm (15¹/₄in). *P:* with rise/fall mechanism £75.

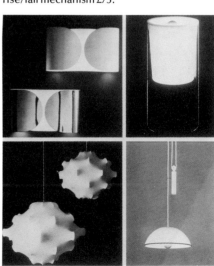

ARGON GALLERY

Unique gallery and shop, devoted exclusively to works of art created in neon and run by two artists who themselves work in this inert gas and others like argon and krypton. Exhibits, and over 300 slides, show the many different ways in which this lovely light form, once solely a commercial medium, can be applied. Work may be commissioned.

ARMSTRONG CORK CO LTD

GRIDMATE lightweight recessed lighting panels for use with this company's ceilings. Fitted with clear prismatic lens covers, they come assembled and ready to clip directly into the matching support grid. *M:* five sizes 60×60–180×180cm (23⁵/₈×23⁵/₈–70⁷/₈×70⁷/₈in). *P:* upon application.

The far more sophisticated LUMINAIRE ceilings integrate lighting, air conditioning and ventilation, and acoustic control. An exposed grid system supports flat or vaulted panels, painted White with slight surface texture. The extent of the lighting area varies according to customers' requirements. *M:* four sizes 150×75–120×180cm (49×29¹/₂–47¹/₄×70¹/₈in). *P:* upon application. See also 'Architectural Ornaments'.

LAURA ASHLEY LTD

Pleated and plain lampshades made from Laura Ashley's famous furnishing cottons. Nine designs are available including florals, fine double stripes and neat geometrics, in colours to suit most schemes. *M:* pleated h 24cm (9³/₈in), plain h 18, 23cm (7¹/₈, 9in). *P:* £12.25, £3.50, £4.25.

Glazed ceramic lamp bases, in two sizes, come in White or Cream, complete with solid brass fittings. *M:* h 20, 28cm (7⁷/₈, 10⁵/₈in). *P:* £8.75, £10.75.

Laura Ashley's pleated shade and large ceramic base

ATRIUM

Small but stunning range of modern lighting. GESTO T2 standard and S1, S2 ceiling lamps are in Black or White stove-enamelled steel with protective glass on the illuminator. The support is chrome plated, with a White, Grey or Black marble stand. *M:* standard h 227cm (7ft 5³/₈in), ceiling h 99, 127cm (3ft 3in, 4ft 2in). *P:* from £400. 250, 500, 750 watts, 1,000 watt (special unit). The 'Pipistrelle' table or standard lamp has a light-diffusing shade in white opal methacrylic, a stainless steel telescopic support, and lacquered base in White, or Dark brown (*M:* h 66–88cm/26–34⁵/₈in, diam 55cm/21⁵/₈in), *P:* £140; 4×25 watts).

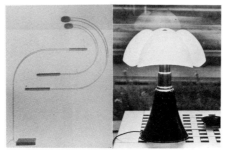

Atrium's GESTO lamps (left), 'Pipistrelle' table lamp (right)

Bamboo and rice paper FAN lighting comes in numerous arrangements for ceiling, floor, wall or table use. Most are supplied in a natural finish, some in Red or Black lacquer. The four-fan 'Yatsuba 1 and 11' wall or ceiling lamps can be dismantled.

The GALGEN range is virtually Minimal Art. Lamps have Red or Black triangular bases and Black supports, both in iron. Shades are net-threaded paper screens, in four simple shapes; two sizes of screens are available for each model. *M:* h 135cm (4ft 5¹/₈in). *P:* £110. 60–100 watts.

Atrium's GALGEN range

RALPH BALL

Marvellous, Minimal kite-like reflectors that seem to float on fine wires strung between floor and ceiling. They can be angled in any direction, positioned anywhere on the low-voltage wires. Colours are Blue, Green, and Silver-grey, or to order. (In addition, please give ceiling height when ordering from this clever designer.) *M:* base unit 8.5×8.5×12.5cm (3¹/₄×3¹/₄×5in), kite reflector 15×15cm (5⁷/₈×5⁷/₈in). *P:* including base, two reflectors and bulbs £95; additional reflectors £20 each.

BAXTER & WOOD LTD

All kinds of reasonably priced lamps and lanterns. Primarily intended for outdoor use, the range includes a number of models that are acceptable inside. They include the 'Cabin Lantern' with a ceiling canopy and chain, and brass finish (*M:* h 33cm/13in, *P:* £15, 60 watts); the 'Leicester Wall Lamp' with a wrought-iron surround and amber glass, finished in weather-resistant Black (*M:* h 40.5cm/16in, *P:* £18.50; 60 watts); the 'Lancaster Torch Lamp' with the same weather-resistant finish and a flambeau globe (*M:* h 48cm/18⁷/₈in, *P:* £13; 40 watts); the 'Emperor Coach Lamp' with a brass canopy topped by an eagle (*M:* h 60cm/23⁵/₈in, *P:* £30; 60 watts); and the 'Carnival Lamp' in weather-resistant brass and Black with 'Arctic' glass (*M:* h 43cm/16⁷/₈, *P:* £9.50; 40 watts). Also the 'London Bridge' four-light lamp post. In weather-resistant Black wrought iron, it has clear, yellow or amber bulged glass.

PRICES AND INFORMATION WERE CORRECT AT THE TIME OF GOING TO PRESS

BEST & LLOYD LTD

Two distinct approaches—traditional and modern—from one firm. Period ceiling and wall-mounted lights come in five styles: Victorian, Art Nouveau (also a table lamp), Adam, Hepplewhite, and traditional 'NO 4'.

Modern lamps for localized lighting, more functional in appearance, include a 'Picture Light' in two sizes, and the similarly styled 'Desk Lamp', both finished in polished brass (*M:* picture light w 30, 55cm/11⁷/₈, 21⁵/₈in, desk light w 30cm/11⁷/₈in, *P:* £32, £46, £46; 60 watts).

'Task Light' has a left- or right-hand mount and is fitted with a fluorescent tube. The flexible 'Cantilever' wall or table lamp has a rotating reflector that pivots about the stem to provide long, low surface brightness wherever the fluorescent tube is directed. It comes in anodized aluminium with a steel base finished in Black. *M:* w 53cm (20⁷/₈in). *P:* £65. 75 watts. The classic 'Bestlite' table or floor lamp is equally adjustable. The reflector, shaped like an egg cup, can be turned back on itself and raised obliquely or vertically while it rotates through 360°. Reflector and base are enamelled in White, Black or Off-white (or to the customer's specifications), tubular parts are finished in brass or chrome.

Best & Lloyd's 'Picture Light' (top), 'Desk Lamp' (bottom)

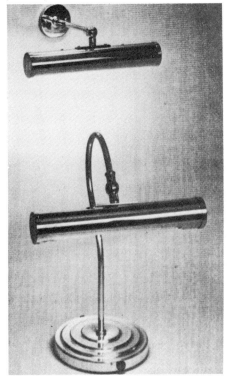

Left: Baxter & Wood's 'Emperor Coach Lamp' (left), 'Leicester Wall Lamp' (centre), 'Carnival Lamp' (right)

Best & Lloyd's 'Cantilever' lamps

G BOCOCK & CO LTD

Unusual lighting, originally designed for use in cabins and saloons, from one of the UK's leading manufacturers of ships' lamps. The range consists of nicely functional brass lights, plus very individual lighting accessories including an extensive selection of shades, globes and chimneys for oil lamps. Most of Bobock's lamps are intended to burn oil, but can be wired for electricity.

'306' has a steel reflector in Black with a White underside (*M:* h 26in/66cm, *P:* £26). There are eight variations of '411', all fitted with a 10in (25.5cm) dome shade (*M:* h 23½in/60cm, *P:* £46.50). Both models come complete with duplex burner, wick and chimney. '3848' has an unusual faceted cap, three scrolled guards and a spherical globe, and is supplied with a wedge chimneyless burner (*M:* h 17in/43cm, *P:* £51). '3884', a four-light pendant (electric only), comes with 4¾in (12cm) White shades (*M:* h 25½in/65cm, *P:* £66). Two- and three-light units are available.

Table lamps come with a burner wick and chimney for oil burning, but can be adapted for electricity. Globes or shades can be fitted. Medium-sized '451 Consul' comes in brass or copper, with a brass trim around the base (*M:* 18¾in/47.5cm, *P:* £12). '455 Monarch', available with clear, opal, or coloured glass shades, is mounted on a stepped marble base in Opal or Green, and has a brass reeded support and capitol (*M:* h 30in/76cm, *P:* £42).

The '3846 Student's Lamp' is in polished brass. It has single adjustable arm, and is fitted with a 7¾in/20cm shade. *M:* h 20in (51cm). *P:* from £41.

The 'Masthead Lamp' in the CANAL BARGEWARE range is a charming reproduction in tinplate. Hand-painted with bright floral designs on a Dark green background, it has a kidney-shaped lens in a brass mounting. It comes with a 1in (2.5cm) burner, wick and chimney, and can be electrified. *M:* h 18½in (47cm) excluding handle. *P:* £55.

Cabin and saloon, or wall-hanging, lamps come in similar designs, generally with opal globes or shades. '435', one of the most unusual, is known as a 'standard size gimbal pattern lamp', and comes complete with burner wick and chimney. A bracket is fitted for electricity. *M:* h 12½in (31.5cm). *P:* £20.

Left to right, from top: Bocock's '455', '411', '3848', '435', '3846', 'Masthead Lamp'

MAURICE BROWN LTD

Good-looking, modern KOSTKA table lamps with ceramic bases finished in a crackle glaze. There's a staggering selection of 30 shapes, including classic urns, jars, spheres and squares as well as the more popular shell and bamboo styles. All have matching fabric shades. Colours are equally wide ranging: White, Ivory, Beige, Caramel, Yellow, Salmon pink, Rust, Red, Plum, Emerald, Pink, Blackcurrant, Brown, Lime green, Celadon green, Pale pink, Blue-grey—50 in all! *M:* h 26–80cm (10¼–31½in). *P:* £16–£70. 60–100 watts. See page 162 for colour illustration.

CANDELL LTD

Enormous range of ornate, but essentially modern, lighting. A good selection of traditional brass, bronze and crystal chandeliers is also available, plus ornate hall lights like 'M216', 'M903' and 'M954' finished in French old gold (*M:* h 100–120cm/3ft 3³/₈in–3ft 11¼in, *P:* £260–£700; 100 watts).

Contemporary fittings include numerous pendant lights. Models 'M1662' to 'M1665' all have a basketwork shade, gold anodized aluminium rim and internal opal glass diffuser (*M:* h 19–26cm/7½–10¼in, diam 18–41cm/7¹/₈–16¹/₈in, *P:* £40–£80; 100 watts). For a really rural look, the 'M792' pendant light comes in Black or Copper-coloured wrought iron with a hand-painted ceramic base and white opal glass shade (*M:* h 90cm/35³/₈in, diam 34cm/13³/₈in, *P:* £70; 100 watts). The 'M884' to 'M886' pendants, also in wrought iron, have a copper reflector, ceramic trim and amber glass (*M:* h 150cm/4ft 11in, diam 40–50cm/15³/₄–19⁵/₈in, *P:* £80–£180; 100 watts).

Candell's 'M1162' to 'M1165' (left), 'M792' (right)

'M857' to 'M860'—two pendants, a wall and a table light—are simpler stunners, finished in polished brass with clear bubble glass globes (*M:* 'M859' table lamp, h 30cm/11⁷/₈in, diam 19cm/7½in, *P:* 'M857'–'M860' £60–£140; 60 watts). Moderately more modern, 'M1463' and 'M1468' ceiling lights come in polished chrome or glass, teamed with suede-textured shades in Brown or Green; a rise-and-fall suspension is supplied (*M:* diam 40cm/15³/₄in, *P:* £95; 60 watts). 'M1469' to 'M1470' in the same finishes plus nickel plate, have Brown or Green suede-textured or White perspex shades (*M:* diam 44cm/17³/₈in, *P:* £90; 60 watts).

For real drama there are strings of glass bubbles. 'M1629', a truly amazing piece, comes in simpler versions or can be wall mounted. Available in clear or amber glass, it's finished in satin or polished aluminium. *M:* h 140cm (55¹/₈in), diam 40cm (15³/₄in). *P:* £250. 40 watts. The 'M1625', or larger 'M1626', table lamps are in a similarly futuristic vein. Also available as pendants or wall lights, they're finished in anodized gold, polished aluminium, chromium plate or polished brass, with clear 'Volcano' glass globes. *M:* h 74–115cm (29¹/₈–45¼in), diam 41cm (16¹/₈in). *P:* £200–£300. 60 watts.

Left to right, from top: Candell's '1470', '1469', 'M1629', and 'M859' in two sizes

Two well-designed modern wall lights are also available. They look great singly, but can also be combined in pairs, threes, fours, etc, and are sold in these variations. 'M920', 'M921', 'M977', and 'M978' are finished in polished aluminium, with white opal glass reflectors (*M:* 'M921' h 31cm (12¼in), diam 16cm (6¼in). *P:* £65. 40 watts. The 'M1637' can also be grouped or used by itself. It's available in White enamelled or gold anodized aluminium, with white opal or topaz 'Volcano' glass. *M:* diam 28cm (11in). *P:* £40. 60 watts.

CASA FINA

Lovely selection of ornamental ceramicware. It includes a large lamp with linen-textured shade, and two light sources, one in the lattice-perforated base (*M:* h 29in/73.5cm, *P:* £63.50, main fitting 100 watts).

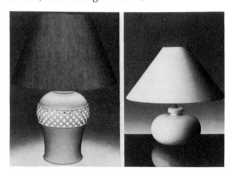

CIANCIMINO DESIGN LTD

Tasteful lamp with a ceramic base and 'coolie' shade, from the most tasteful of shops. The base comes in White, Off-white, and Bright brown; the shade in White card or fabric, or Mint green, Grey-green, Pale blue, Brick red, Coral, Yellow, or Natural laminate. *M:* 15in (38cm). *P:* base £15, shades £5–£9. 100 watts.

COLOURFLAIR FURNITURE

Beautifully traditional TOLE wall-mounted and table standard lamps. (TOLE, an extension of French enamelling developed over the last two centuries, incorporates pleasingly simple hand-painted border motifs.) All 24 styles can be painted to order. *M:* table lamps h 16–29in (40.5–73.5cm). *P:* £60–£140. 100 watts.

CONCORD LIGHTING INTL LTD

Rich and varied selection of functional modern fittings. They include all kinds of recessed downlighters, multiple circuit tracking systems, spotlights and tracklights—even ceiling-mounted projectors and speakers. CONE downlighters are fitted with highly efficient reflectors to minimize the wattage required for lighting. A wide range of 20 fittings is available, most with silver or gold anodized reflectors. *M:* h 27–36cm (10⁵/₈–14¹/₈in). *P:* upon application. 250 watts. Swivelling, directional downlighters come in three styles (*M:* upon application, *P:* upon application).

Three LYTESPAN multiple-circuit systems are designed primarily for commercial use but are very much at home in spacious, modern rooms. 'Tubetrack', the most expensive, can be ordered in Yellow, Red, Dark brown, Green, Black, or White gloss, in minimum lots of 50 lengths. 'Lytespan 3' and 'Lytespan 7' are in satin anodized aluminium only, also to order. A speaker with four-position volume control can be fitted to 'Tubetrack'. *M:* l. 120–360cm (45–135in). *P:* upon application.

Left: Lamps by Casa Fina (left), Ciancimino (right)

A staggering 30 LYTESPOT lamps fit the tracks. Most come in brushed aluminium or White finish. 'Trio' is a small spotlight with a Black or Brown reflector (40 watts). 'Lytesphere Mini', an equally neat spot, comes in polished chrome, White, and Holly green, with an internal aluminium reflector edged in Black (40 watts). 'Lotus' has a unique slip-on adjustable White reflector (60 watts). *M:* diam 12, 13, 18cm (4¾, 5⅛, 7⅛in). *P:* upon application.

'Wall Bullet' is a fully adjustable wall-mounted or pin-up spot. In White, silver or brass it has White moulding and an integral push-button switch. *M:* h 24cm (9¾in), diam 4cm (5½in). *P:* upon application. 100 watts.

Left, left to right, from top: Concord's 'Lytesphere Mini', 'Trio', 'Lotus', 'Wall Bullet'

THE CONRAN SHOP LTD
Comprehensive range of stove-enamelled architectural lighting including spots, pendants and clip-on lights. Not inexpensive, they're beautifully and functionally designed and come in delightful ice cream colours like Peppermint green, Pink, and Peach; also Sea blue, Grey, and Dark green. *P:* £33–£125.

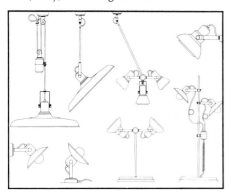

DERNIER & HAMLYN LTD
Gorgeous classical fittings, mainly chandeliers and pendants, from a company that has been making decorative lighting since 1888. Dernier & Hamlyn's products grace many historic and government buildings, underlining the company's unrivalled reputation for elegant traditional design, good service and craftsmanship.

There are 23 ranges, most with 12-, six-, three- and two-light versions. All fittings are finished in polished brass, polished silver, lacquered gilt, or butler's silver; satin brass, satin silver, antique brass and half-finished brass cost an extra 15%. Examples are a 12-light chandelier in polished brass from the DUTCH range (*M:* h 94cm/37in, diam 86cm/33⅞in, *P:* £1,750; 12×25 watts); a 12-light MAZARIN pendant (named after Louis XIV's Chief Minister), the original of which hangs in the Bibliothèque Nationale in Paris (*M:* h 71cm/28in, diam 61cm/24in, *P:* £850; 12×25 watts); a KNOLE eight-light pendant, based on an original at Knole Park near Sevenoaks, Kent, with typically 17th-century pineapple finials and cherubs (*M:* h 48cm/19in, diam 58cm/23in, *P:* £1,350; 8×25 watts); six-light CONTESSA pendant (*M:* h 38cm/15in, diam 50cm/19⅝in, *P:* £360; 12×25 watts); and a 12-light, two-tier DIADEM pendant (*M:* h 63cm/24⅞in, diam 66cm/26in, *P:* £580; 6×25 watts). Most of these are the most expensive models in each range, to give an idea of relative costs.

Table lamps, also classically inspired, are available, plus six lanterns including the three-light, hexagonal '14713' (*M:* h 53cm/20⅞in, diam 46cm/18in, *P:* £625; 3×25 watts).

Dernier & Hamlyn offer a complete restoration service, including any necessary modifications, rewiring and supplying spare parts.

Dernier & Hamlyn's DIADEM pendant

PRICES AND INFORMATION WERE CORRECT AT THE TIME OF GOING TO PRESS

DESIGNERS GUILD
Attractive lighting, displayed in Tricia Guild's charming premises—the perfect complement for their sweet but chic use of antiques with modern, but pastel, fabrics. Ceramic bases come in Blue, Pale green, Apricot, Brick, Off-white, Yellow—and to order, in any colour specified by the customer. Shades can be covered in any Designers Guild fabric, for quintessential co-ordination. *M:* bases h 25–43cm (9⅞–16⅞in), shades diam 45–66cm (17¾–26in). *P:* bases £25–£90, shades £11–£21. 60–100 watts.

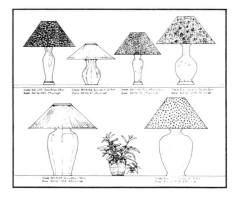

EDISON HALO LTD
Great collection of nicely designed spotlights for surface or track mounting, and compatible tracking systems. The low-profile SINGLE CIRCUIT TRACK, for small spots and a limited number of push-in connectors, comes in a good range of finishes: White enamel, anodized or polished aluminium, Matt black, and teak. For real perfectionists, a RECESSED TRACK in anodized aluminium or White enamel can be adapted to run in lengths, or any regular grid pattern. Both tracks take any of the MINI SPOTS or UNIVERSAL spotlights.

MINI SPOTS come in a great variety of finishes: polished or anodized aluminium, Brown, Matt black, Blue, Gloss white, Yellow, Red, Green, Amber, and Teak (*M:* diam 5cm/2in; 150 watts). UNIVERSAL spotlights are in polished or anodized aluminium, White, and Matt black and can be fitted with colour filters or an anti-glare louvre attachment (*M:* diam 10cm/4in; 150 watts). Both ranges can be fitted with one of four reflectors.

The MAXI, boldly sculptured in die-cast zinc, can be surface or track mounted. Available in White or chrome, in two sizes, it has an adjustable swivel arm that can move through 358° horizontally, 90° vertically. *M:* diam 19.5, 23cm (7¾, 9in). 300 watts.

Five more lighting ranges are available. CYLINDERS comes in three sizes, in polished or anodized aluminium, and White (*M:* h 23–35cm/9–13¾in; 150 watts). CONTINENTALS, in the same finishes, is available in two sizes (*M:* h 23, 28cm/9, 11in; 150 watts). BULLETS, in three sizes, comes in three additional colours: Matt black, Brown, and Green (*M:* h 13–26cm/

5¹/₈–10¼in; 150 watts). SPHERES is available in three sizes and the same colours as BULLETS, plus Yellow, and Red (*M: diam 16–20cm/6¼–7⁷/₈in*; 150 watts). SQUARES, made from extruded aluminium, comes in two sizes, in White, and polished or anodized aluminium (*M: h 23, 33cm/9, 13in*; 100 watts).
Edison Halo also have a very special framing spotlight for picture lighting. It has a double lens, four adjustable shutters to control the light beam, and comes in Matt black.
P: all products upon application.

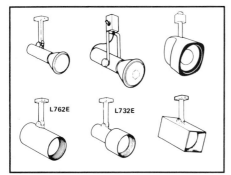

Left to right, from top: Edison Halo's MINI, UNIVERSAL, MAXI, CYLINDER, CONTINENTAL, SQUARE

EMESS LIGHTING LTD

Excellent range of simple indoor fixtures. Solid brass lanterns include 'Mayfair' and 'Hampstead', both with cut-star glass panels. Suitable for entrance halls, they are highly polished, and protected with lacquer. *M:* d 9½in (24cm). *P:* £40, £37. 60 watts. There's also a good selection of pendant lights, most of which can be fitted with any of 18 glass shades in contemporary or traditional styles. GLAZED OPAL ceiling lights are far simpler. Square and round fixtures come in a variety of sizes. *M:* diam 8½–12⁵/₈in (22–32cm). *P:* 10in (22.5cm) £9.50 as illustrated. 100 watts.

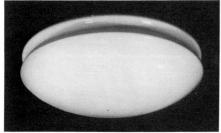

Emess' round GLAZED OPAL ceiling light

The GLASHUTTE LIMBURG range of 96 pendants is distinctively contemporary—a must for fans of modern lighting. Simply designed, but boldly executed, they are wonderful evidence of what can be done with glass. Five examples are: '4225' to '4228' with a brass top, and satin matt opal or pearl raindrop glass shade, in four sizes (*M:* h 23–29cm/9–

11³/₈in, *P:* £85–£130; 150 watts); '1600' to '1684' with an unusual chromium-plated or brass chain and large opal glass shade (*M:* h 27cm/10⁵/₈in, *P:* £125–£155; 150 watts); 'Flora' (1634) in satin matt opal glass with black flex suspension, in four sizes (*M:* diam 20–35cm/7⁷/₈–13³/₄in, *P:* from £59.50; 75 watts); 'Prism' (4215) with Black metalwork and flex suspension and clear crystal glass (*M:* h 30, diam 26cm/11⁷/₈, 10¼in, *P:* £88; 75 watts); and '4162' to '4177', another stunner, with Dark brown metal reflector and either black flex or a finely adjustable rise/fall suspension (*M:* diam 40, 50cm/15³/₄, 19⁵/₈in, *P:* £83–£118; 75 watts).

Left to right, from top: Emess' '1660', 'Flora', 'Prism', '4162'

Emess also excel at wall lights. An overwhelming range of 310 fixtures includes '2956' to '2959'. In satin matt or pearl raindrop glass they are particularly suited to large rooms. *M:* h 21, 30cm (8¼, 11⁷/₈in). *P:* £43–£79. 150 watts. '2338' and '2896' look like a traffic light—evocative of Hollywood in the 1930s. Perfect for lighting mirrors, they're splashproof and come with a gold-plated or chromium surround. *M:* w 38cm (15in), h 13cm (5¹/₈in). *P:* £145 as illustrated. 40 watts. 'The Sphere', an opal or topaz crystal globe with chromium/Black or brass/Black bracket, is available with or without a pull switch (*M:* diam 16, 25cm (6¼, 9⁷/₈in), *P:* £50–£130; 100 watts).
37 table lamps include two unusual all-glass models: '6249' with a white satin opal glass shade and base (*M:* h 30cm/11⁷/₈in, *P:* £93; 100 watts); and '6053', like a large light bulb in opal or topaz raindrop glass, in three sizes (*M:* h 26–46cm/10¼–18in, *P:* £48; 150 watts).
An extensive range of traditional and contemporary outdoor lighting is also available.

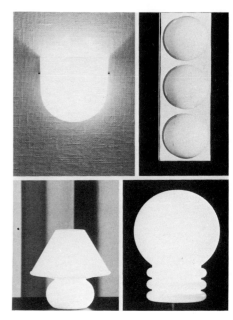

Left to right, from top: Emess' '2956', '2338', '6249', '6053'

ENVIRONMENT DESIGN

Wonderfully modern and pleasingly bizarre lighting from Italy. The justifiably famous FLOS range includes net-draped 'Nuvola' with an inverted triangular centre (*M:* h 60cm/23⁵/₈in, diam 90cm/35³/₈in, *P:* £280; 3×100 watts); the 'Ariette' wall or ceiling light, a piece of modern art in textured fibre (*M:* three sizes diam 80–130cm/31½–51¼in, *P:* £50–£60; 4×40 watts); and 'Tubino', a long, lean desk lamp in Black or White enamelled metal, lit—economically—by a single 8-watt fluorescent tube (*M:* h 29.5 × l. 67cm/15¹/₈×26³/₈in, *P:* upon application); forward-looking 'Taccia', a great uplighter in Black anodized aluminium (*M:* h 54cm/21¼in, *P:* £25; 100 watts); and 'Jucker', like a dwarf visitor from outer space in Red or White enamelled metal (*M:* h 22cm/8⁵/₈in, *P:* upon application; 60 watts).

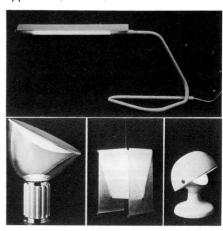

ERCO LIGHTING LTD

Marvellous modern lights from a firm that specializes in fixtures for architects and designers. A great collection of track lighting and spotlight combinations includes spots for clip-fixing, or ceiling or wall mounting, plus colour filters, in numerous styles, for professional and domestic use. One-, two- and three-phase illumination is available. Downlights have reflectors finished in anodized aluminium, silver or gold and can be supplied to fit five different ceiling openings.

Hollywood-style mirror fittings in anodized silver or gold have three, five or ten small, round bulbs and come with or without a press-button switch. A connector for wrapping around the mirrors is also optional. *M:* w 28.5, 57, 120cm (11¼, 22½, 45in). *P:* £15–£45. 40 watts. Other mirror lighting units have opal or crystal glass and electric razor sockets, and are unusually well designed.

Work-place fixtures include '3–23–10' which is available as a desk, clip-mounted or standard lamp (*M:* h 150in/59cm, *P:* £175; 60 watts).

16 styles of pendant light include '2–26–11' in Red or White aluminium with a gold anodized reflector and Black top (*M:* h 32.5cm/15⅞in, diam 36cm/14⅛in, *P:* £40; 100 watts); and '2–20–30' in anodized aluminium (*M:* h 40cm/15¾in, diam 34cm/13⅜in, *P:* £40; 100 watts).

The CONRAN range consists of a standard lamp, two-, four- or six-light pendants, a wall light, a double or track spotlight, and a table lamp. Fixtures are chromium plated with Black edging rings and White aluminium reflectors. *M:* '3–12–05' table lamp h 41.5cm (16⅜in), globe diam 14cm (5½in). *P:* £150. 75 watts.

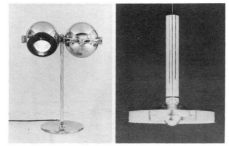

Erco's '2-20-30' (left), CONRAN table lamp (right)

FORMA LTD

Exciting range of progressive Italian lighting from famous manufacturers like Cil, Guzzini, Leucos and Valenti.

Most of the simple pendant lamps in the CIL collection have brass shades, although 'Tamis' features unusual colours like Pink, and Emerald green. Table and standard lamps also reflect this penchant for brass. They include two beautiful desk lights: 'Weimar' with a gilded brass shade and stone base (*M:* h 42cm/16½in, diam 48cm/18⅞in, *P:* £225; 3×40 watts); and 'Vienna', a curvaceous beauty in the same materials (*M:* h 45cm/17¾in, *P:* £290; 60 watts). 'Alugena' comes in numerous ver-

Forma's 'Weimar' (top left), 'Vienna' (top right), 'Alugena' (bottom)

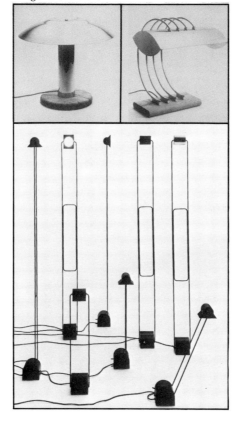

sions, to solve most lighting problems, and is finished in brass, chrome, or Black (*M:* h 60–150cm/23⅝–54in, *P:* £120–£160; 60 watts).

GUZZINI make a comprehensive range of lamps, as well as an excellent track and spot system. 25 ceiling or wall lights include 'Module' with a chromed reflector and nine '5056' or 25 '5058' lights (*M:* 30×30cm/11⅞× 11⅞in, *P:* £47, £150; 25 watts); 'Ping Pong', with a white opal glass sphere, and White plastic handle and pull switch (*M:* h 39cm/15⅜in, diam 26cm/10¼in, *P:* £40; 25 watts); and 'Mezzanotte', which can be rotated to direct the light where you want it, in White aluminium (*M:* diam 24cm/9⅜in, *P:* £40; 60 watts).

30 table standard lamps are available. 'Telescopus' in White aluminium with a concentrically ringed shade also comes in a floor version (*M:* h 43cm/16⅞in, diam 45cm/17¾in, *P:* £46; 3×40 watts). 'Sorella' seemingly defies gravity, in White aluminium (*M:* h 30cm/11⅞in, diam 24cm/9⅜in, *P:* £32; 60 watts). 'Ialea', in diffusing White acrylic, is the most sculptural lamp in the range (*M:* h 22cm/8⅝in, diam 24cm/9⅜in, *P:* £15; 40 watts). Pendant fittings include 'Diaframma' with four metal flaps in Yellow, Green, or White (*M:* h 25cm/9⅞in, diam 26cm/10¼in, *P:* £43; 100 watts).

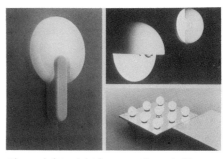

Above, left to right from top: Forma's 'Ping Pong', 'Mezzanotte', 'Module', 'Diaframma', 'Telescopus', 'Ialea', 'Sorella'

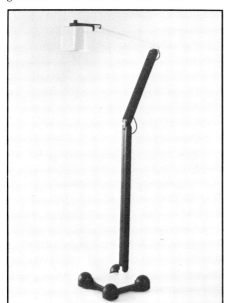

Erco's '3-23-10' standard lamp

Left, left to right, from top: Environment's 'Tubino', 'Taccia', 'Teli', 'Jucker'

VALENTI lighting includes a marvellous range of simple wall lights in plain geometric shapes like spheres, discs and ovals. Also 16 table lamps. 'Pistillo', like a giant flower's pistil, comes in gilded Makrolon or chrome plate and is available in a smaller, wall-mounted version ('Pistillino'). Special low-wattage bulbs with gold or chrome caps are supplied. *M:* diam 60cm (23⁵/₈in). *P:* £35.

'Hebi' is one of a family of very High Tech lamps all with flexible pipe supports. It's available with a clamp, or rubber-covered base, in a multitude of colours: White, Black, Red, Green, Yellow, Blue, Military green, Grape husk, Dark brown, Light brown, Brick red, and Black chromed. *M:* h 60cm (23⁵/₈in). *P:* £55. 60 watts. 'Zeta' comes in a clamp-on version, plus four table, and two wall-mounted, models differentiated by length and the number of sturdy Black segments used to make up their arms. All have a White plastic reflector. *M:* h 40cm (15¾in), diam 27cm (10⁵/₈in). *P:* £85. 60 watts. The 'Aloterra' floor lamp is the answer for anyone who craves lots of light. It comes with one or two revolving independent reflectors, each capable of taking a 500-watt halogen bulb. Made of metal, with melamine reflectors, it is available in Black, and White. A foot-operated dimmer can be supplied. *M:* h 185cm (6ft 1in). *P:* £270, with dimmer £320.

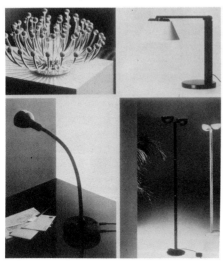

Left to right, from top: Forma's 'Zeta', 'Pistillo', 'Aloterra', 'Hebi' from VALENTI

The LEUCOS collection, mainly in hand-blown glass, is much more flamboyant (and pricey). Pendants come in 27 styles. 'Febo' is a very dramatic Black or White glass hemisphere with bright Yellow, Wine and Red rings at the base (*M:* h 20cm/7⁷/₈in, diam 30cm/11⁷/₈in, *P:* £200–£320; 100 watts). 'Onda' is in clear glass with a fluted edge and frosted cap (*M:* h 40cm/15¾in, diam 30cm/11⁷/₈in, *P:* £265; 100 watts). Also an interesting selection of table lamps.

PRICES AND INFORMATION WERE CORRECT AT THE TIME OF GOING TO PRESS

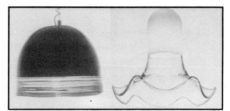

Forma's 'Febo' (left), 'Onda' (right), both from LEUCOS

FRANKLITE LTD
Nice, sensibly priced collection of 20 classically inspired brass chandeliers and matching wall sconces. 'CO 3240/371' comes with three, five or six lights, and as a single light or double wall sconce (*M:* diam 20in/51cm, *P:* £70; 60 watts). 'PE 3420/369' is Victorian-inspired (*M:* diam 19in/48cm, *P:* £64; 60 watts). Globes come in four styles, two in etched glass.

Franklite's '3420/369'

FUTURE TENSE
Neon lighting for domestic as well as commercial use. Virtually any design can be supplied, including figurative light units. Standard colours are Snow white, Standard blue, Mid-yellow, White, Daylight, and Standard green. More expensive, special colours are also available: Ruby red, Lavender, Deep blue, Rose pink, Pale pink, Magenta and Pale blue. *M:* to order. *P:* upon application.

GALLERIA MONTE CARLO
Extremely ornate wall and ceiling fixtures to complement this company's sumptuous bathroom fittings, ceramic tiles, mirrors and wallpapers. Wall lights come adorned with crystal swans, birds, figurines or floral motifs. Most are finished in gold or silver, with mock candle bulbs (40 or 60 watts).

Ceiling lights and pendants are available in nine styles, all of which incorporate some form of crystal. Diffused mirror lighting is rectangular and comes in three lengths. There are four options: crystal beaded panels or frosted glass panels with plain, reeded, or bamboo-shaped metal borders. *M:* w 16, 27, 38in (40.5, 68.5, 96.5cm).

P: all upon application.

GERLIN DECOR
Leaded and stained-glass lighting inspired by the Belle Epoque. The large range includes table lamps on cast-iron bases finished in polished brass, pendants, and wall-mounted lights. *M:* h 15–19in (38–48.5cm). *P:* £31, £53, £56, £52 as illustrated. 100 watts.

DAVID GILLESPIE ASSOCIATES LTD
Several lighting options, all part of this company's stunning range of ZEROSPAN moulded ceiling tiles. The 'ZPLI' chandelier, assembled from 72 cast pendants, is only one of a host of arrangements. Five ceiling-mounted lighting panels and seven down-lighters are also available, integrated with concave, convex or flat ceiling tiles in a prismatic or White matt finish. (Made from Zerodec, a new composite material developed by this firm, fixtures can be painted.) *M:* modules 90×90, 120×120cm (35⁵/₈×35⁵/₈, 47¼×47¼in). *P:* upon application.

GRAFTON INTERIORS
High-quality collection of 200 lamps from Le Dauphin of France. Mainly in lacquer and brass, they are interesting, beautifully made—and tend to be expensive. Table lamps include 'Azincourt' with a Black glass base, and Black glazed cotton shade edged with Amber and Black beads (*M:* h 54cm/21¼in, *P:* £97; 100 watts); 'Hoasin' with Golden birds of paradise on a Black or Maroon base and a slub silk shade (*M:* h 85cm/33½in, *P:* £144; 150 watts); 'Lindos' with water birds from an oriental silk painting nicely reproduced on the base, a brass, ivory or Black surround, and silky shade (*M:* h 65cm/25½in, *P:* £152; 150 watts); 'Mysore' with a tortoiseshell laminate base, slub silk shade and brass feet (*M:* h from 59cm/23¼in, *P:* from £133; 150 watts); 'Warner' a lovely contemporary classic with an inlaid

---

Right: Jane Thomas's pyramid table lamps

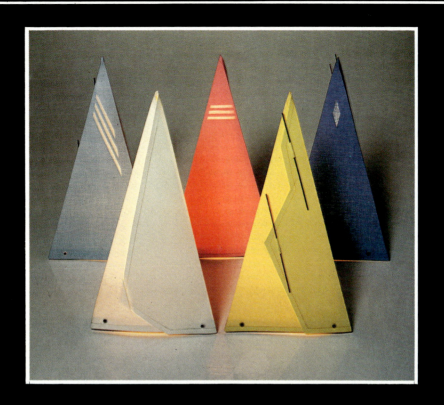

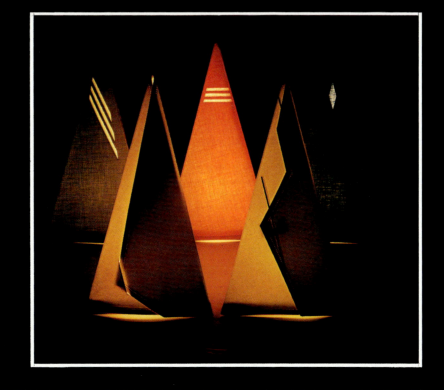

brass rectangle on the base surrounded with Black, Maroon, Brown or Ivory lacquer, and a matching glossy shade (*M:* h 84cm/33in, *P:* £154; 150 watts); and 'Urcay' which has a ceramic base and card shade lined with gold foil (*M:* h 87cm/34¼in, *P:* £148; 150 watts).

Above, left to right, from top: Grafton's 'Azincourt', 'Mysore', 'Hoasin', 'Warner', 'Lindos', 'Urcay'

Grafton's 'Colona', 'Vendôme', 'Coligny', 'Venon'

For less expensive table lamps with a handsome metal colonnade base and matching

Left: Sheila Teague's pleated wall light

pleated poplin or plain 'coolie' shade, there's 'Colona', 'Vendome', 'Coligny', and 'Venon' (*M:* h 39–58cm/15³⁄₈–22⁷⁄₈in, *P:* £37, £67; 100 watts). 'Sim' and 'Sumi', also metal-based, have sweet petal-like cotton shades (*M:* h 33, 43cm/13, 16⁷⁄₈in, *P:* £37, £41; 60 watts). All these lamps come in Black, White, Pale blue, Pale green, Lilac, Rose, Dusty rose, Champagne, Pale yellow, Natural, Ecru, Beige, Salmon, Wine, and Brown.

Grafton's 'Sim'

HABITAT DESIGNS LTD

Good-looking range from a firm that's world famous for sensible, modern design. The 'Metro' wall light has a Black metal frame, and unbreakable Cream or White inset panes, and is also available as a pendant (*M:* w 12in/30.5cm, *P:* £13, pendant £30; 100 watts). 'Cassata' pottery lamps are sweet little classics with matching laminated fabric shades; great value, they come in Grey, Pink, Green, Blue, Vanilla, and Cream (*M:* h 30cm/11⁷⁄₈in, diam 25cm/9⁷⁄₈in, *P:* £8; 100 watts). 'Bulkhead', a ceiling or wall light, is more utilitarian. Available in two shapes, it has an aluminium base with a Red or White steel grille. *M:* diam 20, 22cm (7⁷⁄₈, 8⁵⁄₈in). *P:* £8, £12. 100 watts.

Habitat's 'Metro' (left), 'Bulkhead' (right)

CHARLES HAMMOND LTD

Nice lighting from a well-known interior decorating firm. Two lamp bases are 'Column Lamp' in brass (*M:* h 37cm/14½in, *P:* £40) and 'Crackle Lamp' in textured glass (*M:* three sizes h 35–50cm/13¾–19⁵⁄₈in, *P:* £33–£55); both 150 watts. Classic ginger jar-shaped ceramic bases come in White, Sand, Derby brown, Pale blue, Beige, Apricot, Eucalyptus, Chartreuse, Dark brown, and Black (*M:* h 25, 31, 35cm/9⁷⁄₈, 12¼, 13¾in, *P:* £9–£18; 100 watts). There's also a good selection of standard and 'coolie' shades in White and Cream, or Black, card lined with Gold paper (*M:* diam 12–22in/30.5–56cm, *P:* £6–£22).

OSWALD HOLLMAN LTD

Marvellously modern range of plain but nicely styled BRENDEL & LOEWIG lighting from Germany. The '2532' chandelier in polished brass has 12 lights. (*M:* h 33cm/13in, diam 45cm/17¾in, *P:* £230; 12×40 watts). It is also available with eight lights, and as a three-light wall or table lamp. More functional '4530', in brass, has an acrylic shade in solid Yellow or Brown, or translucent Cognac or White, and a pull flex (*M:* h 34cm/13³⁄₈in, diam 40cm/15¾in, *P:* £44.50; 100 watts).
Table lamps include '6436' with a ten-sided brass or silver base, and artificial silk shade in traditional or 'coolie' shape (*M:* h 67cm/26³⁄₈in, shade diam 48cm/18⁷⁄₈in, *P:* £127.50; 4×60 watts).
'BL 8139' is a wonderfully futuristic wall light with single or double white opal glass bulbs on a brass base, and a pull switch (*M:* h 36cm/14¹⁄₈in, *P:* £52.50; 60 watts).

Left to right, from top: Hollman's '6436', BL '8139', '4530', '2532' from BRENDEL & LOEWIG

HOMESHADE CO LTD

Absolutely gorgeous Baroque, Georgian, Regency and Spanish crystal chandeliers; plus a more usable collection of ceramic chandeliers with matching single or double wall brackets. 'PA 7817/5' and 'PA 7819/2' both have hand-painted decoration and candle drip (*M:* h 16in/40.5cm, diam 18in/46cm; h 12in/30.5cm, diam 13in/33cm, *P:* £110, £45; 5×40 watts). Matching ceramic table lamp bases are also available.
Spanish chandeliers and wall brackets are finished in gold-plate, or gunmetal. 'PA 959/5', an ornate bracket, comes with two, three or five mock candles (*M:* h 22in/56cm, diam 18in/46cm, *P:* £170; 5×40 watts). Four similarly ornate Spanish lanterns include five-sided 'PA 418/1' (*M:* h 12in/30.5cm, diam 9in/23cm, *P:* upon application; 60 watts). See overleaf for illustration.

Left to right: Homeshade's 'PA 7817/5', 'PA 959/5', 'PA 418/1'

HOMEWORKS LTD

Gorgeous glass lamp bases, imported from California by these stylish decorators. Two styles are available, both in clear, or Venetian green glass. The bean jar comes in two sizes, the square-based column in three. *M:* bean jar h 20, 24in (51, 61cm), square base h 20, 28, 36in (51, 71, 91.5cm). *P:* both £120 for largest size. Both 150 watts.

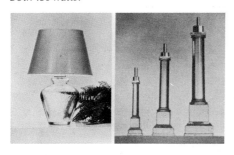

LINOLITE LTD

Functional, nicely designed lighting for awkward places. The SPL PICTURE LIGHT has directional beam control and an adjustable lamp shield that cuts off unwanted light at the top of a canvas, print or photograph. Finished in anodized gilt or chrome, it has a Matt black interior. There's a choice of sizes to suit anything from miniatures to large landscapes; a special arm for extra-deep pictures is available to order. *M:* w 12, 27, 33, 66, 99cm (4¾, 10⅝, 13, 26, 39in). *P:* £13–£32. 60 watts.
CSL SHAVOLITES, with two-pin shaver sockets and cord pull, come with tungsten or fluorescent bulbs (*M:* w 43, 66cm/16⅞, 26in, *P:* £20–£37; 60 watts). They can be mounted in matching NSD LUMINARIES which also give a diffused light.
KY DISPLAY REFLECTORS can be fixed to shelves to highlight collections, or fitted inside cupboards or wardrobes, or above kitchen worktops. In anodized aluminium, they are available with a cord pull, push button, or remote switch. *M:* w 28, 34, 56, 68cm (11, 13⅜, 22, 26¾in). *P:* from £6. 60 watts. The SY STRIPLIGHT, with a polished anodized aluminium spine and white plastic end caps, gives wide angle illumination. The switch can be fixed in one of three positions. *M:* w 34.5cm (13⅝in). *P:* £5.50. 60 watts.

Right (top): Linolite's NSC LUMINAIRE (left), SY STRIPLIGHT (right)

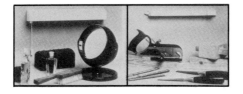

LITA DISPLAY LTD

Really good-looking lighting. Pendants come in 25 permutations including 'Pendolita 6054' with a micromesh perforated metal shade in Red or Black with White (*M:* diam 38cm/15in, *P:* £55; 100 watts); and aluminium and steel 'Pendolita 6043' with a Red or Straw shade that can pivot on the points that attach it to the surrounding ring (*M:* diam 38cm/15in, *P:* £52; 100 watts).
Geometric ceiling lamps, often with white opal glass shades, are similarly simple and stylish. Wall lights include aluminium 'Lirolita 236' finished in White, Orange, Green, or Brown (*M:* d 19cm/7½in, *P:* £13; 2×40 watts); and 'Litaplic 6518', a real piece of sculpture in White or nickel-plated metal, with a pull switch and adjustable depth plate (*M:* diam 36cm/14⅛in, *P:* £35 White, £50 nickel-plated; 2×40 watts).

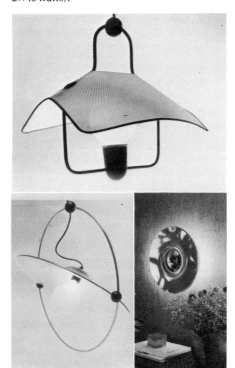

Lita's '6054' (above), '6043' (below left), '6518' (below right)

Lita also excel at table lamps. 'Litapar 132' is a surprising little box lamp in Red, Straw, Pearl grey, or Brown (*M:* d 12 × w 9.4cm/4¾×3¾in, *P:* £20; 100 watts). Globular '950' has a White plastic base and satin opal glass globe (*M:* diam

30cm/11⅞in, *P:* £40; 75 watts). Similar models come with a stand, or a four-pronged base. '951' is a classic beauty with a nickel-plated metal base and white opal polyester shade (*M:* h 60cm/23⅝in, diam 30cm/11⅞in, *P:* £65; 100 watts).

Lita's '951' (left), '950' (top right), '236' (bottom right)

MARLIN LIGHTING LTD

Simple, utilitarian lighting—a favourite with architects. Metal pendants, with white opal liner glasses to provide well-diffused light, come with flex or rise/fall coil suspension.

Marlin's RINGLINE (above left), GLOBE (above right), PAN (below)

The unusual RINGLINE ceiling light, and pendant with flex or rise/fall mechanism, come in Frost white, Chrome yellow, and Flame orange (*M:* diam 15, 29cm/5⅞in, 11⅜in, *P:* pendant £14; 2×75 watts).
The GLOBE wall light rotates on its satin silver mounting to direct light where required. A perfect little bedlight, with removable pull switch, it comes in five colours: brushed silver, Frost white, Signal red, Deep brown, and Chrome yellow. *M:* diam 16cm (6¼in). *P:* £11.75, silver £12.93. 60 watts. The GLOBE also comes in table or floor standard models, and a clamp-on version. PAN, another bedside light, comes in the same colours with the base

finished in Pearl grey. It incorporates a flexible upper tube, sheathed in ribbed Pearl grey plastic, that allows the light to be pointed in any direction. *M:* diam 20cm (7⁷/₈in). *P:* £28.25. 100 watts.

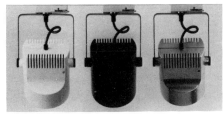

Lita's MAINLINE

There's a seemingly endless choice of track lighting systems including a multi-circuit version, for professional and display purposes, that can be fitted with any of 12 spotlight shapes. MAINLINE, a robust, fully adjustable spot comes in polished silver, Gloss white, Deep brown, and Chrome yellow (*M:* diam 13.5cm/5³/₈in, *P:* polished silver £22.69; 150 watts).

PRISMAX, primarily for industrial use, is an unusual fluorescent lighting system made from one-piece square or rectangular acrylic diffusers on a White metal mount (*M:* 44× 126.5, 156.5cm/17³/₈×4ft 1³/₄in, 5ft 1¹/₂in, *P:* £93, £120; 40 watts).

MIRACLES LTD

Silhouetted table and floor lamps from a firm that specializes in the unusual (including neon lighting designed to clients' specifications). Made in glass and wooden fretwork, by Bugs Young, they are exclusive to Miracles. Glass can be airbrush coloured, to order. *M:* from h 24in (61cm). *P:* £35–£45. 100 watts.

Morgan's 'M12A'

E N MORGAN LTD

Distinctly rustic lighting. Wood candelabra, fitted with mock candles and/or glass globes, include six-light 'M12A' (*M:* diam 71cm/28in, *P:* £70; 6×25 watts). Two-, three- and four-light pendants, single and double wall brackets, and standard and table lamps also come in the same rough-hewn wood look.

NICE IRMA'S FLOATING CARPET LTD

Nice lanterns to complement a floating carpet from Nice Irma. Three styles include a solid brass model with intricate embossed designs and perforations (*M:* 12–15in/30.5–38cm, *P:* £12–£18; 60 watts).

OMK DESIGN LTD

Sleek beauties from a purveyor of the pure modern line. The 'coolie'-shaded SANPAN table lamp is in pressed steel with oven-baked Black or White epoxy finish and optional rise/ fall mechanism (*M:* h 55 cm/21⁵/₈in, diam 52cm/20¹/₂in, *P:* £45; 60 watts). Standard and pendant lamps are also available. RITZ table and standard models are reminiscent of the 1930s with hand-blown glass shades and bases. Table lamps come with white opal glass base and shade, satin matt glass base and shade, satin striped glass base and shade,

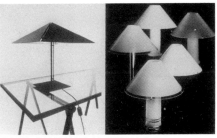

OMK's SANPAN (left), RITZ (right)

chrome/Black base and satin striped shade, or Black base and white opal glass shade (*M:* h 36, 41cm/14¹/₈, 16¹/₈in, diam 33, 45cm/13, 17³/₄in, *P:* £35–£46; 100 watts). Standard lamps have a chrome column and white opal or satin striped glass shade, or a Black or White column with a plain white opal shade (*M:* h 173cm/5ft 8¹/₈in, diam 45/17³/₄in, *P:* £70–£80; 100 watts).

MICHEL RAMON

Absolutely amazing range of beautifully made, but slightly outrageous, table lamps. Vaguely evocative of the Art Nouveau period, when style was all, they're individually imported from France and can to some extent incorporate clients' modifications. Bases, generally in frosted glass, are often patterned and etched to complement fantastically ornate shades made from plain silks and satins, patterned moirés, and florals (often dripping with glass beads and/or baubles). *M:* h 18–30in (46–76cm). *P:* £105–£280. 60–100 watts.

Left to right, from top: Ramon's '206', '401', '708', '447'

RENZLAND & CO LTD

Wrought-iron lighting from a firm that's well known for plant stands, fireplace accessories and hat and coat racks. There are five chandeliers and five wall sconces (single and double), plus standard and table lamps, and lanterns. 'C/21/6', a six-light chandelier, is stove-enamelled in Black or White—great for a conservatory dining table. (*M:* h 16in/40.5cm, diam 20in/51cm, *P:* £19; 6×40 watts). A three-light version is available.

BRUNO RIMINI LTD

Italian ceramic lamps with classical bases and matching shades, both hand-painted with flowers like iris and cherry blossom. 'A2603' comes in Off-white with Pink flowers, Green leaves (*M:* h 21in/53.5cm, *P:* £28; 100 watts). See overleaf for illustration.

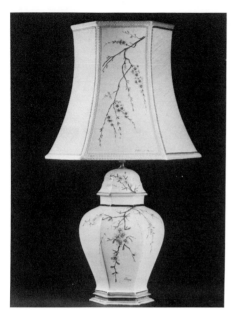

Rimini's 'A2603'

SHANDON CLOCKS LTD

Stunning range of well-made, sensible, and simply executed lights (designed in 1976), from a company that's also well known for its clocks. Made from solid brass, they're either polished then lacquered, or chrome plated. 11 desk or table lamps include the 'SL29' with the sleekest lamp base around—a circular column of brass or chrome, in three heights. Standard lamps, three pendants and nine wall lights are also available—all beautiful (*M:* 'SL11', 'SL17', 'SL23' and 'SL36' h 12–19in/30.5–48.5cm, *P:* £160, £110, £100, £150; 'SL11' 60 watts, 'SL17', 'SL23', 'SL36' 60-watt strip lights).

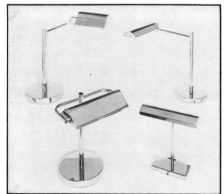

Left to right, from top: Shandon's 'SL11', 'SL36', 'SL17', 'SL23'

SMITHBROOK IRONWORKS LTD

Absolutely enormous range of wrought-iron lighting. Most fittings are in Matt black, some also come in White, or pewter effect from buffing the wrought iron. Five table lamps are

available, one of which holds two mock candles, candelabra style; and nine standard lamps. 'S127 Oxford Bridge' can be raised or lowered (*M:* h 5ft/152.5cm, *P:* £22; 40 watts). 16 pendant styles include three-light 'S475 Cortina', with amber glass globes, also with four, five and six lights (*M:* h 10in/25cm, *P:* £31; 3×40 watts); 'S480 Candle Snuffer', in three-, four- and five-light versions (*M:* h 15in/38cm, *P:* £25, 3×40 watts; 'S483 Jubilee', available with or without amber glass globes, has three, four, five or six lights (*M:* h 15in/38cm, *P:* £25; 3×40 watts); and 'S491 Austrian', for a more up-country look (*M:* h 23in/58.5cm, *P:* £25; 60 watts). The last two can be supplied in pewter effect. All have matching wall sconces, most with double or single lights (*M:* h 5–15in/13–38cm, *P:* £3–£9; 60 watts).

Smithbrook's 'S475 Cortina' (left), 'S483 Jubilee' (right)

SPECTRUM LTD

AB Bruno Herbst fluorescent lighting from Sweden. Exclusive to Spectrum, these beautiful but functional fittings are a High Tech fan's dream come true. Nine hanging strips and six ceiling-mounted lights are available. Most have a White lacquered metal louvre along the base, and come in clear bright colours like Yellow, Red, or Blue, plus Black or White. The 'H172' ceiling-mounted light has slots for upward and downward lighting in the outer reflector, and a ball chain or wire suspension (*M:* w 133–163cm/4ft 4³⁄₈in–5ft 4¼in, *P:* from £55; 60-watt fluorescent tube).

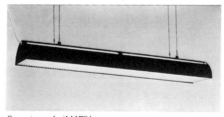

Spectrum's 'H172'

BERNARD SZEPS LIGHTING LTD

Marvellous and diverse selection of traditionally styled lighting. Szeps' own collection of more than 75 table lamps includes models with gilt, porcelain or metal bases, many mounted on alabaster. Unusual examples are: 'W4076' with a Kappa shell shade, bronzed brass base, black stand and dual pull chains (*M:* h 26in/66cm, *P:* £182, 2×60 watts); 'Large Oval Chinese' lamp finished in antique gold, antique silver, bronze, verdigris, Ivory-white

or Red lacquer, with a hand-made lampshade (*M:* h 18½in/47cm, *P:* £113; 150 watts); 'Sphinx' on an alabaster base with a hieroglyphic-decorated shade (*M:* h 22in/56cm, *P:* £100; 100 watts); and 'W4967' with an opal glass shade, bronzed base with Black banding (*M:* h 28in/71cm, *P:* £232; 60 watts).

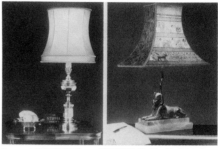

Szeps' 'ST5348' from STIFFEL (left), 'Sphinx' (right)

The imported STIFFEL range of 13 impeccably crafted table lamps includes 'ST5225' with an 'ancient' Grecian urn base in antique brass and White on an alabaster base (*M:* h 27in/68.5cm, *P:* £255; 2×60 watts); and 'ST5348' with a brass base and shantung-texture shade (*M:* h 27in/68.5cm, *P:* £200; 150 watts).

Rather fussier VICTORIANA fixtures, for walls, ceilings and bedsides, are made from brass or gold-plated steel combined with Venetian glass. The '315/8' brass chandelier is teamed

Szeps' '315/8' from VICTORIANA (above), K range (below)

with Bohemian glass—a smashing exception (*M:* h 21in/53.5cm, diam 27in/68.5cm, *P:* £355; 8×25 watts). Classically simple FLEMISH chandeliers are made from brass, then mellowed with a rich gold lacquer or finished in antique brass. Both ranges include matching wall brackets, and optional shades for the mock-candle lights.

The K range has matching solid brass reading and picture lamps, both adjustable for height (*M:* w 10½in (26.5cm), *P:* £515; 60 watts).

SHEILA TEAGUE

Stylish, versatile and inexpensive lighting unit from a young designer better known for her futuristic jewellery. Made from anodized aluminium which has been accordion-pleated, it comes in Red, Dark blue, Turquoise, Gold, Purple, Silver, Black, Pink, Mauve, and Slate grey. *M:* h 12×w 18in (30.5×46cm). *P:* £13. 60 watts. See page 180 for colour illustration.

TEMPUS STET LTD

Very unusual reproduction fittings. 14 wall-mounted candelabra include 'L19' decorated with leaves and fruit in the style of William Kent (*M:* h 33in/84cm, *P:* £120; 2×40 watts); and Queen Anne style 'M15' with central mirror (*M:* h 12in/30.5cm, w 6½in/16.5cm, *P:* £43; 2×40 watts). Smaller, less flamboyant styles are also available. The 'gilded' finish has been developed by Tempus Stet, as genuine gilding would be prohibitively expensive—pure silver is tinted, and aged in a 12-part process to look like gold. In the face of soaring antique prices, this firm makes time stand still with its reproductions.

 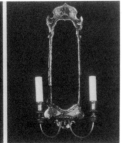

Tempus Stet's 'L19' (left), 'M15' (right)

JANE THOMAS

Amazing pyramid table lamps. Bases are wood, shades are made from glossy glazed chintz, to order in any colour, laminated on card with snappy geometric cut-outs. Fastenings include a titanium hairpin or a little tuck-in flap. *M:* base 20×20×20cm × h 38cm (7⁷⁄₈×7⁷⁄₈×7⁷⁄₈×15in). *P:* £15–£20. 60 watts. See page 172 for colour illustration.

PRICES AND INFORMATION WERE CORRECT AT THE TIME OF GOING TO PRESS

TIVOLI LIGHTING SYSTEMS LTD

Very special, custom-made lighting systems, available only through architects and interior designers. Their sparkling stair curtain, a decorative but practical way to light a stairway, uses low-voltage light tubing containing numerous miniature light bulbs. Powered by a 24-volt transformer, it uses only 5 watts of electricity per metre. All Tivoli systems must be installed by a professional electrician. *P:* upon application.

CHRISTOPHER WRAY'S LIGHTING EMPORIUM LTD

Reproduction Victorian, Edwardian and Tiffany lamps. Christopher Wray, a very famous name in lighting, specializes in turn-of-the-century styles and his three premises contain a vast selection of hand-made lamps and lanterns in solid brass. Handsome modern brass lights are also available.

A staggering array of shades includes ten in brass, six flowery models in French rose glass with curling tinted edges, ten plain glass shades, three in etched glass, four in moulded satin (white) glass, six in cut crystal, six French boudoir and three French Bijou globes, one with etched, scattered stars, plus the flame-like White flambeau-style shades in five sizes. Hand-made fringes, made from real glass beads, come in four patterns on a Black, White, Red, or Green ground. *P:* ft from £7.75 The Wray selection also includes 20 oil lamps with glass or brass shades or globes, and glass or brass bases (*M:* h 20–30in/51–76cm, *P:* £15–£50) and 14 desk lamps. 'Rococo' and 'Art Nouveau' are two of five classical table lamps. There are five 'Ships Gimbal Wall Lamps', five oil lamp wall brackets, and 35 electric wall

Wray's etched shade with hand-made fringes (left), SPRING desk lamp (right)

Wray's White enamelled 'Bird' bracket (left), 'Waterford Hanging Lamp' (right)

lights; also five functional wall lanterns and ten coach lamps. Four stove-enamelled White cast-iron wall brackets, and three hanging lamps designed to hold standard brass oil lamps are particularly pretty. *M:* shades (for bracket) diam 5½–7½in (14–19cm). *P:* £18–£38, wall brackets £25–£50, hanging lamps £65–£85. SPRING LAMPS, with polished brass shell shades, are available as single or double wall or desk lamps (*M:* shade w 9in/23cm, *P:* single wall lamp £22, double £34, single desk lamp £28, double £44). BARN LAMPS in 11 styles include the 'Waterford Hanging Lamp' with twist guard and brass shade (*M:* shade diam 5½–12in/14–30.5cm, *P:* £60; 60 watts). All can be fitted with a number of different coloured shades. Four pendant lights, suitable for Edwardian or Victorian dining areas, are a lot more formal (*P:* £65–£175).

Wray's 'Edwardian' with 'coolie' shade

Two rise-and-fall mechanisms are available: 'Edwardian', shown with a 'coolie' shade (*P:* from £22); and the more functional-looking 'Rolly', with a spring coil (*P:* £95).

The Wray workshop sells replacement parts and shades for oil and gas lamps, and stocks one of the UK's largest ranges of electric bulbs.

INTRODUCTION

This section deals with two different decorative elements, both of which make use of light, and both of which bring a sense of space into your home.

Mirrors can be expensive, but their light-increasing qualities and space expanding make the cost worthwhile. Opposite a window, a mirror will bring light into an otherwise dark interior. A large looking glass – or an entire wall covered in mirror tiles – will double the apparent size of a small room.

This section includes contemporary and period mirrors that range from plain geometrics to perfect reproductions, and also describes some variations: sheet mirrors, tiles and mosaics; versions with tinted or marbled glass; and illuminated models.

Before buying a mirror, check for distortion by looking into it from different distances and angles. The back should be sealed to prevent scratching; an exposed edge should be polished.

If you want to cover an entire wall with mirrored glass, it's worth considering tiles or mosaics. Although they won't appear as streamlined, they're far easier to handle than a single sheet which requires smooth walls, and can break. (The thicker the mirror, the sturdier it will be.)

The next part of this section concentrates on the more decorative aspects of *Glass*, mainly for windows or panels, which exploit the light while highlighting the overall scheme in a room.

A truly extraordinary substance, formed from the most prosaic materials, glass can be exotically ornamental, or unobtrusively functional. Always versatile, it is available in a variety of forms.

Decorated glass can be sandblasted, acid-etched, engraved, appliquéd . . . Stained glass, in its modern form, is steadily growing as a craft; artists will create individual designs for clients as they have through the ages.

Mass-produced window and door glass includes coloured varieties made by fusing glass with a film of metallic oxide, or burning pigment into its surface; and patterned versions created by passing molten glass between textured rollers. Toughened glass, up to five times stronger than normal glass, is heated to near melting point then quickly cooled. Other types are wired glass with a layer of welded wire mesh, and solar glass made in a variety of ways.

The possibilities of glass are almost limitless. Shelves across a window will show off a special collection of ornaments, or support plants. A skylight lets light into the gloomiest room. Textured and/or stained glass can be used as a room divider. Glass is also used architecturally as a decorative element, usually in commercial premises, but also sometimes in domestic settings.

Always make sure that glass is securely installed – and not too subtle (people need to know it's there). Ideally, decorative windows,

panels, etc should be removable so that you can take them with you when you leave. Most panels can be individually framed, with all the advantages of double glazing.

*Prices for individually made glass vary according to technique, size, and the amount of work involved.

See also 'Wall Coverings' for mirror-like reflecting metallic wallpapers.

MIRRORS

ART GLASS LTD
Plain and marbled mirror tiles in an unusual selection of sizes. *M:* 4¼×4¼, 6 × 6, 12×12, 6in (11.5×11.5, 15×15, 30.5×30.5, 15cm). *P:* plain 40p–£1.60 each, marbled 46p–£2.05.

BAKER, KNAPP & TUBBS
'5918' in solid mahogany. An 18th-century reproduction, it has a swan-neck pediment and pierced carving. *M:* w 30 × h 52in (76 × 132cm). *P:* £210.

BAMBOO DESIGNS
Pagoda-top mirror with a bamboo mosaic frame, designed to complement an extensive, well-made range of cane furniture. *M:* w 71 × h 110cm (28 × 43⅜in). *P:* £130. Six similar styles include three inspired by Art Deco. All can be lacquered or painted, to order.

PRICES AND INFORMATION WERE CORRECT AT THE TIME OF GOING TO PRESS

Bamboo Designs' pagoda-top mirror

BRADDELL ENTERPRISES
Delightful 'Nasturtium', hand-printed in three colourways with toning frames in Green lacquered or natural bamboo, or Black lacquered wood. *M:* w 38.5 × h 45cm (15¼ × 17¾in). *P:* £26. Also two larger versions. More than 100 combinations of design, colour and matching frame include 'Trellis', 'Classic' and lace-like Eastern designs, framed in gold-edged Black lacquered wood or gold *faux* bamboo. Special colourways cost £5 extra.

'LLGI' has Gold doves stencilled on a Black lacquered frame. It comes from an unusual range with surround patterns taken from original designs by Lyn Le Grice. *M:* w 64 × h 100cm (25⅛ × 39⅜in). *P:* £145.

Braddell Enterprises' 'Nasturtium'

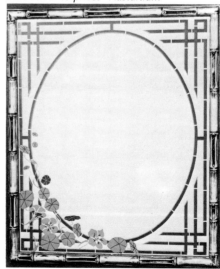

Braddell Enterprise's 'LLG1'

EMESS LIGHTING LTD

Splashproof illuminated mirror, perfect for bathrooms. '2809' comes with one of three surrounds: three-ply satin matt White opal, raindrop-textured glass, or frosted crystal, all with a white metal backplate. *M:* diam 43, 53cm (16⁷/₈, 20⁷/₈in). *P:* £140–£180. 40 watts.

FORMA LTD

Marvellously simple ERO by Valenti. The frame is satinized steel or brass. *M:* diam 55, 75, 100cm (21⁵/₈, 29½, 39³/₈in). *P:* £85–£200, brass 10% extra. A table version comes in highly polished steel or brass.
SPECCHI by Valenti, simply designed with a satinized steel or brass frame, is suitable for almost any room in the house. *M:* 55×55, 70×70cm (21⁵/₈×21⁵/₈, 27½×27½in). *P:* £82, £92. The range also includes rectangular versions.

Forma's ERO (above), SPECCHI (below)

GIORGETTI

'6984' and '6124'. With lacquered or hand-polished solid wood frames, they match Giorgetti's extensive range of rattan furniture. *M:* both w 88 × h 120cm (34⁵/₈ × 47¼in). *P:* '6984' £155, '6124' £160.

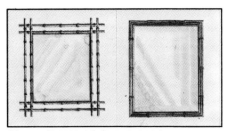

Giorgetti's '6984' (left), '6124' (right)

CHARLES HAMMOND LTD

'Byzantine' mirror from a large and varied Italian-made range. The wooden frame is accented with circles of gold leaf. *M:* w 84 × h 102cm (33 × 40¹/₈in). *P:* £230. A 'Florentine' version is framed in interlocking circles without gold leaf.

Left to right, from top: Charles Hammond's 'Byzantine', 'Octagonal', 'Pier Glass', 'Queen Anne'

Simple but effective, the 'Octagonal' mirror has a frame finished in gesso, oro primo or gold leaf. *M:* w 70 × h 91cm (27½ × 35⁷/₈in). *P:* gesso £55, oro primo £105, gold leaf £140. Two smaller sizes, and an oval version, are available.
A Chinese-style 'Pier Glass' has a gold leaf frame. Normally one of a pair, it's part of an extensive selection of beautifully made reproductions. *M:* w 30 × h 101cm (11⁷/₈ × 39³/₄in). *P:* £200.
A 'Queen Anne' reproduction has bevel-edged glass and a Red or Black lacquered frame painted with delicate Oriental motifs. *M:* w 64 × h 138cm (25¹/₈ × 54³/₈in). *P:* £190.

WILLIAM L MACLEAN LTD

'25-213', a handsome 16th-century reproduction. The solid beech frame is hand-polished to produce an authentic-looking patina. *M:* w 65 × h 75cm (25½ × 29½in). *P:* upon application. See overleaf for illustration.

Maclean's '25-213' (left), '25-223' (right)

Graceful '25-223' is an example of this company's Georgian and Regency reproductions. The simulated bamboo frame, in solid beech, can be hand-tinted to match furniture in Maclean's immense range. *M:* w 40 × h 60cm (15¾ × 23⅝in). *P:* upon application.

MIRACLES LTD
Wonderful mirrors with beautifully worked marquetry frames made from hand-stained woods; an example is illustrated opposite in colour. Each frame sports a secret panel that opens to reveal a secret compartment. *M:* various, as illustrated w 16 × h 24in (40.5 × 61cm). *P:* £125 as illustrated.

OPALS (MIRROR-FLEX) CO
Wonderful MIRROR FLEX for walls, columns, small boxes — even for covering unsightly furniture. Small square mirrors, backed with cloth, bend and curve to reflect a fractured image. Double silvered for maximum brilliance, they come in Shimmering silver, Peach silver or Grey silver; and can be overprinted with Red or Black diamonds, stars or circles. *M:* sheets 12¼×9, 24×18in (31×23, 61×46cm), sectional cuts 1×1–2×½in (2.5×2.5–5× 1.3cm). *P:* sheets £1.25–£5; Peach, Grey silver 20% extra.

REGENCY PARADE
Wall-mounted 'Eco'. Unlit, it looks like a normal smoked glass mirror; illuminated, it becomes an apparently endless tunnel of light. *M:* to order. *P:* upon application.

PRICES AND INFORMATION WERE CORRECT AT THE TIME OF GOING TO PRESS

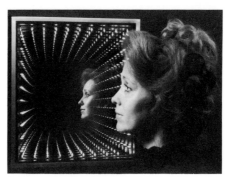

Regency Parade's 'Eco'

ARTHUR E RENOW
'A14' cheval glass, from an extensive range that includes wall, dressing-table, and two cheval standing mirrors; also French-inspired 'A22' and Chippendale-style 'A24'. Wood frames, enriched with gesso, are finished in antique gilt, or gilt and ivory. Like 'A14', most mirrors have bevelled or clean-cut edges. *M:* as illustrated w 16 × h 48in (40.5 × 122cm). *P:* £75.

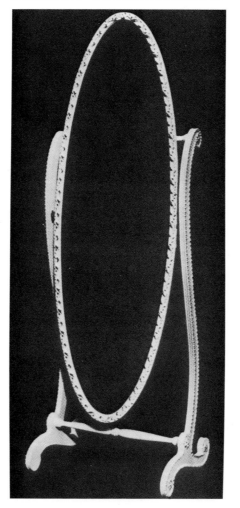

T SAVEKER LTD
Wonderfully functional full-length 'V378' with twin wheel castors. The frame is finished in bronze or chrome. *M:* w 35 × h 120cm (12¾ × 47¼in). *P:* bronze £43, chrome £50. Also a smaller version.

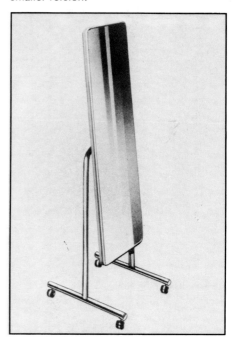

SEKON GLASSWORKS LTD
Delicately tinted COLOURED MIRRORS evocative of the 1930s, in Grey, Bronze, Rose, Peach, Dark brown, Green — and hard-to-find Black. Marble-like 'Antique' glass comes in the same shades. Special colours, to order, include fantastically rich, marbled 'Blue Nimbus'. *M:* to order. *P:* sq ft £5.75–£9.50, 'Antique' £6.50–£11.25.

St Marco's '3015'

Right: Miracles' marquetry-framed mirror

ST MARCO'S
Illuminated '3015' from a firm that's known primarily for beauteous bathroom furniture. Part of the functional MESSINA DARIO range of shaving, magnifying and make-up mirrors, some free standing, it has an expandible wall mount. *M:* diam 20cm (7⁷/₈in). *P:* £75. See overleaf for illustration.

TEMPUS STET LTD
Early English 'M14', one of five reproduction gilt mirrors from a firm that, true to its name, conscientiously recreates beautiful objects from the past. To achieve the quality and depth of real gold leaf — at a fraction of the cost — silver is tinted and aged in a 12-part process before being applied. *M:* w 24 × h 38in (61 × 96.5cm). *P:* £125. Other styles include oval 'M18' with an 'oak leaf' frame, also available in lined oak. All come in any finish, to order.

GLASS

MARK ANGUS
Artist in architectural stained glass. This designer and craftsman sometimes works in the unusual but practical combination of perspex and hand-blown glass. For public or private use, panels can be lit from one side, or both. Mark Angus' work is included in the Victoria and Albert Museum and Ely Cathedral stained-glass collections. *P:* sq ft £25–£35. See page 133 for colour illustration.

CARMINOWE STUDIO
Contemporary stained glass panels specially made for doors and windows in private and commercial buildings. Belinda Underhill will also do repairs. *P:* panels sq ft from £15.

Stained glass by Belinda Underhill at Carminowe Studio

GODDARD & GIBBS STUDIOS
Designers and restorers of ecclesiastical and secular stained-glass windows since 1868, Goddard & Gibbs will also acid etch, sandblast or engrave virtually any item for private customers. Unusually, visitors are welcome at the studio—a bonus that's normally only associated with individual designers and craftspeople. Their creative ability, and the high standard of their finished work, make Goddard & Gibbs one of the world's major commercial studios. *P:* upon application.

Goddard & Gibbs' acid-etched glass with Islamic border design

Example of modern stained glass from Goddard & Gibbs

ROBINA JACK
Stained-glass artisan who accepts any commission that will enrich the environment. Motifs tackled to date include steam engines, polar bears and Islamic themes. *P:* sq ft £25–£30. See opposite for colour illustration.

Opposite page: Tim Plant's hallway mural

PRICES AND INFORMATION WERE CORRECT AT THE TIME OF GOING TO PRESS

JAMES, CLARK & EATON LTD
Useful glass products from a company that's associated to Goddard & Gibbs. They include toughened safety, fire-resistant, bullet-resistant and wired safety glass, the latter in five textures: Georgian wired, wire textured, 'Natur' vertically striated, 'Linkon' with cubical patterns, and 'Neolit' with rectangles on a wavy ground. *P:* upon application.

CATHERINE LALAU-KERALY
Artist in glass who regularly works with architects. Windows and dividing partitions made from sandblasted glass panels are a speciality; also stained-glass free-standing screens that feature abstract geometrical designs rather than figurative motifs. *P:* stained-glass windows sq yd £60. See also 'Partitions'.

PILKINGTON BROTHERS LTD
Enormous range of products. It includes 24 styles of patterned glass, standard wired and mottled wired options, and tinted glass.
Tinted or coated SOLAR CONTROL GLASS reflects and absorbs solar radiation, and cuts down the amount of heat allowed through windows to keep rooms cooler in summer and reduce the glare that can fade fine fabrics. (The most sophisticated glass rejects up to 84% of the sun's heat.) Five types are available: 'Sun Cool', a double glazing unit; 'Antisun' float glass, tinted Grey or Bronze, in a variety of thicknesses; 'Spectrafloat' with a metallic tint just below the surface, in three thicknesses; 'Solar Shield' laminated glass with a central layer of reflective film, in a variety of colours and thicknesses; and 'Reflectafloat' with a silvered mirror exterior.

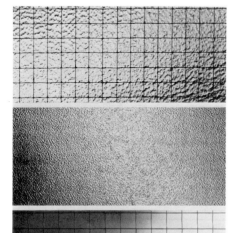

From top: Pilkington's 'Georgian Wired', 'Cast Stippolite', 'Georgian Wired'

From top: Pilkington's 'Cross Reeded', 'Narrow Reeded', 'Pacific' patterns

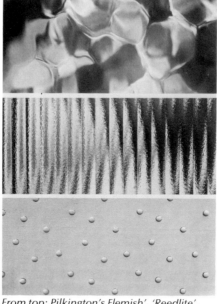

From top: Pilkington's Flemish', 'Reedlite', 'Spotlite' patterns

DIFFUSE REFLECTION GLASS gives a subdued reflection, and is ideal for framing prints, photographs and pictures. Hazard-free LAMINATED GLASS can be patterned, mirrored or tinted, to order.
BULLIONS (olde-worlde Georgian-style ringed glass), for interior or exterior use in period houses, can be supplied with an Amber tint (*M:* standard 14×7¾–23½×18in/35.5×20–59.5×46cm; minimum 5×5in/12.5×12.5cm).
In CHAMELEON GLASS, a revolutionary British invention, electrical impulses create transparent patterns, in blues, greens, purples and browns, that change with the light and the angle of viewing. Available in two designs, this exciting glass can be toughened, silvered, bent, double glazed, or back-painted. *P:* all upon application.

PYROFORM LTD
The wonders of modern science . . . Laser engraving at its finest produces complex, very finely detailed designs that can be executed in wood, acrylic, slate, stone and many other non-metallic substances, as well as glass. Black and white artwork is supplied by the customer. Objects to be engraved must be flat. *M:* maximum 244×122, 15cm thick (8×4ft, 5⅞in). *P:* processed and costed on basis of 15cm (5⅞in) wide strips to any length; minimum £200.

LAURENCE WHISTLER
Specialist in exquisite engraved panels. Expensive, but beautifully detailed, they can be designed as window panes or displayed in more fanciful settings. *P:* £500–£1,500.

WIND'S EYE STUDIOS
Two innovatory craftspeople, Amber Hiscott and David Pearl, who describe themselves as 'artists in architectural glass'. Each piece is designed to meet the specific needs of the space for which it's intended. Techniques include leaded hand-blown antique glass, sandblasted or etched float glass, and glass (or perspex) appliqué for interior screens. *P:* upon application. See page 133 for colour illustrations.

PRICES AND INFORMATION WERE CORRECT AT THE TIME OF GOING TO PRESS

INTRODUCTION

Painting is undoubtedly the cheapest and quickest way to change the atmosphere, or even the apparent shape, of a room.

Before changing an existing scheme, decide which of the predominant colours in furniture, carpets and curtains are most suitable for walls and ceilings. The size and shape of the room will narrow your choice still further: strong, intense colours will create a sense of cosiness in a large room, apparently bringing the walls forward and lowering the ceiling; cool, pale shades give a feeling of space. Light is also important. A sunlit room will accommodate dark shades; warm, light tones are usually best for shaded northern exposure.

If in doubt, stick to one main colour. Apply this rule throughout the house if space is confined: a sunny sitting room emphasized in soft Gold could lead to a hallway in a brighter, yellower, version of the same Gold, and a Beige kitchen.

Aesthetic considerations apart, there are practical benefits in selecting one type of paint in preference to another.

Plastics, or vinyls, have largely superseded traditional cellulose-based paints, and are generally much easier to apply. (Non-drip paints that give a smooth, glossy finish without runs and snags are an offshoot.) They come in matt, silk and gloss finishes. Most other household paints for interior use are waterborne like emulsions, or oil-based like traditional gloss paints. Emulsions are easy to apply, quick drying, and have virtually no smell. Gloss paint, generally tougher, is recommended for windows, skirtings, doors, etc, and comes in full shine, eggshell or silk (mid-sheen) finishes. However, it tends to highlight imperfections, and requires a well-prepared surface — generally an oil-based undercoat — and takes hours to dry.

Modern eggshell or silk finishes can also be water-based, and are more resistant to condensation and wear than water-based matt paints. Most manufacturers produce the 88 British Standard colours, but combine them to achieve their own shades. Paints mixed to order are obviously more expensive than standard ranges. To avoid this extra expense, try creating your own colour by adding a commercial tinter, available in tubes from hardware shops and builders' merchants, to a manufacturer's shade. These strong pigments can be used with water-, oil- and vinyl-based paints, and are perfect for creating a host of pastels from one large tin of White.

Special effect paints can be two-tone, multi-coloured, luminous or textured. This section also includes varnishes, sealers and special finishes.

*Prices are for 2½l (4⅜pt) cans, unless otherwise stated.

See also 'Useful Products'.

ARDENBRITE PRODUCTS LTD

ARDENBRITE spirit-based metallic paint, ready-mixed for brush or spray painting and suitable for virtually any surface—it was used on London's glorious Hammersmith Bridge. Of the highest quality, it dries to a rich sheen, is touch-dry in 15 minutes, and won't be affected by normal heat or condensation. A special thinning medium can be supplied. Eight shiny shades are available: Light gold, Deep gold, Silver, Sovereign gold, Antique gold, Golden brown, Light copper, and Bronze. *P:* 50ml (1¾ fl oz) 75p, 5l (8¾pt) £34.50.

ARTEX PRODUCTS LTD

Textured compounds and paints for light to heavy coverage. Available through builders' merchants, they can produce stippled or combed effects. Some are self-coloured and can be used for overpainting, others come in pastel shades. *P:* standard compound 25kg (55lb) £5.20.

LAURA ASHLEY LTD

Very good range of 23 colours in matt vinyl emulsion and oil-based satin gloss, designed to complement Laura Ashley's extensive collection of pretty, countrified co-ordinates. *P:* gloss 1l (1¾pt) £3, emulsion £4.25. See also 'Ceramic Tiles', 'Wall Coverings', 'Lighting', 'Soft Furnishings'.

BERGER PAINTS

COLORIZER range of 420 colours. Most come in eggshell, but high gloss, plus silk and matt vinyl emulsions are also available. *P:* high gloss £7.43, matt and silk vinyl £6.49½, eggshell £7.76. The more limited MAGICOTE range is in non-drip silk and matt vinyls, and gloss (*P:* high gloss White £4.54, silk vinyl £4.67, matt vinyl £4.59). BROLAC trade paints come in full gloss, P.E.P. (high coverage) emulsion, and satin vinyl in a limited choice of shades. 'Speedon' is a fast-to-apply undercoat. 'Tartartuga', a deeply textured wall finish, can be applied in five different patterns and comes with suitable rollers. The 'Colour Schemer' service costs £3 and offers professional design and decorating advice by way of an information sheet and questionnaire.

BESTOBELL PAINTS & CHEMICALS LTD

CARSONS SUNWAY colours, in a BS4800 trade range of 87 British Standard colours; also the COLORIZER range of 350 shades in seven colour 'families'. Both come in the usual gloss and eggshell plus matt and silk vinyls. A quick-drying high-speed gloss in White only, and an extra-bright aluminium paint, are also available. *P:* upon application.

PRICES AND INFORMATION WERE CORRECT AT THE TIME OF GOING TO PRESS

BLUNDELL-PERMOGLAZE LTD

Paints for the trade, generally available only from builders' merchants. GLOSSY VINYL emulsion, in 21 pale shades, has no residual odour. The gloss absorbs ultra-violet rays that normally cause fading, and so retains its colour longer. Completely washable eggshell is ideal for kitchens and bathrooms. PAMMASTIC emulsion and glossy vinyl, and PERMURA flat vinyl, come in 52 colours. *P:* upon application.

J W BOLLOM & CO LTD

The BROMEL range includes superfine and eggshell enamels, plus standard and flame-retardant emulsions, also in the 104 British Standard colours. A restricted range of shades comes in flat oil paint, vinyl, anti-fungus emulsion, and stoving and cellulose enamel. *P:* enamel 5l (8¾pt) £12.10, emulsion 5l (8¾pt) £9.10. Flame-proofed wall hessians and felt are available to match 80 of the paints in the BROMEL range.

The CONNOISSEUR'S COLLECTION is selected from original colours submitted by professional architects and designers throughout the UK. Generally supplied to the trade only, emulsions and eggshell finishes come in 50 shades, including many dense, hard-to-find colours. In addition, the paints are available off the shelf, and are not mixed on site. *P:* gloss 5l (8¾pt) £16.30, emulsion 5l (8¾pt) £14.40. See also 'Wall Coverings'.

CELMAC DISTRIBUTORS LTD

RENUBATH complete chemical treatment to remove unsightly stains and encrusted scale from sanitaryware. Perfect for hard water areas, it comes in three sizes: 120ml (4¼fl oz), 350ml (12¼fl oz), and 5l (8¾pt). *P:* 350ml (12¼ fl oz) £1.45.

COLE & SON LTD

Unusual and subtle shades from an old-established firm. Matt vinyl comes in 24 very distinctive colours plus White (*P:* 1l/ 1¾pt £2.50, 2½l/ 4⅜pt £6). 'Emulsion Glaze' is available in eggshell and gloss finishes (*P:* ½l/17½fl oz £1.25). Colours can be mixed to customers' specifications. *P:* upon application.

CONNOISSEUR STUDIO (EUROPE) LTD

Three ranges for gilding architectural wood and plasterwork: 'Treasure Gold', 'Liquid Leaf', and 'Treasure Sealer'. All come in eight metallic finishes. *P:* upon application.

CROWN DECORATIVE PRODUCTS LTD

COLOUR CUE range of 980 colours in varied tones and hues, including 80 ultra-deep shades. All come in vinyl, emulsion, eggshell and gloss. *P:* gloss £6.79, silk and matt emulsion £5.64. PLUS TWO consists of 22 matt or silk vinyls with 24 toning shades in full or satin gloss; brochure combines vinyls and gloss paints in colour groups for easier colour scheming. PLUS TWO also includes a high-speed gloss emulsion for wood and metal. *P:* full and satin gloss £7.90, silk emulsion £6.30, matt emulsion £6.15. Crown's Decorative Advisory Bureau, at six regional addresses, provides a complete design service that includes advice on wall coverings, floorings and fabrics. Best of all—it's free.

CUPRINOL LTD
Home-protection products from a famous firm. WOOD PRESERVER comes in four versions: clear is for over-varnishing or polishing; Green is easily recognized, and won't harm plants when it's dry; Light and Dark oak are for staining floors, beams, etc (*P:* 1l (1¾pt) £2.50.
TRANSCOLOR, a water-repellent finish perfect for internal panelling, comes in Pine, Teak, Walnut, Black, Olive, Redwood, Blue, Fir green, Autumn gold, Magnolia, and Indian grey (*P:* 1l (1¾pt) £22).
WOODWORM KILLER gets rid of the little beasts and prevents reinfestation, and two DRY ROT treatments are designed specifically for timber and for masonry. Amazingly, the FIVE STAR wood treatment will do all these jobs: kill dry rot and woodworm, treat wet rot, preserve, and prevent further attacks. *P:* WOODWORM KILLER low odour 1l (1¾pt) £39; DRY ROT timber treatment 2.5l (4³⁄₈pt) £37; FIVE STAR 2.5l (4³⁄₈pt) £38.
INTERIOR WALLS completely seals out damp. Suitable for wet or dry surfaces, it's perfect for a common wall where blame is being disputed. *P:* 500ml (17½ fl oz) £2.30. Sealers include TEAK OIL which enhances the beauty of hardwoods by replenishing natural oils, and BOURNE SEAL, for porous floors like wood, cork and concrete. It gives a tough, non-slip finish; pigmented Red or Grey versions are available for concrete or stone surfaces. *P:* TEAK OIL 125ml (4½ fl oz) 94p; BOURNE SEAL clear 1l (1¾pt) £4.34.

DANE & CO
Fluorescent paint, available in ten Day-Glo colours. It will cover paper, wood, metal, cloth and plaster. *P:* varies according to colour, e.g. 5l (8¾pt) Pink £4.97, Rocket red £5.04, Blaize orange £5.14.

HABITAT DESIGNS LTD
Emulsion paint in 18 colours designed to complement this famous company's fabrics and wallpapers. Gloss comes in seven matching shades. *P:* gloss 1l (1¾pt) £2.75, budget White emulsion 5l (8¾pt) and colours £5.75.

HUMBROL
Tough enamel paint in a wide range of colours, plus some metallic shades which are slightly more expensive. It comes in very small tins for model-makers (so it's less costly to experiment), and in aerosol spray cans. *P:* 15ml (½fl oz) 28p, metallic 30p; 50ml (1¾fl oz) 58p, Golden copper 89p; 125ml (4½fl oz) 89p, Golden copper £1.40.

IMPERIAL CHEMICAL INDUSTRIES LTD
Dulux MATCHMAKER range of 400 colours, all in matt or silk vinyl, undercoat, and in Silthane-based silk and gloss. ICI claim these paints shrug off condensation, can be washed repeatedly and take the roughest wear and tear. *P:* gloss 1l (1¾pt) £3.10, emulsion 2½l (4³⁄₈pt) £5.75. Water-based paints come in 27 silk finish and matching gloss colours, specially designed to harmonize with wall coverings and fabrics (*P:* gloss 1l/1¾pt £3.10, emulsion 2½l/4³⁄₈pt £5.75). ICI also make a universal primer for wood, metal and plaster surfaces (*P:* 1l/1¾pt £5.80), an aluminium sealer for treated wood (*P:* 1l/1¾pt £2.80), a rust-inhibiting metal primer, a primer sealer, an aluminium-finish paint, polyurethane varnishes and a paint brush cleaner.

INTERNATIONAL PAINTS
An unusual range from a firm that specializes in producing the right paint for the job. LIQUID LINO is a tough, low-gloss, floor paint in ten colours. LIQUID SANDER, a revolutionary product, prepares gloss work for repainting *without* sanding. JAPLAC, a quick-drying lacquer for high gloss finishes on wood or metal, comes in ten bright colours including Gold and Silver. For natural wood effects, there's DARKALINE high-gloss stain in beech, teak, mahogany, and three oak shades; and GLOSS VARNISH, a top-quality traditional varnish with exceptional clarity and flexibility. PERMASHINE, a hard, clear polyurethane sealer, is available in super gloss and matt.
For priming, there's a lead-free wood primer suitable for indoors and outside; a rust-resistant metal primer for use as a barrier coat under RADIATOR ENAMEL (a pure White hard-gloss finish that fuses with the metal when heated); and QUICK PRIME, a water-soluble 100% acrylic undercoat. International also make WALL SEAL, a waterproof barrier against damp which can be used on plaster, brick and stone; and TILE RED, a tough protective matt finish, perfect for discoloured roof or floor tiles, brickwork, etc. Finally, MATT BLACK gives a smooth, tough, jet black surface to blackboards, wrought ironwork, darkrooms, beams, etc. A durable high-gloss enamel in the yacht paints division comes in 28 striking colours plus Black and White. Intended for marine use, it's perfect for areas or items that get lots of wear and tear. Compatible undercoats are available.
P: upon application.

PRICES AND INFORMATION WERE CORRECT AT THE TIME OF GOING TO PRESS

IRVINE PAINTS LTD
Brush-applied, multicoloured paints first marketed comparatively recently, available only through trade suppliers. IRFLOK water-based non-flammable gloss paint has remarkable covering power. Designed to coat a huge variety of surfaces, it's available in nine fleck colourways. Special mixes to order.
IRTEK, a less textured vinyl coating, comes in seven two-tone colours. Mixes using two-, three-, and four-colour chips are available on request. Both products require an IRBRASE undercoat.
P: upon application.

JOY PAINT PRODUCTS
Unusual items including a non-radioactive luminous paint which emits a green glow, and a heat-resistant metallic paint in Gold, Silver, Copper, and Bronze shades. Step and tile paint has a glossy, non-slip finish for tile, cement or stone steps and window ledges.
PORCELAINIT is for touching up chips on enamelled surfaces such as washing machines. Blackboard paint, and stove black, a glossy enamel for renovating old grates, are also available.
P: all 250ml (8¾fl oz) sizes, luminous paint (Green) 83p, heat-resistant paint £1.40, tile paint £1.34, PORCELAINIT bottle 53p, blackboard paint £1.05.

JOHN T KEEP & SONS LTD
Glass paint in seven flamboyant enamel colours. It creates a transparent stained-glass effect, but can also be used on metal. *P:* 250ml (8¾fl oz) £1.05.

LANGSTON JONES & SAMUEL SMITH LTD
SIGNPOST PAINTS, an unusually complete range of products, in striking gold and black tins. Marble-hard SUPERTEX, for tough, slightly textured surfaces, contains real marble chips instead of simple sand-based aggregates found in other products. Intended for exterior use, it's available in 12 tasteful shades and is useful to cover concrete blocks, emulsion paint, etc. *P:* £5.28. Gloss, and matt and silk vinyl, paints come in 21 shades (*P:* matt and silk emulsion £5.08). The CRAFTSMAN range consists of all types of wood and metal primers, sealers, varnishes, French polishes, knottings, teak oil, blackboard paint, heat-resisting paint, plus the firm's own paint stripper and white spirit.

LEYLAND PAINT & WALLPAPER LTD
Range of paints from a firm best known for its wallpapers. 30 colours are available in matt or silk vinyl, 20 in gloss. JELLIPEX non-drip paints come in 26 gloss shades, 21 in matt or silk vinyl. Leyland make a general purpose primer and undercoat.
P: upon application.

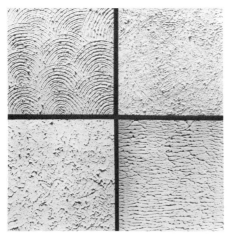

Some textured patterns created with Manders' EASITEX

MANDERS PAINTS LTD

Range of 91 colours plus White, Brilliant white, and Black, in gloss, eggshell and matt vinyl. 27 silk vinyls and several undercoats are also available. *P:* gloss £8.90, matt vinyl £7.20, silk vinyl £7.90. EASITEX, an acrylic-based, textured coating is perfect for applying to badly damaged walls. Various textural patterns can be created (as illustrated) using a brush or roller). *P:* £6.50. Manders have a national network of 52 outlets for paints, wallpapers and all decorating accessories. A technical and after-sales advisory service is available to all customers.

JOHN S OLIVER LTD

Exciting and original colours. Available mainly in matt emulsions, some also come in gloss and eggshell. The range includes muted and bold shades, perfectly presented in a sample book of painted (rather than printed) swatches. John S Oliver will also supply any of the 1,350 Sanderson SPECTRUM paints, and the full BS range, in all finishes. Colours specially mixed to match furnishings are available within four to five days, at extra cost. *P:* gloss £10.90, emulsion £8.70, special colours add £4.

E PARSONS & SONS LTD

Paint-related products from a specialist firm. BLACKFRIAR wood dye, for bringing out the natural grain of new timber, chipboard, etc, before sealing, comes in light, medium and dark oak, walnut, mahogany, teak, and dark Jacobean (*P:* 125ml 60p). Polyurethane stain comes in the same shades, polyurethane varnish in gloss, semi-gloss and matt finishes (*P:* 125ml 75p). Other products include paint remover, cedar dressing, White and Pink wood primers, anti-rust red oxide zinc chromate primer, floor and concrete paints, a Black wrought-iron and a blackboard paint, and a marvellous yacht varnish.

PORCELAIN NEWGLAZE LTD

NEWGLAZE epoxy coating for renovating baths coated with vitreous enamel. Rigorously tested, it's resistant to abrasion and mild chemicals (including many acids). The manufacturers say it has excellent adhesion to porcelain, cast iron, fibreglass, and ceramic surfaces. Colours are Turquoise, Rose pink, Sky blue, Avocado, Primrose, Jade green, Pampas, Sun King, and White. It's a marvellously cheap way of restoring a bathroom to gleaming condition. *P:* two cans that mix together to form epoxy £9.95 (enough for bath).

ARTHUR SANDERSON & SONS LTD

Ingenious Colour Harmony Selector, designed to simplify colour selection and co-ordination. Based on the colour wheel, it gives a choice of over 1,350 colours in the SPECTRUM range, in gloss and eggshell, plus silk and matt vinyl emulsion. Samples from a bank of key colour and tone cards can be made available for home use. *P:* gloss £11.05, matt vinyl emulsion £9.10.

SILEXINE PAINTS LTD

Specialist paints for exterior and anti-fungicidal use, primarily intended for architects, specifiers, etc. The BS4800 range consists of top-quality matt emulsion in 88 BS colours; and vinyl silk in 17 shades from stock. Minimum quantity of 50l (c 10½gal). *P:* upon application.

STERLING RONCRAFT

Excellent range of protective and decorative paints and products. RONSEAL 'Teak Oil', which contains silicone and a preservative to prolong the life of hardwood furniture, is especially suitable for wood subject to drying out as a result of central heating or outdoor weather conditions (*P:* 500ml/17½fl oz £2). 'Hardglaze', a flexible sealer with a transparent, durable, high-gloss finish, is designed for furniture, flooring, etc, that has to take a lot of wear (*P:* 500ml/17½fl oz £2). There are two non-reflective coatings for interior woodwork: 'Mattcoat', and 'Satincoat' which gives a soft sheen finish (*P:* 250ml/ 8¾fl oz £1.16). A non-drip polyurethane sealer is also available. 'Coloured Ronseal' comes in six wood shades and six bright stains. 'Colron' solvent-based wood dyes, in nine wood shades, won't raise the grain, so the surface can be sealed with varnish or wax (*P:* 250ml/8¾fl oz £1.27). 'Ronstrip' paint stripper removes paint without scraping (*P:* 2.5kg/c 5½lb £2.96). 'Speed-strip', a paint-like liquid, gets rid of painted wall coverings, and washable and textured paint (*P:* 1.4l/c 2½pt £4.13). Sterling Roncraft's most useful product for paint-obsessed home decorators is 'Universal Stainer'. Available in ten shades, it will change the colour of matt and silk emulsions, oil and polyurethane gloss paints, varnishes, fillers,

stoppers and wood stains—a real problem-solver for anyone who's bought a large amount of paint, then applied it, only to find it slightly off-colour. 'Universal Stainer' will also tint White. *P:* 50ml (1¾fl oz) 73p. 'Kurust', an all-in-one rust treatment and primer, is perfect for rusty paintwork (*P:* 250ml/8¾fl oz £1.91). 'Kurust Jelly' is designed for rusty metal surfaces that don't need re-painting (*P:* 250ml/8¾fl oz £1.61). 'Fibron', in 13 shades, is a textured spread-on wall fabric, the perfect solution for badly cracked walls. To remove it, soak with water and scrape off. *P:* enough for 20sq ft £6.39.

RICHARD STEVENS WOODSTOVES LTD

THURMALOX DECO KIT of heat-resistant paints to decorate any metal surface that gets hot during use. Perfect for wood or coal stoves, they withstand continuous heat up to 800–1200°F without peeling or chalking. The kit contains 1oz (30ml) jars of Gold, Silver, Green, Blue, Brown, and White paints, one jar each of thinner and eraser, and two brushes. *P:* £7.25. THERMALOX STOVE PAINT is for completely refinishing stoves. It comes in matt and metallic Blue, Green, Black, Brown, and Maroon. *P:* 13oz (364ml) £3.50.

WOOLCO & WOOLWORTHS

WINFIELD COVERPLUS range of household paints, made by a leading British manufacturer (Donald Macpherson & Co Ltd). Great value for money, it comes in 80 colours, in six finishes. A textured vinyl paint, ideal for cracked or uneven surfaces, is also available in six pastel shades. Interestingly, Woolworths put out a 'how-to' brochure on the delights of decorating with stencils. Their promotional picture (illustrated) suggests that all you need to achieve perfection are paint, stencil brush, piece of foam, masking tape, and stencil. *P:* all 1l (1¾pt), gloss £2.39, matt and silk vinyl £2.29.

INTRODUCTION

At a time when land prices are rocketing, with ever more houses and flats to the square mile, it's increasingly important to use space efficiently. Partitions are designed to do just this, with maximum effectiveness.

Easily movable versions on tracks or wheels, or fold-back dividers, will block off areas in a room that's used for more than one purpose. A sliding fabric panel, will shut a bedroom off from a large studio. They can also be regarded as part of the furniture: a screen around a reading spot, for example. More permanent fixed partitions are useful to sub-divide space in a large, high-ceilinged house.

The partitions in this section range from perforated panels in a variety of materials including plastic, acrylic, wood, fabric and metal, to walling substances. Some are self-assembly; others are installed by the manufacturer.

See also 'Blinds', 'Mirrors and Glass'.

CAPE BOARDS & PANELS LTD

MASTERBOARD multi-purpose, lightweight, asbestos-free building board that won't warp, rot, swell or shrink. It can be painted, papered, tiled like plaster, or used for overlaying floor-boards before putting down floor coverings. Conventional woodworking tools are used to cut, shape and drill the board, which is then nailed or screwed into position. *M:* panels up to h 300 × w 120cm (9ft 10^1/8in × 3ft 11^1/4in), 6, 9, 12mm (^{1}/4, ^{3}/8, ^{1}/2in) thick. *P:* 240×120cm× 6mm (7ft 10^1/2 ×3ft 11^1/4in × ^{1}/4in), from £8.

CROYDON DISPLAY GROUP

Amazing WALLSCAN modular system from Sweden. Perfect for covering bad or uneven walls, exposed pipework, etc, it fits into SCANDEX uprights, eliminating the need for expensive battening. Cupboards, shelves, bins, drawers and all kinds of storage units can be incorporated. Panels come in White, or in a variety of finishes from coloured stove enamel to chrome for an extra charge. *M:* w 95cm (3ft 1^3/8in), h to order. *P:* upon application.

FILTRASOL LTD

CONCORDE folding doors. Made from rigid PVC sections with integral hinges and optional locks, they can be made to measure as room dividers. Colours are White, Ivory, Grey, and light or dark woodgrains. Door sizes are standard, or can be made to measure. *M:* h 6^1/2 × w 3, 3^1/2ft (198×91.5, 106.5cm). *P:* upon application.

SUSANNE GARRY LTD

Sheer fabrics, most of them man-made, stretched and framed for use as room dividers. There's a huge range of motifs, mostly floral with wheat sheaves, rushes, bonsai and ferns predominating. Matching opaque furnishing fabrics are also available. *M:* to order. *P:* upon application. See also 'Fabrics'.

Catherine Lalau-Keraly's stained-glass screen

PRICES AND INFORMATION WERE CORRECT AT THE TIME OF GOING TO PRESS

DAVID GILLESPIE ASSOCIATES LTD
Carved redwood screens with a series of small apertures based on squares and other geometric motifs. Ideal for blocking off an area while retaining a sense of spaciousness, they are supplied only in natural untreated wood which can be stained or dyed by the customer. The panels can be carved on one or both sides. Similarly carved metal screens are also available from this innovative supplier. *M:* h 250 × w 100, 1.9cm thick (8ft 2³/8in × 3ft 3³/8in, ³/4in). *P:* upon application.

Gillespie's 'ACR2' redwood screen

HUFCOR (PARTITIONS) LTD
Accordion-pleated partitions. Primarily intended for commercial use, they would be excellent in the home—and rather more durable than some of their domestic counterparts. Acoustical partitions are also available with laminated panels on aluminium frames, or in a material specified by the customer. *M:* to order. *P:* upon application.

CATHERINE LALAU-KERALY
Marvellously different partitions, made to order by a stained-glass artist who has extended her medium to screens. They incorporate wood frames, and glass that has been enamelled, sandblasted, etched, painted and/ or stained. Prices vary, depending on the quality of the glass and the intricacy of the design. *M:* four panels h 200 × w 320cm (6ft 6³/4in × 13ft 1⁵/8in). *P:* £500–£2,000, depending on size, and the amount of work involved. See left for illustration.

W H NEWSON
Great range of PELLA folding doors. Made of high-density particle board, they are faced with mahogany, pine, teak, limba, mansonia, walnut, or oak veneers, and bonded with water-resistant synthetic adhesives. Exclusive inner-spring connectors ensure that they open and close uniformly without bunching, jamming or noise. All doors are available single, as a pair, or as sliding panel doors for recessed installation. Made to order, they come in three styles, two with plain faces, one with striking 'Designer' moulded panels. *M:* to order. *P:* h 6½ft × w 6ft 1in (198×185.5cm) £185.

SCREENLITE double-sided perforated hardboard makes an inexpensive perforated screen, room divider or partition. It can also be used for shuttering, etc. *M:* h 6 × w 2ft, ¹/8in thick (183×61cm, 3mm). *P:* sheet £6.50.

Newson's 'Designer' folding doors from PELLA

Open louvre doors in Canadian fir are supplied as separate panels, or boxed with track and fittings to make two- or four-door installations. Saloon doors are available for Wild West fans. *M:* folding doors h 6½ ×w 2 – h 8 × w 6ft (198×61 – 244×183cm), separate panels h 24 × w 12in – h 6½ft × w 18in (61×30.5 – 198× 46cm); both 1³/8in (3.5cm) thick. *P:* h 4ft ×w 18in (122×46cm) £9.50.
Slightly lower quality ramin hardwood louvre doors, made in the UK, are supplied unfinished (*M:* h 18 × w 12in – h 6½ft × w 30in, 1¹/8in thick/46×30.5 – 198×76, 3cm, *P:* h 4ft × w 18in /22×46cm £8).

Selection of NEWSON's louvre doors in Canadian fir

SILENT GLISS LTD
PANEL GLIDE 2500 combines advanced curtain track technology with the opportunity to display contemporary fabric patterns to their best advantage—in large flat panels. This Japanese-inspired product functions as a roof divider, or screen for windows. Panels can be stacked left or right, drawn from both sides like conventional curtains, or even centre stacked; and can be hand or cord-drawn, or electrically operated. *M:* w 66–70cm (26–27½in), height to order. *P:* upon application.

VISIJAR (PLASTICS) LABORATORIES LTD
GERACRYL heavily patterned extruded acrylic sheet from a company that supplies plastics for virtually every purpose, and is well known for Perspex and other acrylic sheetings. Available in 16 patterns, it's perfect for room dividers and screens, as well as internal doors, stair balustrading and shower surrounds, and is supplied cut to size. Tinted versions include Cathedral yellow 'GC 22' and Bronze 'GC 23'. *M:* to order. *P:* sq m £18–£35.
Polystyrene panels create a similar effect. 13 patterns are available, including plain 'Prismatic', 'Roundel' with concentric circles in clear, Amber, Green, or Bronze, 'Spindrift' woodgrain textures in clear or Bronze, 'Beaded' in White opal, 'Crushed Ice' in clear or Orange, and 'See Thru' in clear or Bronze. 'See Thru' panels are smooth on both sides, all others are smooth on one side with a relief pattern on the other. *M:* h 183 × w 61cm (6ft × 24in). *P:* sq m £3.75–£7.50.

PRICES AND INFORMATION WERE CORRECT AT THE TIME OF GOING TO PRESS

INTRODUCTION

House plants beautify with their foliage, add freshness to any room, and bring some of the outdoors inside, albeit artificially. Practical as well as aesthetically pleasing—they'll humidify a dry, centrally heated atmosphere — at least a few plants are essential to any scheme as a critical look at any successful interior scheme will tell you.

There are two solutions if you don't have a green thumb: have your plants tended by a specialist firm; or install exquisitely 'real' flowers and/or small trees with fabric foliage. (Avoid plastic.)

Use a single, large plant, or a group of three or more, rather than dotting a few smaller specimens around the room. Containers should be as plain as possible to enhance, rather than detract from, the plant/s. At the same time, make sure they are compatible with the rest of the room: brass with traditional furniture, plastic with modern. If in doubt, stick to plain White throughout.

This section concentrates on larger, more unusual stands and planters, rather than the small ceramicware readily available in shops. It includes modern, self-watering indoor/outdoor tubs, fine reproductions, and stands for showing groups of plants.

BAKER, KNAPP & TUBBS

Chinese-inspired planters with proportions and forms based on the designs of Chippendale and his contemporaries in the mid-18th century. The 'Chinese Stand' in pecan with walnut veneer has mitring and fretwork detail typical of 17th- and 18th-century Chinese furniture. (M: w 10½ × d 10½ × h 32in/26.5× 26.5×81.5cm, P: £175). '2613', in walnut, has upturned feet, and characteristic carved Chinese detail on the legs (M: diam 12 × h 42in/30.5×107cm, P: £195).

Baker, Knapp & Tubbs' 'Chinese Stand' (left), '2613' (right)

BY DESIGN

Exclusive range of more than 40 distinctive plant containers. Simple, geometric shapes are made from glass-reinforced polyester, with an easily maintained gloss finish. Perfect for indoor or outdoor use, the planters come in White, or can be made to order in any colour at no extra cost. M: w 51cm (20in) – maximum w 1.5m (4ft 11in). P: £20–£110. An optional inset table top that fits all the containers is an unusual feature. A seat cushion is also available.

CARSON OFFICE FURNITURE LTD

Stylish square, rectangular and circular plastic planters. Suitable for soil or hydroculture, they come in White, or Sandstone with a Brown base. M: square w 20 × d 20 × h 15in (51×51×38cm), rectangular w 36 × d 15 × h 12in (91.5×38×30.5cm), circular diam 15, 22in (38, 56cm). P: square £44, rectangular £48, circular £34, £44.

CLASSIC GARDEN FURNITURE LTD

Two very pretty Victorian-inspired solutions for plant display. Made from cast iron, they are painted White or finished in polished steel. 'C57' is a square or rectangular jardiniere (M: square 25 × 25 × h 31cm, rectangular w 56 × d 35 × h 31cm/9⁷/₈ × 9⁷/₈ × 12¹/₄, 22 × 13³/₄ × 12¹/₄in, P: square £25 painted, £38 polished; rectangle £34, £50). 'C13', a multiflora display stand, evokes days gone by when silks rustled and parrots twittered in turn-of-the-century conservatories; a single-stemmed version is also available (M: h 123cm, single stand h 77cm/48³/₈, 30³/₈in, P: multiflora stand £55 painted, £75 polished; single £36, £55).

Classic Garden Furniture's 'C13' (left), 'C57' (right)

DESIGNERS GUILD

Stands in natural cane, from a selection of cane furniture and antiques in the Guild's flower-filled showroom. Protected by clear lacquer, these can be stained or painted to order. M: cane three-tier stand h 86cm (33⁷/₈in), basket stand h 37cm (28³/₄in). P: £39, £43.

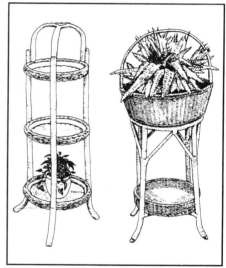

Designers Guilds' three-tier stand (left), basket stand (right)

FORMA LTD

Wonderful 'Fiorera' planter from Italy. Designed for Valenti by Liisi Beckmann and Ezio Didione it comes in White, Green, and Brown. M: diam 50 × h 25cm (19⁵/₈×9⁷/₈in). P: £30.

GROSIFLEX (UK) LTD
Self-watering plant containers in simple geo-metric shapes. EVEREST, made from poly-propylene, consists of four round tubs, four octagonals, and one square and two rect-angular troughs (*M:* octagonal diam 12–24 × h 15–28cm/4³/₄–9³/₈×5⁵/₈–11in, square 20× 20cm/7⁷/₈×7⁷/₈in, *P:* £4.50). RESIDENCE, also in polypropylene, is available as six squares, two round tubs, one trough and two bowls, most finished in White, Brown, Beige, Smoke, aluminium, woodgrain, or cork (*M:* round tubs diam 36 × h 24, diam 47.5 × h 30cm/14¹/₈×9³/₈, 18⁵/₈×11⁷/₈in, *P:* diam 36cm £14). GXP comes in White, Brown, Beige or aluminium-finished PVC, in three troughs, one round tub and two squares (*M:* square 60×60cm/23⁵/₈×23⁵/₈in, *P:* square £61.50).

CHARLES HAMMOND LTD
Tall, elegant marble column for a prize specimen or special bouquet. It comes in White and Grey, and Light or Dark green. *M:* h 105cm (41³/₈in). *P:* £260.

Charles Hammond's marble column (left); Jardine's 'UR7' (right)

JARDINE LEISURE FURNITURE LTD
Weatherproof 'UR7' aluminium jardiniere. Faithfully reproduced from a classic original, it's finished in stain-resistant White paint. *M:* h 42in (106.5cm). *P:* £120.

LESCO ALUMINIUM PRODUCTS
Sleek, straight-sided planters in four sizes. 'P1' is finished in polished chrome or anodized silver or gold, or can be stove-enamelled in White, Brown, Black, Red, or Yellow (*M:* diam 15³/₄ × h 12¹/₂in/40×31.5cm, *P:* £37). 'P2', 'P3', 'P4' and 'P5', in welded steel, come in polished chrome only (*M:* diam 11–18in ×h 10–18in/28–46cm ×25.5–46cm, *P:* £28–£111). Heavy-gauge steel litter bins in Blue, Red, Green, and Black (*P:* £9), and plastic bins in a variety of sizes and colours (*P:* from £2.50) would make excellent and inexpensive plant holders.

OASIS ARTIFICIAL FLORA
More than 100 varieties of beautiful flower arrangements, and over 50 small trees includ-ing bamboo, orange, lemon, azalea, rubber, laburnum, and flowering cherry. Each flower and leaf is made in Provence from the finest silk, then realistically dyed in subtle shades. Oasis will advise on displays, and install on site. *P:* trees from £35, flowers from £15.

PLANTERS HORTICULTURE
Indoor plants from an international company that also offers a comprehensive design, installation and regular maintenance service. Contracts of any size are accepted. A good range of containers made from glass-fibre rein-forced polyester comes in White and all other BS colours. *M:* diam 37.5–46 × h 35–46cm (14³/₄–18 × 13³/₄–18), square 45×45, 60×60 × h 30cm (17³/₄×17³/₄, 23⁵/₈×23⁵/₈ × 11⁷/₈in), rect-angular w 90 × d 30 × h 30–42.5cm (35³/₈× 11⁷/₈×11⁷/₈–16³/₄in). *P:* upon application.

BARRIE QUINN
Original and reproduction ceramic jardinieres from a specialist shop alongside Barrie Quinn's antique shop. These flamboyant plant holders, with rich mouldings, come in often vivid colours but can also be matched to fabrics, wall coverings, etc. *M:* various. *P:* originals £200–£1,000, reproductions £45–£85.

Selection of Barrie Quinn's jardinieres

A C RENTAPLANT
Wide range of plants supplied complete with glass-fibre planters. One of Britain's leading interior planting, supply and maintenance organizations, Rentaplant has its own consul-tants, nursery, and service fleet. Rented plants are automatically tended every three to four weeks, and replaced if damaged; otherwise plants and containers are sold with a main-tenance option. *P:* upon application.

RENZLAND & CO LTD
Sweetly scrolled wrought-iron stand. The height can be adjusted. *M:* h 30–48in (76–122cm). *P:* £18.

SALEMINK LTD
Wondrous collection of brass and copper—perfect planters for anyone who loves the gleam of these metals. They come in virtually every size and shape, all well made and nicely designed: square and rectangular footed troughs, big round buckets, small cache-pots with Blue-and-White china handles, and generous tubs on leonine claw feet. See *Accessories* ('Fireplaces') for illustration and prices.

TEMPUS STET LTD
Tall, fluted Doric column from a firm that specializes in unusual reproductions. Moulded in ground Portland Stone, it is available White, or gilded (*M:* h 51in/129.5cm, *P:* £70, gilded £90). A squatter version comes in White, or with a mock-wood finish (*M:* h 36in/91.5cm, *P:* £57, wood finish £62).

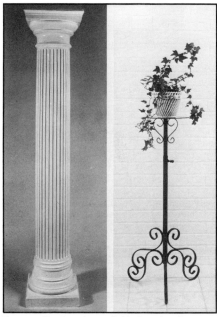

Tempus Stet's column (left); Renzland's wrought-iron stand (right)

ISAAC WEBSTER & SONS LTD
Two unusual 'planters' from a specialist firm that makes stainless steel products for the food, pharmaceutical, chemical and brewing industries. A yeast bin with side handles, and standard taper buckets with or without pouring lips, are ideal for a large plant (*M:* to order, *P:* from £150). A 'tasting stand', to order only, would make an excellent modern jardiniere (*M:* to order, *P:* upon application).

INTRODUCTION

From humble beginnings as stitched together fabric remnants, or painted tarpaulins on the floors of those who couldn't afford silk and wool exotica from the Middle East, rugs have evolved into essential elements in interior decoration.

Over bare floors or wall-to-wall carpeting they provide colour, pull unrelated pieces of furniture together, and can be used to define and highlight space – a perfect application of this is a rug under the dining table and chairs in an open-plan living area. Or a contemporary rug will offset the predominantly period tone of a room filled with traditional furniture. This juxtapositioning of antique and modern is a favourite ploy of Italian designers; success requires skill and a sensitive eye for compatible colours. And, of course, rugs will move with you, unlike wall-to-wall carpets which are never successfully relocated.

As with carpeting, pure wool makes the best rugs – plush, tough, warm (and expensive). Wool and man-made fibre combinations, or 100% cotton, are well worth considering as alternatives. Both types are less expensive, yet relatively static free. Man-made fibres develop an electrical charge, attract dust, are more difficult to clean, and soon lose their looks. Avoid them if you can.

An immense variety of patterns and textures is available, from ornate Orientals, through traditional Greek and Viking rugs, to bolder designs inspired by modern art. Looming styles include long shag piles with all strands cut to the same length, closely cut velours, Wiltons and Axminsters, plus many wonderful effects that can only be achieved on a hand loom. Machine and hand-made rugs are featured in this section.

If your heart is set on a rug that co-ordinates perfectly with your interior scheme, we list several craftspeople who will work to clients' designs. For firms who specialize in made-to-order products see 'Carpeting'.

*Measurements are rounded to the nearest ¼in (6mm).

ARTISAN CARPETS LTD

Gorgeous Greek carpets and rugs. Several times thicker than contract-grade carpets, many can be made to clients' specifications in any size or shape, and any number, or combination, of colours. Delivery is four weeks after the design has been approved. *P:* from sq m £38.

Several extremely high-quality standard designs are also available. All significantly different, they nevertheless show a 'house style': aggressive, asymmetrical designs set against subtly toned base colours. *M:* four sizes 150× 200cm (4ft 11in×6ft 6¾in) to 250×300cm (8ft

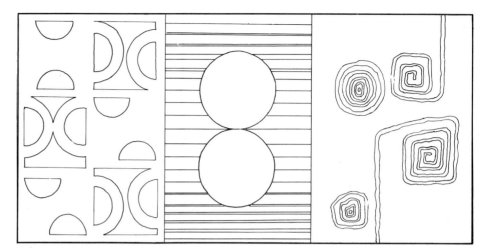

Selection of Artisan's designs

2¼in×9ft 10⅛in). *P:* upon application.
Traditional fluffy white Flokati rugs, in 100% pure wool, come in five sizes as single rugs, or in bales at 7½% discount. *M:* five sizes 70× 140cm (27½in×4ft 7in) 25 per bale to 200× 300cm (6ft 6¾in× 9ft 10⅛in) six per bale. *P:* upon application.

ASSOCIATED WEAVERS LTD

ZARA finely detailed Oriental-style rugs, in a classic Turkish design, with a luxurious velour finish and traditional fringe. They come in five base colours: two Reds, Burgundy, Green, and Blue. *M:* 91.5×133, 200×274cm (3ft× 4ft 4¼in, 6ft 6¾in×9ft). *P:* upon application.

AXMINSTER CARPETS LTD

Bordered carpets and rugs in 100% wool pile. Most of the patterns—'Egyptian' and 'Panel Persian' for instance—are inspired by Middle Eastern designs, but generally geometric in execution. Two exceptions, 'Pompadour' and 'Golden Scroll', are based on swirling floral motifs. Background colours throughout the range include: Olive green, Red, and Brown, plus Fawn, and Mink. 'Egyptian' comes in Gold/Green/Brown on Red, or Gold/Rust/ Olive on Fawn. *M:* Carpets nine sizes 183×274– 229×320cm (6×9–7½×10½ft), but some are unavailable in certain sizes; rugs three sizes 69×137–137×213cm (27½in×4½ft–4½×7ft). *P:* £15.60, £27.50, £48.20.

Detail from Axminster's 'Egyptian'

BLACKWOOD MORTON & SONS LTD

Competitively priced squares and rugs in 40% viscose, 40% wool and 20% nylon. The AXMOR, KELSO and CALEDONIA ranges include Oriental designs, and richly ornate patterns. Base tones are mainly Cream, Brown, and Red. *M:* AXMOR squares four sizes 183× 229–274×366cm (6×7½–9×12ft), rugs five sizes 69×130–137×198cm (27½in×4ft 3¼in– 4½×6½ft), corridor sizes 69×229, 274cm (27½in×7½, 9ft); KELSO rugs five sizes 69×130–183×274cm (27½in×4ft 3¾in–6×9ft, CALEDONIA rugs 69×137cm (27½in×4½ft). *P:* upon application.

BROCKWAY CARPETS LTD

CHAMBORD COLLECTION of rugs and squares in 100% pure wool, woven by craftsmen on traditional Axminster looms. They come in four muted background colours—Rose, Green, Blue, and Beige—with an intricate floral central design and matching borders. *M:* eight sizes 45×70–250×350cm (17¾×27½in–8ft 2¼in×11½ft), circular diam 200cm (6ft 7in). *P:* upon application.

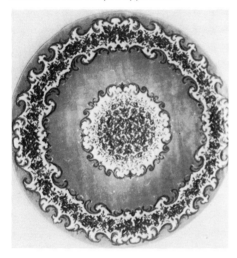

MARY FARMER

Hand-woven tapestries and rugs made to order from the best natural materials available. Bold geometrics predominate, in strong colours. *P:* upon application.

FORBO TAPIJT BV

Classically elegant PARADE rugs from a Dutch firm. Woven from 100% new wool, each design is in a different natural shade. 'Boured', 'Karabesh', and 'Keronan' are highly textured

and thickly shagged. More traditional cut-pile border rugs are also available. 'Topic' has a Greek-key border motif, 'Rubin' a modern rectangle edging, 'Emeril' and 'Jade' have floral motifs, 'Agathe' is edged with a thick plait, and 'Opale' with circular curlicues. *M:* six sizes 130×190–250×350cm (4ft 3¼in× 6ft 2¾in–8ft 2¼in×11½ft), but some designs are unavailable in certain sizes; 'Opale' three sizes diam 170–240cm (5ft 7in–7ft 10½in). *P:* 130×190cm 'Keronan' £50, 'Karabesh' £60, 'Boured' £70; 170×240cm 'Agathe', 'Opale', 'Emeril', 'Jade', 'Rubin', 'Topic' £122.

Left to right, from top: Forbo's 'Topic', 'Rubin', 'Emeril', 'Agathe'

GALLERY JO

Made-to-order hand-knotted or woven rugs, and other wall-hangings in original modern designs. Highest quality natural fibres are used, and the standard of knotting is very strictly maintained—an average of 160 knots to the square inch (6.5 sq cm) virtually ensures that rugs will last forever. *P:* upon application.

GASKELL BROADLOOM CARPETS LTD

Beautiful Good Companions collection in 100% new wool. There are three ranges, in different piles. CUMBRIA, a velvet Axminster, is available in seven geometric, optical, plaid, and Eastern designs with Off-white, Grey, Tan, Gold, Dark brown, and Black, plus six plains in the same colours.
LANCASTRIA, a semi-shag, comes in two American Indian, and several bold modern, designs. NORTHUMBRIA is a thick shag pile in plains, duo-tones, and rather more conservative patterns; 'Kaleidoscope' comes in White, Beige, Tan, Brown, and Black.
M: all above six sizes 69×122–251×351cm (27½in × 4ft–8ft 3in × 11½ft, circular diam 137cm (4½ft), oval l. 198cm (6½ft). *P:* £12–£140, circular £30, oval £36.50.
Two ranges in 'poodle-style' pile that combines loop with velour textures complement the Good Companions collection. CORINTHIAN has 'Kazak', a Middle Eastern-inspired

pattern, 'Versailles' and 'Cameo', similarly styled classics, and two beautifully bold abstracts—'Jupiter' and 'Grand Canyon'. In Cream through Tan tones. *M:* 137×198–251× 351cm (4½×6½ft–8ft 3in×11½ft). *P:* £49–£183.
CRAFTWEAVE comes in striking modern motifs only, in subtle natural shades. *M:* four sizes 137×198–251×351cm (4½×6½ft–8ft 3in× 11½ft). *P:* £82–£265.

Left to right, from top: Gaskell's 'Black Magic', 'Dreaming Spires', 'Navaho', 'Wigwam', all from CUMBRIA

Left to right, from top: Gaskell's 'Beverly Hills' from CUMBRIA, 'Kaleidoscope' from LANCASTRIA, 'Versailles' and 'Grand Canyon' from CORINTHIAN

GILT EDGE CARPETS LTD

SUPER PEERLESS luxurious, plain-coloured Wilton, available as square, round, rectangular, or oval fringed rugs as well as broadloom. They come in ten colours: Soft green, Bright blue, Rose red, Coral, and six natural shades from Dark brown to White ivory. *M:* small rugs two sizes 137×69, 183×91cm (4½ft×27½in, 6×3ft), circles and squares four sizes 137×137–366×366cm (4½×4½–12×12ft), ovals and rectangles three sizes 320×274–457×366cm (10½×9–15×12ft). *P:* circles and squares £50–£400, ovals and rectangles £100–£500.

GRAHAM & GREEN

Beautiful, made-to-order, hand-ruched hearth rugs from a multitude of wonders in this shop off Portobello Road. Practical and original, they incorporate fabrics from the Graham & Green selection, complementing the company's gift and furnishings selection. The example illustrated has Blue trellises and White and Rust flowers on Rust. Similar motifs can be supplied in colours and fabrics selected by the customer. *M:* 24×16in (61×41cm). *P:* £50.

HOMFRAY CARPETS LTD

BRIER PLUS intricately patterned, Oriental-style Axminster rugs. Very competitively priced, they're made in 80% acrylic fibre and 20% nylon. Six well-differentiated designs are available, four with a Red field, two with Brown. 'AN H832' comes in Gold/Rust/Browns. *M:* four sizes 69×130–250×350cm (27½in×4ft 3¼in–8ft 2¼in×11½ft). *P:* £20–£110. See page 199 for 'AN H832' in colour.

SUSIE HONNOR

Hand-loomed woollen rugs with linen warp. Colours are subtly variegated to create a stunning overall effect. Susie Honnor dyes the wools herself so virtually any combination is available. Maximum width is 46in (117cm), but it's possible to sew two rugs together. *M:* 30×60in (91.5×152.2cm) as illustrated. *P:* upon application.

PRICES AND INFORMATION WERE CORRECT AT THE TIME OF GOING TO PRESS

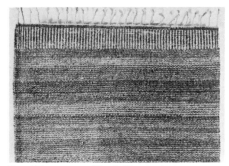

Detail from one of Susie Honnor's rugs

VERNON HOWELL RUGS

Traditional HEMSLÖJD rugs in designs that date back 1,000 years to the first Viking settlements. Hand-woven in coarse wool on a shuttleless loom, these practical rugs are identical on both sides. There are three designs: 'Tulpan' in Grey, Pastel blue, Gold, and Green; 'Hjortron' in Blue, Gold, Peach, Leaf green, and Grey and Red; and 'Gustav' in Grey-green, Oak brown, Gold, and Blue. *M:* three sizes 4ft 7in×6½ft–6½×9ft (139.5×198–198×300cm). *P:* £55–£140. See page 199 for 'Tulpan' in colour.

JAYMART RUBBER & PLASTICS LTD

Chinese natural grass mats from a firm that specializes in economical flooring. Various qualities are available from seagrass through rush to maize and rush, the most expensive. *M:* six sizes 24in×4ft–6×9ft (61×122–183×274.5cm). *P:* sq yd 95p–£2.05. They are supplied only in bales of 10 to 30 mats depending on size. At these prices, who cares about a few extra mats? Also circular rugs (*M:* diam 3, 4ft/91.5, 122cm, *P:* from £2.25).

MARY FOX LINTON LTD

Unusual and beautiful rugs from a well-known interior decorator. Indian dhurries, hand-woven in 100% wool or 100% cotton come in up-dated traditional patterns, or interpretations designed in Mary Fox Linton's studio. Relatively inexpensive, they're wondrously coloured in pastel tones. Wool dhurries can be woven to clients' colour and size specifications. *M:* six sizes 4×6–9×12ft (122×183–274.5×366cm). *P:* wool £150–£600, cotton £90–£400.

Cottagey rag rugs, just like grandmother used to make from scraps, are in 100% cotton, in plain colours or traditional variegated tones. *M:* four sizes 4ft 7in×6ft 6¾in–9×12ft (140×200–274.5×366cm). *P:* £50–£175.

Hand-made needlepoint rugs, in 100% wool, come in a textured floral design in lovely muted tones. These expensive—and absolutely gorgeous—rugs can be custom-made. *M:* 6×4–9×12ft (183×122–274×366cm). *P:* £235–£1,000.

Chain-stitch, crewel-look rugs, in 100% wool,

are available in a good range of muted tones. *M:* 4×6–9×12ft (122×183–274.5×366cm). *P:* £200–£720.

See page 199 for wool dhurrie in colour.

PERSIAN CARPET WHARF

Wide range of Persian and Oriental carpets and rugs. Low overheads, and an astute buying policy, ensure unrivalled value. Rumanian carpets and rugs are Eastern in design, Western in their use of thick wool and pastel colours. Mori Bokharas are less expensive, but still very elegant. They're easily identified by symmetrical rows of Bokhara 'guls' on an open field, usually knotted in Burgundy, Rose, Ivory, Light tan, or Green. The exceptionally durable Afghan rugs are more starkly dramatic, with a central field of Red or Gold, and (typically) an octagonal Afghan 'gul' motif. Inlaid silk prayer rugs have a three-dimensional relief effect in which significant details—often Muslim religious symbols—are highlighted in pure silk. Kashans, the most intricately knotted of all Persian carpets, come in rich deep reds and browns. Sizes and prices vary.

A cleaning and repair service is available.

PERSIAN & ORIENTAL CARPET CENTRE LTD

Marvellous selection, from a prestigious Mayfair company that caters for leading European buyers, including many nearby embassies. It includes rare and delightful antique, and more modern, Persian, Caucasian, Russian and Afghan rugs. The strong, geometric Caucasian designs, in particular, complement both modern and traditional interiors. A good range of Kelims is also available (*M:* 2×3–10×15ft/61×91.5–305×457.5cm, *P:* upon application).

P & O CARPETS LTD

Top quality antique and 20th-century rugs, from Persia, Turkey, Russia, and Afghanistan. P & O operate the only Customs Bonded Oriental Carpet Warehouse in London's West End. Established more than 50 years ago, its main outlets are leading department stores, and specialist carpet shops abroad, but personal shoppers are nevertheless welcome. Sizes and prices vary.

ARTHUR SANDERSON & SONS LTD

Very lovely high quality Axminster rugs in 80% wool and 20% nylon. Three designs co-ordinate perfectly with fabrics, wallpapers, carpets in the Triad collection. 'Acorn' is illustrated with complementary borders, wallpapers and fabrics. Two other designs are available: 'Suki' and 'Honeysuckle'. All come in gorgeous earth shades. *M:* 3×5ft (91.5×152.5cm). *P:* £40. See also 'Carpets', 'Fabrics', 'Wall Coverings'.

Sanderson's 'Acorn'

SHELLEY TEXTILES LTD
Staggering TUMBEL TWIST range of 147 rugs and 21 bathroom sets in plain, washable shaggy cotton. There's a large selection of colours: Bleached white, Ivory, Mushroom, Bleached gold, Laburnum, Old gold, Tangerine, Brandy, Tabac, Havana, Guardsman red, Cerise, Rose pink, Petunia, Violet, Adriatic blue, Horizon blue, Turquoise, Fern, Spring green, Olive green. *M:* six sizes 56×76–76×152cm (22×30in–30in×5ft), circular diam 107cm (3½ft). *P:* £10–£20. Shelley Textiles will supply two widths sewn together (£4 per 3ft/91.5cm of seam), and quote for special sizes. Wall-to-wall carpeting is available in the same twisted pile. *M:* w 56, 68.5, 76, 91.5cm (22, 27, 30in, 3ft). *P:* from m £10.

E N SIMPSON (UK) LTD
Wonderful 'sculptured' rugs and wall-hangings, made to order for interior designers and architects. 50 colours are available in 100% wool, or 80% wool and 20% nylon. Other mixes can be supplied on request. Pile thickness is to the customer's specification. *P:* upon application. See illustration on page 199 for 'Marilyn Monroe' in colour.

THOMSON SHEPHERD (CARPETS) LTD
Multitextured carpets and rugs. TRIBAL SQUARES, inspired by traditional Berber carpets, are woven from 100% undyed wool, in four stunning designs: 'Djebel', 'Highlander', 'Masai', and 'Zanzibar'. *M:* three sizes 4ft×6ft 3in–8ft 9in×11ft 9in (122×190.5–267×358.5xm). *P:* £63–£255.

Thomson Shepherd's 'Zanzibar' from TRIBAL SQUARES

THRESHOLD FLOORINGS LTD
Mats and runners designed to prevent dirt being carried past entrance areas. Made from static-free 60% Evlan and 40% nylon, they're primarily intended for industrial use, but could be a boon in the home. The fibre absorbs up to 38.75% of the pile weight in moisture. This 'barrier' carpeting is available as mats, tiles, and rolls, and comes in slightly speckled colourways: Blue and Brown, Dark brown and Beige, Rust and Brown, Olive green and Brown, and Gold and Brown. *M:* mats three sizes 73×125–146×225cm (28¾in×4ft 1¼in–4ft 9⅜in×7ft 4½in), tiles 50×50cm (19⅝×19⅝in), rolls 13m×w 73, 120, 140cm (42ft 8in×28¾in, 3ft 11¼in, 4ft 7in). *P:* mats £30–£100, tiles sq m £25, rolls m £21–£52.

ROBERT WALLACE DESIGNS
Exciting and beautiful selection of carpets, including the latest V'Soske Joyce productions. The studio is the UK's sole commercial outlet for an organization whose innovatory and sophisticated method of manufacture ensures maximum control over line, texture, and colour—shades can even be matched to carpeting which has been in use several years. Traditional ranges are also available, but Robert Wallace encourages commissions from

Robert Wallace's 18th-century design from a Robert Adam plasterwork ceiling

individual clients—often professional designers with very exact specifications. In addition, a revolutionary process by which carpets can be made without seams in any width up to 30ft (920cm) makes it possible to manufacture to most floor plans. *P:* upon application.

WOODWARD GROSVENOR & CO LTD
Tough, durable, close-pile Oriental reproductions manufactured to a scrupulously high technical standard. There are 100 tufts to every square inch (6.5 sq cm), and at least three strands of backing. Each carpet is endorsed by the weaver responsible. Carpets, intended for loose-laying, come in standard sizes but can be woven extra long. Seven designs are available, most of them in any of five standard shades: Red, Brown, Beige, Salmon, Gold. All carpets can be fringed. *M:* six sizes 3×6–12×15ft (91.5×183–366×457.5cm) but some designs are unavailable in certain sizes. *P:* upon application.

Woodward Grosvenor's 'Kasham'

INTRODUCTION

Almost anything can be shelved, from a television set or stereo to records, *objets d'art* and, of course, books. What's more, modern shelves are available in a wide range of styles and materials, from industrial models in metal through contemporary chrome and glass to more traditional veneered and lacquered versions.

Aesthetics are obviously important, but before making your final choice make sure the shelves will bear the weight you want them to support. As a general rule metal, laminated wood and chipboard make the strongest shelving, followed by glass, metal mesh and wood.

Wall-mounted shelves are usually less conspicuous than free-standing units (which are often works of industrial art in themselves), and ideal for displaying treasured objects. But check that the wall will bear their weight.

This section includes straightforward shelving as well as modular systems with components that can be combined to suit your space and purpose. Storage facilities like drawers, drinks cabinets, etc, are sometimes available for the latter.

See also 'Special Furniture', 'Storage'.

ABSTRACTA CONSTRUCTION LTD

Superb 13mm, 19mm, 25mm, 32mm systems, designed for shops but an inspired choice for anyone who wants a display area. Patented connectors are used to make 90 joints that are as rigid as a weld but much cleaner in appearance. The 13mm (½in) range also allows 1208 connections, and comes in Matt black or polished chrome. The 19mm (¾in) version consists of round chrome tubes; 25mm (1in) tubes have Black connectors that contrast with a satin anodized aluminium square; and the 32mm (1¼in) system has very chunky, chrome-plated tubes and connectors. Shelves are glass, or standard shelving materials. *M:* to order. *P:* upon application.

STRUCTA modular display units, made from toughened glass, have no superfluous components. A transparent plastic locking block at the corner of each module is locked in place with the twist of a screwdriver (or small coin).

Left to right: Close-ups of connectors from Abstracta's 19mm, 25mm, 32mm systems

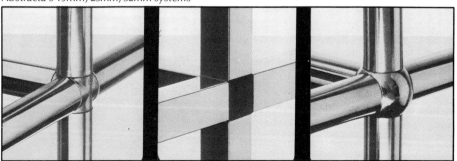

ASTON WOODWARE

PEGGED SHELVES with traditional jointed ends, in natural, waxed or polished finishes. This company makes high-quality, country pub furniture, mainly in oak or elm. *M:* to order. *P:* upon application.

BAKER, KNAPP & TUBBS

Display case for fans of the best in modern design, '1630' has doors in satinized brass and glass, glass shelves and interior lighting. *M:* w 31 × h 84 ×d 15½in (78.5 ×213.5 × 39.5cm). *P:* £1,144.

BEDFORD, STEER, END & CO LTD

Rigid, versatile and easily assembled POSTMASTER modular shelving system that increases in strength the more it's loaded. Finished in hardwearing zinc chrome plate, with a baked-on clear film for extra protection, it comes in 21 shelf sizes for a wide selection of shelving arrangements. Shelf and bin dividers, hooks, castors and wire shelves are available. *M:* vertical supports 34–84in (86.5–213.5cm). *P:*

Baker, Knapp & Tubbs' '1630'

£479 as illustrated. See opposite page for illustration.

STACKMASTER, specifically designed for industrial use, is even stronger (and more expensive).

H BURBIDGE & SON LTD

Self-assembly SPINDLE-FLEX system in natural hardwood that can be painted or stained. Turned supports or 'spindles' screw into the shelves. Six spindle and three finial styles are available; also ten different shelves including rectangles, squares, circles and quadrants. *M:* spindles 14.5, 30, 38cm (5½, 11⅞, 15in). *P:* from 70p each. See illustration opposite.

'Antik' works on the same principle, but has only one spindle style and is finished in a mahogany tone.

CADO FURNITURE UK LTD

CUBEX rectangular units by Hans Nielsen, that can be combined to form shelves, bookcases, room dividers, etc — even flower boxes.

Bedford, Steer, End's POSTMASTER

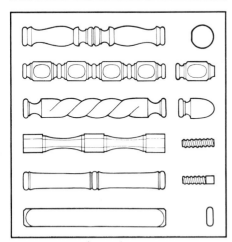

From top: 'Regal', 'Mediterranean', 'Rope Twist', 'Transitional', 'Tropical', 'Modern', all from Burbidge's SPINDLE-FLEX

Available in light pine treated with acid-fast varnish, or scratchproof White lacquer, they can be supplemented with White, Brown, Black or Red sliding doors in two heights, White, Red or Black table tops, and Black back

Cado's CUBEX

panels. No tools are necessary — bases and rectangular panels are joined by patented, Black plastic connectors. *M:* modules w 10¼, 13, 26in × d 11⅞in (26, 33, 66 × 30cm). *P:* 26 × 11⅞in (66 × 30cm) shelf £10 pine, £8 White.
ULTRA modular shelving by Paul Cadovius is ideal for showing a collection. Sections snap together, matching caps plug the join. Finished in teak, pine or mahogany, units can be raised ¾in (2cm) from the ground. Sliding doors are available. *M:* shelves w 33, 72, 142, 212 × d 30, 45cm (13, 28⅜, 55⅞, 83½ × 11⅞, 17¾in). *P:* single shelf 33 × 45cm £8.
'System Cado', also by Paul Cadovius, includes display areas, chests, a desk, record and bar cabinets, wardrobes, even a table. They're designed to be invisibly mounted on wall panels, and come veneered in teak, rosewood, American walnut, mahogany or light oak. Backing panels ⅜in (1cm) thick are attached to the wall with screws on horizontal furring strips — the space between wall and panels provides excellent insulation.

Cado's ULTRA

PRICES AND INFORMATION WERE CORRECT AT THE TIME OF GOING TO PRESS

CIANCIMINO DESIGN LTD

Chic COMO shelving. Clear, or bronze or grey tinted glass shelves are teamed with 1in (2.5cm)-square uprights in satinized chrome-finished solid steel. Top and bottom fittings, and block shelf support are solid brass. *M:* to order. *P:* uprights £6 ft, fittings £10 pair, shelf support £4.50, glass to order, all as illustrated.

Ciancimino's COMO

Ciancimino's DOMENICA

The DOMENICA freestanding system has characteristic and unusual joins that fix five bronzed glass shelves to natural or bronzed anodized aluminium. *M:* w 42 × h 78 × d 13in (107 × 198 × 33cm). *P:* natural aluminium £545, bronzed £620.

Contemporary floor to ceiling GEMINI shelving is based on vertically linked bay units. Beautifully executed, it has natural or bronzed ribbed anodized aluminium supports and bronzed glass shelves. *M:* bay unit w 18 × h 36 × d ^{3}/8in (46 × 91.5 × 1cm). *P:* natural aluminium £330, each additional unit £225; bronzed £420, £275.

Ciancimino's GEMINI

CLASSIC GARDEN FURNITURE LTD

'C60' ornamental aluminium shelf brackets. Enamelled in White only, they're drilled ready for use. *M:* 23 × 18cm (9 × 7^1/8in). *P:* pair £10.

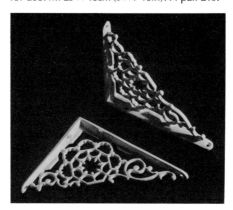

CUBESTORE LTD

CUBESHELF is well-designed and easily fixed. Wall uprights, standard and heavy-duty brackets, shelves and special fittings come in a wide range of lengths, or can be cut to size for awkward spots like alcoves. Uniquely, the uprights project only 10mm (^{3}/8in) from the walls, and have smooth surfaces. Shelves are 18mm (^{3}/4in) chipboard faced in Satin white melamine; optional Brown edgings. Uprights, brackets and fittings are satin anodized aluminium. Screws, wallplugs, etc are supplied with each order. *M:* uprights 24–72in (91.5–183cm), brackets 6–18in (15–46cm), shelves w 36–72in × d 7in (91.5–183 × 17.5cm). *P:* from £1.50, 65p, £2.20.

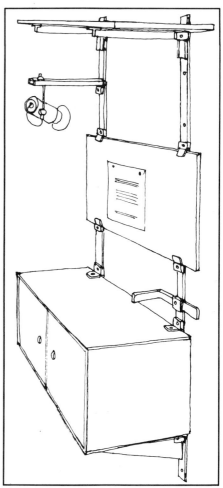

Cubestore's CUBESHELF

Ingenious CUBEKIT system based on a 36.4cm (15in) cube. Assembled by building one box on another, it comes in plain chipboard (for painting, varnishing or colour-staining), or with White or Dark brown melamine-faced door and drawer fronts, panels and edges. Because all parts are interchangeable, Brown doors can be combined with White cubes, White drawers with self-painted Bright blue. Units can face in any direction, so make ideal

Opposite, left to right, from top: Vernon Howell's 'Tulpan' from HEMSLÖJD (detail), E N Simpson's 'Marilyn Monroe', Mary Fox Linton's dhurrie, Homfray's 'AN H832' from BRIER PLUS

room dividers. *M:* wine rack 36.4 × 36.4 × 36.4 (15 × 15 × 15in). *P:* from £17.

Cubestore's CUBEKIT

DE LA PLAIN INTERIORS LTD

GENIA self-assembly modular stacking shelves in pressed metal. Units come in White only, with or without flap doors. *M:* units as illustrated w 100 × h 27/36 × d 27cm (39³/₈ × 10⁵/₈/14¹/₈ × 10⁵/₈in). *P:* £30 without doors.

De la Plain's GENIA

Deliciously slick and simplistic OLINTO shelving in four lacquered shades: Beige, Red, White, and Black. Doors, drawers and marble tops are available. *M:* w 33, 72 × h 72, 146, 332 × d 33, 45cm (13, 28³/₈ × 28³/₈, 57³/₈, 130³/₄ × 13, 17³/₄in). *P:* double cupboard £220.

Left: Interlübke's STUDIMO

De La Plain's OLINTO

DESIGNERS GUILD

CANE SHELF UNIT. Finished in natural clear lacquer, it is also available in coloured lacquers and stains, to order. *M:* w 67 × h 172 × d 36cm (26³/₈ × 67³/₄ × 14¹/₈in). *P:* £215.

CHARLES HAMMOND LTD

Two-tier glass-topped shelving unit or console table. *M:* w 103 × h 86 × d 30cm (40¹/₂ × 33⁷/₈ × 11⁷/₈in). *P:* £195.

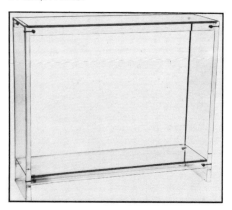

HARRISON-BEACON LTD

Strong, wall-mounted BEACON shelving system in anodized aluminium finished in Gold or Silver. Slotted wall bars come in five heights, shelves in four widths. Two brackets 24in (61cm) apart will support 275lb (123.57kg) on a 6in (15cm)-wide shelf. *M:* wall bars w 15–65in (38–165cm), brackets d 6–14in (15–35.5cm). *P:* bars 85p–£3.60, brackets 6in 60p, 14in £1.20.

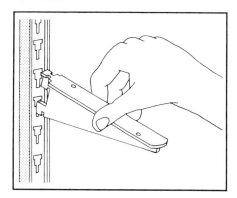

Hippo Hall's ELEPHANT bookcase (described overleaf)

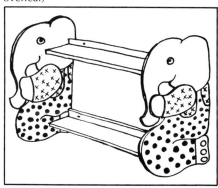

HIPPO HALL
ELEPHANT bookcase, hand-painted in cheerful colours, and supplied in four pieces complete with screws and simple assembly instructions. Panda, lion and bear versions are available. *M:* w 24 × h 22 × d 12in (61 × 56 × 30.5cm). *P:* £40. See overleaf for illustration.

HOUSE OF LAMBETH
Wonderfully innovative and inexpensive self-assembly 'Loop' adjustable shelving, suspended on pre-stretched cords attached to two wall screws. Shelves are self-locked into any position by looping the cord around the dowels. Packs contain four or six matt varnished laminated birch shelves, dowels,

two book ends, two lengths of cord, two screws with collars, and two Rawlplugs; also illustrated assembly instructions. *M:* shelves w 24 × d 8¼in (61 × 21cm). *P:* four-shelf unit £10, six-shelf £12.

KEWLOX FURNITURE LTD
MORESTORE in Dove grey stove-enamelled steel. Designed for industrial use, it's ideal for storage anywhere. Shelves, with stabilizing corner plates, are adjustable at 1in (2.5cm) intervals. Bin units, lateral files and sliding and hinged doors are available. *M:* w 36 × h 78 × d 12in (91.5 × 198 × 30.5cm). *P:* £50.

LIBRARY DESIGN & ENGINEERING LTD
Sturdy SHELVING SYSTEM designed for libraries but equally suitable for home use. Slotted steel uprights, stove-enamelled in

White or any BS colour, are fitted with vinyl-coated sheet steel shelves which accommodate book supports, pamphlet boxes, dividers, pull-out slides, seats, desk units — and more. *M:* uprights h 37–96in (94–244cm); shelves w 30, 36in (76, 91.5cm), d 8, 10, 12in (20.5, 25.5, 30.5cm). *P:* upon application; no minimum order.

MARWIN (HOLDINGS) LTD
LINSHELF shelving in anti-corrosive steel. in Blue stove enamel, it also comes with backs and sides made from weldmesh cladding — very High Tech. Accessories include bases for uneven floors, bracers, label holders and shelf dividers. Special heavy-load shelves are available. *M:*w 36, 72in (91.5, 183cm), h 72, 84, 99in (183, 213.5, 251.5cm), shelf d 12, 15, 18, 24, 36in (30.5, 38, 46, 61, 91.5cm); as illustrated w 36 × h 72 × d 12in (91.5 × 183 × 30.5cm). *P:* £65.

MERROW ASSOCIATES
Marvellously metallic CHEVRON shelves. Eight sizes are available, in polished chromium plate — or with gold-plated steel accents for the same price. *M:* four-shelf unit (left) w 39 × h 57½ × d 14½in (99 ×146 × 37cm). *P:* £220.

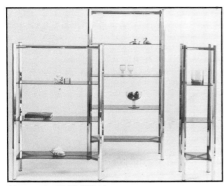

Merrow's CHEVRON

MORESECURE LTD

'Bin Unit' with rolled edges, perfect for a workroom or High Tech kitchen. Stove enamelled, in Dove grey only, it comes in polythene-wrapped packs with all necessary nuts and bolts. Shelves can be fitted at 1in (2.5cm) intervals. *M:* w 36 × h 75 × d 12, 18in (91.5 × 190.5 × 30.5, 46cm). *P:* £65 as illustrated.

Moresecure's 'Bin Unit'

Durable UNIPAK domestic shelving in Dove grey stove enamel. It comes, complete with fittings, as a single tall unit with six shelves, or two lower units each with three shelves — the top one for use as a worktop. *M:* single unit w

34 × h 72 × d 12in (86.5 × 183 × 30.5cm), three-shelf units w 34 × h 36 × d 12in (86.5 × 91.5 × 30.5cm). *P:* two three-shelf units £40.

Moresecure's UNIPAK

NICHOLL & WOOD LTD

Functional ZAMBA in Dove grey or with Orange shelves and Black uprights. It comes in kit form, with shelves, uprights, bracing stays, corner brackets, nuts, bolts and washers, or with components to order. *M:* 'Kit A' as illustrated w 36 × h 75 × d 12in (91.5 × 190.5 × 30.5cm). *P:* £25.

OMK DESIGN LTD

Tubular T SYSTEM with polished chrome or coloured frames, chrome or aluminium joints. Wire mesh backing is optional. Available in three heights, units can be used singly or in combination. Clear or tinted plate glass shelves, bought separately, can be adjusted to one of three heights. *M:* w 85 x h 70, 89, 174 × d 27cm (33½ × 27½, 35, 68½ × 14½in). *P:* upon application.

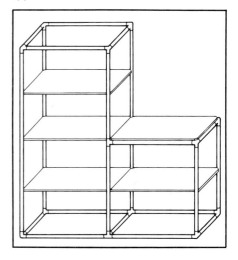

PENTABLOC LTD

PENTABLOC display system based on five-sided block fittings in toughened thermoplastic. Each of two sizes will take any length of ½in (1.3cm) square tubing three ways so that both vertical and lateral supports can be locked into place with one simple grub screw. Aluminium alloy tubing comes in a selection of

durable finishes. Six kits, each containing single and double fittings, tubing, and shelf-retaining clips, are available. *M:* 200cm (78¾in) or to order; Unit A as illustrated w 56 × h 60 × d 16in (142.5 × 155 × 40.5cm). *P:* upon application.

RENZLAND & CO
BRIANCO, an original 1950s design by Heinz Renzland. Versatile steel-ladder uprights, wall mounted or with plastic feet, support grained PVC shelves, drawers, cabinets (some with sliding doors or drop fronts), etc. Black ladders team with units finished in Black oak, Olive-green with Green oak, and Dark brown with Teak. *M:* three-drawer chest w 30 × h 16½ × d 14in (76 × 42 × 35.5cm). *P:* £60.

T SAVEKER LTD
Foolproof ALLWAY modular glass shelving held together with chrome or tough White plastic base and globe connectors. Suitable for lightweight objects only — books could be too heavy. *M:* shelves 25 × 25, 35 × 35cm (9⅞ × 9⅞, 13¾ × 13¾in). *P:* connectors from 28p each, shelves from 88p.

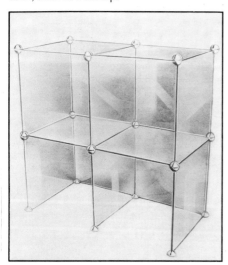

SPECTRUM LTD
Chrome-plated 'Stackmaster' entertainment unit with a central television shelf, from the inexpensive, self-assembly WIRE TECH range. Levelling bolts adjust to uneven flooring. *M:* each section w 75 × h 108 × d 15in (109.5 × 274.5 × 38cm). *P:* £175. Other solutions include small tables, trolleys, wall-mounted shelves, wine rack, room divider, and a kitchen unit with butcher's block top.

TOWNHOUSE INTERIORS
Striking 'LIB5' shelving or display unit. The laminate base, in any colour you like, supports stepped glass shelves with brass or stainless steel frames. *M:* w 200 × h 245 × d 50cm (78¾ × 96½ × 19⅝in). *P:* £1,375.

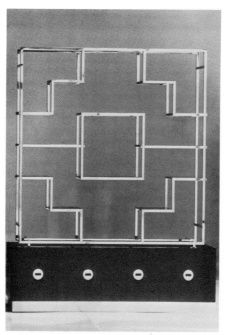

PRICES AND INFORMATION WERE CORRECT AT THE TIME OF GOING TO PRESS

TRANNON MAKERS
Wonderful 'Hanging Shelves' in clear or Red lacquered or Black-stained sycamore; special colours to order. Held together with sprung ash supports, they can be suspended from a picture rail and are easily assembled. *M:* w 60 × h 48 × d 8in (152.5 × 122 × 20.5cm), or to order. *P:* £90.

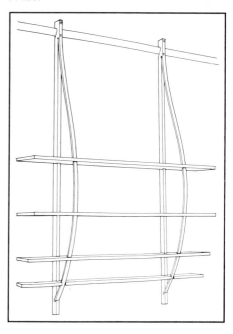

CHRISTOPHER WRAY'S LIGHTING EMPORIUM LTD
HANGING SHELVES in glass with brass supports, suspended from hooks and/or on chains. Inspired by those used in Victorian butchers' and grocers' shops, they're perfect in alcoves, and over bars and beds. *M:* w 30 × h 40 × d 8in (76 × 101.5 × 20.5cm). *P:* £58.

INTRODUCTION

Wall coverings and paintwork, floor coverings and furniture, combine to create a total effect, but soft furnishings provide the comforting highlights and accents in a room.

This rather small section specializes in squishy, sensuous, snuggly, and sometimes silky, cushions, quilts, coverlets, and bedlinen. It's devoted to craftspeople, special lines, and items that you won't find in the more pedestrian retail outlets. Although some are expensive, it might be worth designing an entire room around one of the collector's pieces we feature.

*Bedlinen comes in standard sizes, unless otherwise stated.

ALBARY LINENS

Bedlinen from famous foreign and domestic manufacturers—at discount prices. 95% is in soft but strong percale (50% polyester/50% cotton). American companies include FIELD-CREST, WAMSUTTA, SPRINGMAID, CAN-NON, ST MARY'S, J P STEVENS, MARTEX and DAN RIVER. Designer sheets and matching pillowcases come from leading names like Christian Dior, Yves St Laurent, Bill Blass, Oleg Cassini, Calvin Klein and Zandra Rhodes, in up to 100 prints and 20 plain shades. Some have matching towels, bedspreads, etc.

'Seconds' or irregulars with slight misprints are also available. In addition, Albary will make up curtains, valances, duvet covers, frilled pillowcases, tablecloths, etc, in prints selected by the customer.

P: single sheet £5–£15.

LAURA ASHLEY LTD

Pretty, 'country look' soft furnishings to match fabrics and wallpapers. Laura Ashley have an exclusive collection of traditional patchwork quilts based on squares and rectangles. Remarkably good value compared to similarly complex antique quilts, they come in 15 colours: Dark green, Moss, Apple, Navy, Smoke (blue-grey), Sapphire, Dark brown, Sand, Terracotta, Plum, Poppy, Rose, Burgundy, Apricot, and Ochre. *M:* 150, 240×250cm (59, 94½×98⅜in). *P:* £50, £60.

Extra-wide 100% cotton fabrics are available for making co-ordinating sheets or curtains. Easy-care, with a minimum iron finish, they come in eight flowery designs plus six plains: Cream, Moss, Sapphire, Smoke, Plum, and Rose. *M:* w 230cm (90⅝in). *P:* m £4.95. There's also a quilted fabric for bedspreads, in the same colourways.

Ready-made cushion covers are square or round with frills, and square with piped edges (*M:* frilled 45×45, diam 30; piped 50×50cm/ 17¾×17¾, 11⅞; 19⅝×19⅝in, *P:* £4.25, £3.75, £3.25, plus £2.50 for cushion).

Co-ordinating table linens, garment bags, storage boxes, picture frames and paint are available.

See also 'Fabrics', 'Paint', 'Wall Coverings'.

Selection from Laura Ashley

KIM BENTLEY

Absolutely beautiful hand-dyed silk cushions and quilts—a real exercise in perfectionism. Feather-filled, they're exquisitely coloured in various weight silks with no repeats, so every item is unique. Kim Bentley also makes bedspreads and blinds. *M:* to order. *P:* cushions £23–£25, quilts from £200.

COLOROLL LTD

Bedlinen in a cotton and polyester mixture, to match two wallpaper collections. DOLLY MIXTURES comes in 14 designs with Pink, Brown, Blue, Green, or Gold predominating, on White. 'Pippa', in Pink or Brown, consists of a pair of pillowcases, a single or double sheet, quilt cover, and valanced sheet, and ready-made curtains. (*M:* curtains 46×54, 72; 68×54, 72in/117×137, 183, 173×137, 183cm.) The JOHN WILLMAN range has 12 designs including a White trellis on Brown or Olive-green, teamed with a matching stripe on White. A very dramatic pattern has Pink or Yellow tulips and field flowers on Dark brown. Pillowcases, a single or double quilt cover and valanced sheet, plus ready-made curtains in two sizes, are available. *M:* curtains 68×54, 72in (173× 137, 183cm).

P: pillowcases £7; single sheet £16.25, double £20; single quilt cover £17, double £23; curtains 68×54in (173×137cm) £20.

Coloroll's 'Pippa' from DOLLY MIXTURES (above), 'Lady Marie Green' from JOHN WILLMAN (below)

THE CONRAN SHOP LTD

Exclusive French bedroom linens in 100% cotton. They include single and double sheets, pillowcases, kimonos, and duvet covers with edges bound with plain toning cotton tape. Five small-scale contemporary prints come in soft but not sickly shades. (Three can be bought by the metre.) *P:* single duvet cover £25.50–£28, single sheet £14–£20, pillowcase £5.50, kimono £24, m £6.50.

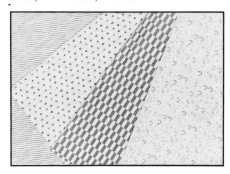

CVP DESIGNS LTD

Lovely, extravagant, one-off cushions made from ZANDRA RHODES' fanciful dress and upholstery fabrics. Expensive but wonderfully flamboyant bedspreads, tablecloths, etc, are made to order. Quilting, appliqué and other touches to clients' specifications. *P:* upon application.

DORMA
Rather lovely collection of bedwear in a cotton and polyester mixture, from a firm whose linen is a household name. Designs in the MARY QUANT collection are 'Mah Jong' with large rectangles made up of smaller rectangles in Navy with Red accents, or Caramel with Blue, both on Stone; 'Fizz' with vertical stripes in Green, Peach, Mauve, Pink, or Blue, fading into stippled stripes which shade into the Stone ground; charming 'Romany' with entwining flowers, in Brown and Orange, Blue and Red, and Green and Pink; and nostalgic 'Wallflower' with small flowers reversing to delicate stripes and florals, in Sepia and Lavender, or Pale blue and Lilac. All designs are available as quilt covers and pillowcases; 'Wallflower' also comes as ready-made curtains (*M:* curtains in four drops: 54, 72, 90, 108in/137, 183, 230, 275cm).

Dorma's 'Mah Jong' by MARY QUANT

Other DORMA ranges include 'Gingham' with neat checks that reverse to lace overlaid with tiny flowers, in Brown, Dark green, Mulberry, or Navy, on White; 'Kimono', an oriental panel pattern in Pink, Grey, Green, and Blue; 'Tickertape', bright stripes in Red, Green, Black, Blue, and Yellow, on White; and 'Geisha', a cascade of flowers tumbling into a magnolia-filled pool, in Mulberry, Brown, and Blue. Plain colours include nine deep-dyed shades and eight pastels. Designs for children are ever-popular 'Betsey Clark' characters, and 'Country Lane', in shades of Green, depicting the antics of rabbits, weasels, badgers, etc.
Most designs come as quilt covers and sheets in three sizes, pillowcases, and ready-made curtains, some are available as comforters and quilted bedspreads. Uniquely, 1m (39³/₈in) squares of 'Gingham', 'Geisha' and 'Romany' come complete with sewing instructions, for making a lampshade, table cloths or place mats, etc, in the HOME SEW PACK. *P:* single sheet £7.75 pastel, £10.50 deep-dyed, £10.50 printed; single quilt cover £16; pair curtains from £20.

Items made from Dorma's HOME SEW PACK in 'Romany' by MARY QUANT

ELLARD SLIDING DOOR GEARS LTD
Tough SLIDING INDUSTRIAL CURTAINS for High Tech fans. Made from rot- and waterproof heavy 100% cotton duck, in White, Green, or Blue, they're ideal for draughtproofing and probably the most durable curtains available. Eyeletted at the top for hanging, and at the sides for lacing if necessary, they have weight pockets along the bottom edge. Running gear—tubular galvanized steel tracks, and steel supports with adjustable cord suspenders that hang the curtain just clear of the floor—can enclose almost any shape or space. Similar curtains are available in fire-resistant cotton duck. *M:* w up to 10ft (305cm) unsupported, to order. *P:* upon application.

KAFFE FASSETT
Beautiful, made-to-order needlepointing by an artist extraordinaire who also paints murals. The illustration shows a rather ordinary

basketweave chair transformed to grace the most chic of sitting rooms. Complex but subtle colour combinations make Kaffe Fassett's work instantly recognizable. *P:* upon application. See also 'Wall Coverings'.

GLORAFILIA
Clever, beautifully prepared needlepoint wall decoration or cushion cover kits with designs by Jennifer Berman and Carole Lazarus. Motifs include flowers, seashells, butterflies, geometrics, townscapes, and birds of paradise. Many designs are linked by theme or colour, to create interesting groupings on a sofa or wall. Circular and octagonal shapes as well as the usual square are also available. Canvases are hand-screenprinted, or painted in oil, to make it easier to stitch accurately. Kits come complete with plaits of wool, needles, Swiss canvas and instructions. Glorafilia will undertake special commissions, and change colours on hand-painted canvases to suit the customer's own colour scheme, or adapt clients' designs. *M:* 10×10–14×14in (25.5×25.5–35.5× 35.5cm). *P:* screenprinted £11–£25, handpainted £13–£37.

LUCY FABRICS
Original screenprinting on quilts and cushions for cat-crazy people. Quilts, made from strong pre-shrunk calico filled with three layers of Dacron, have Blue, Pink, Brown, or Gold cats on a Cream background. Matching, fully lined quilted cushion covers are available. Both can be handwashed or dry cleaned. Lucy Fabrics also make cat-shaped cushions in silk. *M:*

cushion covers 16×16, 18×18in (40.5×40.5, 46×46cm), quilts three sizes single to kingsize, plus cot size. *P:* quilts £45–£70, cot quilt £20, cushion covers £7.50, 'cat' cushions £9–£11.

Selection of Lucy Fabrics' cushions

MAISON DESIGNS

Bright and beautiful BANANA and TURKISH DELIGHT bedlinen in easy-care 50% polyester/50% cotton. BANANA sheets, duvet

Maison Designs' TURKISH DELIGHT (top), BANANA (bottom)

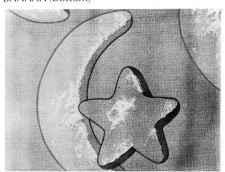

covers and pillowcases have White and Pale green bananas, with Yellow skins, on an Emerald green background. TURKISH DELIGHT has Pink moons and Yellow stars on Bright Blue. *P:* double duvet cover £23, pair pillowcases £6.50.

MIRACLES LTD

Fantastic made-to-order bedspreads and cushions from this company's flock of miracle workers. Appliqué, airbrushing and/or quilting are used to execute favourite motifs like clouds, sunbursts, birds of paradise, plum trees, landscapes and seascapes. *P:* upon application.

WORKSHOP NO. 8

Exquisite patchwork coverlets and cushion covers in pure Haborai silk, made by a three-woman team in Manchester—proof that small is beautiful. Designs are geometric, in a lovely array of shades that can be combined to create a zappy modern effect or a softly pastel feeling. Coverlets and cushion covers are backed with matching cotton to prevent slipping. Workshop No. 8 will make up bedspreads, chair covers, etc, in customers' own fabrics. *M:* coverlets three sizes, single to kingsize, plus cot size, cushion covers 15×15, 20×20in (38×38, 51×51cm). *P:* coverlets £95–£140, cushion covers £7.50–£8.50.

Selection of Workshop No. 8's designs

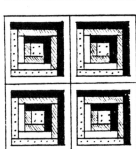
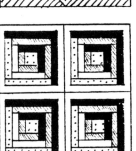
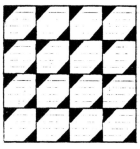
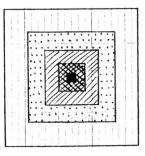

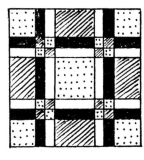
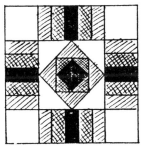
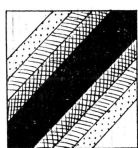
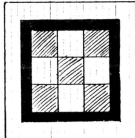

INTRODUCTION

This section is devoted to people and firms who supply individualistic, or unique, furniture. Although pieces are more expensive than their mass-produced counterparts, you don't have to be a millionaire to afford one. Prices compare favourably with similar items at the top end of the market.

Designers/Craftspeople work with specific materials, to their own designs. Although they don't normally make to order, they will design and produce a piece for a specific purpose, and to fit a particular space; and may be willing to adapt their own designs, for example by using a wood requested by the customer.

Made-to-order Furniture deals with people and firms who work in their own medium – bamboo, lacquer, polyurethane, etc – but follow clients' specifications as to size, colour, design, covering and/or finish.

Firms in *Made-to-order Upholstery* supply sofas, chairs, seating units, etc, in the size, and covering, requested by the client.

*Prices vary according to complexity of design, and material used.

Fred Baier's boardroom table

DESIGNERS/CRAFTSPEOPLE

FRED BAIER
Marvellous furniture, somewhere between High Tech and New Wave. This stunning boardroom table, its top veneered in natural sycamore with radial accents stained Bright red, is held rigid by tension wires. Fred Baier also accepts less prestigious commissions. *P:* £3,500.

CABOCHON FURNITURE LTD
Good-looking, functional pieces. The standard range includes mirrors, desks, cabinets, and tables of all sizes. All furniture can be finished in stippled or rag-rolled paint work, or plastic laminates. *P:* upon application.

ASHLEY CARTWRIGHT
Beautifully made furniture, mainly in English hardwoods. This English elm dresser was designed for a client who wanted to combine a display area for a modern ceramic collection with storage space for everyday plates, cutlery, etc. *P:* £1,200.

MARTIN GRIERSON
Distinctive modern furniture made with beautiful natural woods and rich veneers. The dining group illustrated is in oak and Indian laurel. *P:* upon application.

RICHARD HEATLY
Marvellous simple pieces in English and imported hardwoods, predominantly yew, sycamore, cherry and walnut. This yew cabinet with figured cedar internal panelling and concealed lighting, was designed to display carved ivory miniatures from Japan. *P:* upon application.

Martin Grierson's dining suite (left)

PETER MILNE

Utterly uncluttered solid wood furniture for domestic and commercial use. Past commissions undertaken by this designer include music stands, four-posters, jewellery boxes and a boardroom table. The hexagonal six-seater comes in solid brown oak. *P:* £800.

ALAN PETERS

Uncompromisingly modern pieces that often combine metal with fine woods – the illustration shows a collector's cabinet in ebony and satinized aluminium. Limited edition repeats of some of his most highly regarded creations are available – a comparatively recent innovation. *P:* upon application.

PRICES AND INFORMATION WERE CORRECT AT THE TIME OF GOING TO PRESS

MICHAEL SEVERN

Classically sleek acrylic pieces – perfect for uncluttered environments. This clever base and top can be a dining or occasional table depending on how the base is placed. Tough, and difficult to work with, acrylic is a marvellously versatile medium – Michael Severn's creations include a 'traditional' whatnot shelf. Because he uses an oil-based product, his furniture is fairly expensive – but acrylic's 'clean' appeal makes it worth the price. *P:* upon application.

Jane Thomas' cabinet

JANE THOMAS

Delightful, small cabinet from a talented, versatile designer. Originally in ebonized sycamore, and one of a pair designed to house precious jewellery, silver, etc, it comes in a variety of woods including mahogany, padouk and sycamore. *P:* from £400.

MADE-TO-ORDER FURNITURE

ACB DESIGN CONSULTANCY

Exclusive perspex furniture in a choice of 52 colours; also pieces made from clients' designs. The lovely high gloss of this luxury material is protected with glass tops where necessary. The low Black bookcase featured in a Victoria & Albert Museum exhibition. *P:* £250.

BROWNS OF WEST WYCOMBE

High-quality pieces, hand-made by a helpful firm that specializes in chairs. Browns will also restore period furniture. *P:* upon application.

CARVED PINE MANTELPIECES LTD

PINE RANGE shelving units, bookcases, bureaux and wardrobes. In selected Russian pine, they complement panelling and mantels. *P:* upon application. See also *Mantels & Surrounds* ('Fireplaces').

COALBROOK HOUSE (FURNISHING CONTRACTS) LTD

Complete bedroom furnishing service. This specialist firm designs, installs – and builds – the highest quality furniture and fittings, especially four-poster and other period bedsteads; also restoration work. *P:* upon application. See overleaf for illustration.

Coalbrook House's bedroom furniture

ELIZABETH EATON LTD
Furniture finished to clients' specifications. This interior decorator will spatter, stripe, lacquer, or swirl paint on, any piece in her collection (pine or metal, modern or antique), in any colour. The illustration shows a selection of real charmers from her hand-painted range. *P:* upon application.

GRAFTON INTERIORS
OBLIQUE coffee tables with marble insert tops. They can be made in any shape, any combination of metals – and with any built-in electronic gadget/s you feel you need. *P:* upon application.

LAURENT MARCEL
All kinds of beautiful pieces, from small boxes to four-poster beds. This French craftsman works exclusively in Chinese bamboo – sturdier (and more expensive) than cane. The seven-panel screen illustrated is edged with Black lacquered bamboo. *P:* £700. See overleaf for illustration.

OAKENCRAFT
Nicely crafted reproductions in solid oak, waxed to give a mellow patina. Drawer joints are dovetailed, others oak-pegged. Oakencraft will make almost anything, from farmhouse tables with matching dressers to long-case clocks and corner cupboards. *P:* tables from £350, dressers from £400, long-case clocks from £450, corner cupboards from £275.

Selection from Elizabeth Eaton's painted furniture

Oakencraft's cupboard

Stanwater Designs' blanket box

Selection from Stuart Interiors

STANWATER DESIGNS LTD
Beds, mirrors, chests of drawers, blanket boxes, etc, in re-cycled pine, specially hand-painted by former textile designer Jeanette Garsten. *P:* upon application.

PRICES AND INFORMATION WERE CORRECT AT THE TIME OF GOING TO PRESS

Laurent Marcel's screen in Chinese bamboo with mirror panels

Swan Galleries' bookcase

WHITNEY BURN LTD
Absolutely anything is possible from these modern lacquer-masters, who will advise on design or work to order. A polyester lacquer, the shiniest and most practical available, is applied to a wooden base. *P:* upon application.

ARNOLD ZELTER
Music stands and cabinets by a cabinet maker who specializes in furniture for music-making; also long-case clock cases (with movements by Sinclair Harding).
Arnold Zelter works mainly in oak, mahogany, rosewood and walnut, and will incorporate carving and turning.*P:* music stands £86–£480 as illustrated.

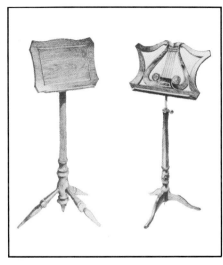

STUART INTERIORS
Reproduction Elizabethan and Jacobean furniture and interior woodwork, with the emphasis on authenticity and traditional craftsmanship. These Somerset-based specialists use mainly English oak or yew with accents in holly, walnut and various fruit woods. The illustration shows some made-to-order beauties: panelling, staircase, oak dining table, and Gothic Windsor chair in yew. *P:* upon application. See previous page for illustration.

SWAN GALLERIES
Bookcases, display cases, corner cabinets, upholstery – even fireplaces and panelling in Siberian pine; elm also available. Pieces can be supplied with flat or pediment tops, glass or wooden shelves, doors or drawers. *P:* upon application. See also 'Architectural Ornaments', 'Fireplaces'.

PRICES AND INFORMATION WERE CORRECT AT THE TIME OF GOING TO PRESS

MADE-TO-ORDER UPHOLSTERY

PERCY BASS LTD
Lovely, traditional sofas as well as custom-made seating – their speciality. Percy Bass will also make curtains, bedspreads, Roman and festoon blinds, swags and tails, and upholstered headboards – even undertake a complete redecoration scheme.

COLOURFLAIR FURNITURE
Nice selection of footstools, chairs, and two- and three-seater sofas in 11 styles including some with long, lean, modern lines. *P:* armchairs from £240, excluding fabric.

CORONFIELD LTD
Sofas and chairs, covered in the client's choice of fabric, made to a submitted design; also 14 standard styles. Other services from this multi-faceted company include making pelmets and curtains, and hanging fabric on walls. *P:* sofa from £300.

PETER DUDGEON LTD
Hand-made seating in 30 styles. Coverings range from average-priced fabrics to exclusive imports. This interior decorator also makes furniture to order, and will re-upholster and do repairs. *P:* sofa from £350.

CHARLES HAMMOND LTD
Ten sofas and nine chairs, covered in any of Charles Hammond's stunning fabrics or the customer's own material. Other soft furnishings to order.

L M KINGCOME LTD
Wide range of hand-made seating. The customer specifies the overall length, and the number of cushions and their filling. Depth, height and the angle of the back can be varied at no extra cost, to fit awkward spaces. Chairs and two- and three-seater sofas are available, covered in any fabric, or ready for loose covers. Most pieces can also be upholstered in suede or leather. Armwraps, extra cushions, braiding, etc, upon request. *P:* two-seater from £300.

Selection of sofas and chairs from Colourflair

GORDON LINDSAY PARTNERSHIP LTD
Seven classical and contemporary made-to-measure sofas and chairs with kiln-dried beech frames; also available in standard sizes. Dacron-wrapped seat cushions are flameproof foam; feathers cost extra. Most styles come as chairs and two- and three-seater sofas,

covered in any of the company's extensive range of fabrics, or your own. Gordon Lindsay will also make matching curtains and/or blinds. *M:* to order. *P:* upon application.

SWAN GALLERIES
Hand-built seating, traditionally made with hair, hessian, cotton, felt, coil springs, feather cushions and beech frames, covered in flameproof calico or fully upholstered in the client's choice of fabric. Nine sofas, with matching pouffes and chairs, are available. *P:* chairs from £320, sofas from £450, both in calico.

TULLEY'S (CHELSEA) LTD
Sofas, chairs and pouffes in ten basic styles. Made to last a lifetime with dowel-secured hardwood frames, and cushions filled with curled feathers, they can be supplied in unbleached calico, with loose covers, or upholstered in one of Tulley's exclusive fabrics. *P:* two-seater sofa £220–£350 in calico.

Selections from Gordon Lindsay (above), Charles Hammond (below)

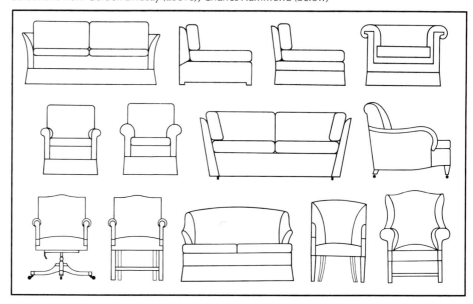

INTRODUCTION

A staircase may not be decoration, but it can be a strikingly decorative element. This section concentrates on examples that will take you in style from one level to another; and includes components like hand-rails, treads and spindles.

ACROW SCULPTURED TUBING LTD

Enormous range of sculptured metal tubing. It's suitable for everything from decorative security bars to lamp bases and, of course, strikingly elegant balusters. Some variations are illustrated—but anything is possible. *P:* upon application.

ALBION DESIGN

Spiral staircase, replica of an ornate Victorian original. Treads and balusters are made of cast

iron, the central post is steel, and the hand-rail wrought iron. It's delivered ready to assemble, primed for undercoating. Non-standard floor to floor heights can be supplied. Gratings, tie-bar plates, balusters, railings and other architectural ironwork also available, to order. *P:* £158 per tread including three balusters.

BIRMINGHAM GUILD LTD

Modern spiral staircases with central support in steel, treads in iroko hardwood, from an old-established manufacturer. Stairs can also be individually designed to suit clients' specifications. *P:* upon application.

CLASSIC GARDEN FURNITURE LTD

Another very attractive Victorian cast-iron ornamental staircase. 'C25' is supplied, complete, to any height; spirals are clockwise or anti-clockwise. *M:* rise 8in (20.5cm), diam 4in (10cm), 6in (15cm). *P:* diam 4in £35 per riser, diam 6in £45 per riser.

CONSCULPT LTD

Spiral staircases, each step moulded in concrete around a central steel tube. Described as 'functional sculpture' the powerful and im-

pressive designs are reminiscent of stone and granite stairs found in ancient castles and manor houses. Finishes include exposed granite stonework, and polished stone giving a terrazzo effect. There is also a modern smooth finish in Grey and White, with or without carpet recesses. All staircases are available in kit form, or Conscult will handle the installation. *P:* £1,000 as illustrated.

CORNISH STAIRWAYS LTD

Spiral stairway system of pre-cast reinforced concrete treads, sleeved around a central steel

core to execute a graceful sweep from floor to ceiling. A dynamic design focus, it's available with a choice of aluminium or wrought-iron balustrades in a wide range of designs and colours. Straight flights also available. *P: treads in White/Grey £33 each, landings (100×100cm/39³/₈×39³/₈in) £90, riser bars £3 each, satin anodized aluminium balustrade £24 per tread.*

JAY CURZONS

Traditional spiral staircases, based on Georgian and Victorian cast-iron originals. Although traditional foundry methods and skills are used, they're cast in aluminium—a unique combination. A replacement service for architectural castings such as railing heads and balustrade panels is available; also many original patterns for brackets, supports and signs. Staircases are supplied with assembly instructions. *P: £550 as illustrated.*

MAGNET SOUTHERNS

Modern metal and hardwood spiral staircase, pre-packed and ready to collect in kit form. Also standard and open tread stairs, and a

From top: Magnet Southerns' 'Mediterranean', 'Traditional', 'Regal', Colonial' spindles

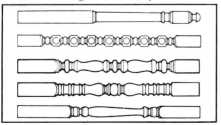

range of traditional turned spindles and rails. Sanded, clear timber spindles come in 'Mediterranean', 'Traditional', 'Colonial', and 'Regal' designs, complemented by a classic hand-rail, bottom rail and bullnose step. Staircases can also be made to order. *P: 12 treads, 13 risers, w 2ft 10in (86.5cm) £125.*

From top: Magnet Southerns' special, standard and open tread stairs

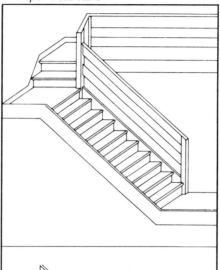

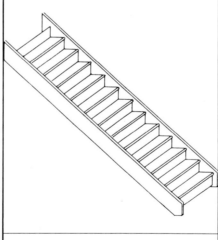

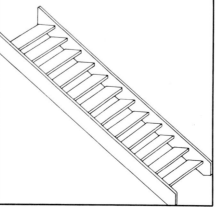

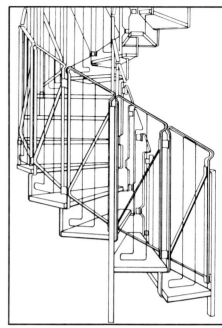

Magnet Southerns' metal spiral staircase

JACK MARSHALL & SUE WIGFIELD

Cast-iron antique and reproduction spiral staircases (*M:* antique w 3–6ft/91.5–183cm, reproduction w 3½, 4, 4½ft/107, 122, 137cm, *P:* £250, £500).

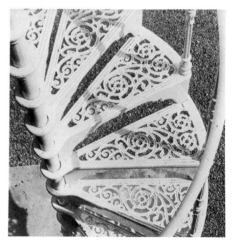

W H NEWSON

Standard staircase with open treads or risers, plus a multitude of accessories. They include newel posts, hand-rails, bottom rails, and four spindles: 'Mediterranean', 'Colonial', Traditional', and 'Regal'. All are made from kiln-dried hemlock, ready to be painted, polished or stained. Larger complementary spindles up to 5ft (152.5cm) high can be used as room dividers. *M: spindle h 1–5ft (30.5–152.5cm). P: £1.30–£6.90. See overleaf for illustration.*

Newson's standard staircase with 'Traditional' spindles

RENZLAND & CO

Simple but elegant spiral staircase, part of a large selection of wrought-iron furniture and accessories. It's shown at its most unadorned, but Renzland will twist and scroll hot metal to clients' specifications. *P:* upon application.

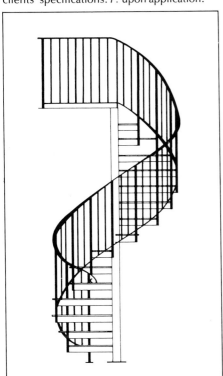

SPIRAL STAIRCASE SYSTEMS

Wide range of spiral staircases including a modern one in pine plywood and Black metal; an ornate antique stair with replica Victorian balusters; and the contemporary DS8, useful if space is at a premium, in ash and ash veneer. Very special staircases in chrome, perspex and stainless steel can be made to order. The company provides a comprehensive service covering initial design work, preparation of working drawings, manufacture, delivery and installation. *P:* upon application.

STUART INTERIORS

Specially designed staircase with newel posts, finials and bosses (and plain, moulded or carved stringers), set off by turned baluster supports under a finely moulded hand-rail. It's just one of many fine products from a specialist firm that prides itself on the craftsmanship and authenticity of its work. Staircases are normally built in the Stuart workshop from solid oak and reassembled for installation. Matching panelling. *P:* upon application.

Spiral Staircase Systems' staircase with replica Victorian balusters (right); Stuart Interiors' oak reproduction staircase (below)

INTRODUCTION

'A place for everything, and everything in its place' need not be an unattainable ideal. A wide choice of storage solutions is available, from a simple pine chest of drawers to a complete wall of mahogany-veneered splendour, designed to house rare books or a collection of netsuke.

Materials include woods, chipboard, cane and wire, and are the most important consideration next to function. A beautifully veneered or lacquered drinks cabinet, for example, is marvellous for anyone who never spills a drink; non-porous plastic laminates are sensible choices for pieces that will be heavily used; glass is easily cleaned and doesn't stain. In addition to modular wall systems and traditional chests, bookcases, dressers and sideboards, this section also describes a host of storage ideas, including a mobile trolley, a bar-refrigerator, and a telescopic wardrobe rail. See also 'Shelving', 'Special Furniture'.

ARAM DESIGNS LTD
Simple SILVER 825 modular units for drawers, cabinets and wardrobes, finished to order in walnut, mahogany, or natural or Black-stained ash. *M:* module as illustrated w 60 × h 146 × d 50cm (23⁵/8 × 57³/8 × 19⁵/8in). *P:* £472–645.

ASKO FINNTERNATIONAL LTD
Infinitely variable BOREAL system based on slatted wall panels. Hanging or free-standing units include shelves, cabinets, drawers, a wardrobe and even a table which can be attached to the panels with metal hooks, at any level. All wooden parts are in natural, Honey brown, Cherry brown, Pale brown or Brown stained birch. Panels are recessed to allow for skirting boards, and easily fixed to the wall with concealed screws. *M:* wall units w 55, 85 × h 55, 205cm (21⁵/8, 33½ × 21⁵/8, 80¾in); tall wall panels as illustrated, w 55, 85 × h 205cm (21⁵/8, 33½ × 80in); glass door cabinet w 85 × d 43 × h 104cm (33½ × 16⁷/8 × 41in). *P:* wall panel £90, glass door cabinet w 85cm £140.

Asko's BOREAL

Modern craftsmanship at its best. Not inexpensive, but very handsome, MIKADO consists of a floor cabinet, chests of drawers, secretaire/bar unit, two cabinets with glass doors, an open shelf, and two sets of shelves. It comes in stained or lacquered birch with highly figured front graining. *M:* floor cabinet w 100 × h 67 × d 44cm (39³/8 × 26³/8 × 17³/8in). *P:* £130.

Asko's MIKADO

ATRIUM
TECTA furniture for devotees of De Stijl, illustrated in colour on page 225. The Mondrian-inspired wardrobe, finished in Red, Yellow, Navy and Cream high-polished lacquer, with Black outlines, is signed with its number and year of production. The storage unit, from a 1923 Per Keller original now in the Schlop Museum, Weimar, can be fitted as a cradle (for a most sophisticated child). Also finished in high-polished lacquer, it comes in Yellow and Red with a White interior and rests on Blue circles. *M:* wardrobe w 83 × h 162 × d 36cm (32⁵/8 × 64 × 51in), unit w 98 × diam 91cm (38½ × 36in). *P:* £1,430, £445.

AUSTINSUITE FURNITURE
Fully assembled DUET units in an unusual, and warm, combination of natural cane and teak-stained wood veneer, with recessed lighting on display shelving. Handles are solid wood. Available as a twin unit which includes illuminated display area, with sliding glass doors, cabinet with drop-down flap, two deep

drawers, and removable shelving; and a single unit (right) that includes a cabinet with drop-down flap, two deep drawers and removable shelving. All units delivered fully assembled and mounted on castors. *M:* single unit w 154 × h 166 × d 43cm (60⁵/8 × 65³/8 × 16⁷/8in). *P:* £110, £575.

Austinsuite's DUET

BAKER, KNAPP & TUBBS
'7736', an ornate Louis XV-style chest in finest white oak. The deep relief carving is characteristic of 18th-century French rural furniture. *M:* w 42 × h 33 × d 18in (106.5 × 84 ×46cm). *P:* £550.

'7737', a fine mahogany Chippendale-style *bombé* chest in the kettle shape, with ball and claw feet. Fittings are solid brass. *M:* w 39 × h 32 × d 20½in (99 × 81.5 × 52cm). *P:* £635.

Other fine reproduction chests include '7731', a bow-fronted beauty in yew inlaid with ebony, with a cross-grained edge and banded top. It has beaded drawers and a pull-out slide. French-style '7742', an oak armoirè, has ornate relief carving on the doors. Authentic in every external detail, its interior is fitted as a home bar with mirrored back, lighted glass shelves and a pull-out mixing shelf. The bottom section contains a wine rack and two shelves. *M:* w 60 × h 85½ × d 17in (152.5 × 217.5 × 43.5cm). *P:* £2,160.

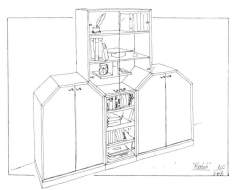

Banks Heeley's KASBAH (above), PASTOE (below)

Baker, Knapp & Tubbs' '7742'

BANKS HEELEY
Stylish KASBAH lacquer units with angled tops. Available in two heights and two widths, in Black, White and/or Burgundy, this extremely well-designed range consists of six shelf-units, six cabinets, drawers and plinths; additional glass shelves can be supplied. *M:* central base unit w 42 × h 84 × d 42cm (16½ × 33 × 16½in). *P:* £45.
Simple but stunning PASTOE units with slick sliding panels that close from top to bottom, or rest in any position. In natural wood with White panels, or finished in White, Black, Grey, Blue or Pink lacquer, they can be used separately or grouped as a wall system. *M:* 'KR137' roll-top cabinet (closed) w 74 × h 135 × d 37cm (29¹/₈ × 53¹/₈ × 19⁵/₈in). *P:* £240.

BLC's STYLE A

BLC TRADITIONAL COUNTRY FURNITURE LTD
Nicely proportioned STYLE A dresser (left, below) from a range of country-style kitchen furniture. Three sizes are available, in matured pine or seasoned beech. *M:* w 72 × h 78, 84 × 90, 96 × 102in (183 × 198, 213 × 228.5, 243.5 × 258.5cm), all × d 24in (61cm). *P:* £325–375.

CLASSIC GARDEN FURNITURE LTD
'C20' Waiting Dog umbrella stand in White, Black or polished cast iron. *M:* w 45 × h 73cm (17¾ × 28¾in). *P:* £35. Three other styles are available, with a Roman cherub, flowery details, or entwined branches.

The 'C67' hatstand, also with branch-like arms, is a Coalbrookdale classic from these specialists in Victorian cast-iron reproductions. In Black only.

CONTINENTAL FURNISHERS
Well-made, uncluttered PINE DECOR in a combination of lacquer-coated solid Scandinavian pine and 2cm (¾in) pine veneer. A wall system that builds into floor-standing units, its 12 components include side panels, shelves, doors, drawers, bar flap and television platform. *M:* side panels h 105, 180, 210cm (41³/₈, 70⁷/₈, 82¾in), shelves, doors w 40, 80cm (15¾, 31½in); two-drawer unit w 40 × h 35 × d 35cm (15¾ × 13¾ × 13¾in). *P:* two drawers £40. See overleaf for illustration.

PRICES AND INFORMATION WERE CORRECT AT THE TIME OF GOING TO PRESS

Continental Furnisher's PINE DECOR

CUBESTORE LTD
Inexpensive storage based on a 16in (40.5cm) cube. CUBEBOX units can be used alone, or stacked together and joined by special plugs to build up to multiples of the basic module. The range includes vertical and horizontal partitions, two and three-drawer units, cupboards, wardrobes with sliding glass doors, and plinths for worktops. All come in 12mm (½in) chipboard faced with White melamine; Bitter chocolate door and drawer fronts cost 10% extra. *M:* six-drawer unit w 16 × h 32 × d 16in (40.5 × 81 × 40.5cm). *P:* £30.

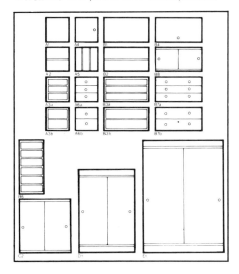

DALVERA
Sleek MALAYSIA sideboard in natural cane with woven cane panels. It also comes in stripped cane, or oak or walnut finish. *M:* base w 181 × h 75 × d 46cm (71¼ × 29½ × 18in), top w 181 × h 137 × d 36cm (71¼ × 53⅞ × 14⅛in). *P:* £500. Matching bedroom and dining-room furniture is available; base and top can be bought separately. See also *Bedroom Furniture* ('Bedrooms').

PRICES AND INFORMATION WERE CORRECT AT THE TIME OF GOING TO PRESS

Dalvera's MALAYSIA

DE LA PLAIN INTERIORS LTD
Mobile 'Carello' bar on castors. The base, in Black or White marble, supports a slick top in White, Black, Beige or Red polyester-lacquered wood. *M:* w 28 × h 19¼ × d 28in (72 × 49 × 72cm). *P:* £245.

MARTIN J DODGE
'H88' Adam-style commode in finest figured mahogany inlaid with exotic woods. Like all this firm's furniture, it's beautifully made. *M:* w 42 × h 38 × d 19in (106.5 × 96.5 × 48.5cm). *P:* £1,750.
Beautifully crafted serpentine-front 'H8' comes in finest solid mahogany, with a brush slide. *M:* w 33 × h 36 × d 16in (84 × 91.5 × 40.5cm). *P:* £1,100. Other pieces from this specialist firm include a simple but stunning sideboard, also with a serpentine front, in solid mahogany with rosewood, satinwood or yew inlaid banding, and a breakfront sideboard. A handsome solid mahogany desk with gold-tooled Green leather top has eight drawers including one for files.

Martin J Dodge's 'H88' (above), 'H8' (below)

ELFA WIRE PRODUCTS (UK) LTD
Modular rack and basket SELF-ASSEMBLY system based on combinations of three units and three basket sizes. Options include trays, a bi-level rack, castors, basket liners, name plates, separate runners for fitting out existing cupboards and hanging rail brackets to hang clothes between storage stacks. Frames are Dark brown, baskets Beige. *M:* modules as illustrated w 18, 21 × h 54 × d 18, 21cm (7⅛, 8¼ × 21¼ × 7⅛, 8¼in). *P:* £25 as illustrated.

FAVORITE INTERIOR

Imposing made-to-measure wardrobe in lacquered solid wood. One of Favorite's plainest pieces — the company's famous for its exquisitely fancy furniture — it can also be painted or left natural. *M:* as illustrated w 126 × h 102 × d 25½in (320 × 259 × 65cm). *P:* £4,500.

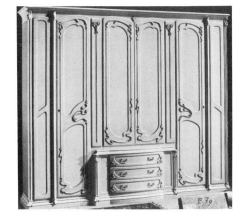

G C FURNISHINGS LTD

'AS 156/25', part of the huge INTERFUNCTION range of drawers, shelves and cupboards. Beautiful, functional, and designed to take the hard knocks of office life, it would work equally well in a domestic setting. Finished in Grey-White or textured 'graphite' laminate, it's edged with a rounded aluminium section rim. *M:* w 156 × h 135 × d 45cm (61³⁄₈ × 53¹⁄₈ × 17³⁄₄in). *P:* Grey-white £325.

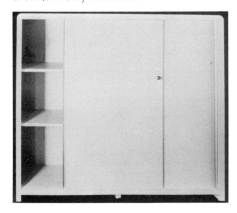

GEORGIAN FURNISHING CO

Imposing Chippendale-style piece with a double domed top, painted side panels. 'L14' comes in Red, Brown or Black lacquer, hand-painted with Gold Oriental motifs. *M:* w 38 × h 80 × d 22in (96.5 × 203.5 × 56cm). *P:* £900. 'A37' is a fine little cabinet. Quartered bamboo veneer, on a solid plywood carcase, gives an unusually interesting texture. Hinges and pulls are solid brass. *M:* w 24 × h 36 × d 18in (61 × 91.5 × 46cm). *P:* £340. See overleaf for illustration.

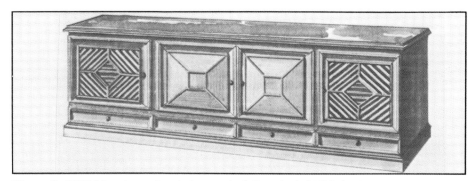

Giorgetti's '6115' (above), see description overleaf; Georgian's 'L14' (below)

Georgian's 'A37'

GIORGETTI

'6115', a perfectly crafted sideboard base made from solid hand-worked wood which can be lacquered or polished. *M:* w 205 × h 78.5 × d 50cm (80¾ × 31 × 19⅝in). *P:* £1,375. A three-door version is available. See overleaf for illustration.

GRAFTON INTERIORS

Chic, but very expensive, MARINARA 16-drawer chest in steel, brass and polivar (plasticized mirror). By L'Anglometallarte, it also comes in steel, brass and bamboo or briarwood. *M:* w 80 × h 166 × d 50cm (31½ × 65⅜ × 19⅝in). *P:* £3,200. Smaller versions are available.
A floor-to-ceiling Louis XV-style ensemble is made up of six units in the enormous and exquisite L'PRESTIGE range by Éléments Jacquelin. In mahogany, cherry, or gilded Pastel green or Ivory, it includes pull-down beds, corner cabinets and dining furniture. *M:* as illustrated w 266 × h 220 × d 53cm (104¾ × 86¾ × 20⅞in). *P:* £1,000.

Grafton's L'PRESTIGE

Grafton's MARINARA

Joyce Hardy's CHICKEN COOP dresser

JOYCE HARDY

Unusual CHICKEN COOP dresser, made to order in solid pine from Victorian Neo-Gothic remnants. *M:* w 54 × h 75 × d 22in (137 × 190.5 × 56cm). *P:* £550. More traditional styles are also available. See also *Dining Tables* ('Tables').

M & IJ HARRISON LTD

Classically-styled chests of drawers from a firm that specializes in reproduction pine country furniture. Fittings are brass. *M:* w 39 × h 39 × d 19, 18 × 39 × 18, 18 × 26 × 18in (99 × 99 × 48.5, 46 × 99 × 46, 46 × 66 × 46cm). *P:* £190, £110, £70.

HOUSE OF LAMBETH

Practical, good-looking STORE AWAY boxes in five sizes. Made from natural or varnished laminated birch, they're supplied flat and are easily assembled — just slot them together. *M:* 35, 45, 60cm cubes (13¾, 17¾, 23⅝in), w 90 × h 45 × d 45, w 70 × h 35 × d 35cm (35⅝ × 17¾ × 17¾, 27½ × 13¾ × 13¾in). *P:* cubes £8.20–£18.20, rectangles £9.40, £16.30.

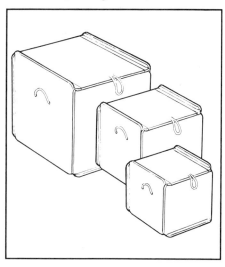

PRICES AND INFORMATION WERE CORRECT AT THE TIME OF GOING TO PRESS

STORAGE

INTERLÜBKE
Exciting STUDIMO wall or free-standing divider system in Cream lacquer, natural or Black-stained ash, or cherrywood or mahogany veneer. Illustrated in natural ash on the cover, in mahogany, in colour, on page 200, it includes cupboards with optional tinted glass fronts, book shelves, fold-down secretaire and fold-away bed. *M:* modules d 36, 60cm (14^1/$_8$, 23^5/$_8$in). *P:* two-drawer unit £54, £2,280 as illustrated.

Other similarly wonderful ranges from this design-conscious German firm are MUTARO faced in lacquer, veneer or fabric, with simple leather strip drawer pulls; stackable MEDIUM PLUS in natural or Black-stained ash, Chinese red, Cream or Grey-white lacquer, and Brazilian mahogany, with slightly dished matching tops with rounded edges, or plain tops in granite or travertine; and ORTUS 33 based on three heights, in Bombay rosewood, cherrywood, and Grey-white, Chocolate brown or Chinese red lacquer.

STORAGE WALLS comes in White laminate-faced wood. Primarily shelving, it also includes a bar unit, fold-out table, etc. *M:* module d 40cm (15^3/$_4$in). *P:* ten-drawer unit £250.

JAYCEE FURNITURE LTD
Solid oak TREVANA units with intricately hand-carved panels. Nine bases and 17 tops are available in three finishes: Old English, Middleton and Antique oak. They include bookshelves, cocktail bars, corner and drawer units, dressers — even wall panelling. *M:* corner unit as illustrated w 71 × h 124 × d 38cm (28 × 48^3/$_4$ × 15in). *P:* upon application.

Interlübke's STORAGE WALLS

Jaycee's TREVANA

LINK 51 LTD
Wall-mounted LINBIN in Blue stove-enamelled steel, fitted with Red, Yellow, Green and/or Beige containers; both in a multitude of sizes. Intended primarily for commercial use, it's perfect for creating order out of chaos in the home. A double-sided version is available; also feet and wheels. Other options include transparent container lids, metal dividers, wire baskets with or without dividers, and metal bulk containers. *M:* rack from w 36 × h 54in (91.5 × 137cm), containers maximum w 10 × h 7 × d 16in (25.5 × 17.5 × 40.5cm). *P:* rack from £40, containers £25 (pack of eight).

WILLIAM L MACLEAN LTD
'I–95', a solid beech buffet cabinet. Part of an enormous range of reproduction Georgian and Regency furniture, it's hand-polished or can be specially coloured for a small sur-

Link's LINBIN

charge. *M:* w 98 × h 89 × d 50cm (38^1/$_2$ × 35 × 19^5/$_8$in). *P:* upon application.

William L Maclean's 'I-95'

MORESECURE LTD
SLIDING DOOR UNIT in Dove grey stove enamel, with six-lever locks. Two heights and various depths are available. *M:* as illustrated w 48 × h 40 × d 18in (122 × 101.5 × 46cm). *P:* £90. See overleaf for illustration.

Moresecure's SLIDING DOOR UNIT

MARTIN NEIL DESIGNS LTD
'MND 80' bar-refrigerator for sitting- or bedrooms, from a firm that specializes in executive furniture. The cabinet, veneered in teak, light oak, American walnut or mahogany, conceals separate bar and refrigeration sections, each with a lock and key. *M:* w 44 × h 31 × d 21in (111.5 × 78.5 × 53.5cm). *P:* £800. A more traditionally styled version has a classical curl mahogany veneer and matching mouldings.

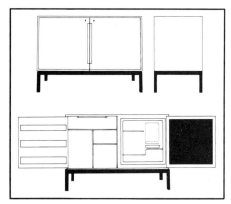

N NORMAN LTD
'Y64', an imposing figured bookcase in warm yew; darker mahogany also available. *M:* w 71 × h 80 × d 18in (180.5 × 203.5 ×46cm). *P:* £1,000.

PANAVISTA LTD
Versatile, space-saving PANAVISTA wardrobe units with made-to-order sliding doors that can even be used to create a small extra room — an en suite bathroom, for example. An ingenious device enables them to adjust to uneven walls or irregular alcoves. Top-hung, so that runners don't get clogged with fluff or grit, the doors are finished in silver or bronze mirror, White satin lacquer, sapele, rosewood or ash veneer protected by satin lacquer, or sapele, teak or Cream vinyl laminate. Internal

Norman's 'Y64'

fittings include rails, drawers, shelves, etc. Units can be self-assembled or installed professionally. *M:* doors up to w 192 × h 98½in (488 × 250.5cm). *P:* White lacquer from £40, ash veneer from £65.

PIRA LTD
Versatile TOTO storage trolley in White, Black, Green, Yellow or Red plastic with an aluminium frame. It can be used as a seat when closed, a worktop, television table, etc, when raised. Options include wire baskets, and a stainless steel tray or chopping board top. *M:* w 40 × h 45–75 × d 40cm (15¾ × 17¾–29½ × 15¾in). *P:* from £48.

PRICES AND INFORMATION WERE CORRECT AT THE TIME OF GOING TO PRESS

Panavista's PANAVISTA

Pira's TOTO

REMPLOY FURNITURE

'A016' three-drawer chest in ash with classically modern Black pulls. *M:* w 43 × h 80 × d 43cm (16^7/$_8$ × 31^1/$_2$ × 16^7/$_8$in). *P:* £97. Two larger sizes are available; also a desk, television cabinet, small cupboard and trolley.

RIPCEL LTD

'SC 01' chest, perfect for a coffee- or side-table, by signpainters who've extended thier craft to chests of drawers, wine holders, clocks, etc. Naval, pastoral, military or hunting

scenes can be adapted to suit customers' needs. *M:* w 33 × h 13^1/$_2$ × d 16^1/$_2$in (84 × 34.5 × 42cm). *P:* £50.

Ripcel's 'SC 01'

T SAVEKER LTD

Space-saving 'V362' telescopic ring stand for clothes, in chromed steel. *M:* diam 60 × h 100–175cm (23^5/$_8$ × 39^3/$_8$–68^7/$_8$in). *P:* £36. Other styles from these shopfitting specialists include bar-top stands, double rings, fixed-arm trouser racks, glider rails, and garment rails (some with castors).

Saveker's 'V362'

SHELFSTORE

Sturdy UNIVERSAL SHELVING SYSTEM in plain or varnished solid Swedish pine. Originally

Shelfstore's UNIVERSAL SHELVING SYSTEM

designed in Sweden in 1948 (for warehouses) it has been continually enlarged and improved to include an extensive selection of components; uprights in eight sizes, shelves in six, writing desks, sloping newspaper supports, drawer units, cupboards, wardrobes, tables, file trays, record holders, strip lights, a single bed, and numerous small accessories. *M:* bunk bed w 100 × l. 200 × h 218cm (39³/₈ × 78³/₄ × 85⁷/₈in). *P:* £235.

SOLENT FURNITURE LTD
Self-assembly SYSTEM IQ in unusual American cherry; doors and drawers can be finished in rattan. Intended mainly for living rooms, it consists of base and corner units, some with glass-doors, open shelves — even a planter. *M:* six-drawer chest w 50 × h 95 × d 42cm (19⁵/₈ × 37³/₈ × 16¹/₂in). *P:* £145.

STAPLES & CO LTD
Marvellously simple yet dramatic DEAUVILLE display cabinet in dark-grained Rio rosewood veneer, by Max Holba. Many matching pieces include chests of drawers, base cabinets, top cabinets with or without glass doors, etc. *M:* base w 85 × h 67.5 × d 47.5cm (33¹/₂ × 26³/₄ × 18⁷/₈in), top w 85 × h 112 × d 25cm (33¹/₂ × 44¹/₈ × 9⁷/₈in). *P:* £430, £460.

Staples' DEAUVILLE (left); Frederick Tibbenham's 'C65' (right)

FREDERICK TIBBENHAM LTD
'C65' corner cabinet, finished in Stuart brown or Warm Jacobean. Like all Tibbenham's oak reproductions it's beautifully made — and cheaper than a comparable antique. *M:* w 27 × h 71 × d 15in (68.5 × 180.5 × 38cm). *P:* £300. A bigger size comes with or without doors; a low version, and a glazed or panelled hanging cabinet are available. Other pieces include wine, gun, television and hi-fi cabinets.
The pleasingly styled 'C35' coffer in oak has carved front panels, is finished in Stuart brown or Warm Jacobean. *M:* w 42 × h 21 × d 18in (106.5 × 53.5 × 46cm). *P:* £220. Two other versions, both more highly carved, are available.

Frederick Tibbenham's 'C35'

VENESTA INTERNATIONAL COMPONENTS LTD
Self-assembly UNIVERSAL LOCKER in chipboard or birch plywood, melamine-faced inside and out to resist humid conditions. The basic unit consists of a single or double locker, the former with a fixed shelf, both with concealed vents. *M:* single w 30 × h 180 × d 58cm (11⁷/₈ × 70⁷/₈ × 22⁷/₈in). *P:* upon application.

WESTRA OFFICE EQUIPMENT LTD
Mobile EUROPA VARIFILE for a study, kitchen — even a dressing room. Frames are finished in Black epoxy, with Grey or Red drawers or trays; tops are White. *M:* w 34¹/₂ × h 28¹/₂ × d 16¹/₂in (87.5 × 72.5 × 42cm). *P:* £105.

Westra's EUROPA VARIFILE

WOOD BROS FURNITURE LTD
Solid oak rug chest-cum-table, hand-carved with authentic Tudor designs. Part of the extensive OLD CHARM range, it comes in light oak, Tudor brown, or special antiqued finish. *M:* w 45 × h 20¹/₂ × d 17¹/₂in (114.5 × 52 × 44.5cm). *P:* £190, antiqued finish £220.

YOUNGER FURNITURE LTD
Spanish-style '403' cabinet in chestnut-veneered ash, from the LA MANCHA range of dining- and living-room furniture. *M:* w 102 × h 60 × d 41cm (40¹/₈ × 23⁵/₈ × 16¹/₈in). *P:* £180. Other storage pieces include a bookcase.

Right: Selection from Atrium's TECTA

INTRODUCTION

Stoves are a special case of combined function and beauty. Efficient, and economical to run, they deserve a place in all decorating schemes, whether for a grand country house kitchen, a suburban home, or one-room city flat.

As fuel and energy conservation becomes more urgent, the size and number of rooms we can afford to heat will diminish further. Certainly, it makes good ecological sense to keep automatic central heating for background warmth and rely on a stove for more immediate heat. The perfect answer to making living rooms comfortable, it will also provide that decorator's delight – a warm, glowing focal point. Similarly, its culinary offshoot, the kitchen range, will not only cook dinner, but also heat space – and even dry the laundry.

Most stoves burn wood or coal, while some can be converted to use peat or even bales of old straw. Kitchen ranges may also be oil or gas fired.

Ideal for anyone who lives in an area where firewood is free, or cheap, stoves and ranges are also perfect for holiday cottages, caravans – even boats – that are only used infrequently. The choice of styles is almost overwhelming, and includes sleek modern beauties from the Scandinavian countries (where stoves are a way of life), marvellously evocative reproductions, and more homely models in cast iron with nostalgic decorations embossed on the doors. (Cast iron, unlike sheet metal, won't warp and doesn't require a firebrick lining.)

This section is divided into *Stoves* which are primarily for heating space, although some are fitted with a hotplate for keeping food or a kettle warm, and sometimes have optional boiler attachments; and *Kitchen Ranges* which are first and foremost for cooking, although they will often heat some domestic water, and sometimes radiators as well.

AGAHEAT APPLIANCES

'Rayburn Open Fire' from a justifiably famous company that makes AGA cookers and numerous heating appliances in addition to RAYBURN fireplaces.

Designed to stand in the chimney recess, away from the wall and surrounding brickwork, it heats by convection as well as radiation. An adjustable plate, concealed in the canopy, restricts the size of the chimney opening to reduce draughts and heat loss. The rate of burning is controlled by a small lever below the decorative front. It will burn solid fuel, oil or gas, as well as heat a domestic water supply.

Left: Agaheat's RAYBURN 'MF'

PRICES AND INFORMATION WERE CORRECT AT THE TIME OF GOING TO PRESS

The grate, with integrated canopy, is loosely based on classical 18th-century designs, and is finished in Matt black with bright metal stars on the canopy and decorative fire front. *M:* w 22³/₈ × h 40 × d 15¹/₄in (57×101.5×38cm) up to 2,250 cubic ft (64 cubic m), w 24³/₈ × h 40 × d 15¹/₄in (62×101.5×38cm) up to 2,500 cubic ft (71 cubic m). *P:* £180–£220.

Agaheat's 'Rayburn Open Fire'

A BELL & CO LTD

One of the first patented wood-burning stoves, designed by inventor Benjamin Franklin in 1741. Made of heavy cast iron, the 'Franklin' has a flat top, two doors with double hinges, and a removable swing-in barbecue grill. The flue pipe can be connected to the back *or* top of the stove. The stove is designed to burn coal slowly, so it may become red hot. *M:* w 38½ × h 32 × d 27½in (98×81.5×70cm). *P:* £280.

CANLIN DEVELOPMENTS

Small, but very graceful, 'Bijou' solid-fuel stove in cast iron. Three splayed feet are an unusual feature, one at the centre back of the

base plate, one each side at the front. Stylized fleurs-de-lis decorate the sides, and the front is embossed with more florals. There are two hotplates for keeping food and drink warm. *M:* w 16 × h 16 × d 12in (40.5×40.5×30.5cm). *P:* £300.

CLASSIC GARDEN FURNITURE LTD

Efficient, decorative and economic EPPING STOVE. Finished in heat-resistant Grey lacquer, it burns solid fuel, wood and kitchen waste. Fitted with an air control to regulate the rate of burning, the cylindrical shape is decorated with an embossed leaf design on the front. *M:* diam 36.5 × h 91.5 (14×36in). *P:* £150.

The CLASSIC COOKER, a functional square number in Black cast iron, has a generously sized oven and a three-piece hotplate. Any solid fuel can be used. *M:* w 56 × h 70.5 × d 37cm (22×27³/₄×14½in). *P:* £130. For real economy there's the ARTIC SLOW COMBUSTION STOVE, cylindrical in shape. Available in four sizes, it will burn any fuel efficiently. *M:* h 51–81cm, diam 23–36.5cm (20–32, 9–14in). *P:* £45–£75.

The ornamental QUEEN STOVE is supplied complete with firebricks, tools, ash tray and stack pipe (*M:* w 46 × h 46 × d 35.5cm (18×18×14in). *P:* £95.

Classic Garden Furniture's QUEEN STOVE

Canlin's 'Bijou' (left)

DALLING ANTIQUES

Gorgeous, antique Continental solid-fuel stoves and cooking ranges. About 60 are usually in stock, including upright stoves in various designs and colours, and some ornate cast-iron models. All stoves are totally refurbished, so they not only look great—they work! *P:* £150–£200.

Two stoves from Dalling Antiques

ESSE, SMITH & WELLSTOOD LTD

Complete range of cooking and heating appliances. The simple, functional ROMESSE comes in six different sizes, and is ideal for workshops and studios. Its body is made of grooved cast-iron sections which fit together without screws or cement. There's no firebrick lining, and the bottom grate is also cast iron. A circular gallery which fits around the outside to support a kettle is an optional extra. The ROMESSE burns anthracite, coke, coal, solid smokeless fuels, wood and refuse sweepings. *M:* h 27½–49½ × diam 14–16in (70–126×35.5–40.5cm). *P:* from £120.
The decorative Victorian/Edwardian 'Dragon' has double glass doors, a decorative scroll design on the feet, corners and top, and is finished in plain iron, Black heat-resisting paint, or Red lacquer-like copper lustre enamel. A cleverly designed, removable scroll conceals a boiling plate for cooking and keeping food hot. Designed for burning

Esse's ROMESSE (left), 'Dragon' (right)

wood, the 'Dragon' can be easily adapted for coal. *M:* w 33½ × h 32 × d 22in (85×81.5×56cm). *P:* from £300. The 'Dolphin', similar to the 'Dragon', has a flat top and smaller base. The 'Queen' solid-fuel stove, finished in Black heat-resisting paint, was originally manufactured in the Victorian era. As with the 'Dragon', an ornamental scroll on the top can be removed to reveal a boiling plate. *M:* w 20 × h 23¾ × d 15in (51×60.5×38cm). *P:* £135. For stove snobs, 'Fame' is a limited edition model from one of the first-ever enclosed fires, manufactured by Smith & Wellstood in c 1870. Finished in Matt black, it has a crested top and is heavily decorated with fleurs-de-lis. *M:* w 30¼ × h 35 × d 20½in (76.5×89×52cm). *P:* wood £430, solid fuel £450. The 'Kali', on the other hand, is incredibly plain. Easy to assemble, it will burn coal, wood or charcoal, is perfect for camping, barbecues, etc—and can be used for cooking in an emergency. It comes in a fine cast iron, in two different sizes. *M:* No 1 w 12¼ × h 7 × d 17in (31×17.5×43cm); No 2 w 12¼ × h 14 × d 17in (31×35.5×43cm). *P:* from £35.

FOSSE WARMAIR LTD

Remarkable DEVILLE FIREPLACE STOVE from France. Designed to give 70% efficiency, compared to 20% from normal fireplaces, it will burn three logs for up to 14 hours. The large firebox also burns other solid fuels. Two styles, both incorporating a grill barbecue, are available: the 'Highlander' with a small overhead hood, and the 'Clansman' with a large hood. *M:* both h 86cm (33⅞in) excluding hood, 'Highlander' 97cm (38⅛in), 'Clansman' 197cm (77½in) with hood. *P:* £570, £630.

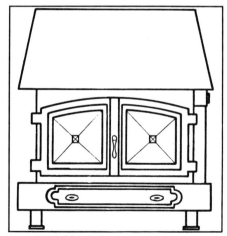

Fosse's 'Highlander'

MARK HAYNES

Great selection of antique stoves and ranges, plus some fireplaces and accessories, many imported from France, Belgium or Holland. All are restored and in guaranteed working order. Installation service available. *P:* from £200.

HOME STOVES LTD

Three reproduction stoves. 'Le Select', cast from an original 1880s design, and the larger 'Le Grand Select', come in solid fuel or slow combustion wood-burning versions. Both are available in Black cast iron (the least expensive), Jade green, Stewpot brown, and French blue (the most expensive). *M:* 'Le Select' w 22 × h 22 × d 14½in (56×56×37cm), 'Le Grand Select' w 27 × h 27 × d 17½in (68.5×68.5×44cm). *P:* £271–£351, £382–£547. 'Poppy', the most decorative model in the Home Stoves range, has panels of Art Nouveau-style glazed tiles at the sides and above and below the door; there's a choice of 'Poppy' tiles in Red and Green on a pale background, and 'Iris' tiles in Blue, Yellow, and Black. Cast-iron relief panels of sensuous, swirling ladies, in Cobalt

Home Stoves' 'Le Select' (above), 'Poppy' (below)

blue, are also available. Designed primarily for solid fuel, the 'Poppy' can also burn wood. *M:* w 19 × h 33 × d 18in (48.5×84×46cm). *P:* £529. All stoves can be fitted with a back boiler for domestic hot water.

Up to 50 antique stoves are usually in stock—all gorgeous, all completely renovated including re-nickelling and new grate systems, windows, and firebricks. Home Stoves will supply spares, and give advice on whether a stove is suitable for a particular room.

INTEROVEN LTD
Large, well-designed range of wood-burners and alternative heating systems. The 'Good-wood Stove', made from ¼in (6mm) thick steel plate, is specially designed for smaller fire-places, and has a built-in boiler. Two large doors accommodate 18in (46cm) logs. *M:* w 21 × h 24 × d 18in (53.5×61×46cm). *P:* £250.

Interoven's 'Goodwood Stove' (above), 'Cosi Comfort Major, Minor' (below)

The very unusual-looking cast-iron 'Cosi Comfort' is delivered in kit form. Quick and easy to assemble, it's economical to run, and will burn coal, coke or peat as well as wood.

Two models, 'Minor' and 'Major', are available. *M:* 'Minor' w 13⅞ × h 45 × d 13¼in (35.5×114.5×33.5cm), 'Major' w 17½ × h 68 × d 25in (44.5×173×63.5cm). *P:* £239, £295.
The most beautifully designed range consists of three 'Rais' stoves, all with unadulterated contemporary good looks. 'No 2' and 'No 6' are square, 'No 3' is round. Designed by Bent Falk of Denmark and manufactured in the UK by Interoven, all have three levels: wood storage (at the base), a wood-burning section, and a slow-cooking plate at the top. *M:* 'No 2' w 62 × h 100 × d 47cm (24⅜×39⅜×18½in), 'No 3' w 70 × h 115 × d 52cm (27½×45¼× 20½in), 'No 6' w 50 × h 100 × d 45cm (19⅝×39⅜×17¾in). *P:* £249–£420.

Interoven's 'Rais No 3'

LE FEU DE BOIS
Wood-burning 'Kamina FL1', with an angled hood, glass-fronted doors and cast-iron body, finished in vitreous enamel, takes approximately 20lb (9kg) of logs; it comes in Olive green, Anthracite grey, Dark brown or Beige, with a low flue adaptor, back boiler and pivoted adjustable grill as optional extras (*M:* w 29 × h 32 × d 15in/73.5 ×81.5 × 38cm, *P:* £285). 'Kaminette' is similar but smaller (*M:* w 28½ × h 29½ × d 14½in/72.5 × 75 × 37cm, *P:* £260). 'Doric', also with an angled hood and glass-fronted doors, is a wood-burning convector in decorated cast iron, with a removable ash pan; colours are Anthracite and Black, and Dark brown (*M:* w 39 × h 31 × d 17½in/98 × 80 × 45cm, *P:* £295).
'Supra', another wood-burning convector, is more box-like, in cast iron with a louvred top (*M:* w 21 × h 13 × d 26in/53.5 × 33 × 66cm, *P:* £155).

Rectangular 'Rosieres 621' burns wood or coal; it has a Brown and Beige exterior, cast-iron body, and sides made from enamelled sheet steel (*M:* w 20 × h 15¾ × d 30¾in/51 × 40 × 78cm, *P:* £190).

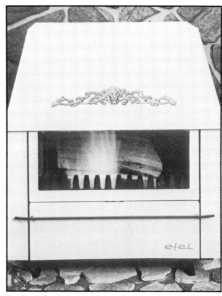

Le Feu de Bois' 'Kamina FL1'

MORLEY MARKETING
Large range of fine, functional New England stoves, imported from the USA, and distributed by Morley. Made by Vermont Castings Inc, in cast iron, they're designed to deliver economical heat for generations. 'Defiant', the largest wood-burner, will take a load of 70lb/31.5kg of dry wood (*M:* w 36 × h 32½ ×d 22½in/91.5×82.5×57cm, *P:* £520). 'Vigilant', so called because it has a thermostat which controls the rate of burning *and* heat intensity, takes a maximum load of 60lb/27kg (*M:* w 28¾ ×h 30½ × d 24¾in/73×77.5×63cm, *P:* £450). 'Resolute', also with thermostatic control, is ideal for smaller homes or cottages; maximum load 50lb/22.5kg (*M:* w 26¼ × h 26 × d 17¼in/ 67×66×43.5cm, *P:* £400). All have optional accessories including bottom and rear heat shields, a warming shelf, trivet, andirons and extendible mitten racks (for drying wet winter gear such as mittens, gloves, socks, etc).
Morley stock a wide range of appliances, including New England, Jøtul, Esse, Sherwood, and 'Le Select' cast-iron stoves; Kamina, Pither Forester, Suddiac, and Falcon convector heaters; Wamsler, Franco-Belge, Kamina Chef, Tirolia, and Tiba cookers with boilers; Wamsler, Franco-Belge, Tasso, Thermorossi, and Gaelwood boilers; and Trianco, Esse, Godwin, and Pither solid-fuel stoves and boilers. Scanfield straw-burning boilers also burn large pieces of wood, tree stumps and wooden pallets. Open grates, dog baskets, fire backs, etc, are displayed in their showroom. See overleaf for illustration.

Morley Marketing's 'Defiant' (top), 'Vigilant' (centre), 'Resolute' (bottom)

NORCEM UK LTD

Enormous, well-designed range of mainly free-standing JØTUL stoves from Norway. Primarily designed for burning wood, most can be converted into coal-burners by adding a special fire basket. Additional fitments for providing cheap domestic hot water are available for some models.

Economical and compact, NO. 1, in Matt black cast iron, is modern in design (*M:* w 27½ × h 34 × d 19½in/70 × 86.5 × 49.5cm, *P:* £315). Three-legged NO. 4, inspired by the Easter Island sculptures, has a flue outlet at the top or back and comes in mottled Dark green or Matt black enamel (*M:* w 24 × h 41 × d 24in/61 × 104.5 × 61cm, *P:* Black £350, Green £390). NO. 7, very simply designed with a conical steel smoke hood that can easily be connected to an ordinary chimney, is in Matt black with a semi-circular spark guard (*M:* w 31½ × h 50 × d 31½in/80 × 127 × 80cm, *P:* £350).

NO. 118 can take logs up to 2ft (61cm) long. Made from cast iron, with typical Norwegian country scenes in relief on the sides, it's finished in Dark green or Matt black enamel. A water-heating kit is available. *M:* w 30½ × h 14 × d 32in (77.5 × 35.5 × 81.5cm). *P:* Black £270,

Norcem's JØTUL NO. 1 (left) and NO. 121 (right)

Green £300. NO. 121 is in cast iron with caribou in relief on the sidewalls. Its combustion system is advanced, with a secondary flow of air channelled around the base. *M:* w 19 × h 32 × d 35½in (48.5 × 81.5 ×90.5cm). *P:* £400.

PETAL AGENCIES LTD

COMBI-STOVES range of convectors, from Denmark. Designed for wood, they can also burn coal; combined with a back boiler, they are highly efficient at heating domestic water and/or radiators. Six models are available, forged in heavy steel with a polished finish and beautifully cast brass handles; coal grates and back boilers are optional extras. Used with slate or marble hearth plates from MARMORINO, they can be placed directly on any floor. No. 1, No. 1K and No. 7 are cylindrical (*M:* h 94–108cm/37–42½in, *P:* £580, £640, £495); No. 3, No. 5 and No. 5K are more box-like (*M:* h 93–106cm/36⅝–41¾in, *P:* £480, £570, £620). Prices include spark arrester, log guard and a 23.5cm (9⅛in) pipe with damper; coal grate £50, back boiler £50.

MARMORINO hearth plates come in a variety of shapes and thicknesses. Slate, an unusual choice, looks wonderful with functional modern stoves. Unlike marble it is comparatively scratch resistant. *M:* various, but standard thickness 1.6–2cm (⅝–¾in). *P:* sq m slate £77, marble £87.

QUEBB STOVES

Five functionally designed British-made, peat or wood-burning stoves with optional water-heating boilers for domestic water supply and/or radiators. The 'Minor' in five sizes is for caravans, boats, etc, with optional boiler, perfect for tight spaces. *M:* w 13½ × h 25 × d 14½in (34.5×63.5×37cm). *P:* £115. The '4.5kW Medium' is suitable for average rooms (10× 10ft/305×305cm to 15×15ft/457.5×457.5cm),

Quebb's '7kW Magnette'

the '7kW Large' for large kitchens, living rooms, studios, workshops. *M:* w 16½ × h 27 × d 27½in (42×68.5×52cm). *P:* £150. The '7kW Magnette', a compact alternative to the 'Large', is available with a double door. *M:* w 16½ × h 27 × w 20½in (42×58.5×52cm). *P:* £150.

SOLAR ECONOMY LTD

Very unusual 'Marlborough' wood-burning stove, designed and manufactured in Britain. Part of the LOGFIRES range, it has a tough steel body with baked-on Jet black finish. *M:* w 24 × h 25 × d 16in (61 × 63.5 × 40.5cm). *P:* £245. Solar Economy also have a comprehensive selection of solar heating panels.

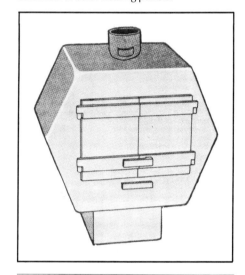

Stove Shop's Swedish pot stove (1890)

STOVE SHOP

Original Danish stoves, many dating from the end of the 19th century. Most are made from cast iron, so are inexpensive to run and highly efficient. All stoves are stripped and renovated, broken or missing parts are replaced and heat-resistant linings renewed. Some are equipped with hotplates while a few larger models also have ovens. Traditional English stoves are also available as well as Swedish and French models. Stove Shop will advise on installation (or do it for you), and will renovate old stoves. *P:* £200–£800.

KITCHEN RANGES

AGAHEAT APPLIANCES

Handsome, sensibly designed oil, gas and solid-fuel kitchen ranges with cast-iron ovens. (Aga may be a household word for the much loved old-fashioned, all-purpose kitchen range, but Agaheat appliances are totally up to date.) Two- and four-oven models are available, in beautiful gleaming colours: Brown, Blue, Green, Cream, Black, Red, and White. Humidity-controlled, the Aga also has a grill pan, and two big hotplates, one fast, one slow. Ovens and hotplates are self cleaning—the cooker remains so hot that spills simply get burned to a very fine carbon dust. What more could you ask? The 'Solid Fuel Aga' burns Sunbrite Doubles, Phurnacite or Anthracite Stove Nuts; the 'Oil Aga' runs on commercial kerosene; and the 'Gas Aga' can be adapted for town, natural or LP gas. With an optional boiler the 'CB' (solid fuel), 'OCB 90' (oil) and 'GCB' (gas) models supply approximately 90 gallons (408.6 litres) of hot water in 24 hours, the 'OCB 135' (oil) up to 135 gallons (612.9 litres). The solid-fuel 'Agamatic' is suitable for a 190-litre (41.8-gallon) indirect cylinder, plus 100 sq ft (9.29 sq m) radiation surface. The gas 'Agamatic G55-65' and oil 'Agamatic P60' can heat a 245-litre (53.8-gallon) indirect cylinder,

Agaheat's 'Agamatic'

plus 275 sq ft (25.5 sq m) radiation surface. *M:* C, CB, OC, OCB, GC, GCB w 38¾ × h 33½ × d 26¾in (98.5×85×68cm). *P:* White £900. Agaheat also distribute RAYBURN cast-iron ranges all with cast-iron ovens. 'Regent' and 'Royal' burn solid fuel, 'OF7' and 'OF22' use oil, and 'G7' and 'G33' are gas fired. 'MF' burns solid fuel and wood. 'MF' can heat 100 sq ft (9.29 sq m) of radiation surface, 'OF22' 120 sq ft (11.1 sq m), and 'G33' 180 sq ft (16.7 sq m), all including pipes. A high output boiler, on all models, heats 100 gallons (454 litres) of water daily. All come in Matt black, White or Cream (with Black top plate) except 'Regent' in White and Cream only. *M:* 'Regent' w 30 × h 37 × d 23in (76×94×58.5cm), others w 33 × h 39¼ × d 22⅝in (84×99.5×57.5cm). *P:* 'Regent' White £500–G33 Cream £1,100. See page 242 for RAYBURN 'MF' in colour.

ESSE, SMITH & WELLSTOOD LTD

Enormous selection of cooking/heating solutions. The 'Doric' solid-fuel cooking range and water heater burns any fuel including wood and peat, and can be supplied with the oven on the left or right. (Perfect for use on yachts, barges and other small craft.) *M:* w 30 × h 30 × d 18in (76×76×46cm). *P:* £350–£500. The larger, double-oven 'Countess' runs on solid fuel. It gives a continuous supply of hot water. *M:* w 33 × h 32 × d 20in (84×81.5×51cm). *P:* £620. Both models have fronts in White vitreous enamel, White acrylic sides, and a top plate in Black vitreous enamel.

'Diamond', the most unusual cooking range, is available with guard rails, pillars and bolt fixings for marine installation. It's finished in plain iron or Black heat-resisting paint. *M:* w

Esse's 'Doric'

24½ × h 22½ × d 19½in (62.5 ×57×49.5cm). *P:* from £260.

Esse's 'Diamond'

FRANCO-BELGE (UK) LTD

Cast-iron stoves. The 'Brule Bois' woodburner, finished in coppertone porcelain, has an exceptionally long firebrick hearth that can take logs 18in (46cm) long and 6in (15cm) in diameter. An adjustable air inlet controls burning rate and heat output. The top hinges up to reveal a ground cast-iron hotplate for slow cooking or plate warming. *M:* w 60 × h 69 × d 35cm (23⅝× 27⅛×13¾in). *P:* £134. The 'Ebene' is similar to the 'Brule Bois' but will burn solid fuel as well as wood. The hotplate lifts so that the stove can be charged through the top. There are Pyrex glass windows on the side. *M:* w 60 × h 72 × d 35cm (23⅝× 28⅜×13¾in). *P:* £208.

MORLEY MARKETING

Wamsler kitchen ranges, manufactured in West Germany (by appointment to the Kings of Bavaria . . .). Morley are sole importers and distributors. The 'Bavarian Double Draught' system, a special feature, incorporates a long flue passage within the range, giving greater efficiency and more consistent oven temperature. The 'K92H Blenheim' has heavy firebrick insulation, a ground steel hotplate, and an insulated cover for heat retention. All metal surfaces are protected against corrosion with vitreous baked enamel, stainless steel or aluminium-coated steel. *M:* as illustrated overleaf w 90 × h 85 × d 60.5cm (35⅜ × 33½ × 23¾in). *P:* £780. The 'Chartwell' is smaller and cheaper (*P:* £560). Both burn most fuels, heat domestic water, and are available in White or Mid-brown enamel finish.

Morley Marketing's 'K92H Blenheim'

NORCEM UK LTD

Three compact JØTUL kitchen ranges from Norway. NO. 380, with two hotplates (8, 11in/ 21.5, 28cm) and a rear chimney, is finished in Matt black and has intricately decorated sides that enhance its old-fashioned appearance (*M:* w 16 × h 27½ × d 32½in/40.5 × 70 × 82.5cm, *P:* £200). NO. 404, made from cast iron, finished in easy-to-clean shiny Black enamel, is equally charming; it has an oven compartment with a baking sheet and pressed steel roasting tin, both enamelled (*M:* w 24½ × h 31½ × d 19in/ 62.5 × 80 × 48.5cm, *P:* £350). Finally, the NO. 602 in cast iron with a Dark green enamel or Matt black finish has a hotplate, and optional decorative top to cover the cooking surface when it isn't in use (*M:* w 12½ × h 25 × d 21½in/31.5 × 63.5 × 54.5cm, *P:* Black £150, Green £170).

Upright, functional NO. 507 will burn coke or wood. In cast iron with a Dark green enamel finish, it has a pony in relief on the front. *M:* w 13 × h 32½ × d 14in (33 × 82.5 × 35.5cm). *P:* £250. NO. 606 is a real piece of nostalgia. In Matt black, it has a chequered top-piece with an arch that enables smoke and hot gases to circulate for extra heat. *M:* h 41 × w 12½ × d 22½in (104.5 × 31.5 × 57cm). *P:* £280. SYSTEM 17, probably the most unusual model, is basically a wood-burning hearth with doors that convert it into a stove. It can be installed in a fireplace, or incorporated in a specially designed chimney breast. *M:* w 29½ × h 36½ × d 17½in (75 × 92.5 × 44.5cm). *P:* £450.

QUEBB STOVES

The '10kW Magnum' for large rooms, halls, and kitchens. It comes with single or double doors, and an optional top-fitting oven. *M:* w 16½× h 27 × d 27½in (42×68.5×70cm). *P:* £170. All in Matt black.

STOVE SHOP

Limited, but beautiful, selection of cooking ranges. Stock varies, but always includes some real gems. The English model illustrated was made in cast iron between 1900 and 1930, with two or sometimes three hotplates. It generally comes in two sizes. *M:* w 72 × h 72 × d 66cm (28³⁄₈×28³⁄₈×26in), w 80 × h 80 × d 72cm (31¹⁄₂×31¹⁄₂×28³⁄₈in). *P:* £200–£250.

More ornate Continental cooking ranges include the fine Flemish cast-iron stove illustrated. Decorated with a profusion of flowery tiles, it's an example of the kind of merchandise available, and has a nickel-plated towel rail and fittings, three hotplates, two ovens, ash box, plate warmer, and draught control. *M:* w 79 × h 90 × d 50cm (31¹⁄₈×35³⁄₈×19⁵⁄₈in). *P:* £700.

Quebb's '10kW Magnum' (right)

Stove Shop's Continental range (below)

INTRODUCTION

There's a table for practically every social occasion: tea for two, bridge for four, dinner for eight – even a children's get-together. And styles range from fine period reproductions to 20th-century classics in chrome and glass and modern marvels in shiny lacquer with gold-plate accents.

Materials, and prices, vary enormously, so before buying a table make sure it will suit your lifestyle. The surface is all-important. Cheaper laminates and lacquers will scratch if heavily used. Glass is beautifully cool looking, fairly tough, and reasonably priced. Solid wood is easier to maintain than dark veneers, which are usually polished and subject to crazing and watermarks (but often less expensive). Softwoods – ash and pine, for example, cost less than hardwoods like mahogany, walnut, and oak.

Before finally buying a table, check that it's the right size for your room. Make an exact copy of the top in paper and lie this on the floor to see how much space it will take up.

If space is at a premium, go for an extendible model, or one that converts from a dining table to a drawing, coffee-, or even billiard table.

This section is divided into *Dining Tables*, normally 29–32in (73.5–81.5cm) high; *Dining Suites* complete with matching storage units and/or chairs; and *Occasional Tables* including coffee-, side, sofa, console and lamp tables.

DINING TABLES

ARAM DESIGNS LTD

Wonderful ALTRA table tops, in any shape or size, in polished plate glass, slate, marble, granite, travertine, plastic laminate, wood veneer, etc. Separate legs (diam 3, 4in/7.5, 10cm) come in polished chromium-plated steel; polished brass or stove-enamelled versions to order. *M:* as illustrated w 36 × l. 72 × h 28½in (91.5 × 182 × 72cm). *P:* £900.

Aram's ALTRA table tops

Gorgeous 'Atlantic' is made from natural or stained ash and veneered in English elm, with solid natural ash edges. *M:* w 122 × l. 203 × h 71, w 240 × l. 800 × h 71cm (48 × 79⅞ × 28, 94½ × 315 × 28in), or to order. *P:* from £1,000.

Aram's 'Atlantic'

'Circline' with plain glass top. Two separate base sections come in polished or satin finish chrome, or Black, Dark red or Sand enamel. A smoked glass version is available. *M:* maximum diam 150 × h 73 cm (59 × 28¾in). *P:* £176–£255.

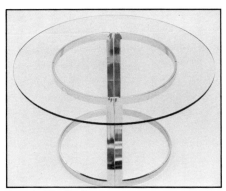

Aram's 'Circline'

ASTON WOODWARE

Reproduction trestle and refectory tables made from carefully dried timbers, mainly elm or oak. Three or four selected boards are

Aston Woodware's refectory table (top), trestle table (bottom)

jointed together with a shrink-cap across the ends, in the traditional manner. Natural or stained, they have a waxed or matt polyurethane finish. *M:* both w 30-33 × l. 60–96in × h to order (76–84 × 152.5–244cm). *P:* elm £250–£600, oak £280–£750.

ATRIUM

'Tau Quadro', an unusual interlocking base with a tinted glass top. The base is glazed or Matt black, chromed or brassed; circular and rectangular tops are available. *M:* 130 × 130 × h 72cm (51¼ × 51¼ × 38⅜in). *P:* £500. Other tables include collapsible 'Ribot' with ash legs and a smoked glass top edged with ash.

BLC TRADITIONAL COUNTRY FURNITURE LTD

Sturdy, hand-made pedestal table. Part of this company's delightful range of kitchen furniture, it comes in matured pine or seasoned beech. *M:* diam 30, 42, 54 × h 30in (76, 107, 137 × 76cm). *P:* all sizes £240.

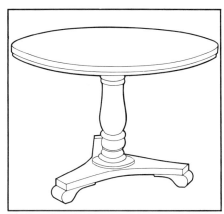

BLC's pedestal table

A hand-made Victorian farmhouse table is in pine or beech. *M:* w 32 × l. 72, 84, 96 × h 30in (81.5 × 183, 213.5, 243.5 × 76cm). *P:* £150–£190. See overleaf for illustration.

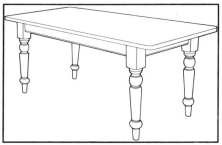

BLC's farmhouse table

CIANCIMINO DESIGN LTD

Classically contemporary beauty. 'Pedestal' has a bronzed anodized aluminium base, mock-marble glassfibre top. *M:* diam 60 × h 29½in (152.5 × 75cm). *P:* £565.

E A CLARE & SON LTD

'President' dining table with a polished oak or mahogany veneered top that is raised and levelled, in two easy movements, to reveal a billiard table complete with real slate bed, natural rubber cushions and a pure wool billiard cloth in traditional Emerald green. Equipment can be stored on the playing surface, under the dining top. The table can be supplied to match existing furniture. *M:* w 35 × l. 65 × 30in (89 × 165.5 × 76cm). *P:* from £1,900. This company also supplies wonderfully

reconditioned and/or rebuilt billiard tables (with new accessories), magnificently carved; also new gaming tables.

THE CONRAN SHOP LTD

'Heron Parigi', a clever, space-saving drawing/ dining table. The White laminate top can be elevated and tilted, or laid flat. The Black wood and metal base is accented with Green details. *M:* w 80 × l. 100 × h 72–92cm (31½ × 39⅜ × 28⅜–36¼in). *P:* £300.

CUBIC METRE FURNITURE

'M3', a well-constructed table, bordered in beech, that gives lots of scope for individual design combinations. Legs are chromed, or Red, Black, Yellow, Green, Blue, or White. Tops come in Grey or White melamine, or three tile arrangements: 'Check', a classic Black and White chequerboard; 'Pasta' with White tiles scattered with Light brown pasta shapes; and 'Rain' with Blue and Green diagonal slashes on White. *M:* w 84 × l. 130 × h 75cm (33 × 51¼ × 29½in). *P:* plain £174, tiled £270. A coffee-table version is available.

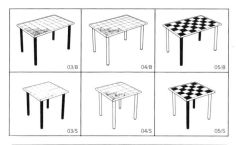

ENVIRONMENT DESIGN

Arrestingly simple 'La Basilica' by Mario Bellini, in natural walnut or acacia, or natural or ebonized ash. Three square column legs

support each end of the slatted top. *M:* w 78.5 × l. 225 × h 74cm (31 × 88⅝ × 29in). *P:* £550. A wider, four-leg version is available.

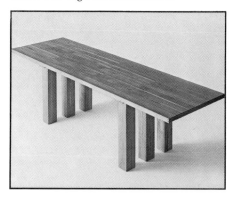

ESTIA DESIGNS LTD

'E32', a clever multi-purpose table that can be tilted, and is adjustable to coffee-, drawing or dining table height. The White melamine top rests on a tubular steel frame finished in Red, Yellow, Green or Brown. *M:* w 32 × l. 60 × h 18–30in (81.5 × 152.5 × 46–76cm). *P:* £40. See also 'Chairs'.

FORMA LTD

'Luego' extending two-flap table. In natural beech, it has a wood-grain laminated top and round legs. *M:* w 75 × l. 110–150 × h 75cm (29½ × 43⅜–59 × 29½in). *P:* £165.
'Blue', a slightly bigger version with rectangular legs, and a fixed-top model, are available.

PRICES AND INFORMATION WERE CORRECT AT THE TIME OF GOING TO PRESS

Forma's 'Luego'

G C FURNISHINGS LTD
Beautifully pure-lined 'K200' conference table. A Minimalist's dream, it's part of the INTER-FUNCTION office furniture range but is equally suitable for domestic use. The Grey-white or textured 'graphite' laminate top is edged with an aluminium-section rim; legs are also aluminium. *M:* w 100 × l. 200 × h 72cm (39³/₈ × 78³/₄ × 28³/₈in). *P:* £400. A larger version is available. See also 'Storage'.

HABITAT DESIGNS LTD
TILE TOP table in natural British Columbian pine, teamed with Pure white ceramic tiles. Two sizes are available. *M:* w 76 × l. 138 × h 76, w 83 × l. 175 × h 76cm (30 × 54³/₈ × 30, 32⁵/₈ × 68⁷/₈ × 30in). *P:* £101, £132. A matching

dresser, also in pine, has White melamine shelves edged with pine, White melamine door and back panels, and a tiled top. The range includes a trolley.

JOYCE HARDY
Made-to-order COUNTRY TABLE from a selection of pieces in re-cycled old pine. *M:* w 33 × l. 72 × h 30in (84 × 183 × 76cm). *P:* £200. These pine-stripping specialists will make virtually anything, from mirror frames to a complete fitted kitchen. See also 'Chairs', 'Storage'.

PETER HAXWORTH & CO LTD
Practical, sensible 'Conference 2000' table. Made by a firm that specializes in custom-built systems for boardrooms, offices, etc, it's equally suitable for dining rooms. The top, veneered in russet-coloured kevasingo or Indian silver greywood, rests on Haxworth's unique 'universal table structure' in chrome-finished steel with a levelling adjustment at all glide positions. The table can be packed flat. *M:* w 100 × l. 200 × h 45–75cm (39³/₈ × 78³/₄ × 17³/₄–29¹/₂in). *P:* upon application.

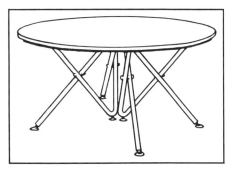

INTERSPACE
Marvellous collapsible 'Plano' in four segments. Made from rigid polyurethane, it comes in White, Red, Green, Beige, Brown, and Black. The base, in polished die-cast aluminium alloy with adjustable nylon glides, has a special locking mechanism to ensure stability. *M:* diam 95 × h 72cm (37³/₈ × 28³/₈in). *P:* £135. A square version is also available.

Interspace's 'Piano'

'TPL' fold-up table from Castelli of Italy, ideal for small areas. Tops, faced in White, Black or Grey plastic laminate, have rounded edges faced with impact-resistant PVC or squared edges with laminate facing. A patented self-locking mechanism ensures efficient folding and unfolding; feet on the chromed tubular legs adjust to uneven floors. *M:* w 80 × l. 140, 160, 200 × h 73cm (31¹/₂ × 55¹/₈, 63, 78³/₄ × 28³/₄in). *P:* £120–£150.

Interspace's 'TPL'

JARDINE LEISURE FURNITURE LTD
Elegant, conservatory-style 'B4', painted stain-resistant White. Part of a range of aluminium garden furniture, its intricate top complements the scrollwork base. *M:* w 37 × l. 74 × h 28¹/₂in (94 × 188 × 72.5cm). *P:* £230. See overleaf for illustration.

PRICES AND INFORMATION WERE CORRECT AT THE TIME OF GOING TO PRESS

Jardine's 'B4'

KINGSHALL FURNITURE LTD
'KB/1' double pedestal table. Part of the KNIGHTSBRIDGE collection of superbly made, hand-finished Georgian reproductions in the finest solid mahogany with mahogany veneers, this extendible table has traditional splayed legs, solid brass claw feet and castors. *M:* w 42 × l. 66–84 × h 30in (106.5 × 167.5–213.5 × 76cm). *P:* £725. The range includes a matching serving table, and sideboard with brass drawer pulls. See also 'Chairs'.

JOHN LARKING
Marvellous Minimalist table in sycamore that reverses to expose a Black-stained sycamore finish. Blue and Green ball hinges, and surface fittings, allow the legs to turn and the square top to flip, giving a completely new table. Ball hinges can be coloured to order. *M:* 90 × 90 × h 71cm (35³/₈ × 35³/₈ × 28in), or to order. *P:* £500.

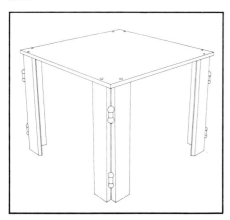

WILLIAM L MACLEAN LTD
Pedestal table in cast resin finished to look like solid beech. Intended for contract use, '26/4003' is a wonderfully childproof 'antique' for family kitchens or dining rooms. *M:* 112× 112×h 71cm (44¹/₈ × 44¹/₈ × 28in). *P:* upon application. Also available with a plain top and simpler base.

OGGI DOMANI
Marble OCTAGONAL table with brass top and base accents. It comes in marvellous shades including Versailles red, Empire or Garmisch black, Louvre purple, Regency green, and Cortina White. *M:* w 50 × l. 180 × h 75cm (19⁵/₈ × 70⁷/₈ × 29¹/₂in). *P:* £550.

OMK DESIGN LTD
Sophisticated 'T20' trestle table by Rodney Kinsman. Frame and legs in square tubular steel, finished in Black or White matt epoxy, support a Georgian-wired, clear or tinted glass top. *M:* w 76 × l. 168 × h 76cm (30 × 66¹/₈ × 30in). *P:* £205 with Georgian-wired top. Trestles can be bought separately. See 'Lighting' for illustration.

PRICES AND INFORMATION WERE CORRECT AT THE TIME OF GOING TO PRESS

PROJECT OFFICE FURNITURE LTD
Rectangular '4710' and circular '4RTO' from a range of well-designed office furniture. Warm oak veneers combine with Dark brown textured PVC panels and frames. *M:* '4710' w 80 × l. 160 × h 72cm (31¹/₂ × 63 × 28³/₈in), '4RTO' diam 120 × h 72cm (47¹/₄ × 28³/₈in). *P:* £120, £150.

T SAVEKER LTD
'V128' table frame in chromed steel, with rubber-padded supports for an inset top. *M:* to order. *P:* upon application.

Saveker's 'V128' (left), 'V3037' (right)

Free-standing 'V3037' table support with a chrome stem, and Black enamelled top and base. *M:* base diam 40, 50, top 30 × 30, h 75cm (15³/₄, 19⁵/₈; 11⁷/₈ × 11⁷/₈; 29¹/₂in). *P:* £26, £32. A version with four glider feet is available; also two with floor-fixed bases. Table tops are not supplied.

SCANDIA
'6284' in solid oak, from a great-looking range of clean-lined furniture in light woods. *M:* w 90 × l. 180 × h 70cm (35³/₈ × 70⁷/₈ × 27¹/₂in). *P:* £240.

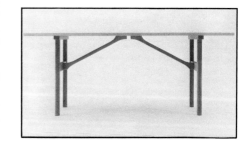

Beautiful EXECUTIVE conference table. The top, made from hundreds of inlaid wood squares, is set in a padouk, mahogany, cherry, ash, teak, walnut or Dark brown Wenge frame. *M:* padouk as illustrated w 96 × l. 196 × h 72cm (37¾ × 77⅛ × 28⅜in). *P:* £990. A wide variety of shapes and sizes is available.

Scandia's EXECUTIVE conference table

STOKECROFT ARTS
Craftsman-made gate-leg table in solid pine. One of many sensible, well-designed pieces, it can be extended by two leaves (maximum length 28in (71cm) each). The centre can be made in any size. *M:* as illustrated w 36 × l. 18–72 (fully extended) × h 29in (91.5 × 46–183 × 73.5cm). *P:* £215.

FREDERICK TIBBENHAM LTD
'T114' pedestal table in solid oak. *M:* w 46 × l. 46–64 × h 30in (117 × 117–162.5 × 76cm). *P:* £350. Rectangular tables from these manufacturers of fine oak reproductions include a lyre-end draw-leaf version, a trestle, and two tavern tables.

WILLIAM TILLMAN LTD
'Model I' Sheraton-style breakfast table in mahogany with rosewood and satinwood cross-banding. *M:* diam 63 × h 28½in (160 ×72.5cm). *P:* £910. A smaller oval table, and a rectangular version, are available. Other exquisite Tillman reproductions include Sheraton and Regency models without cross-banding, and a simple Chippendale-style gate-leg table in solid mahogany.

TOGGLE MOULDINGS LTD
'TO1' made from tough, moulded glass-reinforced plastic. Part of a cheerful range of seats and tables, it comes in Red, White, Yellow, Dark brown, and Light stone; other colours to order. *M:* diam 122 × h 71cm (48 × 28in). *P:* £98. Two lower versions are available.

R TYZACK LTD
'2043' with a solid mahogany top, from a selection of 18th- and 19th-century reproductions. *M:* w 39 × l. 87 × h 30in (99 × 190.5 × 76cm), or to order. *P:* £550.

'2016' on a single pedestal with reeded legs and brass castors. The top is plain Honduras mahogany, with or without satinwood cross-banding, or curl mahogany with boxwood and rosewood cross-banding. *M:* diam 60 × h 29½in (152.5 × 75cm). *P:* mahogany from £550.

Tyzack's '2016'

WOODSTOCK
BUTCHERBLOCK tables in Canadian maple, a wonderfully durable wood that positively glows when it's rubbed with steel wool and a special oil. *M:* round diam 48 × 30in (122 × 76cm), rectangular w 30 × l. 60 ×30in (76 × 152.5 × 76cm), or to order. *P:* upon application. Sideboards, end tables and classic dining chairs are available. See 'Kitchens' for illustration.

YOUNGER FURNITURE LTD
Handsome '408' fold-over centre-leaf table in solid English ash with chestnut veneer. *M:* w 91 × l. 157 × h 72cm (35⅞ × 61¾ × 28⅜in). *P:* £260. Also a larger version. The enormous TOLEDO range also includes two other tables, three chairs and dining-room storage .

DINING SUITES

ASKO FINNTERNATIONAL LTD
Modern bentwood table and chairs in natural or mahogany-stained Finnish birch. KOIVUTARU includes a chair with a high, low or very low back, with or without arms, a table in two sizes for dining, plus three coffee-table versions. *M:* chair as illustrated w 58 × h 86 × d 66cm (22⅞ × 33⅞ × 26in), table diam 115 × h 72cm (45¼ × 28⅜in). *P:* £170, £113. See overleaf for illustration.

Asko's KOIVUTARU

Amazingly futuristic UPO knock-down range consisting of an armchair, stacking chair, cube-based storage cabinet, and three dining tables. Good value, they're in White, Red or Brown injection-moulded thermoplastic. *M:* table 85 × 85 × h 73cm (33½ × 33½ × 28¾in), armchair w 59 × h 78.7 × d 55.5cm (23¼ × 31 × 21¾in). *P:* £114, £40.

Asko's UPO

Pleasing modern versions of a country classic, in solid pine, LAPPONIA chairs and extendible table are both available in a natural or dark-stained finish. *M:* table w 85 × l. 130–180 × h 73cm (33½ × 51¼–70⁷/₈ × 28¾in), chair w 46 × h 88 × d 45.5cm (18 × 34⁵/₈ × 17⁷/₈in). *P:* £160, £70. See 'Kitchens' for illustration.

Atrium's MOUNT table, MONK chairs

ATRIUM

Complementary table and chairs (left, below), radically constructed and sure to be classics. The MOUNT table's leather or lacquer top rests on angled legs that literally lock together. *M:* w 95 × l. 160–255 × h 72cm (37³/₈ × 63–100³/₈ × 28³/₈in). *P:* £496. MONK chairs have leather or canvas seats and backs slung on steel tubes that screw into solid wood supports. *M:* w 52 × h 73 × d 48cm (20½ × 28¾ × 18⁷/₈in). *P:* from £110.

BAMBOO DESIGNS

F RANGE table and chairs from a comprehensive collection of high-quality cane furniture for virtually every room in the house. The table comes in three sizes, chairs in four styles; all lacquered or painted to order. *M:* table 102 × 102 × h 74cm (40¹/₈ × 40¹/₈ × 29¹/₈in), chair w 54 × h 87 × d 58cm (21¼ × 34¼ × 22⁷/₈in). *P:* £500, £145.

BANKS HEELEY

Beautifully simple, comparatively inexpensive, High Tech MONDRIAN 'AY3' table and X–LINE stacking chairs. A clear acrylic sheet

links and stabilizes perforated steel table bases, supporting a glass top screenprinted with a grid design. In Black or White, the table comes in three sizes; also hall and coffee-table versions. Chairs have chromium-plated steel frames, perforated steel seats and backs. *M:* table w 91 × l. 213 × h 91cm (35⁷/₈ × 83⁵/₈ × 35⁷/₈in), chair w 40 × h 76 × d 40cm (15¾ × 30 × 15¾in). *P:* £190, £26. See also 'Storage' for KASBAH units in background.

CARSON OFFICE FURNITURE LTD

LINK '900' conference table with a 1½in (4cm) thick top veneered in pale, pine-like West African anigré. Designed for office use, it could be equally at home in the dining room. Ergonomically correct POLYTROPIC side chairs by Giroflex, with a chrome-finished steel cantilever base, have a one-piece shell upholstered in Dralon; 15 shades include lovely brights and ten subtle woven textures. Armchair versions are also available. *M:* table w 100 × l. 200 × h 72cm (39³/₈ × 78¾ × 28³/₈in) or to order, chair w 43.5 × h 90 × d 43.5cm (17 × 35³/₈ × 17in). *P:* £190 as illustrated, £120.

MICHAEL DAVIS

'TD1' table, 'D1' armchairs and 'CR' trolley in White fibreglass. Designed for patios and conservatories, they also look good in a dining- (or sitting-) room. Upholstery, made from PVC-coated polyester treated with an anti-fungal agent, comes in Grey, Beige, Bright green, Bright yellow, Burgundy, Blue or Brown stripes, on White; frames in White, Grey or Beige. Two larger tables are available. *M:* table diam 42 × h 27in (106.5 × 68.5cm), armchair w 23½ × h 19 × d 26½in (59.5 × 48.5 × 67.5cm). *P:* £120, £70. Similarly beautiful complementary pieces include square, rectangular and side tables, a love seat, ottoman, canopied swing, chaise-longue and double, adjustable chaise.

PRICES AND INFORMATION WERE CORRECT AT THE TIME OF GOING TO PRESS

Michael Davis' 'TD1' table, 'D1' armchairs, 'CR' trolley

ESTIA DESIGNS LTD

Stylish, inexpensive 'E31' integrated table and seat unit, from a sensible supplier. The Red, Yellow, Green or Brown tubular steel frame supports a Finnish birch plywood top, finished in clear polyurethane. Seats are covered in one of a wide range of practical fabrics (details in 'Upholstered Furniture'). Two-, four-, five- and six-seat versions are available. *M:* three-seater as illustrated 58¾ × 58¾in × h to order (147.5 × 147.5cm). *P:* from £90.

ERCOL FURNITURE LTD

OLD COLONIAL range in solid hand-waxed elm, with over six table and 12 chair styles; also five dressers. *M:* table w 32½ ×l. 64–84 × h 28in (82.5 × 162.5–213.5 × 71cm), as illustrated in colour on page 243.

Ercol's PINE LINE

PINE LINE, in solid, hand-waxed pine, has four table and two chair styles, plus five storage solutions. *M:* table w 42½ × l. 53½–73½ × h 28¼in (108.5 × 136–187 × 71.5cm). *P:* both ranges upon application.

GRAFTON INTERIORS

Lustrous MARBELLA table and sideboard, finished in Beige or Black lacquer with brass or gold-plated accents. The table, illustrated with 'Bombay' chairs, comes in five sizes up to 600cm (244¼in) long, the sideboard in three. *M:* table w 100 × l. 200 × h 72cm (39³⁄₈ × 78¾ × 28³⁄₈in), sideboard w 225 × h 76 × d 46cm (88 ⁵⁄₈ × 30 × 18in), both as illustrated. *P:* £790, £1,020.

Grafton's MARBELLA

Stunning MAYA comes in purest White lacquer, or — for even more drama — Black or Aubergine. Table and sideboard come in four sizes; the chair can be upholstered in any fabric selected by the customer. *M:* table w 100

× l. 200 × h 75cm (39³⁄₈ × 86¾ × 29½in), chair w 50 × h 102 ×d 47cm (19⁵⁄₈ × 40¹⁄₈ × 18½in), both as illustrated. *P:* £940, from £250.

Grafton's POSTUMIA

POSTUMIA by Ca'Onorai is Italian walnut with Black anodized aluminium accents, rounded corners. Part of a very sophisticated range of office furniture, this suite would also fit into a more domestic setting; pieces also come in White or Brown laminate with natural aluminium accents. The table is available in three sizes up to 420cm (165³⁄₈in) long; the sideboard illustrated is made up of three out of 28 units. *M:* table as illustrated w 100 ×l. 240 × h 74cm (39³⁄₈ × 94½ × 29¹⁄₈in), sideboard w 300 × h 75 × d 45cm (118¹⁄₈ × 29½ × 17¾in). *P:* £305, £475.

Solid beech REGENCY table, chairs and cabinets are painted to order and striped, by hand, in the customer's choice of colour. Chair upholstery, table length and cabinet size

Grafton's MAYA

are to order. *M:* table as illustrated w 39 × l. 84 × h 29½in (99 × 213.5 × 75cm), chair w 19 × h 32½ × d 19in (48.5 × 82.5 × 48.5cm). *P:* table from £415, chair £140.

Grafton's REGENCY

MAGGIE HARRIS
Nicely executed FRENCH RANGE of Louis XVI-style furniture with reeded legs, hand-painted details and gilding. All pieces can be painted to order. Maggie Harris is primarily a trade supplier, but will sell to private customers who know what they want. *M:* to order. *P:* upon application.

M & I J HARRISON LTD
Well-made ALBERT dresser and table from a firm that specializes in pine reproductions. They are available in standard sizes, or made to

order. *M:* table w 30 × l. 60 × h 30in (76 × 152.5 × 76cm), dresser w 55½ × h 71 × d 19in (139.5 × 180.5 × 48.5cm). *P:* £130, £350. See also 'Kitchens'.

HIPPO HALL
BEAR table with ALLIGATOR and ELEPHANT chairs. Hand-painted in cheerful colours these intriguing pieces should keep children quiet for a few minutes at least. Variations on this theme can be accommodated — Hippo Hall will design virtually anything for kids. *M:* to order. *P:* table from £55.

HOMEWORKS LTD
'DC-166B' chairs and 'ST-325' table, part of the WICKERWORK suite hand-made in Italy. Well constructed and good-looking, unlike many cheaper versions, they come in a natural or Dark brown finish. Loose, reversible chair cushions are plain or tufted. *M:* table w 18 × l. 50 × h 28in (46 × 127 × 71cm), chair w 22 × h 38 × d 22in (56 × 96.5 × 56cm). *P:* £290, £330. A round dining table is available.

INTERSPACE
'Plia' folding and stacking chair and 'T120' table. Frames are chromium-plated steel, or plasticized Red, Green, Brown, White or Black. The chair seat and back is in clear, smoke, Yellow, Blue or Pink translucent 'Cellidor' plastic; Red, Green, Brown, Beige, White or Black polypropylene; or cane edged in wood. Up to four chairs can be hung on a nylon hook that folds against the wall when not in use. The laminated plastic table top is Yellow, Grey, Brown, Black or White; wood costs an extra 30%. Dozens of sizes are available; base variations include hemispheres and arcs. *M:* chair w 47 × h 89 × d 50cm (18½ × 35 × 19⅝in), table as illustrated diam 120 × h 73cm (47¼ × 28¾in). *P:* chair in polypropylene and chrome £23, 'Cellidor' and coloured frame £40; table upon application.

JAYCEE FURNITURE LTD
TUDOR solid oak dresser, lyre-end draw-leaf table and ladderback chairs with upholstered or rush seats. In Old English, Middleton or Antique oak finishes, they're part of an extensive range that includes ten other tables and an additional nine chairs and 12 dressers and sideboards. *M:* dresser w 137 × h 180 × d 43cm (54 × 70⅞ × 16⅞in), table w 81.5 × l. 122–183 × h 76cm (32 × 48–72 × 30in), chair w 51.9 × h 94 × d 42cm (20⅜ × 37 × 16½in). *P:* from £540, £270, £68. Also sitting-room furniture.

PRICES AND INFORMATION WERE CORRECT AT THE TIME OF GOING TO PRESS

KESTERPORT LTD

Sleek BAMBOO table and fabric-upholstered chair, with solid brass tubular frames finished in blackened, glossy 'Ossidiana' or 24-ct gold plate. The table top is 8mm (c $^3/_8$in) thick smoked glass, or covered in baize for card sharps. Matching coffee-tables, trolleys, hatstands, coat hangers, bookcases and mirrors are available. *M:* table w 88 × l. 88, 148, 180 × h 72cm (34$^5/_8$ × 34$^5/_8$ × 58$^1/_4$ × 70$^7/_8$ × 28$^3/_8$in), chair w 44 × h 105 × d 44cm (17$^3/_8$ × 41$^3/_8$ × 17$^3/_8$in). *P:* table £155–£245, gold-plate £195–£290, chair from £94, gold-plate from £108.

Opulent but nice SOTILIA table and chair in highly polished walnut or briarwood with 24-ct gold plate accents. The chair can be upholstered in a choice of fabrics. The range also includes a trolley, console table, hatstand

and small tables. *M:* table w 88 × l. 148 × h 74cm (34$^5/_8$ × 58$^1/_4$ × 29$^1/_8$in), chair w 46 × h 84 × d 46cm (18 × 33 × 18in). *P:* table £230 walnut, £282 briarwood; chair £100.

WILLIAM L MACLEAN LTD

Suite in simulated BAMBOO, for al fresco or indoor dining, from an enormous and beautiful range of Regency reproductions. The table comes in various diameters from 109 to 152cm (43 to 59$^3/_4$in), matching chairs in a variety of styles. *M:* table diam 109 × h 75cm (43 × 29$^1/_2$in), chair w 49 × h 91 × d 51cm (19$^1/_4$ × 35$^7/_8$ × 20in). *P:* upon application. See also 'Chairs'.

MERROW ASSOCIATES

Competitively priced CAMELIA range. The table is veneered in Rio rosewood, American walnut, oak or elm. Chairs, with polished chrome or Black frames, have all-wool upholstered seats and backs in a good range of colours. *M:* table w 30 × l. 81 × h 28$^1/_2$in (76 × 206 ×72.5cm), chair w 20 × h 33$^1/_2$ ×d 21in (51 × 85 × 53.5cm). *P:* table from £385, chair £100 chrome.

Merrow's CAMELIA

Glass-topped CHEVRON table. The polished chrome base has gold-plated accents on the top and bottom stretchers. Matching chairs come in a selection of fabrics, or the customer's own material. *M:* table w 32 × l. 69 × h 28$^1/_2$in (81.5 × 175 × 72.5cm), chair w 19 × h 29 × d 19in (58.5 × 48.5 × 74cm). *P:* £350, £80.

Merrow's CHEVRON

COMO, evocative of the 1930s, with polished chrome frames. The table, veneered in Rio rosewood, oak, elm or American walnut, also comes in a smaller size. Chairs have Black hide or natural canvas seats and backs, ash arms. *M:* table w 39 × l. 72 × h 29in (99 × 183 × 73.5cm), chair w 21 × h 32 × d 22$^1/_2$in (53.5 × 81.5 × 57cm). *P:* £250, chair £100 hide.

Merrow's COMO

N NORMAN LTD

Reproduction 'Y58' chairs, 'Y46W6' figured-front sideboard, and 'Y55V' extendible drum dining table, in yew or mahogany. *M:* table diam 42–78 × h 29in (152.5–198 × 73.5cm), sideboard w 70 × h 35$^1/_2$ × d 17$^1/_2$in (178 × 90.5 × 44.5cm). *P:* from £500, £600.

OGGI DOMANI

Luxurious 'Lively' table and 'Margherita' chairs from Italy. The shape of the table frame, in gold- and chrome-plated steel with Ivory lacquer trims, is echoed in the Gold outline screenprinted on the clear or smoked plate glass top. The high-backed chairs, also with gold- and chrome-plated steel frames, are upholstered in a wide range of fabrics, including silk and velvet. *M:* table w 100 × l 200 × h 73cm (39$^3/_8$ × 78$^3/_4$ × 28$^3/_4$in), chair w 50 × h 112 × d 56cm (19$^5/_8$ × 44$^1/_8$ × 22in). *P:* £475, £170 as illustrated overleaf.

Oggi Domani's 'Lively' table, 'Margherita' chairs

PARNHAM HOUSE
PARNHAM EDITIONS drop-leaf dining table in solid oak, cherry or muninga with a heat-resistant finish. Chairs, in the same woods, have coach-hide seats and backs. Parnham House is the home of some very inventive modern furniture made in the John Makepeace Furniture Workshops. All 'limited edition' pieces are signed by individual craftsmen. *M:* table diam 120 × h 72cm (47¼ × 28⅜in), dining chair w 52 × h 82 × d 49cm (20½ × 32¼ × 19¼in), folding chair w 75 × h 75 × d 45cm (22⅞ × 29½ × 17¾in). *P:* £750, £200, £250.

QUARTO FURNITURE
Simple 'Black Oak' table with chromed tubular legs, and perennially pleasing 'Bauhaus' chairs. The single-flap top, in Black-stained oak, also comes in natural and Brown. *M:* table w 90.5 × l. 136–193 × h 73.5cm (35½ × 53½–76 × 29in), chair w 46 × h 80 × d 42.5cm (18 × 31½ × 16¾in). *P:* table £160, chair £25 without arms. A centre-leaf table has square oak legs.

RENZLAND & CO
Well-designed 'GT112' table and 'CH2G' chairs for tiny kitchens as well as gardens. Great value, they come in White stove-enamelled steel; table top and chair seats and backs are heavy expanded steel. *M:* table 30 × 30 × h 29in (76 × 76 × 73.5cm), chair w 17 × h 31 × d 14in (43.5 × 78.5 × 35.5cm). *P:* £55, £28.

ROOKSMOOR MILLS
CANE SUITE. The unusual table base and bentwood-inspired chairs are stained warm walnut or Ivy green. The table top is heavy smoked glass, cushion covers are Dralon. *M:* table diam 47 × h 29in (119.5 × 73.5cm), chair seat diam 17 × h 43in (43.5 ×109cm). *P:* £200, £60.

SCANDIA
Handsome suite, well-made like all this company's Scandinavian-style furniture. 'MO 2181' and 'MO 2179', from a range of 19 table modules, and 'MO 4551' chairs have oak or beech frames. Table tops are functional but

striking Black linoleum; chairs have Black leather seats, Black-stained backs. *M:* table modules (combined w 180 × l. 270 × h 70cm (70⅞ × 106¼ × 27½in), chair w 61 × h 70 × d 47cm (24 × 27½ × 18½in). *P:* £700, £135.

TURBERVILLE SMITH
Elegant '7915' conference table, with a shelf for papers, etc. Also perfect for dining, it comes in rosewood only. The matching '7918/4' cabinet, with overhead lighting in each section, has smoked glass doors, adjustable glass shelves; and six drawers, two trays and two shelves in the base. *M:* table w 49½ × l. 98 × h 28in (126 × 246 × 71cm), cabinet w 95 × h 75 × d 16in (241.5 × 190.5 × 40.5cm). *P:* £1,100, £2,200.

VERARDO
Dramatic, Italian-made KABUKI suite in Black or beige lacquer. The chair is a strikingly elegant version of a classic Hepplewhite shape, upholstered in a wide choice of fabrics. *M:* table w 98 × l. 182 × h 73cm (38½ × 71⅝ × 28¾in), small two-door cupboard w 90 × h 78 × d 43cm (35⅜ × 30¾ × 16⅞in). *P:* upon application.

Verardo's KABUKI

MISTRAL, another chic, shiny, modern range, is also lacquered in Beige or Black. Like all Verardo furniture it's very well finished.

PRICES AND INFORMATION WERE CORRECT AT THE TIME OF GOING TO PRESS

Right: Dining suite from Ercol's OLD COLONIAL range (see Dining Suites)

WHITE & NEWTON LTD

Graceful but simple teak-finished DROXFORD, by Philip Hussey. The table has a flip-over centre leaf, slightly tapered legs. Chairs can be upholstered in Dralon velvet, or the customer's own fabric. *M:* table diam 46–67 × h 28½in (117–170 × 72.5cm), chair w 19 ×h 38½ × d 16in (48.5 × 98 × 40.5cm). *P:* £230, £110.

WOOD BROS FURNITURE LTD

OLD CHARM reproduction Tudor draw-leaf table similar to a 16th-century piece at Little Moreton Hall, Cheshire, and dresser. Hand-carved in solid oak, both come in light oak, Tudor brown, or special antiqued finish. *M:* table w 30 × l. 48–72 × h 32in (76 × 122–183 × 81.5cm), dresser w 60 × h 77 ×d (base) 18, (top) 12in (152.5 × 196 × 46, 30.5cm). *P:* £265, £600.

Selection of dining furniture from Younger's MANOR HOUSE

YOUNGER FURNITURE LTD

MANOR HOUSE (left, below) in pine and pine veneer, finished in satin lacquer. A refectory-type table is also available. *M:* gate-leg table w 127 × l. 127–180.5 × h 72.5cm (50 × 50–71 × 28½in), splat-back chair w 48.5 × h 98 × d 48.5cm (19 × 38½ × 19in). *P:* £330, £80.

OCCASIONAL TABLES

ARAM DESIGNS LTD

'E1027', a table that's stood the test of time — it was designed by Eileen Gray in 1927. The polished chromium-plated tubular steel frame supports a stove-enamelled sheet steel, or plate glass, top. Height is adjustable. *M:* diam 20 × h 24–39in (51 × 61–99cm). *P:* £125.

Baker, Knapp & Tubbs' '1440'

Opposite: Colourflair's marble tables

BAKER, KNAPP & TUBBS

'1440', rattan sofa table (left, below). Lacquer, in toning vibrant colours, is overlaid on the boldly textured base. *M:* w 16 × l. 54 × h 27½in (40.5 × 137 × 70cm). *P:* £530.

A spider-legged drop-leaf tea table is part of the CHARLESTON range of 18th-century American reproductions. '1932' comes in Black lacquer, hand-painted with Chinoiserie detail. *M:* w 11½ × l. 28 × h 27¼in (29.5 × 71 × 69.5cm). *P:* £690. The original is in a private house in Charleston, South Carolina.

Baker, Knapp & Tubbs' '1932' (left), '1974' (right)

A charming Sheraton-style flip-top table in mahogany veneer with satinwood inlay is also American-inspired.

The '2083' console table, part of the ALESSANDRO range, is made from three joined 'C' shapes. The *trompe l'oeil* goatskin-leather surface is one of many fantasy finishes. *M:* w 16 × l. 78 × h 27in (40.5 × 198 × 68.5cm). *P:* £1,450.

Baker, Knapp & Tubbs' '2083' (left), '5402' (right)

An elegant little lamp table from the FRENCH collection, '5402' is made from pecan wood with walnut veneer. It has sabot feet and a fine brass gallery. *M:* diam 26 × h 24in (66 × 61cm). *P:* £275.

BAMBOO DESIGNS

'414' triangular tables — six form a hexagon. In best-quality cane, lacquered or painted to clients' specifications, they are also available singly. *M:* 53 × 53 × h 41cm (20⅞ × 20⅞ × 16⅛in). *P:* £81 each. Also coffee- and console tables. See overleaf for illustration.

PRICES AND INFORMATION WERE CORRECT AT THE TIME OF GOING TO PRESS

Bamboo Designs' coffee-tables

CADO FURNITURE (UK) LTD
'680' and '681', sleek little end and coffee-tables. Polished chromium-plated steel legs support a White melamine top. *M:* end table w 23 × l. 26 × h 17in (58.5 × 66 × 43cm), coffee-table w 26 × l. 46 × h 17in (66 × 117 × 43cm). *P:* from £90, £100.

CIANCIMINO DESIGN LTD
Sleek CONSOLE table that complements Ciancimino's dining tables and shelving. An optional hotplate makes it perfect for dining rooms. Legs are natural or bronzed aluminium, the top comes in bronzed glass or travertine marble. *M:* bronzed aluminium legs with glass top, natural aluminium with travertine, w 18 × l. 72 × h 32in (46 × 183 × 81.5cm). *P:* £295, £338. *M:* bronzed aluminium legs with travertine top and hotplate, w 16¼ × l. 72 × h 34in (41.5 × 183 × 86.5cm). *P:* £520. See also *Dining Tables*, 'Shelving'.

Ciancimino's CONSOLE table

CIEL (CHRISTOPHER LAWRENCE LTD)
Exquisitely painted, but competitively priced, simple tables. Made to order, they can be finished in any texture, or colour. Special textural effects include marbling, spattering, feathering, and lacquer. *M:* to order. *P:* upon application.

CLASSIC GARDEN FURNITURE LTD
Two tables with ornamental bases and mahogany ('C27') or cast-iron ('C10') tops, from a firm that specializes in cast-iron reproduction Victorian garden furniture. Another 11 styles are available. *M:* 'C27' diam up to 36 in (91.5cm) × h to order, 'C10' diam 24in (61cm) × h 27½in (70cm). *P:* £75, £55.

PRICES AND INFORMATION WERE CORRECT AT THE TIME OF GOING TO PRESS

Classic's 'C27' (left), 'C10' (right)

COLOURFLAIR FURNITURE
Exclusive made-to-order sculptured tables that combine the beauty of classic marble with clean modern lines. Tops, in a variety of shapes, are mounted on bases that range from two interlocking squares to a simple 'V'. The marble can be ribbed, tooled or chamfered to produce unique forms. Three small side tables are available; also two larger coffee-tables with octagonal or rectangular tops. *M:* to order. *P:* side tables as illustrated from £160, larger coffee-tables from £360. See page 244 for two tables in colour.

DE LA PLAIN INTERIORS LTD
Cheap, cheerful and modern AMANTA tables in tough moulded fibreglass. Colours are Black, White, and Dark brown. *M:* w 60 × l. 120 × h 60; 70 × 70 × h 60; 85 × 85 × h 60cm (23⅝ × 47¼ × 23⅝; 27½ × 27½ × 23⅝; 33½ × 33½ × 23⅝in). *P:* £65–85.

De la Plain's AMANTA

GLI SCACCHI is an unusual cubic display of useful modular tables. Made in injection-moulded polyurethane, they come in Black, Red, or Green. *M:* 30 × 30 × h 37; 90 × 90 × h 54cm (11⅞ × 11⅞ × 14½; 35⅜ × 35⅜ × 21¼in). *P:* upon application.

Low, square and rectangular RE QUADRO tables have staggered tops in White, Red, Black or Beige polyester-lacquered wood. Bases are Black or White marble. *M:* 110 × 110 × h 33, w 110 × l. 170 × h 33cm (43⅜ × 43⅜ × 13, 43⅜ × 66⅞ × 13in). *P:* £290, £400.

De la Plain's GLI SCACCHI (above), RE QUADRO (below)

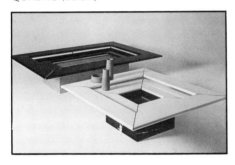

DESIGNERS GUILD
CANE HEXAGONAL table, marvellously evocative of Edwardian conservatories. It comes in natural cane with a clear lacquer finish; special colours and stains available to order, at extra cost. *M:* w 77 × l. 68 × h 42cm (30³/₈ × 26³/₄ × 16¹/₂in). *P:* £105.

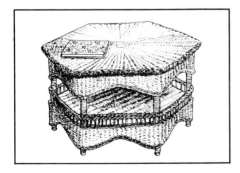

MARTIN J DODGE
Fine extendible 'T30' sofa table in solid mahogany inlaid with rosewood, satinwood, mahogany or yew cross-banding. The wood is polished and waxed, by hand, to a rich Mid-brown. *M:* w 20 × l. 40–60 × h 29in (51 × 101.5–152.5 × 73.5cm). *P:* £800.

Martin J Dodge's 'T30'

DU-AL FURNITURE LTD
Competitively priced CRYSTALINE coffee-table in chrome and smoked glass. *M:* 60 ×60 × h 33cm (23⁵/₈ × 23⁵/₈ × 13in). *P:* £40. A matching rectangular table and bookcase are available.

ESTIA DESIGNS LTD
'E35' and 'E36' supports, for use with customers' own tops. 'E35' is a pair of sturdy trestles that will support anything from a piece of chipboard to a marble slab. Available in Black, White, Red, Green or Brown, each consists of two identical tube frames screwed together, and can be taken apart and stored

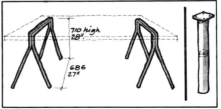

Estia's 'E35' (left), 'E36' (right)

nearly flat. *M:* w 15¹/₂ × l. 27 × h 28in (39.5 × 68.5 × 71cm). *P:* pair £20. 'E36', a set of four fat tubular legs is supplied complete with screws for fitting tops. In the same colours as 'E35', it comes in two heights for low or dining tables. *M:* h 14, 28in (35.5, 71cm). *P:* set £15, £20.

FURNITURE PRODUCTIONS (BRADFORD) LTD
Functional but good-looking WARWICK 235 tubular table with Brown metal frames and Beige laminate top. *M:* 62 × 62 × h 35cm (24³/₈ × 24³/₈ × h 13³/₄in). *P:* £37.

GEORGIAN FURNISHING CO
'A31', a decidedly Oriental table. The solid carcase is veneered with quartered bamboo, decorative fretwork abounds. *M:* w 30 × l. 47 × h 18in (76 × 119.5 × 46cm). *P:* £270. Smaller tables, gaming tables and desks are available in the same style.

Georgian's 'A31'

A butler's table gone mad, 'FBT' is a solid beauty in Indonesian walnut, with fold-out extensions, a removable tray top with hand-carved details on the inside corners, and collapsible legs. Fittings are made from solid brass. *M:* w 21 × l. 30¹/₂–91 × h 30in (53.5 × 77.5–231 × 76cm). *P:* £370. See overleaf for illustration.

PRICES AND INFORMATION WERE CORRECT AT THE TIME OF GOING TO PRESS

Georgian's 'FBT'

Lovely side table. 'TT', veneered in Indonesian walnut with solid brass pulls, has a dished top and graceful cabriole legs, à la Chippendale. *M:* w 15 × l. 34 × h 29in (38 × 86.5 × 73.5cm). *P:* £300.

Georgian's 'TT'

GIORGETTI
Terrific '6144/Q' table for anyone who loves the sinuous curves of Art Nouveau. In solid hand-polished wood, it has a cut crystal top and splayed feet. Very beautiful. *M:* 120 × 120 × h 74cm (47¼ × 47¼ × 29⅛in). *P:* £725.

GIPSY TABLES
Round tables for covering with cloth. This simple but effective way of showing fabric to its best advantage is popular with interior decorators as well as gipsies. Two styles come in two heights and seven diameters. Gipsy will make (and line) the covering, ruffle or braid its edges, and provide a protective glass top. Alternatively, 4m to 5m of your own fabric will do the job, and they'll supply just the top and base. *M:* diam 18–72 × h 24, 30in (46–183 × 61, 76cm). *P:* 'A' £14.50, 'B' £16; unlined made-up cloth £6.60; glass top £7.50.

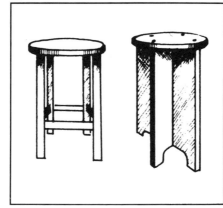

Gipsy's tables

HADDONSTONE LTD
Two XVIII CENTURY LIONS to support a table top — and protect you in your sitting-room.

Made in reconstructed marble by a firm that specializes in garden furniture, they come in a natural or antique finish. *M:* w 11 × l. 24 × h 16in, weight 115lb (28 × 61 × 40.5cm, 51.75kg). *P:* £50 each.

CHARLES HAMMOND LTD
'Cant Corner', an octagonal, glass-topped acrylic lamp table. *M:* 51 × 51 × h 40cm (20 × 20 × 15¾in). *P:* £195. A rectangular coffee-table version is also available from this stylish Sloane Street decorator. See also 'Shelving'.

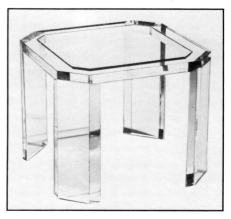

HOMEWORKS LTD
'RT 206' and 'XT 281', two of four wickerwork bases designed and hand-made in Italy. Other round versions, and squares, are available; all in a natural or Dark brown finish. *M:* diam 36 × h 16in (91.5 × 40.5cm). *P:* 'RT 206' £250, 'XT 281' £205. See also 'Upholstered Furniture'.

House of Lambeth's 'Fold Away'

HOUSE OF LAMBETH
Self-assembly 'Fold Away' space-saver (left, below) in laminated birch finished in high-gloss clear varnish. Uniquely, top and supports are linked with a pre-stretched White nylon cord. *M:* w 20 × l. 40 × h 17½in (51 × 102 × 44.5cm). *P:* £13.75.

KESTERPORT LTD
Slick, low SOTILIA occasional tables in walnut with a glossy Black 'Ossidiana' finish, or walnut or briarwood with 24-ct gold-plated edgings. *M:* 88 × 88 × h 42cm, w 63 × l. 118 × h 42cm (34⅝ × 34⅝ × 16, 24⅞ × 46½ × 16½in). *P:* both sizes 'Ossidiana' £130, gold-plated £149 walnut, £159 briarwood.

L M KINGCOME LTD
Slick but classically styled LACQUER TABLE on a metal frame. It can be supplied in any colour, to any size. *M:* as illustrated 23 × 23 × h 15in (58.5 × 58.5 × 38cm). *P:* £200.

PRICES AND INFORMATION WERE CORRECT AT THE TIME OF GOING TO PRESS

KINGSHALL FURNITURE LTD
Simple, pleasing sofa table from an extensive range of military-inspired furniture. 'MO/7D' is veneered in the finest mahogany, accented with solid brass fittings. *M:* w 16 × l. 54 × h 27in (40.5 × 137 × 68.5cm). *P:* £225. Many other styles include coffee- and lamp tables.

WILLIAM L MACLEAN LTD
Chippendale-style '27/99' in solid beech, with glass or painted top. Illustrated in a natural, hand-polished finish. *M:* w 40 × l. 141 × h 75cm (15¾ × 55½ × 29½in). *P:* upon application. The company specializes in high quality French and English reproductions; all their furniture can be finished or painted to order, or simply hand-waxed.

William Maclean's '27/99'

Console table '27/76' is hand-carved beech, with a marble top. *M:* w 50 × l. 168 × h 90cm (19⅝ × 66⅛ × 35⅜in). *P:* upon application.

William Maclean's '27/76'

'28/172' has a lacquered base, available in any colour, and a square glass top. *M:* base h 43cm, top 40 × 40cm (16⅞, 15¾ × 15¾in). *P:* upon application.

William Maclean's '28/172' (left), '28/370' (right)

'28/370', an octagonal table full of Eastern promise, is in simulated bamboo, with tripod legs. *M:* w 56 × l. 56 × h 48cm (22 × 22 × 18⅞in). *P:* upon application.

William Maclean's '27/227'

'28/227', a reproduction Louis XV table in the Grecian style, is made in solid beech. Reeded legs form an elongated 'X'. *M:* w 47 × l. 106 × h 41cm (18½ × 41⅝ × 16⅛in). *P:* upon application.

MARBLE PANELS LTD
Table tops in Marble Panels' own Connemara marble. One of the world's oldest and rarest marbles, it's usually highly marked in Sepia or Dark green tones, with Blue tints. Its high silica content makes it virtually impervious to stains. There's a small range of other marbles such as Rosa Aurora, Pelata, White Sicilian, and Estremoz; also granites including Blue pearl,

Miracles' marquetry table

Sardinia Beige, Baltic brown, and Imperial mahogany. Veneers or solid slabs are available, and a choice of jointing. *M:* in Baltic brown granite as illustrated w 48 × l. 24 × h 17in (122 × 61 × 43.5cm). *P:* £350

MARSHA INTERIORS
Unbelievably shiny, split-level 'Goya' coffee-table from Artedis of France. Part of a range of 40 pieces, including other tables and a chest of drawers, it comes in Red, Brown, Ivory or Black lacquer, or tortoiseshell effect, edged with stainless steel or gold-plated trim. *M:* w 70 × l. 120 × h 38cm (27½ × 47¼ × 15in). *P:* £500.

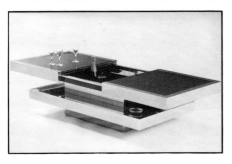

MERROW ASSOCIATES
Stunning DANDELION occasional table with a square bronzed glass top, polished chrome support, and American walnut base. (No sign of dandelions but plenty of triangles.) *M:* 30 × 30 × h 15in (76 × 76 × 38cm). *P:* £150. Also available in Rio rosewood, oak and Canadian elm.

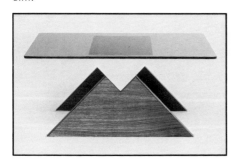

MIRACLES LTD
Made-to-order marquetry table from a firm of miracle workers. Table tops are inlaid with stained, cut woods in motifs chosen by clients. Tigers, seascapes and landscapes are a speciality. All tables have a secret compartment. *M:* to order. *P:* from £150.

N NORMAN LTD
Three reproduction drum tables 'Y50V', 'Y80L' and 'Y22V', in yew or mahogany. The centre one revolves, has a gold-tooled leather top in Green, Gold, Black, Red, Pink or Parchment. *M:* 'Y50V' diam 20 × h 26in (51 × 66cm); 'Y80L' diam 20 × h 26in (51 × 66cm); 'Y22V' diam 19 × h 26in (48.5 × 66cm). *P:* £170–£190. A sofa

Left to right: Norman's 'Y50V', 'Y80L', 'Y22V'

Norman's sofa table

table has graceful reeded legs and brass fittings. *M:* w 20 × l. 34–35 × h 20in (51 × 86.5–89 × 51cm). *P:* £200. Matching dining-room and storage furniture is available.

OGGI DOMANI
Stone table in polished travertine marble, with distinctive concentrically stacked legs. *M:* 110 × 110 × h 25cm (43⅜ × 43⅜ × 9⅞in). *P:* £255. Also available with a plate glass top.

Oggi Domani's stone table

PARNHAM HOUSE
PARNHAM EDITIONS stool (or small side table) in English or exotic woods, and display table in cherry, oak or muninga with a glass top and suede-lined base. From the John Makepeace workshops in Parnham House — one of the most beautiful houses in Dorset, and the birthplace of some of the UK's finest contemporary furniture — they are two of a few signed 'limited editions' for those who can't afford this well-known designer/craftsman's precious one-off pieces. All Parnham House furniture is signed by the craftsman who made it. *M:* stool w 31 × h 25 × d 21cm (12¼ × 9⅞ × 8¼in), table 75 × 75 × h 31cm (29½ × 29½ × 12¼in). *P:* £85, £340.

REMPLOY FURNITURE
Very stylish 'A020' stacking tables. Made in ash, they're perfect for really tight spaces. *M:* 36.5 × 36.5 × h 37.5, 43 × 43 × h 42.5cm (14¼ × 14¼ × 14¾in, 16⅞ × 16⅞ × 16¾in). *P:* two £84. A larger coffee-table is available in ash veneer, or Yellow, Brown or Black melamine.

Remploy's 'A020'

T SAVEKER LTD

Low '417' table frame with bent end rails, special corners, and four rubber rings to hold a glass top. *M:* w 50 × l. 75 ×h 32cm (19⅝ × 29½ × 12⅝in). *P:* £30. Other sizes are possible. Simple, wonderfully inexpensive 'T189' legs for glass-topped tables are in chrome, satin chrome, and bronze- or brass-plated chrome. Each column has a top screw, with protective washers, to fit a 13mm (½in) diameter hole. *M:* diam 5.1 × h 35, 50cm (2 × 13¾, 19⅝in), or to order. *P:* h 50cm £4.50–£5.75.

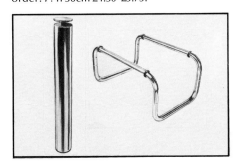

Staples' 'TB1'

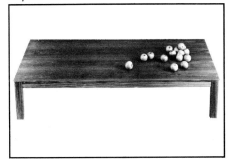

STAPLES & CO LTD

'TB1' (left, below) from the Deauville range by Max Holba, in warm sienna-coloured teak or darker rosewood. *M:* w 75 × l. 168 × h 35cm (29½ × 66⅛ × 13¾in). *P:* £375. Also in two smaller sizes.

SWAN GALLERIES

Competitively priced, marble-topped side table. Almost made to order — customers choose from elm, oak, mahogany and Siberian pine — it also comes with a plain wood top, and/or without drawers. Castors can be supplied. *M:* w 20 × l. 36 × h 30in (51 × 91.5 × 76cm). *P:* upon application. A square version, and lower coffee-tables, are available.

Tempus Stet's 'B19'

TEMPUS STET LTD

'B19' support brackets (left, below), part of a wondrous range of reproductions. Gilt, antique silver, bronze, stone and lead-effect finishes are available. *M:* h 28in (71cm). *P:* gilt £65 each.

Tempus Stet's 'D22'

The 'D22' dolphin table base is from a late 17th-century original belonging to the Duchess of Sutherland. Finishes are gilt-effect, antique silver, bronze, stone and lead-effect. *M:* w 26 × h 28in (66 × 71cm). *P:* gilt-effect £460. Also available singly.

FREDERICK TIBBENHAM LTD

Beautiful 'D31A' four-drawer Georgian side table, from a firm that specializes in fine oak reproductions. *M:* w 18½ × l. 84 × h 30in (47 × 213.5 × 76cm). *P:* £350. A shorter, three-drawer version is available.

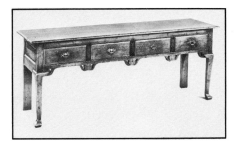

'T14' reproduction Hunt table. Gorgeously simple, but traditional, it's made in solid oak. *M:* w 38–55 × l. 55 × h 21in (96.5–139.5 × 139.5 × 53.5cm). *P:* £175.

Frederick Tibbenham's 'T15' (right)

'T15', a pleasing carved hall table, in solid oak with ringed legs. *M:* w 14 × l. 54 × h 28in (35.5 × 137 × 71cm). *P:* £175.

Frederick Tibbenham's 'T25L'

'T25L', a beautifully simple reproduction coffee-table. *M:* w 21 × l. 48 × h 18in (53.5 × 122 × 46cm). *P:* £120. Five styles of nesting tables are also available.

WILLIAM TILLMAN LTD

'Model CT', a beautifully reproduced Chippendale-style tea table in solid mahogany. *M:* diam 48 × h 28½in (122 × 72.5cm). *P:* £650.

William Tillman's 'CT'

Exquisite 'Model M', a Sheraton-style poker table in mahogany, with a leather top. *M:* diam 57 × h 28½in (144.5 ×72.5cm). *P:* £820.

William Tillman's 'Model M'

'Model O', a fine reproduction coffee-table in mahogany, with serpentine ends and cross-banded top. *M:* w 19½ × l. 45 × h 19in (49.5 × 114.5 × 48.5cm). *P:* £230.

William Tillman's 'Model O'

Tyzack's '2000'

R TYZACK LTD

Fine '2000' table (left, below) with two end drawers, in the Gothic Chippendale style. Three mahogany finishes are available. *M:* w 19 × l. 42 × h 29in (48.5 × 106.5 × 73.5cm). *P:* £280.

'2013' is a mahogany Pembroke table with satinwood cross-banding. *M:* w 19–37 × l. 37 × h 29in (48.5–94 × 94 × 73.5cm). *P:* £330.

Tyzack's '2013'

The '2032A' coffee-table has a beautifully quartered curl mahogany top and reeded legs. *M:* 36 × 36 × h 18in (91.5 × 91.5 ×46cm). *P:* £280. A smaller size is available; also rectangular versions.

Tyzack's '2032A'

TABLES, OCCASIONAL

WOOD BROS FURNITURE LTD
OLD CHARM sofa table in hand-carved oak. One of more than 120 pieces, it comes in a special antiqued finish, light oak or Tudor brown. *M:* w 29¼ × l. 53 × h 20½in (74.5 × 134.5 × 52cm). *P:* from £190. Another 11 table styles are available.

WORKSHOP WONDERLAND
Wonderfully simple 'Plain Square'. Part of an amazing range of 13 laminate tables in a huge variety of colours, it comes in three sizes. *M:* 60 × 60 – 120 × h 120cm (23⅝ × 23⅝ – 47¼ × 47¼in), or to order. *P:* £75–£175. Other shapes include a simple box in five sizes, and a cube in two. There's also a matching planter. All designs, including 'Plain Square', can be made to order in any size.

Workshop Wonderland's 'Plain Square' (below)

WINTHER, BROWNE & CO LTD
Classic 'Tripod' in polished solid Swedish pine. Perfect for staining, stencilling and other applied finishes, it's just one example of Winther Browne's unusual wood products. *M:* diam 50 × h 73cm (19⅝ × 28¾in). *P:* £40.

INTRODUCTION

Soft, resilient and durable, upholstered furniture has been popular for centuries. The Victorian era, in particular, was the heyday of overstuffed chairs and sofas.

These traditional pieces are still made as they were in the 19th century, with elaborately lashed springs and layers of hand wadding. Less expensive modern versions have pre-manufactured spring units and separate rubber webbing, with latex or plastic foam. Rigid foam shells in light, strong, expanded polyurethane or polystyrene are also available. Wool is the most hardwearing covering, rivalled by man-made acrylics; cottons and linens cost less than wool, but don't wear as well. Leather is virtually maintenance-free, but colours aren't always fast. Go for a dark, patterned covering unless the covers are removable and easily cleaned.

This section concentrates on fully upholstered furniture. See 'Chairs' for partially upholstered pieces.

*Prices include covering, unless otherwise stated.

ADEPTUS DESIGNS LTD

Cheap and cheerful, well-designed multi-density foam furniture from the firm that arguably pioneered the use of this material. Double and single convertibles, sofas, chairs and modular units come in 17 styles, covered in tough, natural fabrics like linen, corduroy, velour, wool (and one in Black leather). Colours are mainly clean, clear shades like Greens and Browns, with some small florals. *M:* various. *P:* convertibles from £75, £120, sofa from £170, modular unit from £60.

ARAM DESIGNS LTD

'Bibendum' by Eileen Gray, an unusual Michelin-man chair, upholstered in leather or fabric. Two arcs rest on a pouffe seat. The base is polished chromium-plated tubular steel. *M:* w 36½ × h 28½ × d 31in (92.5 × 72.5 × 78.5cm). *P:* fabric £400, leather £800.

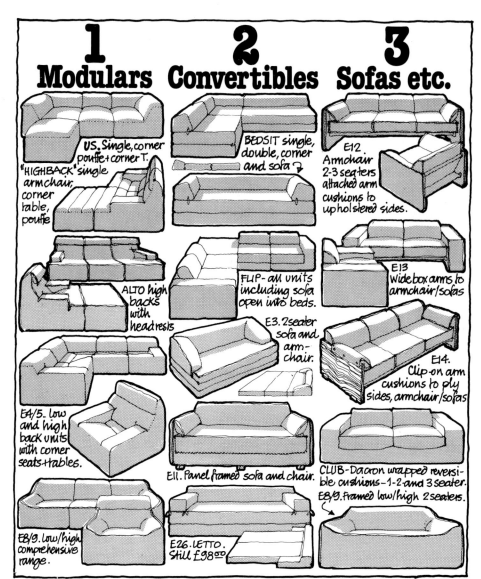

1 Modulars 2 Convertibles 3 Sofas etc.

US. Single, corner pouffe + corner T.

"HIGHBACK" single armchair, corner table, pouffe

ALTO high backs with head rests

EA/5. low and high back units with corner seats + tables.

E8/9. Low/high comprehensive range.

BEDSIT single, double, corner and sofa ?

FLIP- all units including sofa open into beds.

E3. 2 seater sofa and armchair.

E11. Panel framed sofa and chair.

E26. LETTO. Still £98.00

E12. Armchair 2-3 seaters attached arm cushions to upholstered sides.

E13 Wide box arms to armchair/sofas

E14. Clip-on arm cushions to ply sides, armchair/sofas

CLUB-Dacron wrapped reversible cushions-1-2-and 3 seater. E8/9. framed low/high 2 seaters.

Selection from Adeptus

GRAND CONFORT 'love seat' by Le Corbusier, Pierre Jeanneret and Charlotte Perriand that utilizes the marvellous contrast between polished chromium-plated steel and leather. The four loose cushions can be covered in fabric. *M:* w 39 × h 27 × d 25in (99 × 68.5 × 63.5cm). *P:* leather £610. The more compact and cuddly version 'S' has an additional down-filled seat cushion.

The 'Lota', designed in 1924 by Eileen Gray, has its four feather-filled loose cushions and seat mattress covered in fabric, or aniline leather. The fully upholstered base and back support rest on turned feet. Detachable box units, on castors, have Black polyurethane lacquer fronts and backs; sides and tops come in a contrasting colour that could match the upholstery. *M:* w 94½ × h 33 × d 34½in (240 × 84 × 87.5cm). *P:* upon application.

Aram's GRAND CONFORT

PRICES AND INFORMATION WERE CORRECT AT THE TIME OF GOING TO PRESS

Aram's 'Lota'

ARTIMA OF SWITZERLAND

'A–22', 'A–28', A–30', 'A–31' — wonders of modern design. All can be upholstered in a selection of marvellous Artima fabrics. Gorgeously contoured 'A–22', with soft foam layers and upholstery padding on both cushions and arms, can be covered in leather. *M:* w 211 × h 76 × d 94cm (82⁷/₈ × 30 × 37in). A

From top: Artima's 'A-22', 'A-28', 'A-30', 'A-31'

two-seater sofa, armchair and unusual asymmetrical chaise-longue are also available. 'A–28', arguably Artima's most classic piece, has sturdy sides that curve in faintly Oriental style to become graceful arms. *M:* w 170 × h 79 × d 93cm (66⁷/₈ × 31¹/₈ × 36⁵/₈in). It has a matching chair, three-seater sofa and corner unit. 'A–30', upholstered with layers of foam covered with padding, has unconventional soft contours emphasized with leather piping. *M:* w 152 × h 74 × d 93cm (59¾ × 29¹/₈ × 36⁵/₈in). It has a complementary armchair with a matching stool, plus sumptuous two-, three- and four-seater sofas. 'A–31', one of the most comfortable sofas on the market, also has piping accents. It comes in modular end, corner, single and footstool units; leather upholstery is optional. *M:* upon application. Other, more linear, sofas include 'A–26', also with optional leather upholstery, with a built-in extendible tray under each arm. 'A–25' is available fully covered in fabric, or with its wood parts finished in high-polish lacquer; the range also includes an armchair and three-seater. *P:* all upon application.

ASHLEY FURNITURE WORKSHOPS

Two-seater conversation chair upholstered in Florentine tapestry, or one of an extensive

selection of leathers: matt in 120 colours, glazed in 12, and hand-antiqued in 15. Also known as a confidante, companion chair, tête-à-tête or sociable seat, the style dates from the early 19th century. *M:* w 50 × h 35 × d 33in (127 × 89 × 84cm). *P:* £450. Other reproductions in Ashley's beautifully crafted range include two-, three- or four-seater Chesterfield sofas with buttoned or cushion seats, a Cromwellian sofa, and wing chairs. All can be upholstered in any of the company's fine leathers.

The hall porter's chair was originally designed to protect hall porters from draughts. Available with a tufted, or plain, inside hood, it comes in the same leathers as the conversation chair. Stud nails are solid brass. *M:* w 35 × h 69 × d 34in (89 × 175.5 × 86.5cm). *P:* £700. An exclusive facsimile of an early 18th-century sedan chair has a wooden frame covered in leather, the inside upholstered in tufted fabric. Hinges, door furniture and nearly 5,000 stud nails are solid brass; windows are toughened 4mm (c ¹/₈in) glass.

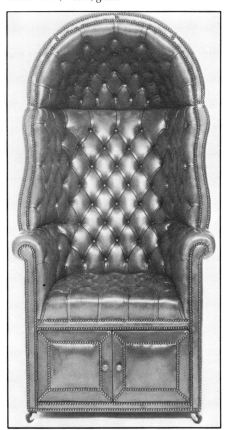

Ashley's hall porter's chair

ASKO FINNTERNATIONAL LTD

KOIVUTARU chair, one of many stunning models from this firm. It has a natural or mahogany-stained frame in laminated Finnish birch slung with Black or Brown canvas. Cushions are covered in matching canvas, fabric, or leather. *M:* w 68 × h 103 × d 97cm (26¾ × 40½ × 38⅛in). *P:* canvas £175, fabric £175–£195, leather £280.

Asko's KOIVUTARA chair

Unusual OCTAVIA sofa and chairs with curved wooden frames in stained or lacquered birch, and fabric or leather upholstery. *M:* chair w 80 × h 83 × d 79cm (31½ × 32⅝ × 31⅛in). *P:* £175.

Asko's OCTAVIA

SETTI versatile fabric-upholstered unit seating in natural pine or stained or lacquered birch. The range consists of unit chairs, with or without backs, corner units, and a single sofa-bed with a flap seat that transforms it into a double bed. Optional clip-on shelves are available. *M:* corner unit 80× 80 × h 68 cm (31½ × 31½ × 26¾in), footstool 79 × 79 × h 38cm (31⅛ × 31⅛ × 15in). *P:* £175, £85.

Asko's SETTI

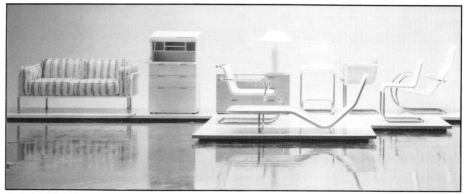

Atrium's TECTA

ATRIUM
Two-seater TECTA sofa, a favourite of Walter Gropius's wife Ilse. It has a chromed tubular frame and natural or Black polypropylene 'wickerwork'. Loose cushions, filled with polyester and Dacron, are covered in fabric or leather. A chair and three-seater version are available. *M:* two-seater w 156 × h 74 × d 71cm (61⅜ × 29⅛ × 28in). *P:* fabric from £875. See also 'Chairs', 'Storage'.
The pleasingly proportioned 900 range, another example of Atrium's fine Continental furniture, has removable leather or fabric coverings. It consists of a two- or three-seater sofa, high- or low-backed armchair, and a pouffe.

BAKER, KNAPP & TUBBS
'887–80', an updated American version of a Regency classic. Details include exaggerated pleats, French seams, and multi-colour rope welt on borders, cushions and the top of the skirt. Ties and tassels extra. *M:* w 80 × h 26 × d 33in (203.5 × 66 × 84cm). *P:* £1,000.

The CHARLESTON range, also American Colonial-inspired, includes a 'Chippendale Bench'. *M:* w 21 × h 17 × d 16½in (53.5 × 43.5 × 42cm). *P:* £344. See page 169 for colour illustration.
Other fine reproductions include the '868/90' sofa and '461' wing chairs shown on the cover. *M:* three-seater w 78 × h 34 × d 24in (198 × 86.5 × 61cm), chair w 32 × h 43 × d 33in (81.5 × 109 × 84cm). *P:* £1,048, £448.

BAMBOO DESIGNS
Fully upholstered DECO RANGE sofa with unusual bamboo and bronze mirror facings. A matching chair, three-seater sofa, tables and screen are available. *M:* two-seater w 170 × h 76 × d 95in (66⅞ × 30 × 37⅜in). *P:* £630.

BRENDON DESIGNS LTD
Comfortable 'Elizabeth' sofa with a beech and steel frame. The suspension system is in the back as well as the base. A total of 38 coverings is available, including a ribbed, high-pile cotton, linen and acrylic fabric. *M:* w 230 × h 102 × d 96cm (90⅝ × 40⅛ × 37¾in). *P:* from £435.

CADO FURNITURE (UK) LTD
Very inviting and well-made easy chair with an adjustable neck pillow, and matching

footstool. '183' by Arne Vodder is upholstered in mock leather, or any of Cado's handsome fabrics. Its frame is varnished blond ash on beech laminate, or beech laminate stained to resemble teak or mahogany. *M:* w 83 × h 86 × d 97cm (32⁵/8 × 33⁷/8 × 38¹/8in). *P:* leather from £420, fabric from £270.

Cado's '183'

An example of the best in modern design, in varnished blond ash. '246' by Arne Vodder has loose reversible cushions, filled with 'Polydown' sheared down and polyether granules, which rest on supports made from 59% cotton, 41% flax. Arms are saddle-stitched hide slings. *M:* w 176 × h 79 × d 73cm (69³/8 × 31¹/8 × 28³/4in). *P:* fabric from £700.

Cado's '246'

CIANCIMINO DESIGN LTD
Stylish but simple little wing chair designed by the owner of this sleek shop. Upholstered in any of the beautifully loomed wools in the Scottish BUTE range, it has a foam and Dacron-wrapped timber frame. *M:* w 36 × h 30 × d 30in (91.5 × 76 × 76cm). *P:* £350.

CLEMENTS INTERNATIONAL UPHOLSTERY LTD
Authentic reproductions of Victorian spoon-backs. Covered in fabric, they are also avail-

Clements' spoonbacks

Ciancimino's wing chair

able in tough but finely grained leather in Gold, Tan, Bronze, Rust red, Brick red, Coffee, Chocolate, Light olive, and Dark olive. (Clements have possibly the largest range of hide-covered furniture in Europe.) *M:* chaise-longue w 66 × h 35 × d 30in (167.5 × 89 × 76cm), armchair w 27 × h 37 × d 31in (68.5 × 94 × 78.4cm). *P:* £650, £370.
Other reproductions, all made to a high standard, include numerous chairs, traditional Chesterfields and wing-backs; also beautifully scaled-down versions of these for children.

COLLINS & HAYES LTD
Ultra-simple sofa. Collins & Hayes specialize in beautifully made, innovative furniture — the best in British design. 'Alto' by Robert Heritage combines a traditional wrap-around drop back with an elegant suspended seat that merges into the arms, and comes in soft aniline leather, or any of the company's fabrics. *M:* two-seater w 149 × h 69 × 90cm (58⁵/8 × 27¹/8 × 36¹/4in). *P:* fabric from £425.
Softly contoured BOLERO by Fred Scott is for people who like their surroundings well-rounded. Designed for relaxing, it's available in a variety of covers including pure new wool,

velvets and leather. Two- and three-seaters are available. *M:* four-seater w 235 × h 76 × d 112cm (92⁵/8 × 30 × 44¹/8in). *P:* from £760.

Collins & Hayes' 'Alto' (above), BOLERO (below)

Imposing CORNICHE by Graham Stewart has comfortable, high backs and large, soft arms. Cushions, made from Dacron-wrapped polyether foam, can be covered in any of the company's fabrics, or leather. An armchair, two- and three-seater sofas, a stool and a matching glass-topped table are available. *M:* two-seater w 168 × h 88 × d 100cm (66¹/8 × 34⁵/8 × 39³/8in). *P:* from £410.

Collins & Hayes' CORNICHE

The 'Jasmine' loose-covered range consists of the same pieces, plus a convertible sofa-bed. There's a wide choice of fabrics, including traditional florals and modern geometrics — with a set of covers from each you can change the mood of a room within minutes.

Chunky, high-backed ECLAIR units are designed, unusually, by a woman (Susan Layton). Made of multi-density polyether foam on a timbered base, they include single and corner units, two- and three-seater sofas, and a footstool. Deep-buttoned quilted covering is available in a wide range of fabrics that includes wools and velvets. *M:* two-seater w 162.5 × h 79 × d 96cm (63¾ × 31⅛ × 37¾in). *P:* from £300. See page 270 for colour illustration of ECLAIR.

Wonderfully geometric OCTAVE is designed by Ronald Carter. Its relatively low back has all ergonomical requirements for back support. It can be covered in Collins & Hayes fabric, or leather. *M:* three-seater w 207 × h 70 × d 92cm (81½ × 27½ × 36½in). *P:* from £728.

Collins & Hayes' OCTAVE

Comfortable, high-backed PASTORALE armchairs by Martin Grierson are from a range that also includes two- and three-seater sofas, and matching stools. The functional-looking quilted covering harmonizes attractively with their soft curves. A wide range of other upholstery fabrics is available. *M:* high-back

Collins & Hayes' PASTORALE

armchair w 83 × h 105 × d 73cm (32⅝ × 41⅜ × 28¾in). *P:* armchair from £400.

'Butterfly', another high-backed range, is foam-covered with loose seat cushions; arms and back arch slightly outwards. Fairly inexpensive, it also comes in an extensive selection of well-designed fabrics, and leather.

Elegant, expensive SERENADE is by Graham Stewart. Inspired by petals, each piece has a beech frame with rattan weave inserts. Soft, lap-over cushions come in a variety of coverings. A two-seater sofa is available. *M:* three-seater w 221 × h 73.5 × d 94cm (87⅛ × 29 × 37in). *P:* from £1,150.

Collins & Hayes' SERENADE

THE CONRAN SHOP LTD

Wonderfully welcoming 'Ballon' and 'Wings' sofas, exclusive to this chic shop. Frames, made of solid beech, formed plywood and tubular steel, are wrapped in polyether foam

Conran's 'Ballon' (above), 'Wings' (below)

and a thick layer of Dacron. Both can be covered in the customer's, or any Conran, fabric. *M:* 'Ballon' w 69 × h 32 × d 37½in (175.5 × 81.5 × 94.5cm), 'Wings' w 71 × h 32 × d 39½in (180.5 × 81.5 × 99.5cm). *P:* £460, £400.

DALVERA

ANTIGUA in peeled or natural cane, or with an oak or walnut finish, in a variety of charming upholstery fabrics. *M:* two-seater w 129 × h 87 × d 84cm (50¾ × 34¼ × 33in), small armchair w 60 × h 77 × d 62cm (23⅝ × 30⅜ × 33in). *P:* £280, £110.

COLLEZIONE THAI two-seater sofa and armchair, with grid frames in natural cane. *M:* two-seater w 152 × h 100 × d 83cm (59⅞ × 39⅜ × 32⅝in). *P:* £410. Also a sofa-bed.

DE LA PLAIN INTERIORS LTD

LE BAMBOLE, cushy numbers from Italy designed by Mario Bellini. Tough steel frames, wrapped in foam and padding, are upholstered in leather or fabric. In addition to modular units and conventional three-piece suite, the range includes a chaise-longue and double and single beds. *M:* two-seater w 169 × h 72 × d 90cm (66½ × 28⅜ × 35⅜in), armchair w 122.5 × h 72 × d 90cm (48⅛ × 28⅜ × 35⅜in). *P:* sofa from £460, armchair from £320. ELETTO by Paola Piva is a beautiful sleek sofa-bed covered in leather, or fabric. Unlike most, it's perfectly acceptable as a bedstead in its own right. Easily converted, it has a structural steel and aluminium body embedded in polyurethane and springs made from plastic-coated steel strips, all wrapped in Dacron and polyurethane. *M:* w 181 × h 75 × d 110–210cm (71¼ × 29½ × 43⅜–82¾in). *P:* fabric £750, leather £950.

De la Plain's LE BAMBOLE (above), ELETTO (below)

DE SEDE UK LTD

'DS-54', a high-backed swivel chair with a down-filled head cushion and leather-covered pedestal. A reclining mechanism that locks into place is optional. *M:* w 88 × h 93 × d 89cm (34⅝ × 36⅝ × 35in). *P:* upon application. A matching footstool is available.

The deceptively simple 'DS-53', also with a high back and optional footstool, has a continuous reclining mechanism. Seat and back are made from a single skin, embellished only with a zig-zag seam stitch.

Incredibly light-looking 'DS-64', like all the de Sede furniture shown here, is upholstered in top-quality, soft-textured leather, polished to repel grease; shades — all beautiful — vary according to range. This Swiss firm specializes in the ultimate leather furniture. A matching easy chair and two-seater sofa are available. *M:* three-seater w 209 × h 76 × d 90cm (82¼ ×30 × 35⅜in). *P:* upon application.

de Sede's 'DS-54' (above), 'DS-64' (below)

Impressively solid 'DS-94' unit seating has a visible seat frame on a set-back base—a distinctive feature. The range consists of a two-seater sofa, chair, footstool, and end, corner and single units. *M:* single unit w 78, 102 × h 85 × d 87cm (30¾, 40⅛ × 33½ × 34¼in), end unit w 90, 127 × h 85 × d 87cm (35⅜, 50 × 33½ × 34¼in). *P:* upon application. Something completely different! Circle-based

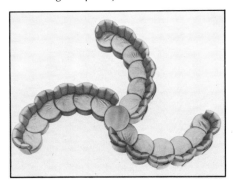

de Sede's 'DS-800' (above), 'DS-94' (below)

'DS-800' units, joined with a pin at the centre of each circle, can curve 26° to the right or left to form concave or convex seating arrangements. All pieces except end units are sickle-shaped. A matching easy chair is available. *M:* unit w 85 × h 78 × d 85cm (33½ × 30¾ × 33½in). *P:* upon application.

DESIGNERS GUILD

Sweet suite. The DAISY armchair and two-seater sofa have beech frames, handsprung seats and backs, and bun front feet. *M:* sofa w 153 × h 78 × d 92cm (161¼ × 30¾ × 36¼in), armchair w 92 × h 78 × d 92cm (36¼ × 30¾ × 36¼in). *P:* £420, £345.

Perfect deep-buttoned HUMPHREY reading chair, and ottoman. They have beech frames with dual sprung units and sprung edges. Covers are fixed. *M:* chair w 92 × h 89 × d 99 (36¼ × 35 × 39in). *P:* £470.

Designers Guild's JUMBO

Wonderfully large, the welcoming JUMBO sofa has a hard beech frame like DAISY and handsprung seat and back; Dacron-wrapped foam cushions have removable cases. *M:* w 230 × h 88 × d 100cm (90⅝ × 39⅜ × 34⅝in). *P:* from £725.

Low, modular LICHTENSTEIN units are untypically modern—Designers Guild is better known for updated country styles. Seat cushions in Dacron-wrapped polyether foam, and back cushions filled with feathers and down, have zips. Special sizes are available, to order. *M:* chair unit (no arms) w 72 × h 75 × d 89cm (28⅜ × 29½ × 35in). *P:* £270.

Designers Guild's LICHTENSTEIN

The comfortable two-seater NELLY sofa has piped, zipped cushions and a base valance. It has a traditional wooden frame with a sprung

Designers Guild's NELLY

unit base on castors. An armchair and three-seater sofa are available. *M:* two-seater w 230 × h 76 × d 91cm (90⅝ × 30 × 35⅞in). *P:* £645.

DESIGNS UNLIMITED LTD
Two-seater BASIS sofa with slim arms that are packaged separately for home assembly. Part of the company's most economical range, it can be covered in a selection of fabrics including textured man-mades, linen unions, small floral or geometric prints, Dralon velvets and herringbone tweed. An armchair and three-seater sofa are available; also armcaps and extra cushions. *M:* two-seater w 51 × h 31 × d 34in (129.5 × 78.5 × 86.5cm). *P:* from £160. Like all Designs Unlimited furniture, it is upholstered in foam and Dralon, and can be high- or low-backed.

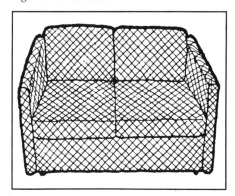

Designs Unlimited's BASIS (above), BIG BOY (below)

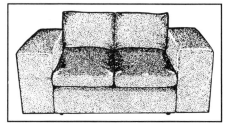

BIG BOY, a low-backed two-seater, with wide, puffy arms and soft, inviting cushions comes in the same fabrics as BASIS. A matching armchair and three-seater sofa are available. *M:* two-seater w 72 × h 30 × d 36in (183 × 76 × 91.5cm). *P:* from £200.

ECLIPSE, a low-backed sofa evocative of the 1930s, has unboltable arms that curve boldly forwards. It is covered in the same fabrics as BASIS. A three-seater sofa and an armchair are available; also armcaps and extra cushions. *M:* two-seater w 61 × h 30 × d 36in (155 × 76 × 91.5cm). *P:* £175.

Designs Unlimited's ECLIPSE

S ENGLENDER & SONS LTD
ODEON, a 1930s design modified for the 1980s. The range comes in a large choice of plain and patterned velvets. *M:* three-seater w 234 × h 76 × d 89cm (92¼ × 30 × 35in), armchair w 117 × h 76 × d 89cm (46⅛ × 30 × 35in). *P:* £590, £320.

ENVIRONMENT DESIGN
Two-seater sofa from the 920 range designed by Afra and Tobia Scarpa in 1965. Covered in fabric, or leather, it has a natural ash, or natural or stained walnut frame. Cushions are polyester-filled. An armchair, three-seater sofa and modular units are available; also small tables in four sizes. *M:* two-seater w 118 × h 42 × d 78cm. *P:* from £400.

LA BARCA is a double sofa for anyone who feels their current couch just isn't big enough. Made from Cassina's wonderfully simple modular units in natural polished ash, it features terrific prop-up tables. Seat cushions are filled with polyurethane foam, back and side cushions with foam and feathers; all have removable covers. Upholstery is fabric or leather. *M:* as illustrated w 237 × h 68 × d 237cm (93¼ × 26¾ × 93¼in). *P:* two units as illustrated £1,370.

Environment's 920 two-seater (above), LA BARCA double sofa (below)

Stylish, sensible LE CORBUSIER furniture designed in the late 1920s. Reproduced by Cassina in Italy, its High Tech look is totally up-to-date. All pieces, including the ultimate chaise-longue, can be upholstered in fabric as well as luxurious leather. *M:* armchair w 76 × h 67 × d 70cm (30 × 26³/8 × 27½in), chaise-longue w 56.4 × l. 160 cm × h variable (22¹/8 × 63in). *P:* leather £360, £400.

Environment's LE CORBUSIER

Beautiful leather-covered MARALUNGA seating is one of the best of its kind on the market. Sofas and easy chairs have a movable headrest

that folds over for a contemporary low-backed look, but provides total support when straight. The range includes two- and three-seater sofas; also a matching footstool. Fabric upholstery is available. *M:* armchair w 98 × h 72–104 × d 85cm (38½ × 23³/8–41 × 31½in). *P:* from £520.

Environment's MARALUNGA

'Tentazione' by Mario Bellini, a luscious little number, comes in leather or fabric. The frame, made from nylon turnbuckles and ash struts fixed to a plywood base, is padded with feathers or Dacron. Two- and three-seater sofas are available. *M:* w 77 × h 83 × d 66cm (30³/8 × 32⁵/8 × 26in). *P:* leather from £295.

Environment's 'Tentazione'

ESTIA DESIGNS LTD
Comprehensive E SERIES no-nonsense furniture, conscientiously designed by Demetri Petrohilos to make maximum use of the multi-density foam upholstery. Competitively priced, it includes fold-out beds and modular units, one with retractable tables, some with tubular supports. Most pieces are exclusive to Estia. There's a wide choice of sensible cover-

ings: wide and narrow corduroys in Rust, Emerald, Brown, and Dark green; Sage green, Brown, Beige, Tan or Grey velour; Beige, Black or Brown linen with a White grid design; quilted Beige cotton; nubbly wool in Tan/Gold and Brown/Rust; and tiny checked velour in Black/White, Brown/Black, Green/Black, and Tan/Black. Linens are plain Beige or Brown; Green, Orange or Brown with a narrow White stripe; and Beige striped in any of these colours. *M:* 'E21' sofa-bed w 74 × h 37⁷/8 × d 33½–75in (188 × 86 × 85–190.5cm). *P:* from £180.

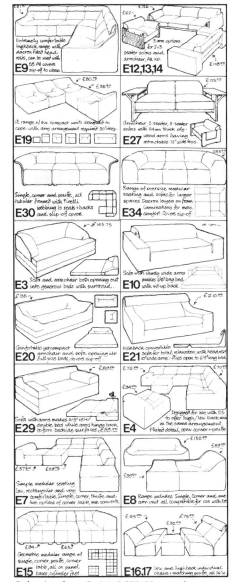

Selection from Estia's F SERIES (see also overleaf)

PRICES AND INFORMATION WERE CORRECT AT THE TIME OF GOING TO PRESS

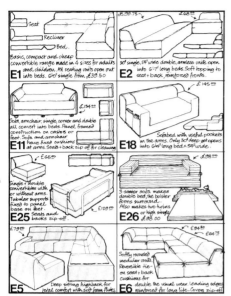

Selection from Estia's E SERIES

FAVORITE INTERIOR
GHIBLI sofa and armchairs. Possibly the ultimate three-piece suite, it's covered in best-quality Dralon, or leather, with walnut accents. A matching coffee-table is available. *M:* sofa w 210 × h 88 × d 100cm (82¾ × 34⅝ × 39⅜in), armchair w 93 × h 88 × d 100cm (36⅝ × 34⅝ × 39⅜in). *P:* three-seater £2,400 in Dralon.

FURNITURE PRODUCTIONS LTD
High-quality, metal-framed armchair from the utilitarian and competitively priced WARWICK range. *M:* w 61.5 × h 91.5 × d 78.5cm (24¼ × 36 × 31in). *P:* from £60. A low-backed version, a chair without arms, and an occasional table are also available. All are upholstered in a tough, subtly striped fabric.

THE FURNITURE WORKSHOP
Good-looking, competitively priced 'Suffolk Recliner', designed by David Wicks. Ergonomically perfect, it adjusts to any angle and is

Furniture Productions' WARWICK

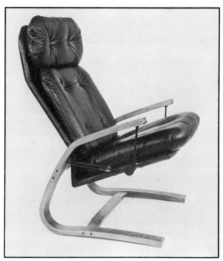

Furniture Workshop's 'Suffolk Recliner'

locked into position by your weight (no knobs or levers); the front height of the seat can also be altered. Upholstery is Black, Chocolate, Coffee or Russet leather; a tough, flameproof acrylic fabric with minute Tan and White checks; or Grey, Beige or Ginger all-wool 'Barvas' tweed from the Isle of Bute. The wood frame is finished in Brown or Black epoxy, or chromium, depending on the fabric. *M:* w 58 × h 106 × d 97cm (22⅞ × 41¾ × 38⅛in). *P:* leather with wood frame £240.

GEORGE GILDER
ZOË sofa from a small but quality-conscious firm. Upholstered in soft fabrics like velvet, Dralon or cord, or with linen union or Sanderson prints loose covers, it has a hardwood frame and Pirelli webbing suspension. Cushions, all with zipped covers, are filled with foam, or feathers at extra cost (£6 per seat, £4 per back). A two-seater sofa, and

chair, are available. *M:* three-seater w 79 × h 31 × d 35in (200.5 × 78.5 × 89cm). *P:* £300 as illustrated.

George Gilder's ZOË sofa

GIORGETTI
'6120', a *bergère* gone wild. One of dozens of styles from this high-quality Italian manufacturer, it has fully upholstered cushions, caned seat and back. Wood trim can be lacquered or polished, fabrics are floral prints or plains. *M:* w 144 × h 86 × d 76cm (56¾ × 33⅞ × 30in). *P:* from £750.

'Hollywood' sofa, evocative of days gone by, covered in fabric, suede or leather. Traditionally upholstered, it has a deeply buttoned back, sprung seat, feather-filled cushions, and hand-made fringes. The leather version comes with visible wooden feet. A three-seater sofa is available. *M:* two-seater w 166 × h 70 × d 89cm (65⅜ × 27½ × 35in). *P:* fabric from £900.

GRAFTON INTERIORS
Silk-upholstered armchair from the ultra-stylized MAYA collection by Westamm. The range includes matching two- and three-seater sofas. *M:* w 120 × h 105 × d 100cm (47¼ × 41⅜ × 39⅜in). *P:* £1,200 as illustrated.

Lovely, overstuffed sofa, upholstered here in hand-painted silk, with little lacquered round feet. Part of the MISTRAL range, it can also be covered in traditional calico or any fabric selected by the customer. An armchair and two- and four-seater sofas are available. *M:* to order. *P:* £1,300 as illustrated.

DENNIS GROVES

Practical and good-looking ZIP range of ultra-stylish, ultra-simple seating. Pieces have tubular frames finished in Black or White epoxy resin (other colours to order), wire mesh supports, Kee Klamp steel fittings, and cast-iron joints. Flame-retardant foam padding is covered in a tough cotton and flax mix with Bright green or Chocolate brown stripes on Beige, or Beige stripes on Orange; or Rust, Bright green or Chocolate corduroy. All units are available with high or low backs. *M:* two-seater w 44 × h 16 × d 29½in (115.5 × 40.5 × 75cm). *P:* £115. There's a 30% reduction if you're prepared to put the components together with a twist of your wrist.

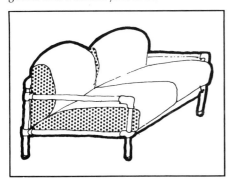

HABITAT DESIGNS LTD

Cheap, cheerful and comfortable 'Chameleon' two-seater for tight spaces and budgets, with an all-beech frame, removable seat cushions, and heavy cotton cover. Its unique feature is that you sew loose covers yourself from a free, full-size paper pattern. They take 9m of plain fabric, 10½m patterned. *M:* w 154 × h 74 × d 86cm (60⅝ × 29⅛ × 33⅞in). *P:* £135.

Habitat's 'Chameleon'

Good-looking 'Lattice' sofa that doubles as a daybed when the back and side cushions are removed. Side and back grid panels are solid birch; polyether foam cushions are covered in Rust, or Rust-dotted Cream, cotton. *M:* w 120 × h 71 × d 78cm (80⅜ × 28 × 30¾in). *P:* £275.

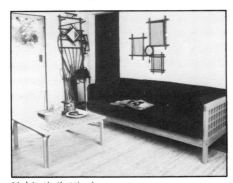

Habitat's 'Lattice'

Adaptable SORBY seating will convert to a bed of any size. Any number of seating units can be combined, and finished with arms from a pack containing two arm panels and two loose cushions. Frames are solid pine, the back panel is chipboard. Foam-filled cushions are covered in Red or Beige quilted cotton. *M:* w 76 × h 69 × d 80cm (30 × 27⅛ × 31½in). *P:* unit £99, arm pack £35.

Sleek, chic and cheap, TECH seating is covered in Beige or Charcoal stain-resistant cotton. Frames are Matt black tubular steel; Dacron-wrapped solid foam cushions rest on seat bases made from ramin slats. *M:* sofa w 145 × h

Habitat's SORBY (above), TECH (below)

76 × d 81cm (57⅛ × 30 × 31⅞in), armchair w 84 × h 76 × d 81cm (33 × 30 × 31⅞in). *P:* £185, £110.

CHARLES HAMMOND LTD

'Louis XV Régence' sofa, illustrated with a fine beech frame and 'Ikat', a striking Lee Jofa upholstery fabric. *M:* w 133 × h 97 × 76cm (52⅜ × 38⅛ × 30in). *P:* £1,100 as illustrated.

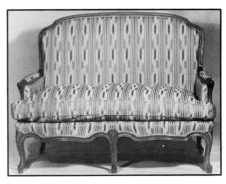

Charles Hammond's extensive range of reproduction Louis XVI furniture also includes a side chair, a *bergère*, a two-seater sofa, a footstool, and three roundback chairs. Frames are hand-finished in the finest beech, and all pieces are supplied painted and upholstered to clients' specifications.

HILLE INTERNATIONAL LTD

'Hexagonal' chairs, designed by Peter Murdoch. Originally designed for reception areas, the witty — but comfortable — shape encourages free-form grouping. The shells, in expanded rigid polyurethane foam, are fully upholstered; loose cushions are reversible. *M:* w 71 × h 57 × d 71cm (28 × 22½ × 28in). *P:* upon application.

Versatile SECTION 3 range, designed by Alan Turville. It consists of an armchair; two wedge-shaped units, one with a wide seat and narrow back, the other with a narrow seat, wide back; and an armless unit. Arms can be fitted between the various pieces. Seating combinations include snakelike curves, straight runs — even a complete circle. *M:* armchair w 56 × h 66 × d 76cm (22 × 26 × 30in). *P:* upon application.

HK FURNITURE LTD

Unique BARBICAN seating, covered in any of nine HK fabrics, the customer's own material, or hide. Virtually a design-it-yourself range, it

HK's BARBICAN

HK's CLOUD

has four cushion widths and four arm shapes, and is upholstered with high-resilience foam and synthetic fleece. *M:* seat unit w 99 × h 75 × d 101cm (39 × 29½ × 39¾in). *P:* as illustrated £3,000.

Very comfortable, futuristic CLOUD is strongly constructed, with a webbed and steel-sprung timber frame; fleece-wrapped foam shapes are inserted into individual pockets over heavy foam underpadding. Coverings as for BARBICAN. *M:* sofa w 263 × h 76 × d 120cm (103½ × 30 × 47¼in). *P:* fabric £1,110.

HOMEWORKS LTD

'SB 107' day-bed and 'SO 178' ottoman by WICKERWORKS, hand-made in Italy. Both come in a natural or Dark brown finish, with loose, reversible buttoned upholstery; also with pleated or tufted and buttoned seats and backs. Five similar sofas, four armchairs, a

chaise-longue and seven side tables are available. *M:* day-bed w 85 × h 29 × d 40in (216 × 73.5 × 101.5cm). *P:* £1,253. See also *Occasional Tables* ('Tables').

BUMPER NO 10 modular seating is available in single, double, triple and corner units with three-tier foam-padded bumpers, or low skirts. Covered in the client's choice of fabric, units can be supplied with hand-webbed, coil-sprung seats. *M:* single unit 31 × 31 × d 35in (78.5 × 78.5 × 89in). *P:* £230.

Homeworks' BUMPER NO 10

PETER HOYTE

Low-lying 'PH32' sling chair on a chromed tubular frame. Upholstery is PVC, Dralon, wool tweed or customer's own fabric. *M:* w 36 × h 30 × d 40in (91.5 × 76 × 102cm). *P:* PVC from £100.

PRICES AND INFORMATION WERE CORRECT AT THE TIME OF GOING TO PRESS

INTERSPACE

Good-looking 'Flexus' reclining chair from a firm that specializes in comfortable office furniture. Ergonomically perfect, with a comfortable head rest, it provides 23 seating angles. High-quality coverings include leather. The matching footstool is optional. *M:* w 97 × h 115 × d 74cm (38¹/₈ × 45¹/₄ × 29¹/₈in). *P:* fabric from £250.

Gracefully curved 'Mondial', resting on steel glides. It comes in a selection of fabrics that complement its simple lines, or can be upholstered to order. *M:* w 95 × h 73 × d 79cm (37³/₈ × 28³/₄ × 31¹/₈in). *P:* from £250.

KNIGHTSBRIDGE UPHOLSTERY

Classically simple CAVENDISH range. Loose covers only are available, in specially selected prints or the customer's own fabric. The range also includes a two-seater sofa, high-back armchair, footstool, and a table with a drop-in glass top. *M:* three seater w 78 × h 32 × d 35in (198 × 81.5 × 89cm). *P:* from £450.

Knightsbridge's CAVENDISH

Country-style PANDORA seating has solid pine frames, covered in printed cotton. Matching scatter cushions are delicately edged with broderie anglaise. The range also includes a convertible three-seater sofa. *M:* two-seater w 50 × h 29 × d 33in (127 × 73.5 × 84cm). *P:* from £235; cushions extra.

Knightsbridge's PANDORA

SCHEHEREZADE is one of the most dramatic sofas on the market. The broad sweeping back and deeply curving arms are equally effective on two- and three-seater versions; an armchair and coffee-table are available. Pieces can be covered in a variety of fabrics from Knightsbridge, or in the customer's own material. *M:* four-seater w 118 × h 33 × d 41in (300 × 84 × 104cm). *P:* from £700; scatter cushions extra.

Similarly sophisticated SAMARKAND, with very broad arms and a deep seat for real comfort, consists of an armchair, and two- and three-seater sofas. *M:* three-seater w 92 × h 34 × d 40in (232.5 × 86.5 × 101.5cm). *P:* from £450.

Knightsbridge's SAMARKAND

Knightsbridge's SCHEHEREZADE

LIFESTYLE DESIGN WORKSHOPS

CANE, one of a number of nicely designed, competitively priced ranges from this company. As with all Lifestyle seating, cushions are filled with highest quality flame-resistant foam, or — unusually — feathers at no extra cost; and all designs can be covered in any fabric selected by the customer. *M:* two-seater w 72 × h 29 × d 29 (183 × 73.5 × 73.5cm). *P:* £485 excluding fabric.

Plain, modular UNIT SEATING. The range also includes an armchair, and two- and three-seater units with or without arms. *M:* single unit without arms 30 × 30 × d 36in (76 × 76 × 91.5cm). *P:* £190 excluding fabric.

PRICES AND INFORMATION WERE CORRECT AT THE TIME OF GOING TO PRESS

WILLIAM L MACLEAN LTD

Louis XV-style armchair, '48/314' is beautifully upholstered, and hand-polished, or painted to order. *M:* w 67 × h 92 × d 78cm (26³⁄₈ × 36¼ × 30¾in). *P:* upon application.

William L Maclean's '48/314'

'49/4006' from the extensive DEAUVILLE range of simulated bamboo furniture in solid beech. This comfortable sofa is finished to order, and upholstered in the customer's choice of fabric. *M:* w 150 × h 100 × d 85cm (59 × 39³⁄₈ × 33½in). *P:* upon application.

William L Maclean's '49/4006'

Beautifully proportioned love seat, with a solid beech frame, from a range of Georgian and Regency reproductions. '49/WM304' is upholstered and finished to clients' specifications. *M:* w 150 × h 86 × d 76cm (59 × 33⁷⁄₈ × 30in). *P:* upon application.

PRICES AND INFORMATION WERE CORRECT AT THE TIME OF GOING TO PRESS

MB's PARTY

William L Maclean's '49/WM304'

MB DESIGN

PARTY by Ekornes, covered in deep-buttoned or patchworked oxhide in a selection of colours. Frames are natural, or Dark brown stained, solid pine. *M:* armchair w 101 × h 72 × d 85cm (39¾ × 28³⁄₈ × 33½in). *P:* £325.

MIRACLES LTD

Very unusual made-to-measure coiled chair made from foam covered with the customer's choice of fabric. *P:* upon application.

NEUROPA LTD

Chic, Italianate '110' sofa from a very British manufacturer. Woodwork is crown ash veneer with solid ash lippings, finished in clear, waterproof, heat-resistant lacquer with Green, Red or Blue perspex, or brass inlay, banding; or Dark brown with Red perspex or brass. Foam and Dacron fibre seats and feather-filled back and side cushions are covered in any of 13 fabrics, or the customer's own material. Woodwork and fabric choices combine to give a total of 78 options. The range also includes an armchair and three-seater sofa; five matching tables are available. *M:* two-seater w 60 × h 36 × d 25½in (152.5 × 91.5 × 65cm). *P:* £500.

OGGI DOMANI

Slick CANARIA with gold-plated steel trim, covered in a selection of fabrics. Unusually, cushion and armrest covers can be removed for cleaning. The range also includes a two-seater sofa. *M:* three-seater w 210 × h 80 × d 100cm (82¾ × 31½ × 39³⁄₈in). *P:* £420.

OMK DESIGN LTD

Stylish CASSIS seating by Rodney Kinsman, upholstered in printed linen, corduroy or velour. One of several self-assembly ranges from this progressive design company, it's made from perforated sheet steel panels with a rigid tubular trim, finished in Black, White, Green, Brown or Terracotta epoxy. A three-

Oggi Domani's CANARIA

seater sofa is available. Components are packed flat for economical transport. *M:* two-seater w 160 × h 74 × d 110cm (63 × 29¹/₈ × 43³/₈in). *P:* £349.

A T RANGE self-assembly tubular chair is by Rodney Kinsman. The polished chrome, or weatherproof nylon-coated, frame is covered in Black or Brown hide, Navy or Oatmeal canvas. *M:* w 75 × h 70 × d 75cm (29¹/₂ × 27¹/₂ × 29¹/₂in). *P:* leather £225. Two- and three-seater sofas are available.

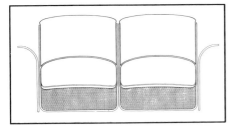

OMK's CASSIS (above), T RANGE (below)

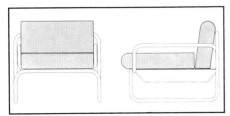

Low-lying UNIT seating is covered in leather, corduroy, velour or the customer's fabric. *M:* single unit (without arms) w 58.4 × h 63.5 × d 86.5cm (23 × 25 ×34in). *P:* from £273.

PARKER KNOLL FURNITURE LTD
Luxurious, traditional 'Bosworth' wing chair. Like all Parker Knoll furniture, it is always eligible for their renovating service. *M:* w 74 × h 101 × d 94cm (29¹/₈ × 39³/₄ × 37in). *P:* from £210.

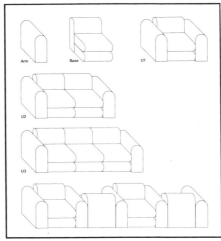

OMK's UNIT

The WAVERLEY suite is covered in Mink velvet, or any of a selection of fabrics. *M:* two-seater w 116 × h 87 × d 84cm (45⁵/₈ × 34¹/₄ × 33in), chair w 68 × h 87 × d 84cm (26³/₄ × 34¹/₄ × 33in). *P:* from £320, £180.

Parker Knoll's 'Bosworth' (above), WAVERLEY (below)

PIEFF FURNITURE LTD
Comfortable velour-covered BOGART seating. The range also includes a two-seater sofa. *M:* three-seater w 240 × h 88 × d 100cm (94¹/₂ × 34⁵/₈ × 39³/₈in). *P:* from £500.

TALIM modular units with quilted cushions covered in Brown suede, leather, or velvet in a choice of colours. Components also include a chair, footstool and table. *M:* corner unit w 80 × h 65 × d 80cm (31¹/₂ × 25¹/₂ × 31¹/₂in). *P:* fabric from £220.

Good-looking VALENTINO. Cubic chrome frames support soft, squishy cushions covered in any of this company's distinctive fabrics, or leather. A matching two-seater sofa, swivel chair and footstool are also available. *M:* three-seater w 239 × h 73 × d 82cm (94¹/₈ × 28³/₄ × 32¹/₄in). *P:* fabric from £650.

QUARTO FURNITURE
Good-looking PRIMO sofa and armchair covered in Dark brown or Creamy beige tailored tweed, with contrast piping. A two-seater sofa is also available. *M:* three-seater w 216.5 × h 71 × d 94cm (85¹/₂ × 28 × 37in). *P:* upon application.

Quarto's PRIMO

RELYON

'Oregon' sofa-bed with an unusual pine and canework frame. Cushions are covered in tweedy Cream on Brown or Brown on Cream windowpane checks; florals also available. *M:* w 165 × h 76 × d 84–198cm (65 × 30 × 33–78in). *P:* £440.

Remploy's 'UC21'

REMPLOY FURNITURE

'UC21', a cottage chair covered in one of three floral fabrics with Dark brown, Tan or Charcoal grounds. *M:* w 78 × h 83 × d 85cm (30¾ × 32 ⅝ × 33½in). *P:* £160. There's also a fully upholstered version.

REST ASSURED LTD

Traditional BALMORAL SUITE with deep-buttoned, hand-pleated back cushions, shaped for extra support. The fringe is optional. *M:* three-seater w 203 × h 79 × d 91cm (79⅞ × 31⅛ × 35⅞in). *P:* from £400.

Attractive 'Topaz' three-seater sofa that becomes a single bed when the L-shaped bolsters are removed; or unfolds to form a

full-size double bed. One of a large range of sofa-beds, it's upholstered in selected grades of foam, the seat and bolsters lined with a soft, fleecy fabric for extra comfort. *M:* w 198 × h 70 × d 81–177cm (77⅛ × 27½ × 31⅞in–70in). *P:* from £250.

SCANDIA

Handsome, beautifully crafted '2192' sofa with a wood frame, fully upholstered in leather. Three- and four-seater versions are available. *M:* w 60½ × h 41¾ × d 35in (153.5 × 106 × 89cm). *P:* £1,360.

SLEEPEEZEE LTD

CUDDLER sofa that converts into a single bed with interior sprung mattress. Coverings include floral linen unions, herringbone tweeds, geometric prints and plain or figured velvets. *M:* w 136 × h 82 × d 90cm (53 × 32½ × 35½in). *P:* from £430. A three-seater/double bed version is available. Other sofa-beds are boxy ALBANY, classic BRIGHTON with a loose-cushioned back, and contemporary, low-backed ROGUE and WARWICK with loose cushions. All except BRIGHTON come as two- and three-seater sofas.

Right: Selection from Baker, Knapp & Tubbs' CHARLESTON

JANE THOMAS

Chic two-seater sofa. The frame in high gloss paintwork matches the softly shining chintz upholstery or the piping accents. Other fabrics to order. As illustrated, the sofa would look marvellous with Jane Thomas's PYRAMID lights (illustrated in colour on page 147). An armchair is available. *M:* two-seater w 160 × h 81 × d 72cm (63 × 31^7/$_8$ × 28^3/$_8$). *P:* £650.

TOGGLE MOULDINGS LTD

'TW4' with a moulded glass-reinforced plastic frame, and matching cushion upholstery. Colours are White, Red, Yellow, Dark brown and Light stone, or to order. *M:* w 81 × h 70 × d 36cm (31^7/$_8$ × 27^1/$_2$ × 14^1/$_8$in). *P:* £58. Also available without upholstery.

R TYZACK LTD

Generously proportioned '1068', upholstered in plain or deep-buttoned hide. *M:* w 32 × h 45 × d 34in (81.5 × 114.5 × 86.5cm). *P:* from £600. A smaller, less curvaceous version is available; also a similar, but more elegant, wing chair. Other Tyzack reproductions include Chesterfields, a 'tub' chair and a Victorian-style spindle-legged chair, both with matching two-seater sofas, and the low-backed GEORGIAN range with deep-buttoned inside back and arms, and cushion seats.

Left: Collins & Hayes' ECLAIR

Tyzack's '1068'

WADE SPRING & UPHOLSTERY CO LTD

MANDARIN, one of some two dozen splendidly traditional ranges — Wade have specialized in high-quality upholstered furniture since 1922. The base, optionally covered with skirts, is made from mahogany. A matching wing chair is also available. *M:* three-seater w 180 × h 72 × d 52cm (70^7/$_8$ × 28^3/$_8$ × 20^1/$_2$in). *P:* from £530. The leather-covered 'Minor' YORK suite also comes in fabric. The range includes a lift-top footstool. *M:* Chesterfield w 183 × h 66 × d 86.5cm (72 × 26 × 34in). *P:* leather £850. YORK also comes in a larger 'Major' version.

Wade's MANDARIN (above), YORK (below)

WELBECK HOUSE (SANDIACRE UPHOLSTERY) LTD

Deep-buttoned chaise-longue, love seat and porter's chair, upholstered in Ice blue, Mink, Bronze, Pale green, Red, Dusty pink, Champagne or Midnight blue Dralon, or any of three striped velours, with bobble fringe trim. The porter's chair can be fitted with a stereo and two speakers. *M:* porter's chair w 35 × h 63 × d 36in (89 × 160 × 91.5cm). *P:* £500. Also wing chairs and Chesterfields.

Classic 'Chatsworth' has an arched back, rolled-over arms and turned wooden feet. It comes with four scatter cushions, in a choice of seven fabrics. Matching four-seater sofa and bed sofa versions. *M:* 80 × h 33 × d 40in (203.5 × 84 × 101.5cm). *P:* £700.

Welbeck's deep-buttoned suite

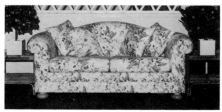

Welbeck's 'Chatsworth'

WESLEY-BARRELL (WITNEY) LTD
Well-designed BLENHEIM sofa-bed with wide, padded arms and foam-filled cushions. A single chair and two-seater sofa are available, both convertible. Options include scatter cushions, a 1¾in (4.5cm) thick foam mattress — and, like all of this company's seating — matching curtains or blinds, to order. *M:* w 81 × h 31½ × d 22in (80 × 206 × 56cm). *P:* £260.

Wesley-Barrell's BLENHEIM

CHESTERFIELD three-seater upholstered in Liberty's 'Ianthe', a tough 54% flax and 46% cotton mixture. Also available deep-buttoned in plain fabrics, this great range also includes wing and low chairs, and a two-seater. Both sofas are available as bed-settees. *M:* w 82 × h 28½ × d 24in (208.5 × 72.5 × 61cm). *P:* £430.

Wesley-Barrell's CHESTERFIELD

Fresh New England colonial-style DELAWARE with reversible seat, back and arm cushions is also available with loose covers and/or feather-filled back and arm cushions. Two- and three-seaters can be supplied as bed-sofas.

WESTNOFA (LONDON) LTD
ORBIT reclining chair that adjusts to body weight, by Ingmar Relling. It has a natural or stained laminated beech frame, leather upholstery. *M:* w 72 × h 95 × d 105cm (28⅜ × 37⅜ × 41⅜in). *P:* from £300. Also available without arms, and as a two-seater sofa.

Westnofa's ORBIT reclining chair

'Panter', a leather-upholstered reclining chair by Arnt Lande. The laminated beech frame comes in five finishes including Black, rosewood and teak. *M:* w 77 × h 94 × d 85–130cm (30⅜ × 37 × 33½–57¼in). *P:* from £380.

ROBERT WHITING DESIGNS LTD
Generously proportioned ADAGIO unit seating with foam-filled cushions and fixed or loose cushion covers. Like all Robert Whiting's ranges it can be upholstered in a variety of fabrics including the company's own prints, or in Chocolate brown, Terracotta, and Oatmeal beige linen union. Similarly, scatter cushions can be supplied with all seating; armcaps are available. *M:* corner unit w 89 × h 74 × d 89cm (35 × 29⅛ × 35in). *P:* £140.

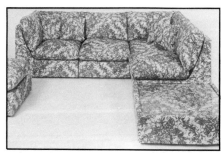

Robert Whiting's ADAGIO

POLLO, with low, clean lines, is available as a chair with optional removable headrest, and two- and three-seater sofas.

BELLAMO with fixed covers, bordered skirts, contrast piping, and hand-quilted seat and back cushions — motifs are outlined with silk thread. Also available with a high back. The range includes an armchair, stool, table and three-seater sofa and sofa-bed. *M:* two-seater w 140 × h 82 × d 90cm (55⅛ × 32¼ × 35⅜in). *P:* £460.

Robert Whiting's BELLAMO

DELFINO three-seater sofa. Available in calico or with loose covers, the range includes a low-backed two-seater sofa or sofa-bed, high-backed three-seater sofa-bed, armchair and stool. *M:* w 140 × h 82 × d 90cm (55⅛ × 32¼ × 35⅜in). *P:* calico from £230.

Robert Whiting's DELFINO

Loose-covered POLLYANNA. Very good value for money, it has a matching three-seater sofa, high- or low-backed armchair, footstool and table. *M:* two-seater w 140 × h 77 × d 87cm (56 × 30⅜ × 34¼in). *P:* £230.

Robert Whiting's POLLYANNA

INTRODUCTION

Successful decorating depends largely on using the right product – and/or the right tool – for a specific job.

Although tools can be expensive, it's important to buy the best you can afford. High-quality items will not only last longer, providing better value in the long term, but will also be more reliable and give better results. But do make sure you really need them, and learn how to use them properly.

This section is devoted to rather unusual products, which you may not know even exist. For convenience, it's broken down into the following parts: *Adhesives; Carpet Protectors; Polishes; Sealants; Miscellaneous* (ranging from exotic veneers to wood fillers); *Tools;* and *Upholstery Supplies.*

ADHESIVES

BOSTIK LTD

Wide range of adhesives from a well-known manufacturer. It includes all-purpose clear BOSTIK 1 (*P:* 62p); BOSTIK 3 contact adhesive for plastic laminates, wood, rubber, metal, leather and woodwork (*P:* 84p); BOSTIK 8 for laying parquet floors (*P:* 85p); and multi-tile BOSTIK 4 for ceramic, metal, mirror and polystyrene tiles (*P:* 70p). BOSTIK 10 HYPER BOND (M 890) will bond anything and achieve final strength within ten minutes (*P:* £1.25). Prices are for the smallest sizes.

CIBA-GEIGY

ARALDITE epoxy resin adhesive. Heat-resistant and waterproof, it forms extremely strong, durable bonds between metal, glass, wood, plastics, rubber, etc. Supplied in two tubes, which must be mixed before use, it takes 12 hours to set so some kind of clamp is necessary. *P:* 30gm (1oz) 95p. ARALDITE RAPID for difficult to clamp jobs, also in two tubes, sets in ten minutes. *P:* 30gm (1oz) £1.12.

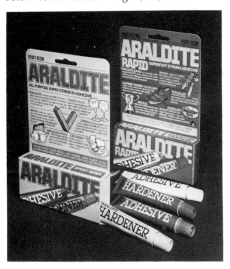

CLAM-BRUMMER LTD

Wide range of CLAM adhesives for general use, carpets and textiles, vinyl flooring and wall coverings, and expanded polystyrene. It includes a wallpaper paste, and 'Gold Label Clam 143' adhesive specially formulated for most types of heavy wall coverings (*P:* ½ l/17½ fl oz 75p). By applying 'Peel' to walls before papering, wallpapers can be peeled off in complete lengths when redecorating, without the need for soaking or scraping. *P:* 1l (1¾pt) £2.20.

DUNLOP SEMTEX LTD

Useful selection of contact adhesives for woodworking and flooring, and a specialist product for cork. Wall and ceiling tile adhesives are also available. *P:* Woodworker 100ml (3½fl oz) 50p; P.V.A. Wall Tile Adhesive 2½l (4⅜pt) £2.50; Ceiling Tile Adhesive ¼l (8¾fl oz) 60p; Cork Adhesive ½l (17½fl oz) £1.

HENKEL CHEMICALS LTD

SOLVITE adhesives. A general-purpose wallpaper paste is suitable for all weights, including washable and vinyl papers (*P:* 2oz/57gm 37½p). There's also a ready-mix adhesive for heavier decorative materials such as hessians, fabric backed vinyls, etc, and a special adhesive for heavyweight wallpapers (*P:* 2¼oz/350gm 98p). The VINYL OVERLAP adhesive bonds overlapping vinyl wallpaper seams quickly and easily (*P:* 2oz/60gm 66p). Other decorators' materials include interior fillers for plaster and wood, wallpaper stripper, and sanding blocks.

PURIMACHOS LTD

FIXATILE heat-resistant tile cement for fireplaces and boiler surrounds. It will

withstand temperatures up to 1,000°C, and provide gas and smoke-tight joints. *P:* 250gm (8¾oz) 85p. KOS fire cement, for use where heat and fumes have to be contained, is ideal for pointing fireplace bricks or sealing fireplaces (*P:* 500gm/17½oz 82p). Purimachos BATH STAIN REMOVER, a specially formulated jelly, removes hard water and rust stains from baths, tiles and taps (*P:* 15oz/428gm tube 68p).

CARPET PROTECTORS

3M UK LTD

SCOTCHGARD CARPET PROTECTOR fluorochemical textile finish, developed for use on carpets by the 3M Company. It protects against dry and water-based soiling, and also resists oil-based soiling – caused by smoke, for example. It is applied to the carpet during manufacture, or to new or freshly cleaned carpets by a 3M-licensed applicator. Treated carpets stay cleaner up to three times longer than untreated ones; protection should last through several cleanings. *P:* upon application.

STAPRO LTD

STAPRO FLUOROCATION PROTECTOR for carpeting and upholstery. It is effective on all colours, including White, and all fibres, except polypropylene. As with SCOTCHGARD, a treated carpet should stay clean up to three times longer than an untreated one. New carpeting obviously benefits most, but existing carpets can be treated, provided they have first been cleaned professionally. STAPRO also reduces the level of static. A same-day service for cleaning and protecting carpets is available. Stapro also provide two flame-retardant treatments. *P:* upon application.

TREWAX MANUFACTURING LTD
'Hydro-Mist-650' hot-water soil extraction cleaner, available for hire from Trewax stockists. It avoids conventional shampoo which can leave behind a residue which in turn attracts dirt. A chemical solution is applied to dissolve dirt, then hot water is sprayed into the fibres, where it merges with the dirt. Both the water and chemical are then vacuumed out at high pressure. The process is suitable for most colour-fast upholstery fabrics, except silk, satin and velvet. The machine weighs only 24lb and can be hired nationwide. *P:* upon application.

POLISHES

A BELL & CO LTD
Liquid wax BELL MARBLE POLISH for use, sparingly, on all marble including floors (*P:* ½pt/280ml £2.75). BELSEALER is for slightly porous surfaces like natural slate (*P:* ½pt/280ml £4.10). BELL 1967 CLEANER is an excellent multi-purpose cleaner and degreaser (*P:* ½pt/280ml £2).

D FARMILOE
'Touch and Go' French polish kit. Each kit contains six bottles of French polish stains – dark and light mahogany, medium and dark oak, and medium walnut and teak – plus wax stopping, in four shades, to fill deep scratches and dents before repolishing. Easy-to-follow instructions are also supplied. *P:* kit £5.65 including postage, bottle of stain 4fl oz (140ml) £1.32.

HENRY FLACK LTD
Very wide range of often hard-to-find polishes, lacquers, sealers, stains, solvents, oils, varnishes, and paint and varnish removers.
It includes HARRACKS high-quality, general purpose wax polish (*P:* 483ml/16¾fl oz 90p), unbeatable BRIWAX hard wax polish in four wood shades plus clear (*P:* 483ml/16¾fl oz £1.50); classic BEESWAX (*P:* 450gm/1lb £3.25); SHERADALE antique wax with beeswax base (*P:* 483ml/16¾fl oz £1.50); and a LIQUID GLASS polish reviver (*P:* 200ml/7fl oz 60p). Because this company is basically a trade supplier orders must be worth at least £10, excluding carriage and VAT.

MARRABLE & CO LTD
Lots of finishing materials, including a very good quality French polish. All are available from the company's trade counter at 22 Bateman's Row, London EC2. *M:* minimum 1l (1¾pt).

PRICES AND INFORMATION WERE CORRECT AT THE TIME OF GOING TO PRESS

SEALANTS

BOSTIK LTD
Fantastically useful sealing strip for gaps around windows and baths. A kind of sticky putty, it doesn't harden or crack and can be overpainted, but its adhesive properties mean it can't be used on surfaces which have to be opened and closed frequently. *M:* 17in (43.5cm). *P:* pack of six strips 80p.

R N BRADLEY
BRYDALE draught excluders. Cut to size with ordinary hand tools before being screwed or nailed to the base of the door, they come with flexible rubber or plastic strips, or brush tufts. *M:* BRYDALE X 3ft (91.5cm). *P:* £8.10. A foam draughtproofing strip for doors and windows, and a more substantial strip with a wipe-clean plastic surface, are also available. *M:* BRYDALE FOAM 20ft (610cm) lengths. *P:* 60p.

SILICONE PRODUCTS
SANITARY 1700, specially formulated for bathrooms, is flexible and mildew resistant. Perfect for high humidity areas, it is available in White only. SILGLAZE, a glazing sealant, weathers outstandingly well. Intended primarily for exterior commercial use, cartridges come in useful and unusual translucent, Black, aluminium, bronze, and White. Quantities are larger than the normal do-it-yourself sizes, but anyone who's serious about sealing should contact this company. *P:* upon application.

SLOTTSEAL LTD
Mail-order selection of draught excluders, all for use on doors. BEADSTRIP and RAILSEAL are also perfect for sliding sash windows, which are otherwise difficult to draughtproof without going to the expense of double glazing. *M:* l. 1m (3ft 3³/8in). BULBSTRIP is ideal for casement and pivot windows (*M:* l. 1m/3ft 3³/8in). WEATHERSTRIP, an aluminium and vinyl doorset, is in natural aluminium for painting, or finished in brass for the outside of external doors. *M:* two strips l. 1.3m (4ft 3¼in), l. 86.5cm (34in). THRESHOLD BRUSH STRIPS for the base of internal and external doors are PVC or aluminium, with nylon brushes (*M:* l. 3ft/91.5cm). *P:* upon application.

MISCELLANEOUS

ART VENEER CO
Comprehensive mail order service for home woodcraftsmen or women. 50 exotic veneers range from afara, ayan, and afrormosia to zebrawood; sample sets of this company's array of exquisite woods will inspire even the most ham-fisted. (*P:* sq ft from 30p–£1.20). Other products include special adhesives, abrasives, polishes and veneer-laying tools;

also marquetry sets and ready-made period inlays and bandings.

Selection of Art Veneer's ready-made period inlays

CLAM-BRUMMER LTD
Wide range of problem-solving BRUMMER STOPPING wood fillers. 'Yellow Label', for interior use, prepares wood for a professional finish and comes in 13 shades (*P:* 65p). 'Green Label' is for use outside, and on yachts (*P:* 86p). 'Rub-in Woodgrain' filler primes, seals and fills in one operation. Suitable for using under any top coat, it's perfect for whitewood (unfinished) furniture, and fibreglass. Six standard wood shades are available, plus neutral for self staining (*P:* £1.12). 'Red Label' filler remains soft and flexible in heat or cold, is completely waterproof, adheres to wood, iron, glass, concrete and fibreglass, and can be coated with paint or varnish (*P:* £1.10). 'Blue Label' metal filler is for smoothing cracks and dents (*P:* 63p). Oil-based 'Woodgrain Filler' seals exceptionally porous surfaces like chipboard (*P:* £1.12). 'Plastic Filler' for holes and cracks in plaster won't shrink, can be used on grouting, and will adhere to bare or painted surfaces. Prices are for the smallest sizes.

DYLON INTERNATIONAL LTD
COLOUR FUN FABRIC PAINT for anyone who yearns to create their own (not too complicated) designs. Suitable for all fabrics, even synthetics, it can also be used with lino and potato cuts for screen printing. The paints come in 12 non-toxic colour-fast colours, including Black and White, which can be mixed to make hundreds of shades. *P:* 25ml (½fl oz) 60p, 1l/1¾pt £13. Other useful products include 'Dygon' colour and stain remover; rain and stain repellents for fabric, and suede and leather; Dylon Super White, Nylon White and Curtain White; and dyes.

Selection of kitchen accessories decorated with Dylon's COLOUR FUN FABRIC PAINT

HARRISON-BEACON LTD
All the small items needed for redecorating. This hardware manufacturer's range includes bolts, catches, chains, hooks, mirror and picture fittings, plumbers' accessories (cistern pulls, plugs, etc), door stops, upholstery nails, castors, curtain wire, nails, screws, etc.

STERLING RONCRAFT
KURUST rust remover and metal primer from a firm that's best known for its RONSEAL wood stains and varnishes. *P:* 125ml (4½fl oz) £1.10. KURUST JELLY is for surfaces that want protection, but don't require painting. *P:* 125ml (4½fl oz) 96p. SPEEDSTRIP wallpaper and paint remover converts paint into a peelable skin; and enables several thicknesses of any wall covering to be stripped after a single application. *P:* 1.4l (c 2½pt) pack covering up to 20sq m (215sq ft) £4.

TOOLS

ATTRACTA PRODUCTS LTD
ROLL ROCKET PAINTING MACHINE to take the mess out of painting. Available by mail order only, it has an airtight, fully enclosed paint reservoir that prevents drips and splashes, and makes paint go further by controlling the flow to the lambswool roller. Suitable for use with any emulsion paint, but not gloss, it will cover a 12 × 9ft (366 × 274.5cm) wall without refilling. *P:* £7.99 plus 65p p&p, including spare roller.

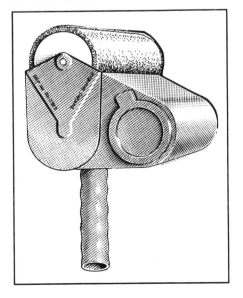

Attracta's ROLL ROCKET (right)

Wallpaper (top) and paint (above) treated with Sterling Roncraft's SPEEDSTRIP

BEAVER INTERNATIONAL PAINTS LTD
'Touch 'n Grip'' abrasive sanding discs. A flat backing pad with a selection of adhesive-coated discs, it fits any do-it-yourself drill, and sands evenly, without distortion. *P:* pad and three mixed discs £3.50.

ROBERT BOSCH LTD
Professional power tools from one of Europe's leading manufacturers. Made from a unique glass-fibre reinforced polyamide, they are lightweight, heat-resistant, and absorb sound. The range includes eight hammer drills, all of which switch to a simple drill action (*P:* £35–£80), and a jigsaw and circular saw. *P:* jigsaw £32, 6in (15.5cm) circular saw £46. A lathe kit is one of the more unusual items. *P:* £54.

BOSTIK LTD
Two riveting tools from a company whose name is synonymous with adhesives. UNIMARK SENIOR, for the more professional do-it-yourself handyman, will set three sizes of rivets (*P:* £12). The UNIMARK POP RIVET KIT is simpler to use, and useful for materials like leather and heavy denim (*P:* £5.50).

BURMAH INDUSTRIAL PRODUCTS LTD
Extensive range of fixings and allied products, made by the well-known Rawlplug Company, a division of Burmah Industrial Products. Products include specialized fixings like gravity or spring toggles or rivets, and METALIDE or DURIUM masonry drill bits, plus glass drills, soldering irons, abrasive discs, and tile and laminate cutters. RAWLANCHOR cavity fitting, designed for use with wood screws, consists of tough nylon flanged tubes split to allow expansion (*P:* six screws from 45p, 100 from £3). The ROTOSAND, a long-lasting solid plastic wheel impregnated with aluminium oxide grit, can be used with any high-speed drill to remove paint, varnish, rust and surface imperfections, gently but effectively (*P:* £2.50).

PRICES AND INFORMATION WERE CORRECT AT THE TIME OF GOING TO PRESS

CEKA WORKS LTD
All the hand and garden tools anyone is ever likely to need, from a long-established company. The range caters both for home handymen and skilled craftsmen, and includes punch pliers for leather, plastic or card (*P:* £4), and impact drivers for loosening or tightening stubborn nuts, bolts, or screws (*P:* £4). A wide variety of scissors, including paper-hanging versions, is also available.

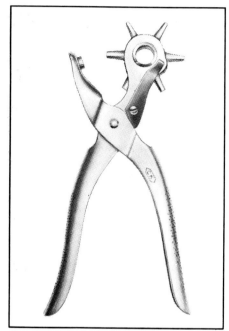

Ceka's '3817' punch pliers

FLORIN LTD
Diverse VITREX equipment for home decorators. Several safety appliances are available: a protective mask comes with five spare filters (*P:* £1.10); also safety goggles, ear protectors, and a face shield. A set of 'odd-job' brushes for painting, glueing, de-rusting, etc, is cheap enough to throw away after use (*P:* £1.35). The long-lasting VITREX tungsten carbide rod saw fits standard hacksaw frames; it cuts ceramic tiles and hard materials from brick to steel easily, and in any direction including slots, angles and curves. *P:* 10in (25.5cm) £2, 12in (30.5cm) £2.50.

MONOCO LTD
High quality MUNDIAL SHEARS scissors and shears, made in Brazil. Paper-cutting scissors with 10in (25.5cm) blades are perfect for paper-hanging (*P:* £3.50).

GRAHAM OXLEY TRADE TOOLS LTD
High-quality wood-working tools made from Sheffield steel. A wide range of chisels, gouges, trade knives and saws is available.

JOHN PALMER LTD
VICTORY brushes for every job from painting and paper-hanging to sweeping chimneys. The range also includes household brooms and, more unusually, feather dusters and corn brooms. *P:* corn broom £1.60.

F PARRAMORE & SONS LTD
PARAMO and CLAY quality tools. They include 13 vices and hammers and 18 screwdrivers, plus saws, trimming knives, drill bits, and filling and stripping knives. Unusual items are an upholsterer's ripping chisel (*P:* £3.60–£5) and spiral ratchet screwdrivers which take an assortment of bits (*P:* £9–£16).

PATON, CALVERT & CO LTD
Popular 'Paintmaster' rollers and trays, widely available from department stores and super-markets. Rollers are short- or long-pile pure wool, or polyester foam (*M:* w 7in/17.5cm). Covers are easily removed for cleaning, and can be replaced. *P:* roller and tray £2.20–£3.50.

PIFCO LTD
Two mains tester screwdrivers from a firm that's well-known for its electrical products. The blades are moulded into the casing, and a neon indicator glows when they touch a live circuit. *P:* 5in (12.5cm) Mains Tester 80p, Senior Mains Tester 95p, Circuit Tester 95p.

STANLEY TOOLS LTD
Huge range of quality hand tools from one of the country's best-known manufacturers, and a good spare part service. Stanley's famous range of small knives with replaceable blades includes trimmers, handles designed to hold small saw blades, knives with retracting blades, front-loading knives for easy blade replacement, models with snap-off blades, a throwaway knife set, and retractable and folding pocket knives. The trimming knife, probably the best known, has an assortment of seven blades for all kinds of jobs. (*P:* £1.40, five blades 40p–55p). Unusual items include a 'Clamp-Web', with 12ft (366cm) of nylon webbing tensioned by easy-action ratchet, to repair sagging chair bottoms (*P:* £5.80).

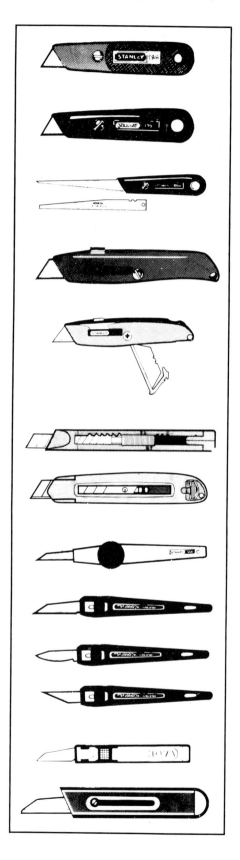

Selection of Stanley Tools' knives (from top): '199' and '199E' trimming knives; saw knife set; knife with a retractable blade; front-loading knife; knives with snap-off blades; craft knife; '5901', '5905', '5903' throwaway knives; nova knife; pocket knife with a retractable blade

PRICES AND INFORMATION WERE CORRECT AT THE TIME OF GOING TO PRESS

UPHOLSTERY SUPPLIES

DANGLES & CO

Hand-made tassels in a great range of colours and styles for light switches, roller blinds, etc. MINI DANGLES come in three styles, LARGE DANGLES in five. Both are available in Black, Dark brown, Navy, Emerald, Gold, Hot pink, Pale pink, and Beige. *M:* MINI DANGLES ¾–2½in (2–6.5cm) plus shank, LARGE 3in (7.5cm). *P:* £2.40–£5.80, £7.

DISTINCTIVE TRIMMINGS CO LTD

Huge stock of furnishing trimmings. Outstanding items include a barrier or staircase rope in acrylic or wool worsted yarn, complete with brass fittings. Curtain tie-backs have single or double tassels, other styles to order. Upholstery fringes come in 27 shades (*M:* w 3in/7.5cm, *P:* from m £1.10), or can be specially dyed (*M:* w 2–10in/5–25.5cm). Tiffany fringe is Black, Brown, or White (*M:* w 6, 12in/15, 30.5cm, *P:* from m £1.80); trellis-headed fringing comes in a very large range of colours. Key and bolster tassels, light pulls, and woven curtain borders are also available. (*M:* w 1¼–3½in/3–9cm, *P:* curtain border from m £2). Other products include decorative hooks, gimps, braids and ruches – but no haberdashery items like bias binding or ribbons. There's no catalogue, but the company offers a postal service. Sample/s will be sent by return post on receipt of a fabric swatch and indication of the type of trimming required, plus a self-addressed stamped envelope.

PRICES AND INFORMATION WERE CORRECT AT THE TIME OF GOING TO PRESS

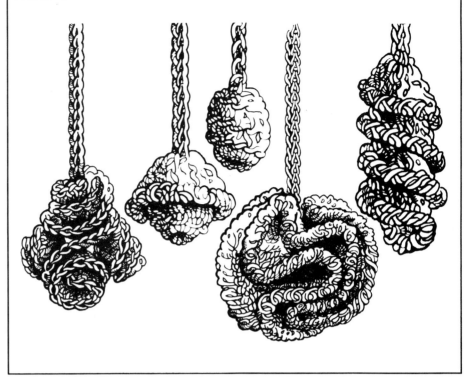

Dangles' LARGE pulls

D L FORSTER LTD

Very varied mail-order range of DELF upholstery sundries – virtually everything that you could ever need, except the fabric. Products range from adhesives through calico and cotton felt, fillings, nails, needles, piping cord, and tools like stretchers and tack removers, to webbing and zips. See overleaf for illustration.

PIRELLI

Rubber seating products, especially useful for renovating sagging frame chairs. 'Sisiara' nylon fabric springing panel for chair seats, rubber back straps, and 'Fabweb' webbing are available, plus staples, clips and hooks, and a webbing tensioner. *P:* upon application. See overleaf for illustration.

TISSUNIQUE LTD

Wondrous range of upholstery trims imported by a company popular with interior decorators. LA PASSEMENTERIE NOUVELLE includes woven cotton braids, fringes, borders, tassels, and much more. They come in standard shades, but specially woven colours cost only 10% extra. Thick, chunky woollen trims are perfect for complementing or accenting nubbly carpets, rugs, and upholstery fabrics. *P:* upon application.

G T YOUNG & CO LTD

Upholstery sundries like twines, needles, baize, webbing and hessian. Cut lengths of flame-retardant fabrics, dust sheets, tarpaulins and plastic sheeting are also available. *P:* upon application.

Selection of trims from Distinctive Trimmings

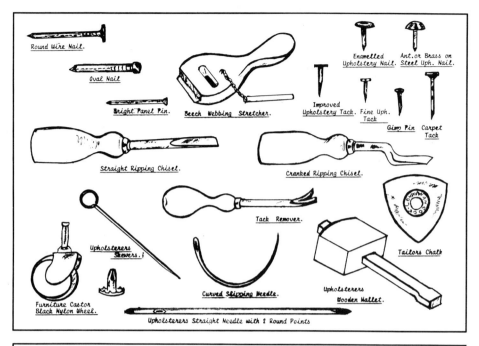

Round Wire Nail.

Oval Nail.

Bright Panel Pin.

Beech Webbing Stretcher.

Enamelled Upholstery Nail.

Ant. or Brass on Steel Uph. Nail.

Improved Upholstery Tack.

Fine Uph. Tack

Gimp Pin

Carpet Tack

Straight Ripping Chisel.

Cranked Ripping Chisel.

Tack Remover.

Upholsterers Skewers.

Curved Slipping Needle.

Tailors Chalk

Furniture Castor Black Nylon Wheel.

Upholsterers Wooden Mallet.

Upholsterers Straight Needle with 2 Round Points

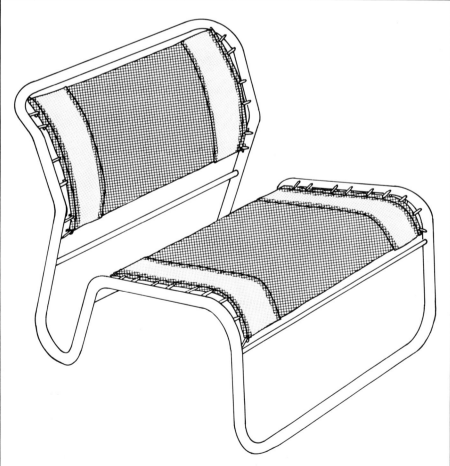

Left, top: Selection from Forster's range of upholstery tools and supplies

Left, below: Pirelli's 'Sisiara' nylon fabric springing panels

PRICES AND INFORMATION WERE CORRECT AT THE TIME OF GOING TO PRESS

Selection of co-ordinating fabrics and wall coverings (right):
Designers Guild's 'Shells' fabric (1), wallpaper (2), from GERANIUM
Elizabeth Eaton's 'Hilda' (3), 'Hilda Border' (4), 'Saighton' (5)
David Sage's 'Condotti' (6), 'Graffiti' (7)
Mary Fox Linton's 'Biron' (8)
Designers Guild's 'Small Peaweed' wallpaper (9), fabric (11), from VILLAGE
Mary Fox Linton's 'Aurillac' (10), 'Blois' (12)
Sartor's 'Maidenhair' (13, 18)
Paper Moon's AFRICA (14, 15)
Sartor's 'Honesty' (16), 'Dragonfly' (17)
Habitat's 'Alphabet' fabric (19), wallpaper (20)
Sartor's 'Chrysanthemum' (22)
Paper Moon's 'Chickens' wallpaper (23), fabric (29), from LA NATURE, 'Stars' wallpaper (24)
Habitat's 'Camargue' wallpaper (25), fabric (26)
Coloroll's 'Picatee' (27), 'Geraldine' (28), both from DOLLY MIXTURES
Paper Moon's 'Check for Chickens' (30)
Elizabeth Eaton's 'Small Grid' from YVES HALLARD (31)
CVP's 'Tassel' (32)
Habitat's 'Alouette' wallpaper (33), fabric (34)
Designers Guild's 'Peaweed' from VILLAGE (35)

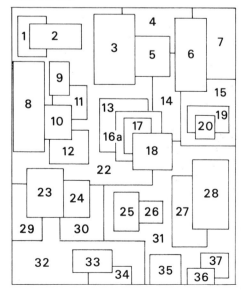

INTRODUCTION

What began as a draught-excluding exercise has become a multi-million-pound industry. In the past, tapestries and leather hangings were used to keep rooms warm, and for wall decoration, in the place of much more expensive paintings. Today, the insulating properties of wall coverings are usually of secondary importance. Decoratively, however, they can make or break an interior scheme, adding life to a dull, featureless room.

Luckily, the choice of designs and materials is almost limitless. Cheerful floral patterns and chic geometrics and stripes are still on the market, but so are rainbows, squiggles, grasses, mock suedes, metallics, faithful period reproductions, and much more.

Materials include practical cork, supplied by the roll, for excellent soundproofing; textured panels specifically for heat insulation; and hardwearing wipeable vinyls, in a myriad designs.

Paper-backed fabrics, including beautiful natural yarns, that create an atmosphere of warmth and cosiness, are also available. These thicker coverings will also disguise unsightly old walls.

Wall coverings are immediate mood setters, so take time over your choice. The size of the repeat is important – a large pattern will overwhelm a small room – so check this with the manufacturer. And remember, the larger the pattern, the more rolls you will need for matching. Before making your final decision, hang samples (the largest available) on the walls concerned.

Prices vary enormously, from paper for as little as £2.50 a roll, to fabrics and contract wall coverings (usually also textile based), both of which are usually bought by the metre. Machine and hand-printed papers are both silkscreen printed, but the latter (some printed from wood blocks) are slower to produce, often involve several complex colour registers, and are therefore more expensive. However, they can frequently be coloured to order.

The first part of this section lists the various wall coverings on the market. Co-ordinates, the second, deals with complementary fabrics and wall coverings. Some consist of groups of papers – as many as seven – that mix with each other and/or match plain or patterned fabrics. In others, larger or smaller versions of a basic motif are available on both fabrics and wall coverings, fabrics only, or wall coverings only. Co-ordination may also be achieved by isolating an element from a complicated pattern. Or the basic design may be unchanged, but come in reverse colourways on the fabric or covering.

To accent a relatively plain paper or fabric, combine it with a border where the ceiling

Selection from TT Design's CHARTERHOUSE collection (see Co-ordinates)

meets the walls, around a door, or in place of picture rails, wainscotting, etc.

For a more individual effect, it's always possible to create your own look by selecting colour co-ordinated fabrics and wallpapers from different manufacturers. See our collage illustrating just this point on page 289.

Whether you decide on total co-ordination, based on a manufacturer's designs, or your own choice, it's wise to carry the same, or a similar, colour scheme throughout your house. Co-ordination has run wild over the last few years, and it's possible to match bedlinen, rugs, blinds, ceramic tiles and paintwork, as well as wall coverings and fabrics. Where relevant, we refer you to these sections at the end of an entry.

Finally, if coverings aren't to your taste, any of the muralists listed in this section will paint your desired fantasy on the walls of your choice.

*Most papers are 20–27in (51–68.5cm) wide, 10m (11yd) long. However, contract quality wall coverings tend to be wider, and are usually sold by the metre.

*In *Co-ordinates* we give prices for 1m (39³⁄₈in) of fabric and one roll of wall covering, unless otherwise stated.

ARENSON INTERNATIONAL LTD

Amazing FABRITRAK system for covering walls with fabric — the perfect solution for anyone who's ever been frustrated by co-ordinates that are supposed to match, but don't. Any fabric from the lightest silk to the heaviest damask can be stretched into place to complete a decorating scheme, and/or disguise unsightly walls. Professional fitting of wall tracks is advised— fabric is inserted with a special tool. Fabrics can be easily removed for cleaning; or re-used elsewhere if the original scheme is changed. Sound and heat insulating materials are available as backing. *P:* m £1.25, locking-in tool £2.50.

MARTHE ARMITAGE

Absolutely exquisite papers hand-printed from hand-cut wood blocks. Colours are mixed for each order, all printed on White grounds. Commissions are accepted; fabric will also be printed on request. *M:* roll w 22, 30in × 11yd (56, 76cm×10m). *P:* roll £11.50–£18.

ARMSTRONG CORK CO LTD

Attractive, acoustical wall panels from a company known for its flooring. SOUNDSOAK, a lightweight mineral board, has a vertically embossed fabric surface in Mist (off-white), Flagstone (cool beige), Wheat, Caramel, Wood (light), and Paprika. Suitable for a single wall, or an entire room, the panels can be applied to almost any surface. *M:* 270×60cm (106¼×23⁵⁄₈in). *P:* upon application.

Hand-printed paper from a selection by Marthe Armitage

JOHN BOATH JNR & CO LTD

Paper-backed textile wall coverings from ESKATEX. They include hessian in 12 colours, and seven nubbly designs: 'Norland 5081' and 'Jutland' in 100% jute; 'Wheatsheaf' in 50% cotton and 50% jute; and finer woven 'Finavon', 'Silva', 'Super Silva' and 'Strand' in man-made fibre and linen mixtures. *M:* pre-trimmed w 90cm × 55m (36in × 60yd 6in). *P:* m £1.50–4.95.

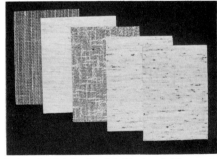

Left to right: John Boath's 'Norland', 'Finavon', 'Wheatsheaf', 'Silva', 'Super Silva' from ESKATEX

J W BOLLOM & CO LTD

Enormous range of flameproof, paper-backed wall felts — a total of 70 colours (*M:* w 31in/78.5cm, 72in/183cm, *P:* decreases with quantity, 1–11m £2.15, 12m £1.95).

Wall hessian comes in 35 shades, and glossy thin plastic sheeting in 50. Emulsion paint is available to match all these colours. J W Bollom also stock a huge array of useful tools and products for decorating and paper-hanging. See also 'Paint', 'Useful Products'.

Cassell's 'Westbourne' on metallic paper

BRYMOR LTD
Natural-looking textured vinyls in soft realistic colours. Nine designs in the MURELLE range include 'Hessian' in eight shades plus White, 'Plaid' in five, 'Grass Cloth', a variegated yarn effect in four, 'Oporto', patchworked cork in four colours, and 'Berber' pattern in six tones. *M:* w 53cm × 10m (20¾in × 10yd 33¾in). *P:* roll £4–£5.75.

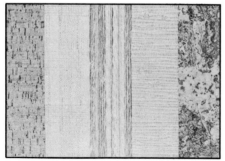

Left to right: Brymor's 'Cork', 'Plaid', 'Berber', 'Grass Cloth', 'Oporto', all from MURELLE

CASSELL WALLCOVERINGS LTD
Wall coverings from a designer who has worked for many famous Californian design houses. Michael Cassell also works in England where he has undertaken the delicate and difficult task of duplicating antique wallpapers for numerous restorations. Most of his 14 designs have a luxurious Oriental flavour. All come in standard colourways, but Cassell pride themselves on printing any shades on paper, fabric, metallic paper, or even mirrors, leather, suede or grasscloth, as well as designing to order. Minimum order is three rolls of any design; trimming and varnishing are optional extras. *M:* trimmed w 27½–28½in × 10yd (70–72cm × 9.1m), marbleized paper w 21½in × 11yd (54.5cm × 10m). *P:* roll £13–£60.

CAVALCADE WALLCOVERINGS LTD
Fantastic and unusual range of paper-backed fabric wall coverings — felt in 35 shades, plus four marbled versions on White, Beige, Aqua, or Wine (*M:* w 79cm × 25m/31⅛in × 27yd 12½in, *P:* m £3.75). Wall hessian is in 30 colours (*P:* m £4.25); CAVALSUEDE, made from 65% rayon and 35% acrylic, is in 15 lovely tones (*P:* m £6.75); and there are 12 variants of textured, patterned metallics (*P:* m £5–£8.50). *M:* all w 135cm × 40m (53¾in × 43yd 27in). Naturally coloured CAVALTEX, for a homespun, tweedy wall texture in 18 patterns, is a mixture of linen, jute and some man-made fibres, with subtle herringbones, stripes, etc. Predominantly neutrals, sometimes accented in Rust, Black, or Green (*M:* w 71cm × 9m/28in × 9yd 30¼in, *P:* m £4.25–£7.75). There are two vinyl ranges: CONFETTI with eight colourways, and FLAX with 12 including White and marvellous pastel shades of Cream, Beige, Greenstone, Sky grey (light grey), Grey, Cotswold (pale peach), and Mid-green, plus four earth tones — Vellum, Yellow (gold), Sienna (bronze), and Oak (darkest brown) (*M:* w 127cm × 30m/50in × 27yd 12¼in, *P:* m £1–£1.50).
Paintable GLASS FIBRE, in five textures, will disguise flawed walls (*M:* w 130cm × 50m/51¼in × 54yd 6¾in, *P:* m £1.30–£1.75).
Papers can be supplied cut to length, and Cavalcade will also supply appropriate adhesives.

COLE & SON (WALLPAPER) LTD
Hand-printed period wallpapers and borders. Gorgeously printed, they feature traditional florals, and classic motifs from Art Nouveau to Gothic *P:* roll £8.50–£30. THE EFFECTS AND STRIPES range is perfect for flawed walls. It includes mottled effects in 15 subtle shades; self-stripes and small all-over checks in six earth tones; and 36 Regency and Georgian dragged stripework textures. Broad or narrow stripes mainly in pastels, or classic combinations like Gold or Black, on White, are also available. *P:* roll £7.30–£11.40. Vinyls, mainly in soft shades, include traditional moiré patterns and stripes, plus self-coloured florals (*P:* m £1.40–£2). *M:* all w 53cm × 10m (20¾in × 10yd 33¾in).
The BORDER COLLECTION, primarily period accents for walls and window and door edgings, blends with Cole paints. There are twisted ropes in seven shades, and a good selection of architectural trims: the famous 'egg and dart' in four colours and 'reed and tie' in three, plus ribbons and bows, floral bands and pretty garlands with wild roses, sweet

Left to right, from top: 'CB 103', 'CB 75', 'CB 120', 'CB 65', 'CB 66', 'CB117' from Cole & Son's BORDER COLLECTION

peas, pansies, or grapes predominating. 'Bamboo Trellis', on a mottled ground, matches papers in the EFFECTS AND STRIPES range. Other motifs are swans, Art Nouveau sailing ships, and Louis Philippe festoons and tassels. *M:* h 3–26.5cm (1⅛–10⅜in). *P:* m 18p–£4.85.

Left to right, from top: 'CB 141', CB 147', 'CB 156', 'CB 137' from Cole & Son's BORDER COLLECTION

Sumptuous SOIRETTE fabric wall coverings from France and Italy consist of silk slubs in 11 shades, nubbly wools in seven, and moirés in 12 (*M:* w 88cm/34½in, *P:* m £5.20–£9.10). SUEDEL has 17 convincing shades in mock suede (*P:* m £5.75), 28 colours in hessian (*P:* m £3–£4). *M:* w 36in (90cm).

Two ranges from the Far East create an exotic and Oriental look: MIKADO paper-mounted linen, silk and cork (*P:* m £3.80–£23.80); and very unusual and beautiful KABUKI with subtly underprinted floral motifs overlaid with naturally textured grasses and sheer textile weaves. (*P:* m £3.40–£5.90). *M:* both w 90cm × 7.3m (36in × 8yd).

REFLECTION has zappy geometrics and abstract flowers on silvery or golden grounds (*M:* w 53, 69cm × 10m/20¾, 27in × 10yd

Cole & Son's 'Donna Maria' from IBERIAN

33¾in, *P:* roll £20–£30 patterned, £11.50 plain silver, £14 plain gold). IBERIAN washable papers, with a highly glazed surface, are perfect for kitchens and bathrooms. 19 patterns and six border designs, based on Portuguese tiles, come in marvellously bold colour combinations plus naturalistic earth tones, all on White (*M:* w 46cm × 10m/18in × 10yd 33¾in, *P:* roll £6.60, border m 40p). The SPECIAL ORDER range of quintessentially traditional patterns is ideal for restoration (*M:* w 53, 69cm × 10m/20¾, 27in × 10yd 33¾in, *P:* roll £12.65–£13.75). Cole will print their own designs in colours specified by clients; minimum order 10 rolls (100m). See also *Co-ordinates*, 'Paint'.

COMMERCIAL PLASTICS LTD

Remarkable, pre-pasted FLOCKS AND FOILS from the vinylized Mayfair collection. Designs are for confident and flamboyant tastes only. Flocks include classic 'Toulouse', 'Hatfield', and 'Chatsworth' with co-ordinating stripes, and more subtle patterns like striped 'Norwegia', mottled 'Harris', and chic 'Herringbone', loose-weave 'Forfair' and linen-like 'Brabant'. Colourways for most designs include Baby blue, Sage green, Ruby red, Bright gold, Mint green, Navy, and Bronze. Pretty-pretty 'Constance' has Pink or Lilac roses with co-ordinating unflocked moiré paper. Designs for Far Eastern fans are 'Rama', a bold trellis; and 'Tisagai', a grass screen overflocked with large leaves. 'Liège', a bamboo trellis on a cork-effect ground, has a complementary plain, unflocked cork paper. *P:* upon application. Polyester foils are equally bold. Most have big flowers or leaves, except 'Sacramento' in Bronze with a marble-like texture. *P:* upon application. *M:* paper w 51cm × 10.05m (20in × 11yd). See also *Co-ordinates*.

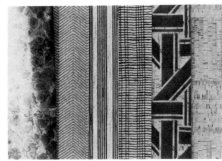

Left to right: Commercial Plastics' 'Sacramento', 'Herringbone', 'Kintyre', 'Forfair', 'Liège', 'Cork Tile' from FLOCKS AND FOILS

CROWN DECORATIVE PRODUCTS LTD

Good selection of vinyls. Favourite motifs in YOUNG GENERATION, for children's rooms, include 'Mr Men', 'Star Trek', 'English Footballers', and 'Captain Beaky' (*M:* w 53cm × 10m/21in × 10yd 33¾in, *P:* roll £3.75–£5).

TILES AND TEXTURES luxury vinyls are perfect for anyone who wants a tiled look but can't afford the real thing. Designs include 'Istria' in Grey/Brown, Pink/Lilac, and Sand/Orange; 'Louise' in Brown/Yellow, Green/Beige, and Lilac/Pink; 'Quinto' in Blue/Turquoise, Beige/Pink/Green, and Brown/Mustard; and 'Ionia' in Beige/Brown, Blue/Brown, and Dark and Light green. *M:* w 53cm × 10m (21in × 10yd 33¾in). *P:* roll £9.50–£11.

Left to right, from top: 'Istria', 'Louise', 'Quinto', 'Ionia' from Crown's TILES AND TEXTURES

DECOROLLER LTD

Now for something completely different — roll-on painted 'wallpaper'. Embossed rollers paint patterns on walls for a fraction of the cost of real papers. Available in more than 50 designs, they can be used with any type of paint: simply use a darker shade to apply the texture. They're the perfect solution for anyone who has painted a room, then wished they'd papered it instead. Mail order only. *P:* £9.20 including postage and packing.

ELIZABETH EATON LTD

Exceptionally wide fabrics, perfect for covering walls. Although the cost per metre seems expensive, the extra width means that 2 or 3 metres will go a surprisingly long way. The fabric can easily be taken off the wall for cleaning — and re-used (for upholstery if required). Two patterns are available, in 100% cotton: a tiny geometric check in Blue, Green, or Red colourways (P: m from £20); and a flamboyant floral print with Dusty rose, or a stronger Red and Purple predominating (P: m £36). Plain fabrics include DUPION made from polyester and Dralon, in 50 colours (P: m £27); the hessian-like OCEAN range in a mixture of linen and cotton, in a huge range of colours (P: m £22); and diamond-weave BLIKO linens in 55 lovely shades (P: m £22). M: w 200cm (78¾in).

The KATZENBACK & WARREN collection has colonial 17th and 18th-century designs in up-to-date colourways (M: w 40–71cm × 4.60–7.30m/15¾–28in × c 5–c 8yd, P: roll £9–£24). 'Winds and Wilds' is one of many bold, but nicely coloured modern jungly prints, some with matching fabrics (M: w 69cm × 4.57m/27in × 5yd, P: roll £13–£16). Excellent vinylized papers include 'One Nice Thing After Another' (M: w 61–70.5cm × 4.57–5.50m/24–27¾in × 5–c 6yd, P: roll £11–£15): and the plain, textured STAMFORD range in virtually every shade imaginable (P: roll £9–£11). M: w 70–73cm × 4.57m/27½–28¾in × c 5yd. See also Co-ordinates.

KAFFE FASSETT

A craftsman extraordinaire who paints, embroiders, does needlepoint, knits, and generally creates beautiful things. His murals reflect his love of subtle colour and contrasting textures, and his interest in detail. P: upon application. See also 'Soft Furnishings'.

Detail from a mural by Kaffe Fassett

GALLERIA MONTE CARLO

Beautifully produced wallpapers designed to co-ordinate with their own hand-painted bathroom basins, but also perfect for adjoining bedrooms. Seven patterns are available, all with abstract flowery configurations, many faintly Chinese in style. M: w 30in × 5yd (76cm × 4.5m). P: upon application. See page 26 for colour illustration of basins.

GERLAND LTD

GERFLEX MURAL flexible vinyl wall sheet, designed to match this company's vinyl flooring — ideal for office corridors or studios, where high traffic is expected. It comes in three marbleized shades: Sage green, Ivory white, and Pearl grey. M: w 150cm × 30m (60in × 32yd 29¼in). P: sq m £2

DAVID GILLESPIE ASSOCIATES LTD

Exciting BONDED TEXTURES panels with sculptured surfaces. Made from real metal particles, or solid colour, reinforced with glass fibre, they can be used indoors or out. They come in 13 low-profile textures that can be finished to simulate bronze, brass, aluminium, slate, etc, or can be ordered in any colour. Vertical and horizontal divisions within the panels are part of the design, making joins less obvious. M: 200×300cm (78¾×118in). P: upon application.

LYN LE GRICE STENCILS

Wonderfully charming stencilled murals by a designer and innovator who has been instrumental in reviving the technique in this country. The gradation of colour within each shape is the result of Lyn Le Grice's unique method of spray painting. She will work on

Detail from a stencilled floor by Lyn Le Grice

rooms of almost any size, including friezes and floors, and on fabrics and furniture. A gorgeously stencilled upper hallway is shown on the cover. P: upon application.

Lyn Le Grice also markets her own stencil kits. COUNTRY COLLECTION contains a festoon of fruit, leaves and ribbons; a circle of leaves and berries; and a basket of fruit. CRAFT KIT has designs suitable for smaller areas — pheasants and bay trees, birds and posies, and a dolphin. Future kits will include animals and an English garden. All available as full kits or individual stencils, and come with full instructions. P: kits £6–£7.50, individual stencils £2.25.

DAVID HAIGH

Specialist service from a small company that uses the traditional French method for applying fabrics to walls. The wall (or ceiling) is battened, and padded, then the fabric is stretched across and tacked down. The finishing touch is a trim of braid edging. David Haigh will supply everything but the fabric, and will also advise on this if desired. P: upon application.

HATEMA (UK) LTD

Enormous range of flame-resistant AEROVYL-S vinyl wall coverings without cotton backing and especially suitable for condensation-prone rooms like kitchens and bathrooms. Their foam content provides effective heat and sound-insulating properties. 23 textures are available, including stucco, hessian, linen, silk, pebbledash, stone, marble, string, wool, and plaster. M: w 130cm (51¼in). P: m £4.

D H HEYWOOD LTD

Beautiful BARRA luxury wall coverings. Made in the UK from 100% new wool, they have a heavy paper backing for easy application. The 25 designs are moth and flameproof. M: rolls w 50cm × 50m (19⅝ × 54yd 24¾in). P: m £7.

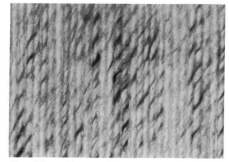

Detail from Heywood's BARRA range

HILL & KNOWLES LTD

An inspiring range of hand-printed borders (and matching emulsion paints). Colour combinations include 16 single shades on White: Black, Bright green, Sand, Mid-brown,

Dark brown, Bright red, Coffee, Navy blue, Stone, Deep terracotta, Light cream, Olive green, Silver, Light terracotta, Yellow, and Light blue. Slightly more complex two-colour designs, also in White, are in Yellow and Brick, Pink and Light green, Blue and green, and Dark and Light coffee; other mixes are White and Olive on Parchment, and White and Terracotta on Aubergine. Stylized lotus flowers in two sizes come in Dusky pink/Coffee on Grey, Lime/Green on Pale yellow, Green/Terracotta on Parchment, Leather brown/Tan on Cream, Light beige/Stone on White, and Dusky pink/Coffee on White. Utterly wonderful to have a picture rail or ceiling moulding for no trouble and little money. *M:* h 1⅝–6¾in (4–17cm). *P:* yd 35p–80p. See also *Co-ordinates*.

Selection of Hill & Knowles' borders

STANLEY J HOLMES & SONS LTD
Traditional embossed borders, some with 'gold' accents to complement matching papers. 16 designs, most with six pastel colour options on White. *M:* border d 3.5cm × 8.2m (1⅜ × 8yd 35in), paper w 52cm × 10m (20½in × 10yd 33¾in). *P:* borders £1.80–£2.90.

MARK AND JEAN HORNAK
Remarkable mother and son team, well known for their skill in trompe l'oeil and gilding, and in painting convincing surfaces resembling porphyry, tortoiseshell, stonework, wood grains, bamboo, etc.
Having worked for years under the aegis of J B Fowler of Colefax and Fowler (Wallcoverings) Ltd, the Hornaks are kept busy with National Trust restoration projects. However, they will undertake domestic items as small as a picture frame.
P: upon application.

Detail from Mark and Jean Hornak's 'marble' columns

LEYLAND PAINT & WALLPAPER LTD
Eight vinyl ranges including WEAVTEX 1 and WEAVTEX 11, two of the most convincing simulations on the market. Florals, hessians, leaves, grasses, bamboos and tweeds are incorporated in these ranges which are more competitively priced than other fabric-backed textured wall coverings. *M:* w 21in × 11yd (53.5cm × 10m). *P:* upon application.
Flowery COUNTRY LADY is available in 100 colourways. PERFECTLY PLAIN is a small collection in subtle colours and soft textures, designed to blend with the patterned ranges. *M:* as above. *P:* upon application. See also *Co-ordinates*.

MARY ANN MACKENZIE
A specialist with a unique talent, Mary Ann MacKenzie paints homely scenes, to gladden rooms and hearts, on boarded-up fireplaces. She will work on site or on a hardboard panel — and will decorate other parts of the house. *P:* burning fire, brass andirons and Burmese cat £300 as illustrated.

Fireplace by Mary Ann MacKenzie

MELODY MILLS LTD
THINK SMALL range of very nice mini-prints and textures on non-shiny vinyl. Blue, Green, Beige, Gold or Lilac predominate in 21 good-looking, appropriately tiny designs. They include 'Pastorale', with poppies, buttercups, cornflowers, harebells and butterflies; 'Rangoon', a neat trellis; 'Ribbons', with nosegays linked by flowing ribbons; and 'Ming', straight from the 'Blue Willow' china pattern. *M:* w 20½in × 11yd/(52cm × 10m). *P:* roll from £3.
COUNTRY STYLE COLLECTION has 16 cottage-perfect designs on vinyl paper. Traditional flower and stripe combinations abound, some with co-ordinating smaller stripes. Colours, always printed on a White textured ground, are Blue, Green, Pink or Apricot, often with metallic gold highlighting the design. A border design in four colourways can be used with any of the wallpapers. *M:* w 52cm ×10m (20½in × 10yd 33¾in), border d 6.5cm (2½in) × 10m (10yd 33¾in). *P:* roll from £1.75, border 75p per coil. See also *Co-ordinates*.

Left to right: Melody Mills' 'Rangoon', 'Ming', 'Pastorale', 'Ribbons', all from THINK SMALL

SALLY MILES MURALS
A talented mural painter who has created a clown-filled nursery, a leafy jungle around a Los Angeles swimming pool, and a gilded oriental scene, for an exotic dining room (*P:* upon application).

MUNDET CORK & PLASTICS LTD

Lightweight JOINITE insulating corkboard imported from Portugal. Both mould and vermin proof, it comes in thicknesses to order from ½ to 12in (1.5–30.5cm). *M:* 36×12, 24in (90×30.5, 61cm). *P:* upon application.

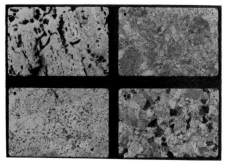

Selection from Mundet's JOINITE

NAIRN COATED PRODUCTS LTD

Good-quality vinyls including flocks, foils, tiles and natural textured effects. NAIRN-FLOCK comes in over 90 colourways including co-ordinating non-flocked vinyls for kitchens and *en suite* bathrooms (*P:* roll £5–£20). CONTEXT, with either a suede or velvet-like texture, is available in four patterns which co-ordinate with a selection of plain coverings. 'Crushed Suede' is in Off-white, Grey, two Blues, two Reds, two Greens, Mustard, and three Browns. *P:* roll £20–£30.
CONTOR TEXTURES has a floral tile, hessian, large and small bamboo fretwork, woven grass, bark, brick, stone, and basketweave (*P:* roll £11). The 27 designs in the MOODS range, generally on a workable small scale, include small and large florals, stripes, abstract leaves, checks, plaids, and floral tiles. The pattern book is divided into seven basic colour groups: Blue, Green, Russet, Brown, Yellow, Peach, and Pink (*P:* roll £9). *M:* all ranges w 52cm × 10m (20½in ×10yd 33¾in).

NORTHERN CORK SUPPLIES LTD

Comprehensive, unusual and competitively priced natural wall coverings, mainly cork-derived. WESTCO cork tiles are 'Electra' with 'broken' natural cork on Black, Green, Blue, Red, Brown or Amber, 'Edipo' with subtle, dark or light vertical striations, and dark, highly textured 'Natural Bark' (*P:* sq yd 86p–97p). AUTUMN has natural cork granules in medium shades (*P:* sq yd 65p); SQUARES is a waxed chequerboard tile (*P:* sq yd £4); the more expensive EMPEROR, also waxed, has alternating bands of cork (*P:* sq yd £4.10). Thin, SLIM CORK wall tiles come in light, medium and dark shades (*P:* sq yd 65p), and BARCE-LONA CORK, in two thicknesses, is in natural only (*P:* sq yd £2.15–£2.40). *M:* 12×12in (30.5× 30.5cm), except 'Electra' 24×12in (61×30.5cm), BARCELONA CORK also 36×12in (90× 30.5cm).

Unusual textile wall coverings include two hessians: COLOURWEAVE in Beige, Sand, Mid-brown, Dark brown, and Indigo (*M:* w 20¾in/53cm, *P:* roll £7); and WINCHESTER in Off-white, Cream, Beige, Tan, Sand, Gold, Leaf green, Dark green, Rust, Coffee, Dark brown (*M:* w 36in/90cm, *P:* sq yd £1.95). CANTERBURY, a two-tone hessian-type weave, combines Tan and White, Beige and Coffee, or Coffee and Off-white; a solid Caramel version is also available (*P:* m £1.40). ELM has the same shades underprinted with a tree design (*P:* m £1.95). MOUNTAIN ASH, CORNISH ELM, and HAREBELL are similar, but overlaid with nubbly spun yarns (*M:* w 90cm × 8.2m/36in × 9yd 35in, *P:* roll £11). FLAXSPUN also has subtle vertical stripes in yarn on plain Green, Coffee, and Creamy white (*P:* m £2.25). TWEEDSPUN, in three tawny tones, is more nubbly than FLAXSPUN (*P:* m £2.60). *M:* w 90cm (36in), except CORNISH ELM, HAREBELL w 53cm (20¾in).
Adhesive and tools are available, and Northern Cork will supply a sample pack for £3.

JOHN S OLIVER LTD

Exclusive hand-printed wallpapers, designed and manufactured by this adventurous company. The BAMBOO COLLECTION is just that — small, medium and large bamboo lattices on foil or mottled grounds, in dozens of colourways. Wild and wonderful motifs in the METALLIC COLLECTION are tiny, complex geometrics, palm trees, zig-zags, polka dots, cats, clouds, mosaics, Islamic stars, bold Art Nouveau-style florals — even Marilyn Monroe

John Oliver's 'Love Birds', 'Star', 'Fadel's Palm' from METALLIC COLLECTION, 'Bamboozle' from BAMBOO COLLECTION

— most available on plain paper or foil. *M:* w 53cm × 10.5m (20¾in × 11yd 17¼in). *P:* roll £18–£40.
There's also a collection by CAROLINE HILL who specializes in stencil effects — prowling leopards, pineapples, fruit trees on a trellis ground, and five-pointed stars (*M:* w 21in × 11yd/53.5cm × 10m, *P:* roll £23–£29).
Finally, for anyone who yearns for 'real' foliage on the wall, the most expensive paper in the shop is scattered with supremely real-looking leaves (*M:* w 36in×8yd/90cm×7.3m, *P:* roll £55). John Oliver will re-colour any design to clients' specifications.
A range of 36 uniquely coloured paints is available; or emulsions can be mixed to match furnishings (at extra cost). See also 'Paints'.

OSBORNE & LITTLE LTD

Enormous selection of more than 600 wall coverings from two brothers-in-law whose first range caused quite a stir in the late 1960s — and eventually won a Council of Industrial Design award. Today's rather more mellow collection includes traditional florals, plus grasses, hessians, and metallics.
Metallic CHROME on gold or silver foil has small geometrics like 'Prism' and 'Scallop', bold stripes and lively florals (*M:* w 20in × 11yd/51cm × 10m, *P:* roll £12–24, except plain silver, gold foil £6).

Osborne & Little's 'Scallop' from CHROME

Expensive but beautiful ORIENTAL GRASS papers come in many colours and textures including the very unusual and natural 'Wood Mosaic' made from thin wood veneers (*M:* w 36in × 8yd/90cm × 7.3m, *P:* roll £24). The airy, country cottage DURO range from Sweden has sweet scattered flowers and dots, birds,

Selection from Osborne & Little's DURO

leaves and stripes in clear, pastel shades, mainly on White (*M:* w 20in × 10yd/51cm × 9.1m, *P:* roll £6).
Special colourways are available to order; minimum ten rolls. See also *Co-ordinates*.

C PAINE & SONS LTD
Delightfully unsentimental papers for children's rooms. Hand-printed, untrimmed and wipeable, they include 'Teddy Bear's Picnic' which can also be applied as a mural, or used as a frieze. Standard colourways are Blue, Yellow, Green, and Red; and Forest, Gold, Lime, and Brown. Special colours cost an extra 25%, minimum order ten rolls. *M:* w 30in × 10yd (76cm × 9.1m). *P:* roll £19.50.

Paine & Sons' 'Teddy Bear's Picnic'

MABEL PAKENHAM-WALSH
Carved wooden panels, beautifully and charmingly executed in bright colours. They can be used as features over doorways, or a frieze. *M:* to order. *P:* upon application.

PEEL & CAMPDEN LTD
SCANDECOR PHOTOWALL collection of photographic scenes and some illustrations reproduced in full colour. Anyone who wants a complete change without moving from home has a choice of 27 designs, on spongeable, lacquered paper. They include sandy beaches edged with swaying palms; autumn forests dappled with Yellows, Reds and Rusts; New York's skyline at night; a sun-drenched primeval glade; and snow-capped mountains reflected in a glacial lake. Most come in three sizes, six are available in 'apartment-size' only. Sailing ships in the sunset, and a wide sandy beach, are on extra-wide papers. *M:* 6ft 4in × 9ft (apartment size), 12ft 8¾in × 4½ft, 12ft 8¾in × 9ft (193 × 274.5, 388 × 137, 388 × 274.5cm). *P:* upon application. PHOTODOOR paper panels with similarly striking imagery are for scene-changing on a smaller scale (*M:* w 33in × 7ft 2in/84 × 218.5cm, *P:* £8.50).

PHOTOGRAPHIC COLLECTIONS (UK) LTD
FRANCIS FRITH COLLECTION of sepia-tinted early 20th-century photographs. Nostalgic images from his travels in Britain and throughout the world are taken from early glass negatives. Framed prints and, more appropriately, murals are available, all made to order. *M:* maximum 40 × 25ft (12.2 × 7.6m). *P:* upon application.

TIM PLANT
Devoted muralist who will paint anything a client desires, indoors or out. A gazebo mural, painted in oils on the walls and ceiling of a staircase, turns it into a garden of delights complete with Italianate vistas. *P:* upon application. See page 182 for colour illustration.

RECTELLA INTERNATIONAL FABRICS
Fantastically comprehensive collection of textile wall coverings. The 50 patterns include

one- and two-colour hessians in Olive, Rust, Dark, Light and Mid-brown, and Beige. Less predictable solutions for bad walls or cold rooms include the following vertical yarn textures: 'Cascade', from 95% viscose and 5% nylon, with White yarns flecked with Brown on a Beige ground; 'Aber', in 100% jute, with Beige yarns striped with Bronze, Green, Gold or Rust accents; 'Shin', 75% viscose and 25% linen, in Beige on White is accented in Bronze, Green, Gold, or Rust; and 'Hardrow', 100% viscose, in Beige on White or Apricot beige on the same ground with co-ordinating 'Bronte', a bamboo-bedecked underprinted paper. 'Grecian', a mixture of 85% jute and 15% linen, is in Beige on Dark brown or Cream. *M:* w 90cm × 5.5m (36in × 6yd). *P:* m £2–£4.

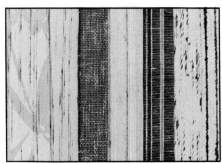

Left to right: Rectella's 'Bronte', 'Hardrow', 'Spacetweed', 'Aber', 'Grecian', 'Cascade', 'Shin'.

RUSSELL & CHAPPLE LTD
Wall coverings from a company that makes stagecloths and backdrops for theatres. The paper-backed HESSATEX range includes dyed hessian in Soft gold, Bronze, Sand, Caramel, Mink, Dark brown, and Olive (*P:* m £1.75); and textured coverings in seven patterns (*P:* m £1.83). *M:* all w 90cm (36in). Discounts are available for orders over 20 metres.

ARTHUR SANDERSON & SONS LTD
High-quality wallpapers and coverings from one of the UK's best-known manufacturers. SCENICS, by James Seeman, is a collection of 24 murals. It includes 'Sherwood Glen', a woody glade in Beige and White; 'Trelliage' with White latticework against Blue, Green or Yellow; 'Aubusson', a large 'tapestry' in Beige or Rust; and 'Horizon', a modern landscape in Grey, Blue or Gold. Matching plain papers are available in all background colours. *M:* h 200cm × 7.1m (78¾in × 7yd 28in). *P:* roll £135–£250.
Textured wall coverings are equally dramatic. They include rich, soft 'Chenille' in ten shades (*P:* m £5.50); 'Tweed', in various effects, in 35 colourways (*P:* m £4.15–£4.85); 'Vertical Yarns' in pastels, neutrals and bright colours (*P:* m £3.10–£3.60); 'Suede Look' in 12 shades (*P:* m £2.45–£4.05); and 'Hessian' in 20 colours (*P:* m £2.45). 'Cork' comes in 26 patterns with a cork

effect, mainly in natural, overlaid on different colours, and sometimes overprinted. *M:* w 65–69cm (25½–27⅛in).

Utterly beautiful 'Oriental' has wafer-thin sheets of wood backed with paper in Beige, Tan, and Grey (*P:* roll £13–£36). 'Moiré' comes in 18 shades, 'Bouclé' in ten (*P:* both roll £7.20). *M:* w 65–69cm × 10.05m (25½–27⅞in × 11yd), except 'Oriental' 7.3m (8yd).

Left to right, from top: Sanderson & Sons' 'Chenille', 'Vertical Yarns', 'Oriental', 'Boucle'

Magnificently printed HANDPRINTS is similarly luxurious, but expensive. Patterns include Art Nouveau designs by William Morris with lilies, peonies, mayberries or daisies, some with complementary borders, foils, Greek keys and Chinese panels *M:* w 65–69cm × 10.05m (25½–27⅛in × 11yd, *P:* roll £9.15–£40, borders £4.55–£13.20. See also *Co-ordinates.*

SOMMER ALLIBERT (UK) LTD
MURAL MOUSSE wall coverings with excellent sound and heat-insulating properties. Made from expanded PVC foam, they are perfect for condensation-prone bathrooms, kitchens and shower rooms; also boats, caravans and swimming pool changing rooms. 13 textures include wood grain, textile, stone, travertine, plaster, etc. Most are in neutrals, but an Olive textile and Pale blue striated plaster effect are available. *M:* w 100cm (39⅜in). *P:* from sq m £4.50.

ROBIN STEWART HANDPRINTS LTD
Beautifully produced, hand-printed wall papers. Eight designs, all available on paper, vinyl, or silvery foil, feature stylized florals, including 'Spring Glory' with daffodils, and lacy 'Tiger Lily', soft textured 'Meadow Flower', woodcut-effect 'Indra'; 'Interspace' and 'Chequers' are neat geometrics. All are beautifully coloured in a choice of six colourways. Special shades can be printed to clients' specifications; 50% extra for 10 to 24

rolls, 25% for 25–49, free over 50 rolls. *M:* w 27in × 10yd (69cm × 9.1m). *P:* roll paper £7–£10, vinyl £9–£11, foil £11–£13.

From top: Robin Stewart's hand-printed 'Acorn', 'Indra', 'Spring Glory', 'Chequers', 'Tiger Lily'

STICKABRICK LTD
Real brick STICKABRICK wall tiles. Easily applied to most surfaces, including plaster, wood, asbestos, ceramic tiles, concrete, plastic, and normal brickwork, they come in good, realistic colours: Brown, Grey, Red, Old English (terracotta), and Russet (sand). Corner tiles are available. *M:* 22×6.5cm (8⅝× 2⅝in), corner tiles 10.5×6.5cm (4¼×2⅝in). *P:* sq m £20, corner tiles (pack of ten) £10.70.

STOREY BROTHERS & CO LTD
Some unusual options from a household name in wall coverings. 38 designs in the JULIETTE ready-pasted vinyl range include seven nostalgic print collages: 'Bubbles' from the Pears soap posters; 'Rhyme Time' period nursery rhyme illustrations; 'Playtime' with romping teddy bears; 'Once Upon a Time' with pictures from the *Flower Fairy* books; 'Isadora' with Art Nouveau posters; 'Chef''s Choice' with kitchen illustrations; and 'Muffet' inspired by the well-loved nursery rhyme. The range also includes mock tiles, garden flowers and small geometrics. *M:* w 53cm × 10m (20¾in × 10yd 33¾in). *P:* roll £6–£11. See also *Co-ordinates.*

Storey Bros' 'Rhyme Time' from JULIETTE

TEKKO & SALUBRA (UK) LTD
Exceptional, exclusive and richly coloured STYLES NOBLES collection of papers. Over 1,200 options are available, based on the finest classic damasks from the great periods of design: the Renaissance, Louis XIII, Louis XIV, Baroque, Regency, Rococo, Chippendale, Louis XVI, Directoire, Sheraton, Louis Philippe, and the Biedermeier. Patterns, divided into these periods, all come in 28 shades, with matching plains; a few are hand-printed in Gold and Silver. *M:* w 80cm (31½in). *P:* m £4–£5.

Lightfast, washable velours or flocked papers, some on moiré grounds, are mainly traditional (*M:* w 80cm/31½in, *P:* m £6.50).

Hand-made, metallicized SALUBRA FOIL panels come in 30 textures, including marvellous mottles, and 15 colours. The unique 'cracked lacquer' surface is the result of an ingenious embossing process. *M:* 300×60cm (118×23⅝in). *P:* panel £15.

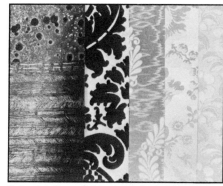

Selection from Tekko & Salubra's SALUBRA FOIL (left, top and bottom), STYLES NOBLES

PRICES AND INFORMATION WERE CORRECT AT THE TIME OF GOING TO PRESS

TARGOS papers, with more naturalistic textures, are 'Ocena' in 12 shades; 'Flax', a muted textile effect, in 14; 'Perl', a pastel series of six shell-like textures with a mother-of-pearl glaze effect; and 'Antique' reminiscent of gold-printed ancient Chinese silk hangings. In MOIRÉ, available in ten colours, the technique for achieving this classical texture has been perfected. TWEED has wood bark textures, in six colours, and RUSTIC papers imitate more expensive textiles with warp, weft and slubs. NATURAL is another rarity: real plaster oil-painted wallpapers; four textures are available, each in three colours. *M:* w 80cm (31½in). *P:* m £2.75–£3.50.

Textile coverings range from fine close weaves to heavy slubs in some 42 yarns; combinations include linen, wool, silk and cotton as well as plain and printed hessians (*M:* w 80cm/31½in, *P:* m £6–£9.50).

TEROYDECOR LTD

Warp-laid wall coverings in 100% pure new wool, plus woven wool versions, both backed with strong paper. Mothproof, and fire and fade-resistant, they can be washed or vacuumed like any wool carpet. Three woven ranges are available from these leading manufacturers who originated this form of covering. All have vertical yarns in various thicknesses — ONE ELEVEN has the thickest yarns, TWO ELEVEN thin ones, and THREE ELEVEN incorporates a combination of the two, as illustrated. Shades are predominantly natural, but ONE ELEVEN includes some tones — Pale rust, Pale emerald, and Pale royal. *M:* w 50, 100cm (19⁵⁄₈, 39³⁄₈in). *P:* m £8–£12.

Selection of Teroydecor's wall coverings

TODAY INTERIORS LTD

Excellent textile wall coverings. Ten collections include strikingly chunky

---

MARAKESH, in wool; varying stripes are available in 28 soft shades, with a plain co-ordinate (*M:* w 50cm/19⁵⁄₈in, *P:* m £6–£7). CHENILLE has sophisticated silky textures with natural slubs, in 13 colourways; heavier CHENILLE ROYALE comes in 19 shades (*M:* both w 100cm/39³⁄₈in, *P:* m £5).

Suede-effect DAYMUR is in 27 colours including flamboyant Navy blue, Pillar box red, and Emerald green; some match the MARAKESH range. Co-ordinating fabrics are available. *M:* paper w 66cm (26in), fabric w 145cm (57in). *P:* paper m £4.60, fabric £7.60.

Silk-textured DELFO has 14 soft Georgian shades; DELFO FASHION comes in ten stronger colours (*M:* both w 100cm/39³⁄₈in, *P:* m £5). Innovative PROFIL VINYL is a chunky 'embroidered' cotton overlay on florals (*M:* w 21in × 11yd/53.5cm × 10m, *P:* roll £16–£19.50).

Today Interiors' CHENILLE ROYALE

T-T DESIGN SERVICES INTL LTD

Wonderful imported wallpapers. Cheerful, chic foils from JOHN T RAISIN have vaguely Oriental motifs and some small-scale geometrics, all printed on amazingly thin paper that can be easily stripped (*P:* roll £6–£12). The huge SANCAR range includes shiny or matt plain vinyls, plus mottled, speckled or stippled papers in every shade under the sun; also a good selection of moirés (*P:* yd 60p–£1). *M:* both w 27in × 5yd (69cm × 4.6m).

GARDEN COURT, is a high-quality mural by Richard Haas in 100% rag paper (which won't rot like canvas), silkscreen printed in 20 colours with washable oil-based paints. This revival of the Second Empire fashion for large-scale murals is the result of T-T's passion for unusual imports. The edition is limited to 200 prints, plus 20 artist's proofs, all numbered and signed by Richard Haas. *M:* 72×96in (183×244cm). *P:* £1,000.

See also *Co-ordinates.*

PRICES AND INFORMATION WERE CORRECT AT THE TIME OF GOING TO PRESS

T-T Design's GARDEN COURT mural

ERNEST TURNER LTD

Fantastically comprehensive collection of wall coverings. Designed for contract use, they would be equally at home in a domestic setting. More than 3,000 options include large and small-scale hessians, wool yarns, cork laminates, grasscloths, glass fibre, suede effects, moirés, silk effects, weaves, tweeds, stripes, linens, textured metallics, foils, and vinyls which reproduce most natural textures. A technical and colour consultancy service is available. *M:* various. *P:* m 80p–£80.

VENILIA LTD

SANDRA vinylized wallpapers in distinctively deep, striking shades like Cobalt, Raspberry, and Gold. Small contemporary designs include 'Razia', 'Talat' and 'Rahat'. *M:* w 53cm × 10m (20¾in × 10yd 33¾in). *P:* roll £5.25–£6.25.

VIGERS STEVENS & ADAMS LTD

Very unusual CORVELLE cork wall coverings. They come in rolls to eliminate the patchwork effect created by tiles. Seven natural tones and patterns are available, some with cork chips, some with cork striations. *M:* w 60cm × 2.5m (23⁵⁄₈in × 2yd 27¼in). *P:* carton containing 7 sq yd £34.50.

WALLPAPER ORIGINALS

Stunning Oriental wall coverings from a specialist firm. 65 ranges include numerous natural grasses, some in very unusual colours like '2019' in Burgundy, '2057' in White backed with metallic gold, and '2112' in Natural with copper foil. '2024' is metallicized mica pebbles, '2022' has cork on coloured or metallic silver foil. Wallpaper Originals will send samples through the post. *M:* w 36in × 8yd (90cm × 7.3m). *P:* roll £19–34.

WATTS & CO LTD
Gorgeous reproduction wallpapers. 30 beautiful and authentic hand-printed designs, many from the original Regency and Victorian pearwood blocks, include a number by the famous Victorian architect Augustus Pugin. Believed lost, they were rediscovered in 1975. Original colourways are available, plus special finishes like metallic or gold-coated background papers. Motifs include abstract flowers as well as pineapples, thistles, oak leaves, bamboo, pears, and an exotic bird of paradise. Some designs have co-ordinating fabrics. *M:* w 53cm × 10.1m (20¾in × c11yd). *P:* roll £14–36.

Left to right, from top: Watts' 'Bird', 'The Pear', 'Pugin Pineapple', 'Pugin Triad'

GORDON WATTS & CO
HACKMAN HALLTEX wall panels with superb heat and sound-insulating properties, developed in Finland to combat exceptionally cold winters. Made from porous wood fibre and finished, for interior use, with a variety of pleasing materials, they can be fitted over existing walls, and ceilings. Panels are grooved for perfect joining. Ideal for pinboards, they're also perfect for attic or cellar studios where temperature control is vital. Finishes include Snow-white textured board, suitable for painting, Natural Japanese grass, Natural linen, Natural, Gold or Green hessian, Natural, Gold or Beige glass fibre, and Estoril cork. *M:* wall panels w 60 × 244cm, up to 545cm to order (23⅝×96 in, up to 15ft 34½in); ceiling w 30 × 305, 366cm (11⅞×10, 12ft). *P:* panel £3.50 hessian, £10 Japanese grass.

WICANDERS (GB) LTD
WALCORK decorative cork wall tiles or panels from a well-known flooring company. 'Cork Bark' and 'Cork Wood' are untreated; other tiles are waxed. A great selection of patterns includes 'Barque' and 'Nova' with Red, Blue, Yellow, Green, Black or Natural backing; 'Corkwood' with dark slabs; 'Squares', a Natural or dark chequerboard design; and 'Stripes' with natural variegations. They also make 'Walbond' special adhesive for fixing tiles to walls. *M:* 30, 60×30cm (11⅞, 23⅝× 11⅞in). *P:* £2.50, 'Cork Bark' £5.

WINTER & CO LONDON LTD
Something for everyone from a versatile manufacturer. Rayon WICOTEX SUEDEL comes in 16 luscious shades, without the sheen or grain of some cheaper suede effects (*P:* m £5.50). WICOTEX HESSIAN 100 is in 15 bright colours and neutrals, including lilac; WICOTEX HESSIAN 200 is a coarser weave in Beige and Off-white on pastel grounds (*P:* m £2.65). *M:* all w 90cm (36in).
An outstanding collection of vinyls will amaze anyone who thought vinyls were always tasteless and never sophisticated. Gorgeous thin-ribbed CORDUROY is in solid colours (Off-white, Cream, Mink, Sand, Teal, Rust, and Brown); co-ordinating RENO comes in Off-white accented with diagonal stripes in the above shades. HERRINGBONE, like a ruched fabric, is in Cream, Beige, Soft sand, Mid-brown, and Pale Green; BURMA is a yarn effect in Rust, Soft gold, Light brown, Cream, and Beige. Mock grass, mock silk and mock moiré are also available. *M:* w 136cm (54in). *P:* m £3–6.
Finally, AMERICAN MYLAR has cheery florals and geometrics on an utterly stable silvery base (*M:* w 69cm/27in, *P:* m £12–£18).

Selection from Winter's AMERICAN MYLAR

CO-ORDINATES

LAURA ASHLEY LTD
Complete, countrified co-ordination at competitive prices. Laura Ashley's now-famous prints come on plain and pleated lampshades, lampbases, patchwork quilts, roller blind kits, and ceramic wall and floor tiles as well as fabrics and wallpapers. There are also fabric-covered picture frames, sewing and trinket boxes, place mats, table cloths, cushion covers, etc—even paint.
Matching wallpapers and 100% cotton fabrics come in 35 designs, based on leaves, flowers, and simple geometrics. Many involve a single colour on Cream or White although there are more dramatic floral combinations on Black, Dark brown, Burgundy, or Navy. There are also plain furnishing cottons in 20 shades. *P:* m £3.25, roll £3.35.
BORDER PRINTS to co-ordinate with most wallpapers are sold in two-roll packs (*P:* pack £1.50).
PVC-coated fabric is available in 11 patterns; double-sided quilted cottons with polyester filling come in nine designs, 12 colour combinations (*P:* m £4.75, £7.50). Wide-width sheeting comes in five plains, 13 patterns, in 100% cotton with an easy-care finish (*M:* w 230cm/90⅝in, *P:* m £6.25); traditional glazed chintz in three flower cluster motifs, nine colourways, all on White (*P:* m £4.25).
M: fabric w 120cm (47¼in), paper w 53cm × 10m (20¾in×10yd 33¾in), border 10m (10yd 33¾in). See also 'Ceramic Tiles', 'Lighting', 'Paint', 'Soft Furnishings'.

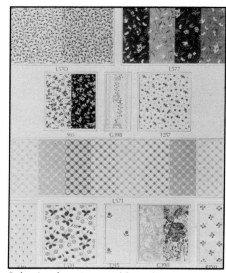

Selection from Laura Ashley's designs

MAURICE BROWN LTD
Impeccable co-ordinates from an enterprising company. The REGENTS PARK COLLECTION has wipeable vinyl wallpapers, ceramic tiles and printed cotton fabric. Ten delightful designs include 'Daisy Sans' with a single

flower; 'Petit Lille', an overall floral with a sweet trellis border; 'Bamboo Shoot', a bolder trellis entwined with leaves; and 'Acacia Key', an all-over maze that complements 'Acacia' with trees on a maze-patterned ground. They all come in Deep blue, Rose, Grass green, Apricot, Emerald, Baby blue, Red, Brown or Yellow, on White. 'Nash Terrace', unusual rounded flowers scattered over a dotted ground, is one of few two-colour designs. It comes in Red/Navy, Pink/Green, Beige/ Green, Orange/Grey, and Lemon/Lime. *M:* fabric w 48in (122cm), paper w 30in × 10yd (76cm×9.1m). *P:* yd £7–£11, roll £11–£20.

Selection from Maurice Brown's REGENTS PARK COLLECTION

American ranges include the very unusual PAUL KAISER collection of custom-coloured fabrics and wallpapers. The vaguely Oriental designs can be executed in any three colours chosen by a client, and before final printing he sends a large sample from America for approval. Fabrics and wallpapers both come in a variety of textures and weights, including sheers, silks, hessians and linens, and moiré, glossy and matt papers. *M:* fabric w 48in (122cm), w 27in × 5yd (69cm × 4.5m). *P:* yd £12, roll £23.

Design from Maurice Brown's MALIBU EAST

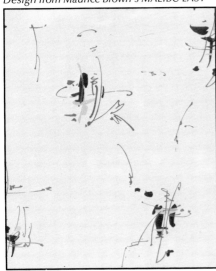

MALIBU EAST, also from America, is really different. Its 20 arty designs, inspired by the spare beauty of Oriental brushstrokes, are adapted to the modern idiom. They include, checks, bold stripes, dots, squiggles and flecks, in Deep navy, Rich red or Dark green, on Beige or Off-white. Fabric is pure cotton, treated with SCOTCHGARD. *M:* fabric w 54in (136cm), paper w 27in×5yd (69cm×4.5m). *P:* yd £10–£13, roll £17–£22.

The HASI HESTER JADE COLLECTION, hand-printed in California, is equally inspiring. It has only four colour combinations but within each there are 35 wallpaper designs and 28 fabric patterns. They include small neat geometrics, bold florals, strict stripes, borders, and the ultimate in modern abstracts — a wonderful range to be used throughout the house. Colour combinations are White/Beige/ Sage green/Dark green, Chocolate/White/ Black/Tan, Teal blue/Navy/Beige/White, and Navy/Rust/White/Beige. Wallpapers are vinylized, fabrics are pure cotton sailcloth or velvet. *M:* fabric w 54in (136cm), paper w 27in × 5yd (69cm × 4.5m). *P:* yd cotton £15–£20, velvet £27, roll £15–£20.

Selection from Maurice Brown's HASI HESTER JADE COLLECTION

COLEFAX & FOWLER DESIGNS LTD
Beautifully re-coloured traditional fabric and wall covering designs, based on 18th- and 19th-century document prints. Fabrics include 40 chintzes, 12 printed cottons and two printed

voiles; nine co-ordinating hand-printed wall-papers are available, seven with matching borders either printed on one side of the paper or sold separately. In the chintz collection, 'Eugenie' has climbing roses, on neutral grounds, in Carmine/Forest/Yellow, Dusky pink/Dull blue/Apricot, and Rust/Light olive/ Peach. Smaller scale 'Leaf' has vertical panels of leaves in Mushroom/Beige, Rose/Rust, Olive/Sage, Turquoise/Pale blue, and Gold/ Yellow, all on White. More contemporary 'Melbury', based on a Regency dress print but looking as fresh as today, comes in Gold/ Yellow, Magenta/Rose, Turquoise/Pale blue, and Grass green/Lime green, on Beige and White. *M:* w 122–136cm (48–54in). *P:* m £12.15– £14.

Printed cottons with co-ordinating papers include 'Bees'; based on a mid-19th-century block print, it looks deceptively modern with Yellow, Gold, Green, Turquoise, Pink or Beige insects on Cream (*M:* fabric w 122cm/48in, paper w 72cm × 9m/28³⁄8in × 9yd 30¼in, *P:* m £8, roll £11.95). Other papers £9–£15 per roll.

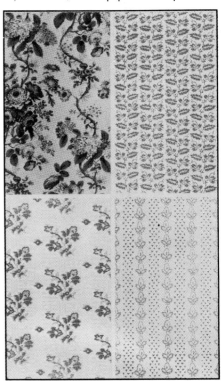

Left to right, from top: Colefax & Fowler's 'Eugenie', 'Leaf', 'Melbury', 'Bees'

COLE & SON (WALLPAPER) LTD
Wonderful co-ordinates from the Continent. French COLLECTION INALTERA has vinyl papers and polyester fabrics in both bold and small-scale florals, some on hard-to-find dark grounds (*M:* fabric w 63in/160cm, roll w 21in × 11yd/53.5cm × 10m, *P:* m £8.50, roll £6–£9). LES ROMANTIQUES DE JULIE with tiny pastel

flowers on Off-white has patterned vinyls and co-ordinating plain papers, with matching fabrics in 100% cotton (*M:* fabric w 130cm/51¼in, paper w 21in × 11yd/53.5cm × 10m, *P:* m £5.50, roll £5.50). GRAND CORNICE, beautifully printed in Italy, in rich colourways, has suitably grand, traditional French chintz motifs; fabrics are 100% cotton (*M:* fabric w 136cm/54in, paper w 73cm × 7m/28¾in × 7yd 23½in, *P:* m £8.25–£9.35, roll £6–£7.70). The bright, contemporary CONSORT COLLECTION features cotton fabrics with plain and stippled papers in Olive, Brown, Coral, Bright turquoise, Bright green, Gold, Red, and Grey (*M:* fabric w 113cm/44½in, paper w 53cm × 10m/20¾in × 10yd 33¾in, *P:* m £5.70, roll £7.30–£9.75).

See also *Wall Coverings*.

COLOROLL LTD

Competitively priced DOLLY MIXTURES co-ordinates, designed by Linda Beard for one of Europe's fastest-growing wall covering manufacturers. They include bedlinen, blinds and curtains. Small florals in gentle but clear colours predominate but some lovely stencil effects and flower and stripe combinations are available, while many patterns come in large and small versions. The 19 wallpapers, some with matching borders, are softly vinylized; fabrics are 100% cotton.

Coloroll's 'Pippa' (left), 'Posie' (bottom right), matching border (top), all from DOLLY MIXTURES

The JOHN WILMAN collection of cottons and pre-pasted vinyls comes mainly in traditional combinations of florals, stripes and birds of paradise. Each wall covering has two or three co-ordinating fabrics. *M:* fabric w 122cm (48in), paper w 52cm × 10m (20½in × 10yd 33¾in). *P:* m £4.25, roll £3–£3.25.

See page 289 for 'Geraldine', 'Picatee' in colour.

COMMERCIAL PLASTICS LTD

Nice collection of ready-pasted, scrubbable vinyls, crease-resistant cotton fabrics, and polyester blinds. Motifs are mainly floral, generally with complementary large and small-scale designs including checks and stripes, so colours can be co-ordinated throughout the house. 'Christina' is in Pink, Blue or Yellow colourways. *M:* fabric w 48in (122cm); wall covering w 21in × 11yd (53.5cm × 10m), blinds maximum w 72in (183cm). *P:* m £4.50; roll from £4; blinds upon application.

See also *Wall Coverings*.

Commercial Plastics' 'Christina'

CVP DESIGNS LTD

Zandra Rhodes AT HOME collection of flamboyant fabrics, and matching wallpapers — exclusive to CVP. Designs, all fantastically confident, feature her famous lily motif, plus swirls, zig-zags and wavy lines in Blue, Peach, Yellow, Russet, Red, Lime green, Soft green; or printed to order. In addition, any design can be supplied on calico, cotton, voile, satin, linen, moiré, or silk.

CVP's own range is based on a lovely knotted and twisted cord design, including a trellis effect. All fabrics come with four co-ordinating wallpapers, one of which always includes a frieze or border. Painted ceramic lamp bases with matching pleated shades, frilly cushions, hand-quilted bedspreads and hand-stencilled wall or blind panels are available.

M: fabric w 48in (122cm), paper w 30in × 10yd (76cm×9.1m). *P:* m £11.50 (cotton, calico) to £23 (silk), roll £16.50. See page 289 for 'Tassel' in colour.

Selection from AT HOME by Zandra Rhodes for CVP

DESIGNERS GUILD

Unmistakable country-in-the-city look. Soft hues, subtle colourations and a distinctively pretty style unify Tricia Guild's fabrics, wallpapers, furniture and soft furnishings.

There are four printed collections and one solid colour range in 100% cotton. And although not all designs come in both papers and fabrics, each collection is so impeccably co-ordinated that it's easy to achieve perfection. The colour range is wide, but muted, including Beiges, Mustards and other neutrals. BEAN AND DAISY designs probably combine the most colours and are the most complex. They include sea shell, daisy, starflower, snowdrop, leaf, and tulip motifs. GERANIUM, in two or three colours, focuses on abstract pebbles and shells, teardrops and lacy leaves. WATERCOLOUR is much more abstract with small spatters, and combines prettily with larger-scale floral patterns like 'Paper Roses', 'Dandelion', and 'Thistledown'.

Left to right, from top: Designers Guild's VILLAGE, BEAN AND DAISY, VILLAGE, GERANIUM

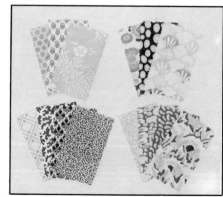

VILLAGE, by far the most graphic range, has squiggly 'Peaweed' on White, 'Tasket', a basket of flowers, neat, geometric 'Crispin', and 'Bindi' with spotted dots. Nubbly UTTER PLAIN in woven cotton comes in 12 pastel shades.
M: fabric w 122cm (48in), paper w 53cm×9–10m (20¾in×9yd 30¼in–11yd), except VILLAGE w 76cm (30in). *P:* m £8–£15, roll £7–£8, VILLAGE m £7.50–£9. See page 289 for 'Shell', 'Peaweed', 'Geranium' in colour.

ELIZABETH EATON LTD
Elizabeth Eaton's own collection of hand-printed fabrics, wallpapers and borders. Suitable for most rooms, it includes 'Hilda', and 'Saighton'. *P:* m £14–£16, roll £12–£15.
Exclusive imported co-ordinates include traditional florals from Hobe & Irwin in America; papers are supplied in double or triple rolls. The Yves Halard range from France is excitingly progressive, in wonderful colours. His COLLECTION QUATRE COINS has three co-ordinating fabrics for each paper; for convenience both paper and fabrics are displayed on the same page in the pattern book. Illustrated from right to left are 'Ariane', 'Daimier' and 'Quadrille'. *P:* m £18, paper roll £18.
M: fabric w 115cm (45in), paper w 53cm × 10–11m (20¾in × 10yd 33¾in–c12yd).
See page 289 for 'Hilda' (with matching border) and 'Saighton' papers, 'Saighton' as 100% linen, QUATRE COINS in colour. See also *Wall Coverings.*

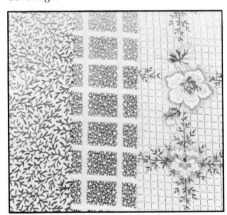

Selection from Elizabeth Eaton's QUATRE COINS by Yves Halard

THE FABRIC SHOP
Two wall covering and fabric collections. 'Maidenhair', 'Dryad' and 'Painted Lady', based on ferns and butterflies, come in Lilac/Lime, Pink/Fuchsia, Blue/Beige, Lemon/Apricot, and Mint/Lime, all on White. 'Diamond Trellis', 'Springtime' and 'Chelsea Green' are mainly small and large-scale floral arrangements also on White, in Pink/Green, Red/Yellow/Green, and Peach/Tan/Grey.

Fabrics are silk, cotton, polished cotton, Terylene, and voile; wall coverings are available as papers or paperbacked hessian. All can be specially coloured, to order; minimum 20m fabric, 10 rolls of wall covering. *M:* fabric w 48in (122cm), wall coverings w 30in × 10yd (76cm×9.1m). *P:* from £7.50, roll £17. These approachable interior decorators also stock other fine national and international ranges; all kinds of soft furnishings including custom-made curtains, bed coverings, etc; and will supply borders and blinds, hang fabrics on walls. Other specialities include patchwork, smocking, quilting, and appliqué. See page 105 for 'Springtime', 'Chelsea Green' in colour.

Fabric Shop's 'Maidenhair'

FOURSQUARE DESIGNS
The ultimate in luxury — but still affordable. The CORNEY & CO range has five floral and geometric designs on natural raw silk, plus a small geometric version of one pattern on 100% cotton. Wallpaper with this 'Little Bark' design on foil or White works with all fabrics. Colours are soft Dusty pink, Beige, Gold, Blue, and Sea green. *M:* fabric w 90cm (36in), paper w 51cm (foil), 76cm (paper)×9.1m (20, 30in×10yd). *P:* m £12, roll £20 foil, £12, £16 paper.

Selection from Foursquare's CORNEY & CO

SUSANNE GARRY LTD
COUNTRY COUSINS co-ordinating nets and curtain-weight fabrics. Sheers, in 50% cotton and 50% polyester, look like fine cheesecloth; the heavier weaves are 100% cotton. Four designs are available, all tiny sprays of flowers, in various colours, scattered on Off-white. *M:* sheer w 270cm (106¼in), cottons w 120cm (47¼in). *P:* m £6, £9.50.

HABITAT DESIGNS LTD
Spongeable wallpapers and 100% cotton fabrics. ALPHABET papers have Bright yellow, Blue or Red letters scattered on White; fabric letters are White on grounds in the same choice of colours. Great value, and great in a child's room. Matching floor cushions also available. *P:* fabric m £2.85, paper m £2.50.
BRIGHTON ROCK, with noughts and crosses inside small square grids, comes in candy colours: Pink, Yellow, Blue and Green (*P:* m £4.10, roll £3.15). CAMARGUE is a sophisticated dot design, in similarly sweet tones: Red, Yellow and Blue, or Baby blue, Yellow and Grass green (*P:* fabric m £3.80, paper m £2.83).
ALOUETTE is completely different — it looks as though a cat had stepped evenly over a Pale blue robin's egg (*P:* fabric m £3.80, paper m £2.83). Habitat also has neat grids, stylized florals, airborne birds and neat stripes to bedeck your walls and soft furnishings – chic but cheap.
M: fabric w 122cm (48in), except ALPHABET w 130cm (51¼in), paper w 53cm × 10.5m (20¾ × 11yd 17¼in).
See page 289 for ALPHABET, CAMARGUE, ALOUETTE in colour.

HILL & KNOWLES LTD
Seven borders that co-ordinate with two fabric and wallpaper patterns, from a wonderfully rich and varied range. 'Emma' has sprays of

twigs, 'Kip' a crisp trellis; both mix and match, as illustrated. In Light terracotta, Sand, Blue, Stone, and Fresh green, on White. *M:* fabric w 122cm (48in), paper w 52cm × 10m (20½in × 11yd). *P:* m £6.75, roll £6, border yd 27p–65p. See also *Wall Coverings.*

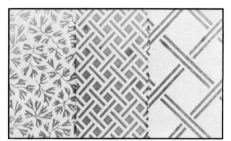

Hill & Knowles' 'Emma' (left), and 'Kip'

DAVID ISON LTD

Overwhelming selection — more than 100 wall coverings and fabrics imported from America. They include bright, cheerful HACIENDA, perfect for children's rooms (*M:* fabric, paper w 54in/136cm, *P:* m £18, roll £16–£19); lovely CHARLES BARONE designs on kraft (brown wrapping) paper, with matching fabrics (*M:* fabric, paper w 54in/136cm, *P:* m £24, roll £20); and Kenneth MacDonald's DESIGN ONE on naturalistic textured grounds (*M:* fabric, paper w 54in/136cm, *P:* m £23, roll £23). ACADEMY HANDPRINTS has wonderful, punky designs in pastels and bright colours (*M:* fabric, paper w 48in/122cm, *P:* m £17, roll £20). NEW CONCEPTIONS by Fine Art is equally zappy, with daring florals (*M:* fabric, paper w 42in/102cm, *P:* m £15, roll £15).

Two of the most unusual collections are James Seeman's DONGHIA with modern abstract flowers (*M:* fabric, paper w 48in/122cm, *P:* m

David Ison's 'Los Palomas' from HACIENDA

£15, roll £17); and LAVERNE MARBLE papers which come as panels, to fit walls, or in strips; matching fabrics are available (*M:* walls maximum 14×75ft/4.3×22.8m, strips w 35in/89cm, *P:* sq ft £4.50).

David Ison's '275' from CHARLES BARONE, '2019' from LAVERNE MARBLE (bottom)

Below, from top: Mary Fox Linton's NANTES, CHARTRES, ARCACHON

MARY FOX LINTON LTD

Marvellously abstract collection of 14 designs from a multi-talented interior decorator. Most are geometric, with some plant-inspired motifs, in colours that range from soft pastels to handsome darks. Fabrics, all upholstery-weight 100% cotton, can be plasticized.

NANTES wallpapers come in Green/Blue, Pink/Brown/Grey, Blue/Orange and Pink/Yellow/Green, all on White. Fabrics are Melon/Pink/Brown, Turquoise/Melon/Blue, and Green/Blue/Turquoise, also on White. CHARTRES wallpapers come in Yellow/White on Yellow, Blue/Brown on Natural, Dark and Light melon on Natural, and Brown/White on Grey. Fabric colourways are Blue/Brown on Natural, Green/Yellow on White, and Light and Dark melon on Natural. ARCACHON has papers in Grey/Beige/Cream, Yellow/Pink/Gold, Red/Brown/Beige, and Rust/Grey/Pink, all on White. Fabrics come in Pink, Beige, Grey, or Blue, also on White.

Special colours can be ordered in both fabrics and papers; minimum order 45m of fabric, ten rolls of wallpaper. Three designs have matching ceramic tiles.

M: fabric w 48in (122cm), paper w 75cm×9.1m (29½in×10yd). *P:* m £6.25–£6.60, roll £11.50 –£16.50. See page 289 for BIRON, AURILLAC, BLOIS in colour.

MACHINKA PRINTS LTD

Decoratively delicious 100% cotton fabrics and vinyl wallpapers. 12 designs are available, on White or one of five pale grounds: Pink, Green, Apricot, Beige, and Yellow. Motifs include trailing morning glories, trellises, butterflies and poppies, in cheerful colours like Grass green, Pink, Red, Lilac, Lavender, and Salmon. *M:* fabric w 48in (122cm), paper w 50in (127cm). *P:* m £5.50–£9; roll £9–£17 depending on the number of colours.
See page 106 for colour illustration.

Selection of Machinka's designs

MELODY MILLS LTD

REFLECTIONS fabrics and vinyls with corner and border pieces to add the finishing touch to walls. Fabrics are all colour- and lightfast 100% cotton; wall coverings are washable, easy to hang, and ideal for hallways, kitchens, bathrooms and children's rooms. There are ten practical yet pretty designs most in both positive and negative combinations, plus eight

Osborne & Little's 'Oakwood' wallpaper, 'Seaweed' fabric (left); small 'Clematis' wallpaper, large 'Clematis' curtain fabric, 'Bark' tablecloth, from FOLIA (right)

Selection from Paper Moon's DURO

border and corner patterns. Motifs include flowers, all-over leaf designs, and bamboo lattices. Colours, all on White, are Summer blue, Caribbean blue, Rose pink, Rust, Spice, Cinnamon, Sand gold, and Cyprus green. *M:* fabric w 120cm (47¼in), paper w 52cm×10m (20½in×10yd 33¾in), 5cm (2in) border. *P:* m £4.50, roll £3.50, 20 corner pieces £1.20. See also *Wall Coverings*.

Selection from Melody Mills' REFLECTIONS

OSBORNE & LITTLE LTD

Beautifully designed selection of more than 600 wall coverings and 125 pure cotton fabrics. Gorgeous HAND PRINT motifs include florals plus swans, palms and sea shells (*P:* m £7–£8, roll £10–£18). Special colours are available to

order; minimum 10yd fabric, ten rolls wallpaper. FOLIA has soft co-ordinating chintzes like 'Wattle' (*P:* m £10, roll £8).
For a more contemporary look, PLANTA has soft plaids and checks, dots and tulips in pastel shades (*P:* m £9, roll £7). V.I.P. from Germany is more abstract — even punky — with bizarre squiggles, spots and curlicues in muted colours like Grey and Beige. Both cottons and sheers are available. *P:* m £10, roll £7.
M: fabric w 48in (122cm), paper w 20in × 11yd (51cm×10m). See also *Wall Coverings*.

PAPER MOON

Overwhelming choice of surface-printed wallpapers and matching fabrics, at amazingly competitive prices. Outstanding are the lively acrylic-coated papers from design-conscious DURO in Sweden, with stencil-like flower effects, borders, clouds, grasses, butterflies, stars, checks, and wavy lines. Primary Reds, Blues, Yellows and Greens abound, but there are also more muted tones for floral border designs. *P:* roll £7.
The papers blend perfectly with BORAS pure cotton fabrics, also from Sweden. Ten similar motifs are available, plus dots, stripes and wavy lines, also in beautifully bold bright colours. *P:* m £7.50.
Original LA NATURE wallpapers and 100% cotton fabrics from France are specifically for kitchens, bathrooms and/or nurseries. 20 designs include chickens, checks and stars in Navy/Red or Olive/Orange on White. *P:* m £6, roll £8.
MATCH papers are charming — simple, country-like prints with dots, stripes and tiny

flowers, often bordered with a band of flowers, co-ordinate perfectly with dotted cotton fabric. Colours are light Grass green, Apricot pink, Sky blue, Red, and Gold yellow. *P:* m £5.50, roll £7.
Amazing ESSEF papers from Germany have large checks, ribbons, bows and zig-zags which, like DURO, co-ordinate with BORAS fabrics. Colours are Hot pink, Lime green, Bright yellow, Cornflower blue, and Aqua. *P:* m £7.50, roll £5.
AFRICA is one of the most unusual collections on the market. Crayon lines in small geometric arrangements could have come straight off some precious tribal vessel, and colourways are almost too wonderful to imagine: Burnt red/Blue/Beige/Grey on Sand, Gold/Burnt red/Cobalt/Green on Off-white, and Cobalt/Brown/Burnt red/Beige on Grey. Fabrics are 100% cotton. *P:* m £6, roll £8.
M: fabric w 60in (150cm), except MATCH w 48in (122cm), paper w 21in × 10m (53.5cm × 10yd 33¾in), except LA NATURE, AFRICA w 21in × 11m (53.5cm × c12yd).
For striking simplicity, MARIMEKKO from Finland features vinyl wall coverings, matching

Paper Moon's 'Tulipani', 'Seitsman', 'Kesakuu' from MARIMEKKO

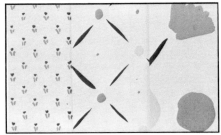

cotton, and some sheer fabrics in both pastel and bright shades. Three designs, from a collection of 20 including florals, stripes, grids and dots, are illustrated: 'Tulipani', 'Seitsman' and 'Kesakuu'. *M:* fabric w 140cm (55in), paper w 53cm × 10.5m (20¾in × 11yd 17⅜in). *P:* m £9, roll £15.
See page 289 for LA NATURE chickens, checks and stars, and AFRICA in colour.

PARKER KNOLL TEXTILES LTD
KIANG collection of silk-textured fabrics, made from 68% viscose and 32% acetate, in 100 plain shades with matching wall coverings in 30 colours. This subtle range also includes co-ordinating quilted fabrics in Off-white, Champagne, Beige, Soft gold, Apricot, Rose, Pale Turquoise, Pale olive, Pale celadon, and Pale forest green. *M:* fabric, wall coverings w 100cm (39⅜in). *P:* fabric m £10.50, wall coverings m £4.

POPPY LTD
Simple, inexpensive co-ordinates from a recently established company that deserves to do well. Fabrics are pre-shrunk, washable Egyptian cottons; their wallpapers, printed by a large manufacturer, are spongeable. YVON is in White on Chocolate, Stone (peachy beige) or Dusky pink. Wallpapers are available in the same shades, on White. TREES fabric has White trees on Bright red, Bright blue, or Forest green; wallpaper comes with Red trees on Grey, Green on Pale green, or Bright blue on Pale blue. HEDGEROW fabrics and papers are more muted, both with Olive, Mulberry or Rust twisting vines on Magnolia (beige).

Left to right, from top: Poppy's YVON paper and fabric, TREES, HEDGEROW

Poppy will also arrange for duvets, curtains, cushions, etc to be made.
M: fabric w 45in (114.5cm), except 'Yvon' w 36in (90cm), paper w 51cm×10m (20in×10yd 33¾in). *P:* m £2.99, roll £2.49, except YVON m, roll £2.29.

QUENBY PRINTS
EDITH DE LISLE wallpapers and complementary cottons include 'Golden Cage', a dotted lattice in White on Mint green, Yellow or Peach, with birds and garlands on the fabric only; 'Apiary', a White honeycomb ground etched on Green, Yellow or Rust, with bees added on the fabric; and 'White Hunter', a key-inspired motif in White on Teal blue, Mid-brown or Stone. The fabrics, much less expensive than Quenby's normal ranges, and just as lovely, are suitable for soft furnishings and loose covers, but not fitted upholstery. *M:* fabric w 45in (115cm), wallpaper w 21in × 11yd (53.34cm ×10m). *P:* m £3.25, roll £3.25.

Quenby's 'Golden Cage'

David Sage's TRELLIS

PRICES AND INFORMATION WERE CORRECT AT THE TIME OF GOING TO PRESS

DAVID SAGE DESIGNS
Not cheap, but good value for great style. This light and airy collection incorporates just about evey motif imaginable, from bamboo, dots and Art Deco designs to flowers and clouds. CAMELLIA, in 100% cotton or cotton satin drill, comes in Yellow, Peach, Grass green, Beige, Grey, Navy, and Rust, on White. TRELLIS, in the same fabrics, is Grass green, Coffee, Peach, Copper, Sky blue, or Rust, also on White. All patterns come in large and small-scale versions with co-ordinating plain shades, and matching wallpapers, some with co-ordinating borders. *M:* fabric w 120cm (47¼in), paper w 69cm×10m (27in× 10yd 33¾in). *P:* m £8–£10, roll £14.50. See page 289 for 'Condotti', 'Graffiti' in colour.

ARTHUR SANDERSON & SONS LTD
Marvellously wide-ranging selection. Wallpapers, fabrics, carpets, rugs, bedcovers — even blinds and paints — can be completely, and relatively inexpensively, co-ordinated as a result of this large firm's superb efforts in recent years.

Sanderson & Sons' 'Cariba' from the TRIAD collection

The designer-quality florals in the TRIAD collection are adventurously coloured; several new designs are added every year, each one seemingly more beautiful than the last. 'Cariba' with trailing entwined branches, comes in Greens/Pinks on Off-white; Strong Greens/Pink on Sky blue, and Greys/Cream/Pink on Antique gold. Three prints have matching White-on-White voiles in 91% polyester and 9% linen, including 'Christobell', with lilies of the valley in Green/Pink, Beige/Pink, and Green/Pale Gold/Turquoise. The four-poster illustrated has swags of matching voile. 'Acorn' and 'Kandahar' wallpapers have complementary borders; 'Border Incident', 'Black Thorn', 'Acorn', and 'Yum-Yum' papers have matching rugs 36×60in (90×150cm). *P:* TRIAD m £5.20, voiles m £4.40, roll £4–£6. Plain fabrics that complement TRIAD prints include linen union BL5900 in 62 colourways (*P:* m £6.50). Co-ordinating stripes — only for the confident — include BEELINE pure cotton fabrics in eight reversible shades (*P:* m £6.50). *M:* all fabrics w 122–127cm (48–50in), TRIAD papers w 27in × 11yd (69cm × 10m).

Sanderson & Sons' 'Christobell' from TRIAD

For small-scale designs in good, slightly muted colours look at the HEIDI collection. Not as sweet as it sounds, but competitively priced and well executed with 12 designs in ten colourways. Each page of the book shows six papers and three 100% cotton fabrics designed to work together. They include 'Franz', 'Gerhard', 'Sophia', 'Frieda', 'Erica', 'Eric', 'Karen', 'Karl'. Fabrics in 100% cotton. *M:* as above. *P:* m £4, roll £3.85.

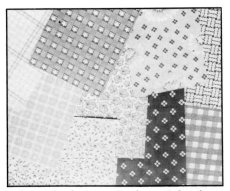

Left to right, from top: Sanderson & Sons' 'Franz', 'Gerhard', 'Sophia', 'Frieda', 'Erica', 'Eric', 'Karen', 'Karl', all from HEIDI

Sanderson also import two co-ordinating collections. MAISON JARDIN from Rasch in Germany has tiny floral and geometric motifs on wallpapers and borders, with complementary plain or patterned cotton chintz and semi-sheer acrylic fabrics. 'Après-Midi', a leaf design on 100% cotton fabric, can be teamed with three related papers: 'Après-Midi'; 'Midi', the same with superimposed poppy and daisy heads; and 'Petite', an all-over design of daisy heads. A bold border with a profusion of poppies and daisies growing in a grassy hedgerow complements all three. Plain acrylic fabric is also available. Colourways are Red poppies and White daisies on White and Green; or Pink poppies and Yellow daisies on White and Brown. *M:* fabric w 117–150cm (46–60in), paper w 53cm (21in). *P:* m £5.20–£11.50, roll £5.75–£10.
The French PAUL GRUIN collection is divided into four themes, each of which runs through washable wallpapers, a related pure cotton fabric, and a striped wallpaper that can be cut into friezes. 'Persian' has seven complementary papers and two printed cotton fabrics in Blue, Red, or Green. 'Japanese' is Pale Grey, Turquoise, or Peach on seven papers and one fabric; 'Fauna and Flora' in Green/Pink or Yellow/Mauve has five papers, one with a frieze of jungle animals, and one fabric; and 'Flowers and Fruit' in Pink/Grey or Blue/Green has eight papers and two fabrics, the latter scattered with strawberries, peaches, and blossom. Seven plain, linen-look companion papers are available. *M:* fabric 117–150cm (46–60in), paper w 53cm (21in). *P:* m £5.20, roll £5.20.
See also 'Blinds', 'Carpets', 'Paint', *Wall Coverings*.

Sanderson & Sons' 'Persian' from the PAUL GRUIN collection

SARTOR

Fresh and pretty fabrics, wallpapers and ceramic tiles. Fabrics, all pure cotton, can be quilted and come in 16 designs, 12 with matching wallpapers. Plant, animal and insect shapes have a definite Oriental flavour, on White (the least expensive), Cream, Peach, or Blue-grey. Special colours are available, to order. FIREFLY, DRAGONFLY, and SWAMP-FLY, all with insects of varying sizes, come in Fuchsia, Beige, Bright or Dark green, Navy, Peach, Blue-grey, and Sky blue, on standard ground colours. Other designs, in the same colourways, include POSY, MAIDENHAIR, FERN, HONESTY, CHRYSANTHEMUM and

Left to right: Sartor's FIREFLY, DRAGONFLY, SWAMPFLY

IRIS. *M:* fabric w 48in (122cm), paper w 30in × 10yd (76cm × 9.1m). *P:* m £6.75–£9.50, quilting sq m £10, roll £8.50.
See also 'Ceramic Tiles' and 'Fabrics'. See page 289 for DRAGONFLY, MAIDENHAIR, CHRYSANTHEMUM, and HONESTY in colour.

STOREY BROS & CO LTD

Marvellous VICTORIA range of pre-pasted vinyls and matching polyester fabrics, plus — a unique feature — matching plain polyester velvets. Small period designs predominate; a few geometrics and stripes in summery shades are also available. *M:* fabric w 130cm (51¼in); paper w 53cm × 10m (20¾in × 10yd 33¾in). *P:* m £2, velvet £7.40, roll £6.30–£7.10. See also *Wall Coverings*.

From left: Storey Bros' '825', '937', from VICTORIA

TAMESA FABRICS LTD

A plethora of neutrals for lovers of paler than pale shades. Silky sheers, nubbly textures, hand-screen prints, embroidered weaves, soft chenilles, textured wallpapers and gorgeous carpets are available. Fabrics are mainly linens, cottons, wool and silk. There are also Greens, Dark browns and other earth tones.
ALBANY and BAMBOO are just two of a selection of large-scale hand-screen prints on Off-white linen in Terracotta, Khaki, Grass green, Bright blue, or Tan. Special colours to order (*P:* m £9–£14). CHECKERS is a softened geometric cotton in Beige, Caramel, Apricot, or Grey-blue (*P:* m £9. Textured linen weaves include SLOANE *P:* m £8). Other fabrics include cotton and linen mixes in plain shades plus stripes and checks (*P:* m £7–£14); unusual chenilles (*P:* £20–£33); and woven silks with abstract or geometric motifs (*P:* £38–£50). *M:* all 127cm (50in).

Tamesa's CHECKERS

Unusually wide textured wallpapers co-ordinate with the fabrics, and are stiffened so that they can be used for roller blinds (*M:* w 42in/107cm, *P:* m £7–£9). See also 'Carpets'. See page 291 for ALBANY, BAMBOO in colour.

TISSUNIQUE LTD

Exquisite, and expensive co-ordinates from the Continent. The Manuel Canovas PERGOLA collection has contemporary small-scale motifs on Off-white, including three-leaf clovers, cornflowers, and cross-hatched lines and tiny leaves, in Grey, Tan, Dark brown, Red, Rust, Apricot, Rose, Bright green, Navy, Sky blue, or Lavender. Fabrics are 100% cotton. *P:* m £12–£16, roll £12.

Selection from Tissunique's PERGOLA by Manuel Canovas

Pierre Frey's LES ENFANTS range of charming prints for children's rooms also has 100% cotton fabrics. Eight designs include scattered mice, stars, turtles, elephants and clowns, in clear, ice-cream colours, with matching stripes in all colourways. *P:* m £15, roll £13–£15. *M:* both ranges fabric w 124.5–152.5cm (49–60in), paper 53cm × 10m (20¾ × 10yd 33¾in).

T-T DESIGN SERVICES (INTL) LTD

One of the most comprehensive and exciting arrays of American co-ordinates this side of the Atlantic. Not just one, but many, looks are available. Their exceptionally high quality is reflected in the prices, which are definitely at the top end of the market. CHARTERHOUSE DESIGNS includes exotic, screen-printed jungle-inspired florals, plus some classical patterns. Less expensive roller-printed papers have similar themes. Architectural 'Versailles Treillage' could transform any room into a gazebo. *M:* fabric w 48–54in (122–136cm). *P:* yd £23–£30, roll £24–£30.

T-T Design's 'Versailles Treillage'

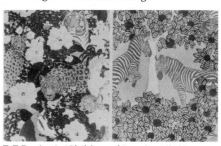

T-T Design's 'Children of Paradise' (left), 'Orange Grove' (right), both from CHARTERHOUSE DESIGNS

The CONNAISSANCE collection consists of washable wallpapers, and complementary polished cottons, vinyl suedes, tough cotton sailcloths, and cotton satins. They include eight beautiful machine-quilted patterns, and three embroidered designs; all can be custom-coloured. *M:* fabric w 48–54in (122–136cm). *P:* upon application, quilted fabrics from yd £30. The I. D. INTERNATIONAL range by Terry della Stuffa features traditional, large-scale florals. All fabrics have a beautiful sheen — the result of an exceptionally heavy glaze. *M:* fabric w 54–56in (137–142cm). *P:* yd £40–£60, roll £25–£30.
ZINA STUDIOS specialize in hand-printed, custom-coloured co-ordinates. Designs are mainly classical with butterflies, flowers, garlands and ribbons predominating. Enlarged single motifs can be supplied, as panels, for chair seats, pelmets, cushion covers, etc. *M:* fabric w 54–56in (136–142cm). *P:* upon application. The masculine DESIGN FRIENDS range is small but beautiful, with wonderfully coloured geometrics. Special colours are available, to order. *M:* fabric w 48in (122cm). *P:* yd £24–£45, roll £24–£45.

Dramatic ALLUME HANDPRINTS are bold, brightly coloured and modern, with some designs on foil papers; fabrics are printed to order (*M:* fabric w 45–58in/115–147.5cm, *P:* fabric upon application, roll £22–£25). The intriguing GILFORD collection includes wet-look papers in every shade imaginable, plus all sorts of suedes, rubbers, mock leathers and simulated furs (*M:* fabric w 54in/136cm, *P:* upon application). Finally, there's the very unusual SOUTH BAY DESIGN CORPORATION range based on geometrical motifs (*M:* fabric w 50–56in/127–142cm, *P:* yd £25–£40, roll £25–£35).
T-T Design Service must be approached through their head office, or leading interior decorators. Quantities are 10m fabric, 15 rolls of wallpaper.
M: all papers w 27in × 5yd (69cm × 4.6m).
See page 280 for CHARTERHOUSE in colour.

VENILIA LTD

Very tasteful LE NOUVEAU ROMANTIQUE range of pre-pasted vinyls and pure cotton fabrics. Small floral and geometric motifs abound, all beautifully coloured and designed to co-ordinate throughout the house so that colour flows from room to room. For example, 'Centre' is a small grid filled with leaves; 'Marina' has bigger leaves of the same shape with clover flowers; 'Tessa' is minute, leafy grids next to thin line grids; 'Livia' has all-over pods on a paler ground; and 'Leda' is plain with a linear texture. All come in Dark green and Rose — plus ten other colour combinations. *M:* fabric 2 130cm (51¼in), wall covering w 53cm × 10m (20¾in × 10yd 33¾in). *P:* m £4.25–£6.95, roll £8.95–£9.95.

Left to right, from top: Venilia's 'Leda', 'Centre', 'Livia', 'Tessa', 'Rahat', 'Talat', 'Marina', 'Razia'

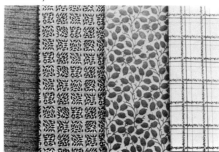

Air Conditioning Advisory Bureau,
30 Millbank, London SW1.
Tel: 01–834 8827

Architectural Association (Inc),
34–36 Bedford Sq, London WC1.
Tel: 01–636 0974

Art Metalware Manufacturer's Association,
27 Frederick St, Birmingham.
Tel: 021–236 2657/9

Association of Master Upholsterers,
Dormar House, Mitre Bridge, Scrubs Lane,
London NW10.
Tel: 01–965 3565

British Adhesive Manufacturers' Associaton,
2a High St, Hythe, Southampton.
Tel: Southampton 842765

British Antique Dealers' Association,
20 Rutland Gate, London SW7.
Tel: 01–589 4128/2102

British Bath Manufacturers' Association,
Fleming House, Renfrew St, Glasgow.
Tel: 041–332 0826

British Blind and Shutter Association,
First Floor, 251 Brompton Rd, London SW3.
Tel: 01–584 5552

British Carpet Manufacturers' Association,
Margam House, 26 St James's Sq,
London SW1.
Tel: 01–839 2145

British Chemical Dampcourse Association Ltd,
4 Burnell Close, Alcester, Warwickshire.
Tel: Alcester 4513

British Floorcovering Manufacturers'
Association,
125 Queens Rd, Brighton, Sussex.
Tel: Brighton 29271

British Horological Institute,
Upton Hall, Upton, Newark, Notts.
Tel: Newark 813795

British Institute of Interior Design,
22–24 South St, Ilkeston, Derbyshire.
Tel: Ilkeston 329781

British Standards Institution,
2 Park St, London W1.
Tel: 01–629 9000

British Wood Preserving Association,
Premier House, 150 Southampton Row,
London WC1.
Tel: 01–837 8217

Building Centre,
26 Store St, London WC1.
Administration Tel: 01–637 1022;
Information Tel: 01–637 8361

Building Centre,
Colston Ave, The Centre, Bristol.
Tel: Bristol 27002

Building Centre,
15–16 Trumpington St, Cambridge.
Tel: Cambridge 59625

Building Centre, Ireland,
17 Lower Baggot St, Dublin.
Tel: Dublin 762745

Building Centre,
113–115 Portland St, Manchester.
Tel: 061–236 6933

The Building Conservation Trust,
26 Store St, London WC1.
Tel: 01–637 1022

Building Centre, Scotland,
6 Newton Terrace, Glasgow.
Tel: 041–248 6212

Building Centre,
Grosvenor House, 18–20 Cumberland Place,
Southampton.
Tel: Southampton 27350/24455

Building and Design Centre,
Hop St, Liverpool.
Tel: 051–709 8484

Building Information Centre,
Cauldon College of Further Education,
The Concourse, Stoke Rd, Shelton,
Stoke-on-Trent, Staffs.
Tel: Stoke-on-Trent 29561

Building Research Station,
Garston, Watford, Herts.
Tel: Garston 76612

Building Research Establishment,
Scottish Laboratory, Kelvin Rd, East Kilbride,
Glasgow.
Tel: East Kilbride 33941

Building Services Research and Information
Association,
Old Bracknell Lane, Bracknell, Berks.
Tel: Bracknell 25071

Carpet Cleaners' Association,
97 Knighton Fields Rd West, Leicester.
Tel: Leicester 836065

Conservation Sourcebook, published by
Crafts Council, 12 Waterloo Pl, London SW1.
Tel: 01–839 1917

Consumers' Association,
14 Buckingham St, London.
Tel: 01–839 1222

The Council of Ironfoundry Associations,
14 Pall Mall, London SW1.
Tel: 01–930 7171

Design Council, The Design Centre,
28 Haymarket, London SW1.
Tel: 01–839 8000

Drycleaning Information Bureau,
178–202 Great Portland St, London W1.
Tel: 01–637 7481

Electrical Floorwarming Association,
5 Roughlea Ave, Culcheth, Warrington,
Cheshire.
Tel: Culcheth 4356

Federation of Master Builders,
33 John St, London WC1.
Tel: 01–242 7583/7

Floor Quarry Association,
Federation House, Stoke-on-Trent, Staffs.
Tel: Stoke-on-Trent 45147

Friends of the Earth,
9 Poland St, London W1.
Tel: 01–434 1684/437 6121

Glazing and Glass Federation,
6 Mount Row, London W1.
Tel: 01–629 8334

Guild of Architectural Ironmongers,
15 Soho Sq, London W1.
Tel: 01–439 1753

The Guild of Master Craftsmen,
10 Dover St, London W1.
Tel: 01–493 7571/2

Hardwood Flooring Manufacturers'
Association,
Clareville House, Oxenden St, London SW1
Tel: 01–839 3381

Heating, Ventilating and Air Conditioning
Manufacturers' Association Ltd,
3 Phoenix House, Heston, Middx.
Tel: 01–897 2848

Institution of Electrical Engineers,
Savoy Place, Victoria Embankment, London
WC2.
Tel: 01–240 1871

Institute of Plumbing,
Scottish Mutual House, North St, Hornchurch,
Essex.
Tel: Hornchurch 51236

Interior Decorators' and Designers'
Association,
24 Ormond St, Richmond, Surrey.
Tel: 01–948 4151

International Wool Secretariat,
Wool House, Carlton Gdns, London SW1.
Tel: 01–930 7300

Kitchen Furniture Manufacturers' Association,
82 New Cavendish St, London W1.
Tel: 01–580 5588

Lofts Conversion Advisory Bureau,
594 Kingston Rd, London SW20.
Tel: 01–542 9095

National Federation of Builders' and Plumbers'
Merchants,
15 Soho Sq, London W1.
Tel: 01–439 1753

Natural Energy Association,
2 York St, London W1.
Tel: 01–486 3356

The Solid Fuel Advisory Service,
The Building Centre, 26 Store St, London W1.
Tel: 01–637 1022

CANE WORK

BUCKINGHAMSHIRE
The Basketmakers' Association,
Bierton House, Dean Way, Chalfont St Giles.
Tel: Chalfont St Giles 2296

Wycombe Cane and Rush Works,
Victoria St, High Wycombe.
Tel: High Wycombe 22610

CHESHIRE
J P A R Steele Antique and Cane Repairs,
22 High St, Warburton.
Tel: Warburton 852261

CUMBRIA
Easedale Antiques,
Easedale House, Grasmere, Ambleside.
Tel: Grasmere 231

ESSEX
The Pump House (Pump House Interiors Ltd)
14 High St, Saffron Walden.
Tel: Saffron Walden 21921

HEREFORD AND WORCESTER
I and J L Brown,
58–59 Commercial Rd, Hereford.
Tel: Hereford 58895

Sidbury Antiques,
61 Sidbury, Worcester.
Tel: Worcester 25461

LONDON
De Villiers Antiques,
311 Fulham Palace Rd, SW6.
Tel: 01–731 3859

H J Hatfield & Sons Ltd,
42 St Michael's St, W2.
Tel: 01–723 8265

The Lots Road People,
91–93 Lots Rd, SW10.
Tel: 01–352 0763

OXFORDSHIRE
Quadrangle Galery,
1 Walton Cres, Oxford.
Tel: Oxford 57035

SURREY
The Jackdaw Antiques,
6 Weyhill, Haslemere.
Tel: Haslemere 51081

CLOCKS

AVON
Lawrence Brass & Son,
93–95 Walcot St, Bath.
Tel: Bath 64057

CAMBRIDGESHIRE
Timecraft,
32 Eltisley Ave, Cambridge.
Tel: Cambridge 350658

CORNWALL
Acanthus Antiques,
33 Fore St, Lostwithiel.
Tel: Bodmin 872435

HUMBERSIDE NORTH
Boothferry Antiques,
104–106 Boothferry Rd, Hull.
Tel: Hull 53272

LEICESTERSHIRE
Loughborough Clock Centre,
221a Derby Rd, Loughborough.
Tel: Loughborough 842376

LONDON
Aubrey Brocklehurst,
124 Cromwell Rd, SW7.
Tel: 01–373 0319

North London Clock Shop Ltd,
70 Mountgrove Rd, N5.
Tel: 01–226 1609

Strike One Ltd,
1a Camden Walk, N1.
Tel: 01–226 9709

NORTHUMBERLAND
Hazel Cottage Clocks,
Hazel Cottage, Eachwick.
Tel: Wylam 2415

SHROPSHIRE
John D I Locke,
'Clocks', Raven Lane, Ludlow.
Tel: Ludlow 4303

SOMERSET
Edward A Nowell,
21-23 Market Place, Wells.
Tel: Wells 72415

SUFFOLK
Clock Antiques,
138 High St, Long Melford.
Tel: Long Melford 2945

SURREY
Roger A Davies, Antiquarian Horologist,
19 Dorking Rd, Great Bookham.
Tel: Great Bookham 57655

WILTSHIRE
Andre David Ltd,
Church House, 26 High St, Bromham, nr
Chippenham.
Tel: Bromham 850347

GILDING

LONDON
Ashby & Horner,
32 Earl St, EC2.
Tel: 01–377 0266

Alexandre Kidd,
67 Castlebar Road, W5.
Tel: 01–997 3896

Alec Ossowski,
83 Pimlico Rd, SW1.
Tel: 01–730 3256

Matthei Radev,
10 Ogle St, W1.
Tel: 01–580 4704

Jill Saunders,
91–93 Lots Rd, SW10.
Tel: 01–352 0763

J Wolff & Son Ltd,
1 Chester Ct, Albany St, NW1.
Tel: 01–935 3636

LAMP RESTORERS

LONDON
W G T Burne Antique Glass,
11 Elystan St, SW3.
Tel: 01–589 1182

N Davighi,
117 Shepherd's Bush Rd, W6.
Tel: 01–603 5357

The Lamp Shop,
24 Bedfordbury, WC2.
Tel: 01–836 3852

David Paton Ltd,
10 Strathearn Place, W2.
Tel: 01–723 0967

W Stitch & Co Ltd,
48 Berwick St, W1.
Tel: 01–437 3776

Christopher Wray's Lamp Workshop,
613 & 615 Kings Rd, SW6.
Tel: 01–736 8434

SUSSEX WEST
David R Fileman,
Squirrels Bayards, Steyning.
Tel: Steyning 813229

METAL RESTORERS

CAMBRIDGESHIRE
Antiques Etc,
18 King St, Cambridge.
Tel: Cambridge 62825

CHESHIRE
Roderick Gibson,
20/24 Hospital St, Nantwich.
Tel: Nantwich 65301

CORNWALL
Old Barn Antiques,
Perranarworthal, nr Truro.
Tel: Truro 863831

Tamar Antiques Restoration,
Tutwell House, Tutwell, Stoke Climsland,
Callington.
Tel: Stoke Climsland 629

ESSEX
Renzland,
London Rd, Copford, Colchester, Essex.
Tel: Colchester 210212

KENT
Darenth Antiques,
Vicarage Hill, Westerham.
Tel: Westerham 63273

LANCASHIRE
Park Galleries Antiques Fine Art and Decor,
167 Mayor St, Bolton.
Tel: Bolton 29827

Jason Trent,
46 Moorgate, Bury.
Tel: 061–761 1986

LONDON
J D Beardmore & Co Ltd,
3-5 Percy St, W1.
Tel: 01–636 1214

R W Crow,
20 Goodge Place, W1.
Tel: 01–636 8741

N Davighi,
117 Shepherd's Bush Rd, W6.
Tel: 01–603 5357

Divertimenti,
68-72 Marylebone Lane, W1.
Tel: 01–935 0689

Garrard,
112 Regent St, W1.
Tel: 01–734 7020

J Grotty & Son Ltd,
74 New Kings Rd, SW6.
Tel: 01–385 1789

Plating and Tinning Service,
125 Broadley St, NW8.
Tel: 01–723 8630

Watts,
7 Tufton St, SW1.
Tel: 01–222 7169

NORTHAMPTONSHIRE
Paul Hopwell Antiques,
30 High St, West Haddon.
Tel: West Haddon 636

SOMERSET
The Flintlock,
17a High St, Glastonbury.
Tel: Glastonbury 31525

SURREY
A E Booth,
9 High St, Ewell.
Tel: 01–393 5245

Murrivan Ltd,
Tamworth Rd, Croydon.
Tel: 01–688 4709

SUSSEX EAST
W H Weller & Son,
12 North St, Eastbourne.
Tel: Eastbourne 23592

TYNE AND WEAR
Country Style,
23–29 High St, Newcastle-upon-Tyne.
Tel: Newcastle 29086

YORKSHIRE WEST
Harewood Antiques,
Harrogate Road, Harewood, nr Leeds.
Tel: Harewood 886327

MIRRORS: RE-SILVERING

LONDON
W J Biles,
79 Woodgrange Rd, E7.
Tel: 01–534 3939

Chelsea Glassworks,
107 Fulham Rd, SW3.
Tel: 01–581 2501

PAINTED FURNITURE

SCOTLAND
Fraser Antiques,
119 High St, North Berwick, East Lothian.
Tel: North Berwick 2722

SUFFOLK
Betty Meysey-Thompson,
10 Church St, Woodbridge.
Tel: Woodbridge 2144

R N Usher,
42 Southgate St, Bury St Edmunds.
Tel: Bury St Edmunds 4838

YORKSHIRE NORTH
Sutton Antiques,
Sutton-on-the-Forest.
Tel: 0347 810249

SECURITY

Adams Rite (Europe) Ltd,
17 Bowater Rd, Westminster Industrial Estate,
London SE18.
Tel: 01–855 0121

Banham's Patent Locks Ltd,
233–235 Kensington High St, London W8.
Tel: 01–937 4311

Bramah Security Equipment Ltd,
31 Oldbury Place, London W1.
Tel: 01–935 7148

Chubb & Sons Lock & Safe Co Ltd,
3 North End Rd, London NW11.
Tel: 01–458 8711

Group 4 Total Security Ltd,
7 Carlos Place, London W1.
Tel: 01–629 8765

Home Automation Ltd,
Pindar Rd, Hoddesdon, Herts.
Tel: Hoddesdon 60355

J Legge & Co Ltd,
Moat St, Willenhall, West Midlands.
Tel: Willenhall 65332

Lockmasters Ltd,
The Bank, Winchester Road, Four Marks,
Alton, Hants.
Tel: Alton 62756

Newman-Tonks Ltd, Hardware Division,
Allesley Street, Birmingham.
Tel: 021–359 4751

Ramicube Ltd,
Mul-T-Lock House, St Michael's Rd,
Bilsborrow, nr Preston, Lancs.
Tel: 01–668 5366 or Brock 40117

Securicor Ltd (Alarms Division),
77 Vicarage Cres, London SW11.
Tel: 01–223 2101

Sentinel Security Service Ltd,
Sensec House, 144 Maidstone Rd, Footscray,
Sidcup, Kent.
Tel: 01–300 0114

Yale Security Products Division,
Wood St,. Willenhall, West Midlands.
Tel: Willenhall 66911

BLIND MAINTENANCE

Contravent Ltd,
1 Eskdale Rd, Uxbridge, Middx.
Tel: Uxbridge 37988

Window Wise Ltd,
94 Church Rd, London N17;
Tel: 01–808 5555.
51 Brimsdown Ave, Enfield, Middx.
Tel: 01–804 2299

Sunvene Ltd,
7 Greenheys Lane, Manchester.
Tel: 061–226 4636

AI (YORKSHIRE) ART GLASS LTD, Providence Buildings, Providence Street, Westgate, Bradford, West Yorkshire, BD1 2PW; Tel: Bradford 32735/6; *Mirrors & Glass*

ABINGDON CARPETS LTD, Nuffield Way, Abingdon, Oxfordshire, OX14 1TE; Tel: Abingdon 27515; London Office: 01-373 7161; *Carpeting (Berber, Flecked, Wilton)*

ABSTRACTA CONSTRUCTION LTD, Eldonwall Trading Estate, Staples Corner, Edgware Road, London NW2; Tel: 01-450 2511; *Shelving*

ACB DESIGN CONSULTANCY, 134 Lots Road, London SW10; Tel: 01-351 4333 (10 lines) & 352 3929; *Special Furniture (Made to Order Furniture)*

ACQUISITIONS (FIREPLACES) LTD, 269 Camden High Street, London NW1 7BX; Tel: 01-485 4955; *Fireplaces (Accessories, Mantels & Surrounds)*

ACROW SCULPTURED TUBING LTD, Ashdon Road, Saffron Walden, Essex CB10 2NG; Tel: Saffron Walden 22444 (12 lines); *Staircases*

W & R R ADAM LTD, Birmingham Road, Kidderminster, Worcestershire, DY10 2SH; Tel: Kidderminster 2247; *Carpeting (Berber, Wilton)*

ADEPTUS DESIGNS LTD, 7 Cubitt Street, London WC1; Tel: 01-837 9133 & 278 5761; *Lighting; Upholstered Furniture*

AEG-TELEFUNKEN, 217 Bath Road, Slough, Buckinghamshire SL1 4AW; Tel: Slough 872101; *Appliances & Kitchen Accessories*

AFIA CARPETS, 81 Baker Street, London W1M 1AJ; Tel: 01-935 0414/5; *Carpeting (Berber, Patterned)*

AGAHEAT APPLIANCES, Glynwed Domestic & Heating Appliances Ltd, PO Box 30, Ketley, Telford, Salop TF1 1BR; Tel: Telford 3973; *Stoves (also Kitchen Ranges)*

AINSTY FACTORING CO LTD, 29/39 Yorkersgate, Malton, N. Yorkshire YO17 0AH; Tel: Malton 2444 (5 lines); *Fireplaces (Mantels & Surrounds)*

ALBARY LINENS, 48 George Street (off Baker Street), London W1; Tel: 01-487 4105; *Soft Furnishings*

ALBION DESIGN, The Studio, Ellington Street, London N7 8PP; Tel: 01-607 4223; *Staircases*

ALBION HARDWARE LTD, Simon House, Sunderland Road, Sandy, Bedfordshire SG19 9QY; Tel: Sandy 80330; *Bathrooms (Accessories); Fittings (Door)*

ALLIANCE FLOORING CO LTD, 36 Maxwell Road, Fulham, London SW6; Tel: 01-736 3811; *Flooring (Cork, Rubber, Wood)*

ALLIBERT (UK) LTD, see **SOMMER ALLIBERT (UK) LTD**

ALLMILMÖ LTD, Station Road, Thatcham, Nr. Newbury, Berkshire RG13 4RD; Tel: Thatcham 68181; *Kitchens*

ALNO (UK) LTD, 164–166 King Street, Hammersmith, London W6 0QU; Tel: 01-748 0671; *Kitchens*

AMTICO (NATIONAL PLASTICS) LTD, London Showroom: 17 St. George Street, London W1R 9DE; Tel: 01-629 6258; *Flooring (Vinyl Tile)*

ANDERSON CERAMICS LTD, Dukesway, Team Valley, Gateshead, Tyne & Wear NE11 0SW; Tel: Gateshead 874511; *Bathrooms (Sanitaryware)*

SALLY ANDERSON (CERAMICS) LTD, Parndon Mill, Harlow, Essex, CM20 2HP; Tel: Harlow 20982; *Ceramic Tiles*

ANGLEPOISE LIGHTING LTD, Enfield Industrial Estate, Redditch, Worcestershire; Tel: Redditch 63771 (4 lines); *Lighting*

MARK ANGUS, Church Road Studio, Combe Down, Bath, Avon; Tel: Combe Down 834530; *Mirrors & Glass*

ANNA'S CHOICE, see **MARGO INTERNATIONAL FABRICS LTD;**

ANTIFERENCE LTD, Aylesbury, Buckinghamshire; Tel Aylesbury 82511; *Fittings (Curtain)*

ANTOCKS LAIRN LTD, Lancaster Road, Cressex, High Wycombe, Buckinghamshire HP12 4HZ; Tel: High Wycombe 24912; *Chairs*

ARAM DESIGNS LTD, 3 Kean Street, London WC2; Tel: 01-240 3933; *Chairs; Lighting; Storage; Tables (Dining, Occasional); Upholstered Furniture*

ARCHITECTURAL HERITAGE OF CHELTENHAM, Bayshill Lodge, Montpellier, Cheltenham, Gloucestershire; Tel: Cheltenham 26567/45589/44165/22191; *Fireplaces (Mantels & Surrounds)*

ARCLINEA UK LIMITED, 12 Cheval Place, London SW7; Tel: 01-584 0646; *Kitchens*

ARDENBRITE PRODUCTS LTD, 57 Farringdon Road, London EC1M 3JH; Tel: 01-405 2487; *Paint*

ARENSON INTERNATIONAL LTD, Fabritrak, 20a Pimlico Road, London SW1W 8LJ; Tel: 01-730 6987/6864; *Wall Coverings*

ARGON GALLERY, 3 Theberton Street, London N1; Tel: 01-359 3845; *Lighting*

ARISTOCAST LTD, Bold Street, Sheffield, Yorkshire S9 2LR; Tel: Sheffield 442423; *Architectural Ornaments; Bathrooms (Sanitaryware); Fireplaces (Mantels & Surrounds)*

MARTHE ARMITAGE, 1 Strand-on-the-Green, Chiswick, London W4 3PQ; Tel: 01-984 0160; *Wall Coverings*

ARMITAGE SHANKS LTD, Armitage, Rugeley, Staffordshire WS15 4BT; Tel: Armitage 490253; *Bathrooms (Accessories, Sanitaryware)*

ARMSTRONG CORK CO LTD, Armstrong House, Chequers Square, Uxbridge, Middx. UB8 1NG; Tel: 01-828 7193; *Architectural Ornaments (Suspended Ceilings); Flooring (Vinyl, Vinyl Tile); Lighting; Wall Coverings*

ARQUATI, Basman Marketing Ltd, 10 Baron Avenue, Kettering, Northants, NN16 8UW; Tel: Kettering 83555; *Fittings (Curtain)*

ART GLASS LTD, Providence Buildings, Providence Street, Westgate, Bradford BD1 2PW; Tel: Bradford 32735/6; *Mirrors & Glass*

ART VENEER CO, Industrial Estate, Mildenhall, Suffolk, IP28 7AY; Tel: Mildenhall 712550; *Useful Products (Miscellaneous)*

ARTEX PRODUCTS LTD, Artex Avenue, Newhaven, East Sussex BN9 9DD; Tel: Newhaven 3100; *Paint*

ARTIMA OF SWITZERLAND, 46 Rochester Row, London SW1P 1JU; Tel: 01-584 1008; *Upholstered Furniture*

ARTISAN CARPETS LTD, 18 Eldon Way, Biggleswade, Bedfordshire SG18 8NH; Tel: Biggleswade 314316; *Rugs*

ASH & CO, 441 Howitt Road, London NW3; Tel: 01-722 2157; *Chairs*

ASHLEY ACCESSORIES LTD, PO Box No 1, Ulverston, Cumbria LA12 9BN; Tel: Ulverston 53333; *Lighting*

ASHLEY FURNITURE WORKSHOPS, 3a Dawson Place, London W2; Tel: 01-229 6013; *Chairs; Upholstered Furniture*

ASKO FINNTERNATIONAL LTD, Victoria Road, Ruislip, Middlesex, HA4 0LF; Tel: 01-841 5291; *Kitchens; Storage; Tables (Dining Suites); Upholstered Furniture*

LAURA ASHLEY, Carno, Powys, Wales; Tel: Carno 671; *Ceramic Tiles; Lighting; Paint; Soft Furnishings; Wall Coverings (Co-Ordinates)*

ASSOCIATED WEAVERS LTD, Toftshaw Lane, Bradford, Yorkshire BD4 6QW; Tel: Bradford 681881; London Office: British Carpet Trade Centre, 99 Kensington High Street, London W8; Tel: 01-937 6606; *Carpeting (Flecked, Patterned, Sculptured Pile, Shag, Wilton); Rugs*

ASTON WOODWARE, Aston Hill (A40), Lewknor, Oxfordshire; Tel: Kingston Blount 51500; *Chairs; Shelving; Tables (Dining)*

ATRIUM, PO Box 48, Harrogate, Yorkshire HG1 5AS; Tel: Harrogate 64317; *Bedrooms (Beds); Chairs; Lighting; Storage; Tables (Dining, Dining Suites); Upholstered Furniture*

ATTRACTA PRODUCTS LTD, 117 Geary Road, London NW10 1HS; Tel: 01-452 1959; *Useful Products (Tools)*

AUSTINSUITE FURNITURE, F Austin (Leyton) Ltd, Argall Avenue, Leyton, London E10 7P2; Tel: 01-539 5566; *Bedrooms (Furniture); Storage*

AXMINSTER CARPETS LTD, Axminster, Devon, EX13 5PQ; Tel: (Sales and order office only) Axminster 33533 (all other departments) Axminster 32244; *Carpeting (Berber, Patterned); Rugs*

BABY RELAX LTD, 113 Wennington Road, Rainham, Essex, RM13 9TL; Tel: Rainham 53344; *Bedrooms (Beds)*

DAVID BAGOTT DESIGN LTD, London Showroom: 266 Old Brompton Road, London SW5; Tel: 01-370-2267; *Bedrooms (Beds, Furniture)*

FRED BAIER, 18 Tichbourne Street, Brighton BN1 1NU; Tel: Brighton 23031/696394; *Special Furniture (Designer Creftspeople)*

G P & J BAKER LTD, PO Box 30, West End Road, High Wycombe, Buckinghamshire HP11 2QD; Tel: High Wycombe 22301; *Fabrics*

BAKER, KNAPP & TUBBS, Showroom: 26 King Street, London WC2; Tel: 01-379 6366; *Bedrooms (Beds, Furniture); Chairs; Desks; Mirrors & Glass; Plants & Planters; Shelving; Storage; Tables (Occasional); Upholstered Furniture*

RALPH BALL, 35a 252 Old Brompton Road, London SW5; Tel: 01-373 6944; *Lighting*

BALTERLEY BATHROOMS LTD, Marlborough Works, Broom Street, Hanley, Stoke-on-Trent, Staffordshire ST1 2EN; Tel: Stoke-on-Trent 21496; *Bathrooms*

BAMBOO DESIGNS, Showroom: 40 Harrowby Street, London W1H 5HX; Tel: 01-723 9371; *Bedrooms (Furniture); Chairs; Mirrors & Glass; Tables (Dining Suites, Occasional); Upholstered Furniture*

BANKS HEELEY, Abbotts Yard, Royston, Hertfordshire SG8 9AZ; Tel: Royston 42346; *Storage; Tables (Dining Suites)*

BARBEE CERAMICS LTD, Merton Works, Church Road, Welling, Kent DA16 3DZ; Tel: 01-855 9644; *Ceramic Tiles*

PERCY BASS LTD, 13 Crescent Place, London SW3 and 18 Walton Street, London SW3; Tel: 01-589 4853; *Special Furniture (Made to Order Upholstery)*

BARKING-GROHE LTD, 5-13 River Road, Barking, Essex IG11 0HD; Tel: 01-594 7292; *Appliances & Kitchen Accessories; Bathrooms (Accessories)*

BAUMANN FABRICS LTD, 17a Newman Street, London W1P 3HD; Tel: 01-637 0253/4; *Blinds (Vertical)*

BAXTER & WOOD LTD, 28/29 Lower Tower Street, Birmingham B19 3NF; Tel: 021-359 4555; *Lighting*

BEAVER INTERNATIONAL PAINTS LTD, Minerva Works, Woodlesford, Leeds, Yorkshire LS26 8PY; Tel: Leeds 826511; *Useful Products (Tools)*

THE BEDCHAMBER, 3 Cadogan Street, London SW3; Tel: 01-589 1860; *Bedrooms (Beds)*

BEDFORD, STEER, END & CO LTD, 74–78 Long Lane, London SE1 4AZ; Tel: 01-403 2400; *Shelving*

A BELL & CO LTD, Kingsthorpe, Northampton NN2 6LT; Tel: Northampton 712505; *Ceramic Tiles; Fireplaces (Accessories, Mantels & Surrounds); Stoves; Useful products (Polishes)*

WM H BENNETT & SONS LTD, 79 Piccadilly, Manchester M1 2BX; Tel: 061-236 3551/2 and 2839; *Fabrics*

KIM BENTLEY, Studio 22, 90 Lots Road, London SW10; Tel: 01-352 7454; *Soft Furnishings*

BERGER PAINTS, Freshwater Road, Dagenham, Essex RM8 1RU; Tel: 01-590 6030; Colour Schemer Service, Berger House, Berkeley Square, London W1X 6NB; Tel: 01-629 9171; *Paint*

BERGLEN ASSOCIATES LTD, Masons House, Kingsbury Road, Kingsbury, London NW9 9NQ; Tel: 01-204 9411; *Appliances & Kitchen Accessories; Bathrooms (Sanitaryware)*

H J BERRY & SONS LTD, Kirk Mills, Chipping, Preston, Lancashire PR3 2RA; Tel: Chipping 226; *Chairs*

BEST & LLOYD LTD, William Street West, Smethwick, Warley, West Midlands B66 2NX; Tel: 021-558 1191; *Lighting*

BESTOBELL PAINTS & CHEMICALS LTD, 131 Western Road, Mitcham, Surrey CR4 3YQ; Tel: 01-648 3422; *Paint*

BILLIB SALES (UK) LTD, Upper Norwich Road, Bournemouth, Dorset BH2 5RA; Tel: Bournemouth 293352; *Clocks*

BIRMINGHAM GUILD LTD, Grosvenor Works, Sherborne Street, Birmingham B16 8HL; Tel: 021-632 6311; *Staircases*

BLACKWOOD MORTON & SONS LTD, Burnside Works, Kilmarnock, Ayrshire KA1 4HB; Tel: Kilmarnock 21100; *Carpeting (Patterned, Shag); Rugs*

BLC TRADITIONAL COUNTRY FURNITURE LTD, Showroom: 53 Fulham High Street, London SW6; Tel: 01-736 4573; Office: The Cliff, Acton Bridge, Nr. Northwich, Cheshire; Tel: Weaverham 853144; *Chairs; Storage; Tables (Dining)*

BLIND ALLEY LTD, Unit 23, Camden Lock Commercial Place, London NW1; Tel: 01-485 8030; *Blinds (Fabric Roller)*

BLOSSOM LTD, 24 Duncan Terrace, London N1 8BS; Tel: 01-837 9192 and 837 5856; *Fabrics*

BLUNDELL-PERMOGLAZE LTD, Sculcoates Lane, Hull, East Yorkshire HU5 1RU; Tel: Hull 3422; *Paint*

JOHN BOATH JNR & CO LTD, Academy Street Works, Forfar, Tayside, Scotland DD8 2EY; Tel: Forfar 63631–2; *Wall Coverings*

G BOCOCK & CO LTD, 17/18 Mott Street, Birmingham; Tel: 021-692 1698; *Lighting*

BOFFI *see* **HOMEWORKS LTD**

J W BOLLOM & CO LTD, Bromel Works, Croydon Road, Beckenham, Kent BR3 4BL; Tel: 01-650 9171; *Paint; Useful Products; Wall Coverings*

BONSACK BATHS LTD, 14 Mount Street, London W1Y 5RA; Tel: 01-629 9981 or 493 3240; *Bathrooms (Accessories, Sanitaryware)*

SAMUEL BOOTH & CO LTD, Cheapside Works, Cheapside, Birmingham B12 0PS; Tel: 021-772 2717/8/9; *Bathrooms (Accessories)*

BOSANQUET IVES LTD, Court Lodge, 48 Sloane Square, London SW1; Tel: 01-730 6241; *Carpeting (made to order)*

ROBERT BOSCH LTD, PO Box 166, Rhodes Way, Watford, Hertfordshire WD2 4LB; Tel: Watford 44233; *Appliances & Kitchen Accessories; Kitchens; Useful Products (Tools)*

BOSTIK LTD, Ulverscroft Road, Leicester LE4 6BW; Tel: Leicester 50015; *Useful Products (Adhesives, Sealants, Tools)*

BOUSSAC DISTRIBUTION (UK) LTD, 299 Oxford Street, London W1R 2EH; Tel: 01-493 8719; *Fabrics*

BOYDEN & CO LTD, Cumberlow Avenue, London SE25 6AE; Tel: 01-771 0141; *Ceramic Tiles*

BRADDELL ENTERPRISES, Cherington, Shipston-on-Stour, Warwickshire CV36 5HS; Tel: Little Cherington 204; *Mirrors & Glass*

R N BRADLEY, Brook Saw Mills, Bradshaw Brow, Bradshaw, Bolton, Lancashire BL2 3EY; Tel: Bolton 51821; *Useful Products (Sealants)*

BRENDON DESIGNS LTD, South Street, Wellington, Somerset TA21 8NN; Tel: Wellington 2216; *Upholstered Furniture*

BRINTONS CARPETS, PO Box 16, Exchange Street, Kidderminster, Worcestershire DY10 1AG; Tel: Kidderminster 3444; *Carpets (Wilton)*

BRITISH THORNTON LTD, PO Box 3, Wythenshawe, Manchester M22 4SS; Tel: 061-998 1311; *Desks*

BROCKWAY CARPETS LTD, Hoobrook, Kidderminster, Worcestershire DY10 1XW; Tel: Kidderminster 4737; *Carpeting (Patterned); Rugs*

MAURICE BROWN LTD, 27 St. John's Wood High Street, London NW8 7NH; Tel: 01-722 3156/3516; *Ceramic Tiles; Lighting; Wall Coverings (Co-Ordinates)*

BROWNS OF WEST WYCOMBE, Church Lane, West Wycombe, High Wycombe, Buckinghamshire HP14 3AH; Tel: High Wycombe 24537; *Special Furniture (Made to Order Furniture)*

BRYMOR LTD, Tonbridge Road, East Peckham, Tonbridge, Kent TN12 5JX; Tel: East Peckham 871384; *Wall Coverings*

T F BUCKLE (LONDON) LTD, 427 King's Road, London SW10 0LR; Tel: 01-352 0952; *Fireplaces (Mantels & Surrounds)*

BULTHAUP UK, 79 Victoria Street, St. Albans, Hertfordshire; Tel: St. Albans 30904/30951; *Kitchens*

H. BURBRIDGE & SON LTD, Oswestry, Shropshire S711 1H2; Tel: Oswestry 5131; *Shelving*

BURMAH INDUSTRIAL PRODUCTS LTD, 147 London Road, Kingston-upon-Thames, Surrey KT2 6NH; Tel: 01-549 5231; *Useful Products (Tools)*

GURDON BURNETT, 20 Rosetti House, Erasmus Street, London SW1; Tel: 01-821 5716; *Clocks*

CLIVE BURR, The Granary Building, Hope Sufferance Wharf, 61 St. Marys Church Street, Rotherhithe, London ST16; Tel: 01-231 2054; *Clocks*

BY DESIGN, Boston Road, Horncastle, Lincolnshire LN9 6JW; Tel: Horncastle 7376; *Plants & Planters*

C & A CEILINGS, Bidder Street, London E16 4ST; Tel: 01-474 0474; *Architectural Ornaments (Suspended Ceilings)*

CABOCHON FURNITURE LTD, 110 Wapping High Street, London E1 9NE; Tel: 01-488 2117; *Special Furniture (Designer Craftspeople)*

CADO FURNITURE (UK) LTD, 5a Portman Square, London W1H 9PR; Tel: 01-486 4931/2; *Bedrooms (Beds); Chairs; Shelving; Tables (Occasional); Upholstered Furniture*

ROSEMARY CAMDEN, Bayham Manor, Lamberhurst, Kent; Tel: Lamberhurst 890 500 or 42 Limerston Street, London SW10; Tel: 01-353 7838; *Fireplaces (Mantels & Surrounds)*

CANDELL LTD, Riverside Works, Broadmead Road, Woodford Green, Essex IG8 8PG; Tel: 01-504 9501; *Lighting*

CANLIN DEVELOPMENTS, Star Foundry, Langley Mill, Nottingham; Tel: Langley Mill 5412 (3 lines); *Fireplaces (Mantels & Surrounds); Stoves*

CAPE BOARDS & PANELS LTD, Iver Lane, Uxbridge, Middlesex UB8 2JQ; Tel: Uxbridge 37111; *Partitions*

CAPITAL CERAMICS, 5/11 Beaumont Road, London E13 8RJ; Tel: 01-471 8121/2; *Ceramic Tiles*

CARMINOWE STUDIO, Belinda M. Underhill, 10 Leechwell Street, Totnes, Devon; *Mirrors & Glass*

THE CARPET MANUFACTURING COMPANY LTD, PO Box 15, Mill Street, Kidderminster, Worcestershire DY11 6XE; Tel: Kidderminster 3434 (16 lines); *Carpeting (Patterned)*

CARPETS OF WORTH LTD, Severn Valley Mills, Stourport-on-Severn, Worcestershire DY13 9HA; Tel: Stourport 4122; *Carpeting (Patterned)*

CARRON CO, Carron, Falkirk, Scotland FK2 8DW; Tel: Falkirk 24999; *Bathrooms (Accessories, Sanitaryware)*

CARSON OFFICE FURNITURE LTD, 1 Beeston Place, London SW1; Tel: 01-828 2087; *Desks; Plants & Planters; Tables (Dining Suites)*

J & A CARTERS LTD, Alfred Street, Westbury, Wilts BA13 3DZ; Tel: Westbury 822203; *Bathrooms (Accessories)*

ASHLEY CARTWRIGHT, 1 Banbury Road, Brackley, Northamptonshire; Tel: Brackley 704104; *Special Furniture (Designer Craftspeople)*

CARVED PINE MANTELPIECES LTD, High Street, Dorchester on Thames, Oxford OX9 8HL; Tel: Oxford 340028 and 28 Beauchamp Place, London SW3 1NJ; Tel: 01-589 5534; *Fireplaces (Accessories, Mantels & Surrounds); Special Furniture (Made to Order Furniture)*

CASA FINA, 9 The Market, Covent Garden, London WC2; Tel: 01-836 0289; *Lighting*

CASSELL WALLCOVERINGS LTD, 5–11 Lavington Street, London SE1; Tel: 01-261 1984; *Wall Coverings*

CASTELNAU MOSAICS & TILES, 175 Church Road, Barnes, London SW13; Tel: 01-741 2452; *Ceramic Tiles*

CATHEDRAL WORKS ORGANISATION, The Cathedral, Chichester, Sussex PO19 1PX; Tel: Chichester 784225; *Flooring (Stone)*

CAVALCADE WALLCOVERINGS LTD, PO Box 78, Croydon Road, Beckenham, Kent BR3 4BL; Tel: 01-650 9171–6; *Wall Coverings*

CEKA WORKS LTD, Pwllheli, Gwynedd LL53 5LH; Tel: Pwllheli 2254; *Useful Products (Tools)*

CELMAC DISTRIBUTORS LTD, Unit 3, Perry Lane, Brentford, Middlesex TW8 0BG; Tel: 01-568 7963; *Paint*

CERAMIC CONSULTANTS LTD, The Old Brewery, Wishward, Rye, Sussex TN31 7DH; Tel: Rye 3038; *Ceramic Tiles*

CERAMIQUE INTERNATIONALE, 47 Cheapside, Bradford, W. Yorkshire BD1 4HP; Tel: Bradford 35441; *Ceramic Tiles*

CHARTA FURNITURE LTD, Westhampnett Mill, Chichester, West Sussex, PO18 0NP; Tel: Chichester 87081/2; *Bedrooms (Beds)*

CHESTER METAL CO LTD, Armstrong 2, Washington, Tyne and Wear NE37 1PB; Tel: Washington 473135; *Fireplaces (Mantels & Surrounds)*

CHLORIDE SHIRES LTD, Guiseley, Leeds LS20 8AP; Tel: Guiseley 73232; *Appliances & Kitchen Accessories; Bathrooms (Accessories; Sanitaryware, Showers)*

CHRISTON CLOCKS LTD, 1350 London Road, Leigh-on-Sea, Essex; Tel: Southend-on-Sea 75000; *Clocks*

CIANCIMINO DESIGN LTD, 307/9 Kings Road, London SW3 5EP; Tel: 01-352 2016/5492; *Chairs; Tables (Dining, Occasional); Lighting; Shelving; Upholstered Furniture*

CIBA-GEIGY, Plastics & Additives Co, Duxford, Cambridgeshire CB2 4QA; Tel: Cambridge 532121 or 30 Buckingham Gate, London SW1; Tel: 01-828 5676; *Useful Products (Adhesives)*

CIEL Christopher Lawrence Textiles & Lighting Ltd, 39 Old Church Street, London SW3; Tel: 01-352 4802; *Blinds (Paper & Wood); Ceramic Tiles; Fabrics; Lighting; Plants & Planters; Tables (Occasional)*

CIL, 149 Upper Richmond Road, Putney, London SW15 2TX; Tel: 01-788 2538/9; *Lighting*

CLADSLATE see **PETIT ROQUE LTD**

CLAM-BRUMMER LTD, Maxwell Road, Borehamwood, Hertfordshire WD6 1JN; Tel: 01-953 2992; *Useful Products (Adhesives, Miscellaneous)*

E A CLARE & SON LTD, 46/48 St Anne Street, Liverpool L3 3DW; Tel: 051-207 1336 (4 lines); *Tables (Dining)*

CLASSICAL DESIGNS, 1387 London Road, Leigh-on-Sea, Essex; Tel: Southend 78392 and 714177; *Architectural Ornaments (Plaster & Plaster Effects, Suspended Ceilings, Wooden Beams, Panels & Mouldings)*

CLASSIC GARDEN FURNITURE LTD, Audley Avenue, Newport, Shropshire; Tel: Newport 813311; *Chairs; Clocks; Plants & Planters; Shelving; Staircases; Storage; Stoves; Tables (Occasional)*

CLEAN BLINDS LTD, Tower Works, Broughton Street, London SW8; Tel: 01-720 5566; *Blinds (Fabric Roller, Venetian, Vertical)*

CLEMENTS INTERNATIONAL UPHOLSTERY LTD, Whitehall Works, Whitehall Road, Ramsgate, Kent; Tel: Thanet 54894; Showroom: 280 Angel Road, Edmonton, London N18; Tel: 01-807 5827; *Upholstered Furniture*

COALBROOK (FURNISHING CONTRACTS) HOUSE, 76-78 High Street, Berkhamsted, Hertfordshire HP4 2BW;Tel: Berkhamsted 5081; *Special Furniture (Made to Order Furniture)*

COLE & SON (WALLPAPERS) LTD, 18 Mortimer Street, London W1A 4BU; Tel: 01-580 5369; *Paint; Wall Coverings (also Co-Ordinates)*

COLEFAX & FOWLER DESIGNS LTD, 39 Brook Street, London W1Y 1AU; Tel: 01-493 2231; *Fabrics; Wall Coverings (Co-Ordinates)*

COLLINS & HAYES LTD, Ponswood, Hastings, Sussex TN34 1XF; Tel: Hastings 430186; *Upholstered Furniture*

COLOURFLAIR FURNITURE, 29 Bruton Street, London W1; Tel: 01-493 2017; *Lighting; Special Furniture (Made to Order Upholstery); Tables (Occasional)*

COLOROLL LTD, Riverside Mills, Crawford Street, Nelson, Lancashire; Tel: Nelson 67777; *Soft Furnishings; Wall Coverings (Co-Ordinates)*

COMBE MANOR FABRICS, 14 Elm Park Road, London SW3 6BB; Tel: 01-351 1688; *Fabrics*

COMMERCIAL PLASTICS LTD, Cramlington New Town, Northumberland NE23 8AD; Tel: Cramlington 713333; *Wall Coverings*

CONCORD LIGHTING INTERNATIONAL LTD, Rotaflex House, 241 City Road, London EC1 1ET; Tel: 01-253 1200; *Lighting*

CONNOISSEUR STUDIO (EUROPE) LTD, PO Box 647, London W1; Tel: 01-727 9177; *Paint*

THE CONRAN SHOP LTD, 77 Fulham Road, London SW3; Tel: 01-589 7401; *Chairs; Fabrics; Lighting; Soft Furnishings; Tables (Dining); Upholstered Furniture*

CONSCULPT LTD, Froghill, Ponsanooth, Truro, Cornwall; Tel: Truro 863578/863590; *Staircases*

CONTINENTAL FURNISHERS, Pine Decor, 2nd Floor, Westgate Arcade, Peterborough PE1 1PY; Tel: Peterborough 46457/267207; *Storage*

COPLEY CRAFTS, Thorney Grange, Spennithorne, Leyburn, North Yorkshire DL8 5PW; Tel: Leyburn 3410; *Architectural Ornaments (Plaster & Plaster Effects)*

CORNISH STAIRWAYS LTD, Commercial Road, Penryn, Cornwall TR10 8AF; Tel: Penryn 74662; *Staircases*

CORONFIELD LTD, 15 Summerstown, Wandsworth, London SW17; Tel: 01-947 9447/8; *Special Furniture (Made to Order Upholstery)*

MICHAEL J COX, Lower Washbourne Barton, Ashprington, Totnes, Devon; Tel: Harbertonford 488; *Bedrooms (Beds)*

C P CARPETS (KIDDERMINSTER), PO Box 21, Stour Buildings, Green Street, Kidderminster, Worcestershire DY10 1HF; Tel: Kidderminster 65311/2; *Carpeting (Made to Order)*

CRAYONNE UK LTD, Windmill Road, Sunbury-on-Thames, Middlesex TW16 7EE; Tel: Sunbury-on-Thames 85644; *Bathrooms (Accessories); Clocks*

CROSBY KITCHENS LTD, Orgreave Drive, Handsworth, Sheffield, Yorkshire S13 9NS; Tel: Sheffield 697371; *Kitchens*

CROYDON DISPLAY GROUP, 229 Green Lane, Ilford, Essex IG1 1XR; Tel: 01-590 3575; *Partitions*

CROWN DECORATIVE PRODUCTS LTD, Crown House, Hollins Road, Darwen, Lancs BB3 0BG; Tel: Darwen 74951; *Paint; Wall Coverings*

CUBESTORE LTD, 38 Grosvenor Road, London W4; Tel: 01-994 6016; *Shelving; Storage*

CUBIC METRE FURNITURE, 17/18 Gt. Sutton Street, London EC1; Tel: 01-251 2437/8; *Tables (Dining)*

CUPRINOL LTD, Adderwell, Frome, Somerset; Tel: Frome 5151; *Paint*

JAY CURZONS, 118-22 Brookside, Stretton on Dunsmore, Nr. Rugby, Warwickshire CV23 9LY; Tel: Coventry 542308; *Staircases*

CVP DESIGNS LTD, 5 Weighhouse Street, Mayfair, London W1; Tel: 01-629 2421/2; Showroom: 01-629 0900; *Soft Furnishings; Wall Coverings (Co-Ordinates)*

CZECH & SPEAKE LTD, 88 Jermyn Street, London SS1; Tel: 01-839 6868; *Bathrooms (Accessories)*

DALLING ANTIQUES, 63 Dalling Road, London W6; Tel: 01-748 5102; *Stoves*

DALVERA, De la Plain Interiors Ltd, 142 High Road, London NW10 2PS; Tel: 01-451 2202; *Bedrooms (Furniture); Storage; Upholstered Furniture*

DANE & CO, Sugar House Lane, London E15; Tel: 01-534 2213; *Paint*

DANGLES & CO, PO Box 12, 4 Hall Lane, Ashley, Market Harborough, Leicestershire LE16 8HN; Tel: Medbourne Green 750; *Useful Products (Upholstery Supplies)*

DAVEY & JORDAN, The Forge, Commercial Road, Penryn, Cornwall TR10 8AF; Tel: Penryn 72282; *Fireplaces (Accessories)*

MICHAEL DAVIS, 111 Mortlake Road, Kew, Richmond, Surrey TW9 4AU; Tel: 01-876 0434; *Tables (Dining Suites)*

DEANS BLINDS LTD, Unit 4, Halesmere Estate, Ravensburg Terrace, London SW18 4SE; Tel: 01-947 8931; *Blinds (Fabric Roller)*

DECOROLLER LTD, 61 Warwick Square, London SW1V 2AL; Tel: 01-834 9791; *Wall Coverings*

DELABOLE SLATE CO LTD, 14 Bassett Street, Camborne, Cornwall TR14 8SP; Tel: Camborne 713120/716471; *Fireplaces (Mantels & Surrounds); Flooring (Stone)*

DE LA PLAIN INTERIORS LTD, 142 High Road, Willesden, London NW10 2PJ; Tel: 01-451 2202; *Bedrooms (Beds); Chairs; Shelving; Storage; Tables (Occasional); Upholstered Furniture*

DEPTICH LTD, 284/288 Western Road, London SW19 2QA; Tel: 01-648 2241; *Bedrooms (Beds)*

DERNIER & HAMLYN LTD, 62 Kimber Road, London SW18 4PP; Tel: 01-870 0011; *Lighting*

DE SEDE LTD, 46 Rochester Row, London SW1P 1JU; Tel: 01-584 1008; *Upholstered Furniture*

DESIGNERS GUILD, 277 Kings Road, London SW3 5EN; Tel: 01-351 1271; *Chairs; Lighting; Plants & Planters; Shelving; Tables (Occasional); Upholstered Furniture; Wall Coverings (Co-Ordinates)*

DESIGNS UNLIMITED LTD, 108 Burley Road, Leeds L53 1JP; Tel: Leeds 440893; *Upholstered Furniture*

DIAS CERAMICA LTD, Kings Arms Lane, Carlisle, Cumbria CA3 8JN; Tel: Carlisle 36366; *Ceramic Tiles*

DISTINCTIVE TRIMMINGS CO LTD, 17 Kensington Church Street, London W8 4LF; Tel: 01-937 6174; also at 11 Marylebone Lane, London W1M 5FE; Tel: 01-486 6456; *Useful Products (Upholstery Supplies)*

DLW (BRITAIN) LTD, Block 148, Milton Trading Estate, Milton, Nr. Abingdon, Oxon OX14 4SD; Tel: Abingdon 831296; *Carpeting (Cord, Tiles, Wilton); Flooring (Vinyl, Vinyl Tile)*

MARTIN J DODGE, Southgate, Wincanton, Somerset BA9 9EB; Tel: Wincanton 32388; *Chairs; Storage; Tables (Occasional)*

DOMUS LTD, 266 Brompton Road, London SW3 2AS; Tel: 01-589 9457/8; *Ceramic Tiles*

DORMA, Newtown Mill, PO Box 7, Lees Street, Swinton, Manchester M27 2DD; Tel: 061-794 4781; *Soft Furnishings*

DORON CLOCKS, 37 Pincott Road, Bexleyheath, Kent; Tel: 01-304 9692; *Clocks*

DU-AL FURNITURE LTD, Du-al House, Byron Road, Harrow, Middlesex HA1 1LY; Tel: 01-863 6611; *Tables (Occasional)*

DUCAL LTD, Moiety Road, London E14 8ND; Tel: 01-987 6609; *Bedrooms (Beds, Furniture)*

PETER DUDGEON LTD, The Old Coach House, 1a Brompton Place, London SW3; Tel: 01-589 6291/2; *Special Furniture (Made to Order Upholstery)*

DUNLOP SEMTEX LTD, 10/12 King Street, St. James's, London SW1Y 6RA; Tel: 01-930 6700; or Chester Road, Erdington, Birmingham B35 7AL; Tel: 021-373 8101; *Carpeting (Tiles); Flooring (Vinyl, Vinyl Tile); Useful Products (Adhesives)*

DUROTANIK, Neucumer Ltd, 39 Landsdowne Road, Croydon, Surrey CR0 2BE; Tel: 01-688 7153/7267; *Architectural Ornaments (Wooden beams, Panels & Mouldings)*

DYLON INTERNATIONAL LTD, Lower Sydenham, London SE26 5HD; Tel: 01-650 4801; *Useful Products (Miscellaneous)*

EASTHAM BURCO see **THOMAS EASTHAM & SON LTD**

THOMAS EASTHAM & SON LTD, Thornton, Blackpool, Lancashire FY5 2SQ; Tel: Blackpool 856771; *Kitchens*

EATON BAG COMPANY, 16 Manette Street, (off Charing Cross Road), London W1V 5LB; Tel: 01-437 9391; *Blinds (Paper & Wood)*

EDISON HALO LTD, Eskdale Road, Uxbridge Industrial Estate, Uxbridge UB8 2RT; Tel: Uxbridge 56561; *Lighting*

ELFA WIRE PRODUCTS (UK) LTD, Tafarnaubach Industrial Estate, Tredegar, Gwent, S. Wales; Tel: Tredegar 5221; *Storage*

ELIZABETH EATON LTD, 25a Basil Street, London SW3; Tel: 01-589 0118/9; *Ceramic Tiles; Fabrics; Special Furniture (Made to Order Furniture); Wall Coverings (also Co-Ordinates)*

ELLARD SLIDING DOOR GEARS LTD, Works Road, Letchworth, Herts SG6 1NN; Tel: Letchworth 2613; *Soft Furnishings*

ELLIOTT-POWELL LTD, 58 Burners Lane South, Kiln Farm, Milton Keynes; Tel: Milton Keynes 567345; *Bathrooms (Sanitaryware)*

J T ELLIS & CO LTD, Crown Works, Wakefield Road, Huddersfield, West Yorkshire; Tel: Huddersfield 39511; *Bedrooms (Furniture); Kitchens*

ELON TILES (UK) LTD, 8 Clarendon, London W11; Tel: 01-727 0884; *Ceramic Tiles; Flooring (Stone)*

EMESS LIGHTING LTD, Station Estate, Eastwood Close, London E18 1BY; Tel: 01-989 6090; *Lighting; Mirrors & Glass*

EMSWORTH FIREPLACES, Station Approach, North Street, Emsworth, Hampshire; Tel: Emsworth 3431; *Fireplaces (Mantels & Surrounds)*

ENGINEERING CONCESSIONAIRES LTD, Glendale Avenue, Sandycroft, Deeside, Clwyd CH5 2QP; Tel: Deeside 533677; *Bathrooms (Accessories)*

S ENGLENDER & SONS LTD, High View Road, South Normanton, Derbyshire DE55 2DS; Tel: Ripley 811508; *Upholstered Furniture*

ENGLISH CLOCK SYSTEMS, Industime House, Chase Road, Park Royal, London NW10 6QE; Tel: 01-965 9011; *Clocks*

ENGLISH ROSE KITCHENS LTD, Warwick; Tel: Warwick 45411; *Kitchens*

ENVIRONMENT DESIGN, Heath Hall, Heath, Wakefield, W. Yorkshire WF1 5SL; Tel: Wakefield 66446/7/8; *Chairs; Lighting; Upholstered Furniture; Tables (Dining)*

ERCO LIGHTING LTD, 38 Dover Street, London W1X 3RB; Tel: 01-408 0320; *Lighting*

ERCOL FURNITURE LTD, High Wycombe, Buckinghamshire; Tel: High Wycombe 21261; *Chairs; Tables (Dining Suites)*

ERICSON BLINDS LTD, Canal Wharf, Langley, Slough, Buckinghamshire SL3 3EN; Tel: Slough 46080/46868; *Blinds (Venetian)*

ESSE, SMITH & WELLSTOOD LTD, Bonnybridge, Stirlingshire FK4 2AP; Tel: Bonnybridge 2171; *Stoves (also Kitchen Ranges)*

ESTIA DESIGNS LTD, 40 Chalcot Road, Promrose Hill, London NW1; Tel: 01-568 2812/3528; *Chairs; Tables (Dining, Dining Suites, Occasional); Upholstered Furniture*

WARREN EVANS, 4a Sans Walk, London EC1; Tel: 01-226 4233; *Bedrooms (Beds)*

FABER BLINDS LTD, Viking House, Kangley Bridge Road, Sydenham, London SE26; Tel: 01-659 2126; *Blinds (Specialist Products, Venetian, Vertical); Fittings (Curtain)*

THE FABRIC SHOP, 6 Cale Street, London SW3 3QU; Tel: 01-584 8495; *Fabrics; Wall Coverings (Co-Ordinates)*

FABRITRAK, see **ARENSON INTERNATIONAL LTD**

D & H FACTORS LTD, 7 Baron Avenue, Telford Way Industrial Estate, Kettering, Northants; Tel: Kettering 82521; *Fittings (Curtain)*

MARY FARMER, Flat 2, 3 Warren Road, Guildford, Surrey GU1 2HA; Tel: Guildford 67825; *Rugs*

D FARMILOE, 'Touch & Go' French Polish Products, 15 Kent Close, Bexhill-on-Hill, Sussex TN40 2LD; Tel: Bexhill 214943; *Useful Products (Polishes)*

KAFFE FASSETT, 62 Fordwych Road, London NW2; Tel: 01-452 3786; *Soft Furnishings; Wall Coverings*

FAVORITE INTERIOR, 123 Bridge Lane, London NW11; Tel: 01-455 0415; *Bedrooms (Beds, Furniture); Storage; Upholstered Furniture*

FEATURE FIRES LTD, 32 High Street, Northwood, Middlesex HA6 1BN; Tel: Northwood 26699; *Fireplaces (Mantels & Surrounds)*

FEBRUARY FABRICS LTD, 10 South Quay, King's Lynn, Norfolk; Tel: King's Lynn 65989 & 65980; *Fabrics*

FILTRASOL LTD, A10 Beaver Industrial Estate, Ashford, Kent TN23 1SH; Tel: Ashford 31055; *Blinds (Fabric Roller, Venetian, Vertical); Partitions*

HENRY FLACK LTD, Borough Works, Croydon Road, Beckenham, Kent BR3 4BI; Tel: 01-650 9171/6; *Useful Products (Polishes)*

FLORIN LTD, 457–463 Caledonian Road, London N7 9BB; Tel: 01-609 0011; *Useful Products (Tools)*

FORBO TAPIJT BV, UK address: Orchard Farmhouse, Filands, Malmesbury, Wiltshire SN16 9NJ; Tel: Malmesbury 3028; *Carpeting (Berber, Shag, Wilton); Rugs*

FORMA LTD, 149 Upper Richmond Road, London SW15 2TX; Tel: 01-733 2538/9; *Chairs; Lighting; Mirrors & Glass; Plants & Planters; Tables (Dining)*

FORMAT KITCHENS, 7b Fox Lane, Palmers Green, London N13 4AB; Tel: 01-886 5599; *Kitchens*

D L FORSTER LTD, 17 Tramway Avenue, Stratford, London E15 4PG; Tel: 01-534 5379; *Useful Products (Upholstery Supplies)*

FOSSE WARMAIR LTD, Old Farm, Norton Road, Iverley, Near Stourbridge, West Midlands DY8 2RU; Tel: Hagley 5898; *Stoves*

FOURSQUARE DESIGNS, 1 Dale Close, London SE3 9BB; Tel: 01-852 7820; *Fabrics; Wall Coverings (Co-Ordinates)*

FRANCO-BELGE (UK) LTD, UA Engineering Ltd, Canal Street, Sheffield, Yorkshire S4 7ZE; Tel: Sheffield 21167/738803; *Stoves (Kitchen Ranges)*

FRANKE AG, UK Sales, 45 Grasmere Road, Gatley, Cheshire SK9 5QB; Tel: 061-428 5978; *Appliances & Kitchen Accessories*

FRANKLITE LTD, 1 Bridgeturn Avenue, Old Wolverton Road, Wolverton, Milton Keynes, Bedfordshire MK12 5QL; Tel: Milton Keynes 316919; *Lighting*

FRANCIS FRITH COLLECTION, see **PHOTOGRAPHIC COLLECTIONS (UK) LTD**

FSI FURNITURE, The Mill, Galgate, Lancaster LA2 0PR; Tel: Lancaster 751820; *Bedrooms (Furniture)*

FURNITURE PRODUCTIONS LTD, 191 Thornton Road, Bradford, W. Yorkshire BD1 2JT; Tel: Bradford 31442; *Tables (Occasional); Upholstered Furniture*

THE FURNITURE WORKSHOP, Forward Green, Stowmarket, Suffolk IP14 5HG; Tel: Stonham 222; *Upholstered Furniture*

FUTURE TENSE, 105 Heath Street, Hampstead, London NW3 6SS; Tel: 01-794 7688; *Lighting*

GAGGENAU ELECTRIC (UK) LTD, Colville Road, London W3 8BL; Tel: 01-992 5095/6; *Appliances & Kitchen Accessories*

GALLEON-CLAYGATE LTD, 216–218 Red Lion Road, Tolworth, Surbiton, Surrey KT6 7RB; Tel: 01-397 3456; *Fireplaces (Mantels & Surrounds)*

GALLERIA MONTE CARLO, 66/67 South Audley Street, London W1Y 5FE; Tel: 01-493 6481/2; *Bathrooms (Accessories, Sanitaryware); Ceramic Tiles; Fittings (Cabinet, Door); Lighting; Wall Coverings*

GALLERY JO, 65 Quarry Street, Guildford, Surrey; Tel: Guildford 62218; *Rugs*

SUSANNE GARRY LTD, 152a Walton Street, London SW3; Tel: 01-589 0459; *Blinds (Fabric Roller); Fabrics; Partitions; Wall Coverings (Co-Ordinates)*

GASKELL BROADLOOM CARPETS LTD, Wheatfield Mill, Rishton, Blackburn, Lancashire BB1 4NU; Tel: Gt. Harwood 885566; *Carpeting (Berber, Patterned, Tiles); Fabrics; Rugs*

GAUTIER LTD, Brett House, Park Parade, Harlesden, London NW10; Tel: 01-965 6703; *Bedrooms (Furniture)*

GAYLINE LTD, Salem Terrace, Llwynpia, Glamorgan CF40 2BR; Tel: Llanrisant 433232; *Blinds (Fabric Roller, Venetian, Vertical)*

G.C. FURNISHINGS LTD, 41 Berners Street, London W1P 3AA; Tel: 01-580 1218; *Desks; Storage; Tables (Dining)*

GEBA KITCHENS LTD, Brent Cross Shopping Centre, London NW4 3FE; Tel: 01-202 5133; *Kitchens*

GENERAL WOLFE ANTIQUES, General Wolfe Inn, Laxfield, Suffolk; Tel: Laxfield 374; *Bedrooms (Beds)*

GEORGIAN CARPETS LTD, Clensmore Mills, Kidderminster, Worcestershire DY10 2LH; Tel: Kidderminster 69921; *Carpets (Wilton)*

GEORGIAN FURNISHING CO, 96–98 Middlesex Street, London E1; Tel: 01-377 2515; *Bedrooms (Beds); Chairs; Desks; Storage; Tables (Occasional)*

GERLAND LTD, 90 Crawford Street, London W1H 2AP; Tel: 01-262 2016; *Carpeting (Tiles); Flooring (Rubber, Vinyl, Vinyl Tile); Wall Coverings*

GERLIN DECOR, Showrooms: 346/8 Oxford Road, Reading, Berkshire and Prospect Street, Caversham; Tel: Reading 594659; *Lighting*

GEORGE GILDER, 80 London Road, Stony Stratford, Buckinghamshire MK11 1JH; Tel: Milton Keynes 564867; *Upholstered Furniture*

DAVID GILLESPIE ASSOCIATES LTD, Dippenhall Crossroads, Farnham, Surrey GU10 5DW; Tel: Farnham 723531; *Architectural Ornaments (Suspended Ceilings); Lighting; Partitions; Wall Coverings*

GILT EDGE CARPETS LTD, PO Box 15, Mill Street, Kidderminster, Worcestershire DY11 6XQ; Tel: Kidderminster 3434; *Carpeting (Cord, Patterned, Wilton); Rugs*

GIORGETTI, Agent: Ian R. Smith, 42 Sunnydale Avenue, Patcham, Sussex BN1 3NR; Tel: Brighton 559134; *Bedrooms (Furniture);*

Mirrors & Glass; Storage; Tables (Occasional); Upholstered Furniture

GIPSY TABLES, 20 Harbledown Road, London SW6; Tel: 01-731 0703; *Tables (Occasional)*

GLAMORLINE LTD, see **SOUTH WALES BLIND CO LTD**

GLORAFILIA, 10 Winterstoke Gardens, London NW7 2RA; Tel: 01-954 5745; and 58 Stanmore Hill, Stanmore, Middlesex; *Soft Furnishings*

GLYNWED BATHROOM & KITCHEN PRODUCTS LTD, see **LEISURE KITCHEN PRODUCTS**

GLYNWED DOMESTIC & HEATING APPLIANCES LTD, PO Box No. 30, Ketley, Telford, Salop TF1 1BR; Tel: Telford 3973; *Stoves (Kitchen Ranges)*

GODDARD & GIBBS STUDIOS, 49 Kingsland Road, London E2; Tel: 01-739 6563; *Mirrors and Glass*

FREDA GOITEIN, Top Farm, Broadway, Worcestershire; Tel: Broadway 3375; *Ceramic Tiles*

GOODFELLOWS CLOCKS, Penmellow Works, Trenant Industrial Estate, Wadebridge, Cornwall PL27 6HB; Tel: Wadebridge 2115; *Clocks*

GRABER, Marvic Textiles Ltd, 41/42 Berners Street, London W1P 3AA; Tel: 01-580 7951; *Fittings (Curtain)*

GRAFTON INTERIORS, 117 Highgate Road, London NW5; Tel: 01-267 6088; *Bedrooms (Beds, Furniture); Ceramic Tiles; Chairs; Lighting; Special Furniture (Made to Order Furniture); Storage; Tables (Dining Suites); Upholstered Furniture*

GRAHAM & GREENE LTD, 4 & 7 Elgin Crescent, London W11; Tel: 01-727 4594; *Fabrics; Rugs*

GRANT SLIDES LTD, Kingsnorth Industrial Estate, Wotton Road, Ashford, Kent; Tel: Ashford 22675/6/7; *Fittings (Cabinet, Door)*

G B GREEN & VERONESE, 24 Edison Road, London N8 8AE; Tel: 01-348 9262; *Architectural Ornaments (Plaster & Plaster Effects)*

GREENCRAFT, Tom Green (Joinery) Ltd, Ingatestone, Essex CM4 0AZ; Tel: Ingatestone 4141; *Kitchens*

THE GREENSWARD COMPANY, The Old Hall, Langham, Oakham, Rutland, Leicestershire; Tel: Oakham 2923/56031; *Carpeting (Indoor/Outdoor)*

GREENWOOD & COOPE LTD, Registered office: Brookhouse Mill, Greenmount, Bury, Lancashire BL8 4HR; Tel: Bury 488 2241 (7 lines); Southen Area Sales Office & Warehouse: Cormar Centre, Wested Lane, Kent; Tel: 82 67141; *Carpeting (Cord, Shag)*

ELEANOR GREEVES, 12 Newton Grove, Bedford Park, London W4 1LB; Tel: 01-994 6523; *Ceramic Tiles*

LYN LE GRICE STENCILS, Wells Head, Temple Guiting, Gloucestershire GL54 5RR; Tel: Guiting Power 200; *Wall Coverings*

MARTIN GRIERSON, Barley Mow Workspace, 10 Barley Mow Passage, Chiswick, London W4 4PH; Tel: 01-994 6477; *Special Furniture (Designer Craftspeople)*

GROSFILLEX (UK) LTD, Garden Furniture Division, 10 Chandos Road, London NW10 6NF; Tel: 01-965 2268; *Plants & Planters*

DENNIS GROVES, 9 Sicilian Avenue, London WC1; Tel: 01-405 5603; *Bedrooms (Beds); Upholstered Furniture*

GROVEWOOD PRODUCTS LTD, Tipton, West Midlands DY4 7UZ; Tel: 021-557 3955; *Kitchens*

PETER D. GURNER DESIGNS LTD, 27 Sackville Street, London W1X 1DA; Tel: 01-437 7677; *Bathrooms (Accessories, Sanitaryware)*

HABITAT DESIGNS LTD, 28 Neal Street, London WC2H 9PH; Tel: 01-240 3474; *Bathrooms (Accessories); Bedrooms (Beds); Blinds (Paper & Wood); Ceramic Tiles; Kitchens; Lighting; Paint; Tables (Dining); Upholstered Furniture; Wall Coverings (Co-Ordinates)*

HADDONSTONE LTD, The Forge House, East Haddon, Northampton NN6 8DB; Tel: East Haddon 365; *Tables (Occasional)*

HAG (UK) LTD, 14-16 Bruton Place, London W1X 7AA; Tel: 01-499 4421/6532; *Chairs*

DAVID HAIGH, 9 Crescent Grove, London SW4 7AF; Tel: 01-622 8775; *Wall Coverings*

CHARLES HAMMOND LTD, 7b Harriet Walk, London SW1X 9JQ; Tel: 01-235 0634; *Architectural Ornaments (Wooden Beams, Panels & Mouldings); Chairs; Desks; Fabrics; Mirrors & Glass; Lighting; Plants & Planters; Shelving; Special Furniture (Made to Order Furniture); Tables (Occasional); Upholstered Furniture*

JOYCE HARDY, Hacheston, Nr Wickham Market, Suffolk; Tel: Wickham Market 746485; *Chairs; Storage; Tables (Dining)*

MAGGIE HARRIS, 569 Kings Road, London SW6; Tel: 01-736 0007; *Tables (Dining Suites)*

M & I J HARRISON LTD, 71/73 Lower Parliament Street, Nottingham NG1 3BB; Tel: Nottingham 52059; *Clocks; Desks; Kitchens; Storage; Tables (Dining Suites)*

HARRISON-BEACON LTD, Bradford Street, Birmingham B12 0PE; Tel: 021-773 1111; *Bathrooms (Accessories); Fittings (Cabinet, Curtain, Door); Shelving; Useful Products (Miscellaneous)*

HART OF KNIGHTSBRIDGE, 3 Beauchamp Place, London SW3 1NG; Tel: 01-584 5770; *Fireplaces (Mantels and Surrounds); Architectural Ornaments (Wooden Beams, Panels & Mouldings)*

NICHOLAS HASLAM LTD, 65c New Kings Road, London SW6 4SG; Tel: 01-736 6083; *Fabrics*

H A S TEXTILES LTD, 299 Oxford Street, London W1R 2EH; Tel: 01-493 9622-4; *Fabrics*

HATEMA (UK) LTD, 70/72 Old Street, London EC1R 9AN; Tel: 01-253 6433/4; *Carpeting (Shag); Wall Coverings*

PETER HAXWORTH & CO LTD, 17 Islip Road, Oxford OX2 7SN; Tel: Oxford 511831; *Tables (Dining)*

MARK HAYNES, The Arcade, Camden Passage, Upper Street, London N1; *Stoves*

HEAL & SON LTD, 196 Tottenham Court Road, London W1A 1BJ; Tel: 01-636 1666; *Fabrics*

HEATHERLEY FINE CHINA LTD, Unit 3, Ferry Lane, Brentford, Middlesex TW8 0BG; Tel: 01-568 7963; *Bathrooms (Accessories); Fittings (Cabinet, Door)*

RICHARD HEATLEY, Hill Oak Farmhouse, Bishop's Frome, Worcester; Tel: Munderfield 285; *Special Furniture (Designer Craftspeople)*

HENKEL CHEMICALS LTD, Road 5, Industrial Estate, Winsford, Cheshire CW7 3QY; or Tretol House, The Hyde, London NW9; Tel: 01-205 6004; *Useful Products (Adhesives)*

HEUGA UK LTD, Heuga House, 1 Oxford Road, Aylesbury, Buckinghamshire HP19 3EP; Tel: Aylesbury 84631; *Carpeting (Tiles)*

D H HEYWOOD LTD, Elliott House, Greenacres Road, Oldham, Lancashire OL4 1AD; Tel: 061-652 1245; *Wall Coverings*

HILLE INTERNATIONAL LTD, 132 St Albans Road, Watford, Hertfordshire WD2 4AG; Tel: Watford 42241; *Chairs; Upholstered Furniture*

HILL & KNOWLES LTD, 1 Bridge Street, Richmond, Surrey; Tel: 01-948 4010; *Wall Coverings (also Co-Ordinates)*

HIPPO HALL, 65 Pimlico Road, London SW1; Tel: 01-730 7710; *Bedrooms (Beds); Shelving; Tables (Dining Suites)*

HK FURNITURE LTD, Omega Works, Hermitage Road, London N4 1NA; Tel: 01-800 5458; *Upholstered Furniture*

OSWALD HOLLMAN LTD, 208 Kent House Road, Beckenham, Kent BR3 1JN; Tel: 01-778 5888/7994; *Lighting*

STANLEY J HOLMES & SONS LTD, Vale Mill, Chamber Road, Hollinwood, Oldham, Lancashire OL8 4PG; Tel: 061-624 3427 & 8351; *Wall Coverings*

HOMESHADE CO LTD, Queens Yard, Whitepost Lane, London E9 5EN; Tel: 01-985 8543/4; *Lighting*

HOME STOVES LTD, 113 Warwick Avenue, Maida Vale, London W9; Tel: 01-289 1667; *Stoves*

HOMEWORKS LTD, Dove Walk, 107a Pimlico Road, London SW1; Tel: 01-730 9116; *Architectural Ornaments (Wooden Beams, Panels & Mouldings); Carpeting (Patterned); Chairs; Fabrics; Kitchens; Lighting; Tables (Dining Suites, Occasional); Upholstered Furniture*

HOMFRAY CARPETS LTD, Riding Hall Mills, Halifax, West Yorkshire HX3 9XG; Tel: Halifax 65722; *Carpeting (Cord); Rugs*

HOPE WORKS LTD, Pleck Road, Walsall WS2 9HH; Tel: Walsall 27175/6/7; *Fittings (Door)*

SUSIE HONNOR, 3 The Howard, Hallbankgate, Nr. Brampton, Cumbria; Tel: Hallbankgate 474; *Rugs*

MARK & JEAN HORNAK, 10 Exeter Mansions, 106 Shaftsbury Avenue, London W1; Tel: 01-734 7391; *Wall Coverings*

HOUSE OF LAMBETH, 220 Farmers Road, London SE5 0TW; Tel: 01-582 2767; *Shelving; Storage; Tables (Occasional)*

VERNON HOWELL RUGS, 16-20 Quay Street, Haverfordwest, Dyfed SA61 1BA; Tel: Haverfordwest 4499; *Rugs*

PETER HOYTE, Millbridge, Frensham, Farnham, Surrey GU10 3DJ; Tel: Frensham 3373; *Upholstered Furniture*

HUBBINET FURNITURE LTD, Progress Works, Eastern Avenue West, Romford, Essex RM7 7NU; Tel: Romford 62212; *Bedrooms (Furniture)*

W A HUDSON LTD, 115-125 Curtain Road, London EC2A 3QS; Tel: 01-739 3211; *Blinds (Fabric Roller); Fittings (Curtain)*

HUFCOR PARTITIONS LTD, Castle Donington, Nr Derby; Tel: Derby 810576/812390; *Partitions*

HUMBROL, Marfleet, Hull HU9 5NE; Tel: Hull 701191; *Paints*

HUNTER-DOUGLAS LTD, 15-16 Bellsize Close, Walsall Road, Norton Canes, Cannock, Staffordshire WS11 3TQ; Tel: Cannock 75757; *Fittings (Curtain)*

HYGENA LTD, PO Box 18, Kirkby Industrial Estate, Liverpool L33 7SH; Tel: 051-548 3505; *Kitchens*

IDEAL STANDARD LTD, PO Box 60, Kingston upon Hull, E Yorkshire HU5 4JE; Tel: Hull 46461; *Bathrooms (Accessories, Sanitaryware)*

ILFORD PARQUET CO LTD, 701 High Road, Seven Kings, Ilford, Essex IG3 8RH; Tel: 01-590 3147; *Flooring (Wood)*

IMPERIAL CHEMICAL INDUSTRIES LTD, Paints Division, Wexham Road, Slough, Buckinghamshire SL2 5DS; Tel: Slough 37644; *Paint*

INSTAFLOW LTD, Instaflow House, Dellbow Road, Central Way, Feltham, Middlesex; Tel: 01-751 3117; *Bathrooms (Showers)*

INTERLÜBKE LTD, 239 Greenwich High Road, London SE10 8NB; Tel: 01-858 3325; *Bedrooms (Furniture); Storage*

INTERNATIONAL PAINTS, 24/30 Canute Road, Southampton, Hampshire SO9 3AS; Tel: Southampton 24712; *Paint*

INTEROVEN LTD, 70-72 Fearnley Street, Watford, Hertfordshire WD1 7DE; Tel: Watford 46761; *Fireplaces (Accessories); Stoves*

INTERSPACE, Rosemont Road, London NW3 6NE; Tel: 01-794 0333; *Chairs; Tables (Dining, Dining Suites); Upholstered Furniture*

IRVINE PAINTS LTD, 3 Dunlop Drive, Meadowhead Industrial Estate, Irvine, Ayrshire; Tel: Irvine 212315; *Paint*

DAVID ISON LTD, 50-54 Charlotte Street, London W1; Tel: 01-636 3541 (4 lines); *Wall Coverings (Co-Ordinates)*

ROBINA JACK, 27 Shirlock Road, London NW3; Tel: 01-267 3863; *Mirrors & Glass*

GEORGE JACKSON, Rathbone Works, Rainville Road, London W6 9HD; Tel: 01-385 6616/7/8; *Architectural Ornaments (Plaster & Plaster Effects); Fireplaces (Mantels & Surrounds)*

JAMES, CLARK & EATON LTD, Southern Industrial Area, Bracknell, Berkshire RG12 4UU; Tel: Bracknell 24733; *Mirrors & Glass*

JARDINE LEISURE FURNITURE LTD, Rosemount Tower, Wallington Square, Wallington, Surrey SM6 8RR; Tel: 01-669 8265; *Chairs; Plants & Planters; Tables (Dining)*

JAYCEE FURNITURE LTD, Bexhill Road, Brighton, Sussex BN2 6QQ; Tel: Brighton 34081 (5 lines); *Chairs; Desks; Storage; Tables (Dining Suites)*

JAYMART RUBBER & PLASTICS LTD, Factory No. 5, Headquarters Road, West Wilts Trading Estate, Westbury, Wilts; Tel: Westbury 864926; *Carpeting (Coir, etc, Indoor/Outdoor); Flooring (Rubber); Rugs*

JBD FURNISHINGS (SALES) LTD, 13 Eccleston Street, London SW1; Tel: 01-730 7951; *Upholstered Furniture*

H & R JOHNSON TILES LTD, Highgate Tile Works, Tunstall, Stoke-on-Trent ST6 4JX; Tel: Stoke-on-Trent 85611; *Ceramic Tiles*

JOY PAINT PRODUCTS, Turnbridges Ltd, 72 Longley Road, London SW17; Tel: 01-672 6581; *Paint*

JUNEGRADE LTD, Unit 6, Limberline Spur, Hilsea, Portsmouth, Hampshire; Tel: Portsmouth 62821; *Bathrooms (Accessories)*

JUST DESKS, 20 Church Street, London NW8; Tel: 01-723 7976; *Chairs; Desks*

JUST DOORS, Unit 2, Limborough Road, Wantage, Oxon; Tel: Wantage 65850; *Kitchens*

KEDDY HOME IMPROVEMENTS LTD, 198 High Street, Egham, Surrey; Tel: Egham 7357; *Fireplaces (Mantels & Surrounds); Stoves*

KEE SYSTEMS LTD, see **GROVES, DENNIS**

JOHN T KEEP & SONS LTD, 15 Theobald's Road, London WC1; Tel: 01-242 0313; *Paint*

KESTERPORT LTD, 197 Kingston Road, Ewell, Epsom, Surrey KT19 0AB; Tel: 01-394 2896; *Bedrooms (Furniture); Tables (Dining Suites, Occasional)*

KEWLOX FURNITURE LTD, 46 Bideford Avenue, Perivale, Middlesex; Tel: 01-997 5444; *Shelving*

L M KINGCOME LTD, 304 Fulham Road, London SW10 9EP; Tel: 01-351 3998; *Special Furniture (Made to Order Upholstery); Tables (Occasional)*

KINGSHALL FURNITURE LTD, 427 Wherstead Road, Ipswich, Suffolk IP2 8LH; Tel: Ipswich 216052/3; *Bedrooms (Furniture); Desks; Chairs; Tables (Dining, Occasional)*

KNIGHTSBRIDGE UPHOLSTERY, Thornton Road, Bradford BB1 2JT; Tel: Bradford 31442; *Upholstered Furniture*

KWC SALES, see **BERGLEN PRODUCTS LTD**

LABLANC LTD, 11-15 William Road, London NW1 3ES; Tel: 01-388 6951/5; *Bedrooms (Furniture)*

LADYLOVE KITCHEN UNITS, Preston & Rowland Ltd, Century House, Widnes, Halton, Cheshire WA8 6QY; Tel: 051-423 2551; *Kitchens*

CATHERINE LALAU-KERALY, 29 Colville Terrace, London W11; Tel: 01-229 2540; *Mirrors & Glass; Partitions*

LANGLEY LONDON LTD, 161-3-5-7 Borough High Street, London SE1 1HU; Tel: 01-407 4444; *Ceramic Tiles*

LANGSTON JONES & SAMUEL SMITH LTD, (Signpost Paints), Haverhill, Suffolk CB9 8PQ; Tel: Haverhill 3611; *Paint*

JOHN LARKING, Flat 3, 290 Muswell Hill Broadway, London N10; Tel: 01-883 0684; *Tables (Dining)*

CHRISTOPHER LAWRENCE TEXTILES & LIGHTING LTD, see **CIEL**

WILLIAM LAWRENCE & CO LTD, Colwick, Nottingham NG4 2EH; Tel: Nottingham 249861; *Bedrooms (Furniture)*

LE FEU DE BOIS, 77 Heath Road, Twickenham, Middlesex TW1 4AW; Tel: 01-891 4313/4; *Stoves*

LEICHT FURNITURE LTD, Leicht House, Lagoon Road, Orpington, Kent BR53 QG; Tel: Orpington 36413/4; *Kitchens*

LEISURE KITCHEN PRODUCTS, Glynwed Bathroom & Kitchen Products Ltd, Meadow Lane, Long Eaton, Nottingham NG10 2AT; Tel: Long Eaton 4141; *Appliances & Kitchen Accessories; Bathrooms (Sanitaryware, Showers); Kitchens*

LESCO ALUMINIUM PRODUCTS, Wincheap Industrial Estate, Canterbury, Kent CT1 3RH; Tel: Canterbury 54646; *Plants & Planters*

JOHN LEWIS LTD, Oxford Street, London W1; Tel: 01-629 7711; *Ceramic Tiles*

LEYLAND PAINT & WALLPAPER LTD, Northgate, Leyland, Preston, Lancashire PR5 2LT; Tel: Leyland 21481; *Paint; Wall Coverings*

LIBRARY DESIGN & ENGINEERING LTD, 44 Gloucester Avenue, London NW1 1AA; Tel: 01-722 0111/4; *Shelving*

LIFESTYLE DESIGN WORKSHOPS, The Angel Yard, High Street, Highgate Village, London N6; Tel: 01-341 1284; *Upholstered Furniture*

B LILLY & SONS LTD, Baltimore Road, Birmingham B42 1DJ; Tel: 021-357 1761; *Fittings (Cabinet, Door)*

GORDON LINDSAY PARTNERSHIP LTD, 9 Bedford Corner, The Avenue, London W4; Tel: 01-995 5446/7/8; *Special Furniture (Made to Order Upholstery)*

LINK 51 LTD, Link House, Uxbridge Road, Hayes, Middlesex UB4 8JD; Tel: 01-573 7700; *Storage*

LINOLITE LTD, Pier Road, Feltham, Middlesex TW14 0TW; Tel: 01-890 8142; *Lighting*

MARY FOX LINTON LTD, 1 & 35 Elystan Street, London SW3; Tel: 01-581 2188/9; *Carpeting (Patterned, Sculptured Pile); Ceramic Tiles; Fabrics; Rugs; Wall Coverings (Co-Ordinates)*

LITA DISPLAY LTD, 75 Newman Street, London W1P 3LA; Tel: 01-636 2148/9; *Lighting*

VINCENT LLOYD (PARTITIONS) LTD, Unit 4, Kent Street Industrial Area, Kent Street, Leicester LE5 3BD; Tel: Leicester 25023; *Chairs*

LUCY FABRICS, Churchview Cottage, Cookley, Halesworth, East Suffolk IP14 0GW; Tel: Ubbeston 274; *Soft Furnishings*

LUMITE CEILINGS, Station Works, Datchet, Slough, Buckinghamshire SL3 9EE; Tel: Slough 49511 (10 lines); *Architectural Ornaments (Suspended Ceilings)*

LUXAFLEX LTD, Hunter Douglas Ltd, Wellington House, New Zealand Avenue, Walton-on-Thames, Surrey KT12 1PY; Tel: Walton-on-Thames 28822; *Blinds (Fabric Roller, Venetian, Vertical)*

MACHINKA LTD, Fourth Floor, Block A, Pall Mall Depositories, 126-128 Barlby Road, London W10 6BL; Tel: 01-960 8646; *Wall Coverings (Co-Ordinates)*

HUGH MACKAY & CO LTD, Head Office: PO Box 1, Durham City DH1 1SH; Tel: Durham 64444; London Showroom: Roman House, Wood Street, London EC2Y 5BU; Tel: 01-606 8491; *Carpeting (Berber, Made-to-Order, Patterned)*

MARY ANN MACKENZIE, 13A Ascham Street, London NW5; *Wall Coverings*

WILLIAM L MACLEAN LTD, 119-131 London Road, Brighton, Sussex BN1 4JH; Tel: Brighton 695411; *Bedrooms (Beds, Furniture); Chairs; Desks; Mirrors & Glass; Storage; Tables (Dining, Dining Suites, Occasional); Upholstered Furniture*

MAGNET SOUTHERNS, Head Office: Magnet Joinery Ltd, Keighley, West Yorkshire; Tel: Keighley 61133; *Architectural Ornaments (Wooden Beams, Panels & Mouldings); Staircases*

MAISON DESIGNS, Sheldon Corner, Chippenham, Wiltshire SN14 0RF; *Soft Furnishings*

MAJESTIC SHOWER CO LTD, 2 The Square, Sawbridgeworth, Herts CM21 9AE; Tel: Bishops Stortford 725500; *Bathrooms (Showers)*

MANDERS PAINTS LTD, PO Box 9, Mander House, Wolverhampton, West Midlands WV1 3NH; Tel: Wolverhampton 20601; *Paint*

MANHATTAN, Dennis & Robinson Ltd, Blenheim Road, Churchill Industrial Estate, Lancing, West Sussex BN15 8UH; Tel: Lancing 5321; *Bedrooms (Furniture); Kitchens*

MARBLE HILL GALLERY, 72 Richmond Road, Twickenham, Middlesex; Tel: 01-892 1488; *Fireplaces (Mantels & Surrounds)*

MARBLE PANELS LTD, Sherborne House, 16 Imperial Square, Cheltenham, Gloucestershire GL50 1YU; Tel: Cheltenham 582577/8; *Flooring (Stone); Tables (Occasional)*

LAURENT MARCEL, L A M Bamboosmith, 51 Westover Road, London SW18; Tel: 01-730 3215; *Special Furniture (Made to Order Furniture)*

MARFINITY LTD, West Works, 141 West Road, Shoeburyness, Essex SS3 9EF; Tel: Southend-on-Sea 588 688; *Bathrooms (Showers)*

MARGO INTERNATIONAL FABRICS LTD, Belford Mills, Kilmarnock, Ayrshire KA1 3JP; Tel: Kilmarnock 20115; *Fabrics*

MARLBOROUGH CERAMIC TILES, Marlborough, Wiltshire SN8 2AY; Tel: Marlborough 52422; *Ceramic Tiles*

MARLIN LIGHTING LTD, Hampton Road West, Feltham, Middlesex TW13 6DR; Tel: 01-894 5522; *Lighting*

MARRABLE & CO LTD, Delamare Road, Cheshunt, Waltham Cross, Hertfordshire EN8 9SP; Tel: Waltham Cross 37361; *Useful Products (Polishes)*

PARKER KNOLL FURNITURE LTD, PO Box 22, Frogmoor, High Wycombe, Bucks; Tel: High Wycombe 21144; *Upholstered Furniture*

PARKER KNOLL TEXTILES LTD, PO Box 30, West End Road, High Wycombe, Buckinghamshire HP11 2QD; Tel: High Wycombe 22301; *Fabrics; Wall Coverings (Co-Ordinates)*

PAR-K-PLY LTD, Lydney, Gloucestershire; Tel: Lydney 2213; *Flooring (Wood)*

PARNHAM HOUSE, Beaminster, Dorset DT8 3NA; Tel: Beaminster 862204; *Tables (Dining Suites, Occasional)*

F PARRAMORE & SONS LTD, Tools Division, Caledonian Works, Chapeltown, Sheffield, Yorkshire S30 4WZ; Tel: Sheffield 460141; *Useful Products (Tools)*

E PARSONS & SONS LTD, Blackfriars Road, Nailsea, Bristol BS19 2BU; Tel: Nailsea 4911; *Paint*

PATON, CALVERT & CO LTD, Binns Road, Liverpool L13 1BU; Tel: 051-228 2721; *Useful Products (Tools)*

PATRICKS OF FARNHAM, Guildford Road, Farnham, Surrey GU9 9QA; Tel: Farnham 722345; *Bathrooms (Sanitaryware); Fireplaces (Mantels & Surrounds)*

PEEL & CAMPDEN, 4 Ashbourne Parade, Finchley Road, London NW11 0AD; Tel: 01-455 3044; 458 5585/6; *Blinds (Fabric Roller, Specialist Products, Venetian); Carpeting (Indoor/Outdoor); Wall Coverings*

PEL LTD, Oldbury, Warley, West Midlands B69 4HN; Tel: 021-552 3377; *Chairs*

PENTABLOC LTD, Thornsett Works, Thornsett Road, London SW18 4EW; Tel: 01-874 5726; *Shelving*

PERKINS & POWELL LTD, Cobden Works, Leopold Street, Birmingham B12 0UJ; Tel: 021-772 2306; *Fittings (Cabinet, Door)*

PERMA BLINDS LTD, Prospect Row, Dudley, West Midlands DY2 8SE; Tel: Dudley 214231; *Blinds (Specialist Products, Venetian, Vertical)*

PERSIAN CARPET WHARF, Registered Office: North Quay, Regents Canal Dock, Mill Place, Commercial Road, London E14; Tel: 01-589 4225; *Rugs*

PERSIAN & ORIENTAL CARPET CENTRE LTD, 63 South Audley Street, London W1Y 5FB; Tel: 01-629 9670; *Rugs*

PETAL AGENCIES LTD, Whitney Cottage, Broad Chalke, Nr Salisbury, Wiltshire, SP5 5EH; Tel: Broad Chalke 338; *Stoves*

ALAN PETERS, Aller Studios, Kentisbeare, Cullompton, Devon; Tel: Kentisbeare 251; *Special Furniture (Designer Craftspeople)*

PETIT ROQUE LTD, 5a New Road, Croxley Green, Rickmansworth, Hertfordshire WD3 3EJ; Tel: Rickmansworth 77968 & 79291; *Fireplaces (Accessories, Mantels & Surrounds); Flooring (Stone); Wall Coverings*

PETRATE LTD, Unit 21, Eldon Way, Crick, Northampton NN6 7SL; Tel: Crick 822118/9; *Bathrooms (Accessories, Sanitaryware, Showers)*

PHOTOGRAPHIC COLLECTIONS (UK) LTD, The Francis Frith Collection, Lower Sandhurst Road, Finchampstead, Berkshire RG11 3TH; Tel: Yateley 872862; *Wall Coverings*

PIEFF FURNITURE LTD, Portersfield, Cradley Heath, Warley, West Midlands B64 7BQ; Tel: Cradley Heath 64891; *Upholstered Furniture*

PIFCO LTD, Failsworth, Manchester M35 0HS; Tel: 061-681 8321; *Useful Products (Tools)*

PILKINGTON BROTHERS LTD, St Helens, Merseyside, Lancashire WA10 3TT; Tel: St Helens 28882; *Mirrors & Glass*

PILKINGTON'S TILES LTD, PO Box 4, Clifton Junction, Manchester M27 2LP; Tel: 061-794 2024; *Ceramic Tiles*

PIRA LTD, 10 Hoxton Square, London N1 6NU; Tel: 01-739 7865; *Desks; Storage*

PIRELLI, GRG Division, Derby Road, Burton-on-Trent, Staffordshire DE1 0BH; Tel: Burton-on-Trent 66301; *Useful Products (Upholstery Supplies)*

TIM PLANT, 7 Bramham Gardens, London SW5; Tel: 01-370 2945; *Wall Coverings*

PLANTERS HORTICULTURE, 35A Gloucester Road, London SW7 4PL; Tel: 01-581 2983; *Plants & Planters*

DANIEL PLATT & SONS LTD, Brownhills Tileries, Tunstall, Stoke-on-Trent ST6 4NY; Tel: Stoke-on-Trent 86187; *Ceramic Tiles*

P & O CARPETS LTD, 5A Aldford Street, London W17 5PS; Tel: 01-629 9678; *Rugs*

POGGENPOHL UK LTD, 226 Tolworth Rise South, Surbiton, Surrey KT5 9NB; Tel: 01-337 8697; *Kitchens*

S POLLIACK LTD, Railway Street, Slingsby, York YO6 7AN; Tel: Hovingham 431 or 347; *Bathrooms (Accessories; Sanitaryware); Ceramic Tiles*

M A POPE (FIREPLACES) LTD, Rear of 62-64 High Street, Barnet, Hertfordshire; Tel: 01-449 5893; *Fireplaces (Mantels & Surrounds)*

POPPY LTD, 44 High Street, Yarm, Cleveland TS15 9AE; Tel: Eaglescliffe 782101; *Wall Coverings (Co-Ordinates)*

PORCELAIN NEWGLAZE LTD, 111 Fulham Road, London SW3; Tel: 01-584 8203; *Paint*

PRIOR UNIT DESIGN, A P & P M Hammick, Woodbury, Exeter, Devon; Tel: Woodbury 32237; *Kitchens*

PROJECT OFFICE FURNITURE LTD, Hamlet Green, Haverhill, Suffolk CB9 8QJ; Tel: Haverhill 5411; *Tables (Dining)*

PROWODA LTD, Headbrook, Kington, Herefordshire HR5 3DZ; Tel: Kington 230789; *Appliances & Kitchen Accessories*

PURIMACHOS LTD, 14 Waterloo Road, Bristol BS2 0PG; Tel: Bristol 298021; *Useful Products (Adhesives)*

PURITAN FORGE LTD, PO Box 287, London SE23 3TN; Tel: 01-699 1854; *Fireplaces (Accessories)*

PYROFORM LTD, 9 Holkham Road, Orton Southgate, Peterborough, Huntingdonshire PE2 0TF; Tel: Peterborough 236665; *Mirrors & Glass*

QUADRANT 4 *see* **MICHAEL SEVERN**

QUARTO FURNITURE, Lower Bristol Road, Bath, Avon BA2 1ET; Tel: Bath 331818; *Tables (Dining Suites); Upholstered Furniture*

QUEBB STOVES, Haymarket Stores, 4 Market Street, Hay-on-Wye, Herefordshire HR3 5AF; Tel: Hay-on-Wye 338; *Stoves (also Kitchen Ranges)*

QUENBY PRINTS, Shop: 194 Ebury Street, London SW1; Tel: 01-730 4946; *Fabrics; Wall-coverings (Co-Ordinates)*

BARRIE QUINN, 1 Broxholme House, New Kings Road, Fulham, London SW6; Tel: 01-736 4747; *Plants & Planters*

RAINBOW PRODUCTS LTD, Ocean House, Beechmore Road, London SW11 4ET; Tel: 01-720 7181; *Bathrooms (Sanitaryware)*

MICHEL RAMON, 5 Perth Close, Bramhall, Stockport, Cheshire SK7 1LQ; Tel: 061-440 8949; *Lighting*

RECTELLA INTERNATIONAL FABRICS, Rectella House, Railway Road, Chorley, Lancashire; Tel: Chorley 72211; *Wall Coverings*

M R RECTOR LTD, Rectella House, Railway Road, Chorley, Lancashire PR6 0HL; Tel: Chorley 72211; *Fabrics*

REGENCY BATHROOM ACCESSORIES LTD, Unit 5, Bromford Road Industrial Estate, West Bromwich, West Midlands; Tel: 021-544 6633/4; *Bathrooms (Accessories)*

REGENCY PARADE, Limco House, High March, Daventry, Northamptonshire NN11 4HD; Tel: Daventry 77444; *Mirrors & Glass*

RELYON, Price Brothers & Co Ltd, Wellington, Somerset TA21 8MM; *Upholstered Furniture*

REMPLOY FURNITURE, 415 Edgware Road, London NW2 6LR; Tel: 01-452 8020 (30 lines); *Tables (Occasional); Storage; Upholstered Furniture*

ARTHUR E RENOW, 3 Rosebank Yard, Rosebank Road, Harwell, London W7 2EU; Tel: 01-567 9821; *Mirrors & Glass*

A C RENTAPLANT, Acorn Nursery, Barrow Lane, Cheshunt, Waltham Cross, Hertfordshire EN7 5LL; Tel: Waltham Cross 27333; *Plants & Planters*

RENZLAND & CO, London Road, Copford, Colchester, Essex CO6 1LG; Tel: Colchester 210212; *Fireplaces (Accessories); Lighting; Plants & Planters; Shelving; Staircases; Tables (Dining Suites)*

REST ASSURED LTD, Bembridge Drive, Northampton NN2 6NB; Tel: Northampton 716000; *Upholstered Furniture*

RICO TILES, c/o Classical Designs, 1387 London Road, Leigh-on-Sea, Essex; Tel: Southend-on-Sea 78392 & 714177; *Architectural Ornaments (Wooden Beams, Panels & Mouldings)*

BRUNO RIMINI LTD, 10 Ringwood Avenue, London N2 9NS; Tel: 01-444 6716/883 2740; *Lighting*

RIPCEL LTD, Dane John Works, Gordon Road, Canterbury, Kent; Tel: Canterbury 54667; *Storage*

RMC PANEL PRODUCTS LTD, Waldort Way, Denby Dale Road, Wakefield, Yorks; Tel: Wakefield 62081; *Blinds (Specialist Products)*

JAMES ROBERTSHAW & SONS (1954) LTD, Albion Works, Larkhill, Farnworth, Bolton, Lancashire BL4 9LB; Tel: Bolton 74764; *Blinds (Fabric Roller, Paper & Wood)*

ROOKSMOOR MILLS, Bath Road, Nr Stroud, Gloucestershire GL5 5ND; Tel: Amberley 2577 (3 lines); *Bedrooms (Beds); Carpeting (Coir etc, Cord, Wilton); Tables (Dining Suites)*

ROTHLEY BRASS, Merrivale Street, Wolverhampton, West Midlands; Tel: Wolverhampton 27532; *Fittings (Door)*

ROYAL DOULTON SANITARYWARE LTD, Whieldon Road, Stoke-on-Trent, Staffs ST4 4HN; Tel: Stoke-on-Trent 49191; *Bathrooms (Sanitaryware, Showers)*

RUSSELL & CHAPPLE LTD, 23 Monmouth Street, London WC2H 9DE; Tel: 01-836 7521; *Fabrics; Wall Coverings*

E RUSSUM & SONS LTD, 29 Bridgegate, Rotherham S6O 1PL; Tel: Rotherham 65373; *Carpeting (Coir etc)*

RAGNO ITALIAN CERAMIC TILES LTD, Eldonwall Estate, Eldon Way, Crick, Northamptonshire NN6 7SL; Tel: Crick 822129; *Ceramic Tiles*

DAVID SAGE DESIGNS, Showroom: 40 Harrowby Street, London W1H 5HX; Tel: 01-723 9371; *Wall Coverings (Co-Ordinates)*

SALEMINK LTD, Kilmallock, Co Limerick, Ireland; Tel: Kilmallock 219; *Fireplaces (Accessories); Plants & Planters*

SALTREE VERTICAL BLINDS LTD, 152 High Street, Harborne, Birmingham B17 9PN; Tel: 021-427 6148/5898; *Blinds (Vertical)*

T F SAMPSON LTD, Creeting Road, Stowmarket, Suffolk IP14 5BA; Tel: Stowmarket 3535; *Blinds (Paper & Wood, Venetian)*

ARTHUR SANDERSON & SONS LTD, 52 Berners Street, London W1A 2JE; Tel: 01-636 7800; *Paint; Rugs; Wall Coverings (also Co-Ordinates)*

SANDERSON CARPETS see **THOMAS SHEPHERD (CARPETS) LTD**

IAN SANDERSON TEXTILES LTD, 3 Bromley Place, Conway Street, London W1; Tel: 01-580 9847; *Fabrics*

SANDTEX, Blue Circle Group, Special Products Division, Portland House, Stag Place, London SW1E 5BJ; Tel: 01-828 3456; *Paint*

SARTOR, 42 Pimlico Road, London SW1W 8LP; Tel: 01-730 6607; *Ceramic Tiles; Lighting; Wall Coverings (Co-Ordinates)*

T SAVEKER LTD, Phillips Street, Birmingham B6 4QL; Tel: 021-359 5891; *Chairs; Fittings (Door) Mirrors & Glass; Shelving; Storage; Tables (Dining, Occasional)*

SCANDIA, Per Jorgensen (Scandia) Ltd, Dorton Park, Dorton, Aylesbury, Buckinghamshire HP18 9NR; Tel: Aylesbury 237561; *Tables (Dining, Dining Suites); Upholstered Furniture*

JAMES SECCOMBE LTD, 18 Broadground Road, Lakeside, Redditch, Worcestershire B98 8YP; Tel: Redditch 21010; *Bedrooms (Beds)*

SEKON GLASSWROKS LTD, Essian Street, London E1 4QE; Tel: 01-790 5001/3792; *Mirrors & Glass*

HENRY SERVENTI LTD, 38 Barretts Grove, London N16 8AL; Tel: 01-249 0131; *Chairs*

MICHAEL SEVERN, Quadrant 4, Shakenhurst, Cleobury Mortimer, Nr Kidderminster, Worcestershire; Tel: Clows Top 300/406; *Special Furniture (Designer Craftspeople)*

SHANDON CLOCKS LTD, 33-39 Beadnell Road, London SE23 1AA; Tel: 01-699 9403; *Clocks; Lighting*

SHASTON FURNITURE LTD, Station Road, Semley, Shaftesbury, Dorset; Tel: Shaftesbury 3447; *Bedrooms (Furniture); Kitchens*

SHELFSTORE, 59/61 New Kings Road, London SW6 4ST; Tel: 01-736 5823; *Bedrooms (Furniture); Shelving; Storage*

SHELLEY TEXTILES LTD, Barncliffe Mills, Shelley, Huddersfield, Yorks HD8 8LU; Tel: Kirkburton 4336 (5 lines); *Rugs*

CHRISTINA SHEPPARD, 3 Doughty Street, London WC1; Tel: 01-405 9966; *Ceramic Tiles*

SIEMATIC UK LTD, 11-17 Fowler Road, Hainault Industrial Estate, Ilford, Essex IG6 3UU; Tel: 01-501 2216; *Kitchens*

SILENT GLISS LTD, Star Lane, Margate, Kent CT9 4EF; Tel: Thanet 63571; *Bathrooms (Accessories); Blinds (Paper & Wood, Vertical); Partitions*

SILEXINE PAINTS LTD, 80 Abbey Road, Barking, Essex IG11 7BY; Tel: 01-594 3871; *Paint*

SILICONE PRODUCTS, Silicone House, Cranfield Road, Lostock, Bolton, Lancashire BL6 4QD; Tel: Bolton 692531; *Useful Products (Sealants)*

D & J SIMONS & SONS LTD, 122-8 Hackney Road, London E2; Tel: 01-739 3744/5/6/7/8; *Architectural Ornaments (Wooden Beams, Panels & Mouldings)*

E N SIMPSON (UK) LTD, Ensign Works, Cullingworth, Bradford, W Yorks; Tel: Cullingworth 273670; *Rugs*

SITTING PRETTY LTD, 131 Dawes Road, London SW6; Tel: 01-381 0049; *Bathrooms (Accessories)*

SLEEPEEZEE LTD, Morden Road, Merton, London SW19 3XP; Tel: 01-540 9171 (15 lines); *Bedrooms (Beds); Upholstered Furniture*

SLOANE SQUARE TILES, 4b Symons Street, Sloane Square, London SW3; Tel: 01-730 4773; *Ceramic Tiles*

SLOTTSEAL LTD, Brook Street, Tring, Hertfordshire HP23 5EF; Tel: Tring 5303; *Useful Products (Sealants)*

SLUMBERLAND LTD, Prince of Wales Mill, Vulcan Street, Oldham, Lancashire OL1 4ER; Tel: 061-652 5131; *Bedrooms (Beds)*

SMALLCOMBE (IMPEX) LTD, 5a Crammavill Street, Grays, Essex; Tel: Grays Thurrock 77181; *Clocks*

JAMES SMELLIE LTD, Ivanhoe Works, Stafford Street, Dudley, West Midlands DY1 2AD; Tel: Dudley 52320; *Fireplaces (Accessories, Mantels & Surrounds)*

H & E SMITH LTD, Britannic Works, Broom Street, Hanley, Stoke-on-Trent, Staffordshire ST1 2ER; Tel: Stoke-on-Trent 21617/8; *Ceramic Tiles; Fireplaces (Mantels & Surrounds)*

PETER SMITH ASSOCIATES LTD, Highworth, Swindon, Wiltshire SN6 7AQ; Tel: Swindon 763042; *Carpeting (Coir, Indoor/Outdoor)*

SMITHBROOK IRONWORKS LTD, Smithbrook, Cranleigh, Surrey GU6 8LH; Tel: Cranleigh 2744; *Lighting*

SMITHS INDUSTRIES CLOCK COMPANY, Wishaw, Lanarkshire, Scotland ML2 0RN; Tel: Wishaw 73461; *Clocks*

SOLAR ECONOMY LTD, Balksbury Hill, Upper Clatford, Andover, Hampshire; Tel: Andover 51522; *Stoves*

SOLAR FIREPLACES LTD, Canning Street, Fenton, Stoke-on-Trent, Staffordshire ST3 3NF; Tel: Stoke-on-Trent 314331; *Fireplaces (Mantels & Surrounds)*

SOLARBO FITMENTS LTD, PO Box 5, Commerce Way, Lancing, West Sussex BN15 8TF; Tel: Lancing 63451/7; *Kitchens*

SOLENT FURNITURE LTD, Pymore Mills, Bridport, Dorset DT6 5PJ; Tel: Bridport 22305; *Bedrooms (Furniture); Kitchens; Storage*

SOMMER ALLIBERT (UK) LTD, Berry Hill Industrial Estate, Droitwich, Worcestershire WR9 9AB; Tel: Droitwich 4221 (10 lines); *Bathrooms (Accessories); Carpeting (Cord); Flooring (Vinyl); Wall Coverings*

SOUTH WALES BLIND CO LTD, Tonypandy, Glamorgan CF40 2JS; Tel: Tonypandy 3454; *Blinds (Fabric Roller, Venetian, Vertical)*

SPACE-SAVING BED CENTRE, 3-14 Golden Square, London W1R 4EP; Tel: 01-734 4246/7; *Bedrooms (Beds)*

SPECTRUM LTD, 53 Endell Street, London WC2H 9AJ; Tel: 01-836 1104; *Appliances & Kitchen Accessories; Bathrooms (Accessories); Lighting; Shelving*

SPIRAL STAIRCASE SYSTEMS, The Mill, Glynde, Lewes, Sussex; Tel: Lewes 159341/2; *Staircases*

STAG CABINET COMPANY LTD, Haydn Road, Nottingham NG5 1DU; Tel: Nottingham 37605; *Bedrooms (Furniture)*

STANLEY CURTAIN COMPANIONS LTD, Elizabethan Way, Lutterworth, Leicestershire LE17 4ND; Tel: Lutterworth 56111; *Fittings (Curtain)*

STANLEY TOOLS LTD, Woodside, Sheffield, Yorkshire S3 9PD; Tel: Sheffield 78678; *Useful Products (Tools)*

STANWATER DESIGNS LTD, Stedham, Midhurst, Sussex; Tel: Midhurst 2578/4900; *Special Furniture (Madeto Order Furniture)*

STAPLES & CO LTD, Staples Corner, Edgware Road, North Circular Road, London NW2 6LS; Tel: 01-452 1144; *Bedrooms (Beds); Storage; Tables (Occasional)*

STAPRO LTD, 15 Ditchling Rise, Brighton, Sussex BN1 4GL; Tel: Brighton 680133; *Useful Products (Carpet Protectors)*

BRUCE STARKE & CO LTD, PO Box 92, Brentwood, Essex CM14 4AF; Tel: Brentwood 218833; *Carpeting (Coir etc)*

STARLING MANTELS LTD, Unit 3, Nelson Road, Townstal Industrial Estate, Dartmouth, Devon TQ6 9LA; Tel: Dartmouth 4271; *Fireplaces (Mantels & Surrounds)*

STATELY HOME KITCHENS LTD, Coronation Parade, 54 Cannon Lane, Pinner, Middlesex HA5 1HW; Tel: 01-866 0973/4; *Kitchens*

STERLING RONCRAFT, Chapeltown, Sheffield, Yorkshire S30 4YP; Tel: Ecclesfield 3171; *Paint; Useful Products (Miscellaneous)*

RICHARD STEVENS (WOODSTOVES) LTD, The Warehouse, Coach Lane, Redruth, Cornwall; Tel: Redruth 218434; *Paint; Stoves (also Kitchen Ranges)*

ROBIN STEWART HANDPRINTS LTD, 48a Parkholme Road, London E8 3AQ; Tel: 01-249 1870; *Wall Coverings*

STICKABRICK LTD, The Green Road, Ashbourne, Derbyshire; Tel: Ashbourne 2118; *Wall Coverings*

ST MARCO'S, 45 Sloane Street, London SW1; Tel: 01-235 4832-3; *Bathrooms (Accessories, Sanitaryware); Mirrors & Glass*

A F STODDARD & CO LTD, Glenpatrick Carpet Works, Elderslie, Johnstone, Renfrewshire PA5 9AJ; Tel: Johnstone 21121; *Carpeting (Cord, Flecked, Wilton)*

STOKECROFT ARTS, 88-94 Caledonian Road, London N1 9DN; Tel: 01-278 6874; *Bedrooms (Beds); Tables (Dining)*

STONEHAM & SON (DEPTFORD) LTD, Powerscroft Road, Footscray, Sidcup, Kent DA14 5DZ; Tel: 01-300 8181; *Kitchens*

STOREY BROS & CO LTD, White Cross, Lancaster, Lancashire LA1 4XH; Tel: Lancaster 65288; *Wall Coverings (also Co-Ordinates)*

STOVE SHOP, Camden Lock, Chalk Farm Road, London NW1; Tel: 01-969 9531; *Stoves (also Kitchen Ranges)*

STUART INTERIORS, Drayton, South Petherton, Somerset TA13 5LR; Tel: S Petherton 40349; *Architectural Ornaments (Wooden Beams, Panels & Mouldings); Bedrooms (Beds); Chairs; Fireplaces (Mantels & Surrounds); Special Furniture (Made to Order Furniture); Staircases*

SUNSTOR LTD, Farlington, Portsmouth, Hampshire PO6 1SE; Tel: Portsmouth 373411; *Blinds (Fabric Roller)*

SUNVENE LTD, 7 Greenheys Lane, Manchester M15 6NQ; Tel: 061-226 4636; *Blinds (Fabric Roller, Venetian, Vertical)*

SUNWAY, Bestobell Home Products, Farnburn Avenue, Slough SL1 4XU; Tel: Slough 38221; *Blinds (Fabric Roller)*

SURREYBOARD CO LTD, 119 Downhills Way, London N17 6AW; Tel: 01-889 0974; *Flooring (Wood)*

SWAN GALLERIES, 57 The High, Oxford OX1 4AS; Tel: Oxford 42748; *Fireplaces (Mantels & Surrounds); Architectural Ornaments*

(Wooden Beams, Panels & Mouldings); Special Furniture (Made to Order Upholstery); Tables (Occasional)

SWEDISH VALVE CO LTD, 195 High Street, Egham, Surrey TW20 9ED; Tel: Egham 33851; *Bathrooms (Accessories)*

SWISH PRODUCTS LTD, Tamworth, Staffordshire B79 7TW; Tel: Tamworth 3811; *Fittings (Curtain)*

MICHAEL SZELL LTD, 47 Sloane Avenue, London SW3 3DH; Tel: 01-589 2634; *Fabrics*

TAMESA FABRICS LTD, 343 Kings Road, London SW3 5ES; Tel: 01-351 1126/9; *Carpeting (Sculptured Pile); Wall Coverings (Co-Ordinates)*

TARIAN DESIGN LTD, 120 Whitchurch Road, Cardiff, South Glamorgan CF4 3YL; Tel: Cardiff 371246; *Fabrics*

TASIBEL (LONDON) LTD, 450 High Road, Ilford, Essex IG1 1UN; Tel: 01-478 8201; *Carpeting (Coir etc)*

SHEILA TEAGUE, 45 Charlotte Road, London EC2; Tel: 01-729 5363; *Lighting*

TEKKO & SALUBRA (UK) LTD, Alan Richards, 9 Queen Street, Oldham, Lancashire OL1 1RD; Tel: 061-665 3362; *Wall Coverings*

TEMPLETON CARPETS, 525 Crown Street, Glasgow, Scotland G5 9XR; Tel: 041-429 6111; *Carpeting (Patterned, Wilton)*

TEMPUS STET LTD, Ingestre Court, Ingestre Place, London W1R 4AL; Tel: 01-251 3695; *Lighting; Mirrors & Glass; Plants & Planters; Tables (Occasional)*

TEROYDECOR LTD, 10 Vincent Street, Bradford, West Yorkshire BD1 2NT; Tel: Bradford 35431; *Wall Coverings*

THEALE FIREPLACES LTD, High Street, Theale, Reading, Berkshire; Tel: Reading 302232; *Fireplaces (Mantels & Surrounds)*

JANE THOMAS, 80 Castellain Mansions, Castellain Road, London W9; Tel: 01-286 4324; *Lighting; Special Furniture (Designer Craftspeople); Upholstered Furniture*

THOMAS & WILSON LTD, 454 Fulham Road, London SW6 1BY; Tel: 01-381 1161/7; *Architectural Ornaments (Plaster & Plaster Effects)*

THOMSON SHEPHERD (CARPETS) LTD, Seafield Works, Dundee, Scotland LDD1 9PS; Tel: 645111; Showrooms: 112 High Holborn, London WC1V 6JS; Tel: 01-242 1378; Pall Mall House, 24 Church Street, Manchester M4 1PN; Tel: 061-834 5252; *Carpeting (Berber, Patterned, Flecked, Wilton); Rugs;*

3M UNITED KINGDOM LTD, 3M House, PO Box 1, Bracknell, Berkshire RG12 1JU; Tel: Bracknell 26726; *Useful Products (Carpet Protectors)*

THRESHOLD FLOORINGS LTD, Vorda Works, Highworth, Swindon, Wiltshire SN6 7AJ; Tel: Swindon 763042; *Rugs*

FREDERICK TIBBENHAM LTD, Fairview Estate, Farthing Road, Ipswich, Suffolk IP1 5AP; Tel: Ipswich 47242; *Chairs; Storage; Tables (Dining, Occasional)*

TIDMARSH & SONS LTD, 1 Laycock Street, London N1 1SW; Tel: 01-226 2261; *Blinds (Venetian)*

TIELSA (UK) LTD, Alston Road, Barnet, Hertfordshire EN5 4HS; Tel: 01-440 9319/8665; *Kitchens*

TIFFANY KITCHENS, Hartley Morris Ltd, 4 High Street, Esher, Surrey; Tel: Esher 64350; *Kitchens*

WILLIAM TILLMAN LTD, Crouch Lane, Borough Green, Kent TN15 8LT; *Chairs; Desks; Tables (Dining, Occasional)*

TINTAWN LTD, Richfield Avenue, Reading, Berkshire RG1 8NZ; Tel: Reading 56321/581511; *Carpeting (Berber, Patterned, Shag, Wilton)*

TISSUNIQUE LTD, 10 Princes Street, Hanover Square, London W1R 7RD; Tel: 01-491 3386 (office); 01-408 0671 (showroom); *Fabrics; Wall Coverings (Co-Ordinates); Useful Products (Upholstery Supplies)*

TIVOLI LIGHTING SYSTEMS LTD, c/o Philip Henderson Co, 27 John Adam Street, London WC2 6HX; Tel: 01-930 0348; *Lighting*

TODAY INTERIORS LTD, Corringham Road, Gainsborough, Lincolnshire DN21 1QB; Tel: Gainsborough 4721; *Wall Coverings*

TOGGLE MOULDINGS LTD, 1 New Road, Newhaven, East Sussex BN9 0EG; Tel: 4227/8/9; *Tables (Dining); Upholstered Furniture*

TOMKINSONS CARPETS LTD, 18 St Martins Le Grand, London EC1A 4EH; Tel: 01-606 3371/3; *Carpeting (Patterned)*

TOWNHOUSE INTERIORS, 259 Lowndes Street, London SW1; Tel: 01-235 3180/3189; *Shelving*

TRANNON MAKERS, Llaws-y-Glyn, Powys SY17 5RH; Tel: Trefeglwys 313; *Bedrooms (Beds); Chairs; Shelving*

TRETFORD CARPETS LTD, Lynn Lane, Shenstone, Lichfield, Staffordshire WS14 0DU; Tel: Lichfield 480577; *Carpeting (Cord)*

TREWAX MANUFACTURING LTD, Craddock Road, Luton, Bedfordshire; Tel: Luton 599571; *Useful Products (Carpet Protectors)*

CHRIS TRIPPEAR, Shap Wells Cottage, Shap, Near Penrith, Cumbria; Tel: Shap 264; *Special Furniture*

T-T DESIGN SERVICES (INTL) LTD, 56 Goodwins Court, 55/56 St Martins Lane, London WC2 4LL; Tel: 01-846 7360; *Wall Coverings (also Co-Ordinates)*

TUFTED CARPET TILE LTD, Silverwood, Graigavon, County Armagh, Northern Ireland BT66 6LN; Tel: Craigavon 41324/5/6/7; *Carpeting (Tiles)*

TULLEYS (CHELSEA) LTD, 289/297 Fulham Road, Chelsea, London SW10 9PZ; Tel: 01-352 1078; *Special Furniture (Made to Order Upholstery)*

TURBERVILLE SMITH, 16/17 Hay Hill, Berkeley Square, London W1X 7LJ; Tel: 01-499 1638/9; *Carpeting (Made to Order); Tables (Dining Suites)*

ERNEST TURNER (NORTHDOWN HOUSE) LTD, 72-78 Brewery Road, Kings Cross, London N7 9NE; Tel: 01-609 4201/8; *Wall Coverings*

TWYFORDS LTD, PO Box 23, Stoke-on-Trent, Staffordshire ST4 7AL; Tel: Stoke-on-Trent 29531; London Office: The Bathroom and Shower Centre, 204 Great Portland Street, London W1V 6AT; Tel: 01-388 7631; *Bathrooms (Accessories, Sanitaryware, Showers)*

R TYZACK LTD, Kitchener Road, High Wycombe, Buckinghamshire HP11 2SJ; Tel: High Wycombe 23265/20993; *Chairs; Desks; Tables (Dining, Occasional); Upholstered Furniture*

UAS ENGINEERING LTD, Canal Street, Sheffield, Yorkshire; Tel: Sheffield 738804; *Bathrooms (Sanitaryware)*

ULSTER CARPET MILLS LTD, Castleisland Factory, Portadown, Craigavon, Northern Ireland BT62 1EE; Tel: Craigavon 34433; *Carpeting (Patterned)*

UNIFLEX FURNITURE LTD, Lea Valley Trading Estate, London N18 3LH; Tel: 01-807 1077; *Bedrooms (Furniture)*

VALFORM, Landsdown Industrial Estate, Cheltenham, Gloucestershire GL51 8PL; Tel: Cheltenham 20483; *Partitions*

VALLI & COLOMBO LTD, St Mary's Chambers, Station Road, Stone, Staffordshire ST15 8AS; Tel: Stone 817331; *Fittings (Cabinet, Door)*

VENESTA INTERNATIONAL COMPONENTS LTD, West Street, Erith, Kent DA8 1AA; Tel: Erith 36900; *Storage*

VENETIAN BLIND SERVICES (STAFFS), Oakdale Trading Estate, Ham Lane, Kingswinford, Brierley Hill, West Midlands DY6 7AY; Tel: Brierley Hill 5440/6074 & 87161; *Blinds (Specialist Products)*

VENILIA LTD, 1 Preston Road, off Elgar Road, Reading, Berkshire RG2 0BG; Tel: Reading 864442; *Wall Coverings (also Co-Ordinates)*

VERARDO, 36 The Precinct, Letchworth Drive, Bromley, Kent BR2 9BE; Tel: 01-460 5790 & 01-464 8605; *Bedrooms (Beds, Furniture); Tables (Dining Suites)*

VERINE PRODUCTS & CO, Folly Faunts House, Goldhanger, Maldon, Essex CM9 8AP; Tel: Maldon 88611; *Fireplaces (Mantels & Surrounds)*

VERTIKA INTERNATIONAL LTD, Sutton Mill, Cross Street, Macclesfield, Cheshire SK11 6TF; Tel: Macclesfield 611622; *Blinds (Vertical)*

VIGERS STEVENS & ADAMS LTD, Leadale Works, Craven Walk, London N16 6BY; Tel: 01-800 1290; *Flooring (Cork, Wood); Wall Coverings;*

VISIJAR (PLASTICS) LABORATORIES LTD, 1 Pegasus Road, Croydon Airport, Surrey CR9 4PR; Tel: 01-686 6341; *Partitions; Useful Products (Draught-proofers)*

VIXEN-SMITH LTD, Cove, Nr Tiverton, Devon EX16 7RU; Tel: Bampton 430; *Blinds (Fabric Roller, Vertical)*

VOGUE BATHROOMS, Bilston, Staffordshire WV14 8UA; Tel: Bilston 43121; *Bathrooms (Sanitaryware)*

WADE SPRING & UPHOLSTERY CO LTD, Wellington Street, Long Eaton, Nottingham NG10 4HT; Tel: Long Eaton 2135; *Upholstered Furniture*

WALCOT RECLAMATION, 108 Walcot Street, Bath BA1 5BG; Tel: Bath 310182; *Fireplaces (Mantels & Surrounds)*

WALDMANN LIGHTING, Burwood Lighting, Market Street, Exeter, Devon; Tel: Exeter 59367; *Lighting*

ROBERT WALLACE DESIGNS, 1-2 Alfred Place, Store Street, London WC1 7EB; Tel: 01-580 5376; *Rugs*

WALLPAPER ORIGINALS, Mosley Street, Manchester M2 3LG; Tel: 061-228 2542; *Wall Coverings*

MR WANDLE'S WORKSHOP, 200-202 Garratt Lane, London SW18 4ED; Tel: 01-870 5873; *Fireplaces (Mantels & Surrounds)*

WATTS & COMPANY LTD, 7 Tufton Street, London SW1P 3QB; Tel: 01-222 7169/2893; *Fabrics; Wall Coverings*

GORDON WATTS & CO, Kern House, 36-38 Kingsway, London WC2B 6HA; Tel: 01-405 8372/9; *Wall Coverings*

ISAAC WEBSTER & SONS LTD, Brow Works, Hipperholme, Nr Halifax, Yorkshire HX3 8BD; Tel: Halifax 203255/6; *Plants & Planters*

WELBECK HOUSE (SANDIACRE UPHOLSTERY) LTD, Bridge Street, Sandiacre, Nottingham NG10 5BH; Tel: Sandiacre 394500; *Upholstered Furniture*

WESLEY-BARRELL (WITNEY) LTD, 3 Bridge Street, Witney, Oxfordshire; Park Street Factory, Charlbury, Oxfordshire; Tel: Charlbury 810481; *Upholstered Furniture*

WESTNOFA (LONDON) LTD, Allard House, 18 Verney Road, London SE16 3DH; Tel: 01-639 8746; *Chairs; Upholstered Furniture*

WESTRA OFFICE EQUIPMENT LTD, The Green, Southall, Middlesex UB2 4DE; Tel: 01-574 3424; *Storage*

LAURENCE WHISTLER, The Old Manor, Alton Barnes, Marlborough, Wiltshire SN8 4LB; Tel: Woodborough 515; *Mirrors & Glass*

WHITELEAF FURNITURE, Goodearl Risboro Ltd, PO Box 2, Princes Risborough, Buckinghamshire HP17 9DP; Tel: Princes Risborough 3311; *Kitchens*

WHITE & NEWTON LTD, Dunbar Road, Portsmouth, Hampshire PO4 8EZ; Tel: Portsmouth 732255; *Tables (Dining Suites)*

ROBERT WHITING DESIGNS LTD, Rollesby Road, Hardwick Industrial Estate, King's Lynn, Norfolk PE30 4JQ; Tel: King's Lynn 64361; *Upholstered Furniture*

WHITNEY BURN LTD, 174 Estcourt Road, London SW6; Tel: 01-385 8324/8677; *Special Furniture (Made to Order Furniture)*

WICANDERS (GREAT BRITAIN) LTD, Maxwell Way, Crawley, Sussex RH10 2SE; Tel: Crawley 27700; London Showroom: First Floor, Building Centre, 26 Store Street, London WC1 7BT; Tel: 01-636 5959; *Flooring (Cork, Wood); Wall Coverings*

S C WILLIAMS & CO LTD, 129-131a Stafford Road, Wallington, Surrey SM6 9BN; Tel: 01-647 4322; *Blinds (Vertical)*

THE WILTON ROYAL CARPET FACTORY LTD, Wilton, Salisbury, Wiltshire SP2 0AY; Tel: Salisbury 274 2441; *Carpeting (Made to Order, Sculptured Pile, Wilton)*

WINCHMORE FURNITURE LTD, Mildenhall, Suffolk; Tel: Mildenhall 712082; *Kitchens*

WIND'S EYE STUDIOS, Gloucester Place, Swansea, Glamorgan SA1 1TY; Tel: Swansea 467485; *Mirrors & Glass*

WINTER & CO LONDON LTD, Glebe Road, Huntingdon, Cambridgeshire PE18 7DZ; Tel: Huntingdon 55321; *Wall Coverings*

WINTHER, BROWNE & CO LTD, 119 Downhills Way, Tottenham, London N17 6AW; Tel: 01-889 0971; *Bathrooms (Accessories); Fittings (Cabinet, Curtain); Tables (Occasional)*

WOOD BROS FURNITURE LTD, London Road, Ware, Hertfordshire SG12 9QH; Tel: Ware 3147/8; *Bedrooms (Beds); Clocks; Desks; Storage; Tables (Dining Suites, Occasional)*

WOODFIT LTD, Whittle Low Mill, Chorley, Lancashire PR6 7HB; Tel: Chorley 72 79521; *Fittings (Cabinet, Door); Kitchens*

WOODSTOCK, Albion Yard, Balfe Street, London N1 9ED; Tel: 01-837 1818; *Kitchens; Tables (Dining)*

WOODWARD GROSVENOR & CO LTD, Green Street, Kidderminster, Worcestershire DY10 1AT; Tel: Kidderminster 745271; *Rugs*

WOOLCO & WOOLWORTHS, F W Woolworth & Co Ltd, 242 Marylebone Road, London NW1; Tel: 01-262 1222; *Paint*

GEORGE WOOLLISCROFT & SON LTD, Melville Street, Hanley, Stoke-on-Trent, Staffs; Tel: Stoke-on-Trent 25121/2; *Ceramic Tiles*

WORKSHOP NO 8, 126 Portland Street, Manchester; Tel: 061-236 6802 (Mon, Wed, Fri); *Soft Furnishings*

WORKSHOP WONDERLAND, Panbeon Ltd, Anthorpe Works, Anthorpe Road, Meanwood, Leeds, West Yorkshire LS6 4JB; Tel: Leeds 784535; *Kitchens; Tables (Occasional)*

WORLD'S END TILES, 9 Langton Street, London SW10; Tel: 01-351 0279; *Ceramic Tiles*

CHRISTOPHER WRAY'S LIGHTING EMPORIUM LTD, 600-604 King's Road, London SW6; Tel: 01-736 8434; *Clocks; Lighting; Shelving*

F WRIGHTON & SONS LTD, Billet Road, London E17 5DW; Tel: 01-527 5521; Domestic Sales: Tel: 01-531 7211; *Kitchens*

B & P WYNN & CO, 18 Boston Parade, Boston Road, Hanwell, London W7 2DG; Tel: 01-567 8758; *Appliances & Kitchen Accessories; Bathrooms (Sanitaryware)*

YOUGHAL CARPETS LTD, Showroom: The Colonnades, Porchester Road, London W2; Tel: 01-229 3674; *Carpeting (Patterned)*

YOUNGER FURNITURE LTD, Monier Road, Bow, London E3 2PD; Tel: 01-985 4755; *Storage; Tables (Dining, Dining Suites)*

G J YOUNG & CO LTD, Ogilvie Road, High Wycombe, Bucks; Tel: High Wycombe 23912-3; *Useful Products (Upholstery Supplies)*

ARNOLD ZELTER, Valley Workshops, East Runton, Cromer, Norfolk; Tel: Cromer 512049; *Special Furniture (Made to Order)*